W9-CJS-969

ECONOMIC ANALYSIS

Kenneth E. Boulding

ECONOMIC ANALYSIS

THIRD EDITION

HARPER & BROTHERS   NEW YORK

330.1
B 763

ECONOMIC ANALYSIS, THIRD EDITION

Copyright, 1941, 1948, 1955, by Harper & Brothers
Printed in the United States of America

All rights in this book are reserved.
No part of the book may be used or reproduced
in any manner whatsoever without written per-
mission except in the case of brief quotations
embodied in critical articles and reviews. For
information address Harper & Brothers
49 East 33rd Street, New York 16, N. Y.

C-I

Library of Congress catalog card number: 55–6344

To ELIZABETH ANN BOULDING

CONTENTS

x   CONTENTS

FIGURES

The purpose of this book is twofold. It is intended as a text from which the student can learn and the teacher can teach the methods and results of economic analysis. It also seeks to be a contribution to the development and systematization of the body of economic analysis itself. These purposes are not separate. The task of presenting a systematic, orderly, and accurate account of economic analysis is identical with the task of preparing the material for teaching. It must be emphasized, however, that the purpose of this work is not primarily to entertain the student, or to enable him to regurgitate appropriate material into examination books, or to learn a few pat phrases, or to indoctrinate him with an abstract discipline which he will never use. Economics is like photography in this respect, that underexposure is less desirable than no exposure at all; and it is to be feared that too many half-exposed students are produced by our institutions of higher learning. The picture of economics held in their minds is a blurred and confused one, and what they have learned is not sufficiently accurate to serve as a tool for the analysis of practical problems. It is hoped that the student who survives this book will at least have come to regard economic analysis as a discipline useful in the interpretation and solution of numerous problems of life and thought, and will be able to add its methods to the cutting tools of his mind. Hence this is a work for the serious student, and not for the course-taster.

Economics presents a peculiar problem of exposition in that its various parts are much more closely related than is the case in many studies. Unless the student catches some vision of the whole great globe of analysis, therefore, he is likely to miss the significance of each part that he studies. It is the experience of most economists that on first approaching the subject it seems to be a hopeless confusion of unrelated principles. After a certain period of study, however, it may happen that the student experiences an illumination, often quite sudden, of the true nature and relationships of the subject, and from that time forth every part that he studies falls into its proper place and the sub-

ject is seen as a closely integrated whole. For this reason I have divided
the work into two parts, each of which contains about enough material
for a half-year's course of study. In the first part I have endeavored to
range over the whole field of economic analysis, using the simplest possible weapons of analysis, so that the student may obtain a rough outline of the whole picture. In this part, therefore, I treat the concepts
of demand and supply curves as self-evident, without discussing the
marginal analysis which underlies them. With the concepts of demand
and supply as the principal instruments of analysis, I outline the main
principles of price determination and of distribution. In this part also
I consider the theory of money, banking, international trade, and the
business cycle, still confining myself to the tools of demand and supply.

In the second part I give in detail the marginal analysis underlying
the demand and supply curves, including the theory of the individual
firm, of consumption, of imperfect competition and monopoly, together with a discussion of the theory of capital. With the foundation
laid in Part I the student will be able to integrate this more difficult
material into his studies as he goes along. In this part I have followed
the practice of segregating the more difficult material into separate
chapters. Hence this part can be studied on two levels: the student
can go through it on an elementary level, or he can take the more
advanced material in his stride.

The arrangement of this work thus is not according to subject
matter, as usually seems to be the case, but according to the methods
of analysis used. The old fourfold division—production, consumption,
distribution, and exchange—has almost completely disappeared. Instead we have a twofold division: into the part of the analysis which
can be conducted with the aid of the demand and supply concepts, and
the part that requires the concepts of the marginal analysis. A surprising amount can be accomplished with the aid of demand and supply
analysis alone. Determination of prices, the elementary theory of distribution and exchange, the elementary theory of money, international
trade, and the business cycle can be discussed without once using the
word "marginal." Therefore, this word so full of torment for the be-
ginner does not occur in Part I. In Part II all this analysis can be
elaborated; demand curves can be derived from utility or from production functions, supply curves from cost curves, and the whole theory
of the individual firm can be worked out. A possible defect in this
method is that the theory of monopoly and imperfect competition must
be postponed to Part II. Nevertheless, there are sound reasons for
this; a student who is introduced to the modern theory of the market

and the individual firm before he receives a thorough grounding in supply and demand analysis is often inclined to lose sight of the broad principles governing the whole economy through his absorption with the study of special cases. The conclusions of the analysis of perfect competition are modified, but not superseded, by the introduction of more complex and realistic assumptions; and the student will perceive more clearly the implications of these modifications if he knows what they modify.

The method of this work, therefore, is somewhat new; it may be called the "implemental" method, as it seeks to classify the various topics of analysis according to the analytical tools or implements used. It is thus hoped that the student will come to regard these tools as instruments, not as playthings. To this end I have introduced a system of discussion of practical problems which has, I believe, some claim to novelty. Instead of having one volume on "principles" and another volume on "problems," as is usually the case, and where all too frequently the "problems" have little or nothing to do with the "principles," I have integrated principles and problems throughout. That is, after each theoretical section in which the student has been introduced to a tool of analysis, there will be found a section dealing with those practical problems to which the tools thus far acquired can be applied. For example, after the chapter on the determination of prices in a competitive market, I discuss immediately the practical problems of organized competitive markets, such as the foreign exchange market, the capital market, and the commodity markets. After the section on normal demand and supply curves I have two chapters of problems which may be solved with the aid of these concepts, and so through the book.

In selecting these problems I have sought to choose those which provide the best illustrations of the principles involved, rather than those whose interest centers merely in their topicality. It is my belief that a work on principles should compete with neither the popular magazines nor the encyclopedias. Consequently I have not endeavored to write a compendium to current economic problems, for the reason that by the time the student has to face economic problems those of today may no longer be current. It seems to me more important to give the student a training which will fit him to understand the problems of the world of his maturity rather than of his youth. Consequently it is more important to give him a rigorous training in methods of analysis than to prime him with personable current opinions. It also seems to me that it is unwise to crowd a principles course with masses of factual material in special studies—labor, marketing, etc.—merely for the sake of giving the work an air of factuality. The place for such factual studies is later in the student's career, when he has acquired the techniques for interpreting the monstrous riddle of the factual material.

No advanced mathematical knowledge is required for this work. A knowledge of plane geometry will carry the student through all except the advanced chapters in Part II. Even in these chapters a nodding acquaintance with solid figures is all that is required. Any material involving algebra or the calculus is carefully segregated in appendices.

K. E. B.

Hamilton, New York
March, 1941

PREFACE TO THE THIRD EDITION

In the fourteen years which have elapsed since the publication of the first edition, there have been many changes in my own thinking and in the interests and activities of economists. These changes are reflected, at least in part, in the extensive revisions which I have felt obliged to make in this work. Its essential structure remains much the same as in the first edition, the reorganization into four parts which was effected in the second edition being carried over to the present.[1] In detail and even in content, however, there have been many changes.

Part I, the first twelve chapters, has suffered the least change. There is something remarkably sturdy about demand and supply analysis, and it has stood up well amid the changing fashions of the day. I have made a few changes in the third edition—a greater emphasis on dynamics in the section on allocation (Chapter 10), and a greater stress on the "absolute" elasticity concept rather than on the Marshallian concept.

Part II, Macroeconomics, has undergone the most change. It was expanded and made into a separate part in the second edition, and has been almost completely rewritten for the third edition. I have some hope that this part has now reached the level of maturity that demand and supply analysis has enjoyed for many years. Just as price theory revolves around the simple basic model of an equilibrium of demand and supply, so macroeconomics now revolves around an equally simple basic model of production, consumption, and accumulation. Chapters 13–15 of the second edition have been rewritten and expanded into Chapters 13–16 of the third edition. The appendix to Chapter 14 is new. Chapters 17, 19, 21, and 22 of the third edition correspond roughly to Chapters 16, 17, 18, and 19 of the second, though all have been rewritten and much new material incorporated. Chapters 18 and 20 of the third edition are new.

---

[1] In reading the preface to the first edition it should be noted that Part I of the first edition corresponds to Parts I and II of the present edition, and Part II of the first edition corresponds to Parts III and IV of the present edition.

Part III, Elements of the Marginal Analysis, has also been extensively rewritten for the third edition, and what amounted to little more than a rearrangement in the second edition now represents a substantial change in focus, especially in the direction of greater generality. Some economy in presentation has been achieved by amalgamating the discussions of perfect and of imperfect markets, and by exhibiting the perfect market as merely a special case of the imperfect market. Chapters 25 and 26 are almost entirely new, and all the other chapters have much new material and extensive rearrangements.

In Part IV, also, the argument has been condensed somewhat by concentrating on the imperfect market as the general case, so that Chapters 34 and 35 of the third edition represent a complete rearrangement of Chapters 31 and 32 of the second edition. Chapters 36 and 37 correspond closely to Chapters 33 and 34 of the second edition. Chapter 37 of the second edition has been eliminated, and Chapters 35 and 36 have been extensively revised as Chapters 38 and 39 of the third edition.

It is hoped, therefore, that the present edition represents an improvement in the balance of the work. Macroeconomics now takes a firmly equal place with microeconomics. There is more attention to problems of dynamics and growth. Marginal analysis has been moved in the direction of greater generality. Economics, however, does not stand still, and especially in the area of the theory of the individual organization, where the most rapid progress is observable at the present time, it is difficult to know how much of current advances should be incorporated in a work of this kind. Thus I have decided not to attempt the incorporation of such recent advances as linear programming, organization theory, decision theory, and operations research, in spite of the fact that many of these advances stem directly from the marginal analysis and the theory of maximization. These topics still lie somewhat too close to the frontier for the settled and domestic environment of a textbook, and I have thought it wise to exclude them at this time.

I must again express my thanks to the large number of students, colleagues, and correspondents who have contributed to the making of this book.

K. E. B.

Palo Alto, California
March, 1955

PART I

DEMAND AND SUPPLY

CHAPTER 1

THE TASK AND METHOD OF
ECONOMIC ANALYSIS

What Is Economic Analysis?

A distinguished economist,[1] on being asked to define the subject matter of his science, once replied, "Economics is what economists do." There is truth in the parry, for the boundaries of any branch of study are seldom quite clear, and topics which it contains at one time may be excluded at another. Consequently, any short definition of the boundaries of economic analysis is unavoidably inadequate. To define it as "a study of mankind in the ordinary business of life"[2] is surely too broad. To define it as the study of material wealth is too narrow. To define it as the study of human valuation and choice is again probably too wide, and to define it as the study of that part of human activity subject to the measuring rod of money is again too narrow.

Economic Phenomena

Nevertheless, we are all aware of a broad class of facts which may be described as "economic." There are, for instance, three types of human activity which readily fall into such a category: production, consumption, and exchange. Acts of transforming raw materials and labor into products, or acts of transporting products to places where they are wanted, are clearly matters of interest to the economist. Similarly, acts of consumption—the burning of coal, the wearing of clothes, the eating of foods—are of interest to the economist, as presumably all commodities are ultimately destined for consumption. Finally, acts of exchange probably constitute by far the greater part of the phenomena subject to economic investigation. Indeed, it is

[1] Professor Jacob Viner.
[2] Marshall, *Principles of Economics,* p. 1.

3

hardly too much to say that the study of exchange comprises nine-tenths of the economist's dominion. The purchase and sale of a commodity or a security is easily recognized as an exchange in which usually one form of property—money—is given in exchange for some other form of property. It is perhaps less generally recognized, but nevertheless easily perceived, that the hiring of labor, the leasing of houses or land, and even the borrowing or lending of money are also acts of exchange. When labor is employed, hours of labor are exchanged for money, and the wage of labor is the price of the commodity bought and sold in this transaction. When property is leased, the services of the property are bought and sold for money, and rent is the price of these services. When money is borrowed, in the immediate present money is given by the lender in exchange for a "security," i.e., for a promise on the part of the borrower to pay money in the future. If we consider the borrowing and repayment as part of the same transaction, it appears as an exchange of present money against future money.

Economic Quantities

In all the events noted above certain quantities or magnitudes appear, and these also are a principal object of economic inquiry. Economists do not merely note idly that there is production, consumption, and exchange; they concern themselves with the *quantities* produced, consumed, and exchanged. The output, consumption, and accumulated stocks of wheat; the price of butter; the wages of bricklayers; the rent of apartments; the interest on bank loans; the tax on tobacco; the tariff on cloth—all such quantities are of interest to the economist. These things we call *economic quantities*. Their collection is the task of economic statistics and economic history, and their interpretation is the principal task of economic analysis.

Economic Organisms

A third object of economic analysis is found in the organizations and institutions which direct economic activity. Who produces, who consumes, who exchanges? All acts are of course acts of individuals, but frequently individuals act on behalf of some organization. A housewife buys for a family, a purchasing agent for an orphanage, a buyer for a department store. A manager lends for a bank, a personnel director hires for a corporation, an official borrows for a government. These organizations or institutions, on whose behalf their agents buy and sell, borrow and lend, hire and fire, are *economic organisms.* They have a being and patterns of behavior independent in some degree of the persons who direct them. They have personalities, even if they are not persons, and decisions are made on their behalf. The study of their behavior therefore constitutes another important part of economic analysis.

The Task of Interpretation

We have now indicated the broad field of fact within which economic analysis functions. We have yet to define the specific task of economic analysis itself. The purpose of any analytical treatment of material is to provide a body of principles according to which facts can be selected and interpreted. The complaint is frequently heard that people want "facts," not "theories." The complaint may be justified in protest against theories which have no basis in fact, but usually it arises from a misunderstanding of the true relationships of facts and theories. Theories without facts may be barren, but facts without theories are meaningless. It is only "theory"—i.e., a body of principles—which enables us to approach the bewildering complexity and chaos of fact, select the facts significant for our purposes, and interpret that significance. Indeed, it is hardly too much to claim that without a theory to interpret it there is no such thing as a "fact" at all. It is a "fact," for instance, that Oliver Cromwell had a wart on his nose. But what constitutes this supposed "fact"? To the chemist it is a certain conglomeration of atoms and molecules. To the physicist it is a dizzy mass of unpredictably excitable electrons. To the biologist it is a certain impropriety in the behavior of cells. To the psychologist it may be the key to the interpretation of Cromwell's character, and a fact of overwhelming importance. The historian may consider it an insignificant detail or an important causative factor, according to whether he follows economic or psychological interpretations of history. To the economist the wart may be of negligible importance unless Cromwell were prepared to pay a good round sum for its removal. What, then, is the "fact" about the wart? It may be any or all of the above, depending on the particular scheme of interpretation into which it is placed.

The Selection of Facts of Economic Significance

It should now be evident that any "fact" contains a great deal more than any single field of inquiry requires. The first task of economic analysis, therefore, is to select from economic events and facts those elements which are significant in relation to the general scheme of economic analysis itself. Consider, for instance, an event such as an exchange. Lest we forget the origins of economics as the science of household management, let us take as our illustration the purchase of two pounds of butter by a housewife, Mrs. Jones, for $1.60, at a definite moment in history. The example is humble, but the event is representative of transactions everywhere, whether on the floor of the stock exchange, in the sanctum of the bank, or in the mart of merchandise.

Facts in an Act of Exchange

Relevant Facts. When Mrs. Jones buys her two pounds of butter, then, we observe first that there are two persons participating in the event, the buyer and the seller. We observe also that there are two physical objects involved. One is the butter, which passes from the possession of the storekeeper to Mrs. Jones. The other is the $1.60, which passes from the possession of Mrs. Jones to the storekeeper. An exchange, therefore, consists of two reciprocal transfers of ownership. At least three economic quantities are involved in the event: the quantity of butter (two pounds), the quantity of money ($1.60), and the *ratio* of these quantities, $1.60 for two pounds, or, what is the same thing, 80 cents per pound. The ratio of the quantities exchanged is the *price*, or exchange ratio. In transactions involving money and a commodity it is usually expressed as the price per unit of commodity and is equal to the quantity of money exchanged divided by the quantity of commodity exchanged. Eighty cents per pound, therefore, is the price of butter. We have now selected, from this event, the aspects which most concern the economist. Other aspects of the event are relevant to him principally because of the bearing they exercise on the three quantities mentioned above. Thus the pleasant smile and winning manner of the storekeeper or the attractiveness or location of the store may be important for the economist, but their importance arises principally because they may help to explain why the price of butter in one store differs from the price in another.

Irrelevant Facts. In describing this apparently simple event, however, the economist has already abstracted from reality the portions which interest him most, and even in simple description he is dealing not with mere facts but with selected facts. There are innumerable other facts about the event which interest other people. The public health officer may be most interested in the chemical and bacteriological composition of the butter, the artist may be most interested in the pictorial possibilities of the scene, the novelist may be most interested in the emotions of the participants, the numismatist may be most interested in the exact inscriptions on the coins transmitted from one hand to the other, the linguist may be most interested in the exact words spoken, the costumier may be most interested in the clothes worn, and the store cat may be most interested in the aroma of fish in Mrs. Jones' shopping bag. All these things are facts about the event we are describing, and it is evident that we have by no means exhausted the list. Indeed, to describe the simplest event completely would require volumes of words and months of investigation. Those, therefore, who cry, "Give me facts, not theories," must beware lest their request be taken too seriously. Taken literally it could be answered only by such a flood of irrelevancy as to obliterate the facts completely. The very concept of relevancy implies the existence of theory, for all facts are relevant only in relation to some body of principles.

Economic Analysis as the Interpretation of Economic Quantities

We see by the above illustration that the most significant aspects of any economic event, for the economist, are the economic quantities concerned in it. The greater part of economic analysis, indeed, is concerned with investigating the nature of economic quantities, the relationships existing between them, and the forces which determine them. In describing the above event we selected as a fact significant for the economist that the price of butter was eighty cents per pound. A major task of economic analysis is to explain *why* the price of butter is eighty cents per pound and, of course, why all prices, wages, incomes, interest rates, and other economic quantities are what they are. Its task, therefore, is not primarily that of description, although the mass of recorded fact provides much of its raw material. Description is particularly the task of the historian and the statistician, although it must not be thought that history or statistics consist merely in the recording of fact. History and statistics themselves need principles of interpretation, and it is the task of economic analysis to provide the necessary body of principles. The student must not expect to find in this volume a complete discussion of all the economic phenomena of history or of the problems of that small part of history called "today." Such studies are the discourses of economics; economic analysis is its grammar. It consists of a body of general principles and of a discipline of logic which may be applied to the interpretation of all economic problems, past or present. Although it has been developed largely with reference to a free capitalistic society and consequently is particularly concerned with the problems of capitalism, it rests on a broad foundation of the study of human nature, and its most fundamental propositions can be applied to all conditions of mankind.

Economics and Welfare

To this point we have defined the main task of economic analysis as the explanation of the magnitudes of economic quantities. The student will find also that the main part of this, as of most other works on the subject, is concerned with the theory of the determination of prices, wages, interest rates, incomes, and the like. He may well inquire, therefore, in the midst of so much mathematics, whether the first task of economics is not the investigation of wealth, or welfare. Some economists have endeavored to restrict the boundaries of the science to the investigation of those quantities which are numerically measurable. Well-being, under such a restriction, would not be part of economics at all. Professor Robbins, for instance, in defining economics as "the science which studies human behavior as a relationship between ends and scarce means which have alternative uses,"[3] seems to deprive economics of the right to study welfare, for welfare is an "end" in itself. Nevertheless, economists have always been interested in problems of wealth and welfare. Adam Smith, founder of the science, bravely called his masterpiece *An Inquiry into the Nature and Causes of the Wealth of Nations;* and though it may be argued that the most important part of his work deals not with wealth at all but with the equilibrium of prices, nevertheless he not only concerns himself with wealth but openly advocates certain measures, such as free trade, which he believes will lead to an increase in wealth. His lineal successors—Mill, Marshall, Pigou, and the modern welfare economists— likewise concern themselves with problems of wealth and welfare. It is evident, therefore, that whether or not the study of welfare is within the province of economic analysis, it is certainly adjacent, and subject at least to its imperial dominion.

Prices and Satisfactions

Indeed, it is impossible to explain even the determination of prices without some reference to the concept of well-being. In attempting to define the quantity of any commodity we are constantly forced to recognize that commodities are wanted not for their own sakes but for the sake of some satisfaction derived from their use or consumption. The moment any idea of "quality" enters into our discussion of

[3] *The Nature and Significance of Economic Science,* 2nd ed., p. 16.

the nature of commodities we are involved immediately in a discussion of the well-being, or satisfactions, which commodities create. There is no satisfactory test of quality except the test of intelligent preference. If, out of a proper experience of each kind, Mrs. Jones chooses butter "A" instead of butter "B," when the price of both is the same number of cents per pound, we can assume that for Mrs. Jones butter "A" has the higher quality. For someone else, however, butter "B" might have the higher quality. Chemical and physical standards of quality are important, but they can never be wholly satisfactory, if only because "quality" is ultimately not a material property but a psychological property.

The Limitations of Economics

It is impossible for us to exclude problems of welfare, of wants and their satisfactions, from the subject matter of economics. Nevertheless, these problems are of peculiar difficulty, and we shall reserve them as far as possible to the later stages of our discussion. Even then the propositions which emerge from our analysis may seem to the student vague and unsatisfactory. But it is well to realize that economic analysis alone does not provide the ultimate answers to what is right or wrong in individual or political conduct, and gives no magic formula by which schemes for the betterment of mankind are to be tested. It is not, for instance, the business of the economist as such to decide whether large armaments are necessary, whether a marriage is successful, a religion efficacious, or even whether a law is wise. The principal attention of the economist is directed to the area in which values can be measured in numerical terms, and consequently he cannot claim jurisdiction over the great region of valuation where such imponderable realities as friendship, patriotism, sincerity, and loyalty are assessed. In all political questions such imponderable valuations are of vital importance, and economic analysis is an important witness, but is not the sole judge.

This is not to say, of course, that the economist denies validity to the imponderables. He recognizes them and, indeed, uses them in explaining the magnitude of the ponderables. It is impossible to explain differences in wages, for instance, without reference to imponderables such as danger, enjoyment of work, pleasantness of associations, loyalty to employers, and so on. Nor is it proper to draw a sharp line between ponderable and imponderable values, between gain and glory. The concepts of economic analysis—concepts, for instance, of choice, of exchange, and of price—apply to the imponderable values as much as to the ponderables, though of course in a less measurable fashion. Every man has his price, even if that price be in some exceptional cases infinite. Glory may be purchased by the sacrifice of ease, just as guns may be purchased by the sacrifice of butter. Love and loyalty are treasuries which may be exhausted by too many claims, as many nations have found to their cost. We will probably exert ourselves more to rescue a friend than to rescue a stranger. The propositions of economics, therefore, though quantitatively applicable only where valuations can be expressed in numerical terms, extend wherever choices are made, be they between butter and eggs or between good and evil. But the economist studies the choices; he does not judge them, except in so far as they are made without proper knowledge of the possible alternatives. His main responsibility to the statesman or to the reformer is to show clearly the nature of the choice to be made, particularly in its quantitative aspects. The responsibility for the choice itself, however, always rests with the individual who makes it. Whether there are absolute standards by which choices themselves may be valued is an interesting question. But it is not one that can be answered by the methods of economic analysis.

THE METHODS OF ECONOMIC ANALYSIS

We now have a rough idea of the questions to be answered. We must next inquire by what methods the answers are to be found. It is clear at the outset that the experimental method, so fruitful in the natural sciences, is of strictly limited application in the social sciences. The experimental method consists essentially in bringing about certain preconceived events in a highly simplified environment. The chemist, for instance, studies a reaction by bringing his chemicals together in a controlled environment with known impurities or with none. An experiment, therefore, is an event or series of events in which only relevant elements are present, or in which, at least, the irrelevant elements are known. It is possible occasionally to perform controlled experiments in the social sciences. For example, the effect of a milk diet on school children can be determined by observing two groups of children, similar in all respects except diet. One group may be given a diet which includes extra quantities of milk, the other may receive a regular diet, and the differences in progress can then with some security be attributed to the milk. Experiment in economics, however, is of limited importance. It is impossible, for instance, to determine the effect of high interest rates on the conduct of business men by dividing them into two groups and subjecting one group to a high rate of interest and the other group to a low rate.

The Statistical Method

In these circumstances we are forced back on two other methods of gaining knowledge. The first of these is the statistical method. The second we may call the method of "intellectual experiment." The statistical method is in a sense a substitute for the method of controlled experiment—a poor substitute, but the best we have. We cannot, as we have just seen, divide people into two groups in order to find their exact reaction to various changes. What we can do, however, is to observe similar groups of people at different times and under different circumstances, and then record both the difference in the circumstances and the difference in the behavior which we may expect the circumstances to effect. Then we may *tentatively* suppose that the change in circumstances "caused" the change in behavior.

Its Limitations. It is important to realize, however, that statistical information can only give us propositions whose truth is more or less probable; it can never give us certainty. Statistics, for instance, tell us that in the years when the price of sugar has in fact been high, the consumption of sugar has in fact been low. From this statement it may seem that we can jump straight to the important proposition that *if* the price of sugar is high, *then* the consumption *must* be small. This conclusion (which is, of course, the generalization at which we really want to arrive) does not inevitably follow from the historic, statistical facts. It may be that things other than the price of sugar affect its consumption, and that it was these other things which made the consumption low in the years when the price of sugar happened to be high.

Statistics vs. Experiment. This illustrates the difference between the statistical method and the experimental method. In an experiment we can actually keep out of our test tubes the "other things" in which we are not for the moment interested, but in statistical work either we have to take the "other things" specifically into account— which, of course, makes the problems more difficult—or we must hope that the "other things" remain constant, or nearly so, during the period of years under investigation. The most dangerous fallacy in statistical investigation is that of assuming that if two things have been observed together in a few instances, they *must* of necessity be causally connected. Because two young people are constantly found in each other's company, it does not follow in the least that they cannot be separated. The same holds true of two statistical series.

The Method of Intellectual Experiment

We shall return later to the uses of the statistical method in economics. For the most part, however, we shall be using the method of "intellectual experiment" in this study. The essential *problem* of economic analysis is, as we have seen, to study the nature and the relationships of the various economic quantities—prices, wages, and the like. The actual world of economic quantities and relationships, however, is almost unbearably complicated. It is impossible to follow through immediately, without considerable training, all the ramified economic effects of even the simplest event. Under these circumstances what we do is to postulate, in our own minds, economic systems which are simpler than reality but more easy to grasp. We then work out the relationships involved in these simplified systems and, by introducing more and more complex assumptions, finally work up to the consideration of reality itself.

Analogy with Mathematics

This method is similar in a great many respects to the method of pure mathematics. In mathematics we start with some very simple propositions to which we can give assent without any difficulty, e.g., that a straight line cuts each of two parallel straight lines at the same angle. Starting from these propositions we can train ourselves by processes of "proof" to perceive more complicated propositions which we could not otherwise "see," as, for instance, that the sum of the three angles of a triangle is equal to two right angles. Similarly, in "pure" economics we also start from simple assumptions and deduce from them conclusions which *necessarily* follow. The propositions of pure economics, therefore, are all *hypothetical* propositions; that is to say, they all take the form, "*If* A and B and C are true, *then* X and Y and Z will be true."

Non-Euclidian Economics

In this sense it would be quite possible to build up any desired system of economics, depending on the initial assumptions taken. Just as it is possible to have non-Euclidian geometries in mathematics —that is, geometries whose fundamental axioms do not correspond to the facts of our ordinary experience—so there can be non-Euclidian systems of economic relationships in economics, whose fundamental axioms do not correspond to the facts of our experience. In ordinary economics we assume that an enterprise wishes to make as great profits as it can. There is nothing to prevent our assuming, however, that firms wish to make fixed profits, or that they wish to make the value of the product as great as they can, or that they wish to make their average cost of production as small as they can. By assuming these different things, we shall of course get different conclusions, but the same method of analysis applies to them all. Naturally, however, we are more interested in those assumptions which correspond most closely to reality as we know it, i.e., to the system in which we live. But it is important to realize that the method of economic analysis is not confined to one particular system. Indeed, economic analysis perhaps can make contributions to the study of noncapitalist economic systems quite as significant as those it makes to the study of capitalism.

Economic Analysis as a "Map" of Reality

The method of economic analysis, then, is to start with very simple assumptions concerning human behavior, then to discover what consequences would follow for the economic system as a whole if these assumptions were true. In this way we can build up a picture of a *simplified* economic system. Having mastered this simple picture, we can then proceed to bring it into closer relation to real life by introducing qualifications of our original assumptions and seeing how they affect the picture as we see it. But never do we come to "real life," however closely we may approach it, for reality is always more complex than the economist's picture of it. This fact frequently makes students feel that economic analysis is "unrealistic," because the world with which it deals seems to be so much simpler than the real world. To think this, however, is to misunderstand the whole nature of economics. Economic analysis is not a perfect picture of economic life; it is a *map* of it. Just as we do not expect a map to show every tree, every house, and every blade of grass in a landscape, so we should not expect economic analysis to take into account every detail and quirk of real economic behavior. A map that is too detailed is not much use as a map. This is not to say, of course, that all the economic "maps" have been good maps, for many of them have falsified even the broad outlines of reality. But it is a map that we are looking for, and not a detailed portrait. Consequently, we should not look to economic analysis for intimate details as to how to run a business or a bank, any more than we should expect to find in it the technical details of manufacture or mining. It is not even the business of the economist to give detailed advice to the statesman. His business is to take the system which the business man, the banker, the worker, and even the statesman see only in part and visualize it as a whole, even though in seeing the whole he inevitably misses some of the detail.

QUESTIONS AND EXERCISES

1. A knowledge of ballistics (the theory of moving balls) would not necessarily help a tennis player, although he constantly practices by a kind of instinct the principles laid down therein. Does the same apply to the relations between economic analysis and the practice of business? If so, is this any argument against studying either ballistics or economics?

2. Is a *price* a sum of money?

3. Suppose the price of chocolate was 5 cents per bar. Suppose now that the manufacturer made the bar bigger but still charged only 5 cents per bar. Would you say that the price of chocolate had fallen? Now suppose that instead of making the bar bigger the manufacturer made it *better* (i.e., made it taste better) and again charged only 5 cents per bar. Has the price of chocolate fallen now?

4. If a Packard costs twice as much as a Ford, does that mean that there is twice as much automobile in a Packard as there is in a Ford? If this were true, would the prices of all cars really be the same?

5. Write out formal definitions, in your own words, of the following terms: economic analysis; price; economic quantities; exchange; experiment.

6. Which of the following would you classify as economic quantities? (a) The average wage. (b) The number of senators in Congress. (c) The salary of the President of the United States. (d) The price of eggs. (e) The number of days in a month. (f) The number of unemployed workers. (g) The basic rate of income tax. (h) The number of pages in this book.

7. The physical sciences are commonly supposed to be more successful than the social sciences. Why?

CHAPTER 2

SPECIALIZATION AND EXCHANGE: THE TASK OF ECONOMIC ORGANIZATION

In the preceding chapter we observed that most of the economic quantities in which we are interested are associated in some way with acts of exchange. It will not surprise us, therefore, if the first stage in our inquiry consists of an examination of this apparently simple phenomenon. We shall ask three questions: *Who* exchanges? *What* is exchanged? and *Why* are things exchanged?

Who Exchanges? "Economic Organisms"

We saw in our preceding example that Mrs. Jones and the storekeeper made an exchange of $1.60 for two pounds of butter. The answer to the question *Who* exchanges? would seem to be simple: Mrs. Jones on the one hand and the storekeeper on the other. But the matter is not so simple as that. Perhaps Mrs. Jones is buying for her family, or perhaps she runs a boardinghouse and wants the butter for her paying guests. The storekeeper also may not be acting merely in his personal capacity. He may be acting as a representative, who is selling not for himself but for the store. This is obviously true if the storekeeper is an employee. It is also true even when the storekeeper is an independent grocer working for himself, for his activities as a private individual must be distinguished from his activities as a seller of commodities over the counter. It should now be clear that exchanging, i.e., buying and selling, is something which is done not only by individuals in a private capacity. It is usually done, in fact, by individuals who *represent* some institution or organization, such as a family, a church, an orphanage, a bank, a store, or a mill, or who represent themselves in some capacity such as a worker or a landowner. These organizations or capacities which people represent when they buy or sell, we have called *economic organisms*. Economic life

15

consists very largely of the behavior and interactions of these organisms.

Types of Economic Organisms

Let us now return to Mrs. Jones. She buys butter in her capacity as a housewife, not in order to sell it again but in order to consume it. The butter finds its ultimate end and goal on the table of the Jones family. When the storekeeper originally bought the butter, however, he bought it not for his own use but in order to sell it again. Moreover, we may suppose that he sold the butter to Mrs. Jones for a price somewhat higher than the price he paid for it. The difference between the two prices represents something else which he has sold to Mrs. Jones—his *services* as a retailer, which he did not buy from anyone else. It seems here as if there are three fairly distinct classes of economic organisms.

Firms. First, there are organisms such as stores, manufacturing companies, and so on, which buy in order to sell again, and which sell in order to be able to buy again with the money received. These are called *firms,* or *enterprises.*

Ultimate Consumers. Then there are organisms which buy not in order to sell again but in order to consume and enjoy; families and orphanages fall in this class. These are the *ultimate consumers.*

Original Producers. There are also organisms which sell what they have not bought but have produced themselves. The workman who sells his labor, the landowner or mineowner who sells the use of his land or his mines, fall in that class. These may be called the *original producers.* There is bound to be some difficulty of terminology here, for the word "producer" is frequently associated with a certain type of *firm.* By an original producer, however, we mean not a firm in the strict sense of the word but the seller of a commodity or a service which is the source of the seller's net income. In some cases the commodity sold by an original producer is sold directly, as when a worker sells his labor. In other cases the commodity is sold indirectly, as when an independent storekeeper "sells" his services by selling goods at a price higher than the price he paid for them.

Individuals Have More Than One Capacity

Every individual who has to spend money in the purchase of commodities for consumption is an ultimate consumer. Every individual who receives a money income not derived from gift or charity is also an original producer in the sense used above. We obtain our personal income by selling something we have not previously bought, such as the services of our bodies or the services of other property which we own. Many individuals also act as representatives of firms as well as original consumers or original producers. A farmer, for instance, will buy food for his cattle as a representative of his business or firm. In this case it is the "farm" rather than the farmer which makes the exchange. He will buy food for himself and his family in his capacity as an ultimate consumer. He will supply labor, and may supply land, to his farm in his capacity as an original producer. In practice, he may not keep separate accounts for these three capacities. In principle, however, we must keep the distinction clear between the accounts of the farm as a business and the accounts of the farmer as a supplier of labor or land to the farm and as a consumer.

Types of Exchanges

We can now distinguish several types of exchanges, according to the types of economic organisms participating in them. First, there are exchanges between ultimate consumers, as when two boys swap marbles for stamps in the schoolyard, or when Mrs. Jones exchanges some of her surplus butter with Mrs. Smith next door for some of Mrs. Smith's surplus bread. These exchanges are not very important. Indeed, they can only be regarded as accidental, for if Mrs. Jones bought her butter with the *intention* of selling it to Mrs. Smith she would be acting as a firm and not as an ultimate consumer at all.

The most important exchanges are those between firms, those between firms and ultimate consumers, and those between firms and original producers. When the storekeeper buys butter from a wholesaler, there is an exchange between firms. When Mrs. Jones buys butter from the store, there is an exchange between a firm and an ultimate consumer. When the store buys the services of a clerk, there is an exchange between a firm and an original producer. There may also be exchanges between ultimate consumers and original producers, as when Mrs. Jones hires a man to mow the lawn. These exchanges, while common, do not account for a very large proportion of things exchanged. In the great majority of cases a firm, or a series of firms, acts as an intermediary between the original producer and the ultimate consumer.

What Is Exchanged?

This bring us to our next question: *What* is exchanged? Again the answer might seem to be simple, but again it proves to be more complicated than it looks at first sight. In the vast majority of the exchanges with which we are familiar the objects exchanged are physical goods or services on the one side, and money—dollars and cents—on the other side. An exchange in which both the things exchanged are physical goods or services is called a *barter* exchange. This is occasionally found in the schoolyard or across the garden wall, but it is not important except in primitive society. About the only important examples of barter exchanges in the modern world are those involved in sharecropping, in which the landowner exchanges the services of land for a part of the physical crop, and those in certain international agreements where there is direct bartering—for instance, of Brazilian coffee for German machinery.

A Commodity as a "Bundle of Services" of Original Agents Paid for Out of the Price

To return to our original example. Mrs. Jones, who has just bought her two pounds of butter, now has $1.60 *less* than she had before, and two pounds of butter *more* than she had before, while the storekeeper has $1.60 more than he had before, and two pounds of butter less. But the storekeeper has presumably bought the butter from someone else —a wholesaler, let us say, for $1.20. What he has "really" sold Mrs. Jones, then, is $1.20 worth of "wholesale butter" plus 40 cents' worth of his own retailing services. But of course the wholesaler did not make the butter; he bought it, say, from a creamery for 80 cents, and spent 20 cents for transport and 20 cents for his own expenses. So what Mrs. Jones has bought is evidently 80 cents' worth of butter-at-the-creamery, plus 20 cents' worth of transport service, plus 20 cents' worth of wholesaler service, plus 40 cents' worth of retailer service. But do we even stop there? The creamery perhaps paid the farmer 70 cents for milk, and paid 10 cents for manufacturing. The farmer, in producing the milk, spent perhaps 25 cents for feed, 10 cents for his cows, 15 cents for hired labor, and 20 cents for his own labor. It seems, therefore, that what Mrs. Jones has "really" bought is not merely $1.60 worth of butter, but 40 cents' worth of retailing, 20 cents' worth of wholesaling, 20 cents' worth of transport, 10 cents' worth of buttermaking, 25 cents' worth of cattle feed, 10 cents' worth of the using up of cows, 15 cents' worth of hired farm labor, and 20 cents' worth of farmer's labor. Mrs. Jones would indeed be surprised to learn that all this—and more—was wrapped up in that innocent package of butter. However, a moment's reflection will show us that, in one sense at least, what we are "really" buying when we buy any commodity is a little bit of the services of all the retailers, wholesalers, transport workers, stevedores, processors, farmers, miners, and what not that have gone to make it up, together with the services of all the land and equipment which they have used, and of all the managers who have organized them. Some of these services may have been performed at the moment of purchase, some a few days before, some weeks, some éven years or decades before.

We can look at the same phenomenon in another way. Consider not the butter but the $1.60. Who gets the $1.60? In the first instance, of course, it goes to the storekeeper, but it does not all stay with him. He keeps 40 cents of it to pay for the services which he has performed, and passes on $1.20 cents to the wholesaler, who in turn keeps his share and passes the rest on to the transporter, and so back to the creamery, the farmer, the farm laborer, the landlord, and all the other people involved.

All Exchanges Can Be Analyzed into the Exchange of Services for Services

Even now we have not finished. Where did the $1.60 *come from?* Where did Mrs. Jones get it? The answer may be, of course, from her husband. But still the question remains, how did Mr. Jones get the $1.60? Perhaps he earned it by selling his services as a barber. Our simple exchange, therefore, of $1.60 for two pounds of butter seems to have been resolved into an exchange of $1.60 worth of haircutting against $1.60 worth of a remarkable collection of services of all kinds of original producers, ranging from retailers to landowners. Thus it seems that all exchanges are in a sense "barter" exchanges between original producers, effected through the intermediary of firms of all descriptions, and through the operations of the peculiar stuff known as *money.*

Money as a "Veil"

This was what the older economists meant when they spoke of money as a "veil" that hid the real operations of the economic system. The too rigorous adoption of this point of view led them to neglect the very important effects which money itself has on the economic system. Nevertheless, the concept of a "barter system" is useful in avoiding certain crude fallacies which are frequently made by politicians and others unversed in thinking about society. We must get a picture of the economic order as a system in which each individual exchanges his services, or the services of things he owns, for the services of other people, or of the things they own, even though these services may not be direct but may be wrapped up in the parcels that we call "goods."

Specialization Is a Prerequisite of Exchange

This brings us to another very important proposition concerning exchange. It is clear that no exchange could take place if everyone had, or made, the same things. If there were only one commodity—say, butter—there would be no exchange, for obviously it would be silly to exchange butter for butter. It is possible to imagine a society in which each family owns a plot of land on which they raise all their own food, make all their own clothes, dig or cut all their own fuel, and entertain themselves with all their own songs. In such a society, where each family lived like the Swiss Family Robinson, there would be no exchange in the ordinary sense of the term. There would be for each family a choice of alternatives in production, in many ways analogous to exchange. They might, for instance, have to give up building a house in order to find the time to build a boat, and we might perhaps say that the house they might have had is in a sense "exchanged" for the boat which they in fact make. But exchange in the sense of a transaction between two parties always implies a difference in the possessions or abilities of the parties concerned. Unless different individuals possess different things, the exchange of goods is impossible, or at least futile. Unless different individuals perform different tasks, the exchange of services is impossible.

This doing of different things is called *specialization,* and it plays a very important part in economic development. Instead of each sitting under his own vine and his own fig tree, caring for all his own wants by himself, as soon as there is anything we can call society at all, one man will begin to grow vines and another to grow figs, and they will exchange wine for figs. Even in savage societies there are specialized crafts—the tentmaker, the fisherman, the hunter, the weaver. In complex societies there are thousands of different occupations—some 200,-000 in the United States alone! Each one of these occupations means that somebody is devoting the bulk of his available time to a single form of service, and exchanging that service, or its products, for the products or services of innumerable other people. One proposition should now be clear: Exchange cannot take place unless there is specialization, for there would be nothing to exchange; but specialization without exchange would be useless, for the tailor would starve and the farmer go naked. *Exchange without specialization is impossible; specialization without exchange is silly.* This is a proposition the im-

portance of which extends far beyond the field usually covered by economics; it applies, for instance, to the question of specialization in
knowledge and discovery. If specialization in the sciences is carried to
the point where exchange of ideas becomes impossible—where each
man is so specialized that he can understand only himself—then specialization has become silly. We need middlemen in the sciences to
perfect the system of exchange of ideas as much as we need them in economic life to facilitate the exchange of goods and services.

The Importance of "Middlemen"

This proposition can be used immediately to explode a common
fallacy—that middlemen, or distributors, are "unproductive." This
fallacy is current in agricultural circles; the farmer frequently feels
that he is the "real producer" because he produces the physical commodity, and consequently he feels that the middlemen and distributors are parasites. But it is no use for the farmer to produce milk if he
cannot exchange that milk for other things. Milk-on-the-farm is a
different commodity from milk-on-the-doorstep, and the people who
get the milk from the farm to the doorstep—and, indeed, the housewife who gets the milk from the doorstep to the pudding—are just
as much "producers" as the man who gets it from the udder to the
bottle. Circumstances may arise, of course, in which middlemen are
too well paid for the services which they render, but this does not
mean that these services are valueless.

Why Do People Exchange? Because Both Parties Benefit

There remains the third question: *Why* do people exchange? The
answer is simple: because people want to exchange—that is, of course,
if there is no compulsion present. Ruling out difficult cases like the
payment of taxes or the granting of forced loans where the exchange
is not free, we can formulate the proposition that no exchange will
take place unless both parties to it feel, at the time, that they will
benefit from it. Unless Mrs. Jones feels that she wants two pounds of
butter more than she wants $1.60, and unless the storekeeper feels that
he wants $1.60 more than he wants two pounds of butter, the exchange
will not take place. Even if one party thinks he will benefit and the
other party does not, there will be no exchange, for though an offer
may be made it will be refused. An exchange, therefore, is not so
much an equality (two pounds of butter = $1.60) as *two inequalities*.
Mrs. Jones thinks two pounds of butter are worth more to her than

$1.60, and the storekeeper thinks that $1.60 is worth more to him than two pounds of butter.[1]

How Can Both Parties Benefit? Because of Differences in Valuation

The question at once arises: How can this be? How is it possible for something to be "worth more" to one person than to another? We shall find the answer in a proposition which forms one of the primary axioms of economic analysis. Stated in a rather crude, non-mathematical form it is as follows: The more of anything we have (under the condition that the quantities of all the other things we have remain the same), the less we want more of it.[2] If we had only two ounces of sugar a week, we should greatly welcome an extra ounce. If, however, we had a hundred ounces of sugar a week, an extra ounce would make very little difference to us. The more sugar we have, the less we want an extra ounce of it. The less sugar we have, the more we want an extra ounce of it. This again is an obvious truth, once it is stated. Again, the failure to understand it causes trouble and confusion.

Fallacy of "Intrinsic Value"

Popular economic discussion often assumes that things have an "intrinsic" worth. As soon as we perceive the truth of the above proposition, however, it becomes clear that what a thing is worth to us depends on how much of it we have, and that therefore the "worth" is not anything "in" a commodity. It is not a physical property of an object like weight or volume, but is simply "how we feel about it." Things are "valuable" because somebody thinks they are, and for no other reason whatever. This is true, as we shall see, even of gold—a commodity which people are inclined to think has an "intrinsic" value. Gold, like everything else, is valuable only because people think it is.

---

[1] This proposition may seem almost too obvious to be worth stating, but it is surprising what trouble has been caused in economic thought by the failure to realize its truth. Thus Karl Marx argued that as an exchange is an equation (e.g., $1.60 = 2$ lbs. butter), the two things that are equal must have a common attribute. If a pound of apples is equal to a pound of oranges, we mean that they are equal in respect to some attribute common to both—in this case, weight. If, then, $1.60 is equal to two pounds of butter in "value," there must be some attribute, common to them both, which gives them their value. The common attribute, he decided, was labor. This error, which runs through the whole "classical" school of economics, might have been avoided had there been a more adequate interpretation of the phenomenon of exchange.

[2] This is the principle which usually goes under the name of the "law of diminishing marginal utility." As, however, the mathematical discussion of this problem presents some difficulty, it will be reserved for a later chapter (Chapter 32).

Exchange Possible, Even Where People Have Identical Tastes, Where Quantities Possessed Differ

We can now see how exchange can be possible, even between people who have identical tastes. Suppose Mrs. Jones has laid in a great deal of butter, and Mrs. Smith next door has laid in a great deal of bread, and all the shops are shut. Then we may imagine Mrs. Jones knocking at the Smiths' back door and asking, "Will you give me a loaf of bread for a pound of butter?" Mrs. Smith replies that she would be delighted. *Because* Mrs. Jones has a lot of butter, the loss of a pound does not mean a great deal to her. *Because* she does not have very much bread, an extra loaf of bread *does* mean a good deal to her. So she is willing to give up a pound of butter, which she does not want very much, for a loaf of bread, which she wants rather more. Mrs. Smith is in the opposite situation. Because she has so little butter, an extra pound means a great deal to her. Because she has so much bread, one loaf less means very little. Consequently, she also is glad to make the exchange, and to give up the loaf which she wants little for the butter which she wants more. We thus see how, even if Mrs. Jones and Mrs. Smith were identical in their *tastes* regarding bread and butter, they might still find exchange desirable if they possessed at the start different quantities of the things to be exchanged.

How Specialization Gives Rise to Exchange

There should now be no difficulty in seeing exactly why exchange takes place in economic life generally. Because each individual is specialized, if there were no exchange he would have a large quantity of the thing in which he specializes. The farmer's barns would burst with corn, the tailor's shelves be stuffed with suits. Because, therefore, we each have a relatively large quantity of the things in which we specialize, we are eager to get rid of them in exchange for the other things which we do not have, just as Mrs. Jones was eager to get rid of some of the butter of which she had plenty for the bread of which she had little. A dairy farmer and a baker are perpetually in the position of Mrs. Jones and Mrs. Smith, for one has a continual surplus of butter, the other a continual surplus of bread. This does not mean, of course, that we must exchange everything we have, for neither exchange nor specialization is usually carried to the extreme. The dairy farmer will keep some butter for his own use; the baker will keep some bread. Exchange will stop when either of the parties feels that the loss involved in giving up a little more of what he has is just balanced by the gain involved in getting a little more of the thing received in exchange. Mrs. Jones will be willing to go on exchanging butter for bread as long as she feels that an extra loaf of bread is worth more to her than the butter she gives for it. As she goes on exchanging she finds her stock of butter dwindling and her stock of bread increasing. This means that extra butter means more to her and extra bread less, so that the moment will soon arrive when the additional bread ceases to mean more to her than the relinquished butter. At that moment she will say to Mrs. Smith (unless, of course, Mrs. Smith has anticipated her), "Thank you, I think that's all I want now" and the exchange will stop.

But Why Do We Specialize?

Thus, if we have specialization, we shall also have exchange. We have not yet answered the question: Why do we have specialization? Why do we bother with this extraordinarily complex system of exchange? Why do we not each cultivate our own garden and provide for our own wants directly by our own labor? Such is largely the case in savage society. Even in the feudal period each village grew its own food, brewed its own drinks, made its own clothes, and built its own houses. Today, even our breakfast table is loaded with products from all over the world, and many of the things that our grandparents did for themselves are now done for us by other people. Mother no longer cuts father's hair, and she sends out the wash to the laundry.

Because Specialization Makes Us Richer. A general answer to this question is, of course, that by specialization and exchange of the specialized products we can satisfy our wants better than if we all lived like Robinson Crusoe. This fact was observed by the founder of economics, Adam Smith. Popular recognition of the principle can be seen in the proverb "Jack of all trades and master of none." If there are two castaways on a desert island instead of one, specialization will soon begin. Each will find that there are certain tasks in which he excels, and each will specialize in these tasks and perform them for both. One may be more successful at fishing than the other; he will catch enough fish for both. The other may be more successful in building huts; he will build huts for both. Thus they will both have more fish and better huts than if each tried to catch fish and built a hut for his own use. Exactly the same principle applies in a more complex form to any society. If we all lived like Robinson Crusoe we should all be extremely poor. It is only because we have this complex system of specialization and exchange that we can enjoy the conveniences and luxuries of modern life.

Two Kinds of Specialization

1. *Of Products.* Specialization takes two forms: the specialization of *products,* which we may call external specialization, and the specialization of *processes,* which we may call internal specialization. We could imagine a society in which each man specialized in making a given product but in which each man performed all the processes necessary for its production. Even today that is approximately true of some occupations. A farmer, for instance, often performs almost all the operations connected with the production of his products: he raises seed, sows it, cultivates the soil, reaps his crop, stores it, feeds it to his cows, milks his cows, and bottles their milk. Such external specialization is the first to arise, and this in itself, of course, is sufficient to bring about exchange.

2. *Of Processes.* In modern industrial society, however, another kind of specialization is important, in which a man confines himself not merely to the production of a single product but to a single *operation* in that production. The automobile industry is a good example of this internal specialization. Each worker in an automobile plant performs a single, simple task and consequently becomes highly proficient at it. By "mass production" in this way we can produce a great many more automobiles than we could if one man tried to perform all the operations necessary in their production. Internal specialization still involves exchange, but the thing exchanged is not a product which the individual makes, but a service which he renders. Mr. Smith, who works in the automobile factory, exchanges, in effect, with society at large a certain quantity of his service of screwing nuts for the food, clothing, and other consumables which he buys with his wages.

The Principle of the Best Alternative

The general principle governing exchange and specialization may be called the *principle of the best alternative.* It may be stated roughly thus: In his endeavor to obtain the commodities he desires, an individual has two possible alternatives. He can either produce the commodities for himself directly, or he can produce some other commodity and exchange it for what he wants. Which alternative he will choose will depend on which is the easier way of getting the commodity he wants, for it is the easier way that he will follow.

Exchange Is Indirect Production

It is important to realize that exchange is an *alternative way* of producing something. If I want a suit of clothes I can either buy the cloth and make the suit myself or I can earn money (by performing some services for society) and pay a tailor to make the suit for me. The first would be direct production; the second would be production through exchange. Instead of spending my time and energies on making a suit myself, I would do something else with my time and energies and exchange that "something else," through the mechanism of money, for the suit I want. If I am an indifferent tailor, I may find that by working for a hundred hours I could make myself a rather unsatisfactory suit of clothes. However, by working for a hundred hours at the occupation in which I am skilled—say, haircutting—I could earn perhaps $120 with which I could pay a tailor to make me *two* suits of clothes of much better cut and quality than I could make by myself. In this case it is obvious that production through exchange is much more effective than direct production. On the other hand, I would be unlikely to go to a dentist to have my teeth cleaned every morning, even though he might clean them more quickly and more efficiently than I could myself, because I would feel that to earn the money with which to pay the dentist I would have to put in more time and effort than is necessary to clean my teeth for myself.

The Principle of Comparative Advantage

In this connection it is important to notice that specialization and exchange will take place even in the case of an individual who could produce the commodity obtained in exchange more efficiently than the person from whom he obtains it. For instance, a doctor who is an excellent gardener may very well prefer to employ a hired man who as a gardener is inferior to himself, because thereby he can devote more time to his medical practice. Suppose that the doctor could keep his garden in good shape by working for one hour a day, and that the hired man took three hours to do the same amount of gardening. If the hired man was paid $1 an hour and the doctor earned $10 an hour, it might still pay the doctor to work at his profession for the hour which he otherwise might have spent in the garden, and to pay the hired man $3 for his three hours of work. In that case, by working at his profession instead of in the garden the doctor would gain $7. To put the same problem in another way: the doctor could do his gardening in an hour if he worked at it directly. By working at his profession, however, for eighteen minutes, he will have earned enough to pay for three hours of the hired man's time. Consequently he can do his gardening in eighteen minutes by staying in his office, as against the hour it would take him if he were out in the garden itself! In this particular case the situation may be complicated by the fact that the doctor may like gardening for its own sake. But this complication does not affect the fundamental principle. If the doctor is fond of gardening he may prefer an hour of direct gardening to eighteen minutes of indirect gardening, but it remains true that for him medical practice may be an indirect method of horticulture.

Extent of Specialization Depends on the Extent of the Market

There is one more proposition to state concerning specialization and exchange. It is that the *extent* of specialization depends on the ease with which things can be exchanged, or, as it has been phrased, by the "extent of the market."[3] The main things affecting the ease with which things are exchanged are first, the density of the human population, and second, the ease or difficulty of transportation. Obviously, if large numbers of people are closely packed together, and if the means of transportation of commodities and of persons are good, it will be easier to make exchanges than it would be among a widely scattered population separated by high mountains and deserts. Robinson Crusoe does not specialize, only because the means of transportation between him and the outside world do not exist. In a remote mountain village where transportation is difficult and the population is small, specialization will not be carried on as far as it is in a great city like New York. We should not expect to find economists, opticians, gem cutters, or patent lawyers in a mountain community in Tennessee. We should expect to find them in New York City. A highly specialized occupation can exist only where its products are available to a large number of people, for the average quantity of the product taken by any individual is small. An eye specialist, for instance, might find a comfortable practice in a community of 100,000 people when he would be idle most of the time in a community of 5000.

Specialization and Transportation

Any improvement in the means of communication will, therefore, probably result in an extension of the degree of specialization and in the volume of exchanges. The great cities of the present day owe their existence to the development of our world system of transportation. London and New York, for instance, could not exist unless they could draw food supplies from all over the world, and unless they could send products all over the world in return. Even Robinson Crusoe would probably begin to specialize in the production and export of

[3] Adam Smith, *The Wealth of Nations,* Book 1, Chapter 3.

coconuts if communications were established between his island and the outside world.

The Ratio of Exchange and Alternative Cost

From the principle of the best alternative can be deduced the general law which governs the ratio of exchange between commodities in a society where there are no hindrances to the movement of resources between various occupations and employments. This law states that the ratio of exchange of two commodities in the market always tends to be equal to the ratio of the quantities which can be produced by an identical expenditure of economic resources. This latter ratio is frequently called the "alternative cost" ratio. Suppose, for instance, that with a given quantity of resources a society could produce either 50 bushels of wheat or 1 ton of steel. Then the alternative cost of steel in terms of wheat is $\frac{1}{50}$ tons per bushel, and the alternative cost of wheat in terms of steel is 50 bushels per ton, meaning that, given the full employment of resources, an extra 50 bushels of wheat can only be produced at the cost of *not* producing 1 ton of steel, and an extra ton of steel can be produced only at the cost of not producing 50 bushels of wheat. The society has the *alternative,* with a given unit of resources, either to produce 50 bushels of wheat or 1 ton of steel; thus the "cost" of producing 1 ton of steel is the 50 bushels of wheat that had to be given up in order to produce the steel, and the "cost" of producing 50 bushels of wheat is the ton of steel that could not be produced by the resources used in producing wheat.

If then the alternative cost of wheat in terms of steel is 50 bushels per ton, it can be shown that provided resources can easily be shifted from wheat production to steel production, the market prices of wheat and steel must be in the proportion of 50 bushels to 1 ton. For if it were possible to exchange wheat for steel in the market at a ratio of, say, 60 bushels to 1 ton, people could get more wheat with a unit of resources by producing steel and exchanging it for wheat than by producing wheat directly. In this case by direct production a unit of resources would only yield 50 bushels of wheat, but by employing the resources in making a ton of steel and exchanging it for wheat in the market, 60 bushels of wheat could be obtained. It is evident that in such a situation people would abandon wheat growing and turn their resources into steel production. This very movement of resources, however, by creating a scarcity of wheat would raise its price, and by creating a surplus of steel would lower its price; and this movement would go on until the ratio of exchange in the market was equal to

50 bushels per ton, at which point there would be no advantage in transferring resources from wheat to steel production and the movement would cease. Similarly, if the price in the market were 40 bushels per ton when the alternative cost was 50 bushels per ton, it would pay to divert resources into the wheat industry, and purchase steel with the wheat, rather than to make steel directly. The wheat industry will grow, and the price of wheat fall, and the steel industry will decline, and the price of steel rise, until once more the market ratios are 50 bushels per ton.

Assumptions Under Which Ratio of Exchange Equals Alternative Cost

The extremely abstract assumptions of the above argument must be noted carefully. It assumes full employment and perfect mobility of resources. It is, therefore, a long-run argument, and the tendency for market prices to be equal to alternative costs is only a long-run tendency. If, indeed, there are obstacles to the movement of resources from one occupation to another, whether due to monopoly, to distance, to regulation, or any other cause, then the adjustment of market prices to alternative costs may be delayed indefinitely. Nevertheless, the principle is not shaken—the tendency exists, even if the resistance to it is too great for any movement to take place. The absence of a current between two points does not indicate an absence of potential difference between them, as long as there is great resistance to the passage of a current. It is because the resistance to the transfer of resources is likely to be smaller over long periods than over short periods that we refer to the above tendency as "long-run."

It should be observed that the principle of the equality of price with alternative cost does not assume that the alternative cost ratios are constant. It is quite possible for the adjustments to be made both in market price and in alternative cost. Thus in the above example, where the market price is assumed to be 60 bushels per ton and the alternative cost ratio 50 bushels per ton, the movement of resources from wheat into steel productions may well have a twofold effect. Not only will the market price of steel in terms of wheat fall to 59, 58, 57 bushels per ton, but it is quite possible that the alternative cost will rise from 50 bushels per ton to 51, 52, 53, as the movement of resources goes on. In the diminution of wheat production the worst wheat-growing lands and the least efficient farms will be abandoned first, and hence wheat production will concentrate more and more in more efficient hands, and a unit of resources will produce more and more wheat as production declines. In steel production, on the other hand, the expansion of production may lead to smaller efficiency as worse ores and less suitable labor have to be employed; therefore, as the industry expands, a unit of resources will produce less and less. As long as the market ratio differs from the alternative cost ratio, and resources are mobile, the movement will go on; it is only when these two ratios are equal—say, at 54 bushels per ton—that the movement will stop. In the example it was assumed that an expansion of an industry lowered and its contraction raised the efficiency of the use of resources, but even this assumption is not necessary. Even if the reverse were true, it would still be the case that a divergence between market price and alternative cost would tend to bring about a movement of resources that would lessen this divergence.

QUESTIONS AND EXERCISES

1. Some economists have argued that since nothing was *created* in an act of exchange (as exchange merely means a change in ownership of commodities already in existence), exchange could not add to wealth. Do you think this is correct? If not, how would you answer this argument?
2. State and prove at least five propositions concerning exchange and specialization.
3. What is meant by the statement that an exchange in which money is one (or both) of the things exchanged is not a *complete* exchange? What is a complete exchange?
4. How would you classify the following exchanges according to the character of the economic organisms performing the exchanges?
   a. The hiring of a teacher by a school.
   b. The purchase of a piece of candy by a schoolboy.
   c. The purchase of books by a school.
   d. The exchange of tops for whistles by two schoolboys.
   e. The renting of a stream to a fisherman.
5. Why do some people shave themselves, while some have themselves shaved by a barber?
6. Does the wealth of a person affect the proportion of real income obtained by exchange, i.e., would you expect a wealthy person to do more or less for himself than a poor person?
7. Would you expect to find that a greater proportion of things made are sold (exchanged) in a wealthy society than in a poor one?
8. Danish butter producers in normal times eat very little butter. They use margarine to spread on their bread although they produce some of the best butter in the world. Is this stupid behavior? Or is there a good reason for it?
9. The wheat farmer is the product of the railroad and the steamship. Discuss.

CHAPTER 3

SOME APPLICATIONS OF THE
ELEMENTARY THEORY OF EXCHANGE

Economic Conflict. Community of Interest in the Fact of Exchange

One important practical application of the principles of the last chapter is to the discussion of the problem of economic *conflict*. Is there any possibility of conflict arising in exchange? How are people's interests affected by the act of exchange or by the quantities arising therefrom? We have seen that an exchange cannot take place unless both parties gain, or at least think they gain. There is evidently, therefore, a certain community of interest in exchange. This in itself is an important conclusion, for it is commonly believed that in trade—especially in international trade—one party must gain and the other party must lose. But if one party to a prospective exchange thinks he will lose by it, he will not enter into the exchange at all. This is true even in an exchange which is commonly regarded as an occasion for conflict—the exchange of labor for money between employers and employed. Even here there is a community of interest in the exchange in the sense that unless both parties believe themselves to be benefited, the exchange will not take place. A wage bargain cannot be struck, in the absence of coercion, unless the employer prefers buying the labor to buying any of the other things for which he could spend the money, and unless the worker prefers to spend his time working for a wage rather than in any other way.

Conflict of Interest About the Ratio of Exchange: The Range of Mutual Benefit

But this is not the whole of the matter. There may be a community of interest in the *fact* of exchange. There is always a conflict of interest, except in some rare cases, about the *ratio* of exchange—i.e., about the *price,* the terms on which the things are exchanged. Generally speak-

31

ing, in the case of any given exchange there is a certain range of prices within which the exchange will take place but outside of which one of the parties will feel that he does not benefit by the exchange. To return to our friends Mrs. Jones and the storekeeper. There must be some price for butter *above* which Mrs. Jones will not buy; suppose

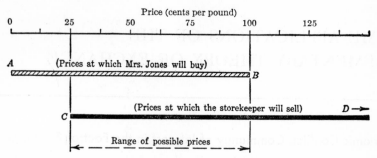

FIG. 1.   The Range of Mutual Benefit.

this is $1 per pound. At any price below $1 Mrs. Jones will buy this particular two pounds of butter, but at any price above it she will not. There is also some price for butter *below* which the storekeeper will not think it worth his while to sell; at any price below, say, 25 cents per pound he will prefer to keep the butter in his shop, or keep it for his own use. Consequently, at a price below 25 cents or above $1 per pound this particular transaction cannot take place. At any price between 25 cents and $1 per pound the transaction may take place, as both parties feel they benefit. We may represent this situation diagrammatically as in Fig. 1. The line *AB* represents the prices at which Mrs. Jones is willing to buy the two pounds of butter in question; the line *CD* represents the prices at which the storekeeper is willing to sell. Only at those prices where the lines overlap, between *C* and *B*, is an exchange possible, for only at those prices will both parties feel that they gain. The *amount by which* the parties to the exchange feel that they gain depends, however, upon exactly *where* the price falls within this range. If the price is $1 a pound, Mrs. Jones will feel that she barely gains anything by the exchange, and the storekeeper will gain much more than the minimum which would persuade him to make the exchange. If the price is 25 cents a pound, Mrs. Jones will gain greatly by the exchange while the storekeeper will feel that it is only just worth while making. Clearly, the nearer the price is to 25 cents a pound, the more will Mrs. Jones gain by the exchange, and the less will the storekeeper gain. The nearer the price is to $1 a pound, the more the storekeeper will gain and the less Mrs. Jones will gain. Mrs. Jones, therefore, who is buying, wants the price to be as low as possible, and the storekeeper, who is selling, wants it to be as high as possible.

Most Economic Conflicts Are of This Type.   This principle applies to any exchange whatever and accounts for a large part of the real conflict of interest in economic life. Thus in the exchange between employers and employed, even though both benefit, the worker will benefit more if the wage is high, the employer more if the wage is low. In the exchange of the products of any one industry—say, farming—the producer wants a high price, the consumer wants a low price, even though over a wide range of prices, the farmer prefers to sell his crops rather than to try to spend his time making manufactured goods at home, and the industrial population prefers to sell its products rather than to try to grow its food in its own back yards.

"Vertical" and "Horizontal" Conflicts

Just as we classified exchanges according to the character of the exchangers involved, so we can classify conflicts in exchange. Corresponding to exchanges between firms and original producers, especially workers, we have what is usually called the "class" conflict—the conflict, for instance, between the working class, interested in high wages, and the employing class, interested in low wages. Corresponding to exchanges between ultimate producers and ultimate consumers are what may be called "vertical" conflicts of interest. Thus all the people concerned with coal mining—miners, operators, owners—have a common interest in maintaining a high price for coal, as compared with all people not in the mining industry, who have a common interest in keeping the price of coal low. These vertical, or group, conflicts may be in practice much more important than the "horizontal," or class, conflicts. Very few acts or lines of policy will affect wages or profits as a whole, but it is easy to organize lines of action which will affect *particular* prices, *particular* wages, or *particular* profits. The organization of monopolies is one of the principal weapons of this group conflict.

Tariffs as an Example.   Tariff policy is also intimately bound up with group conflict. A duty on the import of shoes may improve the lot of people in the shoe industry, as it may, at least for a time, enable them to raise the price at which they can sell shoes. This increase in the price of shoes, however, will injure all the people who buy shoes.

Here is a clear conflict of interest between a "group" in society—all those concerned with making shoes—and those outside the group. The groups are frequently well organized and able to exercise political pressure, but the "people outside the group," i.e., everybody else, are not organized—everybody being nobody in particular! Consequently, a great deal of legislation is passed which makes us on the whole poorer because it makes a small group richer. The effect on the small group is obvious, and the small group is organized to exert pressure on legislatures. The effect on the rest of us is diffuse and not always immediately apparent, and so does not influence lawmakers as it should.

The Determination of Price: "Higgling"

We have seen that in most acts of exchange there is a certain *range* of prices within which the exchange may take place. The question naturally arises: What determines the exact position of the price within this range? In our example we supposed the price of butter to be 80 cents a pound, although we saw that even if it were as high as $1 or as low as 25 cents the exchange would still take place. Why, then, should not the price of butter be 90, or 50, or 40 cents a pound instead of 80? The rest of this book is little more than an attempt to answer this question. However, there are one or two things that we may say about it now. One answer is of course that the price may be decided by "higgling and bargaining."

Mrs. Jones might come into the shop, see the two pounds of butter nicely wrapped on the counter, and say to the storekeeper, "That's a nice package of butter you have there; I'll give you 80 cents for it." Now the storekeeper would be willing, if necessary, to sell the butter for 80 cents (i.e., 40 cents a pound), but of course he would like to get more for it if he could. So, suspecting that Mrs. Jones would give more for it if pressed, he might say, "I'm sorry, Mrs. Jones, but I couldn't think of selling it under $2 this morning." Mrs. Jones' reply might be, "Don't be absurd; I'll give you $1.20 for it," and the storekeeper again might say, "Well, I'll come down to $1.80, but no further." Mrs. Jones might answer, "A dollar fifty is absolutely the limit," and the storekeeper might follow with, "I could let you have it for $1.70 and no less." Then Mrs. Jones might say, "Let's split the difference and call it $1.60," and the storekeeper would say, "Done!" A few things are sold in this way, even in western countries—antiques and rugs, for instance. In Oriental countries a great many more things are sold thus; and although to us it may sound ridiculous to higgle for butter in the manner described above, in some countries even the ordinary day-today purchases are made in this way. Even two or three hundred years ago the practice of higgling was much commoner in western countries.

Collective Bargaining

Perhaps the most important example of higgling today is that known as "collective bargaining." Collective bargaining is the name given to the process of deciding a price between *organized* groups of buyers and sellers. It is found when a trade union bargains with an employers' association or even with a single employer. In this case the trade union is "selling" a certain "commodity"—the labor of its members—which the employers are buying. The object of the collective bargain is to set a price which will prevail in all purchases of labor of the type in question. Collective bargaining is also to be found between producers of raw materials and the users of those raw materials. In the milk industry, for example, we frequently find collective bargaining between the organized farmers who sell milk and the organized distributors who buy it. In this case also the purpose of the bargain is to determine the price at which all the individual sales shall be made. The opposite of collective bargaining is, of course, individual bargaining, in which each individual buyer or seller makes his own arrangements as to the price and the other terms on which the transaction shall be made.

Conditions of Settlement of a Collective Bargain. The process of higgling just outlined is essentially similar to what occurs when collective bargains are made. It may happen that the highest price at which one party will buy is less than the lowest price at which the other party will sell. Under those conditions no bargain will be effected and there will be a "strike," or else a breakdown of collective bargaining altogether. If the highest wage that an employer would pay were $1.60 an hour, and if the lowest wage that a trade union would accept were $1.80 an hour, it is clear that no settlement would be reached. Either there would be no exchange at all (i.e., a strike) or the men would go behind the back of the trade union and make individual bargains with the employer. If the men remained loyal to the union, the strike would go on until one or other of the parties changed its mind about its extreme price. In this case the strike might go on until either the employer raised the highest wage that he was willing to pay to $1.80 an hour or more or the union lowered the lowest wage at which the men were willing to work to $1.60 an hour or less—or, of course, until both made a corresponding shift.

The Custom of the Fixed Price

We see, therefore, that the business of higgling forms an important part of our method of determining prices. Nevertheless, in most of our ordinary transactions higgling plays no part. Naturally we ask, "Why is this?" One possible answer is: custom. It is customary for most sellers to set a fixed price at which they are willing to sell, to make that price known beforehand publicly so that all potential buyers know it, and then to allow the buyers to take advantage of the price or not, as they wish. This custom originated partly as a result of a moral feeling against the appearance of lying and cheating which is always present in higgling. The early Quakers, for instance, in the seventeenth century set a fixed price for their goods and refused to higgle about the price, for they felt that to ask a price at first which was higher than the price they expected to receive was untruthful. But the spread of the custom was undoubtedly due to the fact that higgling is for most people a troublesome waste of time. People preferred to deal with storekeepers who did not higgle but set a fixed price at which the customer could buy or not as he pleased. Gradually, therefore, the custom became almost universal, so much so, in fact, that we now seldom realize how much a matter of comparatively recent habit it is.

Many Buyers and Sellers

As a general rule, the custom of the fixed or "quoted" price can flourish only where there is a large number of buyers or sellers. Higgling is a method of determining prices most frequently used where there is only one buyer and one seller in the market, or where, as in the case of collective bargaining, there is an organized group of buyers facing an organized group of sellers. However, a seller who is faced with a large number of potential buyers and repeats his transactions frequently with different buyers is likely to quote a price without higgling. In quoting his price the seller takes account of the prospective volume of sales at the price quoted, and in that sense the buyers assist in determining the price. The buyers' part is not, however, the active part of higgling but the passive part of deciding how much to buy at the set price. This is the situation usually found in retailing, and frequently in manufacturing.

In other markets, notably in the market for standardized agricultural commodities like wheat or cotton, the price is quoted by the buyer. In this case the seller has the option to sell or not to sell at the price quoted, and this power of the sellers again plays a decisive part in determining the price which the buyers will quote. It will be observed that where the custom of a fixed price prevails, it is generally the "middleman" who quotes the price. The consumer at one end of the chain and the "producer" at the other end have the power merely to take or to leave the exchange offered by the middleman, be he retailer or wholesale merchant. This does not mean, however, that the middleman has arbitrary power over prices. If he offers to buy at a price which is "too low," not enough people will offer to sell to him. If he offers to sell at a price which is "too high," not enough people will offer to buy from him. The power of the buyers to refuse to buy, or of the sellers to refuse to sell, is therefore the real factor which determines the price fixed by the middleman.

Auction Sales

An interesting example of a situation in which we have many buyers and a single seller is the auction sale. This is a method of determining prices commonly used in the sale of objects which cannot be standardized, such as cattle, vegetables, wool, or household goods and equipment. In the ordinary type of auction an article is put up for sale by the auctioneer—suppose it is a cow at a cattle auction. The auctioneer then invites "bids" from the people who have come to the auction. He may start at $30; someone in the crowd nods to show that he is willing to buy at that price. Someone else, however, thinks the cow is worth (to him) more than $30; he bids $35, someone else bids $40, and so on until no further bids are received. The cow then goes to the person who has made the last—and therefore the highest—bid.

Determination of Price in an Auction.   It should not be difficult to formulate a principle by which the price is determined in such a sale. The price of any article sold will be the next price above the greatest price which the second most eager buyer will give. This principle may sound a little strange at first, but it should be grasped easily. For any given article put up for sale the buyers can be ranged in the order of their eagerness to buy—their eagerness to buy being measured by the greatest price they are willing to pay for the article. Thus one buyer might be willing to buy the cow at any price below $30, another at any price below $35, another at any price below $40, and so on up the scale until we get to the most eager buyers of all—one who will buy it at any price below, say, $50, and another who will buy it at any price below $60. As the bidding goes on and as the price rises gradually, all the less eager buyers drop out until the price is $50.

when only the two most eager buyers are left. At the next price rise—
say, to $55, if it is the convention to raise the bids by five dollars at a
time—the second most eager buyer, who will buy below $50 but not
above, drops out, leaving only the most eager buyer, to whom the
cow is sold. Notice, however, that the price is not necessarily the
greatest which the most eager buyer would be willing to pay; in this
case he would have been willing to pay $60, but in fact has to pay only
$55, for that is the price which knocks out his nearest competitor.

The Dutch Auction.   An interesting variant of the auction is the
"Dutch auction" in which the bids come down from a high price instead of rising from a low price. Cheap-Jacks in fairs sometimes use
this method. Department stores occasionally use what is essentially
a variant of it by reducing the price of certain goods by so much each
day. In Holland this method of auction is used extensively in the sale
of agricultural commodities. As there organized, it has the advantage
of dispensing with the services of an auctioneer. The buyers sit at
desks facing a dial, like a clock, on which prices are indicated instead
of hours. The sale is begun by starting the hand of the "clock" at
some price well above that which is expected. Every few moments the
hands move to another and lower price. At each buyer's desk there is
a button which will stop the "clock" when pressed. When the hands
move down to a price which he wishes to pay, the buyer presses the
button and so stops the "clock." In this case we may expect the button
to be pushed by the most eager buyer at a price which is just about the
highest he is willing to pay, for in this case the most eager buyer does
not know what prices the other buyers are willing to give. He does
not know, indeed, until he stops the "clock," that he is in fact the most
eager buyer, for each buyer fears that someone may slip in ahead of
him. Thus we might suppose in this case that each buyer has in his
mind a price at which he will bid; one will bid at $60, another at $50,
another at $48, and so on. Suppose the "clock" starts at $80, and ticks
away—$80, $75, $70, $65; still nothing happens. Then at $60 the most
eager buyer pushes the button. He gets the cow; the others do not.
The most eager buyer does not wait till the price falls to $55, because
he is afraid some other buyer will get in first.

Small Range of Price in an Auction.   In both these cases there is
an interesting fact. Although in the case of an exchange between *two*
bargainers the price can lie within a certain range, the actual price
depending only on the relative bargaining skill or bluffing powers of
the two bargainers, in this case, where we have a large number of
buyers, the price appears to be quite definite. There is no range over

which it may vary, or at most only a small range between the highest prices of the most eager and the second most eager buyers. This is a very important result of quite general application. Wherever we have a large number either of buyers or of sellers, or of both, the price will be quite definite—or, as we say, "determinate"—in spite of the fact that there may be, as in the case of the auction, no custom of charging a fixed price.

International Trade

Another important application of the theory of exchange is to problems of international trade. What we have done so far, little as it is, will enable us to clear from our minds a good many of the illusions that cling to this topic. In the first place, we have seen that for society as a whole exchange is essentially the exchange of goods and services for other goods and services. Money is only an intermediary in the "swapping" of the specialized services of producers. This is as true of international trade as it is of domestic trade, and realization of that fact will at least enable us to avoid the spectacular error in the remark (which may be attributed to any politician whom you dislike) that "when we buy from abroad we get the goods but the foreigner gets the money; when we buy at home we have the goods and have the money too."

Result of a Purchase from Abroad. It is, of course, perfectly true that the initial result of a purchase from abroad—let us say, of a bicycle from England—is that some American owns a bicycle which he did not have before and has, say $80, less than he did before, while some Englishman owns one bicycle less and $80 more than he had before. But this, as we can readily see, is not the end of the matter. We are now sufficiently trained in economics to inquire, "What does the Englishman do with the $80?" The answer is, generally speaking, "The same as an American would do with $80." He may, of course, eat it, or put it in a stocking, or burn it, or lose it. These things, however, are unlikely. What we should expect him to do is to spend it. If he spent it on buying a sewing machine from America, obviously, in an international sense, the exchange is complete. The English bicycle has been bought with an American sewing machine, and money has merely played the part of a go-between in this transaction. Actually, the situation is likely to be much more complicated. The Englishman may spend the $80, or its equivalent in English money, on buying an English sewing machine; but then we still have to ask, "What will the English sewing machine seller do with the $80?" Perhaps he will buy coffee with it from Brazil, and then the Brazilian may buy with it a machine from America. Sooner or later, the money will come back to roost; sooner or later, it will buy American goods. In the absence of borrowing or lending, the only way to buy goods or services is with other goods and services; and this applies to international trade as much as to trade in general. In other words, over a long period of time, imports can only be bought with exports. As we shall see, there are a good many exceptions and qualifications to be made in this statement; but if we hang on to it now, it will at least save us from falling into the grosser misunderstandings about the nature of international trade.

APPENDIX TO CHAPTER 3

ADVANCED APPLICATIONS OF THE THEORY OF EXCHANGE

Absolute Advantage in International Trade Is Not Necessary

Another frequent misunderstanding about the nature of international trade is to be found in the statement that "only those things should be imported which we cannot make for ourselves." This would confine international trade to those commodities in which each country had an *absolute* advantage. Thus Brazil would export coffee to the United States only because the United States cannot grow coffee, and the United States would export automobiles to Brazil only if Brazil could not possibly make them herself. Our analysis shows, however, that this is not so. There does not have to be an absolute advantage in order to make trade profitable to both parties. That is to say, in order to get a mutual benefit from trade it is not necessary for each party to be more efficient than the other in making the things that he produces. Any one party will benefit from trade if he can obtain a commodity more cheaply, in terms of the expenditure of his resources, when he "produces" it by exchange than when he produces it directly.

The "Best Alternative" in International Trade

The principle of the "best alternative" applies, therefore, to international trade. England, for instance, can either grow her food directly or make cotton goods and steel and exchange them for food. That is to say, England can "grow" her food in steel and cotton mills as well as on farms. If the price of food in terms of manufactured products is such that England finds that with a given amount of resources she can produce more food in factories than on farms, she will benefit by producing the food in factories; i.e., by specializing in manufactures and exporting them in exchange for food. Thus, suppose that England can produce both wheat and steel more cheaply than Argentina. It might still be to the advantage of each country to specialize and exchange their specialized products, if England could get wheat more cheaply, in terms of real resources, by producing steel and exchanging it for Argentinian wheat, and if at the same time Argentina could get steel more cheaply, in terms of real resources, by producing wheat and exchanging it for English steel. Suppose that with one "unit" of resources England could produce either 50 bushels of wheat or 1 ton of steel. If the price of steel in terms of Argentinian wheat were 50 bushels of wheat per ton of steel it would pay England equally well to obtain wheat either in international trade or by domestic production. With one unit of resources she could obtain 50 bushels of wheat either by growing it at home on farms or by making a ton of steel and exchanging it. But if the price of steel were higher than this—say 60 bushels per ton—she could obtain, with one unit of resources, 60 bushels of wheat by international trade and only 50 bushels by growing it on farms at home. It will pay England to produce wheat by international trade, therefore, as long as the price of steel is greater than 50 bushels per ton. Suppose, now, that in Argentina one unit of resources will produce 40 bushels of wheat or half a ton of steel. In this case it will pay Argentina to produce steel on her wheat farms by international trade, rather than in her foundries, as long as the price of steel is *below* 80 bushels of wheat per ton of steel. If the price of steel is 60 bushels per ton, with one unit of resources Argentina could produce two-thirds of a ton of steel if she grew wheat (40 bushels) and exchanged that for steel at 60 bushels per ton. She would only get half a ton if she produced steel directly.

Comparative Advantage

Under these circumstances it is evident that at any price between 50 bushels per ton and 80 bushels per ton international trade and specialization will benefit both countries, for England will find it cheaper to grow wheat in steel mills than on farms, and Argentina will find it cheaper to make steel on farms than in steel mills. In the above example, however, we have not assumed that England has an "absolute" advantage in steel and Argentina an "absolute" advantage in wheat. Indeed, we assumed that England had an absolute advantage in both wheat and steel, for a unit of resources will produce more steel in England than in Argentina (1 ton as against $\frac{1}{2}$ ton) and more wheat also in England than in Argentina (50 as against 40 bushels). It is, therefore, not the absolute advantage which determines the profitability of trade, but what is called the "comparative advantage." Steel has a greater advantage over wheat in England than it has over wheat in Argentina.

The "Alternative Cost"

The ratio of the quantities of two commodities produced by a unit of resources is called (p. 28) the "alternative cost" of these commodities. In the above example, we assumed that one unit of resources in England would produce 50 bushels of wheat or 1 ton of steel. The "alternative cost" of steel in England is therefore 50 bushels of wheat per ton. That is, in order to produce an extra ton of steel, resources must be used which would otherwise have been able to produce 50 bushels of wheat; in effect, 50 bushels of wheat have been given up in order to obtain the ton of steel. In Argentina, on the other hand, the alternative cost of steel is 80 bushels of wheat per ton. Within the limits set by the alternative costs of steel in the two countries a price can be found at which specialization and trade are profitable to both sides. If the alternative cost of steel in terms of wheat were the same in both countries, no matter what the absolute advantages, trade would not be profitable. Thus, if in England one unit of resources would produce either 50 bushels of wheat or 1 ton of steel, and in Argentina one unit of resources would produce either 25 bushels of wheat or half a ton of steel, no trade would result, although England would have an absolute advantage in both commodities.

Effect of Costs of Transport

In the above example we assumed implicitly that there were no costs of transport. If there are costs of transport they limit the range of prices within which trade is profitable. Suppose that it cost the equivalent of 1 bushel of wheat in every 9 to transport wheat from Argentina to England, and the equivalent of 1 ton of steel in every 10 to transport steel from England to Argentina. Now if England is to trade, 1 ton of steel in England must produce at least 50 bushels of wheat in England by trade. But 1 ton of steel in England is equivalent to $\frac{9}{10}$ ton in Argentina because of the cost of transport of steel, and $(50 \times \frac{9}{8})$ or $56\frac{1}{4}$ bushels of wheat in Argentina become 50 bushels in England when the cost of transport $(56\frac{1}{4} \times \frac{1}{9} = 6\frac{1}{4}$ bu.) is deducted. If 1 ton of steel is to bring 50 bushels of wheat to England by trade, then the price of steel in Argentina must be $(50 \times \frac{9}{8})$ bushels for $\frac{9}{10}$ ton, or 62.5 bushels per ton. And if 80 bushels of wheat are to bring back 1 ton of steel to Argentina, the price of steel in London must be $(80 \times \frac{8}{9} \times \frac{9}{10})$, or 64 bushels per ton. If the wheat price of steel is between 62.5 bushels per ton and 80 bushels per ton in Argentina or, what is equivalent, between 50 bushels per ton and 64 bushels per ton in England, trade will be profitable to both sides. Without costs of transport, trade would take place if the price were between 50 bushels and 80 bushels per ton in either place.

The "Barter Terms of Trade," and the Gain from Trade

The actual ratio at which the goods are exchanged in international trade is called the "barter terms of trade." In the above example, if there were no costs of transport, the barter terms of trade could lie anywhere between 50 and 80 bushels of wheat per ton of steel. At any price within this range trade will benefit both parties. But the gain will not necessarily be equally distributed. If the barter terms of trade were 51 bushels of wheat per ton of steel, England would only just find it worth while to trade; but Argentina, being able to get a ton of steel for 51 bushels of wheat by trade instead of having to give up 80 bushels in direct production, would benefit a great deal. Similarly, if the barter terms of trade were 79 bushels per ton, England would benefit greatly, Argentina very little. Here is an example of the economic conflict pointed out earlier—conflict about the ratio of exchange even when there is community in the fact of exchange.

QUESTIONS AND EXERCISES

1. An important distinction is often made between "money" income and "real" income. From what you now know of the nature of exchange, what do you think that distinction would be?
2. "Everybody wants a low price for the thing that he buys and a high price for the thing that he sells." How does this principle apply to (a) trade union activity, (b) tariff legislation, (c) complaints about the "cost of living"?
3. Construct formal definitions of the following expressions: (a) international trade, (b) a tariff, (c) collective bargaining, (d) sale by auction, (e) economic conflict.

4. "The more eager people are to buy anything, the higher will be its price." Illustrate the operation of this principle with reference to (a) sale by auction, (b) sale by higgling (or collective bargaining).

5. "Economic conflict is only apparent when there is a small number of buyers and sellers." Do you agree? If so, would you say that collective bargaining increases economic conflict?

6. Suppose that one unit of resources in the United States could produce 1 ton of steel or 100 yards of silk, and one unit of resources in Japan could produce $\frac{3}{4}$ ton of steel or 90 yards of silk. What would be the "alternative prices" of steel in terms of silk in the United States and in Japan? If there were no costs of transport would there be international trade? If so, in what range of prices (of steel in terms of silk) would trade be possible? Suppose that it cost 1 yard of silk in every 15 to transport silk from Japan to the United States, and that it cost 1 ton of steel in every 21 to transport steel from the United States to Japan. What is the range of prices within which trade would be possible?

7. A tariff is an artificial increase in the cost of transport. Suppose that in the above case there were no costs of transport. What would be the effect of the imposition of a tariff on silk by the United States equivalent to 1 yard of silk in every 10 yards imported? What would be the smallest tariff on silk that would be prohibitive—i.e., that would prevent trade altogether?

CHAPTER 4

PRICE DETERMINATION IN PERFECTLY COMPETITIVE MARKETS

The Competitive Market: Definition

We have now studied two situations in which prices may be decided—one, where two individuals or groups bargain with each other, and the other, sale by auction. We must now consider a third very important situation in which prices are decided: the *competitive market*. A competitive market may be defined as a large number of buyers and sellers, all engaged in the purchase and sale of identically similar commodities, who are in close contact one with another and who buy and sell freely among themselves. Let us examine each of these four conditions more carefully.

1. *Large Number of Buyers and Sellers.* What is meant by a "large" number of buyers and sellers? There is no definite answer in terms of numbers, of course—we cannot say that 1000 is a "large" number but 999 is not. It is important, however, to appreciate the significance of "largeness" as applied in this connection. The number of buyers and sellers must be so large in a "perfectly" competitive market that the ordinary transactions of any single one of them do not appreciably affect the conditions under which other transactions are made. Obviously, the smaller the number of sellers selling any given commodity, the greater will be the effect of the transactions of any one seller on the fortunes of the others. Where we have only two or three sellers of clothes in a community, if one has a bargain sale the fortunes of the others are pretty sure to be affected. Where, however, we have a large number of sellers selling the same thing, any increase in sales on the part of one of them will probably not affect the fortunes of any single one of the others to any great extent. If seven million farmers are all selling wheat, however much Farmer Giles increases his sales the sales of his neighbors will not be appre-

ciably affected as a result, because the total effect is spread over such a large number of people.

2. *A Homogeneous Commodity.* The second condition of a competitive market is that the units of commodity bought and sold by all buyers and sellers shall be identically similar. When this is the case, the commodity is described as "homogeneous." That is to say, the commodity sold by one seller must not be different, in the mind of a buyer, from the commodity sold by any other seller. This condition is present only when the commodity is a substance of definite chemical and physical composition, such as salt, tin, or specified grades of wheat or cotton. Then the buyer—or seller—is influenced in his choice of a seller—or buyer—only by considerations of price.

3. *Close Contact of Buyers and Sellers.* A competitive market is also one in which the buyers and sellers are in close contact. This means that there must be *knowledge* on the part of each buyer and seller of the prices at which transactions are being carried on, and of the prices at which other buyers and sellers are willing to buy or sell. It means also that there must be opportunity to take advantage of that knowledge. If nobody knows what prices the automobile dealers of a certain town are charging for their cars, then these dealers do not form a perfectly competitive market. If the people in one village know that the stores in the next village sell groceries much cheaper than their own stores, but the roads are blocked so that no one can get over, then the stores of these two villages do not compete with each other.

4. *No Discrimination.* The fourth condition is that the buyers and sellers must buy and sell freely among themselves. This means that they must be willing to enter into transactions with all and sundry. When a buyer announces that he is willing to buy or a seller announces that he is willing to sell at a certain price, these gentlemen must be willing to buy and sell openly to *all* comers. There must be nothing of the business of taking Mr. Jones to the back of the shop and telling him that as a special favor he will be given a 10 per cent cut.

Competition a Matter of Degree

It should now be clear that "competition" in a competitive market is a matter in which there can be degrees. A "perfectly" competitive market would presumably be one in which there was an infinite number of buyers and sellers, dealing in an absolutely homogeneous commodity, with perfect knowledge on the part of all, and with complete openness in all transactions. In an absolute sense such a market could not, of course, exist. Nevertheless, there are many commodities, especially those bought and sold on organized "exchanges" like the Stock Exchange or the Cotton Exchange, in which the market is "perfect" enough to make the conclusions derived from the study of a perfect market practically useful. The market in most commodities falls away from this "perfection" to a greater or less degree. We shall return to the study of these imperfectly competitive markets later. Meanwhile we shall investigate how prices would be decided, and what forces would affect them, in a perfectly competitive market.

Price Depends on Eagerness to Buy and Sell

It seems obvious that prices are going to be concerned in some way with the *eagerness* of people to buy or sell. We have seen already that in the case of an auction, the more eager people are to buy, the higher the price of any commodity put up for sale is likely to be. We should expect this principle to be generally true. We may formulate it by saying that the more eager people are to buy a commodity, the higher will be its price, and the more eager people are to sell a commodity, the lower will be its price. If people as a whole want a thing very badly the price will be high, for the people who do not have it will be willing to give a lot for it, and the people who have it will not be willing to let it go unless they get a good deal for it. Likewise, if people as a whole want a certain thing but little, the people who have it will be willing to let it go for a little, and the people who do not have it will not be willing to pay very much for it.

The Measurement of "Eagerness"

Our next task is to try to reduce these broad principles to *measurable* terms. It is all very well to talk loosely about people's eagerness to buy or sell, but we cannot be content with that. A device is necessary which will enable us to *measure* how eager people are to buy or sell, and to be quite accurate, for instance, about what we mean by people being "more eager" or "less eager" to buy or sell.

Can It Be Measured by Quantities Offered or Demanded? In order to do this we shall have to introduce a new idea into our concept of exchange. Up to now we have assumed that the quantities of goods to be exchanged were fixed, and have argued as if—to return again to our old friend, Mrs. Jones—the only possible exchange were of two pounds of butter for money, and the only question, whether the exchange took place or not. Similarly, in the case of an auction, a given article is "put up for sale" and is either sold or not sold. In any given transaction of this kind there is no question of the *quantity* of the commodity to be bought or sold. In a competitive market, however, it is evident that the question may not be merely, "Shall I buy this given commodity or shall I not?" The question is more often, "Shall I buy two pounds of butter at this price, or one pound, or half a pound, or three pounds?" The introduction of the idea that the *quantity* of a given commodity which people are willing to buy or sell may vary gives us a clue to the accurate description of the concept of "eagerness" to buy or sell. Can we measure the eagerness of people to buy or sell anything by the *quantities* which they are willing to buy or sell? A man who is willing to buy a large quantity of a commodity is presumably more eager to buy it than one who is willing to buy only a small quantity.

No, Because These Depend on the Price. However, the matter does not end there. The quantity of a commodity which people are willing to buy or sell depends, among other things, on the price of the commodity. A man may buy more hair oil *either* because there is a cut in the price of hair oil which tempts him to buy more, *or* because he has fallen in love with a girl who is particular about untidy hair, *or* because he has had a raise in pay. It is clearly going to be necessary to distinguish between these various situations, for we should not use the same word indiscriminately to describe them all. There is something about the increase in the purchases of hair oil resulting from falling in love which differs from the increase in purchases resulting from a fall in the price of hair oil. Indeed, it would probably not be stretching the meaning of words too far to say that the increase in purchases which was a result of falling in love was a "real" increase in the eagerness to buy, whereas the increase which resulted from the fall in price of the hair oil was not so much an increase in the eagerness as in the opportunity to buy.

We would not be justified, then, in taking the simple "quantity" which people are willing to buy or sell as a measure of their eagerness to buy or sell, for people may become willing to buy or sell larger or smaller quantities *merely* because there is a change in the price of the commodity concerned. It is not enough to say, "This man is eager to buy doughnuts, for he is willing to buy sixteen of them in a week." If the price of doughnuts were forty cents a dozen these purchases might not be at all remarkable. But if the price were a dollar apiece, the willingness to buy sixteen in a week might indicate a passion for doughnuts that verged on insanity.

The Individual "Market Schedule"

The eagerness of any individual to buy or sell may be indicated by a *schedule* showing how much he will be willing to buy or sell at *various prices*. To make the illustration more concrete, suppose we consider the situation of a single wheat merchant, on a particular day, in the Chicago wheat market. He has in his possession, or at his command, a given stock of wheat—let us say 5000 bushels. He also has in his possession, or at his command, a certain sum of money—let us say $10,000. The problem is, *how much* wheat will he sell (i.e., turn into money) or how much will he buy (i.e., how much money will he turn into wheat)? Now a number of things may affect his decisions as to how much wheat to buy or sell. The weather, the crop reports, even his own state of health, may make him more or less eager to buy or sell. The problem under consideration here, however, is what determines the *price* of wheat. We must therefore concentrate our attention on the effect exercised by the price, and by the price alone, on the quantity which he will buy or sell. In order to do this we must suppose all other things except the price to remain constant during the day, and inquire under these circumstances what quantities the merchant would buy or sell at various hypothetical prices. At very high prices he would probably be willing to sell a large quantity; at lower prices he would probably wish to sell less; at a still lower price he would probably wish neither to buy nor to sell, being satisfied with his present stock; at yet lower prices he would be willing to buy, and at very low prices he would buy a great deal. These facts can be expressed in the form of a schedule, or table, as in Table 1.

TABLE 1.   The Individual Market Schedule

If the Price of Wheat Were (per Bushel)	He Would Be Willing	
	To Buy	To Sell
$1.20	0	5,000 bu.
1.10	0	2,000 bu.
1.00	0	0
0.90	3,000 bu.	0
0.80	12,500 bu.	0

We should read this schedule: "If the price of wheat were $1.20 a bushel, he would not be willing to buy any but would be willing to sell 5000 bushels. If the price of wheat were $1.10, he would not be willing to buy any but would be willing to sell 2000 bushels; if . . . etc." Of course there should also be places on the schedule for other prices—$1.19, $1.18, and so on—but we leave these out for the sake of simplicity.

This is the *market schedule* of the individual in question. It tells us exactly how much wheat he will be willing to give or to take in exchange for money at some hypothetical prices of wheat. It also tells us how much money he would be willing to take or give for wheat at some hypothetical prices. Thus at a price of $1.20 he would be willing to take $6000 in exchange for wheat (5000 bushels at $1.20 per bushel), at a price of $1.10 he would be willing to take $2200 in exchange for wheat, and so on.

In this particular case our "marketer," as we may call him, has only 5000 bushels of wheat and $10,000 in money. Consequently, he cannot offer more than 5000 bushels of wheat, no matter how high the price goes, and he cannot offer more than $10,000 of money, no matter how low the price goes. In Table 1 we have supposed that he reaches the limit of his wheat offer at $1.20. At all prices above this he will still offer only 5000 bushels, as he has no more than this to offer. We have supposed also that at a price of $0.80 he has reached the limit of his money offer at $10,000 (corresponding to the 12,500 bushels which he would buy at that price). At prices below this he will presumably still be willing to offer $10,000 for wheat, but he cannot offer more if that is all the money he can command. Below $0.80 he will always buy $10,000 worth of wheat—i.e., 14,285.7 bushels at a price of $0.70, 16,666.7 bushels at a price of $0.60, 20,000 bushels at a price of $0.50, and so on.

Graphic Representation. It is often convenient to represent schedules like that in Table 1 by means of a graph or chart. A graph is merely a convenient, shorthand way of expressing the facts or circumstances which are set forth in a schedule. Both a schedule and a graph express a *relationship* between two quantities or, as we call them, "variables." Both a schedule and a graph are merely a shorthand way of writing a large number of conditional sentences of the form, "If *this* quantity were this much, then *that* quantity would be that much." We have already seen how to read the market schedule in this way; graphs should be interpreted similarly.

The market schedule of Table 1 can be expressed on a graph by measuring, as in Fig. 2, the *price* vertically above the base line *AA* and the *quantity* which would be bought or sold at each price horizontally from the axis *OC*. Quantities bought are assumed to be *positive;* following the usual mathematical convention these will be measured to the right of *OC*. Similarly, quantities sold are *negative,* and will be measured to the left of *OC*. On such a figure, therefore, any point represents a combination of a certain price with a certain quantity bought or sold. We may read the point *P,* for instance, as

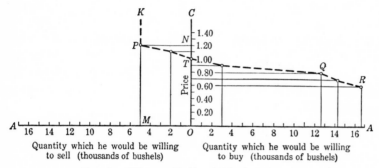

FIG. 2.   The Individual Market Curve.

an expression of the fact that at a price of $1.20 per bushel, represented by *MP* (or *ON*), our marketer will wish to sell 5000 bushels of wheat, represented by *NP* (or *OM*). The point *Q* expresses the fact that at a price of $0.80 he is willing to buy 12,500 bushels—and so on for all the other points.

The Individual "Market Curve"

If all the points on the graph which correspond to the market schedule of Table 1 are connected by a line, *KPTQR,* we shall have a line on the graph which tells us exactly the same set of facts as the market schedule. This is called the *market curve* of the individual marketer. It may be described as the curve which shows the relationship between the price and the quantity which he is willing to buy or sell at each price.

Market Schedule of an "Eager Buyer"

Every individual in the market on any particular day will have his own market curve expressing his eagerness to buy or sell. The market curves of these various individuals will not necessarily be the same; indeed, as we shall see, it is only because the market curves of various individuals are different that any transactions take place in the market at all. The question arises, therefore, how can we express the "eagerness" of people to buy or sell in terms of these market curves? What will happen, for instance, to the market curve of an individual if for some reason he becomes more eager to buy (which is the same thing, of course, as becoming less eager to sell)? This will mean that *at each price* he will be willing to buy a *greater* quantity (or sell a smaller quantity) than he did before. His market schedule, instead of being as it was in Table 1, may now be as in Table 2. At a price of $1.20,

TABLE 2.   Market Schedule of an Eager Buyer

If the Price of Wheat Were (per Bushel)	He Would Be Willing	
	To Buy	To Sell
$1.20	0	2,500
1.10	0	0
1.00	4,000	0
0.90	11,000	0
0.80	12,500	0

whereas before he was willing to sell 5000 bushels, now he is more cautious; he is willing to sell only 2500. At a price of $1.10, whereas previously he was willing to sell 2000 bushels, now he is not willing to sell anything. At a price of $1, whereas previously he was not willing either to buy or sell, now he is willing to buy 4000 bushels, and so on for all other prices.

Market Schedule of an "Eager Seller"

In a similar way, if for any reason he becomes less eager to buy (or, what is exactly the same thing, more eager to sell), this means that at each price he will be willing to buy a smaller quantity (or sell a larger quantity) than he did before. His market schedule may now be as in Table 3.

TABLE 3.   Market Schedule of an Eager Seller

If the Price of Wheat Were (per Bushel)	He Would Be Willing	
	To Buy	To Sell
$1.20	0	5,000
1.10	0	5,000
1.00	0	2,400
0.90	0	0
0.80	4,500	0
0.70	14,000	0

Graphic Illustration.   The market curves corresponding to the schedules of Tables 1, 2, and 3 are shown in Fig. 3. We see immediately that an increased eagerness to buy is reflected in a "rise" in the market curve, and an increased eagerness to sell is reflected in a "fall" in the market curve. Curve $KP'T'Q'R$ is the market curve corresponding to Table 2, the "eager buyer." Curve $KP_1T_1Q_1R$ is

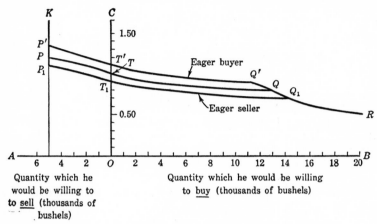

FIG. 3.   Market Curves of Eager Buyers and Sellers.

the market curve corresponding to the "eager seller" of Table 3. Curve $KPTQR$ corresponds to our original schedule, Table 1.

Derivation of Market Demand and Market Supply Schedules from Individual Market Schedules

With the information given merely by the market schedules or curves of *all* the individuals in the market we can now proceed to deduce what will be the market price of the commodity and what will be the quantity exchanged. Suppose as an example that there are five marketers. Such a market would not of course fulfill the conditions of a perfectly competitive market, but for the sake of simplicity of arithmetic we shall assume first a relatively small number of buyers and sellers. The processes can easily be extended to any number whatever. Let us suppose that the market schedules of each one of these marketers is represented in Table 4. For the sake of convenience we shall represent a quantity which people are willing to buy, by a (+) sign, and a quantity which people are willing to sell, by a (−) sign.

Mr. A is a very eager seller. He will sell something even if the price is as low as $0.80, and it has to fall almost to $0.70 before he will be persuaded to buy. Mr. E, on the other hand, is a very eager buyer.

Even a price as high as $1.10 will find him still willing to buy a small quantity. The other marketers range somewhere in between.

TABLE 4.   Derivation of the Market Demand and Supply Schedules

Price (per Bu.)	Quantity Which Each Marketer Would Buy (+) or Sell (−) at That Price					Demand	Supply
	A	B	C	D	E		
$1.20	−5,000	−3,000	−1,500	−1,000	− 500	0	−11,000
1.10	−3,000	−2,000	− 500	− 200	+ 100	+ 100	− 5,700
1.00	−2,000	−1,500	− 200	+ 100	+ 500	+ 600	− 3,700
0.90	−1,000	− 800	+ 200	+ 600	+1,000	+ 1,800	− 1,800
0.80	− 500	+1,000	+1,500	+2,000	+3,000	+ 7,500	− 500
0.70	+ 500	+1,500	+2,000	+3,000	+5,000	+12,000	0

The Market Demand Schedule.   The seventh and eighth columns of the table are of the utmost importance. The first is obtained by adding up all the individual amounts which the marketers are willing to *buy* at each price. Thus, at a price of $1.20 there are no buyers at all and nothing will be bought. At a price of $1.10 Mr. E will buy 100 bushels, but nobody else will buy. At a price of $1 Mr. E will buy 500 bushels. Mr. D will buy 100 bushels, making 600 bushels in all. At a price of $0.90 Mr. E, Mr. D, and Mr. C are all willing to be buyers, and will buy together 1800 bushels, and so on. This schedule shows the relation between the price of the commodity and the total quantity of that commodity which all the people in the market will buy at each price. It is called the *market demand schedule* for the commodity.

The Market Supply Schedule.   The last column is obtained by adding up all the separate amounts which the marketers are willing to *sell* at each price. Thus a price of $0.70 is so low that no sellers will be found. At a price of $0.80 there will be one seller, Mr. A, who will sell 500 bushels. At a price of $0.90 Mr. A and Mr. B between them will be willing to sell a total of 1800 bushels, and so on. This schedule shows the relation between the price of the commodity and the total quantity which people are willing to *sell* at each price. It is called the *market supply schedule* of the commodity. The market demand schedule is an expression of the general willingness to buy on the part of the people in the market. The market supply schedule is an expression of the general willingness to sell.

The Condition for an Equilibrium Price

We now come to what is perhaps the most important proposition in the whole of economic analysis, the key that unlocks the doors to a vast number of problems. Unless the price in the market is such that the quantity of the commodity which people want to buy is equal to the quantity which people want to sell, there will be a tendency for the price to change. If the market price is such that sellers in the market as a whole wish to sell more than buyers in the market wish to buy, then the price must fall. If the market price is such that buyers as a whole wish to buy more than sellers wish to sell, then the price must rise. The price at which the quantity of the commodity that the sellers wish to sell is just equal to the quantity that the buyers wish to buy is called the *equilibrium price*. It is that price which "clears the market."

The Meaning of Equilibrium

The word "equilibrium" is one that will recur very frequently, and consequently it may be advisable to pause for a moment and examine what it means. The word comes from two Latin words meaning an equal balance. Anything is in equilibrium when the forces acting on it are such that it has no tendency to change its condition. A book at rest on a desk is in equilibrium relative to its surroundings, for it has no tendency to change its position. On the other hand, a book falling through the air is not in equilibrium; the forces acting upon it do not balance, and therefore it changes its position. Similarly in economic life we say that any quantity—e.g., a price—is in equilibrium if there are no forces acting upon it, on balance, tending to change it one way or another.

The Equilibrium Price and the Actual Price

The equilibrium price is not necessarily the actual price existing at a given instant of time. A price may exist—i.e., there may be transactions taking place at a certain ratio of exchange—and yet there may be forces operating in the market which tend to bring about a change in that price. In the same way a book falling through the air could be photographed at any moment and we should see that it had a definite position—say, four feet above the floor. This would not be an equilibrium position, however, because the book would be moving away from it. The equilibrium position would be on the floor below.

It is possible, even, that we may *never* reach the equilibrium price, that in fact no actual price is ever an equilibrium price. Before the forces which would bring together the actual and the equilibrium prices have had time to work themselves out, it is quite possible—indeed, almost inevitable—that the circumstances will have changed, and with them the equilibrium price. To go back to an analogy: the pursuit of the equilibrium price by the actual price is rather like the activity of a dog chasing a rabbit. The position of the rabbit at any one moment is the *equilibrium* position of the dog, for that is the spot where the dog wants to be, the spot toward which all the forces acting on the dog are driving him. Nevertheless, the dog may never reach the rabbit because by the time he has reached the rabbit's original position the rabbit is no longer there, and the dog starts off to a new "equilibrium position." In much the same way the actual price at any moment may be moving toward an equilibrium price which itself changes as the actual price approaches it. But the fact that the equilibrium price may not be the actual price does not mean it is not important. The rabbit in the above illustration is absolutely necessary for the explanation of the dog's behavior, even if it is never caught.

At Equilibrium Price All Sellers Can Find Buyers, and All Buyers, Sellers. Let us now go back and examine the significance of the equilibrium price in our wheat market. In Table 4 this price is clearly $0.90, where the total amount that the sellers want to sell is 1800 bushels and the total amount that the buyers want to buy is also 1800 bushels. Mr. A and Mr. B sell their wheat to Mr. C, Mr. D, and Mr. E. It should be observed that we do not make any assumptions regarding the persons or the amounts involved in any individual transaction. All we assume is that all buyers can find enough sellers to fill their requirements, and all sellers can find enough buyers to fill their requirements. Perhaps in the above case Mr. A will sell to Mr. E the whole 1000 bushels which he offers, and Mr. B may sell 200 bushels to Mr. C and 600 to Mr. D. Perhaps Mr. A will sell 500 bushels to Mr. E and 500 bushels to Mr. D, and Mr. B will sell 200 bushels to Mr. C, 100 to Mr. D, and 500 to Mr. E. Obviously, there are many possible combinations of individual transactions. It will not matter to any of the marketers which combination is finally reached, for if the price is $0.90 per bushel, everyone will be able to buy or sell the quantity he desires.

If Price Is Above Equilibrium Price, Some Sellers Cannot Find Buyers and Will Cut Prices. Now, suppose the price at which transactions are being made in this case is not $0.90, but $1. We see from

Table 4 that at this price buyers will be willing to buy only 600 bushels and sellers will want to sell 3700 bushels. It will be easy enough for the buyers to be satisfied for they will soon find sellers to sell them all they want. But when that is done there will still be a number of sellers who have *not* sold all they want. Suppose that Mr. D and Mr. E buy the 600 bushels they want from Mr. A. That still leaves Mr. A with 1400 bushels that he would like to sell, Mr. B and Mr. C with 1500 and 200 bushels respectively which they would also like to sell, but for which they cannot find buyers.

What, then, is going to be the response of sellers who cannot find buyers for what they want to sell? The answer is, clearly, to cut their prices. Rather than not sell anything at a price of $1, or not sell as much as they wish, Messrs. A, B, and C will lower their prices in the hope of attracting buyers. As they lower their prices, the quantity they are willing to sell declines while the quantity the buyers are willing to buy increases. If they lower the price to $0.90, as we have seen, the quantity that people are willing to buy will increase to 1800 bushels, the quantity that people are willing to sell will decrease to 1800 bushels, and neither buyers nor sellers will go unsatisfied.

If Price Is Below Equilibrium Price, Buyers Will Raise Prices. Similarly, if the price in the market is $0.80, buyers (B, C, D, and E) will wish to buy 7500 bushels; sellers (Mr. A) will be willing to sell only 500 bushels. After Mr. A has sold his 500 bushels, there will still be unsatisfied buyers who wish to buy a total of 7000 bushels at that price. Again, what will happen in these circumstances is that the buyers will *raise* the prices at which they are offering to buy, in the hope of attracting more from the sellers. As they raise the price, however, the quantity that they wish to buy declines, the quantity that sellers wish to sell increases, and some who were buyers before now become sellers, until we find at a price of $0.90 that the amount the sellers offer is equal to the amount the buyers wish to take, and none will go unsatisfied.

Thus, from the market schedules of the individual buyers, and from them alone, we have been able to deduce the price at which the transactions in the market will take place, and also the volume of transactions, i.e., the quantity bought and sold—in the case of Table 4, 1800 bushels.

Graphic Illustration.   The graphic method of statement can also be used in this case. In Fig. 4 the price is measured vertically from the base. The quantity bought or sold is measured horizontally. We can represent both the demand and the supply schedules of Table 4 on the one figure. *DD'* represents the demand schedule; it is called the *market demand curve,* and may be defined as the curve showing the relationship between the price of a commodity and the quantity which people in the market are willing to *buy* at each price in a given period of time. The demand curve usually slopes downward to the right with the conventional coordinates. This indicates the fact that

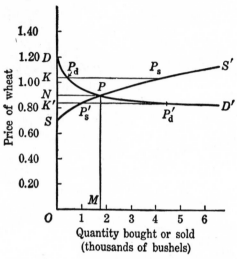

Fig. 4.   Market Demand and Supply Curves.

the higher the price, the less will people be willing to buy, and the lower the price, the more will they be willing to buy.[1] *SS'* represents the supply schedule of Table 4; it is called the *market supply curve.* It may be defined as the curve showing the relationship between the price of a commodity and the quantity which people are willing to *sell.* On this figure it usually slopes upward to the right, indicating the fact that at higher prices people are willing to sell greater quantities of a commodity than they are at lower prices. The point where these two curves intersect, *P,* shows the equilibrium price *(MP* or *ON)* and the quantity *(NP* or *OM)* which will be bought and sold at this price, for this is the only price at which the quantity people wish to buy is equal to the quantity people wish to sell. At any price above this— e.g., *OK*—the quantity people want to buy—(KP_d) is less than the quantity people want to sell (KP_s). At any price below *ON*—say, *OK'*—the quantity people want to buy $(K'P'_d)$ is greater than the quantity people want to sell $(K'P'_s)$. If the price is "too low," buying is too much encouraged, selling too much discouraged. If the price is

[1] This proposition is frequently called the "law of demand."

"too high," selling is too much encouraged, buying too much discouraged.

The Market Identity

By making certain simplifying assumptions a very useful identity can be derived showing what determines the market price. It is assumed that there is a given quantity of money, M "dollars," and a given physical quantity of commodity, A "bushels," present in the market in the possession of the marketers. We assume that the result of the transactions of the "day" is simply to redistribute the ownership of this money and commodity among the various marketers concerned; no new stocks either of money or of commodity are supposed to come on the market. Now let us assume that the marketers as a whole wish to hold a certain proportion, r_m, of their assets in the form of money, and a certain proportion r_a in the form of the commodity. The name "preferred liquidity ratio" may be given to r_m; if it were, say, 10 per cent, or $\frac{1}{10}$th, that would mean that the people in the market, on the whole, wanted to hold $\frac{1}{10}$th of the value of their total assets in the form of money. If, for instance, the total amount of money held by them was $100,000, they would not be satisfied unless the total value of their assets was $1,000,000. Similarly, r_a may be called the "preferred commodity ratio." If the commodity is, say, wheat, a preferred wheat ratio of $\frac{1}{5}$th would mean that the market would not be satisfied unless one-fifth of the value of its assets were held in the form of wheat.

Now, let the total value of all assets held by the marketers be T. The total value of the stock of commodity, A, is $p_a A$, where p_a is the money price of the commodity. Then by definition we have:

$$r_m = \frac{M}{T} \text{ and } r_a = \frac{P_a A}{T}$$

Eliminating T between these two equations we obtain:

$$P_a = \frac{M r_a}{A r_m}$$

This may be called the *Market Identity*.

Significance of the Market Identity

In order to bring out the significance of this fundamental identity let us consider an arithmetical example. Suppose first a case in which there are only two kinds of assets—money and a commodity—call it "wheat." Suppose there are 50 million bushels of wheat in the market and 10 million dollars of money. Suppose also that the liquidity preference ratio is 0.2 and the commodity preference ratio 0.8. The two preference ratios in this case must add up to 1, for if there are only two kinds of assets, to say that we prefer to hold 20 per cent of our assets in one form is the same as to say we prefer to hold 80 per cent of our assets in the other form. Then the following table shows the condition of the market on the assumption of various prices for wheat.

TABLE 5.   The Market Identity

Price of Wheat (p_a)	Value of Wheat (p_aA) Mill. Dollars	Value of Money M	Total Value of Assets $(p_aA + M)$ Mill. Dollars	r_m	r_a
$1.00	50	10	60	0.167	0.833
0.90	45	10	55	0.182	0.818
0.80	40	10	50	0.2	0.8
0.70	35	10	45	0.222	0.778
0.60	30	10	40	0.25	0.75

It is evident that only at the price of $0.80, given by the market formula, is the total value of assets such that the ratio of money to total assets or of commodity to total assets is what the market wants. If the price were above this level, say at $1 per bushel, the value of the stock of wheat, and therefore the value of the total assets of the market, would be "too high," relative to the quantity of money held. That is to say, there would be an excess of people in the market who felt that they held too much commodity and not enough money, and who would, therefore, be "eager sellers." An individual, of course, increases his money holding by selling and increases his commodity holding by buying. The situation would be like the price OK in Fig. 4, and the excess of sellers would soon force down the price. Similarly, if the price were 60 cents, there would be an excess of people who wanted to increase their commodity holdings and lower their money holdings, and these "eager buyers" would force up the price. The situation would be like the price OK' in Fig. 4. Thus we see that the function of "clearing the market" can also be expressed in another form, and we can say that the function of price is to adjust the value of assets to those proportions which best satisfy the market. The value of assets depends on their price; a rise in the price raises and a fall lowers the total value of assets. A rise in price, therefore, lowers and a fall raises the proportion of the total value of assets held in the form of money.

QUESTIONS AND EXERCISES

1. What does the phrase "a lessening of competition" mean?
2. Would we be justified in constructing demand and supply schedules in the way we have done if (a) there were only a small number of buyers and sellers; (b) all transactions were quite private, so that no one person in the market knew what prices were being offered and taken by others in the market; (c) the commodity were of a large number of grades and qualities? If we could construct supply and demand schedules in any of these three cases, could we still use them to determine the market price?
3. In a perfectly competitive market we have assumed that all transactions take place at the same price. What characteristics of a perfectly competitive market justify us in making this assumption?
4. How would you expect a general rise in the eagerness to sell to affect (a) the price and (b) the quantity bought and sold of a commodity sold in a perfectly competitive market? Analyze in detail, using supply and demand curves.
5. We have assumed that "selling" is a kind of "negative buying." Would a negative price have any meaning? If so, what? What would be the meaning of the "price of money" in terms of wheat, if the price of wheat in terms of money were 90 cents per bushel?
6. Construct a market schedule from Table 1, showing what amounts of *money* the marketer in question will be willing to give or to take in exchange for wheat at various prices of wheat.

    Now take the schedules of our five marketers in Table 4, and transform these similarly into market schedules for money. From these derive the demand schedule of "money for wheat," showing how the amount of money which people will *accept* in exchange for wheat will vary with the price of wheat. Derive also the supply schedule of "money for wheat," showing how the amount of money which people will *offer* will vary with the price of wheat. From these demand and supply schedules of money for wheat deduce (a) the equilibrium market price of wheat and (b) the amount of money that will change hands in exchange for wheat.
7. Draw the supply and demand curves of the individual marketer in Table 1.
8. Suppose a market with two commodities, A and B, one form of money, M, and no other assets. The quantity of money is $8,000,000, the quantity of A is 12,000,000 bushels, and the quantity of B, 5,000,000 tons. Let the preferred liquidity ratio, $r_m = 0.2$, the preferred commodity

ratios $r_a = 0.3$, and $r_b = 0.5$. Construct tables showing the total value of assets for various prices of A and B, and show that the only prices which satisfy the above conditions are those given by the market identities.

9. Prove, by means of the market identity, that (a) a change in the quantity of money, other things being equal, will affect all prices; (b) a change in the quantity of a single commodity will affect the price of that commodity, but of no other, as long as there is no change in the preference ratios; (c) a change in the preference for one commodity, other things remaining the same, will not only affect its own price but will also affect the prices of other commodities. (Note that the sum of the preference ratios must be equal to 1.)

CHAPTER 5

SUPPLY AND DEMAND IN A COMPETITIVE MARKET

Prices and Quantities Determined by "States of Mind"

The concepts of supply and demand are very powerful weapons of analysis. We shall use them first to investigate the question, how do *changes* in the states of mind of the people in a market affect the price of the commodity and the quantity of it which is exchanged? We have seen that the price and the quantity of commodity exchanged in a market on a given day depend *solely,* in the first instance, on the states of mind of the people in the market, as described by their market schedules. We can therefore attribute any change in the price or the quantity sold to a change in the state of mind of the marketers. Of course these states of mind are not self-subsistent fantasies, unconnected with any other facts of the system. Indeed, a great deal of our inquiry will be spent in seeking out the underlying causes of the states of mind of people who buy and sell. But these underlying causes, such as, for instance, costs of production or the tastes of consumers, affect prices and quantities only because they affect the states of mind of people who buy and sell. The market schedules of individuals, and the demand and supply schedules which are derived from them, are merely convenient ways of describing those states of mind that are the immediate determinants of prices.

A General Increase in the Eagerness to Buy a Commodity

Let us consider the effects on the price of a commodity, and on the quantity exchanged, of a general increase in the eagerness to buy. This will be reflected by a "rise" in the market schedules of the individual marketers. Each marketer will now be willing to buy more, or to sell less, than he did before. Let us suppose that Table 6 shows the market schedules of the five marketers of Table 4, page 54, after

TABLE 6.   Market Schedules in an "Eager Buyers' Market"

Price (per Bu.)	Quantity Which Each Marketer Would Buy (+) or Sell (−) at That Price					Quantity De-manded	Quan-tity Offered
	A	B	C	D	E		
$1.20	−3,000	−2,000	− 500	− 200	+ 100	+ 100	−5,700
1.10	−2,000	−1,500	− 200	+ 100	+ 500	+ 600	−3,700
1.00	−1,000	− 800	+ 200	+ 600	+1,000	+ 1,800	−1,800
0.90	− 500	+1,000	+1,500	+2,000	+3,000	+ 7,500	− 500
0.80	+ 500	+1,500	+2,000	+3,000	+5,000	+12,000	0

there has been a general increase in the eagerness to buy or, what is the same thing, a general decrease in the eagerness to sell. Comparing this table with Table 4, we see that at each price each marketer will buy more, or sell less, than before. At $1.20, for instance, marketer A is now willing to sell only 3000 bushels, whereas previously he would have sold 5000; marketer E will actually buy 100 bushels, whereas previously he would have wished to sell 500 bushels.

Leads to an Increase in Price.   What has happened to the demand and supply schedules? Table 4 shows that at a price of $1.20 a quantity of 11,000 bushels will be offered for sale, but nothing will be demanded. After the change (Table 6) at this same price only 5700 bushels will be offered for sale, and 100 bushels will be demanded. The result of the change in the market schedules has been, therefore, that at each price more is demanded and less is offered than before. The equilibrium price has risen from $0.90 to $1, for $1 is now the price at which the quantity offered and the quantity demanded are equal.

Does Not Necessarily Lead to Any Change in the Quantity Exchanged.   In the above example, although the equilibrium price has risen, the quantity which will be exchanged at the equilibrium price has not changed. Our five marketers would exchange 1800 bushels among themselves even if each one were to become a more eager buyer. This conclusion follows because there has been a special kind of rise in the market schedules which we shall call a "pure" rise. Comparing Tables 4 and 6 we see that the "shapes" of the market schedules have not changed. Indeed, all that we have done to make Table 6 is to move the schedule of prices in Table 4 one row downward. Mr. A, for instance, in Table 4, is willing to sell 3000 bushels at $1.10. In Table 6 he sells 3000 bushels only when the price is $1.20. In Table 4 he sells

2000 bushels at $1, and in Table 6 he sells 2000 bushels only at $1.10. If we have an irregular rise in the market schedules, it does not necessarily follow that the quantity exchanged will be unaltered.

Graphic Illustration. Fig. 5 shows the effect of a pure change in the market schedules on the market supply and demand curves. As before, the price of wheat is measured vertically, and the quantity bought and sold horizontally. Then the "old" demand curve is *DD'*,

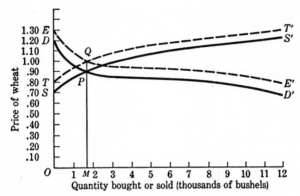

FIG. 5.   Effect of Increased Eagerness to Buy.

the "old" supply curve is *SS'*, as in Fig. 4. After the pure rise in the market schedules the demand curve is *EE'*, the supply curve is *TT'*. These are the graphic descriptions of the demand and supply schedules of Table 6. The point of intersection of the demand and supply schedules, i.e., the point where the quantity offered and the quantity demanded are equal, has moved from *P* to *Q*. The equilibrium price has changed from *MP* to *MQ*. The quantity which will be exchanged, however, has not changed, being *OM* in both cases.

A Pure Fall in Market Schedules Causes a Fall in Price

In an exactly similar way a "pure" fall in the market schedules brings about a fall in the equilibrium price but no change in the quantity exchanged. If the situation in Table 6 were the original situation, Table 4 would represent the market schedules after a "pure fall." The price would have fallen from $1 to $0.90, the quantity remaining the same at 1800 bushels. Or in Fig. 5, if *EE'*, *TT'* represented the original supply and demand curves, *DD'*, *SS'* would represent the supply and demand curves after a pure fall in the market schedules.

The "Total Market Schedule"

There is no harm in looking at a thing from more than one point of view, especially when the thing in question is one of the most important features of the economic landscape. We may therefore pause for a moment to look at the problem of the effect of a change in market schedules in another way. Table 7 shows the demand and sup-

TABLE 7.   The Total Market Schedule

Price (per Bu.)	Quantity Demanded	Quantity Offered	Excess Demand (+) or Excess Supply (−)
$1.20	0	−11,000	−11,000
1.10	+ 100	− 5,700	− 5,600
1.00	+ 600	− 3,700	− 3,100
0.90	+ 1,800	− 1,800	0
0.80	+ 7,500	− 500	+ 7,000
0.70	+12,000	0	+12,000

ply schedules of Table 4. For each price, we have found the "excess demand" or the "excess supply," as the case may be. The excess supply is found by subtracting the total quantity demanded by the market from the total quantity offered, where the total quantity offered is the greater. The excess demand is found by subtracting the total quantity offered from the total quantity demanded, when the total quantity demanded is the greater. Algebraically, the excess demand (+) or supply (−) is the sum of the quantity demanded (+) and the quantity offered (−).

It will be seen from Table 7 that at the equilibrium price the excess demand (or supply) is zero. This is another way of stating the proposition that at the equilibrium price the quantity offered and the quantity demanded are equal. The schedule of excess demand or excess supply may be called the "total market schedule," as it is calculated by taking the algebraic sum of the quantities in all the individual market schedules at each price.

If now there is a pure rise in all the individual market schedules there will also be a rise in the total market schedule. This is shown in Table 8, where we calculate the total market schedule corresponding to the market in Table 6.

Graphic Illustration.   In Fig. 6 the price of wheat is measured vertically, and the quantity which will be in excess demand or supply, horizontally. Quantities in excess demand are measured to the right

Table 8.   Total Market Schedule in an Eager Buyers' Market

Price (per Bu.)	Quantity Demanded (Bu.)	Quantity Supplied (Bu.)	Excess Demand (+) or Excess Supply (−) (Bu.)
$1.20	+ 100	−5,700	− 5,600
1.10	+ 600	−3,700	− 3,100
1.00	+ 1,800	−1,800	0
0.90	+ 7,500	− 500	+ 7,000
0.80	+12,000	0	+12,000

of the origin, *O,* and quantities in excess supply to the left of *O,* following the convention that quantities demanded are positive and quantities offered are negative. Then *MPM'* is the curve corresponding to the total market schedule of Table 7. It may be called the *total market curve.* The equilibrium price, *OP,* is found at the point *P,* where the total market curve cuts the price axis *OY.* This is the price

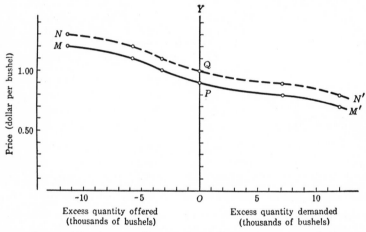

Fig. 6.   Effect on the Total Market Schedule of an Increased Eagerness to Buy.

at which the excess demand (or supply) is zero. *NQN'* is the total market curve after the rise in the eagerness to buy. It corresponds to the total market schedule of Table 8. It will be seen immediately from this figure that any rise in the total market schedule causes a rise in the price, and any fall in the total market schedule causes a fall in the price. What is perhaps more important, a rise in price *can occur only* as a result of a rise in the total market schedule, and a fall in price can occur only as a result of a fall in the total market schedule.

The rise or fall in the total market schedule need not, of course, be a pure rise or fall. When there is a pure rise or fall, the *shape* of the market schedule does not change; it rises or falls as a unit. In that case the quantity exchanged is not affected. But any change in the individual market schedules which results in a generally increased eagerness to buy and a generally diminished eagerness to sell, whether the changes are "pure" or not, will raise the price of the commodity.

What Determines the Volume of Transactions?

Let us now see if we can isolate the factor that determines the quantity exchanged—i.e., the volume of transactions. Let us first consider an extreme case in which the market schedules of all the people in the market are identical.

Table 9 shows a market in this condition. The equilibrium price

TABLE 9.   Market Schedules in a Market Where There Is No "Divergence"

Price (per Bu.)	Quantities Which the Various Individuals Will Buy (+) or Sell (−)					Total Quantity Supplied	Total Quantity Demanded
	A	B	C	D	E		
$1.20	−1,000	−1,000	−1,000	−1,000	−1,000	5,000	0
1.10	− 600	− 600	− 600	− 600	− 600	3,000	0
1.00	− 300	− 300	− 300	− 300	− 300	1,500	0
0.90	0	0	0	0	0	0	0
0.80	200	200	200	200	200	0	1,000
0.70	400	400	400	400	400	0	2,000
0.60	700	700	700	700	700	0	3,500

in this case is $0.90, but the total quantity which will be bought and sold at this price is zero! We may illustrate this situation in Fig. 7, where *TS* is the supply curve and *TD* is the demand curve corresponding to the situation above. The demand and supply curves intersect at the point *T,* where the price is *OT* and the volume of transactions is zero.

It is evident, therefore, that there will be no transactions at all in a market where the schedules of all the marketers are identical. We can go further than this. Even if the individual market schedules are not identical, there will be no transactions if the price at which each marketer will neither buy nor sell is the same in all the schedules. Thus in Table 9, as long as at a price of $0.90 none of the marketers were willing to buy or sell even the smallest quantities, it would not matter what the offers to sell at higher prices might be, or the offers to purchase at lower prices, for there would still be no transactions.

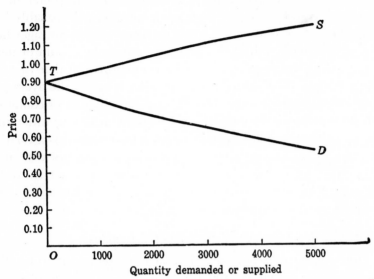

Fig. 7.   Supply and Demand in a Market Without "Divergence."

Divergence of Attitude

That feature of a group of market schedules which gives rise to a volume of transactions we may call "divergence of attitude." The volume of transactions depends therefore on the divergence of attitude in the market, as described by the market schedules. If the market shows a wide divergence of attitude, with one group of eager buyers and another group of eager sellers, there will be a large volume of transactions. If there is little divergence of attitude, if all the people in the market are about equally eager to buy and sell, there will be a small volume of transactions.

What Makes an "Eager Buyer"?

What creates this "divergence" in the market schedules? To answer that question we must first answer the question, "What makes any particular marketer an 'eager buyer' or an 'eager seller'?" A marketer will be an "eager buyer"—i.e., his market curve will lie relatively "high," for one of two reasons. He may have a strong *preference* for the possession of the commodity rather than for the possession of money. When a buyer buys a certain quantity of commodity, he changes the form of his possessions, for he diminishes the quantity of money which he owns and increases the quantity of commodity. If a buyer has a strong preference for the possession of the commodity, he will probably be an eager buyer. If he has a strong preference for holding his possessions in the form of money, he will probably be an eager seller. The second reason why a marketer may be an eager buyer is that he may have in his possession a relatively large sum of money and a relatively small quantity of the commodity. In that case even if his preference for holding the commodity is below the average, he may still be a relatively eager buyer; for if the quantity of commodity which he possesses is very small, he will want to buy in order to increase that quantity. On the other hand, a buyer who has a relatively large stock of the commodity and a relatively small stock of money will probably be an eager seller, for he will want to get rid of part of his stock of the commodity and so increase his stock of money, even if the price of the commodity is low.

What Makes for Divergence of Market Schedules?

1. *Divergence of Preference.* We have, therefore, a strong divergence of market schedules, and therefore a large volume of transactions, when there is a strong divergence of preference in the market and also when there are great differences in the quantity of the commodity possessed by people in the market. If one group of marketers has a strongly marked preference for holding their possessions in the form of wheat, and another group has a strongly marked preference for holding their possessions in the form of money, then the divergence of preference in the market will be great and the volume of transactions will also be great. There will be a large number of buyers who wish to increase their holdings of wheat, and of sellers who wish to increase their holdings of money, when the price is in equilibrium. If, on the other hand, there is not much divergence of preference in the market, if every marketer has about the same degree of preference for wheat or for money, the volume of transactions will be small.

2. *Divergence in the Quantities Possessed.* Similarly, if there is a great divergence in the relative quantities of wheat and money held by the marketers, there is also likely to be a great divergence in the market schedules and therefore a large volume of transactions. If some marketers hold a large quantity of wheat, and some hold a small quantity, then the former will be eager sellers and the latter eager buyers; and at the equilibrium price there will be a large number of both buyers and sellers. If, however, at the equilibrium price all the

marketers are pretty well satisfied with the quantities they possess, the volume of transactions will be small.

This Is True Even in Isolated Exchanges. This result is what we should expect from our preliminary study of exchange. We saw that Mrs. Jones was able to exchange her butter for Mrs. Smith's bread because there was a divergence of opinion between them about the relative value of butter and bread. The greater this divergence, the greater will be the volume of transactions between them. This divergence of opinion, again, depends on two factors. The first is the divergence of *preference* between the two ladies. If Mrs. Smith is passionately fond of butter, for which Mrs. Jones cares very little, and if Mrs. Jones is passionately fond of bread, for which Mrs. Smith cares very little, then Mrs. Jones, who has the butter, will give up a large quantity to Mrs. Smith, who has the bread. The second factor is the divergence of the *quantities possessed* by the two ladies. If Mrs. Smith possessed no butter and Mrs. Jones possessed no bread, the volume of transactions between them will be greater than if they each possessed roughly equivalent quantities of both bread and butter.

Effect on Price of an Increase in the Quantities Possessed

We can now apply our analysis to the problem of the effect of a change in the total quantities, either of the commodity or of money, which are held by the people in a market. Up to now we have assumed that the total quantity of commodity, and of money, held by all the marketers does not change in the course of the transactions of the "day." All that happens is that some units of the commodity, and some units of money, change owners. In any actual market, however, the quantity of commodity, and even the quantity of money, held by the marketers is constantly changing. On the wheat market, for instance, wheat is continually coming into the market from the farms where it has been produced, and is continually being taken out of the market into consumption. The next step in our analysis is therefore to answer the question: what happens to the price, and to the volume of transactions, when there is a change in the *total* holdings of the commodity, or of money?

We have seen that the greater the quantity of commodity held by any individual, the "lower" will be his market schedule—i.e., the more eager will he be to sell, and the less eager to buy. If, therefore, there is a general increase in the quantity of wheat held by people in the wheat market, there will be a general fall in market schedules.

and this will lead to a fall in the total market schedule and a fall in the price of wheat. Similarly, if there is a decrease in the quantity of wheat held by people in the market, there will tend to be a rise in the price of wheat.[1]

Effect on the Volume of Transactions

What, now, will be the effect on the volume of transactions of an increase in the total quantity of wheat held? This question is not quite so easy to answer, and may not admit of a definite solution. If the extra quantity of wheat comes only into the hands of marketers who are already eager sellers, there will be an increase in the divergence of the market schedules, for the market schedules of the owners of the new wheat will fall, while those of the other marketers will be unchanged. But if the new wheat comes into the hands of marketers who previously were relatively eager buyers, the fall in their market schedules will lessen the divergence of market schedules. In the first case there will be an increase, in the second case a decrease, in the volume of transactions. To put the matter in another way: It is evident that there will be some distribution of quantities of wheat in the hands of the various marketers which will lead to a zero volume of transactions, all marketers being satisfied with the amount of wheat which they possess when the price is in equilibrium. If the increased quantity of wheat falls into the hands of those marketers who already have more wheat than they want (the eager sellers), the volume of transactions will be increased, for the eager sellers will sell the new wheat, as well as the quantity which they would otherwise have sold, to the eager buyers. If, however, the new wheat falls into the hands of those who have less wheat than they want (the eager buyers), it will help to satisfy their desire for wheat, and they will buy less from the eager sellers than they otherwise would have done.

Similarly, when wheat is taken out of the market, the effect will

---

[1] The relation between the quantity of commodity and the price can be seen even more clearly from the Market Identity, $p_a = \dfrac{Mr_a}{Ar_m}$. If there is no change in the quantity of money or in the preference ratios, an increase in the quantity of commodity, A, will cause a proportionate decrease in price—in other words, the total value of the commodity (p_aA) will remain unchanged. It should be observed, however, that if the increased quantity of commodity causes an *expectation* of falling prices, the commodity preference will decline and the liquidity preference increase, as people come to prefer to hold their assets in the liquid form, which, when prices are falling, is rising in purchasing power. If this happens, a rise in the quantity of commodity in the market will bring about a more than proportionate fall in price, the total money value of the commodity actually declining as its physical quantity increases.

certainly be a rise in the equilibrium price. There may be either an increase or a decrease in the volume of transactions, according to which group of marketers loses the wheat.

Effect of a Change in the Quantity of Money

A change in the quantity of money possessed by the marketers will have an effect on the price opposite to the effect of a change in the quantity of the commodity. If there is an addition to the total quantity of money held in the market, the result will be a general increase in the eagerness to buy, a rise in market schedules, and a rise in the price of the commodity. If there is a decrease in the total quantity of money held in the market, there will be a fall in the price of the commodity. The effect of a change in the quantity of money on the volume of transactions again depends on how the "new" money is distributed.

Arbitrage

There is yet another phenomenon to study in connection with the formation of prices in a competitive market. This we may name "arbitrage." It may be defined as the process of increasing the value of one's possessions by buying a commodity at one time or place and selling it at another time or place *at a higher price*. In a sense, as we shall see, all enterprise is arbitrage; for the moment, however, we shall confine the term to the buying and reselling of some physical commodity.

Suppose, for instance, that in one corner of a wheat market transactions are going on at 90 cents per bushel while in another corner they are going on at 80 cents per bushel. It would clearly pay anyone who was aware of this to buy in the "cheap" market and sell in the "dear" market. If, for instance, a man has $1000, he can buy 1250 bushels of wheat with it in the 80-cent market. He can then take the wheat over to the 90-cent market and there exchange his 1250 bushels for $1125. His original $1000 has now grown into $1125; he has increased the value of his possessions by $125, and has made a profit of 10 cents on every bushel of wheat bought and sold. Now, however, observe what happens to the two "corners" of the market when our enterprising friend plunges into them. Into the "cheap" corner has entered an eager buyer, and the price in that corner will therefore rise. Into the "dear" corner has entered an eager seller, and the price in that corner will therefore fall.

Arbitrage Prevents Permanent Price Differences.   Our friend, therefore—whom we may call an *arbitrageur*—has by his very act of arbitrage raised the cheap price and lowered the dear price, and so has made any subsequent act of arbitrage less profitable. The act of arbitrage itself, therefore, tends to do away with the price differences which make it possible. Nevertheless, in most markets these differences are always being recreated, and consequently arbitrageurs can make a living. It is their operations, however, which prevent any great divergence from the rule of "one price in all transactions in one market at one time."

Arbitrage When There Are Costs of Transport. Where the two parts of a market are geographically separate, there may be a certain cost of transport of the commodity between the two parts. In this case the effect of arbitrage is to ensure that the difference in price between the two markets shall not appreciably differ from the cost of transport of a unit of the commodity between them. Thus, we may regard the Chicago wheat market and the Liverpool wheat market as essentially part of a single world market in wheat. Wheat normally flows from Chicago to Liverpool, and the price of wheat on the Liverpool market in normal times tends to be greater than the Chicago price by an amount equal to the average cost per bushel of transporting wheat from Chicago to Liverpool. Let us suppose that the cost of transporting wheat from Chicago to Liverpool is $0.30 per bushel. Then when the price in Chicago is $0.90 per bushel we should expect the price in Liverpool to be $1.20 per bushel. If in these circumstances the price in Liverpool were $1.15 while the price in Chicago were $0.95, it would not pay anyone to buy wheat in Chicago and ship it to Liverpool. Consequently, people on the Chicago market as a whole would be less eager to buy. Also, as wheat kept coming into the Chicago market from the wheat fields, the market would become even more eager to sell and less eager to buy, and the Chicago price would fall. At the same time, in Liverpool there would be no wheat coming in from Chicago; as the stocks of wheat fell off (because of wheat passing into consumption), the price would rise. By the time the difference between the Chicago and Liverpool prices had reached $0.30 per bushel, wheat would begin to flow again from Chicago to Liverpool.[2] The exporter-buyers would come on to the Chicago market and would prevent the price from falling further there and the importer-sellers would come on to the Liverpool market and prevent the price from rising further there.

---

[2] In the "cost" of transportation we include the normal profits of the merchants and businesses concerned, so that the price differential does not have to be *more* than $0.30 per bushel in order to make it profitable to ship wheat from Chicago to Liverpool.

Similarly, if the difference in price between the Liverpool and Chicago markets were $0.40, it would be very profitable to buy wheat in Chicago, transport it to Liverpool, and sell it there; consequently, there would be a rush of buyers on the Chicago market—which would raise the price there—and a rush of sellers on the Liverpool market—which would lower the price there. The price in Chicago would rise and the price in Liverpool would fall until the difference between them was again $0.30 per bushel.

Arbitrage Makes for Consistency in Exchange Ratios. Arbitrage is also very important in establishing *consistency* in the exchange ratios existing among three or more markets. Suppose, for instance, to develop our example further, that in Chicago wheat is exchanged against dollars, that in Liverpool it is exchanged against shillings, and that in New York shillings are exchanged against dollars. Here we have three markets: the Chicago wheat market, the Liverpool wheat market, and what we call the "foreign exchange" market where dollars and shillings are exchanged. Let us suppose, to make the arithmetic easier, that there are no costs of transport for any of these things between the various markets. Suppose now that in the Chicago market wheat is exchanging for $0.90 to the bushel, in the Liverpool market it is exchanging at a rate of 4 shillings to the bushel, and in the foreign exchange market shillings are exchanging for dollars at a rate of 4 shillings to 1 dollar. If this is the case, it will be possible to make profits by buying wheat in Chicago for dollars, then buying shillings with the wheat in Liverpool, and then buying dollars again with the shillings in the foreign exchange market. Thus, if I took $900, bought 1000 bushels of wheat in Chicago, sold it for 4000 shillings in Liverpool, and then sold my shillings for $1000 in the foreign exchange market, my original $900 would have grown to $1000; I would have made $100 profit. As long as it is possible to make profits by these three-cornered transactions, we say that the exchange ratios are not *consistent*.

Now, however, observe what this act of three-cornered arbitrage will do. By bringing a new buyer of wheat into the Chicago market it will raise the price of wheat there, say, to $0.95 per bushel. By bringing a new seller of wheat into the Liverpool market it will lower the price there, say, to 3.895 shillings per bushel. By bringing a new buyer of dollars into the foreign exchange market it will raise the price of dollars, say, to 4.1 shillings per dollar. With these prices it is no longer possible to make profits by buying and selling among the markets. If I now take $950, buy 1000 bushels of wheat with it, get 3895 shillings for my wheat at Liverpool, and exchange my 3895 shillings for dollars at 4.1 shillings per dollar, I will get only $950 back again; no profit. In this case also the act of arbitrage tends to

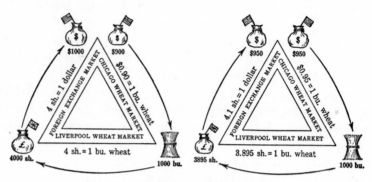

FIG. 8.   Three-Cornered Arbitrage.

bring the exchange ratios (i.e., the prices) in the various markets into line again. These processes may perhaps be brought more vividly to mind by the illustration in Fig. 8.

Speculation Is Arbitrage Through Time

The idea of arbitrage will also help us to explain another phenomenon which many have found puzzling—the phenomenon of *speculation*. By speculation we mean essentially the phenomenon of buying something cheap at one *time* and selling the same thing dear at another time. Speculation, therefore, may be defined as "arbitrage through time"; instead of buying in one place and selling in another we now buy at one time and sell at another. Of course all buying and selling of the same commodity, where the purchase and the sale do not occur at the same time, is in a sense speculation. Nevertheless, we can distinguish broadly between profits which are made because the same thing has different prices in different places and profits which are made because the same thing has different prices at different times. Just as there is a cost of transport of things through space so there is a cost of "transport" through time; as we have to pay charges for the transport of wheat from Chicago to Liverpool, so we have to pay charges for the "transport" of wheat from September to March. Holding wheat in a warehouse is essentially transporting it from one date to another; and the costs of storage, of insurance, of interest charges and other charges, correspond in this case to the costs of shipping, insurance, and other charges in the other. Just as in the case of space arbitrage we should usually expect it to result in an equality between the average cost of transport between two places and the difference in price between the two places, so in the case of time arbitrage we should expect, for instance, the price of wheat in September to differ from the price of wheat in March by a sum equal to the average cost of holding the wheat for that period.

Effect of Uncertainty of the Future.   There is, however, one fundamental difference between arbitrage through space and arbitrage through time. In the case of arbitrage through space the prices in the various markets are *known*. In the case of arbitrage through time the price at the present moment, or at past dates, is known, but the price at future dates cannot be known; it can only be estimated. It is hardly an exaggeration to say that the fact that the future cannot be known with certainty lies at the root of most of the troubles of the present economic system.

Application to Seasonal Fluctuations.   In the case of seasonal fluctuations of prices the uncertainty of the future is not so great that we cannot make reasonably good estimates. Consequently, arbitrage through time operates fairly well in the case of seasonal variations. In the case of a commodity like wheat, the bulk of the world's harvest comes on the market in September. The wheat is consumed, however, at a fairly steady pace throughout the year. The greater part of the crop, therefore, has to be stored for various periods. Ideally, about a twelfth would have to be stored for one month, another twelfth for two months, and so on. But if the price of wheat at later dates than September does not exceed the price of wheat in September by at least the cost of storage, it will not pay dealers and speculators to store wheat. If, for instance, it cost 1 cent per bushel per month to store wheat, we should expect the October price to be 1 cent per bushel greater than the September price, the November price to be 2 cents per bushel greater than the September price, and so on. If the differences were greater or less than this, arbitrage through time would tend to rectify the situation. If in the above case the December price were only 2.5 cents above the September price, the owners of wheat would hold it off the market in the hope of still higher prices in January or later. This would raise the price till it stood at 3 cents above the September price. If, on the other hand, the December price stood at 4 cents above the September price, owners of wheat who otherwise would hold their wheat for later dates would be tempted to throw it on the market to gain the additional profit. This would lower the price till again it stood at 3 cents above the September price.

Generally speaking, in the case of agricultural commodities which are storable and which have a "crop" that comes on the market all at once, we find that the price is lowest at the time of the crop and rises gradually through the year until the next crop comes on the market. This does not always happen; in some years, for instance, the price of potatoes falls sharply even between one crop and the next. But this is always because of some misjudgment on the part of the dealers and owners of the crop.

Application to Commodity Speculation. If we had accurate knowledge of future events the principle of "arbitrage through time" would apply even to fluctuations covering long periods of time. For instance, it is well known that the output of agricultural commodities varies from year to year; in some years we have a poor crop, and in other years we have a good crop. If the crop could not be stored for any length of time, of course, the whole crop would either have to be eaten or go to waste in the year in which it was produced. In a year of a large crop, therefore, we should expect to find a low price, and in a year of a small crop we should expect to find a high price. If, now, we suppose that the commodity can be stored fairly easily, it will pay speculators to buy the commodity in years when the price is low (i.e., when the crop is large) and to sell the commodity again in the years when the price is high (i.e., when the crop is small). In this way the action of speculators tends to make the price vary less from year to year. In the years of good crops they take some of the crop off the market in order to store it for a later year; this has the effect of making the price higher than it otherwise would be. In the years of poor crops the speculators bring out what they have stored and place it on the market; this has the effect of making the price lower than it otherwise would be. If speculators had perfect knowledge of the future, we would expect them to take just so much off the market in years of good crops and to put just so much on the market in years of lean crops, so that the difference in price between the good and the lean years would be just sufficient to make it worth while to store and hold the commodity between the good and the lean years. If, to take a very simple case, we knew that a good year was always followed by a lean year, and the cost of holding, say, wheat for a year was 12 cents per bushel, then we should expect the price in the good year to be 12 cents per bushel lower than the price in the lean year.

In fact, unfortunately, things do not always work themselves out in this simple way. The action of the speculators can be based only upon *estimates* of what the future is going to bring. Consequently, if these estimates are wrong—as they may well be—the result of speculation may be very different from what we have indicated here. To this problem, however, we shall return later.

QUESTIONS AND EXERCISES

1. The following table shows the individual market schedules of eight marketers, A, B, C, D, E, F, G, and H.

Price (per Bu.)	Quantity Which Each Would Buy (+) or Sell (−) at Each Price (Thousand Bushels)							
	A	B	C	D	E	F	G	H
$1.20	+ 1	0	− 3	− 5	−10	−20	−25	−23
1.10	+ 4	+ 2	+ 2	0	− 3	−11	−18	−16
1.00	+ 9	+ 7	+12	+ 6	+ 5	0	− 9	− 9
0.90	+16	+11	+25	+13	+14	+10	0	− 4
0.80	+23	+16	+40	+22	+24	+16	+ 3	− 1

a. Derive and draw the market demand and market supply curves, and the total market curve for this market, and derive from them the equilibrium market price and the volume of transactions at this price. (Assume that the market is perfectly competitive.)

b. Suppose now that H drops out of the market. How would you describe this change in the situation? Draw the supply and demand curves and the total market curve for the market as it now stands, with only A, B, C, D, E, F, and G left in it, on the same diagrams on which you drew the supply and demand curves and the total market curve for the eight marketers. How would you describe the change in these curves? What difference has the removal of H made to the price and to the volume of transactions?

c. Repeat part (b) of this question, on the assumption that not H but A has dropped out of the market, and that therefore only marketers B to H remain.

2. Suppose each of the marketers in the example above suddenly became willing to buy or sell *double* the quantities which they had before (i.e., suppose that each of the quantity figures in the table were doubled). What would happen to:

a. The demand and supply curves.

b. The total market curve.

c. The market price.

d. The volume of transactions.

3. In exercise 2 the change in the individual market schedules changed

both demand and supply curves. Why? Under what circumstances could the market demand curve change without a change in the supply curve, or the market supply curve change without a change in the demand curve?

4. Would it be possible to have a pair of supply and demand curves which did not intersect anywhere? Construct a numerical system of market schedules in which this would be the case. What would be the significance of such a condition?

5. Explain in your own words exactly why you would expect the price of wheat in Liverpool to be greater than the price of wheat in Chicago.

6. During the last century important wheat fields have been developed in the southern hemisphere, in Australia and in South America. Remembering that the months of harvest in the southern hemisphere are February and March, what effect would you expect this development to have on the seasonal variation in the price of wheat, assuming that there is a competitive market and that wheat can be stored without difficulty?

7. Read the Book of Genesis, Chapters 41 and 47. Discuss, with these chapters in mind, the problem of the nature, functions, and desirability of speculating in grain.

8. Suppose that no expenses were involved in holding wheat, and that knowledge of the future were perfect. In this case the action of speculators would result in the price of wheat being constant from year to year. Why, exactly? Would this mean that the *incomes* of farmers were constant from year to year also?

CHAPTER 6

SOME APPLICATIONS OF SUPPLY AND DEMAND ANALYSIS

The concepts and principles of the two preceding chapters have many important applications to practical problems. Before we proceed to further forms of analysis, it will repay us to consider some important aspects of economic life to which the theory of a competitive market can be applied.

THE FOREIGN EXCHANGES

The Meaning of National Currencies

One aspect of the world of today which many people find puzzling is the question of the foreign exchanges. With the aid of the analysis in the previous chapters this apparent mystery becomes understandable. It is a well-known fact that the world is divided into a number of nations, each of which has a monetary unit of its own. The United States has its dollar, Great Britain its pound, France its franc, Germany its mark, and so on. A unit of any one of these currencies represents a tacit undertaking, on the part of the people of the countries concerned, to supply the owner with an amount of goods or services equal in value to the money he owns. If I own a dollar bill, I can go to any American who offers goods for sale to the public and obtain from him a dollar's worth of goods in exchange for the dollar. If I own a pound note, I can go to any Britisher who offers goods or services for sale to the public, and obtain from him one pound's worth of his goods or services. But if I go to an American and offer him a pound note, or if I go to a Britisher and offer him a dollar bill, I will be unlikely to get goods and services in exchange. Frequently, however, we find Americans, with nothing but dollars in their possession, who wish to buy goods and services from Britishers, and who consequently must change their dollars into pounds before that can be done. An American tourist, for instance, must transform some of his dollars into pounds before he can buy British hotel services and British meals. There will also be Britishers who wish to buy goods and services from Americans, and who have to transform their pounds into dollars before this can be done. Or perhaps there are American manufacturers who have sold their goods in Britain and received pounds in return, who wish to bring these pounds home and spend them in America; they must transform them into dollars. Or there may be British manufacturers who have sold goods in America, and who wish to transform into pounds the dollars which they have received.

The Foreign Exchange Market

The foreign exchange market, then, is an arrangement whereby dollars can be transformed into pounds, and pounds can be transformed into dollars. Just as the wheat market is an arrangement whereby people who have money and want wheat can meet people who have wheat and want money, so the foreign exchange market is an arrangement whereby people who have pounds and want dollars can meet people who have dollars and want pounds. The "dollars" and "pounds" in question are not, of course, necessarily dollar bills and pound notes; for the most part they consist of "bills of exchange," which are *orders to pay* dollars or pounds. As we shall see later, these amount to practically the same thing as dollars or pounds in any other form, so that we can neglect the form for the moment.

The Foreign Exchange Rate

The "foreign exchange rate" is the ratio of exchange in transactions taking place in the foreign exchange market. It is, in other words, the "price" of one currency in terms of the other. If we say that the price of wheat is 90 cents per bushel, we mean that anyone can take 90 cents to the wheat market and get a bushel of wheat in return, or anyone can take a bushel of wheat to the market and get 90 cents in return. Similarly, if the "price" of dollars is £0.357, or about 7 shillings per dollar in the foreign exchange market—or if, what is the same thing, the "price" of pounds is $2.80 per pound, anyone can go to the market and find a trader there who will give him $2.80 for every pound he offers, or £0.357 for every dollar he offers.

The Foreign Exchange Market as a Competitive Market

If, then, the foreign exchange market is a competitive market, the principles which apply to the competitive market in general should apply to it. For instance, an increased desire on the part of the people in the market to get rid of dollars should cause the "price" of dollars in terms of other currencies to fall; but an increased desire to acquire dollars should cause the price of dollars to rise. We could interpret the day-to-day fluctuations in the foreign exchange rates therefore just as we could similar fluctuations in the price of wheat—as being due to changes in the market schedules of the people who are in the market.

Application of Principle of Clearing the Market

The principle of "clearing the market" can be applied to the foreign exchange market, as to any other; the "equilibrium" ratio of exchange is that at which the quantity of each currency which the marketers wish to sell is equal to the quantity of each currency which the marketers wish to buy. In the dollar-pound market, for instance, we can postulate market schedules for each marketer showing how many dollars he will buy and sell at each "price" of dollars. From these market schedules we can derive the market demand and supply schedules for dollars, and from these deduce the equilibrium price and the quantity which will be exchanged at that price. Or, as a demand for dollars is exactly the same thing as a supply of pounds, and a supply of dollars the same thing as a demand for pounds, we could deduce demand and supply schedules for pounds which would equally well give us the equilibrium price and the quantity exchanged. These principles are illustrated in Table 10. Column 1 gives

TABLE 10.   The Equilibrium of the Foreign Exchanges

1	2	3	4	5	6
	Number of Dollars	Number of Dollars	Number of Pounds	Number of Pounds	
Price of Dollars (£ per $)	Demanded (Mill.)	Offered (Mill.)	Offered (Mill.)	Demanded (Mill.)	Price of Pounds ($ per £)
0.333	12	8	4.00	2.66	3.00
0.345	11	9	3.79	3.10	2.90
0.357	10	10	3.57	3.57	2.80
0.370	9	11	3.33	4.07	2.70
0.385	8	12	3.08	4.62	2.60

the price of dollars. Just as the price of wheat in terms of pounds is the number of pounds which exchange for 1 bushel, so the price of dollars is the number of pounds which exchange for 1 dollar. Column 6 is the price of pounds—i.e., the number of dollars which will exchange for one pound. Each figure of column 6 is the reciprocal of the corresponding figure of column 1. Column 2 gives the number of dollars demanded at each price. In column 4 essentially the same set of facts is expressed in the form of the number of pounds offered for dollars at each price. The number of pounds offered at each price is equal to the number of dollars demanded at that price, multiplied by the price of dollars. If, for instance, at a price of £0.357 per dollar a man wants to buy $2.80, to get the $2.80 he must offer £1. A demand for $2.80 and an offer of £1 are therefore exactly the same thing if the ratio of exchange is $2.80 per pound. Column 3 shows the number of dollars offered at each price, column 5 the corresponding number of pounds demanded.

Demand and Supply in the Foreign Exchange Market

Columns 1 and 2 form the demand schedule for dollars, and columns 1 and 3 the supply schedule for dollars. Columns 6 and 5 form the demand schedule for pounds, columns 6 and 4 the supply schedule for pounds. The equilibrium price is clearly £0.357 per dollar, or $2.80 per pound. These supply and demand schedules give us sufficient equipment to analyze the effect of any external changes on the foreign exchanges. If for instance the number of dollars possessed by the people in the market increases, our analysis of the preceding chapter indicates that the marketers will be willing to offer more dollars, and to demand fewer, at each price. The equilibrium price of dollars will therefore fall. Likewise, if the number of dollars possessed by the marketers diminishes, the price of dollars will rise.

The "Offer Ratio" Equal to the Price in Equilibrium

We can, however, effect a certain simplification in the exposition of problems of the foreign exchanges if we make an assumption which is not wholly true, but not far from the truth. It is that in any given period of time there will be a certain number of pounds which are in the market "looking for dollars" and which will be offered no matter what the price, and also a certain number of dollars "looking for pounds" which will also be offered no matter what the price. The demand and supply schedules corresponding to this situation are shown in Table 11.

Table 11.   Equilibrium of the Foreign Exchanges with Fixed Supplies

1 Price of Dollars (£ per $)	2 Number of Dollars Demanded (Mill.)	3 Number of Dollars Offered (Mill.)	4 Number of Pounds Offered (Mill.)	5 Number of Pounds Demanded (Mill.)	6 Price of Pounds ($ per £)
0.333	10.71	10	3.57	3.33	3.00
0.345	10.36	10	3.57	3.45	2.90
0.357	10.00	10	3.57	3.57	2.80
0.370	9.64	10	3.57	3.70	2.70
0.385	9.29	10	3.57	3.85	2.60

In this table there are 10 million dollars in the market looking for pounds, and 3.57 million pounds looking for dollars. In this circumstance the ratio of exchange will be equal to the ratio of the quantities of the two currencies being offered. We need merely write $10,000,000 = £3,570,000, or $2.80 = £1, to obtain the exchange ratio immediately, The ratio of the quantities of the two exchangeables offered in a market may be called the "offer ratio." Turning to either Table 10 or Table 11, we see that at the equilibrium price, the price is equal to the offer ratio, and at no other price is this true. At £0.333 per dollar in Table 10, for instance, the offer ratio is $\frac{£4.00}{$8.00}$ or £0.20 per dollar. Only at the equilibrium price is the offer ratio $\left(\frac{£3.57}{$10.00}\right)$ equal to the price (£0.357 per dollar). This is a perfectly general principle, and is in fact an alternative way of stating the principle of "clearing the market."

Effect of Changes in Trade Situation on Exchange Rates

This principle gives us an easy way of telling how any particular change in the trade situation will affect the exchanges, for the foreign exchange rate will always tend to be equal to the ratio in which the two currencies are "looking for each other" in the market. If the rate is $3.00 to £1, there are three times as many dollars looking for pounds as there are pounds looking for dollars. All that is necessary, then, in investigating the effect of some event on the foreign exchanges, is to ask what will be the effect of this event on the number of pounds looking for dollars on the one hand, or on the number of dollars looking for pounds on the other hand.

Examples: 1. *A European War.* One or two examples should make the principle clear. Suppose that Britain gets into a war and suddenly increases her purchases of munitions from the United States.[1] The purchases are made with pounds, which come into the possession of the American manufacturers. These manufacturers do not want pounds; they want dollars. Consequently, the pounds become "pounds looking for dollars" on the foreign exchange market. If previously in each period there were £10,000,000 and $44,000,000 looking for each other on the foreign exchange market and finding each other at a rate of £1 = $4.40, now there are £11,000,000 looking for dollars but only $44,000,000 looking for pounds, for nothing has yet happened to increase that figure. The exchange rate will therefore move to £11 = $44, or £1 = $4.00. The excess of pounds on the market has made pounds cheaper; instead of having to pay $4.40 for one we can now buy one for $4.00

2. *An International Loan.* Now suppose that the British government raises a loan on Wall Street of $5,000,000. Naturally, it will want these dollars turned into pounds and will put them into the foreign exchange market with this in mind. Again, suppose that previously there were £10,000,000 looking for dollars and $40,000,000 looking for pounds. Now there are the same number of pounds looking for dollars—£10,000,000—but as a result of the loan there are $45,000,000 looking for pounds. The exchange rate will therefore move to £1 = $4.50; i.e., the increase in the number of dollars on the market will make dollars cheaper, pounds dearer. In a similar way we can analyze the probable effects on the foreign exchanges of any event we may mention.

The Case of More Than Two Currencies. Arbitrage

In the foregoing analysis we have assumed, in effect, that there were only two countries—the United States and Britain. In fact, of course, there are many more countries and many more currencies. Our analysis will also enable us to deal with this problem. In each market the exchange rate will be in equilibrium at that point where it is equal to the ratio of the quantities of currencies "looking for" each other. As between the different markets the exchange rates will be kept *consistent* by means of the operations of arbitrage. The last chapter showed how arbitrage made for consistency in exchange ratios between three markets—a wheat-dollar market, a wheat-pound

---

[1] The average price of a pound sterling in New York in August, 1939, was $4.623. In September, 1939, it was $4.041. This fall was not, of course, due wholly to an immediate increase of purchases made by Britain in America after the declaration of war; part of the fall may have been due to speculative anticipation of increased purchases, part to the regulative activity of the Exchange Equalization Funds.

market, and a dollar-pound market. In exactly the same way arbitrage makes for consistency in the exchange rates in, say, the dollar-pound market, the pound-franc market, and the franc-dollar market.

Suppose, for instance, that exchange rates in London, Paris, and New York are as follows:

$$\text{London} \quad \$2.70 = £1$$
$$\text{Paris} \qquad\quad £1 = 957\text{fr}$$
$$\text{New York} \qquad\quad 957\text{fr} = \$2.90$$
$$(330\text{fr} = \$1.00)$$

It is evident that a trader could take $2.70 in London, buy £1 with it there, take the pound to Paris and buy 957 francs there, then take the francs to New York and buy $2.90, thus making $0.20 on the transaction, assuming no costs of transport or exchange. These transactions in themselves, however, will change the exchange rates. Because people are throwing dollars on the London market and buying pounds there, dollars will become cheaper and pounds dearer. Similarly in Paris francs will become dearer and pounds cheaper, and in New York francs will become cheaper and dollars dearer. The final result may then be as follows:

$$\text{London} \quad \$2.80 = £1$$
$$\text{Paris} \qquad\quad £1 = 952\text{fr}$$
$$\text{New York} \qquad\quad 952\text{fr} = \$2.80$$
$$(340\text{fr} = \$1.00)$$

At these rates of exchange arbitrage is no longer profitable, for $2.80 in London becomes £1, which becomes 952 francs in Paris, which becomes again $2.80 in New York. The rates therefore are consistent.

Inconsistency Due to Cost of Transport and Exchange

We have assumed· in this that there are no costs of transport or of exchange. In fact, there are small costs involved in transferring funds between various markets and in making the necessary exchanges. Consequently, a certain amount of inconsistency in the exchange rates is possible without giving rise to arbitrage transactions, for unless the gross profit to be made by arbitrage is at least equal to the expenses of performing the operation, the operation will not be performed. In the first example above, for instance, if the cost of performing the operation described were $0.20 or more, there would be no arbitrage, and the rates would therefore be consistent in the sense of not being subject to change through arbitrage. Thus where there is a certain cost of operation of arbitrage, there exists a certain range of variation of the exchange rates within which arbitrage will not take place and within which, therefore, the relative exchange rates may vary freely.

Example. To take a simple example, suppose that in New York the pound-dollar ratio is £1 = $2.80, and that in London the pound-dollar ratio is £1 = $2.85. If no expenses are involved, it would clearly be profitable to take $2.80 in New York, buy £1 with it, take the pound to London, and there change it for $2.85, making a profit of $0.05 on each $2.80 thus exchanged. These transactions would soon do away with the difference in rates. The extra dollars coming into the New York market would make dollars cheaper, moving the rate, say, to £1 = $2.82; the extra pounds coming into the London market would make pounds cheaper there, moving the rate, say, to £1 = $2.82 —and arbitrage would cease. But if the cost of making these exchanges amounts to $0.05 on each $2.80 involved, it will not pay to perform the transaction unless the difference between the two exchange rates amounts to more than $0.05 for each $2.80. If, for instance, the rate in New York were £1 = $2.80 and the rate in London were £1 = $2.86, it would then pay to ship pounds from New York to London, and dollars from London to New York, even if the cost of doing this were $0.05 for each pound shipped. Similarly, if the rate in New York were £1 = $2.80 and the rate in London were £1 = $2.74, it would then pay to ship pounds from London to New York and dollars from New York to London, even if it cost $0.05 to make the shipment. The rates in London and New York, therefore, may differ in this case by as much as 5 cents in $2.80, either way, before arbitrage will occur.

THE GOLD STANDARD

Another mystery which we can now clear up is that of the gold standard. The gold standard is simply a law, passed by the legislative authority of a country like any other law, which says that some authority in the country (usually the Central Bank or the Treasury of the government itself) shall be obliged to exchange gold for the money of the country, and the money of the country for gold, at a *fixed legal rate.* Under the old free gold standard, for instance, the Bank of England was compelled by law to buy gold from anyone who offered it at a price of £4.2409 per fine ounce, and to sell it at a price of £4.2477 per fine ounce to anyone who demanded it. Similarly, the United States Treasury was compelled by law to buy and sell gold at a price of $20.67 per ounce. There are thus two essential features of a gold standard—a fixed legal price for gold, and some arrangement for making that price effective, i.e., for enabling people to buy and sell gold at that price.

Any Commodity Could Hypothetically Be a Standard

There is no absolute reason why gold should be chosen as a standard. At certain periods in the world's history, especially during the nineteenth century, it has been found to be a convenient standard, but it is quite possible to use other metals. A silver standard, for instance, would mean that the price of silver was fixed by law and that some authority was compelled by law to buy and sell silver at this price. It is possible also to imagine the use of nonmetals as standards. If, for instance, Congress passed a law which compelled the Department of Agriculture to exchange pigs for dollars and dollars for pigs at a fixed legal price of, say, $5 per pig, anyone who had a pig could present it to the Department of Agriculture and receive $5 in return, and anyone who had $5 could present that to the Department of Agriculture and get a pig in return. Then we would be on a pig standard. It would be excessively inconvenient, for the Department of Agriculture would have to keep a reserve of pigs in the basement, no doubt to the discomfort of the human inhabitants, and it would be even more awkward to use pigs in the settlement of international balances—but at least it would be a standard.

Exchange Rates Fixed Between Two Gold Standard Countries

Now, when two countries are on the gold standard, the principle of arbitrage operates to make it impossible for the exchange ratio of the two currencies in the foreign exchange market to differ appreciably from the ratio of the fixed prices of these currencies in terms of gold. If (to use simple figures for the sake of the arithmetic) the United States Treasury were compelled to buy and sell gold for dollars at a rate of $35 per ounce of gold, and the Bank of England had to buy and sell gold for pounds at a rate of £12.5 per ounce of gold, the exchange rate between dollars and pounds in the foreign exchange market could not vary very much from the rate of £12.5 = $35 or £1 = $2.80. For suppose that in the foreign exchange market in any one day there are £10,000,000 looking for $30,000,000, so that the equilibrium rate is £1 = $3. At this rate a person wishing to buy pounds with dollars would not buy them in the foreign exchange market at all. By taking $2.80 to the Treasury in New York he could get 0.08 ounces of gold, and by crossing the Atlantic to London and presenting this gold to the Bank of England he could get £1 for it.

Thus by using gold as an intermediary he could get his pound for $2.80 instead of having to pay $3 as he would in the foreign exchange market. This would remove dollars from the foreign exchange market until there were only $28,000,000 looking for the £10,000,000, and the rate would be $2.80 = £1.

Conversely, if we suppose that on a given day there are only $25,-000,000 looking for pounds, and £10,000,000 looking for dollars, the rate in the foreign exchange market will be $2.50 = £1. But if this is the case it will pay anyone who wants dollars for his pounds to take each pound to the Bank of England, get 0.08 ounces of gold for it, ship that gold across the Atlantic to New York, and get $2.80 for it there. Thus he would get $2.80 for each pound instead of $2.50 in the foreign exchange market. But if people bought their dollars through the intermediary of gold, pounds would be removed from the foreign exchange market until the rate in the foreign exchange market was again £1 = $2.80. We should recognize this procedure as merely a special case of the principle of three-cornered arbitrage discussed earlier—a special case which arises because in the pound-gold and the dollar-gold markets the price is fixed by law.

The Gold Points

In the preceding example we assumed that there were no costs of transport of gold between the financial centers. Of course, actually there is a small cost of transport, which introduces the possibility of apparent "inconsistency" in the exchange rates and the gold prices. Suppose that it costs $0.02 to transport 0.08 ounces of gold across the Atlantic in either direction between New York and London. If, then, a man bought 0.08 ounce of gold with £1, shipped the gold to New York, and there bought dollars with it, he would receive a net sum of only $2.78 for his £1, for out of the $2.80 received for the gold at the United States Treasury he would have paid $0.02 for transport. Similarly, a man would have to take $2.82 in New York in order to obtain £1 in London through the intermediary of gold. Gold will not move from one center to the other, therefore, as long as the exchange rate in the market lies within the range from $2.78 to $2.82 per pound. These limits are called the "gold points." If the price of pounds rose above $2.82 in the market, gold would begin to flow from New York to London, for it would be cheaper to buy pounds indirectly through buying gold in New York and selling it in London. This rate, therefore, is the gold export point for New York, the gold import point for London. Similarly, if the price of pounds in the market fell below $2.78, it would pay to buy dollars by shipping gold to New York. This rate is the gold import point for New York, the gold export point for London.

THE SECURITIES MARKET

From our present vantage point we can also gain some insight into the operations of another important feature of economic life—the securities market. Any market is a place where things are exchanged. The first step to the understanding of a market is to answer the question, "What is exchanged in it?" The things that are exchanged in the securities markets are not commodities but rights, expectations, or claims. In these transactions it may be that only a few pieces of engraved paper actually change hands. It may be, even, that the transactions consist of an exchange of abstract rights recorded only in the books of a banker or a stockbroker. These rights are of many kinds. They may, however, be divided into two broad classes, one of which we shall call "securities," the other, "money." As a first approximation to an understanding of the securities market we shall assume that it is an organization through which securities are exchanged for money. It is an organization whereby people who have money and want securities are enabled to meet people who have securities and want money, and so effect the exchanges which both parties desire.

What Is a "Security"?

But what is a "security"? What do we buy when we give up money for a security? A security is a *right* to certain future benefits, when viewed from the side of its owner. It is an *obligation* to grant certain future benefits to the owner, when viewed from the side of the issuer. It would perhaps be even more accurate to describe a security as an *expectation*. The owner of the security expects to receive certain benefits in the future. The issuer of the security expects to grant certain benefits. The benefits in question usually consist of sums of money. They do not, however, have to consist of *definite* sums of money. The possessor may merely gain a right to share in residual profits, or to participate in the control of a corporation.

Kinds of Securities

1. *Bonds.* There are many different kinds of securities. They can be divided, however, into two broad classes—"bonds" and "stocks." A bond is a promise, or an obligation, to pay certain definite sums

at definite future dates to the person who owns it. In the technical language of the market the word "bond" is usually confined to those securities which oblige the issuer to pay a series of equal annual or semiannual payments, culminating in a much larger payment known as the "redemption" of the bond. A security, for instance, which conferred on its owner the right to receive $50 on the first of January each year for the next ten years and a further payment of, say, $1000 at the end of the ten years would be a "bond." For want of a better term, however, we may broaden the term "bond" to mean any security which consists of an obligation to pay definite sums on definite future dates. A promissory note, therefore, would be a "bond" in this sense, for the issuer of the note is "bound" to pay, let us say, a single sum of $1050 twelve months from the present date. A bank loan would be a "bond" of the person to whom it is issued, for he gives his promise to pay the bank a stated sum on a stated date in return for a sum of money in the present.

2. *Shares of Stock.* At the other extreme is a type of security known as a *share of stock,* represented in its purest form by what is known as an "ordinary" or "common" share. This is not an obligation to pay a series of definite sums at definite future dates, nor does its owner expect to receive a series of known sums in the future. It is an obligation to pay a definite share of the residual profits of a business. Consequently to its owner it represents at any one moment a series of expected future payments whose magnitude depends on the expectation which he entertains as to the future profitability of the business. A given ordinary share, therefore, may represent a different series of expected payments in the mind of each person in the market. One person may be optimistic about the future of the business. He thinks it will make large profits in the future, and so for him the ordinary share represents an expected series of large payments. Another may be equally pessimistic. For him, the same share will represent an expected series of small payments, or perhaps of no payments at all. In so far as all future events are uncertain, all securities, whether stocks or bonds, may mean different expectations to different people. In the case of a bond, however, the expected payments are limited on one side by the contract written in the bond and on the other side by the possibility of the repudiation of this contract at some future date. If I have a bond which gives me a right to receive $50 for ten years, I shall not expect to receive more than this. I may, of course, receive less if the bond is repudiated. But the possibility of variation in the payments from an ordinary share is much greater.

3. *Preference Shares.* Midway between the bond and the ordinary share comes a class of security known as the "preference share." This has something of the character of a bond in that it represents an obligation of the issuer to pay not more than a stated sum each year. A "7 per cent" preference share with a nominal value of $100 would entitle its owner to a maximum of $7 per year. If, however, the profits of the issuing company do not justify this payment, it does not have to be made. In this sense it is like an ordinary share.

Other Benefits

The future benefits expected by the owner of a security may include certain "nonmonetary" benefits. An ordinary share, for instance, usually entitles its owner to a voice in the management of the issuing company. A bond normally gives no such right, except when a company defaults on its bonds and is reorganized. Nonmonetary benefits may be important in determining what various people will pay for a security.

The Price of Securities Determined Like Any Other Price

What is meant by the "price" of a security? A price is a ratio of exchange; that is, the ratio of the quantities of things exchanged in a transaction. In order to be able to measure the price of a security in any transaction, we must be able to measure both the quantity of the security and the quantity of the thing given in exchange. The thing given in exchange is almost invariably money of some kind. The "barter" of securities for securities may sometimes occur, but it is rare. We can easily measure the quantity of money as a sum of "dollars." The "quantity of security" is generally measured in conventional units of some nominal value; e.g., "thousand-dollar bonds." Each of these conventional units, however, may represent a different expectation, a different series of expected future benefits, at various times or even in the eyes of various people at one time.

If any security is present in the market in a large number of identical units and has a large number of buyers and sellers, it will have a competitive market. In that case its price will be determined according to the general principles which govern such a market. Its equilibrium price will be that at which the quantity of the security offered for sale is equal to the quantity demanded for purchase. For any such security we can draw demand and supply curves, as in Fig. 4, page 58, derived from the market schedules of all the people in the market. Its equilibrium price will then be given by the point of intersection of these demand and supply curves. Alternatively, we could draw the total market curve for the security, as in Fig. 6, page 67, to find the price at the point where there was no excess demand or supply.

Why Does the Price of a Security Change?

If the price of such a security changes, it must be because of a change in the market schedules of the people in the market, leading to a change in the total market curve. What may cause these market schedules to change? That is to say, what may cause a change in the general eagerness to buy or sell any given security? One thing which may cause such a change is a revision in the expectations of future benefits from a security. Suppose, for instance, that it becomes generally believed in the market that a certain government is about to default on its bonds. The expected sum of future payments from these bonds becomes smaller, no matter what the face value of the obligation. As a result, people become more eager to sell them, less eager to buy them. The total market curve will fall, and with it the equilibrium price will fall. Or, to put the same matter in another way, the fact that people are now less eager to buy the bonds means that the demand for them has fallen; their demand curve has moved to the left. People are also more eager to get rid of them, so their supply has risen; their supply curve has moved to the right. We see from Fig. 5, page 65, that this means a decline in the equilibrium price.

Similarly, if there is a favorable revision of the expected future payments from a security, there will be a rise in the demand for it, a fall in the supply of it, and its price will go up. Ordinary shares are more susceptible to changes of this sort than bonds, as revisions in the expectations of future profit of a company have to be made frequently. A rise in the price of an ordinary share may therefore mean solely that the market as a whole takes a more cheerful view of the prospects of the issuing company. A change of this kind may be called a change in the "quality" of a security. In a corresponding way, if the quality of any commodity rises, its price per unit of quantity may be expected to rise.

Changes in the Price of Fixed Expectations

Securities do not change in price merely because of changes in their "quality," however. Their prices are subject to frequent fluctuations which have nothing to do with changes in their expected future payments. These are brought about by variations in the relative desire of people in the market to hold *money* as against securities. Whenever a security is bought, the buyer relinquishes a certain quantity of money and acquires an equivalent quantity of the security. The seller relinquishes a certain quantity of the security and acquires an equivalent quantity of money. A sale of securities therefore is the same thing as a "purchase" of money, and a purchase of securities is the same as a "sale" of money. A "demand" for securities is the same thing as a "supply" of money, and from the demand curve for a security we can construct a supply curve of "money offered for the security" which will describe exactly the same set of facts. If, for instance, at a price of $100 per unit 500 units of a security should be demanded, this means also that (100 × 500), or $50,000, will be offered in exchange for the security at that price. Similarly, a "supply" of a security is the same thing as a "demand" for money.

Equilibrium Price

The equilibrium level of the price of securities on any one "day" is that level, therefore, at which there is no *net* desire on the part of the people in the market to increase their holdings either of money or of securities. If at a certain price an individual wishes to buy securities, he must be dissatisfied with the distribution of his total funds between securities and money. He must feel that he has too much money and too few securities, and consequently he wishes to increase the amount of securities and to decrease the amount of money which he holds. Similarly, if an individual wishes to sell securities at that price, he must want to increase the amount of money and to decrease the amount of securities which he holds. If, now, the price of securities is such that the desire to get rid of securities and acquire money on the part of some individuals is just balanced by the desire to get rid of money and acquire securities on the part of others, there will be equilibrium. But if at the existing price there is on balance a *general* desire to increase holdings of money and to decrease holdings of securities, then the price of securities must fall.

Increased Demand for Securities or Money

The assumption in this argument, it should be noticed, is that the total quantity both of securities and of money in the possession of the marketers is fixed, so that transactions do not change this total quantity but merely change its ownership. In short periods this assumption is substantially true; over longer periods it is of course much less accurate. In short periods, then, any general increase in the desire to hold securities cannot be satisfied by an increase in the *quantity* of securities held, for the total quantity of securities is assumed to be fixed. It can be satisfied only by an increase in the money *value* of the securities held, i.e., by a rise in the price of securities. Similarly, any increase in the desire to hold money cannot be satisfied by an increase in the *quantity* of money held; it can be satisfied only by an increase in the "value" of the money held in terms of securities, i.e., by a fall in the price of securities.

Example. Suppose that the people in the market on a given day possess $10,000,000 of money and 1,000,000 "units" of securities. Suppose that the price of securities is $50 per unit, so that the total value of the securities held is $50,000,000. Now let there be an increased desire to hold securities, which is the same thing as a desire on the part of the market as a whole to increase its holding of securities, i.e., to acquire securities. The price of securities will rise, let us say, to $60 per unit. The value of the 1,000,000 securities held will now be $60,-000,000 instead of $50,000,000. The rise in the desire to hold securities has resulted in an increase in the *value*, not in the *quantity*, of the securities held. On the other hand, suppose there is an increased desire to hold money—i.e., to acquire money by selling securities—on the part of the market as a whole. The price of securities will fall, let us say, to $40 per unit. Previously the $10,000,000 of money in the market was worth 200,000 units of securities; now it is worth 250,000 units. The increased desire to hold money has resulted not in an increase in the quantity of money held but in an increase in the value of that money. This is a principle of very general importance, as we shall see later.

Effect of Increase in the Quantity of Securities or Money Held

Just as in the case of the wheat market an increase in the quantity of wheat held by the people in the market is likely to depress the price of wheat, so an increase in the quantity of securities held by the people in the market is likely to depress the price of securities. And again, just as an increase in the quantity of money held by people in the wheat market is likely to raise the price of wheat, so an increase in the quantity of money held by people in the stock market is likely to raise the price of securities. Both these propositions, of course, depend on the assumption that the fundamental desires to buy and sell do not change. If, for instance, the government presented $1000 in cash to each person in the stock market one morning, that in itself would have the effect of raising the price of securities. But an event so odd might conceivably scare the wits out of the very people who were the recipients of this bounty, and so increase greatly their desire to get rid of securities and to hold money in readiness to flee so crazy a country. Consequently, the net effect *might* be to lower the price of securities, though in fact this is unlikely.

Self-Justifying Fluctuations

In all respects so far, the principles underlying the wheat market, the foreign exchange market, and the securities market have been exactly parallel. There is, however, a phenomenon especially characteristic of the securities market, which depends upon the peculiar nature of the things exchanged in that market. This we may call the phenomenon of "self-justified anticipations." It arises from the fact that a "security" is not something which exists merely in the present; it is an expectation of receiving future payments. A security also is something which can be *sold* in the future, and the money received from any future sale is part of the anticipated future payments from the security. Suppose I bought a bond for $1000 which promised to pay me $50 a year forever. (Such a bond is called a "perpetuity.") If I anticipated selling the bond for $1100 in two years, then, in effect, the payments which I expect from it are not $50 a year forever, but $50 next year and $50 + $1100 the year after. Obviously, therefore, the greater I expect the price of the bond to be in two years, the more money I expect to receive from it, and consequently the more money will I be willing to pay for it now. So if I expect the price of the bond in the future to be greater than it is now, I shall be more willing to buy the bond than if I expected the price in the future to be less than it is now—in spite of the fact that the bond still represents an obligation on the part of its issuer to pay $50 a year to its owner forever. This means that if people in the market as a whole expect the price of securities to rise, they will be more eager to buy securities than if they expect the price to fall.

Expectations Justify Themselves

Notice, however, the consequence of this. If people expect the price of securities to go up, they will become more eager to buy securities and to get rid of money, and *consequently the price of securities will rise.* The very expectation of a rise tends to bring it about. Similarly, if people expect the price of securities to fall, they will become more eager to sell securities and to acquire money, and therefore the price of securities *will* fall. This is what we mean when we say that anticipa-

tions are "self-justified." The very fact that a certain thing is anticipated by a large number of people tends to bring it about. This accounts for the great magnitude of the ups and downs on the stock
market, although there are also other causes at work.

The "Bull Market"

If for some reason people expect the prices of securities to rise, rise
they will. Suppose now that people find in the fulfillment of their
expectations justification for believing in the continuance of the rise.
Then the continued belief in a future rise in prices will cause prices to
rise still further. This is the phenomenon known as a "bull market."
The New York Stock Exchange between 1927 and 1929 provides a
good example. Prices rise because people think they are going to rise,
and people think they are going to rise because they are rising. However, prices cannot go up forever, and the time must eventually come,
even in the most bullish of bull markets, when people in large numbers begin to doubt whether the rise can continue. The moment they
do this, they will wish to sell securities and to acquire money, for now
it is money, not securities, which is expected to appreciate in value.

The "Bear Market"

Now take the reverse condition. Because prices have fallen, people
expect them to fall further. Hence the desire to sell securities grows
as prices drop, and prices will go on dropping until people believe
that they can go no further. Then when prices are so low that most
people believe they cannot fall further, the drop will be checked. A
new rise may then begin, and the vicious cycle starts all over again.

Fluctuations Due to Predominance of Speculation

Here is an example of speculation—i.e., arbitrage through time—
failing utterly to perform its proper function. Instead of smoothing
out the fluctuations of prices, as it does usually in the case of commodity markets, it leads to an increase in the magnitude of these
fluctuations. It is not difficult to see why this is so. In some markets
the speculators play only a relatively small part. Most of the transactions take place between people who buy the commodity not to sell
again but to use in some way, and who use the money obtained from
the sale of the commodity not for its repurchase but for other purposes.
In that case the action of speculators, and the beliefs of speculators
about future prices, will not greatly affect the total desire to buy and
sell in the market as a whole, for most of the people who are buying

and selling are doing so for present purposes rather than for the future. Then speculation may reasonably be expected to lessen the fluctuations of price through time. If, however, the bulk of the transactions is between people who buy and sell not to hold or use the commodity but to sell it again—that is, if the majority of the marketers are speculators—then their actions may very well set up wide fluctuations of prices through the principle of self-justifying expectations which has just been explained. Speculation in this case will increase the fluctuations of price through time. Most of the commodity markets, fortunately, probably belong to the first class. The securities market, unfortunately, seems to belong to the second class. A great many of the purchases of securities on the securities market are made not with a view to holding or "consuming" the securities bought but with a view to selling them again. Similarly, most of the sales of securities are made with a view to getting money with which to buy other securities. Speculation in "active" periods accounts for by far the greater number of transactions in the security market and consequently gives rise to the disastrous fluctuations of which we are all to well aware.[2]

The Futures Market

There is one further phenomenon, often puzzling to the layman, which can be explored with the aid of our analysis of the market. This is the phenomenon of the "futures" market, and the related problem of "hedging." We have seen how in the securities market present money can be exchanged for promises to pay money in the future. So in the commodity markets money can be exchanged for promises to "pay," or deliver, commodities in the future. Indeed, a promise to pay money in the future can be exchanged for a promise to deliver, say, wheat in the future. These obligations are in fact a peculiar kind of "security" and are knowns as "futures." If I buy "May futures" in the wheat market, I have in effect bought a "security" consisting of the obligation of the seller to deliver to me a certain quantity of wheat

[2] The "market identity" provides a convenient way of expressing the phenomenon of the securities market. If S is the quantity of any given security and M is the quantity of money in the possession of the people in the market, and if r_m is the preferred liquidity ratio and r_s the preferred security ratio, then we have as on page 59, the price of the security, $p_s = \dfrac{Mr_s}{Sr_m}$. An improvement in the "quality" of a security—i.e., an optimistic change in the expectations of future receipts from it—will increase r_s and so increase p_s. An increase in "liquidity preference"—i.e., an increased desire to hold money—increases r_m and so diminishes p_s. An increase in M or a decrease in S, other things being equal, will increase p_s. The principle of self-justifying anticipations arises because the expectation of a rise in p_s will of itself increase r_s and so will increase p_s: if, therefore, a rise in p_s creates expectation of a further rise, the further rise is likely to take place.

next May. A "future contract," then, is a kind of promissory note, the promise being to pay not money but some commodity. Usually, what is given in exchange for this promise to pay "wheat" is a promise to pay money. That is, a promissory note in wheat is really exchanged for a promissory note in money.

Example. Suppose, for instance, that in December I buy 1000 bushels of "May wheat" at $0.90 per bushel. This is known as "buying futures." What I have done is to exchange my promise to pay $900 to the seller next May in return for his promise to deliver to me 1000 bushels of wheat next May. If I "sell futures"—for instance, if I sell 1000 bushels of May wheat at $0.90 per bushel—I have exchanged my promise to deliver 1000 bushels of wheat next May in return for the buyer's promise to deliver $900 next May.

Speculation in Futures

The price of current wheat is called the "spot price." This is the ratio of exchange between "present" wheat and "present" money. Suppose, now, that a dealer expects the spot price of wheat next May to be $1 per bushel, and suppose that he can buy May futures for $0.90 per bushel. In these circumstances he will think it profitable to buy May futures. He exchanges his promise to pay $900 in May for a right to receive 1000 bushels of wheat in May. When May comes around, he fulfills his part of the bargain, pays $900, receives 1000 bushels of wheat, and then sells this wheat for $1000 in the spot market. Thus he makes $100 profit on his transaction. By purchasing May futures at an earlier date he is enabled to come gathering wheat in May at a price which is lower than the spot selling price, and so he makes a profit.

If, on the other hand, the dealer expected the spot price next May to be $0.80, with May futures now selling for $0.90, he would think it profitable to *sell* May futures. He gives his promise to pay 1000 bushels of wheat in May in exchange for the promise of the buyer to pay $900 in May. If his expectation as to the spot price is correct, when May comes he will be able to buy 1000 bushels in the spot market for $800, and to deliver these bushels to the buyer of futures for $900, according to his contract. People who expect the spot price in the future to be greater than the futures price now will therefore be likely to buy futures now, and those who expect the spot price in the future to be less than the futures price now will be likely to sell futures now. Any futures transaction, therefore, is the result of a difference of opinion between the buyer and the seller. The buyer thinks the spot price in the future will be relatively high, and the seller thinks it will be relatively low.[3]

The Purpose of the Futures Markets

Just as bonds on the securities market may change hands many times before the obligation which they represent is fulfilled by the original issuer, so "futures," which are essentially "commodity bonds," can also be exchanged many times before the contract which they represent is fulfilled. The professional speculator in the wheat market may seldom, if ever, handle wheat or make actual deliveries of wheat. He spends his time, and makes his income, if any, by selling and buying the futures contracts themselves. Nevertheless, these complicated arrangements serve really to organize "arbitrage through time" as a specialized function. Their purpose is to separate the function of "carrying" the commodity through time, i.e., of owning and storing it, from the function of bearing the *risks* of price changes. The market in futures enables the speculator to speculate on future price changes without compelling him to own and store the commodity. It also enables the owner and storer of the commodity to escape the risks of speculating on future price changes.

Hedging

The process whereby the owner and storer of a commodity escapes having to speculate on its future price is known as "hedging." A farmer, for instance, may have 10,000 bushels of wheat in his barn in September which he does not wish to sell until May. If he merely holds the wheat until he sells it in the spot market in May, he is in effect speculating on the spot price of wheat in May. If that price is high, he will do well; if it is low, he will do badly. He can lift some of the burden of this uncertainty from his mind by selling "May futures." If May futures stand at $0.90 per bushel, he can enter into a contract with a buyer of futures, binding himself to deliver 10,000 bushels of wheat in May, and binding the buyer to pay in exchange $9000 in money in May. Then no matter what the spot price is when May arrives, the farmer is certain to receive $0.90 per bushel for his wheat. The uncertainty of the future price is lifted from his mind. This does not mean, of course, that he will necessarily gain by the

[3] In so far as futures contracts are not held to maturity, the expected trend of price of the futures contract itself, rather than the expected spot price at the time of maturity, may be the main factor affecting the market demand and supply.

transaction. If in fact the spot price in May turns out to be $1, the farmer would have done better to hold his wheat and sell it in the spot market. Nevertheless, he is protected against a fall in the spot price. It should be noticed that while hedging eliminates speculation from the hedger in so far as it eliminates the uncertainty of the future price, it is not altogether independent of the "profit" motive. A person hedges because he fears a fall in the future spot price more than he hopes for a rise. The holders of wheat will be much more likely to hedge when they are fairly sure of a fall in the spot price than when they are fairly sure of a rise. If, in fact, the holders of wheat were absolutely sure that the spot price in the future would be higher than the futures price now, they would not hedge.

Relation Between "Spot" and "Futures" Prices

The price of a commodity in either spot or futures contracts depends on the supply and demand curves in each case. The price of "spot" wheat, for instance, depends on the eagerness of the market to buy or sell wheat in current contracts. The price of futures for any month depends on the eagerness of the market to buy and sell the contracts which comprise these "futures." The current spot price may be greater or less than the current futures quotation. The possibility of storing a commodity, however, sets a lower limit to the spot price relative to any given futures quotation. If the spot price is below this limit, it will pay dealers to buy the commodity in the spot market and to sell contracts to deliver the commodity in the future, i.e., to sell futures, for they will be able to make profits by holding the commodity for future delivery. The extra buyers in the spot market will bring about a rise in the spot price, and the extra sellers in the futures market will bring about a fall in the futures price, until the minimum difference is once more established. The minimum difference is fixed by the cost of carrying the commodity from the present date to the date when future delivery must be made.

Suppose, for instance, that it cost $0.10 in warehouse, insurance, interest, and other charges to carry a bushel of wheat from September to May. If the price of May futures in September was $1.11, when the spot price was $0.99, a dealer could make a profit of $0.02 per bushel by buying spot wheat in September, selling May futures in September, and holding the wheat bought in September until he had to deliver it to meet his futures contract in May. The cost of the wheat to him in May would be the cost in September, plus the carrying charge, or ($0.99 + 0.10)—$1.09 per bushel. In this case there would be a rush to buy wheat in the spot market in September which would force the spot price up, say, to at least $1. There would likewise be a corresponding rush to sell May futures in September which would force down the price of May futures to at most, say, $1.10. When the difference between the spot price and the price of May futures is less than $0.10, this particular form of "arbitrage" ceases.

Comparison with "Arbitrage"

We see, therefore, how the fact that there is a certain "cost of transport" of wheat from September to the following May tends to set a limit to the amount by which the May futures price can exceed the spot price in September. This limit is closely analogous to the limit on the amount by which, say, the Liverpool price of wheat exceeds the Chicago price, placed by the fact that there is a certain cost of transport of wheat from Chicago to Liverpool. Holding a commodity is indeed nothing more than "transporting" it from one *time* to another, as the very expression "carrying" the commodity indicates. As we saw in the preceding chapter, speculation is essentially "arbitrage through time," for it consists ultimately of trying to buy things when they are cheap and trying to sell them when they are dear. But there is one important difference between space arbitrage and time arbitrage. Transport in space can take place in both directions. Gold, for instance, can be transported with equal ease from New York to London or from London to New York. Hence there is both an upper and a lower limit to the variation in the price of a commodity in one center relative to that in another. The dollar price of gold in London can be neither much greater nor much less than the dollar price in New York, these limits being set by the cost of transport of gold across the Atlantic. Transport through time, however, can take place only in one direction—from the past to the future, never from the future to the past. We can take wheat from September to the following May. We can under no circumstances take it from May to the previous September. Therefore, although the cost of carrying wheat through time tends to set a limit on the fall of the spot price below the futures price, there is no upper limit set by this kind of "arbitrage." If wheat is very scarce in September, but on account of good harvests in the southern hemisphere it is expected to be very plentiful in May, the spot price of wheat in September may exceed greatly the price of May futures in September. The willingness of people to buy May futures depends on what they think the spot price will be in May, not on what the spot price is in September. If the prospect of a plentiful supply of wheat in the following May induces a belief that the spot price next May will be low, the price of May futures will also be low.

"Short Selling" and "Margin Buying" in the Securities Market

A phenomenon somewhat analogous in principle, if not in mechanism, to the "futures" contracts in the commodity markets is also found in the securities market, where it is known as "short selling." A speculator in the securities market "sells short" when he contracts to deliver stock to a buyer at some future date at a price fixed in the present. The seller hopes that at the future date the "spot" price of the stock will be less than the price at which he has contracted to deliver it. Generally speaking, therefore, the short seller is a "bear"— i.e., he expects the price of securities to fall.

The "bulls"—those who expect the price of securities to rise—may also indulge in a practice somewhat analogous to the "futures" contract known as "buying on margin." This is in effect a contract to deliver *money* at a future date in return for stock purchased in the present. The "margin buyer" is one who buys stock in part with borrowed money. To borrow money is of course to contract to deliver money at some future date. When or before that date arrives, the buyer hopes to be able to sell his stock at a higher price than that at which he bought. Suppose, for example, that a speculator buys 100 securities in September at a price of $80 per security. He pays the seller, let us say, $4000, and contracts to pay him $4120 in the following March. He has in effect, though not in legal form or conventional terminology, sold "March futures" in money. If when March comes around the "spot" price of his securities is $90 per unit, he can sell his 100 securities in the spot market for $9000, pay the $4120 according to his contract, and have $4880 left. The $4000 which he paid out in September has grown into $4880 in March, and his investment has shown a handsome profit. But if the spot price of the security in March had been $70 per unit, he would have realized only $7000 in March, and after fulfilling his contract to deliver $4120 he would have had only $2880 left. His initial capital of $4000 would have shrunk, and he would have suffered a loss.

The Decline of the Futures Contract

One of the interesting social phenomena of the nineteen thirties and forties has been the decline of the futures contract and its gradual replacement in one field after another by some form of governmental price fixing. In the foreign exchange market the futures contract has been reduced to insignificance by exchange control, and in the securities market margin buying and short selling alike have been subjected to gradually increasing restrictions and have become of less importance. In the commodities market "price supports" (governmental obligations to prevent the price falling below a certain level by commodity purchase) and price ceilings (the prohibition of transactions above a specified price) have introduced an element of short-run price stability which has made for a decline in the futures contract. Similarly, in the foreign exchange market futures contracts only develop when there is substantial uncertainty about the course of exchange rates over the next few months. In the days of the gold standard there was little such uncertainty, and at present the almost universal direct control of exchange rates likewise does away with short-run fluctuations in exchange rates. In the securities market the decline of short selling and margin buying has been accomplished mainly by direct restriction. This decline of the futures market is part of a general tendency to substitute regulated prices or government purchase for the operations of the free competitive market. Much of the dissatisfaction with the free market must be attributed to the instability of prices in it. There is a real question, however, as to the extent to which governmentally supported and regulated markets can be made sensitive to changing conditions. The mere fact that the state takes over the task of price stabilization does not mean that the risks of faulty pricing are eliminated; it merely means that the losses due to faulty pricing no longer fall on those who have made the mistaken decisions but are spread in some rather arbitrary way over many groups in society. It is a moot point whether governmental pricing may not in fact lead to errors even more costly than those of the free market.

QUESTIONS AND EXERCISES

1. Construct definitions, in your own words, for the following expressions: (a) The gold standard. (b) The foreign exchange market. (c) The securities market. (d) Bonds. (e) Shares. (f) The "futures" market.

2. Suppose British capitalists lent a sum of £50,000,000 to the government of Argentina, to build a railroad, and suppose that the Argentine government spent half that money in buying equipment from the United States and the other half in paying Argentine labor. Trace the effects of such a transaction on the ratios of exchange between (a) pounds and Argentine pesos, (b) pesos and dollars, (c) dollars and pounds. Assume that there is a free market in all these currencies and that there is no gold or other standard.

3. Suppose the British government imposed a tax on all gold coming into

the country. Assuming that both Britain and the United States were on the gold standard, what difference would this tax make to the operation of the foreign exchange market?

4. In 1934 the United States Treasury raised the price at which it offers to buy and sell gold from $20.67 to $35 per ounce. What effect would you expect this "devaluation" (as it is called) to have upon (a) the price of gold in London, and (b) the dollar-pound ratio in the foreign exchange market, on the assumption that Britain is on a gold standard, or that Britain is not on a gold standard?

5. Write a short essay on "Speculation."

6. "The price of a security can fall for two reasons: either because people have an increased desire to hold their resources in the form of money or because people have a lessened confidence in the future of the security." Discuss and explain this statement.

7. As long as the foreign exchange market is a free competitive market the national economic systems of the various countries will move together; a stock market boom in New York will tend to bring about a similar boom in London. Why, exactly? Trace all the steps in this process.

8. What common elements are there in the phenomena of the commodity markets and of the securities markets?

9. "A supply of commodities or of securities is the same thing as a demand for money." Explain carefully what is meant by "supply" and "demand" in the above statement, and illustrate by constructing an arithmetical example.

10. In 1946 the Canadian Exchange Control raised the price at which it bought and sold United States dollars from $0.90 Canadian to $1 Canadian. In the New York market the price rose only to about $0.97. Explain this difference carefully, in terms of the fact that the Canadian Exchange Control only sells strictly limited quantities of United States currency.

CHAPTER 7

PRODUCTION AND CONSUMPTION. THE CONCEPT OF "NORMAL" PRICE

So Far We Have Assumed No Change in the Quantities of Goods or Money Possessed by Marketers

Up to now our formal analysis has been confined to the case of a market in which the total quantity of things exchanged remained constant. That is to say, we have considered literally the exchange of goods for money, or of one money for another money, or of present money for future money, or of future money for future goods. We have supposed that in all these exchanges the final result is merely a change in ownership of the things concerned. In the wheat market, for instance, we have supposed that at the beginning of a "day" there is so much wheat and so much money in the possession of the marketers, and that at the end of the day some of the wheat and some of the money have changed owners. We have then considered what forces determine how much wheat and how much money shall change owners, and at what prices.

Now We Must Observe the Phenomenon of Flows On and Off a Market

Even in our previous discussion, however, we have not been able to leave the matter there, for wheat comes on the market and is taken off the market. It is this phenomenon of a *flow* of a commodity on and off a market which we must now consider. Where do new stocks of a commodity come from? The answer is, from production. The farmer grows his wheat and harvests it, the miner digs his coal, the ironworker smelts his iron, and so on. All these activities continually add to the quantity of the commodity in existence. Every time a farmer harvests a bushel of wheat, he adds one bushel to the quantity of wheat owned by someone. Every time the miner raises a ton of coal, he adds one to the number of tons of coal in the possession of the owners of coal. Stocks of commodities, however, do not merely accumulate; we do not produce for the purpose of piling up monstrous piles of stuff. Out of the stocks of commodities we are continually drawing, and stocks continually disappear. Where do they go? The answer is, into consumption. We burn coal, we eat bread, we wear out clothes, buildings, roads, and all the million and one things which we possess. This drain into consumption must constantly be made good from production. Indeed, the purpose and end of production, of the creation of new stocks of commodities, is to enable us to consume—that is, to destroy these stocks of commodities in a useful and appropriate manner.

Production, Consumption, and Stocks

We must get a picture of the production and consumption of any given commodity—let us say, wheat—as a process something like the flow of water into and out of a tank. The quantity of water in the tank

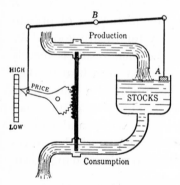

FIG. 9. How Price Regulates Production and Consumption.

corresponds to the quantity of the commodity in existence at a moment of time —1,000,000,000 bushels of wheat, say, in the various storehouses of the world. From the production of farms wheat is constantly being added to the total stock; this corresponds to the flow of water into the tank. The flow is not of course regular, for at harvest time it is very large and at other times very small. However, we may call the rate of flow, averaged over a number of years, the *rate of production*, measured not in bushels but in *bushels per year*.

Wheat is also continually flowing out into consumption, corresponding to the flow of water out of the tank. This flow may also not be quite regular, though it will be more regular than the flow of production. The average rate of flow may be called the *rate of consumption*, measured also in bushels per year. Fig. 9 may help to visualize this process.

Production Must Equal Consumption in the Long Run

It is evident that over a number of years the average rate of production and the average rate of consumption must be about equal.

If production is greater than consumption, more will be added to the stock than is taken away, and the stock will grow. But a stock cannot grow forever. It is not merely that there are physical limitations on the growth of a stock of commodities, set in short periods by the capacity of warehouses. There are psychological limitations on the growth of such a stock, set by the fact that if the stock gets too large people cannot be found who are willing to own it. Our "tank" has therefore a limited capacity, and if more continually runs in than runs out, it will sooner or later be filled to overflowing. Similarly, if consumption is persistently greater than production over a given period, the stock must decline. But the stock cannot decline forever, for a limit is reached when the stock is reduced to nothing. If more runs out of a tank than runs in, the tank will empty itself until nothing remains. After that it is impossible for more to run out than runs in. evidently, there must be some arrangement in our society whereby the rate of production of each commodity can be made equal to its rate of consumption.

The Normal Price

In a free capitalist society this equalization of the rates of production and consumption is brought about through the effect of *prices* on these quantities. It is clear that in a general way a high price will encourage production and discourage consumption, while a low price will discourage production and encourage consumption. For each commodity, therefore, under given conditions, there must be some price which will make the rate of production and the rate of consumption equal. This price is called the "normal" price. It is not one which is necessarily present in any actual exchanges—i.e., it does not have to be the same as the "market price." However, if the market price is such that, other conditions remaining the same, the rate of production of a commodity will be persistently above its rate of consumption, then the market price is *above* the normal price. At this price production is too much encouraged, consumption not encouraged enough, so that there is a persistent tendency for stocks to pile up. If, however, the market price is such that, other conditions remaining the same, the rate of production of a commodity is persistently *below* its rate of consumption, then the market price is below the normal price. At such a price production is too much discouraged, consumption too much encouraged, and the stocks of the commodity show a persistent tendency to decline. If the market price were equal to the normal price, however, and all other conditions remained the same, there would be no tendency on balance, over a period of years, for stocks of the commodity either to increase or to decrease, although of course there might be seasonal and other variations in short periods.[1]

To return to our analogy of the tank, the price of a commodity may be compared to a valve regulating the flows of production and consumption, as in Fig. 9. If it is turned to "high," the production flow is turned on and the consumption flow is turned off. If it is turned to "low," the production flow is turned off and the consumption flow on. The "normal" position is that at which, in spite of seasonal or other spurts and jets, the tank over a long period shows no signs of draining away or of overflowing.

The mechanism relating the stocks and the price is illustrated in Fig. 9 by the float A and the bar B; as stocks rise, the float rises and depresses the price; as stocks fall, the float falls and raises the price. It is evident that a mechanism such as Fig. 9 is self-regulating, the float acting as a "governor." There will be some level of stocks, price, consumption, and production at which the system is in equilibrium. If stocks rise above that level, the rise in stocks will depress the price; the fall in price will shut off production and turn on consumption and so reduce stocks. A similar correction takes place if stocks fall below the equilibrium level.

Relation Between Rates of Production and Consumption and the Normal Price

In order to determine the normal price of any commodity, then, we must know what will be the rates of production and consumption at each of a series of possible prices. The table showing the rate of production at a number of hypothetical prices is called the *normal supply schedule*. The table showing the rate of consumption at a number of hypothetical prices is called the *normal demand schedule*. These schedules are illustrated in Table 12.

This table must be interpreted carefully. It should be read as follows: if the price of wheat were $1.30 per bushel over a considerable period of time, and if all the other factors affecting the production of wheat were to remain constant, then the production of wheat would eventually settle down to a rate of 140 million bushels a year. If the other factors affecting the consumption of wheat were to remain con-

---

[1] This proposition is strictly true only in a society which is not advancing in wealth and population. In a progressing society the stocks of commodities would ordinarily grow with the growth of the society. In a progressing society, therefore, the "normal" price of a commodity is that which induces a small excess of production over consumption, sufficient to allow for "normal" growth in stocks.

TABLE 12.   Normal Demand and Supply Schedules

Price (per Bu.)	Rate of Production (Bushels per Year) (Millions)	Rate of Consumption (Bushels per Year) (Millions)
$1.30	140	60
1.20	100	66
1.10	70	70
1.00	50	74
0.90	30	78
0.80	10	80

stant, the consumption of wheat would eventually settle down to a rate of 60 million bushels a year. So for all the other lines of the table. It is important to observe the phrase, *if the other factors affecting the production (or consumption) of wheat were to remain constant.* Price is not the only thing, by a long way, which affects the production or consumption of a commodity. The prices of things which go to make it, the prices of commodities related either in production or in consumption, the temperament and tastes of the people, the incomes of the people, the techniques of production of the commodity in question and of other commodities, even the weather—all these things affect the rate of production and consumption of a commodity. Nevertheless, to separate out the effects of price, we must suppose that all these other things do not change, and then ask what happens when price alone changes. This is what we are doing in Table 12.

The Determination of Normal Price

In Table 12 it is clear that the normal price is $1.10, for this is the only price at which the rate of production is equal to the rate of consumption, both amounting to 70 million bushels a year. That is, if the average market price over a number of years is $1.10, and other conditions do not change, there will be no persistent tendency for stocks of the commodity to pile up or to drain away, though they may show fluctuations from year to year.

Our next task is to consider by what mechanism the conditions affecting the normal price act upon the actual price in the market. Suppose that in the present example the market price is averaging around $1.20 over a considerable period of time. At this price the production of wheat is highly profitable, and the high price attracts many producers into the field. The rate of production settles down to 100 million bushels a year. The high price, however, acts to discourage consumption, and the rate of consumption settles down to only 66 million bushels a year. If the high price is maintained for some years, the rate of production will gradually rise and the rate of consumption will gradually fall until eventually production exceeds consumption by 34 million bushels a year. That is to say, this amount will be added each year to the total stocks of wheat. Now, as we have seen, the greater the quantity of wheat held by its owners, the less willing are they to buy it and the more willing are they to sell it. As the total stock of wheat rises, therefore, the market curves of most of the wheat marketers will fall, the total market curve will fall, and the market price will fall. So if the market price is above the normal price, it will not be long before the accumulation of stocks forces the market price down. And if the market price is below the normal price—e.g., $1 in Table 12— consumption will outrun production, the total stock of the commodity will decline, and the decline in the stock will raise the market price. The market price, therefore, constantly fluctuates about a level which is the normal price, for whenever the market price differs from the normal price a force comes into play to pull the market price back. Statistically, the "trend" value of the market price is an approximation to the normal price, for the normal price is that toward which the market price is tending.[2]

Graphic Illustration. Normal Demand and Supply Curves. This principle can be illustrated graphically by plotting the price against the rates of production or consumption as in Fig. 10, where Table 12 is so illustrated. These curves are usually called "normal" demand and supply curves. It will be seen immediately that they appear very similar to the "market" demand and supply curves which were evolved in Chapter 5. It is important, however, to distinguish between them. Market demand and supply curves represent the relation between the possible prices on one "day" and the quantities which people will offer for sale or desire to purchase at these prices. The "normal" demand

---

[2] It should be observed that the normal price is determined from the normal supply and normal demand relationships alone, and does not depend on the market equation relationship between stocks and price. Once the normal price has been determined, however, the normal level of stocks follows from the market identity, $p = \dfrac{Mr_a}{Ar_m}$. If we rewrite this in the form $A = \dfrac{Mr_a}{pr_m}$ it will be seen that the exact relationship between A and p depends on the quantity of money and on the commodity and liquidity preferences. In the long run the commodity preference ratio, r_a, will depend mainly on the technical conditions of production, and especially on the average time interval between production and consumption; the longer this interval, the more necessary is it to hold stocks of the commodity, the greater will be the long-run value of r_a, and the larger the normal stocks of the commodity.

and supply curves refer to the relationship between possible average prices over long periods of time and the eventual rates of production and consumption which will be attained at each of those prices if "other things" do not change. In the case of market demand and supply curves it can seldom be assumed that the demand curve and the supply curve are "independent." That is, any change in the market situation will nearly always affect *both* the demand *and* the supply curves, because generally speaking a market is not divided sharply into "buyers" and "sellers" but is composed of marketers any one of whom may buy or sell if the price is suited to his taste. In the case of "normal" demand and supply curves, however, it can often be assumed without difficulty that the curves are independent. That is, it is reasonable to suppose that there can be conditions which will change the position of the normal demand curve *without* changing the position of the normal supply curve. For instance, there might well be a decrease in the willingness of people to consume wheat, reflected in a shift to the left of the normal demand curve, which did not in any way affect the willingness of producers to produce wheat.

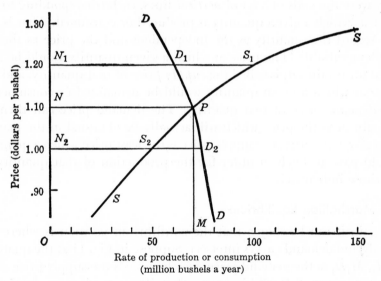

FIG. 10.   Normal Demand and Supply Curves (Quantity-Dependent).

Equilibrium Where Normal Demand and Supply Curves Intersect. We can interpret Fig. 10, then, as follows: SS is the normal supply curve and DD the normal demand curve. These intersect at P, the point where the rate of consumption is equal to the rate of production, both being equal to OM ($= NP$). The normal price is MP

($= ON$). If the average price over a period is greater than ON—say, ON_1—then the rate of production, N_1S_1, will be greater than the rate of consumption, N_1D_1. The difference, D_1S_1 is the rate at which stocks of the commodity are increasing. When stocks are increasing, however, the price will be forced down. But if the price is below the normal price—say, equal to ON_2—the rate of production, N_2S_2, will be less than the rate of consumption, N_2D_2. The difference, S_2D_2, is the rate at which stocks of the commodity are decreasing.

Supply Price and Demand Price

Another approach to the description of the equilibrium of normal price follows the lines laid down by Alfred Marshall.[3] In the above analysis we have treated price as the independent and quantity supplied or demanded, produced or consumed as the dependent variables. We have looked at the supply and demand curves as if they were the ends of a set of *horizontal* lines, each corresponding to the quantity produced or consumed at a given price. This is the method of Walras and Hicks.[4] It is also possible however to look at the same curves as if they were the ends of a set of *vertical* lines, each corresponding to the price at which a given quantity is produced or consumed. That is, we can regard the quantity as the independent and the price as the dependent variable. The price at which a given quantity would be supplied (or produced) is called the *supply price* of that quantity, and the price at which a given quantity would be demanded or consumed is the *demand price* of that quantity. The demand price can then be thought of as the price which will actually be obtained in the market for a given quantity; the supply price is the least price which a quantity would have to fetch in order for the production of that quantity to continue indefinitely.

The Marshallian Equilibrium

Again it can be shown that the equilibrium position is where the supply and demand curves intersect. Suppose in Fig. 11 at the quantity OM_1, M_1D_1 is the demand price, which exceeds the supply price M_1S_1 by an amount S_1D_1. This means that if the rate of production is OM_1, M_1D_1 will be the price actually received, as this is the price at which the whole production can be sold, but M_1S_1 is all that is necessary to induce producers to produce this amount. The production of this particular commodity therefore will be unusually profitable, and

[3] A. Marshall, *Principles of Economics,* 8th Ed. (London, 1922), Book 5.
[4] See Appendix, p. 890.

will remain so as long as the demand price remains above the supply price. If however the production of this commodity is unusually profitable, its output will expand as new producers are attracted into the industry and as old firms expand. As the output expands however

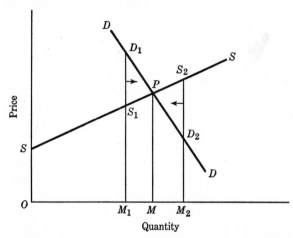

Fig. 11.   Normal Supply and Demand Curves (Price-Dependent).

from OM_1 to OM the demand price falls and the supply price rises, and at OM the supply price and the demand price are equal. At this point therefore the industry is normally profitable; its output can be sold at a price which just induces the existing output to continue. Beyond the point M, at an output, say, of OM_2, the demand price M_2D_2 is below the supply price M_2S_2. This means that the industry is abnormally unprofitable, for its output is so large that it cannot be sold except at a price which is less than what would be required to make the industry normally profitable and so perpetuate the existing output. The output will therefore decline until again it reaches OM, where there is neither excess demand price nor excess supply price. The equilibrium is clearly stable.

The equilibrium positions of the price-dependent and the quantity-dependent approaches are similar, though not always identical, as we shall see later. In most simple problems the differences can be neglected. The dynamic assumptions of the two systems, however, are quite different. The quantity-dependent approach relies on the movements of price to reach equilibrium, and the price-dependent approach relies on the movements of quantity. In practice of course both may move—a disequilibrium situation may express itself both in movements of price under the impact of changing stocks, and in the movements of output under the impact of changing profitability.

Effect of a Rise or Fall in Demand

It is evident now that an increase in the willingness to produce or to consume will be reflected in our curves. An increase in the willingness

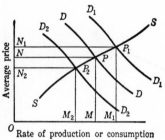

FIG. 12. A Change in Demand.

to consume (called a "rise in demand") means that *at each price* the rate of consumption will be greater than it was before. A *rise* in demand means, therefore, a movement of the whole demand curve to the right. Similarly, a fall in demand means a movement of the whole demand curve to the left, for a fall in demand indicates that *at each price* consumers are willing to consume less than before.

The effect of a rise or fall in demand, the supply curve being unchanged, is illustrated in Fig. 12. Let SS be the normal supply curve, DD the original normal demand curve. An increase in demand for the commodity in question would be indicated by a shift of the demand curve to a position such as D_1D_1. The normal price would increase from PM to P_1M_1, and the rate of production and consumption would increase from OM to OM_1. A decrease in the demand for the commodity would be indicated by a shift of the demand curve to a position such as D_2D_2. The normal price would then decrease from PM to P_2M_2, and the rate of production and consumption would decrease from OM to OM_2.

Effect of a Rise or a Fall in Supply

An exactly analogous concept is that of a rise or fall in supply, or in the willingness to produce. A rise in supply means an increase in the willingness of producers to produce, reflected in a willingness to produce more *at each price*

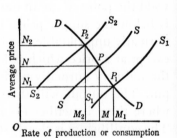

FIG. 13. A Change in Supply.

than they did before. A rise in supply, therefore, is reflected in a shift of the whole supply curve to the right. Similarly, a fall in supply signifies a shift in the whole supply curve to the left.

The effect of a rise or fall in the supply, the demand being unchanged, is illustrated in Fig. 13. Let DD be the normal demand curve, SS the original supply curve. A rise in supply will be reflected in a shift of the supply curve from position SS to S_1S_1. The normal price will decrease from PM to P_1M_1; the rate of production or consumption will increase from OM to OM_1. A fall in supply will be reflected in a shift of the supply curve from SS to S_2S_2. The normal price will now *increase* from PM to P_2M_2; the rate of production or consumption will *decrease* from OM to OM_2.

General Method for Finding Effects of Shifting Demand or Supply

Any case involving shift in demand or supply curves, either singly or together, can be analyzed in a similar manner. To take a single example, suppose there is a large rise in demand coupled with a small rise in supply. The "original" demand and supply curves are DD and SS in Fig. 14, the "new" demand and supply curves are $D'D'$ and $S'S'$. The coordinates of the point of intersection of the "old" curves, P, show the original price, PN, and the original volume of transactions at that price, ON. The coordinates of the point of intersection, P', of the "new" curves show the "new" price, $P'N'$, and the "new" volume of transactions, ON'. In this case evidently a large

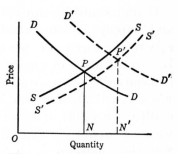

FIG. 14.   A Change in Demand and Supply.

rise in demand and a small rise in supply result in a rise in price, from PN to $P'N'$, and a rise in the volume of transactions, from ON to ON'. In all such problems a solution can quickly be found by comparing the coordinates of the point of intersection of the "original" demand and supply curves with the coordinates of the point of intersection of the "new" curves.

Changes in Demand Price and Supply Price

In the above section we have visualized changes in demand and supply as shifts in the curves to the right or to the left, indicating a change in the quantities demanded or supplied *at each price*. The same shifts in the curves, however, can be described as movements "up" or "down," indicating changes in the demand or supply price of each quantity. Thus in Fig. 14 we see that the shift in demand from DD to $D'D'$ is at once a shift to the right and a shift upward. It represents an increase in the quantity demanded at each price and in the demand price of each quantity. In the case of supply, we see that the shift from SS to SS' represents an increase in the quantity supplied at each price, but a *decrease* in the supply price at each quantity—that is the shift to the right is also a shift "downward." There is no inconsistency in this, for the shift of the supply curve represents an increased willingness to supply, and this can be described either as a willingness to supply more at any given price or as a willingness to supply any given quantity for less. The situation, however, is superficially confusing, and for this reason the student is advised to think of a rise in demand or supply as a movement to the right, rather than as a movement up or down.

Difficulties of Terminology

Certain confusions are apt to arise also because the terms "demand" and "supply" are often used, even by economists, in two senses. They may refer either to the whole schedule of prices and quantities—that is, to the demand or supply functions or curves—or they may be used to mean a single quantity demanded or supplied at a given price. Thus when we talk about a "rise in demand" or a "rise in supply," we generally mean a shift in the whole curve or schedule to the right. In this sense we would say that "a rise in demand causes a rise in price." Sometimes however we say (carelessly) that a "fall in price causes a rise in demand." Here we mean by demand not the whole function, but the *quantity demanded*. We are thinking of a movement along a given demand curve, and not a movement in the curve itself. Similarly a "large supply" may simply mean that the quantity supplied happens to be large because the price is high, whereas a "rise in supply" means that the whole supply curve has shifted and that more will be supplied at *each* price. Confusion will be avoided if the student substitutes the expressed "demand function" or "quantity demanded" in place of the ambiguous term demand, and similar expressions for supply.

Description of Supply and Demand Curves

There is another point of technical terminology which may seem cumbersome, but which is nevertheless necessary for the understanding of the writings of economists. Up to now we have assumed that there is a certain relationship between the price and the quantity demanded, called "demand," and between the price and the quantity supplied, called "supply." We have not said very much about the character of these relationships, apart from assuming that a high price means a large quantity supplied and a small quantity demanded, and that a low price means a small quantity supplied and a large quantity

Ratio of change of quantity
                                    price

demanded. For many problems, however, it is important to know, at least roughly, *how much* a change in price affects the quantity supplied or demanded. There is a great difference between a commodity like wheat, for instance, in which the rate of consumption is but little affected by the price, and a commodity like passenger travel on the railroads, in which a fall in price may result in a large increase in the quantity demanded.

Elasticity of Demand or Supply

In order to describe this characteristic of demand and supply relations, economists have invented the concept of *elasticity* of demand or supply. It measures the *responsiveness* of the quantity demanded or supplied to changes in the price. We have already visualized the relationship between price and quantity as a causal one; a rise in price, for instance, calls forth an increase and a fall in price brings about a decrease in the quantity supplied. The *elasticity* measures the degree to which price is effective in calling forth or holding back the quantity. The relation between price and the quantity supplied is rather like the relation between a whistle and a dog—the louder the whistle, the faster comes the dog; raise the price and the quantity supplied increases. If the dog is responsive—in economic terminology, "elastic"— quite a small crescendo in the whistle will send him bounding along. If the dog is unresponsive, or "inelastic," we may have to whistle very loudly before he comes along at all. We need, therefore, a quantitative measure of this "responsiveness" of quantity to changes in price. One such measure is the "elasticity."

Marshall's Concept of Elasticity

At the outset of the discussion of elasticity we face a certain difficulty in that the usual definition of elasticity in economics, which was originated by Marshall,[5] is not for most problems the most useful one. Marshall defined elasticity as the ratio of the proportional change in quantity (demanded or supplied) to the proportional change in price. The simplest way to visualize the meaning of the Marshallian elasticity is to define it as the percentage change in the quantity (demanded or supplied) which would result from a 1 per cent change in price.[6] If

[5] Marshall, *Principles of Economics*, p. 102.
[6] This definition is open to some mathematical objections, which are treated in the appendix to this chapter. It is, however, sufficiently accurate for all practical purposes, and it gains in clarity what it loses in accuracy.

the elasticity of supply of a given commodity is 2.5, that means that a 1 per cent increase in the price will eventually result in a 2.5 per cent increase in the quantity supplied. If the elasticity of demand for a commodity is −0.6, that means that a 1 per cent increase in the price will eventually result in a 0.6 of 1 per cent *decrease* in the quantity demanded.

Five Cases of Elasticity

It is customary to distinguish five important cases of elasticity.

1. A *perfectly elastic* demand or supply is one in which an infinitesimally small change in price will cause an infinitely large change in the quantity demanded or supplied. The elasticity in this case is infinite.

2. A *relatively elastic* demand or supply is one in which a given change in price will produce a finite but more than proportionate change in the quantity. A supply is relatively elastic if, for instance, a doubling of the price will more than double the quantity supplied, or if a 1 per cent increase in price will produce a more than 1 per cent increase in the quantity supplied. The numerical value of the elasticity is between 1 and infinity. Algebraically, it is between +1 and +∞ in the case of supply, and between −1 and −∞, in the case of demand.

3. *Unit elasticity* of demand or supply is found where a given change in price produces an equal proportionate change in the quantity. In this case, if the price doubles, the quantity supplied will double, or if the price doubles, the quantity demanded will halve. A 1 per cent rise in price will produce a 1 per cent rise in the quantity supplied or a 1 per cent fall in the quantity demanded. The numerical value of the elasticity is 1. The algebraic value is +1 in the case of supply, −1 in the case of demand.

4. A *relatively inelastic* demand or supply is one in which a given change in price produces a less than proportionate change in quantity. In this case a 1 per cent rise in price will bring about a less than 1 per cent rise in the quantity supplied or a less than 1 per cent fall in the quantity demanded. The numerical value of the elasticity is between 0 and 1. The algebraic value is between 0 and +1 in the case of supply and between 0 and −1 in the case of demand.

5. A *perfectly inelastic* demand or supply is one in which a change in the price produces *no change* in the quantity. The quantity demanded or supplied is completely unresponsive to changes in price. The numerical (and algebraic) value in this case is zero.

The "Absolute" Elasticity, or Slope

For many problems however, the simpler concept of the absolute change in the quantity which results from a unit absolute change in price is more useful. This we may call the "absolute" elasticity or the "slope" of the demand or supply curves. At any point it is measured by the gradient or slope of the curves. A "steep" curve in this sense is "inelastic"—a unit change in price produces only a small change in quantity; the quantity, that is to say, is unresponsive to changes in the price. A "flat" curve on the other hand is "elastic"—a unit change in price produces a large response in the form of an increase in quantity.[7]

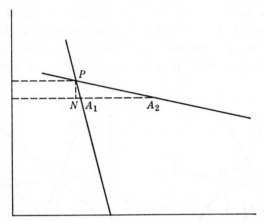

FIG. 15.   Absolute Elasticity.

Thus in Fig. 15 PA_1 is an "inelastic" demand curve and PA_2 an "elastic" curve. A unit fall in price, PN, causes a small increase in quantity, NA_1 in the first case and a large increase, NA_2, in the second case.

The term "elasticity" is so well established in its Marshallian sense that it seems inadvisable to change its meaning. At any given point in the figure, also, a change in the slope signified a similar change in the elasticity. Nevertheless the "flatness" or "steepness" of the curves does not always coincide with the elasticity. At high prices quite steep curves may be relatively elastic, for when the price is high and the quantity small, a unit change in quantity represents a large percentage change, and a unit change in price represents a small percentage change. Suppose, for instance, that at a price of $100 per ton, 1 ton

---

[7] Students whose wits desert them in examinations may find it helpful to remember that *I*nelastic curves look something like a letter I!

will be bought and that at $99 per ton 2 tons will be bought. The $1 per ton change in price is a 1 per cent change; the 1 ton change in quantity is a 100 per cent change, and the demand is therefore highly elastic. Similarly at very low prices and large quantities almost all demands will be relatively inelastic.

Elasticity Determines Effect of Change in Demand or Supply

We shall find many illustrations of the use of the elasticity concept in the following chapter. At this point, however, we can use it to establish two important propositions relating to the effects of changes in demand or supply. The first is that the greater the elasticity of supply, the greater will be the proportionate change in quantity, and the less will be the proportionate change in price, produced by any given change in demand. The second is that the greater the elasticity of demand, the greater the proportionate change in quantity, and the less the proportionate change in price, produced by any given change in supply.

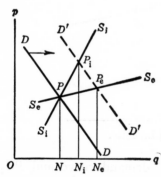

FIG. 16.   Effect of a Change
in Demand.

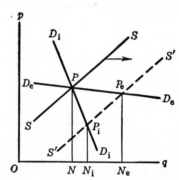

FIG. 17.   Effect of a Change
in Supply.

These propositions are proved in Figs. 16 and 17. The price is measured vertically and the quantity produced or consumed horizontally, according to the usual convention. Then in Fig. 16 DD represents a demand curve, S_eS_e an elastic supply curve. PN is the equilibrium price, ON the equilibrium quantity. Suppose, now, that there is a rise in demand, the demand curve shifting from the position DD to the position $D'D'$. Then if the supply curve is elastic, S_eS_e, there will be a small rise in the equilibrium price, from PN to P_eN_e, and a large rise in the equilibrium quantity, from ON to ON_e. If, however, the supply curve were inelastic, such as S_iS_i, the new equilibrium price would be P_iN_i, and the new equilibrium quantity would be ON_i. In this case the rise in demand evidently results in a large rise in price and a small rise in the quantity.

Fig. 17 shows, similarly, the results of an increase in supply, from SS to $S'S'$. If the demand is elastic, D_eD_e, the price will fall a little, from PN to P_eN_e, and the quantity will rise greatly, from ON to ON_e. If the demand is inelastic, D_iD_i, the price will fall greatly, from PN to P_iN_i, and the quantity will rise but little, from ON to ON_i.

Absolute Elasticity Formulae for Changes in Demand and Supply

Similar propositions can be established relating to the absolute elasticities or slopes. Indeed, in this case the effect can be expressed in a simple formula. In Fig. 18 PP' is a straight-line supply curve, PM and $P'M'$ successive positions of a straight-line demand curve. P and P' are the successive positions of equilibrium. The increase in demand, ΔD, is measured by PM'—that is the increase in the quantity that will be demanded at each price. The increase in output is PN; the increase in price NP'. Then we define the absolute elasticity of demand, $e_d = -\dfrac{NM'}{NP'}$, and the absolute elasticity of supply, $e_s = \dfrac{PN}{NP'}$. Then we have

$$\Delta D = PM' = PN + NM' = e_sNP' - e_dNP'$$

Whence the increase in price, $\Delta p = NP' = \dfrac{\Delta D}{e_s - e_d}$, and the increase in quantity, $\Delta Q = PN = \dfrac{e_s\Delta D}{e_s - e_d}$. Thus with ΔD and e_d given, the smaller is e_s, the larger is Δp, and the smaller is ΔQ. It is worth noting, how-

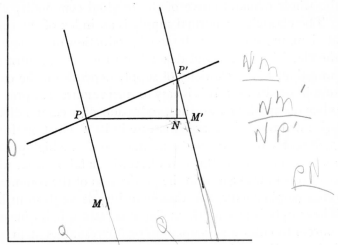

FIG. 18.   Absolute Elasticities and the Effect of a Change in Demand.

ever, that the effect of a given change in the demand curve depends on the elasticity of demand as well as of supply. The elasticity of demand, it should be observed, is negative, as an increase in price is accompanied by a *fall* in the quantity demanded. The more elastic the demand, therefore, the larger is the numerical value of $e_s - e_d$, as e_d is a larger negative number, and therefore the smaller are *both* ΔQ and Δp.

Factors Underlying Demand and Supply

It will not be possible to discuss fully the factors which shape the demand and supply curves until the analysis has been taken much further. Nevertheless, there are a few propositions of great importance in this connection which should be stated at this point, even if we cannot prove them formally.

The elasticity of demand for a commodity depends primarily on the extent to which *substitutes* are obtainable. If a commodity has good substitutes, a rise in its price will divert the expenditures of consumers to the substitutes, and their purchases of the original commodity will decline sharply. If its price falls, consumers who previously bought the substitutes will be attracted to the cheaper commodity, and their purchases will rise sharply. The demand will therefore tend to be elastic. If, on the other hand, a commodity has poor substitutes, consumers will be unable to respond to a rise or fall in its price, and the demand will tend to be inelastic. It is assumed that the prices of the substitutes remain the same. This assumption is necessary to the discussion of elasticity; for if the prices of substitutes change, the whole demand curve of the original commodity changes.

The elasticity of normal supply is an index of the ease or difficulty of changing the total volume of production of a commodity. Just as the elasticity of demand depends on the ease of substitution in consumption, so the elasticity of supply depends on the ease of substitution in production. If it is easy to turn resources at present engaged in other occupations into the production of a commodity, a rise in its price will result in a large increase in its production, for a good many resources will substitute the production of the high-priced commodity for their present employment. Likewise, a fall in price will cause many resources now engaged in the production of the commodity to turn to other employments, and there will be a large drop in its production. The supply is elastic. If, on the other hand, it is difficult for new resources to enter an occupation, or for resources at present employed in it to shift to other occupations, the supply will tend to be inelastic.

Changes in Demand or Supply

Changes in demand or supply are due to many factors. A rise in demand may be due to an increase in the intensity of desire for the commodity, as for ice cream in hot weather. It may also be due to an increase in the money incomes of buyers, for the more money a buyer has to spend, the more of any commodity is he likely to buy at each price. It may also be due to a rise in the prices of other commodities, and especially to a rise in the prices of close substitutes. If the price of beef rises, consumers are likely to buy more pork than before, at each price of pork. It may even be due to a fall in the price of "complementary" commodities the consumption of which assists the consumption of the original commodity. A fall in the price of automobiles, for instance, by increasing the purchases of automobiles will increase the demand for tires and gasoline. In like fashion, a fall in demand may be due to a decline in the intensity of desire for the commodity, to a fall in money incomes, to a fall in the prices of substitute commodities, or to a rise in the price of complementary commodities.

An increase in supply may be due to a decline in the intensity of desire of producers for their own product. If milk producers decide to drink less milk themselves, the supply of milk will probably increase. It may also be due to a decline in the money costs of production of the commodity. If the costs of production of milk fall, more milk will be supplied at each price than before. A fall in the costs of production may take place either because of technical improvements or other economies, or because of a fall in the prices of the factors of production—e.g., a fall in wages or rents. A fall in the price of a substitute which is alternative in production may also cause the supply of a commodity to increase, for the production of the substitute will be less profitable and resources previously employed in making the substitute will turn to the now relatively high-priced commodity. Commodities may also be complementary in production, in which case the production of one assists the production of the other. Thus a by-product of cheese production, whey, is a useful raw material in the production of hogs. A rise in the output of a commodity will raise the supply of products which are complementary to its production. Thus a rise in cheese production is likely to increase the supply of hogs through the intermediary of an increased supply of whey. In like fashion a decrease in supply may be due to an increase in the desire of producers for their own product, to a rise in the costs of production, to a rise in the price of commodities substitutable in production, or to a rise in the output of commodities complementary in production.

QUESTIONS AND EXERCISES

1. From Table 12, page 111, derive an "excess consumption curve" corresponding to the excess demand curve of Chapter 5. What is the exact meaning of this curve? How can it be used to determine the normal price? Can you define the normal price in terms of this curve?
2. What will be the effect on the price and the rates of production and consumption, of the following?
   a. A rise in demand and an equal rise in supply.
   b. A rise in demand and an equal fall in supply.
   c. A large rise in demand and a small fall in supply.
   d. A small rise in demand and a large fall in supply.
3. Comment briefly on the truth or falsehood of the following statements:
   a. A rise in demand always means an increase in the elasticity of demand.
   b. If the consumption of wheat this year is greater than the consumption of wheat last year, either the demand for wheat has risen or it is inelastic.
   c. The demand for a commodity is elastic if a rise in the price causes a fall in the quantity demanded.
   d. If both the demand and the supply for a commodity were perfectly elastic, there would be no single normal price.
4. What would you expect to be the effect on the normal demand and supply curves for *milk* of the following?
   a. A decline in the birth rate.
   b. The discovery of a very superior breed of milch cow.
   c. A great rise in the price of beef.
   d. Increased taxation of the middle classes.
   Deduce the effects on the price of milk and on the rate of production and consumption of each of these four changes taken separately.
5. What do you think would be the effect of the great hurricane of 1938 in New England on the price of (a) firewood and (b) building timber?
6. Prove, by means of graphic analysis, the following propositions:
   a. A change in demand will cause no change in the price when the supply of a commodity is perfectly elastic.
   b. A change in demand will cause no change in the quantity supplied when the supply of a commodity is perfectly inelastic.
   c. A change in supply will cause no change in the price when the demand for a commodity is perfectly elastic.
   d. A change in supply will cause no change in the quantity bought when the demand for a commodity is perfectly inelastic.
   e. When the demand for a commodity is relatively inelastic, a fall in

supply will increase the price and decrease the quantity supplied, but the decrease in quantity will be proportionally smaller than the increase in price.

f. When the supply of a commodity is relatively elastic, a fall in demand will decrease both the price and the quantity supplied, but the fall in price will be proportionally smaller than the fall in quantity.

7. Discuss the following propositions:

a. The causes which operate to produce a rise in demand will also usually operate to produce a fall in supply.

b. Demands and supplies which are inelastic are less likely to rise or fall than those which are elastic.

8. Suppose we have straight-line demand and supply curves, with absolute elasticities of 1000 bushels per dollar per bushel for supply and −100 bushels per dollar per bushel for demand. Suppose now that there is a rise in demand of 1100 bushels at each price. How great will be (a) the change in price (b) the change in the quantity produced or consumed? What assumptions are made in this problem?

APPENDIX TO CHAPTER 7

THE MATHEMATICS OF ELASTICITY

THE GEOMETRY

The Elasticity of Supply

A simple geometrical construction will show at once whether a supply curve at any point is relatively elastic, relatively inelastic, or has unit elasticity. All that is necessary is to draw the tangent to the curve at the point in question. If this tangent passes through the origin, the supply curve at the point of tangency has unit elasticity. If the tangent cuts the vertical (price) axis, the curve is relatively elastic. If the tangent cuts the horizontal (quantity) axis, the curve is relatively inelastic. Thus Fig. 19 shows a supply curve, QPR. At point Q the elasticity of supply is greater than 1, i.e., the curve is relatively elastic, for the tangent QH cuts the price

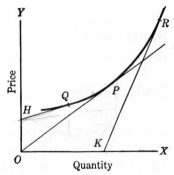

FIG. 19.   Elasticity of Supply.

axis, OY. At point P the curve has unit elasticity of supply, for the tangent at P, OP, goes through the origin, O. At point R the elasticity of supply is less than 1, i.e., the supply is relatively inelastic, for the tangent RK cuts the quantity axis, OX.

The proof of these propositions is contained in Fig. 20. PP' represents a small linear segment of a supply curve. The elasticity of supply

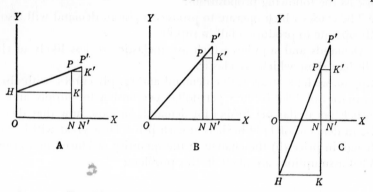

FIG. 20.   Proof of Elasticity Propositions.

e, at point P is the *relative* increase in the quantity supplied divided by the *relative* increase in price. Draw perpendiculars PN, $P'N'$ to meet the axis OX at N and N'. Let $P'P$ be produced to meet the axis OY at H. Drop perpendiculars HK to PN, and PK' to $P'N'$. Then:

$$e = \frac{\dfrac{NN'}{ON}}{\dfrac{K'P'}{NP}} = \frac{PK'}{K'P'}\cdot\frac{NP}{ON} = \frac{HK}{KP}\cdot\frac{NP}{HK} = \frac{NP}{KP},$$

for $NN' = PK'$, $ON = HK$, and by the properties of similar triangles $\dfrac{PK'}{K'P'} = \dfrac{HK}{KP}$. In Fig. 20A, where OH is positive, $\dfrac{NP}{KP}$ is greater than 1, for NP is greater than KP. In Fig. 20B, H coincides with O, and K with N. $KP = NP$, and the elasticity is unity. In Fig. 20C, OH is negative, KP is greater than NP, and the elasticity, $\dfrac{NP}{KP}$, is less than 1.

The Elasticity of Demand

Fig. 21 shows a simple geometrical method for finding the elasticity of demand at any point on a demand curve. Let PP' be a small segment of the demand curve DD, so small that PP' can be taken to be a straight line. Then the elasticity of demand, ϵ, is again equal to the relative change in quantity divided by the relative change in price. That is,

$$\epsilon = \frac{\frac{NN'}{ON}}{\frac{PK}{NP}} = \frac{KP'}{PK}\cdot\frac{NP}{ON} = \frac{NG}{PN}\cdot\frac{NP}{ON} = \frac{NG}{NO} = \frac{PG}{PF},$$

for $NN' = KP'$, and by the properties of similar triangles $\dfrac{KP'}{PK} = \dfrac{NG}{PN}$.

FG is the tangent to the demand curve at the point P.

To find whether a demand curve is relatively elastic or relatively inelastic at any point, P, then, we draw the tangent at that point, cutting the price axis at F and the quantity axis at G. Then if PG is longer than PF the demand is relatively elastic. If PG is shorter than PF the demand is inelastic. If PG is equal to PF the elasticity of demand is unity. A demand curve of unit elasticity throughout would be a rectangular hyperbola. We should not ordinarily expect, however, to find demand curves with constant elasticity over any considerable portion of their length. Any demand curve is bound to intercept both axes, for there must be some price, be it ever so high, at which no quantity of the commodity will be

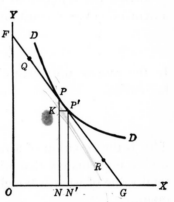

FIG. 21. Elasticity of Demand.

bought, and even at a zero price only a finite quantity will be bought. In such a case the demand will be relatively elastic near the price axis —i.e., at high prices—and relatively inelastic near the quantity axis— i.e., at low prices. Suppose that FG in Fig. 21 represented a straight-line demand curve. At point Q the elasticity of demand is equal to $\dfrac{QG}{QF}$, and is clearly greater than 1. At point R the elasticity of demand is $\dfrac{RG}{RF}$, and is clearly less than 1. At a point which bisects line FG the elasticity of demand will be unity.

THE CALCULUS

The demand curve can be represented algebraically by a functional relationship between the price, p, and the quantity which people will buy at each price, q. Thus:

$$q = F(p). \tag{1}$$

The elasticity of demand, ϵ, is given by the formula:

$$\epsilon = \frac{\frac{dq}{q}}{\frac{dp}{p}} = \frac{p}{q} \cdot \frac{dq}{dp}. \tag{2}$$

In the case of demand the derivative $\frac{dq}{dp}$ is almost invariably negative; i.e., a rise in price brings about a fall in the quantity demanded; ϵ, therefore, is also negative.

Solving the differential equation (2) we have, as the equation of a demand curve of constant elasticity, ϵ,

$$p^{-\epsilon} q = \text{Constant}. \tag{3}$$

In the case of unit elasticity of demand $\epsilon = -1$, and equation (3) becomes

$$pq = \text{Constant}. \tag{4}$$

This is the equation of a rectangular hyperbola. From this equation we see immediately that when the elasticity of demand is unity the total value of what is bought (pq) is independent of the price or the quantity.

The supply curve can also be represented by equation (1), and the elasticity of supply by equation (2), if q now represents the quantity which people will produce or offer for sale at price p. The derivative $\frac{dq}{dp}$ and the elasticity e are now positive, i.e., a rise in price encourages production. The solution of equation (2) may be written:

$$q = Kp^{e}. \tag{5}$$

This is the equation of a supply curve of constant elasticity, e. If the supply curve has unit elasticity this equation becomes:

$$q = Kp. \tag{6}$$

The curve is then a straight line passing through the origin.

The definition of elasticity given by formula (2) shows what is known as the "point" elasticity. The definition on page 129 defines an "arc" elasticity—i.e., an elasticity over a certain range of values of price and quantity, or over a certain "arc" of the demand curve. In general terms we may define the arc elasticity between the values p, q, and $p + \Delta p$, $q + \Delta q$, in any one of four possible ways:

$$\text{(i)} \quad \frac{p}{q} \cdot \frac{\Delta q}{\Delta p}$$

$$\text{(ii)} \quad \frac{p + \Delta p}{q} \cdot \frac{\Delta q}{\Delta p}$$

$$\text{(iii)} \quad \frac{p}{q + \Delta q} \cdot \frac{\Delta q}{\Delta p}$$

$$\text{(iv)} \quad \frac{p + \Delta p}{q + \Delta q} \cdot \frac{\Delta q}{\Delta p}$$

$$\left. \right\} (7)$$

The ambiguity arises because we can measure a *proportional* change with reference to either the original or the final value of the variable. If, for instance, a price changes from 50 to 60, we could reckon this change as either a change of 10 on 50, or 20 per cent, or a change of 10 on 60, or 16⅔ per cent. The smaller the absolute change, the smaller the difference between the two modes of reckoning. It does not matter very much which of the four formulae we choose. Formulae (ii) and (iii), however, have the virtue that a unit arc elasticity of demand gives a constant total value, as does a unit point elasticity. For if the elasticity in formulae (ii) and (iii) is -1 we have: $p\Delta q + q\Delta p + \Delta p\Delta q = O$, and therefore $(p + \Delta p)(q + \Delta q) = pq$.

QUESTIONS AND EXERCISES

1. a. Prove that any demand curve which intersects the axes cannot have constant elasticity throughout.

   b. Prove that at a price so high that no quantity is bought, the demand is perfectly elastic, and that at zero price the demand is perfectly inelastic.

   c. Prove that any supply curve which is a straight line passing through the origin has unit elasticity, no matter how steep it is.

2. The following is a demand schedule:

Price:	20	30	40	50
Quantity:	100	80	60	40

Calculate the arc elasticity in each of the three ranges of the schedule, by each of the four formulae on this page, equation 7.

Assume that the schedule represents a straight-line demand curve with the equation (p = price, q = quantity), $2p + q = 140$. Calculate the point elasticity from equation (2), page 130, at the intermediate points of the three ranges shown—i.e., at $p = 25$, $q = 90$; $p = 35$, $q = 70$; and $p = 45$, $q = 50$.

Tabulate all the results for purposes of comparison.

CHAPTER 8

SOME FURTHER APPLICATIONS OF SUPPLY AND DEMAND ANALYSIS

Elasticity and Change in Total Value

The classification of demand curves into those with elasticity greater than, equal to, or less than one is important in regard to the impact of changes in price or quantity on the *total value* of the commodity produced or consumed, or on the total revenue derived from its sale. The total value of production (or consumption) is the quantity produced (or consumed) multiplied by the price. The total revenue from sales is likewise the total quantity sold multiplied by the price. When the elasticity of demand is numerically greater than 1, a fall in price is associated with a more than proportionate rise in quantity. Hence a fall in price (or a rise in quantity) is associated with a *rise* in the total value or revenue. Thus suppose the original price and quantity were $2 per bushel and 100 bushels. The total value or revenue would be $200. Now suppose the price falls to $1.90 but the quantity expands in a greater proportion—say to 120 bushels. The rise in quantity more than compensates for the fall in price, and total revenue rises from $200 to $228 (1.90 × 120).

Similarly, when the elasticity of demand is numerically less than 1 a fall in price is associated with a *less* than proportionate rise in quantity, and the total value or revenue falls. If in the above example the fall in price from $2 to $1.90 produced a rise in quantity only from 100 to 104 bushels, total revenue would *fall* from $200 to $197.60. If the elasticity is exactly 1, a fall in price is associated with an equal proportional rise in quantity which just compensates for the fall in price, and total value or revenue is unaffected.

Illustration by Graphs

These principles are illustrated graphically in Fig. 22. Fig. 22A shows an elastic demand curve. A fall in price from ON_1 to OH_1 re-

132

sults in an increase in the quantity bought from OM_1 to OK_1. The value of the amount purchased, or the total amount of money spent, at the price ON_1 is $N_1P_1 \times P_1M_1$, or the area $OM_1P_1N_1$. The total amount of money spent at the price OH_1 is $H_1Q_1 \times Q_1K_1$, or the area $OK_1Q_1H_1$. The latter area is clearly greater than the former.

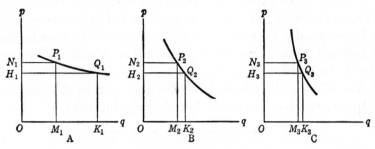

FIG. 22.   Elasticity and Gross Income.

Fig. 22B shows a demand curve of unit elasticity. As before, at a price of ON_2 the total amount spent is equal to the area $OM_2P_2N_2$, and at a price of OH_2 the total amount spent is $OK_2Q_2H_2$. In this case these two areas are equal.

Fig. 22C shows a demand curve which is relatively inelastic. As before, at a price of ON_3 the total amount spent is equal to the area $OM_3P_3N_3$, and at a price of OH_3 the total amount spent is equal to $OK_3Q_3H_3$. In this case the latter area is clearly less than the former.

Practical Application

Perishable Crops.   This discussion may have seemed abstract. Nevertheless, it is of the utmost importance—especially to the farmer. For it means that if the demand for his product is inelastic, a good harvest with a large crop may actually bring in less money than a poor harvest with a small crop; the good harvest may be a disaster for farmers in general. This is particularly the case with perishable commodities, of which the whole crop must be sold at the time of the harvest. Suppose, for instance, that Fig. 22C represented the demand for strawberries, that in one year the harvest was OM_3, and in the next year it was slightly larger—say, OK_3. If the whole harvest had to be sold, so that the supply curves were perfectly inelastic in each year, the price in the first year would be ON_3, and in the second year OH_3. The good harvest would have resulted in a smaller total value of the crop, and therefore a smaller total gross income for the strawberry farmers. If the demand for strawberries had been as represented in

Fig. 22B, the total value of the crop would have been quite independent of its quantity. If the demand had been elastic, as in Fig. 22A, a good crop would have brought in a greater gross return than a poor crop.

Storable Crops. Crops which can be stored, such as wheat, are less likely to have a relatively inelastic demand, for here the demand in any one year comes not only from consumers but also from speculators. Consequently, even though a fall in the price of wheat in any one year may not greatly encourage consumption, it will encourage purchases by speculators. The demand for a single year's wheat crop is therefore likely to be relatively elastic. But even in this case the demand over, say, ten years may be relatively inelastic.

THE STABILITY OF PRICES

Another problem on which supply and demand analysis can throw considerable light is that of the stability of prices. We have already seen (page 122) that a change in demand will cause a large change in price if the supply is inelastic and a small change in price if the supply is elastic. We also saw that a change in supply will cause a large change in price if the demand is inelastic and a small change in price if the demand is elastic. Now, a change in the equilibrium price can come about only as a result of a change in demand, in supply, or in both. It follows that the greater the elasticity of both demand and supply, the less chance will there be of wide fluctuations in price. If both demand and supply are highly elastic, then a change in either demand or supply, or both, will result in only a small change in price. If demand and supply are highly inelastic, then a change in either, or both, will result in a large change in the price. This proposition is illustrated in Fig. 23. Fig. 23A shows the effect of a change in both demand (from *DD* to *D'D'*) and supply (from *SS* to *S'S'*), when both demand and supply curves are elastic. The fall in price (from *PN* to *P'N'*) is a small one. Fig. 23B shows the corresponding effect when both demand and supply curves are inelastic. The fall in price in this case is clearly much larger.

Verbal Proof

It is not enough, of course, to follow the argument "on the curves." Indeed, at this stage the reader may well be warned against thinking too much in terms of curves themselves and not enough in terms of what they mean. The logic of the proposition, however, is clear. In order to satisfy, let us say, an increase in demand we should expect to find an increase in the quantity supplied. If this increase can be obtained easily—that is, if a slight rise in price is sufficient to call forth a large increase in the quantity supplied, supply being elastic—there will be no need for the price to rise much. But if the increase in the quantity supplied cannot be obtained easily, supply being inelastic,

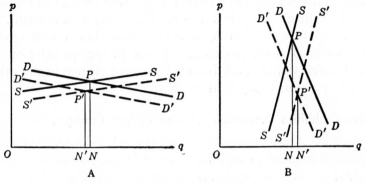

FIG. 23.   The Stability of Prices.

the price will have to rise a good deal in order to restrict consumption and encourage production. If the supply were perfectly inelastic, so that a fixed quantity would be supplied no matter what the price, a rise in demand would force the price to rise to the point where the quantity demanded was the same as before.

Stability of Demand and Supply

It is evident from the above that the stability or instability of prices depends also on another factor, which we may call the *stability* of demand or of supply. A demand curve may be said to be stable if the quantity which would be bought at any given price is not much affected by changes in the factors which determine it, such as incomes, fashions, and the prices of other commodities. Similarly, a supply curve may be said to be stable if the quantity which would be supplied at each price is not much affected by changes in the factors which determine it. Commodities differ substantially in the stabilities of their demands and supplies. Necessities and conventional necessities tend to be more stable in demand than luxuries and fashion goods. Perishable consumers' goods also tend to be more stable in demand than durables.

Income Elasticity and Cross Elasticities

No single measure of the stability of demand or supply can be given, as changes in the demand and supply curves are the result of changes in a complex and heterogeneous system of economic quantities. We can, however, define certain particular measures of stability relating the quantity demanded, price being constant, to income or to the prices of other commodities. Thus the *income elasticity of demand* may be defined as the percentage change in the quantity demanded which would result from a 1 per cent change in money income, other quantities, prices, and the like being held constant. Similarly, the *cross elasticity* of demand for commodity A with reference to commodity B is the percentage change in the quantity of A demanded which would result from a 1 per cent change in the price of B, all other factors being held constant.[1]

Relative Stabilities Determine Price or Output Changes

The effect of any change in one of the other determinants of the quantities demanded or supplied, such as income, on the equilibrium price and quantity depends mainly on whether demand is more or less stable than supply in respect of the determinant in question. Thus, in Fig. 24, suppose that in each case D_0, S_0 are the demand and

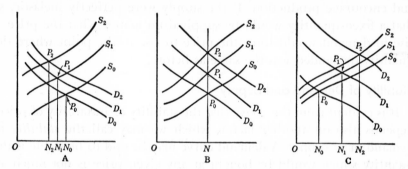

FIG. 24.   Relative Stabilities of Demand and Supply.

supply curves for some commodity when income $= I_0$; D_1, S_1 are the demand and supply curves when income $= I_1$; D_2, S_2 are the demand and supply curves when income $= I_2$, and so on. We suppose that $I_0 < I_1 < I_2$. In Fig. 24A we have supposed that the income elasticity (i.e., the stability with respect to income) of demand is less than that of supply. In other words, rising incomes affect the quantity supplied more than they affect the quantity demanded. In this case it is clear that rising incomes raise the price but lower the output of the commodity; at income I_0 price is $P_0 N_0$, output ON_0; at income I_1 price is

[1] Income and cross elasticities can also be defined in absolute terms. Thus the absolute income elasticity would be the change in the quantity demanded per unit change in income.

P_1N_1, output is ON_1, and so on. In Fig. 24C the reverse situation is shown, in which the income elasticity of demand is greater than that of supply. In this case a rise in incomes leads to a rise in the output as well as a rise in price. In Fig. 24B the income elasticities of supply and demand are equal. In this case it is evident that the effect of a rise in income is to raise the price but to leave the output unchanged. It is clear that the same type of analysis can be used to discuss the effect of changes in any other variable of the system—e.g., quantity of money, prices of other commodities. As we shall see later, this type of analysis is of great importance in the theory of money and employment.

PRICE FIXING AND STABILIZATION

Inelastic Demands Lead to Pressure for "Stabilization"

One of the difficulties of our present system is that many commodities, especially agricultural commodities, have rather inelastic demands and supplies, and therefore changes in the underlying conditions of demand or supply for these commodities cause quite disproportionate changes in price, with a consequent disruption of the flow of incomes. There is consequently much political pressure for a policy of stabilizing prices—especially agricultural prices—by government action. The so-called "valorization" schemes in tin, rubber, and coffee, the "ever normal granary" and the crop-restriction schemes of the New Deal, were all attempts to "stabilize" something, whether prices or incomes.

Most "stabilization" schemes in practice have also been concerned with another, and more sinister, objective than stabilization alone—that of obtaining monopoly prices and profits for their beneficiaries. Although the objective of stabilization is not necessarily inconsistent with the objective of monopoly profit, in practice the attempts to obtain monopoly profits without fulfilling the necessary conditions have frequently been responsible for the breakdown of schemes of stabilization. Indeed, a study of these schemes and their misfortunes is one of the best ways of demonstrating the necessity for economic analysis. We shall not take time to discuss the historical details. We shall, however, state some general principles.

The Failures of Price Fixing

The first principle is that any attempt to fix a price by authority, without control of either production or consumption, is doomed to failure unless, of course, the price fixed happens to be the price which would have been established in the unregulated market. History is strewn with the wrecks of such attempts at the fixing of prices. A government "fixes prices" when it passes a law forbidding any transactions in which the price is different from the one specified by the law. The result is that either the law is evaded or the transactions cease to take place—or the government is forced to interfere drastically with the production or consumption of the commodity. This is abundantly illustrated by the history of price fixing, for instance, during the world wars. Many governments at first essayed to stop the rising price of foodstuffs by decree. What happened? In some cases commodities disappeared from the market altogether. If the price which the government fixed was below that at which the most efficient producer found that it paid to produce, then there was simply no further production.

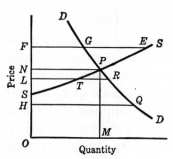

Graphic Illustration. This is illustrated in Fig. 25. *SS* and *DD* are the normal supply and demand curves; *ON* (= *MP*) is the normal price. Suppose the government made it illegal to sell the commodity at a price above *OH*. At

FIG. 25. Results of Price Fixing.

this price producers would not find it worth while to produce anything, and although consumers would be willing to consume a quantity equal to *HQ*, this quantity would not be forthcoming and their desire would have to go unsatisfied. The commodity in this case would disappear from the market altogether, unless it was "bootlegged."

"Shortages" and Rationing

Now suppose that the legal maximum price is fixed at *OL*. At this price a certain amount, *LT*, will be produced. This is all that will be available for consumption. However, people will wish to buy more than *LT* at the price—in fact, they will want an amount equal to *LR*. What will happen? The first buyers will be satisfied. But after the early birds have bought all the available supplies there will be a number of people who would like to buy, who cannot find any of the commodity to buy, and who are prevented by law from doing the natural thing, which would be to bid up the price. The result is a "shortage." Nothing perhaps illustrates better the function of prices in a free market than the difference between a "scarcity" and a "shortage." If a com-

modity becomes scarcer in an unregulated market, the result is a rise
in its price to the point where purchases accommodate themselves to
the smaller amounts forthcoming. The commodity does not disappear
from the market; stocks are always available for purchase by those
who are fortunate enough to be able to afford the high price. If, however, the law prevents the price from rising to this equilibrium level,
stocks disappear from the market as buyers snap them up faster than
they are being replaced. Hence the commodity becomes available only
at certain times, or certain places, or to certain favored people; for
instance, it may only come into the stores on Fridays, or it may only
appear in certain stores, or the storekeeper may keep it under the
counter for his favorite customers. The rate of purchase is forced
down to the rate at which the commodity is reaching the market not
by the restrictive operations of high prices but by direct restrictions
of one sort or another on the ability to purchase.

Rationing

Probably the most equitable method of direct restriction of purchases is "rationing." The government issues ration coupons entitling
every individual to just so much of the rationed commodity and no
more. If rationing is to be successful, the total ration in any period
must be about equal to the quantity coming on the market for sale.
Purchases are then restricted not by the price, for at the controlled
price we suppose that purchasers would wish to buy more than their
ration coupons allow; the restriction of purchases is effected by the
necessity of paying for the commodity not only with money but with
the ration coupon as well. Thus, instead of some consumers getting
all they can afford and others getting none, as in an unregulated
"shortage," most consumers get rather less than they would be willing
to buy at existing prices but nobody needs to go completely unsatisfied. Rationing and price control are therefore a more satisfactory way
of dealing with emergency scarcities, such as those created by war,
than the method of allowing prices to rise freely; in the latter case the
rich may bid the prices of basic necessities up to the point where they
are out of reach of the poor.

Rationing, however, has difficulties of its own. Any attempt on the
part of government to allocate commodities on a basis of "need" is
bound to be very crude. Equal distribution is not equitable if needs
are different. Consequently, once rationing is extended from commodities where needs are approximately equal, such as sugar, to more
complex commodities such as gasoline, clothing, and the like, the

system inevitably becomes more and more complicated, with different rations for different classes of people. The wider the field of rationing the more difficult it is to apportion successfully. Thus it is a recognized principle of food rationing that at least one basic source of calories, such as bread or potatoes, must be left uncontrolled, in order to enable individuals to adjust their caloric intake to their various individual requirements. The development of the "points" rationing system in World War II is an interesting further application of pricing principles. Consumers were given ration coupons ("points") entitling them to purchase a whole range of commodities—e.g., canned goods or clothing—at "point prices" which were changed from time to time by authority as experience showed that consumption was outrunning production, or the reverse. In this case the ration coupon itself became a kind of supplementary money, and the price in terms of ration coupons rather than the money price performed the function of adjusting consumption to available supplies. The ultimate logic of such schemes would seem to be to have a special kind of money, issued to all persons equally, for the purchase of those commodities which are regarded as the basic necessities of life.

The Theory of the Black Market

An almost inevitable consequence of price control and rationing is the development of a so-called "black market"—i.e., an illegal market in which transactions take place above the legal price. Supply and demand curve analysis can throw a good deal of light on this phenomenon. The situation is illustrated in Fig. 26. S and D represent the normal demand and supply curves as they would be in the absence of any regulation. PN would then be the unregulated price. We now suppose that price control is imposed, and that OR becomes the legal maximum price. At this price only RT will be supplied; if buyers were free to buy without restriction at this price, they would buy RV. Conditions must develop, therefore, which prevent buyers from buying more than RT; i.e., there will be shortages or rationing. Now suppose that, as a result of the unsatisfied demand (measured by the quantity TV), a black market develops. We can postulate a "black market supply curve," TS_B, lying to the left of the normal supply curve TS. As operations in the black market involve a certain cost and risk above what would be necessary in a free market, suppliers are not to be found willing to supply as much at each price in the black market as would be done in the free market; in other words, because of the higher costs it now takes a higher price to call forth any given quantity than it did before. The higher the costs of black market operation, the steeper will TS_b rise. We can similarly postulate a black market demand curve, $T'D_b$. Even at the legal maximum price (OR) we may suppose that not all potential buyers are willing to buy in the black market, so that the quantity demanded in the black market at the price OR is not the total unsatisfied demand quantity, TV, but a

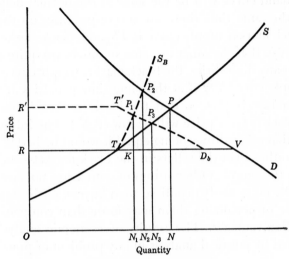

FIG. 26.   The Black Market.

smaller quantity TD_b. The higher the price the less will be demanded in the black market, until at some price, OR', nothing will be demanded in it. Then the black market price is P_1N_1, and the quantity bought and sold in the black market is TK, RK being the total quantity in the legal and the black market combined, and RT the quantity in the legal market.

One or two interesting conclusions follow from the figure. The first is that the black market price may easily be less than the "normal" price which would have been established in a completely unregulated market, though it can be more.[2] The second is that the average price in the legal and the black market together is likely to be lower than the "normal" price, so that even if a black market develops as a result of price control the resulting average price is less than that which would have obtained in a perfectly free market. Only if the black

[2] A. F. W. Plumtre has pointed out that the black market demand curve may rise more sharply than indicated here and cross the regular demand curve. In such a case the black market price might well be higher than the original price. See A. F. W. Plumtre, "The Theory of the Black Market: Further Considerations," *Canadian Journal of Economics and Political Science*, Vol. 13, No. 2, May, 1947, p. 280.

market demand and supply were extremely inelastic could the reverse be the case. The third conclusion is that the more penalties and obstructions placed on the *buyers* in the black market and the fewer penalties placed on the *sellers*, the lower the black market price is likely to be. If we suppose that there are no penalties of any kind, legal or moral, attached to purchases in the black market, the black market demand curve will be the same as the normal demand curve, DP_2. If at the same time there are severe penalties on the sellers, so that the black market supply curve is TS_B, the black market price will be high (P_2N_2). If at the other extreme suppliers are quite unmolested and without any disabilities, the black market supply curve will be the normal supply curve TS; if at the same time penalties are placed on the black market buyers, so that the black market demand curve is D_bT', the black market price will be low (P_3N_3). The inference would seem to be that other things being equal it would be better to penalize the buyers rather than the sellers in the black market—the housewife rather than the grocer. Other things of course are not usually equal; sellers may be more easily penalized than buyers, for instance, and the political ease of penalizing them may more than compensate for the economic disadvantages. The results of economic analysis must be supplemented by political analysis in any problem of practical policy.

Fixing Prices Above Normal

At the other end of the problem we can illustrate, again with reference to Fig. 25, what happens when some authority tries to fix a price which is *above* the normal price. Suppose that the curves on Fig. 25 represented the supply and demand curves for coffee; suppose that coffee could only be sold by a single selling agency, and that the agency fixed the price at an amount equal to OF. At this price the total consumption would be FG, the total production would be FE, and stocks of coffee would pile up in the hands of the selling agency. What, then, must the agency do? Either it must destroy the surplus coffee or it must take steps to restrict production to an amount equal to FG—i.e., to prevent producers from supplying as much as they wish at the price. The Brazil coffee valorization scheme in the twenties chose to destroy coffee by dumping it into the sea.

TAXES AND TARIFFS

Another question on which supply and demand analysis can throw light is that of the effects of taxes and tariffs on particular commodities.

A Specific Tax

Condition Before Tax Is Imposed. Let us consider first the effect of a specific tax on a commodity which is produced wholly within the country imposing the tax. A specific tax is one in which a definite sum must be paid to the state on each unit of the commodity sold, no matter what the price of the commodity. Suppose, for instance, that cigarettes were neither imported into nor exported from the United States, but were produced solely for the home market. In Fig. 27 the

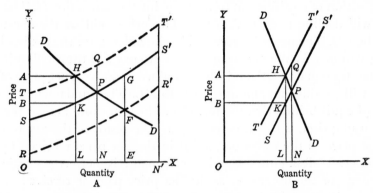

FIG. 27.   Effect of Specific Taxes and Subsidies.

curve *DD* represents the relation between the price which the consumer pays over the counter and the quantity which consumers will buy at each price, in a given time. *SS'* represents the relation between the consumers' price and the quantity which producers and sellers would be willing to produce and sell in that same time. These curves show the situation before the tax is imposed. The price will be *NP;* the quantity produced and consumed will be *ON.*

Condition After Tax Is Imposed. Now let us suppose that a tax equal to the distance *ST* is imposed. The result is a "fall" in the supply curve *SS'*, which now moves to a position *TT'*. The significance of this movement should be noted carefully. It means that because of the tax, at any given consumers' price a smaller quantity will be supplied than before, or, what is the same thing, that in order to induce suppliers to provide any given quantity, consumers must pay a higher price than formerly. Before the tax was imposed, when consumers paid a price equal to *NP*, a quantity *ON* would be forthcoming. Now consumers would have to pay a price equal to *NQ* in order to induce producers to produce a quantity *ON*, where *PQ* is equal to the tax *ST*. For when consumers pay a price *NQ*, producers receive a net price, after they have paid the tax, of only NP. If, then, the paying of the tax does not in itself affect their underlying willingness to produce, a "producers' price" of NP will call forth from producers a quantity ON as before. As this is true for any output, the new "supply curve," TT', will be such that at any output, ON', the new consumers' price needed to call forth that output, $N'T'$, will exceed the old consumers' price needed to call forth that output, $N'S'$, by the amount of the tax, so that $S'T'$ must be equal to ST.

Result of the Tax. The result of the tax will therefore be to change the position of equilibrium from the point P to the point H. The output will decline from ON to OL. The price paid by the consumer will be LH. The net price received by the seller, after the tax has been paid, will be LK. When consumers have to pay LH they will only buy an amount equal to OL, and when producers receive a net price of LK they will produce an amount equal to OL. The fundamental condition of equilibrium, that the rate of production should equal the rate of consumption, is therefore observed. The result of the tax is a rise in the price to the consumer, a fall in the net price received by the producer. Unless either supply or demand is perfectly elastic the "burden" of the tax, as far as the net price paid or received is concerned, will be divided between the producer and the consumer. The consumers' price will rise, but by a smaller amount than the tax; the producers' net price will fall, but also by a smaller amount than the tax. This does not mean, however, that the "real burden" of the tax need be divided in this way.

Result of Tax When Demand and Supply Are Inelastic. The effect which the tax will have upon the *output* of the commodity will depend upon the elasticities of its demand and supply. The more *inelastic* the demand and the supply of the commodity, the smaller will be the fall in output caused by any given tax. This is illustrated in Fig. 27B, where the letters have the same significance as in Fig. 27A but the demand and supply curves are highly inelastic. It will readily be seen from the figure that the fall in output, LN, in Fig. 27B is much less than in Fig. 27A. This explains why commodities with an inelastic demand or supply are best suited to taxation, for with a commodity of this type the tax will produce only a small contraction in the industry taxed, with little dislocation.

Subsidies

The effect of a specific subsidy or "bounty," which is the direct opposite of a tax, can also be illustrated in Fig. 27. A subsidy, of course, is merely a "negative" tax. That is to say, instead of taking something away from the price paid by the consumer, the government adds something to that price. The net price which the producer receives will exceed the price which the consumer pays by an amount equal to the subsidy. The result of this will be that producers will supply a larger quantity at each consumers' price than before; i.e., the supply will have risen. The supply curve (Fig. 27A) will move from position SS' to position RR', where at any output, ON', the difference ($S'R'$) between the old price, $N'S'$, and the new price, $N'R'$, is equal to the amount of the subsidy. The new point of equilibrium is F. Under the warm sun of the subsidy, therefore, the total output will expand from ON to OE; the price paid by the consumer will fall from NP to EF; the net price received by the producer will rise from NP to EG. The difference between the consumers' price and the producers' price, FG, is the amount of the subsidy per unit of output. The more inelastic the demand and supply curves, the smaller will be the expansion of output. Subsidies will therefore be most effective in causing the expansion of an industry where the demand and supply curves are elastic.

An Ad Valorem Tax or Subsidy

We can also apply this analysis to the case of an "ad valorem" tax or subsidy. An ad valorem tax is one in which the tax paid on each unit of the commodity is not a fixed quantity, but is some fixed proportion of the price of the commodity. The general sales tax is of this kind. It is a fixed percentage of the price of the commodity, so that the greater the price, the greater the amount of the tax paid. In Fig. 28, DD' and SS' are the original demand and supply curves for a commodity. ON is the output, NP the price. Now suppose that a tax equal to 25 per cent of the consumers' purchase price is imposed. This will mean,

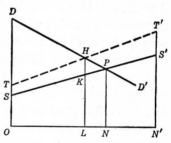

FIG. 28.   Effect of an Ad Valorem Tax.

as before, that at any given consumers' price, producers will be willing to sell less than before, as they will receive not the price the consumer pays but this price less the tax. The supply curve, therefore, will move to the left, indicating a fall in supply, from position SS' to position TT'. To construct this new supply curve, consider first the meaning of any point S' on the old supply curve. It means that if consumers paid a price equal to $N'S'$, producers would be willing to produce an amount equal to ON'. Now when the tax is imposed, a consumers' price of $N'T'$, where $S'T' = 25$ per cent of $N'T'$, will result in a producers' price of $N'S'$ as before. Consequently, after the tax is imposed, consumers will have to pay a price equal to $N'T'$ in order to call forth an output of ON'. T' therefore is a point on the new supply curve. As $S'T'$ is one-quarter of $N'T'$, it follows that $S'T'$ is one-third of $N'S'$. So in order to draw the new supply curve each price ordinate must be increased by one-third of itself.

Effect of an Ad Valorem Tax. The new point of equilibrium is H; the effect of the tax is to cause a decline in output from ON to OL. The consumers' price rises to LH; the producers' price falls to LK. The amount of the tax is KH, which is equal to 25 per cent of LH. The effects of an ad valorem subsidy may be analyzed in the same way.

The Yield of Taxes and the Expense of Subsidies

Our analysis also throws light upon the problem of the yield of commodity taxes. In Fig. 27, page 143, the total revenue produced for the government by the tax KH is equal to $KH \times OL$, or the area of the rectangle $AHKB$, for this is equal to the tax per unit of commodity multiplied by the total number of units produced. It is evident from the figure that a given tax will be more productive of revenue if the demand and supply curves are inelastic than if they are elastic, for in the former case there is little shrinkage in production. The area $AHKB$ is smaller in Fig. 27A than in Fig. 27B. Similarly, the expense of a subsidy will be greater, the more elastic the demand and supply curves of the commodity subsidized.

An interesting problem which can be solved if we know the demand and supply curves is that of the most productive rate of taxation. It is evident from Fig. 27A that the area $AHKB$ will be small both when KH is small and when KH is large. There will be some intermediate value of KH at which the area $AHKB$ is a maximum. This is the most productive tax rate. If the tax rate is greater than this value, the total revenue from the tax will be increased by reducing the tax—a phenomenon of not infrequent occurrence in the history of taxation. It can also be seen from the figure that the more inelastic the demand and supply, broadly speaking, the greater will be the maximum yield of a tax. It does not follow, of course, that the tax rate which gives the maximum yield is the "ideal" rate, for in evaluating the benefits of a tax the effect on the industry, as well as the revenue to the government, must be taken into consideration.

Effect of Tariffs

We can now go further and consider the effects not only of purely internal taxes but also of tariffs on specific articles. Suppose the world is divided into two countries, the United States on the one hand and the "rest" on the other. In Fig. 29A are the supply and demand curves

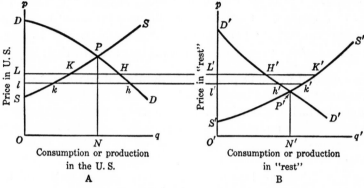

Consumption or production
in the U. S.
A

Consumption or production
in "rest"
B

FIG. 29.   Trade Between Two Countries.

(*DD* and *SS*) of the commodity in question for the United States. In Fig. 29B are the supply and demand curves of the "rest" of the world, for the same commodity, *D'D'* and *S'S'*. It is important to see clearly what these curves mean. *DD* expresses the relation between the price which United States consumers have to pay and the quantity which they will buy at each price. *SS* expresses the relation between the price which United States producers receive and the quantity which they will be willing to produce at each price. *D'D'* expresses the relation between the price which foreign consumers have to pay and the quantity which they will be willing to buy at each price. *S'S'* represents the relation between the price which foreign producers receive and the quantity which they will be willing to produce at each price.

Conditions of Equilibrium in International Trade

We can then state the conditions of equilibrium as follows: (1) United States producers must be able to sell an amount exactly equal to what they are willing to produce. (2) Foreign producers must also be able to sell, to the United States or to foreign consumers together, an amount equal to what they are willing to produce. (3) The exports of the commodity from one country must be equal to the imports of it into the other country, for these are exactly the same thing. To say the "rest" exports 10,000,000 bushels to the United States is to say the

United States imports 10,000,000 bushels from the "rest." (4) If there are no internal taxes, the difference between the price of the commodity in the United States and the price in the "rest" of the world must be equal to the cost of transport per unit of commodity between them. This follows from the principle of arbitrage previously considered.

1. *Without Tariffs or Transport Costs.* If there are no tariffs and no cost of transport, the price of the commodity in the United States will be the same as the price in the "rest" of the world. If this price is Ol, equal to $O'l'$, then from the curves it is evident that:

lk = amount that would be produced in the United States at that price;
lh = amount that would be consumed in the United States at that price;
kh = rate at which stocks will diminish in the United States at that price if there are no imports;
$l'k'$ = amount that will be produced in the "rest" of the world at that price;
$l'h'$ = amount that will be consumed in the "rest" of the world at that price;
$h'k'$ = rate at which stocks will increase in the "rest" of the world at that price if there are no exports.

In the world as a whole, therefore, stocks will be diminishing at a rate equal to $kh - k'h'$. In this case, if the price is Ol, world stocks are evidently going to diminish; hence, as we have seen, the price must rise. It will rise to OL, where,

LK = amount which will be produced in the United States;
LH = amount which will be consumed in the United States;
$L'K'$ = amount which will be produced in the "rest" of the world;
$L'H'$ = amount which will be consumed in the "rest" of the world;
$KH = K'H'$ = amount which will flow from the "rest" of the world to the United States.

At this price the United States will consume more than it produces, but the difference will be made up by imports. The "rest" of the world will produce more than it consumes, but the difference will be made up by exports. By moving the line lk' up and down parallel to itself we can find the place where $KH = K'H'$; this will give us the position of equilibrium.[3] It will be seen that relatively speaking the demand is smaller and the supply is greater in the country *from* which the commodity is exported than in the country *to* which the

[3] A more accurate geometrical method for finding the equilibrium price is as follows: Construct the *total* "world" demand and supply curves by adding the quantities demanded and the quantities supplied in both "countries" at each price. The point of intersection of the "world" demand and supply curves gives the world equilibrium price.

commodity is exported. This is what we should expect. We observe also that the price in the United States, *OL*, is less than it would be if there were no trade (*NP*), while the price in the "rest" of the world (*O'L'*) is greater than it would be if there were no trade (*N'P'*).

2. *With Transport Costs.* Now imagine a condition in which there is a cost of transport. This is illustrated in Fig. 30. Here the curves and symbols have the same meaning as in Fig. 29, except that there

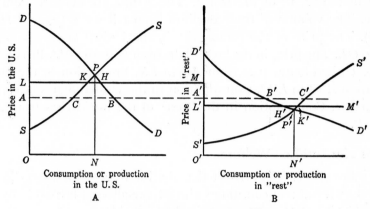

Consumption or production
in the U. S.

A

Consumption or production
in "rest"

B

FIG. 30.   Effect of a Tariff.

is now a cost of transport equal to *L'M* per unit of commodity. The price in the United States (*OL* = *O'M*) must now be greater than the price in the "rest" of the world (*O'L'*) by an amount equal to *L'M*. The equilibrium position is then the one illustrated in the figure, where *LK* and *LH* represent the production and consumption in the United States, *KH* represents the imports into the United States, *L'K'* and *L'H'* represent the production and consumption in the "rest" of the world, and *K'H'* represents the exports to the United States. *KH* must equal *K'H'* in equilibrium, just as in the previous case.[4]

A Tariff as an Artificial Increase in Transport Costs

We can now see immediately what will be the effect of a tariff on imports (or a subsidy on exports). Suppose that originally there were

---

[4] The following is a useful construction for finding the equilibrium price in this case. Let the price in the "rest" of the world be the "world price." Construct demand and supply schedules for the United States in terms of the world price by subtracting the cost of transport from each U.S. supply price or demand price. Thus if the cost of transport is $3 per unit, and if at a U.S. price of $10, 100 units will be demanded, then as the U.S. price must be $3 above the world price, in this case 100 units will be demanded in the United States at a world price of $7. Adding together the quantities demanded and supplied in both the U.S. and the rest of the world at each world price gives us the world demand and supply schedules. The point of intersection of the world demand and supply curves, drawn from these schedules, gives the world price. The U.S. price will be higher than this by the amount of the cost of transport.

no costs of transport, so that in Fig. 30 the equilibrium price in both countries was OA, or $O'A'$. The imports into the United States, CB, would be equal to the exports from the "rest" of the world, $B'C'$. Now suppose that the United States imposes a tariff, in the shape of a specific import tax, equal to $L'M$ per unit of the commodity. $L'M$ is then the "cost of transport" per unit between two countries, OL is the equilibrium price in the United States, $O'L'$ the equilibrium price in the "rest" of the world. The results are evident from the figure. The volume of trade declines from CB (or $B'C'$) to KH (or $H'K'$). The price of the commodity in the United States rises from OA to OL. The price in the "rest" falls from $O'A'$ to $O'L'$. Production in the United States rises from AC to LK. Production in the "rest" falls from $A'C'$ to $L'K'$. Consumption in the United States falls from AB to LH. Consumption in the "rest" of the world rises from $A'B'$ to $L'H'$.

Effects of a Tariff on Welfare

In a broad way it is evident that the interests of producers in the United States, and of consumers abroad, are affected favorably by the tariff. The interests of consumers in the United States and of producers abroad are affected unfavorably. The same result would be brought about by any increase in the cost of transport, whether due to an import tax imposed by the importing country, or to an export tax imposed by the exporting country, or to a change in the techniques of transportation. This analysis does not by itself give us sufficient information to pass judgment on any particular tariff, for it does not tell us how great are the benefits and losses involved. The very fact, however that to discuss tariffs properly we must treat them as artificial increases in the cost of transport should make the tariff enthusiast pause. Tariffs, as Bastiat pointed out, are "negative railways." Just as railways are a device to lessen the cost of transport between two places, so tariffs are a device to increase it. A consistent advocate of tariffs, then, would at least prove his consistency if he were also prepared to advocate a return to the horse and buggy.

The Tariff and Elasticities

It should be observed that the effects of a tariff depend largely on the absolute elasticities or slopes of demand and supply in the two countries. The effect on the *price* of the commodity will be greatest in the country with the most inelastic demand and supply curves. In Fig. 30 for instance, the demand and supply curves for the United

States are more inelastic than the demand and supply curves for the "rest." Consequently, a relatively large rise in price in the United States, *AL*, is necessary to reduce imports to *KH*, when in the "rest" a relatively small fall in price, *A'L'*, will reduce exports to *H'K'*. The effect on the quantities produced and consumed in the two countries will likewise depend on the elasticities of supply or demand. The more inelastic the supply curve, the smaller will be the change in the quantity produced. The more inelastic the demand curve, the smaller will be the change in the quantity consumed. If the supply of the commodity in both countries were perfectly inelastic, the imposition of a tariff would merely cut down consumption in the importing country and expand consumption in the exporting country, without affecting the volume of production at all.

Price Stabilization by Purchase and Sale Policy ("Pegging")

Supply and demand analysis is useful in interpreting the effects of attempts to fix prices by a policy of purchase and sale by government or other authority. There are many examples of such policies. A monetary standard is essentially an undertaking on the part of some central authority to buy or sell the standard commodity at a fixed price in unlimited quantities. Any "pegging" operation, whether of foreign exchange rates, government bond prices, or agricultural prices, similarly involves an undertaking by some authority to buy unlimited quantities of the "pegged" item at the fixed price. Pegging generally involves purchase rather than sale by the authority because the pegged price is usually above the price that would obtain in the free market.

An offer to purchase unlimited quantities at a set price represents a perfectly elastic demand for the purchased item. The effect is illustrated in Fig. 31. Suppose a law were to be passed compelling the Treasury to buy all of some commodity—say silver—offered to it at a fixed price, *OF*. *DD'* and *SS'* represent the commercial demand and supply

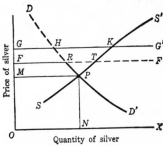

Fig. 31. Effect of Treasury Purchases of Silver.

curves for silver. *FF'* is the Treasury demand curve. In the absence of treasury action the price will be *NP*, and the quantity put on to or taken off the market will be *MP*. Under the purchase policy, however, the demand curve becomes *DRF'*, the price rises to *OF*, a quantity *FT* is offered on the market, *FR* is taken off the market by private purchasers, and RT is the rate at which Treasury purchases will be made. If the Treasury price is raised to OG Treasury purchases will rise to HK, private purchases will shrink to GH, and total output onto the market will rise to GK. Only if the Treasury price were OM would there be no Treasury purchases.

All This Analysis Assumes Supply and Demand Fixed

In all this supply and demand analysis one word of warning must be given. We have assumed in these examples that the changes which have been considered do not alter the position of the supply and demand curves themselves. This condition must always be kept in mind, as in a great many problems it does not hold. If, for instance, the imposition of a tax on cigarettes actually made people dislike smoking because it was associated with the unpleasant act of paying taxes, we should have to modify our analysis. Again, in considering the effects of various changes, such as a tax or a tariff, through time, we must remember that the supply and demand curves are constantly changing as time goes on and conditions of tastes or of techniques change.

Difficulties of Dynamic Analysis

An even more important limitation on demand and supply analysis is apparent when we discuss the dynamics of the movements toward equilibrium, for the process of moving toward equilibrium may itself change the position of the supply and demand curves. If for instance a fall in price produces the expectation of a further fall, as we have seen on page 97, the demand curve itself may fall as people hold off purchases or consumption in the expectation of finding the commodity cheaper later. Similarly the supply curve may rise (move to the right) as suppliers seek to forestall the expected lower price by producing or selling now while the price is still relatively high. Thus as a price moves downward toward equilibrium from a position of excess supply (say from ON_1 in Fig. 10, page 113) the movement itself may push both supply and demand curves "downward" toward the quantity axis, and the equilibrium position itself retreats in front of the pursuing price. Similarly an upward movement of price from a position of excess demand may push the equilibrium price upward. These movements are of course only temporary; eventually the dynamic shift of the curves will slow down and the divergence between the actual and the equilibrium price will disappear. When this happens, however, the demand and supply curves themselves will revert to their "normal" positions and the process starts all over again, setting up what is called an "expectational" cycle. These cycles are discussed more fully later (pages 426–428).

These dynamic effects are important in understanding the theory of price control, for in a basically inflationary situation price control may operate not merely to suppress the symptoms and so create "shortages"; it may also destroy expectations of rising prices, and hence may lower the supply and demand curves themselves below where they would otherwise have been. The effect may only be temporary, and it will not be able to deal with great inflationary pressure, but it is an important element in the explanation of the success of price control, for example in World War II.

It is evident that these modifications do not destroy the basic usefulness of supply and demand analysis. It must be used warily and with a constant sense of its limitations, but the simple equilibrium analysis always provides the base from which dynamic analysis must take its flight.

QUESTIONS AND EXERCISES

1. In our discussion, page 133, of the relation between the size of the total crop of strawberries and the price, we assumed that the supply of strawberries at the time of the harvest was perfectly inelastic. What do we mean by this? What conditions would we have to assume for this to be true? Is it likely to be absolutely true? If not, can you reframe the argument in terms of a supply curve that is not perfectly inelastic?

2. Prove that a tax on a commodity will raise the price to the consumer by the amount of the tax per unit if, and only if, the supply of the commodity is perfectly elastic.

3. Mr. Protectionist: "A tariff will not raise the price to the home consumer, for in order to sell his products the foreigner will have to accept a lower price for himself."

   Mr. Free Trader: "On the contrary, a tariff will always raise the price which the home consumer has to pay by the amount of the tariff, for the foreign manufacturer must get his old price or he will not go on producing."

   Under what circumstances may (a) either one or (b) neither of these two statements be correct?

4. Suppose you were asked to draw up a system of duties on imports with a view to making as little change in the volume of imports or exports as you could. What kind of commodities would you choose to place the tariff on, and what kind would you leave free?

5. Suppose the Treasury was compelled to buy and sell silver at a price which was below the normal price of silver in the commercial market. What would be the effects, if any, of this policy?

6. Suppose that both Britain and the United States are on the gold standard, the price of gold in Britain being £12.5 per ounce and the price in the United States being $35 per ounce. Suppose that the cost of transport of gold across the Atlantic is $0.25 per ounce. Then show that in the foreign exchange market there will be a perfectly elastic demand for pounds at a price of $2.78 per pound, and a perfectly elastic supply of pounds at a price of $2.82 per pound. Show by means of a diagram (plotting the price of pounds against the quantity offered or demanded) that in such a case no matter what the "commercial" demand or supply of pounds, the price cannot go above $2.82 or below $2.78.

Repeat the proof in terms of the demand and supply of dollars.

7. Between 1942 and 1951 the U.S. Treasury supported the market in government bonds by buying bonds whenever the price fell below a level which would yield the rate of interest deemed appropriate. Illustrate the effects of this policy by means of supply and demand analysis.

8. Under the agricultural price support program the Department of Agriculture found itself owning an unmanageable surplus of potatoes. In the following period price supports on potatoes were abandoned and yet potato prices were high. How do you explain these phenomena according to demand and supply analysis?

9. Suppose the following schedules represented the demand and supply schedules for a commodity in two countries, A and B:

Price (per Ton)	Quantity Which Will Be Produced in A (Million Tons)	Quantity Which Will Be Consumed in A (Million Tons)	Quantity Which Will Be Produced in B (Million Tons)	Quantity Which Will Be Consumed in B (Million Tons)
$ 0	0	220	0	90
1	0	200	0	80
2	0	180	10	70
3	0	160	20	60
4	0	140	30	50
5	0	120	40	40
6	20	100	50	30
7	40	80	60	20
8	60	60	70	10
9	80	40	80	0
10	100	20	90	0
11	120	0	100	0

a. Calculate the *total* supply schedule, showing the quantities which producers of both countries together will produce at each price; also the total demand schedule, showing the quantities which consumers of both countries together will consume at each price. Draw the curves corresponding to these schedules and the four schedules of the table.

b. What would be the normal price in each country, assuming that there was no trade?

c. What would be the normal price in both countries, assuming that trade were possible without cost of transport? What would be the volume of imports and exports at this price? What would be the consumption and the production in each country?

d. Suppose the cost of transport were $1.50 per ton. What would then be the normal price in each country, the volume of imports and exports, of consumption and production, in each country?

e. What would be the smallest specific tariff which would be prohibitive—i.e., which would cut off trade altogether—assuming that there is no cost of transport?

f. Why is the effect of an increase in the cost of transport greater on the price in B than on the price in A?

10. Suppose that e_s and e_d are the numerical values of the absolute elasticities of demand and supply for a commodity. Suppose a specific tax of T per unit is levied on the commodity. Then show that the decline in quantity, ΔQ is $\dfrac{T e_d e_s}{e_d + e_s}$. What are the formulas for the rise in the consumers' price and for the fall in the producers' price? Assume linear demand and supply functions.

11. The price of a commodity is $1. Compare the results of (a) a specific tax of 10 cents and (b) a 10 per cent ad valorem tax on the quantity produced and on the consumers' and producers' prices. Why do the results differ?

A P P E N D I X   T O   C H A P T E R   8

MORE ADVANCED ILLUSTRATIONS OF THE USE OF SUPPLY AND DEMAND ANALYSIS

THE STABILIZATION OF INCOMES

Stabilizing Price Does Not Stabilize Incomes

A more advanced problem in the theory of stabilization concerns the policy of a government which desires to stabilize not the *price* of a farm product but the *total value* of the crop. We can easily see that stabilizing the price of a crop through "time arbitrage" does not necessarily stabilize the incomes of the farmers. If the price of wheat were constant from year to year, then in a year of poor crop the gross incomes of wheat farmers would be low, and in a year of good crop the gross incomes of wheat farmers would be high.

Gross Incomes Constant Only if Elasticity of Demand Is Unity

If, now, the elasticity of demand for the wheat crop of each year were unity, this would mean that no matter what the size of the crop, the gross incomes of the wheat producers (i.e., the total value of the crop) would be constant. In years of small harvest the price would be just high enough to compensate for the smallness of the crop, and in years of good harvest the price would be just low enough to compensate for the largeness of the crop. If the elasticity of demand for the crop of any year, therefore, were unity, there would be no need for any government interference in order to insure stable gross incomes for the producer.

If, however, the elasticity of demand for the crop of any particular year were greater than unity (i.e., if the demand were relatively elastic), a small crop would bring in a smaller income than a large crop. Hence, in years of small crop the government—if it wished to stabilize the gross incomes of farmers—would have to take supplies off the market and thereby raise the price. But in years of large crop the income of farmers will be larger than normal, so that the government will have to put still further supplies on the market and so lower the price.

If the demand for the crop were relatively inelastic, a small crop would bring in a *larger* income than normal, as we have seen, and the government would have to put supplies on the market, and so lower the price, in order to bring the farmers' income back to normal. But with a large crop, the farmers' income would be smaller than usual, and the government would have to take supplies off the market in order to raise the price and consequently the farmers' income. This shows how important the distinction between a relatively elastic and a relatively inelastic demand can be. In the case of an elastic demand the government must increase both gluts and scarcities, and in the case of an inelastic demand it must diminish both gluts and scarcities, in order to achieve the same result—a stable farm income.

Graphic Illustration. This argument is shown graphically in Fig. 32. Fig. 32A shows a demand curve of unit elasticity EE'. No matter what the size of the crop, be it small (OH) or large (OK), the total value of the crop is the same. In the first case, it is $OHEF$; in the second case, it is $OKE'G$—an exactly equal area.

Fig. 32B shows a relatively elastic demand curve for the crop, DD'.

Suppose in this case that the average crop over a number of years is OT, and the average price TR; the average value of the crop, i.e., the average income from the crop, is therefore equal to $OTRS$.[5] Then through the point R draw a curve ERE', of unit elasticity. (This is a rectangular hyperbola.) If, then, the crop is abnormally large (say, equal to OM) the price which the farmer should receive in order to

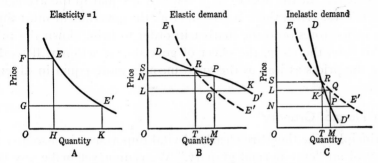

FIG. 32.   The Stabilization of Gross Income.

give him his average income will be MQ, where Q is on the curve EE'. The price which would obtain in the absence of government intervention would be MP, where P is on the demand curve DD'. In order that the price MQ may hold in the market, the government must sell out of its previously accumulated stocks an amount equal to QK, so that the total amount on the market in that year is LK. Thus the farmers' income will be equal to the crop (OM) multiplied by the new price (MQ), or the area $OMQL$, which is equal to $OTRS$ (the average income) by the construction of the curve EE'. If the government had not thrown the amount QK onto the market, the price would have been MP and the farmers' income $OMPN$, which is greater than normal. Similarly, in a year of short crop the government must in this case actually take some of the crop off the market and so raise the price even above what it would have been. The effect of government intervention in this way would be to increase price fluctuations but to do away with fluctuations in the total value of the crop.

Fig. 32C shows an inelastic demand for the crop, DD'. Again through the point R, where SR (or OT) is the crop and TR the price, which

5 To find the "average price," TR, and the "average crop," OT, we do not take the arithmetic mean of all the prices or of all the outputs in the period under review, for the product of these arithmetic means will not give the average gross value. Instead we must calculate the gross value of the crop in each year, and take the arithmetic mean of these figures. This is the "average gross value." Then from the demand curve we must find the output and the price which yields this "average gross value." OT is the output and TR the price so discovered.

yields the average gross income, $OTRS$, we draw a curve of unit elasticity, EE'. Now, when there is a large crop, OM, the farmers' income, in the absence of regulation, will be $OMPN$, which is smaller than the average income, $OTRS$. Consequently, the government must take off the market an amount equal to QK, leaving an amount LK which will sell for a price OL, thus making the farmers' income equal to $OM \times OL$, or the area $OMQL$—which is equal to the average income $OTRS$. When there is a small crop, the government must throw some of its stores onto the market in order to bring down the price. In this case, therefore, the effect of government action will tend to make the prices as well as the gross incomes more equal in different years.

"Ever Normal Granary"

Principles like these are clearly of vital importance in assessing any policy of an "ever normal granary." We cannot yet make any final judgment on such a policy. However, we can perhaps see that there is more justification for it in the case of commodities with a relatively inelastic demand than in the case of commodities with a relatively elastic demand. In the first case such a policy not only will equalize incomes but will diminish the fluctuation of prices. In the second case making incomes more equal actually necessitates an increased fluctuation of prices.

Does Private Speculation Stabilize Farm Income?

An interesting problem of a similar type concerns private speculation. How far would the activities of *private* speculators, apart from government intervention, serve to increase or diminish the fluctuation of farm income? It was explained in Chapter 5, page 78, that if time arbitrage is properly carried out and there is a reasonably accurate and widely known expectation of future events, speculation will tend to diminish the year-to-year fluctuation of the price of a storable commodity, such as wheat. Speculators will buy up part of the crop in years of big harvest in order to sell it in years of small harvest. This will diminish the fluctuation in price from year to year. Whether these operations will reduce the fluctuations in farm income from year to year will depend on how elastic is the demand curve of the market apart from the speculators, and on how much their operations in fact reduce the price fluctuations.

The demand curve of the market without speculators—DD in Fig. 33A—is the curve showing the relation between the size of the crop and the price at which it could be sold, if it all had to be sold for consumption within the year. Speculators take part of the crop off the market in years of good harvest when the price is low and put it back on the market in years of poor harvest when the price is high. They have the effect, therefore, of diminishing the fluctuations in price. The demand curve in the presence of speculators—*EE* in Fig. 33A—will be more elastic than in the absence of speculators. A small crop (*ON*) would command a price *NP* in the absence of specu-

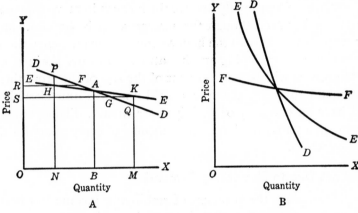

FIG. 33.   Speculation and Gross Income.

lation. Speculators, however, sell from their stocks an amount *HF*, making the total sales to nonspeculators equal to *RF*, and the price equal to *OR*, or *NH*. A large crop, *OM*, would command a price *MQ* in the absence of speculation. Speculators, however, buy up and store an amount *KG*, making the total sales to nonspeculators equal to *SG*, and the price *OS*, or *MK*.

With Inelastic Demand. Now if the demand of the market without speculators were relatively inelastic, as *DD* in Fig. 33B, the action of speculators would make this demand more elastic. If the demand in the presence of speculators had unit elasticity, *EE*, the speculation would diminish not only the fluctuations of prices but also the fluctuation in the total value of the crop, for in this case the size of the crop would not affect its value. If, therefore, the speculators push the demand curve from the position *DD* to a position between *DD* and *EE*, they will have diminished the fluctuations in gross income. But if they push the demand curve into a still more elastic position—for example, *FF*—they may actually increase the fluctuations in the gross income. Such fluctuations will be in the opposite direction to those in the market without speculators. A small crop now brings a smaller gross income than a larger crop.

With Elastic Demand. With the demand curve in the absence of speculation relatively elastic, as it is drawn in Fig. 33A, the presence of speculation will make the demand still more elastic. In this case speculation as always will decrease the fluctuations of price. But it will of necessity increase the fluctuations of gross income.

Gross Income and Net Income

A large crop will probably involve the farmers in more expense than a small crop, for even though the acreage sown is the same, and the larger crop is due solely to the benevolence of the elements, there will be extra charges for reaping and handling. To insure that the *net* income of growers will be independent of the size of the crop, then, the total demand curve for the crop should not have unit elasticity, but should have an elasticity of slightly more than 1. Then a large crop will bring in a somewhat larger gross income to compensate for the increased expenses.

Fluctuations Due to Fluctuating Demands

Up to this point the problem of stabilizing income has been discussed on the assumption that demand is stable and that therefore fluctuations in prices or incomes from year to year are due to changes in output. For some periods (e.g., 1923–1929) this may have been approximately the case. In other periods, however (e.g., 1929–1948), price fluctuations have been due mainly to changes in demand itself arising from changes in income, and the fluctuations of output have been secondary. The problem of stabilizing gross income of producers when demand is fluctuating is illustrated in Fig. 34. OR represents the annual output of the commodity, in this case assumed to be constant. RP is that price which will yield the "average" income which it is desired to stabilize, $ORPS$. If the demand curve passes through P, as DP, the income is average and no action is necessary. If the demand is greater than DP, say DP_1, in the absence of governmental action the price will rise to RP_1 and income will be above average. To bring the price (and therefore the income, as output is assumed stable) down to the average price RP the stabilization authority must put an amount PQ_1 on the market, increasing total sales to SQ_1. If the demand is below average, say DQ_2, the price in the absence of regulation will be RP_2. The authority will have to take an amount PQ_2 off the market, reducing total sales to consumers to SQ_2. If the fall in demand is very great, say to DQ_3, stabilization of gross income will be impossible, as no amount of restriction of sales to consumers will raise the price sufficiently to bring income up to the "average." In Fig. 34 the assumption has been made that the shifts in demand are due to cyclical changes in income, not to changes in tastes, hence, the shifts in demand do not affect the amount of the commodity that would be bought at zero price, OD, and all the demand curves pass through D. This is the most

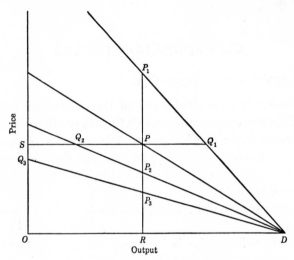

FIG. 34.   Stabilization with Fluctuating Demand.

likely case, as a cyclical shift of tastes is difficult to imagine. However, it is evident that if any commodity were subject to regularly fluctuating tastes, the same type of analysis could be applied.

Criticism of "Buffer Stocks" Plan

It will be observed that the attempt to apply an "ever normal granary" (sometimes called a "buffer stocks" plan) under circumstances of fluctuating demand would require the augmentation of consumption in years of good demand and its restriction in years of poor demand. As years of good demand are the "boom" years and years of poor demand are "depression" years, the result of the ever normal granary plan would be to feed the boom by starving the depression—a most undesirable result. The stability of one element of the economy—the income of producers of the particular commodities stabilized—would be obtained only at the cost of unstabilizing what may be a much more important element in the economy—consumption. Particularly in the case of foodstuffs the "buffer stocks" method of stabilization might well prove disastrous if the cause of instability were unstable demand. If the economy is going to be unstable, it is much better for the instability to be reflected in farm income than in food consumption. Only if the basic cause of unstable farm incomes is fluctuating crop outputs is there much to be said for the "buffer stocks" plan, and only then if the demand is inelastic, so that the operation of the plan tends toward stabilizing prices and consumption as well as producer income.

CROP-RESTRICTION POLICIES

The United States Cotton Restriction

We have already examined some of the difficulties into which a "restriction" scheme may run, especially where there is no effective control of the volume of production. We may now examine an extension of this problem, of considerable practical importance—the case in which a government enforces the restriction of production within its own boundaries of a crop with a world market and with other centers of production. The cotton policy of the New Deal is a case in point.

In Fig. 35, as usual, price is indicated along the axis OY and the quantities produced and consumed, or the rates of production and consumption, along OX. Suppose the figure refers to cotton. Then let $S_u S'_u$ be the normal supply curve for cotton, for producers within the United States. Let $S_f S'_f$ be the normal supply curve for cotton for "foreign" producers—i.e., all producers outside the United States. Then the total supply curve for cotton, $S_f S_t S'_t$, is obtained by adding, for each price, the quantity which will be produced by the United States producers to the quantity which will be produced by foreign producers. Thus, the meaning of these curves is that at any price, OY, American producers will produce at a rate equal to YS'_u, foreign producers will be willing to produce at a rate YS'_f, and therefore the total rate of production at that price will be $YS'_u + YS'_f = YS'_t$.

The normal price will be given at the point Q_t, where the total supply curve cuts the total demand curve, $D'D$. ON $(= MQ_t)$ is the normal price: NQ_t $(= OM)$ is the total quantity produced. NQ_u is the quantity produced in America and NQ_f is the quantity produced abroad.

Now suppose that the American government effectively prevents American producers from producing any quantity greater than LR_u.

The American supply curve then becomes the dotted line $S_uR_uR'_u$. Under the restriction scheme, if the price falls below OL, at which the American producers will normally produce the allotted quantity LR_u, they will automatically lower their production, following the supply curve R_uS_u. If the price rises above this, they are prevented from expanding their output by government authority, and therefore their supply is perfectly inelastic. The foreign supply curve presumably remains the same. The *total* supply curve then becomes the dotted line $S_fS_tR_tR'_t$, where $R_tR'_t$ is parallel to the foreign supply curve $R_fS'_f$. The normal price rises to HP_t $(= OK)$, P_t being the point

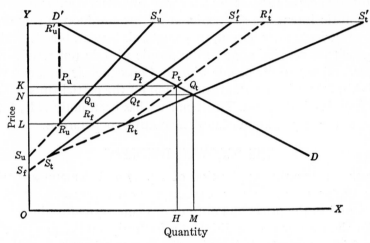

FIG. 35.   Restriction of Part of a Crop.

where this new total supply curve cuts the total demand curve. Then the American production has fallen from NQ_u to KP_u; foreign production has expanded from NQ_f $(= Q_uQ_t)$ to KP_f $(= P_uP_t)$. Whether the total gross income of the American producers has risen or fallen depends, of course, on the actual shape of the curves. In this case it is evident that the gross income of American producers has declined sharply from $(ON \times NQ_u)$ to $(OK \times KP_u)$, and the gross income of foreign producers has increased from $(ON \times NQ_f)$ to $(OK \times KP_f)$. Unless the shape of the supply and demand curves is very peculiar indeed, there must always be a gain in the gross income of the foreign producers, for the price and also the quantity they produce increase. For the American producers the price increases but the quantity produced diminishes. Unless the diminution in quantity is very small, therefore, they are unlikely to gain in gross income. A scheme like this is unlikely to increase the gross income of American producers unless

(1) the foreign supply is very inelastic or (2) the legal maximum American crop is very little less than the normal crop.

If there is any elasticity of supply for foreign production, the result of an American crop restriction is that the foreign producers increase their production to make up in part the deficiency in the American crop. Consequently, the foreign producers get most of the benefit of the increased price. This particular analysis has a good many applications. It applies not only to government restriction but to any attempt to gain monopoly prices by restriction of only a *part* of the total production, whether on the part of a government, a steel combine, or an agricultural cooperative. It explains why voluntary combinations of a monopolistic intent are so fragile. If all the producers of one commodity restricted their output, they might all benefit, but the bulk of the benefits of restriction go to the people who do not restrict their outputs, and not to the people who do. Consequently, in any scheme of this kind there is a constant temptation for the participants to break away from it—if they can. This tendency has been noticeable, for instance, in the organization of milk marketing cooperatives.

THE "COBWEB THEOREM"

Another interesting application of supply and demand analysis is to the explanation of certain curious cyclical movements which are to be found in the prices and outputs of many agricultural commodities. In the case of commodities like fresh vegetables, potatoes, and pigs, a fairly regular cycle is noticeable. In one year the quantity supplied is small and the price is high. The high price encourages producers to plan for an increase in production, which, however, matures in the next year or the year after. When this increased production comes on the market, the price is forced down. Consequently, many producers go out of production; and when their decisions are made effective—in another year or two—the quantity supplied is again small and prices are high, and so the cycle goes on.

Fig. 36 illustrates this process. Here *DD* represents the relationship between the quantity supplied in any one "year" and the price which must be charged in order to sell that quantity. *SS* represents the relationship between the price in any one "year" and the quantity which will be produced in the "year" *following*—the "year" being the period of time between the decision to produce and the completion of production. These, it should be noticed, are not the usual supply and demand curves; they have a special meaning of their own, appropriate to the problem in question.

Suppose in one year there is a production equal to OA. The price will be AC, according to the meaning of the curve DD. If the price in that year, however, is AC, the production in the second year will be FE, according to the meaning of the curve SS. Therefore, the price in the second year will be HG. The production in the third year will be LK. If $LK = OA$, the cycle will start all over again and will be repeated indefinitely, as long as the conditions which define the curves

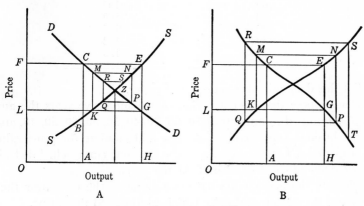

FIG. 36. The Cobweb Theorem.

remain the same. But if the shape of the curves is such that, as in Fig. 36A, LK is greater than OA, the cycle will be repeated, following the path $KMNPQRS$ . . . etc., with ever diminishing range. In practice, of course, long before the cycle has a chance to be repeated the character of the curves themselves may change, but it is important to see what would happen if conditions did not change. Eventually, in this case we will reach the center, Z, and equilibrium will be established. If, however, after the end of the first cycle the production in the third year, LK, were less than that in the first, OA, the cycle would go on with ever increasing amplitude, following a course such as $CEGKMNPQRST$, as in Fig. 36B. Again, this cannot go on forever. Either it will come to a position of neutral equilibrium, following the same path in every cycle, or the whole position of the curves will change. This theorem is usually called the "cobweb theorem," from the nature of the diagram which illustrates it.

QUESTIONS AND EXERCISES

1. Suppose that the following schedule represents the total demand curve of all private individuals for wheat in any given year:

If the Total Output Is (Million Bushels)	The Price Will Have to Be (Cents per Bushel)
110	60
100	70
90	82
80	92
70	100
60	105
50	109
40	116
30	132
20	158

a. Plot this demand curve on squared paper.

b. Now suppose that over a period of ten successive years the annual "crop" amounted to outputs of 80, 60, 70, 40, 50, 80, 60, 50, 40, and 70 million bushels, respectively. Calculate and tabulate the gross value of the crop in each of these years, if the demand curve scheduled above was the demand curve of each of the ten years.

c. Calculate the *average* annual gross value of the crop over the ten years, and the output and price which would yield this value.

d. Construct a schedule showing what price would have to be received for each of the outputs in the schedule in order to make the gross value of the crop in each year equal to the average annual gross value. Plot this schedule on the same paper as the demand curve. It will be a curve of unit elasticity.

e. From the demand curve find the total amount which must be offered on the market in order to fetch the prices discovered in part (d). From these amounts make a schedule showing how much the government would have to buy or sell for each total output.

f. Draw up a schedule showing how much the government would have to buy or sell in each of the ten successive years of part (b). Notice that the government would have to sell a total greater than the amount which it would have to buy over the ten years. Does this mean that stabilization of the gross value of a crop is impossible?

2. Under what circumstances do you think that government interference with speculation in commodities is justified?

3. Prove that if the supply of foreign cotton is perfectly elastic, a restriction of the United States crop will not affect the price of cotton but will merely cause an increase in the foreign output exactly equal to the amount by which the United States crop has been restricted.

4. What conditions of supply and demand are likely to lead to fluctuations of price around an equilibrium level rather than to the establishment of a price at an equilibrium level?

5. Suppose that in Fig. 36 (A and B) the supply curve shows the relationship between the price in one year and the amount of production in the next year. Starting in both A and B with a production equal to OA, plot in each case two diagrams, one showing the fluctuation of price from year to year, the other showing the fluctuation of output. Measure the number of years along the horizontal axis, and the price or output along the vertical axis.

6. Discuss the problem of the stabilization of producer income when *both* output *and* demand fluctuate.

7. In the "cobweb Theorem" diagram (Fig. 36) suppose that p_0 is the excess of the actual over the normal price at C, p_1 at G, p_2 at M, and so on. If the demand and supply functions are linear, with absolute elasticities of e_d and e_s, show that $p_1 = \dfrac{e_s p}{e_d}$, $p_2 = \dfrac{e_s^2 p}{e_d^2}$, and so on. From this show that the "cobweb" will be converging, neutral, or diverging according as $e_s \underset{>}{\overset{<}{=}} e_d$.

CHAPTER 9

THE PRINCIPLE OF EQUAL ADVANTAGE

The Allocation of Resources

In any advanced economic system there exists a high degree of *specialization* of resources. That is to say, our resources—labor, land, equipment—are divided among a large number of different industries. Each industry puts out a product or a group of related products which it exchanges for the product of other industries. It is no exaggeration to say that the principal problem of economic life is to determine *how big* each of these industries, these specialized employments of resources, shall be. How much of each commodity should be produced? How many men should be employed in each occupation? How much land should be devoted to corn? to cabbages? to skyscrapers? These are the fundamental questions of economic life, and all economic systems are attempts to answer them.

Allocation in a Planned Economy. In the completely "planned" economy—the extreme case of which would be a slave society governed by a small class of rulers—these questions are decided by the will of the ruler. The dictator of a totalitarian communist state decrees that a steel factory shall be built, and it is built, no matter what the feelings and desires of those who build it or of those who will use its products. The general of an army disposes of the resources at his disposal without inquiring whether Private A likes cooking or Private B likes killing.

Allocation in a Free Economy. In a "free" economy this is not so. A free economy is an economic system in which any individual is allowed to put the resources which he owns to any use he thinks fit, provided he does not thereby violate the property rights of others. In such an economy there is no "economic dictator" who decrees that so many men shall become barbers and so many lawyers, or that so many acres of land shall be used for corn and so many for houses. Neverthe-
168

less, the interacting wills of all the individuals in such a society succeed in effecting an apportionment of resources among the various employments.

The Principle of Equal Advantage

This apportionment is governed by a principle which we may call the *principle of equal advantage*. It may be stated thus: If the owners of any resources think that they can be put to better advantage in some other use than the one in which they are employed, these resources will be transferred from the less advantageous to the more advantageous use. The process of transfer will generally have the effect of making the occupation *into* which resources have been transferred *less* advantageous than before; it will make the occupation *out of* which resources have been transferred *more* advantageous than before. As long, therefore, as there are people who believe that the resources they own, whether these be their own bodies or some other object, will yield them a greater advantage in an occupation different from that in which they are at present employed, then resources will be transferred from one occupation to another. In this statement, it should be noticed, we use the word "advantage" deliberately, for it includes both monetary and nonmonetary advantages. We do not assume that people are moved only by differences in monetary reward. Indeed, as we shall see, permanent differences in monetary rewards between different occupations may be explained by assuming that people are in fact moved by nonmonetary considerations.

Equilibrium: Advantages Equal in All Employments

A position of "equilibrium" in the distribution of economic resources means a situation in which there is no tendency for resources to move from one occupation to another, on balance. In equilibrium, that is to say, the proportion of resources devoted to the various industries does not change. In the present chapter a state of perfect competition is assumed. The exact meaning of this concept will be discussed later. For present purposes it is enough to know that it assumes there are no restrictions on the migration of resources from one occupation to another. Under these circumstances the economic system will be in equilibrium only when the advantage derived from the employment of resources in all occupations is the same. For if this were not so, resources would move from the occupations of low advantage to those of high advantage. This movement would raise the advantage in the former occupations and lower the advantage in the latter, until all occupations offered equal advantages. At this point there would be no incentive to a further transfer of resources, and the system would be in equilibrium.

Example: The Geographic Distribution of Doctors. We may illustrate this principle first by a simple example. How does it come about that the number of doctors in any one town is roughly proportionate to its size and wealth? How does it happen that a village of 2000 people may have only four doctors and a town of 20,000 people may have forty? There is no authority of government which sets out to achieve this desirable result; there is no official who says to the medical students, as they come fresh from the schools, "Lo, you must go to Oskaloosa and you to Kankakee." It is the operation of the great and universal principle of equal advantage which brings this about. It is evident that as a general rule the more doctors there are in any one town, the less advantageous will be the lot of each. If there are four doctors practicing in a village, the incursion of a fifth will unquestionably bring down the average remuneration of doctors in that village, unless the newcomer strikes a wholly new demand for his services. The incursion of a sixth will bring that remuneration down still further; a seventh might bring all the doctors to scraping, and an eighth to penury. On the other hand, if one doctor leaves a community, the remuneration of the others is likely to increase. There may be exceptions to this rule, but we shall not consider them now, for in the mass they will clearly be unimportant.

Consider, then, the situation of a young doctor just starting out in practice. Where is he most likely to go? To a place which is already overstaffed with doctors? Surely not. He will seek a place where doctors are relatively few, and where therefore their remuneration may be expected to be relatively high. Similarly, if a doctor residing in a place where there is a surplus of doctors hears of an opportunity in a place which has too few, he will be likely to take the opportunity, because thereby he may hope to better himself. Even in so altruistic a profession as that of medicine, therefore, it is the "advantage motive" which by its slow but persistent pressure constantly pushes doctors out of places where there are too *many* to make what they consider an average living, into places where they are so *few* that they make what is considered a better than average living. This force does not act rapidly. Indeed, for long periods we may find places which have too many doctors and places which have too few. But like the pressure of water on the rocks in a stream, even though it does not always cause change immediately, it infallibly determines the direction of change when it comes. Just as we never find streams washing stones uphill, so we never find the force of advantage pushing people from occupations which they think are better into those which they think are worse.

The Allocation of Resources in General

Unprosperous Industries Decline. The same principle applies, in a rather more complex manner, to the distribution of resources in general. Is an industry unprosperous? That is a sign that it is "too big" relative to what it ought to be. Is an industry abnormally prosperous? That is a sign that it is "too small" relative to what it ought to be. What will happen? Resources will leave the unprosperous industry. Firms in that industry will close down, workers will be thrown out of employment or forced to accept low wages; profits and wages will be low and unemployment may be high. Consequently, the industry will decline. Those workers who can get out will do so. The workers who die off will not be replaced, for the new, young workers will not be attracted into the declining industry. Capitalists who can get their capital out of the industry will do so, and new capital will not flow in. Consequently, the output of the industry will be smaller. If the underlying conditions of demand and supply do not change, the price of the product of the industry will rise. If, then, the industry decreases in size sufficiently, its prosperity will rise until it is "normal" once more. Then the decline will cease. The industry will be in equilibrium.

Prosperous Industries Grow. Now imagine an industry which is unusually prosperous. Profits are high, wages are high, it is easy to get employment. What will be the result? Workers will be attracted into it, and new firms will enter it. Its output will increase, and therefore the price of that output will fall. The industry will become rather less prosperous. It will continue to expand until it becomes just "normally" prosperous, when it will cease to attract resources into it and will stop growing. It will then be in equilibrium.

The Adjustments of the Whole System

We must therefore picture the industries of our economic system: some declining under the shadow of adversity, some expanding under the sun of prosperity, some perhaps remaining stationary. But the expanding ones will not expand forever, for the very prosperity which induced their expansion will decline as the industry grows. Likewise those which contract will not contract forever, for by their very contraction they tend to rectify the situation which made them un- prosperous.

Results of a Change in Tastes

We can illustrate this process best, perhaps, by considering the effects of a change in the things which ultimately determine how resources are divided. Consider a system which is in equilibrium—that is to say, all industries are just normally prosperous, no industry is more prosperous than another, and therefore there is no tendency for resources to move from one industry to another. Now suppose that there is a change in the tastes of consumers—for instance, that a change in fashion causes a marked shift in consumers' demand from silk goods to cotton goods. The results of this shift will depend on the period of time taken into account. We may consider three broad stages. First, there is the immediate, or *"impact" effect*. Second, there are the changes which will take place during the period of adjustment, or the *adjustment effects*. Third, there is the effect on the final position of equilibrium; this is the *final effect*.

In considering these effects we shall assume that the other factors affecting economic life remain unchanged. In fact this will never be the case. Nevertheless, this assumption is necessary in order to separate the effects of the particular change in tastes which we are considering from the effects of all other independent changes.

The Impact Effect. In considering the impact effect we shall assume that over a very short period of time the supply of both cotton and silk is perfectly inelastic. Let us also assume that there is no holding of supplies for future sale, so that all that is produced in a given "week" must be sold in that week. These assumptions are rather unrealistic, but they can be relaxed at a later stage. We are considering the effects of a known shift in demand from silk to cotton, which takes place in a certain "week," and which persists thereafter indefinitely. This situation is represented in Fig. 37.

In Fig. 37A, dd' is the demand curve for cotton in the week before the change. That is, it shows the quantity of cotton which will be bought in that week at each hypothetical price. The total quantity of cotton coming on the market to be sold in that week is represented by os. It will have to be sold at a price sp. The perfectly inelastic supply curve for that week is ss'. Now suppose that in the next week the demand for cotton has risen to ee'. The quantity coming into the market is assumed to be unchanged. The price at which that quantity can be sold, however, has now risen to sq.

Similarly, in Fig. 37B the original demand for silk is DD', the weekly quantity of silk coming into the market is OS, the inelastic supply curve for silk is SS', and the new, decreased demand for silk is EE'. The result of the fall in demand is a fall in the price from SP to SQ.

The impact effect of a shift in demand from silk to cotton is therefore a fall in the price of silk and a rise in the price of cotton. These new prices will persist as long as the demands remain at their new levels, and as long as the quantities coming onto the market in each week do not change.

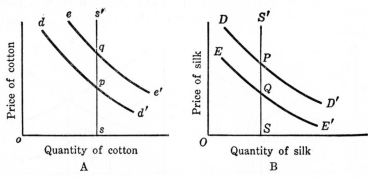

FIG. 37.   Impact Effect of a Shift in Demand.

Intermediate Effects.   However, the quantities coming onto the market *will* change. Under the stimulus of a high price of cotton new producers will enter the cotton industry, new workers will find employment in producing cotton, new land will be put down to cotton, and new cotton factories will be built. The output of cotton will increase. In each "week" after the initial change in demand an increase may be expected in the quantity of cotton placed on the market. This increase may be very slow at first, for it takes time before the effect of a higher price will show itself. Producers cannot enter an industry in the twinkling of an eye; plans have to be made, new fields must be plowed, new men must be trained, new warehouses and factories must be built, new machines must be constructed. All this takes time. Nevertheless, there will be a persistent tendency for the quantity of cotton placed on the market in each week to increase. But this increase will not go on forever, because if the demand remains unchanged at ee', the price in successive weeks must fall. This is illustrated in Fig. 38A. Again, dd' is the old demand for cotton, and ee' is the new, increased demand. The quantity placed on the market in the week of the change is os_0. The price at which this quantity sells, after the rise in demand, is s_0q_0. Under the stimulus of this high price, however, in the next week a slightly larger quantity, os_1, will be placed on the market. This will sell at a rather lower price, s_1q_1. In the second week a still larger quantity will be placed on the market, os_2. This will fetch a still lower price, s_2q_2. So, as the weeks go by, the quantity placed on the market will increase under the stimulus of the high price, but the very increase in the quantity supplied will bring about a steady decline in the price.

Final Effects. This movement, however, will not go on forever. As the price falls, the force which makes for an increase in the weekly quantity supplied will also decline. Eventually there will come a week, f weeks from the initial change, when the force of expansion

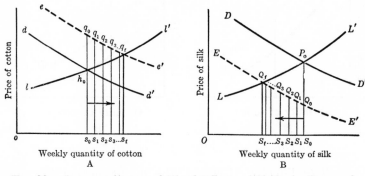

Fig. 38.   Intermediate and Final Effects of Shifts in Demand.

has worked itself out completely. The cotton industry will then be just normally profitable again, and the weekly quantity supplied, os_f, will show no tendency to increase in successive weeks thereafter. The price will be s_fq_f. This is the normal price under the new conditions. It is the price at which, when all necessary adjustments have been made, the industry will neither expand nor contract. The point q_f, therefore, must lie on the "normal" supply curve for cotton, ll', for any point on the normal supply curve shows what rate of production will be permanently maintained, without tendency to rise or fall, at the price which it indicates. Similarly, as the point h_0 represents the point of long-run equilibrium before the change in demand, this point also must lie on the normal supply curve. The output os_f and the price s_fq_f represent, therefore, the final effects of the original change in demand, the point q_f being the point of intersection of the new demand curve with the normal supply curve ll'.

Effects in a Declining Industry. In an exactly similar manner we can analyze the effects of the change in demand on the silk industry in

Fig. 38B. In the week of the change there is a quantity OS_0 placed on the market and selling at a low price, S_0Q_0. This low price will cause a decline in the industry. The output of successive weeks will fall from OS_0 to OS_1, OS_2, etc. This decline, however, will not go on forever, for as the output declines the price will rise from S_0Q_0 to S_1Q_1, S_2Q_2, etc. As the price rises the industry will become relatively less unprosperous, and the force making for its decline will weaken. Finally, the output reaches OS_f, sold at a price S_fQ_f, at which the industry is once more normally profitable, and the decline will cease. The normal supply curve, LL' as before, must pass through points P_0 and Q_f.

Final Results of the Initial Change. The final results of a shift in demand from silk to cotton, then, are (1) a rise in the price of cotton, which will be greater the more inelastic is the normal supply curve for cotton; (2) a fall in the price of silk, which will be greater the more inelastic is the normal supply curve for silk; (3) a rise in the output of the cotton industry, due to an increase in the quantity of resources devoted to cotton production; (4) a decline in the output of the silk industry, due to a decrease in the quantity of resources devoted to silk production.

Effect of a Change in Techniques

We have seen how a shift in demand affects the distribution of resources, acting through the mechanism of prices and their effect on advantage. Let us now see how a change in *techniques* will affect prices, advantage, and the distribution of resources. Suppose that the tastes of consumers in respect to cotton remain constant, but that an improved method of growing or manufacturing cotton and cotton goods is discovered, so that a given quantity of cotton or cotton goods can be produced with the expenditure of a smaller quantity of resources than before—i.e., with less labor, less land, and so on. This situation may be represented in Fig. 39.

As before, we measure the price of cotton along OY and the quantity which will be demanded or supplied in a week along OX. DD' is then the normal demand curve for cotton, representing the relation between the price and the quantity which will be bought in each week. This is assumed to be constant. LL' is the normal supply curve before the change, representing the relation between the price and the quantity which will continue to be supplied in each week at each price.

Impact, Intermediate, and Final Effects. Now suppose there is an improvement in techniques. The first result will be that cotton production will become abnormally advantageous, for the producers are still getting the same price for their cotton as previously, but they can produce it with greater ease and therefore with less expense than they previously could. Consequently, the industry will grow. New producers will be attracted into it. As the weeks go by the output will increase from OS_0 through OS_1, OS_2, etc., to OS_f. As the output increases, however, the price at which it can be sold will fall from S_0P_0, through S_1P_1, S_2P_2, etc., to S_fP_f. As the price falls the stimulus to expansion will decline until eventually the final output OS_f is reached,

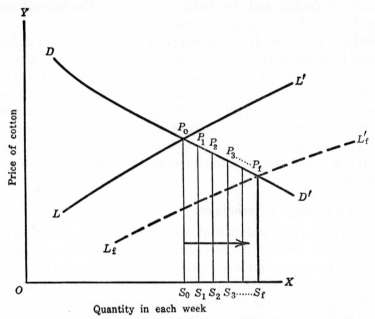

Fig. 39.   Effect of Change in Techniques.

where in spite of the improvement in techniques the industry is once more normally profitable and the output ceases to expand. OS_f, then, is the new normal output; S_fP_f is the new normal price. It follows that there must be a new normal supply curve, $L_fL'_f$ which cuts the demand curve at the point P_f. That is to say, the improvement in techniques has brought about a rise in normal supply. The quantity which producers will supply, or the rate of production which will finally be reached after all adjustments have been made, will be greater for each price than it was before. This is precisely what we should expect.

Effect on Demand for Other Commodities. It is interesting to consider what will be the effect of this improvement in the techniques of cotton production on the demand situation of other commodities. We have seen that the improvement causes a fall in the price of cotton and a rise in the total consumption. If the elasticity of demand for cotton is unity, this fall in the price of cotton will not affect the total amount which consumers will spend upon cotton, for the fall in the price will be matched by a proportionate rise in the amount purchased. If, however, the demand for cotton is relatively elastic, the fall in price will result in a greater proportionate increase in the quantity bought, and therefore the amount spent by consumers on cotton will increase. This means that the consumers of cotton will have rather less to spend upon other things. Consequently, their demand for "other things" will decline. That is, if the prices of "other things" did not change, consumers would be willing to buy rather less of them in the mass.

Any decline in demand is most likely to fall on those things which are close substitutes for cotton.[1] Consumers will be buying an increased quantity of cotton and spending more money on cotton. We should therefore expect them to spend rather less money and buy rather smaller quantities of the "substitute commodities"—silk, wool, etc. —and possibly to reduce slightly their expenditures and purchases in the case of less related commodities. Thus an improvement in the techniques of cotton production might easily reduce the demand for silk and hence might reduce both the price and the output of silk. Nor is this the end of the adjustments. Consumers' expenditures on "other things" will decline, but if the demand for cotton is elastic, the producers of cotton as a class will have a larger gross income. This may result in an increased expenditure on the part of the cotton *producers* on "other things," which may in part offset the decline in consumers' expenditures for them. It will be unlikely, however, to offset the decline completely in the case of each commodity concerned. For instance, if consumers of cotton as a whole are richer than the producers, we should not expect the increased demand of the producers to counterbalance the decreased demand of the consumers in the case of silk, but it might very well do so, and more, in the case of wool.

Other Effects. It is evident that here we are running into a series of ramifications of our analysis which we cannot pursue very far without a much greater body of factual information than we possess. Nevertheless, it is important to realize that these ramifications exist;

---

[1] Even if there is unit elasticity of demand for cotton, a fall in the price of cotton is likely to bring about a *redistribution* of the demand for other things, even though the total amount spent on them remains the same. For this reason there may be a decline in demand in this case for cotton substitutes and a rise in demand for things which are complementary or even independent in demand.

that supplies react on demands and demands on supplies through an immense chain of related commodities, until the final consequences of a single change in the circumstances of production or consumption of even one commodity permeate the whole economic system, echoing and re-echoing ever more faintly from one effect to another until they finally die away.

Cost, Supply, and Price

We shall not yet venture far into the field of problems involving the concept of "cost." But the student should now have some appreciation of the relation of cost to price, even though we cannot examine the various cost concepts in any great detail at this stage.

Let us suppose a very simple case in which there are a number of firms producing an identically similar product, and in which each firm produces a definite amount at a definite cost of production per unit. The cost of production per unit is called the "average cost," and it is defined to include all those payments which are necessary in order to keep the firm in operation. It includes "normal profits"— i.e., the sum which it is necessary to pay to the owner of the capital invested in the firm in order to persuade him to keep his capital in the business. The average cost as thus defined differs from the cost concept of the accountant, which does not include profit; but it has the great advantage that it is equal to the "supply price" of the firm's output, in the sense that if the price of the product falls below the average cost, the firm will go out of business. Only the output of which the average cost is equal to or less than the actual price of the product will be produced, for it will not pay to produce if the average cost is greater than the price.

The Average Cost Distribution

We can now draw up a table showing the distribution of firms according to their average costs. Let us suppose that an investigation of a milk industry has revealed the results shown in Table 13. From this table the supply curve for milk can immediately be derived. If the price is below 20 cents, presumably no milk will be supplied, as there are no firms with costs low enough to make the production profitable. At a price of 20 cents, three firms will find it profitable to produce, and will produce 180,000 gallons. At a price of 21 cents these 3 firms will continue in production, of course, for if it pays them to produce at 20 cents, it will all the more pay them to produce at 21 cents. But at 21 cents 5 more producers find it profitable to produce; these add

TABLE 13.   A Cost Distribution

Average Cost (Cents per Gal.)	Number of Firms	Total Output (Thousand Gals.)
20	3	180
21	5	300
22	10	600
23	11	630
24	20	1100
25	18	900
26	9	400
27	4	150
28	1	30

300,000 gallons to the total output, which is therefore equal to 180,-000 + 300,000 gallons, or 480,000 gallons. At 22 cents ten more producers come into the field, adding another 600,000 gallons, making 1,080,000 in all. So we construct the whole supply schedule, as in Table 14A, by adding the successive increments of output produced at successively higher costs.

TABLE 14.   Cost and Supply

A		B	
Price (Cents per Gal.)	Output (000 Gals.)	Price (Cents per Gal.)	Output (000 Gals.)
20	180	20	0
21	480	21	180
22	1080	22	480
23	1710	23	1080
24	2810	24	1710
25	3710	25	2810
26	4110	26	3710
27	4260	27	4110
28	4290	28	4260
		29	4290

The relation between cost and supply is now clear. Suppose, for instance, that there was a general rise in the cost of production of milk, so that the costs of each producer rose by 1 cent per gallon. It would now take a price of 21 cents to persuade the three lowest-cost producers to produce their 180,000 gallons, 22 cents would be necessary to attract the next 300,000 gallons, 23 cents for the next 600,000, and so on, as in Table 14B. It is evident that the rise in costs has led to a fall in the quantity that would be supplied at each price—i.e., to a fall in supply. It follows that a rise in costs—unless demand is perfectly elastic—will lead to a rise in the price because of the fall in supply.

It is important to realize that the connection between "cost" and "price" is always of this indirect nature. There is no law which says that because a commodity has cost $40 per ton its price must be $40 per ton. If a man builds a house at the South Pole at a cost of a million dollars, the mere fact that it cost a million dollars would not enable him to receive that much for it. But there is, nevertheless, a close relationship between costs of production and price. The price of a commodity depends on its demand and supply curves, and the position of its supply curve depends on its costs of production.

Effect of Output on Supply. Industries of "Decreasing Cost"

We should notice briefly at this point a problem the full solution of which we must again leave until later. The tools of analysis now in our hands, however, will at least enable us to state the problem, and its importance in the interpretation of many economic phenomena is too great to allow us to neglect it even at this stage.

We have assumed that the normal supply curve described the quantity of a commodity which producers were willing to produce at each hypothetical price. We saw in the previous section that these quantities will depend on the costs of production of the commodity; the higher the costs of production of a commodity, the smaller will be the quantity produced at any one hypothetical price. Suppose, now, that the output of an industry *itself* affected the costs of production of that industry's product. For instance, a large industry is presumably more efficient than a small one and consequently, merely because an industry is large, its costs of production decline. This is the phenomenon called by Marshall "external economies." It is an application of the general principle that the degree of specialization is determined by the extent of the market. In a large industry the specialization of processes and the specialization of firms themselves may be developed to a greater extent than in a small industry. Special machines, special tools, special processes may be possible in a large industry which a small industry is not big enough to support. An expansion of such an industry will thus *lower* its whole schedule of costs and will itself increase the quantity of product which the industry is willing to sell at each hypothetical price. In this case it is possible that a rise in demand, although it will at first cause an increase in the price of the product, will also cause an increase in output, a lowering of costs, and therefore a "rise in supply" and possibly a fall in price. Where a rise in demand can in this way cause a fall in price, the industry is said to be one of "decreasing cost."

QUESTIONS AND EXERCISES

1. Does the principle of equal advantage mean that money wages, money profit, and money rents will be equal for all workers, all employers, and all landowners in all industries in a state of equilibrium?

2. Prove: (a) If the normal supply curve of an industry is perfectly elastic, the final result of an increase in demand for the product of that industry will be not to raise the price of the product but to increase the output of the industry.

   b. If the normal demand curve for an industry is perfectly elastic, the final result of an improvement in the technique of production will be not to lower the price of the product but to increase the output of the industry.

3. In the analysis of this chapter we have assumed that after a disturbance, prices and outputs move slowly toward the position of new equilibrium and then stop. Under what circumstances might prices and outputs shoot beyond the equilibrium point and then oscillate backward and forward about it? Would this be a likely case?

4. Analyze as far as you can, making clear your assumptions as you go along, the economic effects of the prohibition of the manufacture and sale of alcoholic beverages.

5. Suppose that a much better and cheaper way of producing gasoline is discovered. What will be the probable effects of this discovery on (a) The gasoline industry. (b) The coal industry. (c) The railroad industry. (d) The tourist industry?

6. "A tax is an increase in the cost of production of a product." On this assumption, analyze the effect of a tax on the price of a product. Does your analysis differ essentially from that on pages 142–146?

CHAPTER 10

SOME APPLICATIONS OF THE PRINCIPLE OF EQUAL ADVANTAGE

THE EXPLANATION OF DIFFERENCES IN MONETARY REMUNERATION

One important application of the principle of equal advantage is in explaining why the wages of different forms of labor are different, why the profits of capital in various industries are different, and why the rents per acre of different plots of land are different.

Wage Differences

Let us consider first the question of labor. Why does a garbage collector receive, let us say, only $60 per week while a film star receives $10,000 per week? This difference in monetary remuneration is one of the most striking facts about our economic system. How, the student may well ask, can we reconcile this obvious fact with any principle of equal advantage? There are two parts in the answer to this question. The first is that the monetary remuneration is not the whole of the advantages and disadvantages of an occupation. There are other advantages or disadvantages, such as the pleasantness or danger of the work, the constancy of employment, the security of income, the attractiveness of the place in which the worker must live, the agreeableness of his workfellows, and so on. Suppose that there were two occupations with the same monetary remuneration which did not have equal nonmonetary advantages. If this were the case, people would move into the occupation with the greater nonmonetary advantages and out of the occupation with the smaller nonmonetary advantages, until the money wage in the first occupation was so much less than the money wage in the second that there was no temptation, on the balance, for people to move from one to the other. If two occupations, A and B, are equally easy of access, we may write:

182

Nonmonetary advantages of A + monetary advantages of A
= Nonmonetary advantages of B + monetary advantages of B

and therefore in those occupations in which the nonmonetary advantages are high the monetary advantages (i.e., the wage) will tend to be correspondingly low.

Immediate Nonmonetary Advantages

Nonmonetary advantages and disadvantages are of two broad kinds. The first may be called the *immediate* advantages and disadvantages. There are some occupations which are immediately and obviously more pleasant than others. Other things being equal, therefore, we should expect these pleasant occupations to be paid less. A good example is found in the difference in the remuneration of professors and lawyers. The occupation of a teacher is, by and large, a pleasant one. He lives usually in agreeable surroundings, works among congenial associates, has a good deal of leisure, has long vacations, exercises a little brief authority over his students, and has opportunities for molding young and immature minds. The occupation of a lawyer, although attractive to some, frequently involves work in a crowded and unpleasant environment, a meticulous attention to detail, association with unsavory characters, difficult moral problems, uncertain income, and so on. We should not be surprised to find, therefore, that although the professions of university teaching and of the law require about the same amount of native ability and about the same amount of expensive education, the remuneration of a university teacher is generally much less than that of a lawyer. The explanation is clear. If the monetary remuneration of these two professions were about the same, education would seem more attractive than the law. The number of professors or would-be professors would grow, either by direct transfer or by a surge of new graduates into teaching, and the number of lawyers would undergo a relative decline, again either by direct transfer or because of a drying up of the stream of young blood. Consequently, the remuneration of lawyers would increase, and that of professors diminish, until there was no longer a force making for the increase of one profession at the expense of the other.

"Whole-Life" Nonmonetary Advantages

The other class of nonmonetary advantages may be called the "whole-life" advantages. In comparing the total advantage or disadvantage of one occupation against another, not only must we consider the state of affairs during a single period of employment; we must consider the process of education which led up to that employment and the ultimate consequences which will follow from it. This accounts very largely for the difference in remuneration between the skilled occupations and the unskilled. In order to get into a skilled trade, and still more in order to get into a profession, a process of education, more or less painful and expensive, must be undertaken. This must be offset by the advantages to be enjoyed once the skill has been obtained, and accounts for the fact that the monetary remuneration of skilled occupations is generally higher than that of unskilled occupations. Suppose, for instance, that of two equally pleasant and equally well-paid occupations, one involved a long and expensive process of training while the other could be entered without delay. It is clear that there would be nothing to attract people into the skilled occupation as against the unskilled. The numbers in the skilled occupation would decline and in the unskilled would increase; the money wage in the skilled occupation would rise and in the unskilled occupation would fall; until finally there would be sufficient difference between them to prevent any further transfer of numbers from the skilled to the unskilled trade. The difficulty and expense of training, therefore, can be likened to a wall around the occupation; there must be a sufficient difference between the money wage inside the wall and that outside to induce enough people to go to the trouble of climbing it.

In a similar way we must assess the consequences of following any occupation. If it is dangerous, or unhealthy, or a "blind alley" occupation leading nowhere, then the wage will have to be higher than in those occupations which are similar in other respects, in order to attract people over this barrier.

Nonmonetary Advantages Explain Differences in Money Wages

So much, then, for the first part of our answer to the question of why different occupations are paid differently. Even if everybody knew what the nonmonetary advantages and disadvantages of all occupations were, and if everybody were free to go into that occupation which he knew would satisfy him best, there would still be differences in monetary reward. That is to say, a system of money wages is possible in which there are different money wages in different occupations, and yet nobody wants to move from one occupation to another even if he knows all about the relative advantages, and is free to move.

Other Sources of Wage Differences

However, there is yet another source of actual differences in monetary rewards. People may be ignorant and may move into an occupation because they think they would be better off in it, when actually as events turn out they are worse off. Also, people may be prevented by some means outside their control from moving into some occupation which they would like to enter if they could. These two factors we may label "ignorance" and "immobility."

Ignorance.   Ignorance in this connection has two aspects. There is the ignorance of the advantages and disadvantages of the occupation itself. Generally speaking, people are inclined to underestimate the nonmonetary advantages and disadvantages when they are taking up an occupation. This is not surprising, for the money rewards are usually fairly well known, while the nonmonetary rewards are elusive, and to take them into one's calculations requires the exercise of some imagination. Consequently, in occupations with marked nonmonetary disadvantages the wage is frequently lower than it would be if people were fully aware of the circumstances. This is particularly the case with dangerous occupations; for a few paltry dollars the lowly and the uneducated can easily be induced to barter their lives. The sand hog or the steeple jack may get a money wage which is greater than the average of his class, but he pays for it dearly. There is also ignorance of one's personal abilities. This usually takes the form of a persistent overestimate of one's skill, charm, and good fortune. Consequently, in occupations which require considerable personal ability for real success, and which offer glittering prizes to the successful, there is all too frequently a large penumbra of failures—larger than there would be if people at the outset had a truer estimate of their abilities and chance of fortune.

"Native" Immobility.   Immobility also has many facets. Of these, perhaps the most important is native ability. Skill is not merely a matter of education; it is also a matter of inherent capacity. Some occupations—notably those which are among the most highly paid—require a degree and kind of native capacity that is extremely rare. In these the remuneration may be very high indeed without attracting other people into the occupation—simply because the other people who might come into the occupation do not exist. This is the case with film and stage stars and with many, if not all, highly paid executives. It also accounts in part for the high remuneration of the professions, of bankers, and of people in positions of trust.

In answer to the question of why a garbage collector receives $60 per week and a Gable $10,000, we may say that anyone can become a garbage collector, but there is only one Gable. If the number of garbage collectors were so small that each one received $10,000 per week, there would be a wild rush into the garbage-collecting business, which would very rapidly bring down the remuneration of the garbage collectors. The number of Gables is so small that he in fact may receive $10,000 per week. But there is no rush of males into the Gable business, for the peculiar quality of charm he possesses is, fortunately or unfortunately, confined to him alone.

Geographic Immobility

Another important fact making for occupational immobility is the difficulty most people find in changing their place of residence. Many ties bind people to the localities in which they live. A well-established habit of life, a congenial circle of friends and associates, familiar surroundings, children at school, and sometimes the ownership of a house all conspire to make it difficult to uproot a worker from one locality and transplant him to another. Consequently, when the employments of a particular region fail, it is hard to shift populations from the depressed area to one where the opportunities for employment are greater. Wider variations in the real advantages of occupations in different regions may persist, therefore, for a long time. The difficulties of "depressed areas," such as, for instance, many coal-mining regions, are a case in point. Adjustment takes place, it is true. The young workers move away, leaving an even more hopeless residue behind them. But the process of adjustment is so slow that it may never catch up with the swiftly changing pattern of economic opportunity.

Specificity

Yet another important element in the occupational immobility of resources we may call their *specificity*. Once resources have been applied to a specific use, it may be difficult, or even impossible, to transfer them to another. Once we have devoted some of our resources to building a shipyard, there is virtually nothing we can do with it but build ships; we cannot spin cotton with it, or build houses with it, or grow strawberries with it. Similarly, once we have devoted some of our resources to the training of a naval engineer, we shall find it hard to use him for any other purpose than for building ships; it will be difficult to use him for preaching sermons, or for weaving rugs, or even for washing dishes.

There are two ways of effecting the transfer of some specific resource from one occupation to another. First, there is the possibility of direct transfer. A factory built for one purpose may be used for another, skill acquired for one job may be carried over into another, or a tool used in one occupation may be used in another. Second, there is the possibility of indirect transfer through obsolescence and replacement. A surplus of shipyards cannot be adapted to spinning cotton, but the resources which would otherwise have been used in replacing these shipyards as they wore out can be devoted to building cotton mills and to making spinning machines. If there is a surplus of naval engineers there may be nothing else to do with them but pension them off. But the young men who are coming up can be turned toward other professions—young men who otherwise would have gone into naval engineering. Through obsolescence, therefore, and the kindly and reformative hand of death, the transfer even of the most specific resources can be achieved. This process, however, takes a long time. It may take a lifetime, or even longer, and meanwhile real differences in advantages between different occupations may persist.

Artificial Restrictions

Finally, there are those hindrances to the mobility of resources between different occupations which may be traced to artificial restriction and regulation, whether of governments or of other organizations. We have seen that the entry of new members into any occupational group will generally have the effect of lowering the average remuneration of all the members of the group. This is no doubt why all professions and trades, at all times, feel themselves to be "overcrowded": it is because if more people come into them, those already established will probably be worse off. What is more natural, therefore, than to find that those who already enjoy the benefits of a favored occupation seek to preserve those superior advantages for themselves by making it more difficult for other people to enter the occupation? So trade unions of the "craft" type seek to prevent the entry of too many people into the craft by imposing arduous and often unnecessary apprenticeship conditions or by demanding high membership fees. Professional associations, under the respectable guise of establishing "standards," frequently impose a long and costly ritual of education and preparation upon the neophyte. Nations favored with great natural resources and relatively small populations, with a consequently high standard of life, shut off immigration in an attempt to preserve that high standard of life against the leveling which might result from the transfer of population from the poor countries to the rich.

These Principles Apply Also to Capital and Land

Practically everything we have said in explaining the differences in monetary rewards among the different occupations of labor can also be applied to explaining the differences in monetary rewards in the different occupations of capital and land. The same principle of equal advantage applies, modified by difficulties of mobility. If all the occupations of capital—i.e., if all the different ways in which money could be invested—were equally safe, equally reputable, equally convenient, and so on, we should expect the rate of profit in each to be the same. If this were not so, capital would move from the less profitable to the more profitable occupation. This movement in itself would raise profits in the less profitable and lower them in the more profitable occupation, until the profits in all occupations had come to equality. Then there would be no further tendency for capital to move from one occupation to another.

Nonmonetary Advantages

The principle is again modified by two conditions. The first is that the monetary rewards are not the only inducements which entice capital into one occupation or drive it from another. A "disreputable" occupation, like the liquor trade or the white slave trade, may persistently make high profits, if these high profits are not sufficient to tempt new investors in over the barrier of disreputability; and it is a strange paradox that the greater the disreputability of a business, the greater are its money profits likely to be. Likewise, risky occupations of capital may also make high profits, if the general temper of the people is to avoid risk. But if (as may very well have been the case in western capitalism) the people are largely infected with the gambler's temperament, so that risk becomes a pleasure rather than a burden, then risky occupations may on the average make smaller money profits than safe occupations.

Natural Immobility

The second modification refers to the problem of mobility. There may be cases in which the owners of capital would like to transfer their capital from one use to another, but for some reason or other they cannot do so. This immobility of capital may exist for "natural" reasons. It may be, for instance, that a special degree of investing skill is required in some occupations, which therefore can command a higher rate of profit than normal without attracting more capital into them. It may be that capital can only be employed in some occupations in very large quantities, and that therefore any fine adjustments of the quantity of capital are not possible. This is likely to be the case in what are often called "natural monopolies" like railroads. A single railroad built between two places may yield profits greater than the average. Nevertheless, if another railroad were built to run alongside of the first, and in competition with it, it might well be that the profits of both railroads would be reduced to a point far below normal. It is the fact that we cannot have railroads in small quantities which makes this possible. If we could build half a railroad, we might find that with one and a half railroads between two places the profits would be normal, whereas with one railroad they are abnormally high and with two railroads they would be abnormally low. In this case the fact that half a railroad is actually worse than no railroad at all will prevent the influx of capital into this occupation even when the profits are above normal.

Artificial Immobility

The difficulties in the way of moving capital from one occupation to another may also be "artificial," i.e., created by the action of government or other authority. If the employment of capital in a particular occupation requires the use of a patent, it may thereby be confined to one particular group of persons. Governments may grant monopolies in certain occupations to favored groups and may prevent the entry of other persons into these groups by law. Or a private group may establish a monopoly through the control of some essential raw material, or through the threat of price wars, or through special favors from transportation companies, and so on. The factor of geographic mobility may also enter into the picture in the case of capital. The owners of capital may prefer to have their capital at home rather than abroad. If this is the case, we should expect to find a higher rate of profit on foreign than on domestic investments.

Application to Land

Nonmonetary Advantages.   The principle of equal advantage even applies to the case of land, although here the element of immobility is so important that it has obscured the real similarity between the case of land and the case of other sources of income. But even so, if all acres of land could be equally well applied to any occupation, we should expect the remuneration of each acre to be the same, for otherwise acres would be transferred from the poorly paid to the well-paid occupations until all were rewarded equally. Why, then, do not all acres obtain the same remuneration? The answer is much the same as that to the question, "Why do not all hours of labor receive the same remuneration?" In the first place, there may be some nonmonetary advantages in the use of land. These would explain, for instance, why the owner of an estate may use some of his land for a private park and garden, even though it brings him no monetary return, or why a fox-hunting squire might prefer a tenant who paid less rent but did not object to hunting, as against one who paid more rent but did object to hunting. This element in the case of land, however, is of little importance, especially in America.

Immobility. The second part of our explanation of differences in remuneration—summed up in the word "immobility"—is of profound importance in the case of land. The principal feature of land which distinguishes it from other sources of income is its geographic immobility. An acre is where it is, and it can be nowhere else. Consequently, if the *position* of any acre results in its obtaining a large remuneration, that remuneration cannot be threatened by the influx of acres from outside. The number of acres in the entertainment business in New York is very small, and consequently the owner of each acre can obtain a very high price for the use of its services. The same principle, therefore, that explains how a film star comes to receive a salary so much greater than the meager wage of a garbage collector also explains how an acre of land on Broadway rents for an amount so remarkably in excess of the rent of an acre of northern woods. Just as there are factors which prevent garbage collectors from becoming film stars, so there is a factor which prevents acres in the Adirondacks from taking wings and flying down the Hudson Valley to Broadway. This fact is the sheer geographic immobility of land. The owner of land in the Adirondacks would no doubt *like* to employ his land in the entertainment business on Broadway. He is prevented from doing so because he can neither bring the crowds which constitute the peculiar advantage of Broadway to the Adirondacks, nor take the Adirondacks to the crowds.

SOME DYNAMIC ASPECTS OF ALLOCATION

Up to this point we have considered the allocation problem on the whole from the point of view of "comparative statics"—that is, by comparing two positions of equilibrium having different underlying determinants. There are, however, some important problems which belong to the field of dynamics proper, either because they involve cumulative and irreversible changes or because the conditions of equilibrium are disturbed so frequently and regularly that the stationary position is never reached. We shall illustrate these problems by three examples: the mining industry, agriculture, and the problem of interregional differences in wealth and income.

Mining—a Suicidal Industry

Take first the case of mining. Mining is the process of taking some form of raw material out of the earth, such as coal, oil, metals or metal ores, salt, clay, or gravel. The dominating feature of the mining industry over a long period of time is that the material once extracted from the earth is never replaced. Consequently, as all deposits of material in the earth are in the last resort limited, mining is an industry which is perpetually committing suicide. The history of a mining community will always take this form: discovery of the deposits, opening up of the deposits, boom period, settling down perhaps into a steady output; gradual exhaustion of the deposits leading to greater difficulties of extraction, a final decline, and then the extinction of the industry in that particular location. The peculiar social problems of mining communities arise very largely from this fact of impermanence. Because of it, mining communities are generally ugly, rough, flimsy, and exciting. It is evident that what is most needed in the mining industry is mobility. Like the Arabs, miners should be able to steal silently away once the mine which gave them livelihood is exhausted. Unfortunately, this is not always the case, and the elements of immobility which we have discussed make the problem of the declining mining community a particularly intractable one. The soft-coal industry is an important case in point.

Agriculture

Agriculture does not present the problem of exhaustion of resources, except in the special case of "soil mining" where the fertility of the soil is not maintained. By proper treatment the fertility of land, in the absence of climatic changes, can be maintained indefinitely. Agricultural communities are therefore likely to be more stable, more settled, less "tough," than mining communities. Nevertheless, in a progressive society agriculture presents a special problem. As a society progresses in wealth the proportion of its total resources which it needs to spend upon agriculture inevitably declines. This is because agriculture, for the most part, provides basic necessities like food and raw materials for clothing. The richer a society becomes, the less is the proportion of its resources which it must spend on these basic necessities and the greater is the proportion which it can afford to spend on luxuries—on automobiles, radios, and so on. In very poor societies almost the whole population must be engaged in agriculture, or at least in food production. In rich societies the food producer can produce enough food not only for himself and his family but for several other people besides—people who are employed in producing manufactured commodities.

Consequently, in rich societies agriculture forms a much smaller proportion of the total activity than it does in poor societies. As a society gets richer, the *relative* magnitude of agriculture—and indeed of all the industries producing basic necessities—must decline. Now, the way in which a competitive society engineers a relative decline in any industry is by making it relatively unprofitable; people are squeezed out of a declining industry by the fact that it is uncomfortable. But in a progressive society, as we have just seen, agriculture must always be declining relative to the other occupations and must always be in process of absorbing a smaller proportion of the whole of economic activity. In such a society agriculture must always be in the uncomfortable position of being "squeezed." The "squeeze" may be masked for some time by the fact that it is only a relative decline that is necessary. We may even find, as in the western world of the nineteenth century, that the whole realm of economic activity is expanding so rapidly that agriculture also expands—witness the great geographic expansion of the United States. Nevertheless, in such a situation the nonagricultural occupations expand still further, and the *proportion* of resources engaged in agriculture declines.

Interregional Differences in Income and Wealth

A striking feature of the present world economy is the great differences in per capita wealth and income among various nations and regions. Thus in the United States per capita real income is at least thirty times what it is in some parts of Asia and Africa, and though statistical comparisons of highly different cultures are very inexact, the differences are so great by any measure that they represent almost different orders of magnitude. In part these differences are due to differences in population density and are perpetuated by both natural barriers to migration (costs of transport, upheaval, and resettlement) and by artificial barriers in the form of restrictive immigration laws.

Looking at the problem as a whole, however, it is clear that the differences in regional incomes are not *mainly* due to differences in population density but to differences in *rates of economic growth.* The "rich" areas are those in which capital has been accumulating, techniques improving, and consequently income increasing at a faster rate than population, especially in the past two hundred years. The "poor" areas are those in which income has not been increasing, over the long pull, as fast as population, and there are even some declining areas (of which China over the past two hundred years seems to have been an example) where total income has increased more slowly than population, and so per capita income has actually declined.

The extraordinary differences which may arise in relatively short periods because of differences in average rates of growth are shown in Table 15, which shows by what proportion an initial quantity will

TABLE 15.   Growth Schedules

Rate of Growth (Per cent per annum)	0	1	2	3	4
Proportional growth in					
50 years	1	1.649	2.718	4.482	7.389
100 years	1	2.718	7.389	20.08	54.60
200 years	1	7.389	54.60	403.4	2981.0

grow in 50, 100, and 200 years at steady (exponential) rates of growth from 0 to 4 per cent per annum. Thus a nation or region in which the rate of growth of per capita income is 2 per cent per annum will have a per capita income 54.60 times that of a stagnant region in only 200 years!

Migration and Economic Growth

Because of the enormous cumulative impact of quite small differences in rates of economic growth, the effects of migration may be quite different from what they would be in a static world in which misallocation was the principal source of differences in income. Immigration frequently stimulates the growth of per capita income in the recipient region, and emigration may even lower the rate of growth in the donor regions. Furthermore, if the population growth of a region is limited mainly by infant mortality due to malnutrition, emigration may do little to relieve the population pressure, for the adults who leave the region may release enough food to enable even more children to survive than is necessary to replace the emigrants. The region thus becomes an inexhaustible spring of emigrants!

Conclusion: The Stability of Capitalism Depends on Mobility of Resources

This brings us to a final conclusion of great importance. It is that a free capitalism of the type we are describing will operate much more satisfactorily in a society in which wealth and especially population are increasing than in a society in which wealth and population are stationary or are decreasing. This conclusion rests upon the general assumption that it is easier to make any industry expand than it is to make it contract. This again rests on the proposition that the hindrances to the mobility of resources between different occupations are based on the difficulties of getting resources out of the old occupations rather than upon the difficulty of getting resources into the new occupations. If a free capitalism is to operate satisfactorily, there must be sufficient mobility of resources between various industries to enable the relative sizes of the industries to adjust to changing conditions of demand or of techniques. That is to say, if fashion decrees that we shall wear cotton instead of silk, there should be a rapid and easy adjustment of the system in the direction of a relative expansion in the cotton industry and a relative decline of the silk industry. If we discover in the automobile a more convenient method of transport than the railroad, the railroad industry should undergo a swift and painless decline and the automobile industry a swift and painless rise. Otherwise—if resources cannot be shifted from one industry to another—there is likely to be unemployment both of men and of equipment. If a large soft-coal industry, built up to meet a large demand for soft coal, becomes "too big" because of the introduction of more convenient fuels, it should be possible to effect a swift transfer of soft-coal miners into other fields. Otherwise the decline in the demand for soft coal will result not in an increase in the production of something else but in sheer unemployment. If there is nothing to be done with certain resources but produce soft coal, and soft coal is no longer wanted, then the soft-coal miners and mines must be left unemployed. Not all our unemployment problem is of this kind by any means, as will be seen, but at least a substantial part of unemployment is due to this factor of immobility.

Adjustments Easy in an Expanding Society, Difficult in a Contracting Society

When a free capitalistic society is expanding in wealth and population, the necessity for making *absolute* contractions in any industry is much less than when such a society is stationary. Are we threatened with agricultural overproduction? Then hold the agricultural horses for a few years and soon the new mouths will come along and solve the problem for us. Is there a shift in demand from coal to oil? Well, keep the youngsters out of the coal industry—send them to the oil fields—and we may hope that even if the demand for coal declines relatively, it will not decline much in an absolute sense. Running a progressing, free economy is rather like running with a team of wild horses; the main problem is to keep the various industries in line relative to each other. With all industries increasing, then, if one gets too far ahead its relative position can be adjusted by preventing it from forging ahead quite as rapidly as the others; this is not too difficult. If, however, it is necessary to keep in line a stationary row of wild horses by backing the ones that are too far forward and pulling out the ones that are too far behind, the task is likely to be more difficult. An industry, like a horse, is usually much better constructed for going forward, however slowly, than for going backward.

The difficulties which the western world faced in the great depression of the 1930's were not unconnected with a decline in the rate of growth of population. At that time it looked as if we were approaching a more stationary society, both in population and in the rate of growth of income and capital. In 1955 the picture looks very different. Birth rates have risen, population growth has been much greater than was expected, and the great depression is seen as an interruption in the growth of the western economy, not as a turning point. The problems of adjustment—for instance, from peace to war and back to an uneasy peace again—have been much easier in consequence than they would have been in a more stationary economy. Growth, however, cannot proceed for ever, and though the problems of the stationary economy can be postponed, they cannot be postponed indefinitely. Sooner or later we will have to reckon with them.

Qualitative Decline of a Declining Industry

One further aspect of the problem of the declining industry should perhaps be mentioned—the problem of the *quality* of the resources which are likely to be left in it. When an industry is declining, it is the energetic workers and the enterprising employers who leave it and strike out for fresh industries. This leaves behind the rather less energetic and enterprising to breed the next generation. Consequently, a declining industry is likely to suffer in a qualitative as well as quantitative sense. It will lack leadership, it will run on old routines, and the quality of its personnel will be inferior, at least in some respects, to that of newer industries which can afford the pick of the brains and talent. A declining industry frequently does not adapt itself to new situations as well as it might, simply because there is greater scope elsewhere for the brains that might make this adaptation. The same may be true of a region or nation which is a source of emigrants. It is frequently the most vigorous and energetic who emigrate, leaving behind the somewhat less vigorous (or troublesome!) to reproduce the culture in succeeding generations.

QUESTIONS AND EXERCISES

1. Some years ago the Home Owners Loan Corporation issued a statement advising workers to buy their own homes, as being the best and safest investment which they could make, and on the same day the Department of Labor issued a statement warning workers against buying their own homes, as that would lead to too much immobility. Comment on this paradox, indicating which type of worker should follow the first advice and which the second.

2. Make a classified list, as exhaustive as you can, of all the factors which explain why wages are unequal in different occupations. How many of these factors can you apply to explaining why (a) the profits of capital and (b) the rent of land are different in different occupations? Are there any factors which are peculiar to capital or land?

3. "It is nonsense to suppose that higher wages are paid for unpleasant work, when a professor gets more than a street sweeper." Criticize this statement.

4. What would you expect to be the effect of the provision of free public education up to the college level on the difference between the remuneration of the "white-collar" worker and the ordinary laborer?

5. The monetary advantages of a college education probably do not cover its expense. Does this mean that a college education is worthless?

6. The birth rate in the country is usually considerably higher than that in the towns. How would this fact react upon the wages of the agricultural laborer?

7. Discuss the effects of occupational *prestige* on the differences in monetary remuneration of various classes of labor, bearing in mind that the prestige of an occupation frequently depends on the monetary reward itself, i.e., the higher the monetary reward, the greater the prestige.

CHAPTER 11

THE ELEMENTARY THEORY
OF DISTRIBUTION

Our first survey of the economic landscape would be incomplete if we did not include some sight of the territory known as "distribution." Traditionally, economics has been divided into four provinces —production, consumption, distribution, and exchange. The boundaries of these ancient provinces are now but little recognized, for exchange seems to have conquered them all. Nevertheless, there remains a not insignificant field to which the name "distribution" may still be given. We shall not be able to explore it thoroughly without the assistance of the concepts of marginal analysis to be developed in Part III. But with the use of supply and demand alone we shall at least be able to make a rough map of the country.

Various Meanings of "Distribution"

The word "distribution," like many others, may mean a number of things. In the phrase "the distribution of commodities" it refers to the process of transporting commodities from their places of origin to their final consumers, or what is known as "marketing." "The distribution of resources" means the division of resources among various industries in accordance with the principles of the last two chapters. When we refer to the "theory of distribution," however, as a branch of economic analysis, we refer not to the above problems but to the problem of the distribution of wealth and income. It is that part of the subject which seeks to answer questions like: "Why does Mr. X get $10,000 a year while Mr. Y gets $500 a year?" "Why are some people rich and some people poor?" "What determines the way in which wealth and income are apportioned among the people?" These questions form the subject matter of the theory of *personal* distribution. In seeking to answer them, however, we run into further questions:

197

"Why is the wage of this man $80 per week?" "Why is the rent of this house $500 per year?" "Why is the rent of this plot of land $5.00 per acre-year?" These questions all concern the *prices* of the things that people sell in order to obtain their incomes. The theory which sets out to answer them goes by the name of the theory of "functional" distribution, for in it we ask not what determines the total rewards of individual persons but what determines the rewards (prices) of the functions which are performed by these persons, or by the property they own.

Functional and Personal Distribution Compared

Starting with the problem of personal distribution, we may ask what determines the total income of any individual? Suppose that John Jones receives an income of $7500 in a certain year. What are the sources of this income? Suppose he has a job which brings in $5000 a year, owns two houses which bring in a net $1200 a year, and owns land which brings him $1300 a year. It is evident that his income can be divided into two parts. What he derives from the labor of his body or mind is one, and what he derives from his property is another. Evidently, owning property, provided the services of the property are valuable, entitles one to income. Indeed, if we widen our definitions sufficiently, we can see that all income is essentially derived from the ownership of property. Income from the sale of the services of mind and body is not generally regarded as income from property. Yet a little reflection will show that it is, because our own bodies are property from which we obtain income. In a slave society this fact is very evident, for there the owner of the slave receives the income which the slave earns. A slave does not obtain income any more than a cow does. Both receive maintenance, both are domestic animals, and the income they earn belongs to their owner. In a nonslave society each man owns his own body—i.e., each man is his own "slave." Consequently there is no market in bodies, only in the services of those bodies, and people do not usually think of their bodies as "property." But the fact that each man owns his own body does not make that body any the less "property," and does not make the income derived from it any the less income from property.

Income Determined by Amount of Property and the Price of Its Services

The income of any individual, therefore, is determined by two things: the amount of property he owns and the price of the services of that property. To find the income of an individual two lists are necessary—one, a list of the property he owns, including his own body; the other, a corresponding list of the services derived in a given period of time from each item of property. The quantity of each service multiplied by its price is the income obtained from it. In the case of John Jones, the list might read as follows:

Property	Service in One Year	Price of Service	Income Derived from Sale of Service
One body	50 weeks	$100 per week	$5000
Two houses	12 months	$ 50 per month per house	$1200
260 acres of land	260 acre-years	$ 5 per acre year	$1300
		Total	$7500

It is evident that two things will cause John Jones to have more income. One is an increase in the amount of his property and the other is an increase in the price of the services of the property he already owns. The link between the problems of personal and of functional distribution lies, therefore, in the distribution of property.

Inequality of Personal Incomes

We can now see what factors make for greater or less equality in personal incomes. The more equal the distribution of all forms of property, the more equal will be the distribution of income, if there is a uniform price for the services of each form of property. Also, the greater the price of the services of those forms of property which are widely distributed, the more equal will be the distribution of income. A society in which property is concentrated in the hands of a few will be a society with very unequal incomes. The extreme case would be a slave system in which all the property of the society, including the bodies of the workers, belonged to a small ruling class. On the other hand, where property is widely distributed incomes will be more equal. A peasant economy in which each man owns his own farm and implements is one with a relatively equal distribution of income. An economy of great landed estates worked by landless laborers is one in which incomes are relatively unequal.

That form of property in a free society which is most widely distributed is the property each man has in his own body. An increase in the price of the services of human bodies, therefore—i.e., in wages —at the expense of the price of the services of other forms of property —i.e., rents—will usually lead to a more equal distribution of income. Even if there were no change in the distribution of property, a general rise in wages would make the poor richer, and a general fall in rents would make the rich poorer.

What Determines the Distribution of Property?

The distribution of property is the result of historical processes and accidents, and the study of the laws which govern these processes belongs rather to the social historian than to the economist. The institutions of society in regard to inheritance, taxation, and the rights of property are particularly important in determining the historical trend toward concentration or dissemination of property. If primogeniture is the rule, we may expect the process of inheritance to lead to the concentration of property in the hands of a small ruling class. In that case the property of the father passes down undivided to the eldest son, and the younger sons get little. The English "squirearchy" is a good example. If, however, an inheritance is divided equally among all the children of a family, property will become more and more widely distributed and we may expect to see a system of peasant proprietorship, as in France. If the wealthy classes have few children, as each generation of inheritors arises property will become more concentrated; but if the rich have many children and squander their wealth, property will be disseminated. Revolutions, wars, taxes, and inflations disseminate the property of the old ruling classes, but may re-establish concentrations in the hands of the *nouveaux riches*.

It is difficult to make any general rules. If Aunt Jemima leaves her millions to her nephew Archibald, who marries the wealthy Rosalind and has only one son, we see wealth concentrating dangerously in the hands of Junior. If, however, Aunt Jemima leaves her millions to a Home for Waifs, or distributes them widely among a vast host of distant and needy relatives, her demise leads to a less concentrated distribution of wealth. Before the vagaries of Aunt Jemima the economist is helpless; he can observe, but he cannot prognosticate.

Concentration or Dissemination?

The available statistical evidence is inconclusive. There is certainly no evidence of any necessary movement toward either the concentration or the dissemination of wealth. Favoring the increasing concentration of wealth are two facts: one is that the wealthy have fewer children than the poor, and the other is that the wealthy find it more easy to save out of their incomes than the poor. It is no hardship for a rich man to save half or three-quarters of his income, but it is privation for a poor man to save a tenth of it. Nevertheless, there are also powerful forces making for the dissemination of wealth. The children of the wealthy may be few, but they are also frequently corrupted by too great fortune. The excesses and follies of a grandson may often dissipate the painfully accumulated fortune of a grandsire. All that is saved is not retained, and the greater the fortune, the greater the risk of loss. A man with thousands may conserve them carefully, but a man with millions may squander them in wild ventures, feeling that with so much he can afford to lose. The liberality of benefactors and the requisitionings of the tax gatherer alike serve to break up large fortunes. In our day the inheritance tax is perhaps the most potent force opposing the concentration of wealth, and nothing breaks down a large fortune more quickly than a rapid succession of deaths among its inheritors.

Functional Distribution as a Part of Price Theory

The economist, then, cannot make many conclusive generalizations about the distribution of property. It is otherwise when we come to consider the problem of functional distribution. Here the economist is immediately at home, for the problem of functional distribution is merely part of the general theory of *prices*. The wages of labor, the rents of land or of capital equipment, are prices, the prices of the services of property. These prices are established in acts of exchange, different perhaps in appearance but similar in reality to the exchange of Mrs. Jones's cents for the storekeeper's butter. When a worker is employed, he gives up a certain commodity—a "week's labor"—and receives in return a sum of money. When a house is rented, the owner gives up a certain commodity—the use of the house for a month— and receives in return a sum of money. The principles which govern exchange and the determination of prices apply also to these exchanges and these prices. We can use the weapons of supply and demand in solving problems relating to wages or to rents just as we can in solving problems relating to the price of butter.

Factors of Production

The prices which form the subject matter of the theory of functional distribution are the prices of the *services* of property, not of the property itself from which the services are derived. These services are usually called the "factors of production," although this term is sometimes carelessly used to mean the property from which the service is derived. Thus, labor is a factor of production derived from the human body. Land service is a factor of production derived from land. The services of houses, of machines, and of other material equipment are factors of production derived from the forms of property which yield them. There is, indeed, a relation between the prices of the services of any particular piece of property and of that property itself. The price of a house or a piece of land depends on the rent which it is expected to yield. We shall investigate this relationship in a later chapter. Meanwhile, it is important to notice that it is the price of the *services* of property, that is, of the factors of production, which concerns us here. To make the discussion more vivid we shall take labor as a typical factor of production and conduct the rest of this chapter's argument in terms of the problem of the determination of wages. The principles enunciated in this case, however, apply also to the prices of other services, like those of material property, subject, of course, to the peculiar circumstances of each case. They do not necessarily apply to the problem of the determination of the rate of interest. That is a special problem which we must leave until we have seen something of the theory of money.

The Determination of Wages in a Competitive Market

The "equilibrium price" of the services of any form of property bought and sold in a competitive market is determined by the familiar principle of "clearing the market." The equilibrium price is that at which the quantity of the service which its owners are willing to offer is equal to the quantity of the service which its employers are willing to take. Take, for example, the case of a particular form of labor, such as weaving. For a given place and a given period of time a demand schedule can be constructed showing the relation between the price of weaving (i.e., the hourly wage of weavers), and the number of hours of weaving that will be purchased at each hypothetical price by the employers. Similarly, a supply schedule can be constructed, showing the relation between the hourly wage of weavers and the number of hours of weaving which they will offer at each wage. Then, as we have seen before, unless the wage is at the point where the quantity of labor offered by the workers is equal to the quantity of labor which employers are willing to take, there will be forces coming into play to move the wage nearer the equilibrium level. If the wage is above the equilibrium level, there will be some workers who are willing to work at that wage but who cannot find employment. If the market is a competitive one, they will undercut the workers already in employment. The wage will fall. As it falls, employers will offer rather more

employment, and some workers will be attracted away into other occupations, until finally a wage is reached at which all who wish to be
employed at weaving will be employed.

Similarly, if the wage is "too low," employers will want more labor
than the workers are willing to offer, and there will be a "shortage
of labor." Consequently, if there is a competitive market, those employers who cannot get the labor they require will raise wages in
order to attract workers. This will force the other employers to raise
their wages, and so wages generally will rise until more workers are
attracted into weaving, fewer weavers are demanded, and the equilibrium wage is again reached.

Effect of Monopolies

If there are monopolies either on the side of labor or on the side
of employers, it does not necessarily follow that the wage will tend
to be where the quantity of labor which employers will take is equal
to the quantity which workers will offer. Suppose, for instance, that
there is a strong trade union of weavers, strong enough to prevent
the employment of any nonunion men. Then the union may force the
wage up to the point where there is a large number of workers who
would like to obtain employment in weaving at the prevailing wage
who cannot find employment at that wage, and yet who cannot gain
employment by offering to work for less because the union will not
allow individual bargaining. Similarly, there may be an employers'
association, or an understanding among employers, which will keep
the wage down to a point where some employers feel a shortage of
labor. In their own private interest these employers may wish to bid
up the wage which they offer; but because of their agreement with
other employers they prefer to suffer a shortage of labor rather than
to overcome the shortage by raising wages.

Importance of Elasticities of Demand and Supply

Evidently in this case as in the case of any price, the elasticities of
demand and supply play a great part in determining the flexibility
of wages and the power of monopolistic combinations to raise or lower
them above the equilibrium level. If the demand for any particular
kind of labor is very inelastic, the wage is likely to be much more
flexible than if the demand is elastic, for the principles which were
developed in Chapter 8 hold here also. If the demand for weaving is
highly inelastic, a weavers' union will be able to raise the wage of
weavers without materially affecting the volume of their employment.

If, on the other hand, the demand for their labor is elastic, any attempt to raise wages above the equilibrium level will result in a large fall in employment. Likewise, if the supply of a particular kind of labor is inelastic, a combination of employers to force down wages is much more likely to be successful than if it is elastic. For with an inelastic supply of labor a low wage will create but little scarcity of labor. But if the supply of labor is elastic, an attempt by a combination of employers to force the wage below the equilibrium level is almost sure to fail. With an elastic supply, a low wage means a severe labor shortage, and some employer will be tempted to raise wages in the attempt to obtain the labor he needs.

What Determines the Demand for Labor, etc.?

A complete study of the forces which determine the elasticity and the extent of the demand and supply of factors of production must wait till Part III. At least four important propositions, however, concerning the demand for a factor of production can be enunciated at this point. These propositions will be discussed in connection with the demand for labor, but they all apply equally well to the demand for anything purchased by an enterprise, whether labor, land services, or raw materials.

The Demand for Labor Is a Derived Demand

In studying the causes affecting the demand for labor the first fact which springs to our notice is that the demand for labor is usually a *derived* demand. That is to say, the people who buy labor do not generally buy it for its own sake. They buy it because with its aid they can produce or acquire some further commodity for which there is a demand, and which can therefore be sold. There is a demand for weavers because of the demand for cloth. There is a demand for automobile workers because of the demand for automobiles. Likewise there is a demand for the services of land because of a demand for the things which land will grow, and a demand for the services of machines because of a demand for the product of these machines.

First Proposition. The first proposition follows from this fact that the demand for labor is derived. It is that *an expected rise in the demand for a product will cause a rise in the demand for the type of labor which produces the product.* If it is expected, for instance, that at each price of cloth more will be demanded than before, then at each price of weaving, i.e., at each hourly wage of weavers, more hours of weaving can be sold than before. The full proof of this proposition must be left until later. It can be seen immediately, however, that the proposition is a reasonable one. For suppose the demand for cloth increases. Then, unless the supply of cloth is perfectly inelastic, its production will also increase. An increased production of cloth will necessitate an increased employment of weavers even at the old wage. That is to say, the demand for weaving will have increased.

Uncertainty of Future Demand. It should be observed that it is the *expected* demand for a product that helps to determine the demand for the labor producing it. When labor is employed, the product which justifies that employment is not yet produced. It will not be finished and sold until some time in the future, a time which may be long or short. When labor is employed, then, it is not because of the present demand for its product, but because the employer expects that there will be a demand for the product at the time when it comes on the market. The expectation may be fulfilled or it may not. If a change takes place in the demand for weaving, it is because of a change in the opinion of employers regarding the demand for cloth in a few weeks or months. The employers may be right or wrong, but it is their opinion, and not the accuracy of that opinion, that determines the demand for weaving.

Second Proposition. The next three propositions concern the *elasticity* of demand for labor. Our second proposition is the following: *The smaller the part played by a factor of production in the production of a commodity, the more inelastic is the demand for it likely to be.* If a factor of production plays only a small part in the making of the final product, a fall in the price of the factor will cause little change in the price or output of the final commodity and therefore little change in the quantity of the factor bought. If there were only one kind of paint which could be used on automobiles, and if the price of this paint were halved, there would be very little effect either on the price or on the output of automobiles, or on the quantity of paint bought by the automobile manufacturers, for paint is a very small part of the total cost of a car. If, however, the wages of automobile workers were halved, there would be a very appreciable effect on the price and the output of cars, and on the employment of the workers, for labor plays an important part in the production of automobiles.

Third Proposition. The third proposition is: *The more elastic the demand for a product, the more elastic is likely to be the demand for the types of labor which go to make the product.* This proposition rests on the assumption (whose exact proof we must again leave until later) that the lower the price of any type of labor, the greater will be the supply of any product which it goes to make. Suppose, for instance, that the wages of automobile workers are reduced. If all other things remain the same, this will have the effect of making the production of automobiles more profitable. Even if the price of automobiles remains the same, the output of the industry will expand. There will be an "increase in supply," for what we mean by an "increase in supply" is an increase not merely in the quantity supplied but in the quantity supplied at each price. Unless the demand is perfectly elastic, then, this increase in supply will lower the price of automobiles, as in Fig. 13, page 116. It will also lead to an increase in the total output, which, however, can usually be obtained only by an increased employment of labor. We started, then, with the assumption of a fall in the wage of automobile workers. Our argument has led to the conclusion that in the absence of other changes this will bring about a rise in their employment. This is what is meant by a "demand" for labor.

The elasticity of demand for labor is the percentage increase in employment which results from a 1 per cent fall in the wage. The demand for labor, therefore, is more elastic, the greater the increase in employment which follows from a given fall in the wage. If the demand for automobiles is elastic, the increase in supply which we noted will bring about a relatively large increase in the total output and therefore a large increase in the employment of labor. If, however, the demand for automobiles is inelastic, the increase in supply caused by the fall in wages will have little effect on the output and on the amount of employment. That is, the more elastic the demand for automobiles, the more elastic will be the demand for automobile workers.

Fourth Proposition. Finally, the fourth proposition is: *The better, and the cheaper, the substitutes for a factor of production, the more likely is it to have an elastic demand.* Suppose that machines can easily be substituted for labor and labor for machines. Then if the price of labor is raised, machines will tend to take its place; if the price of labor is lowered, it will take the place of machines. A lowering of the wage will result in a sharp increase in employment, for an extra quantity of labor will be required to replace the discarded machines. Similarly, a raising of the wage will result in a sharp decrease of employment, for the high-priced labor will be replaced by machines. In this case the demand for labor is elastic. If, on the other hand, a factor has no substitutes in any particular process, i.e., if it is completely indispensable, a rise or fall in the price of the factor will affect its employment only in so far as it affects the general output of the product. The demand for labor will be more inelastic.

Diagrammatic Representation of the Propositions on Elasticity. The last three propositions relating to the elasticity of demand for labor (or any other service) may be illustrated by Fig. 40. The elasticity shows how much a change in the wage (the price of labor) affects the amount of employment. There are three steps connecting these two quantities, each corresponding to one of our three propositions. The wage affects the supply curve of the product, the supply curve of the product affects the output of the product, and the output of the product affects the amount of employment. These influences are

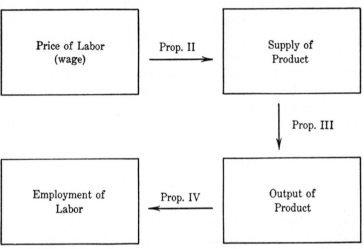

FIG. 40.   Effect of the Price of Labor on Its Employment.

shown by the arrows in the figure. The stronger each of the three influences represented by the arrows, the greater will be the effect of a change in the wage on the quantity of employment, i.e., the more elastic will be the demand for labor. The strength of the first influence, that of the price of labor on the supply of the product, depends on how important a part labor plays in the process; the more important the part, the greater the influence. This is Proposition II. The strength of the second influence, that of the supply of the product on the output of the product, depends on the elasticity of demand for the product, as we saw on page 206. This illustrates Proposition III. Finally, the influence which the output of the product exerts on the employment of labor depends on the degree to which labor is substitutable for other factors. If labor cannot be substituted for other services, a change in output must produce a proportionate change in the employment of labor. If labor can be substituted easily for other services, then a rise in wages, leading to a decline in output, will produce a greater proportionate decline in employment, for not only will there be a smaller output but each unit of it will be produced with a smaller amount of labor than before. This illustrates Proposition IV.

The Supply of Labor

Our preliminary survey of the forces affecting the demand for labor, or for other services, is now complete. Our next task is to consider some questions relating to the *supply* of labor and of other services. The supply of labor means the relationship between the price of labor and the quantity of labor offered for sale at each hypothetical price. Usually this is a direct relationship, in which a greater quantity of labor of a particular kind is called forth at a high wage rather than at a low wage. Under certain circumstances, however, an inverse relationship is possible, in which a higher wage calls forth less labor than a lower wage.

Two Factors in the Supply of Labor

Labor is usually measured by *hours* of work. Other methods of measurement have been devised by the exponents of the so-called "scientific management," methods which attempt to take into account the intensity as well as the duration of labor. These refinements will not concern us, important as they may be in practice, for no matter how labor is measured, the ensuing principles are valid. We shall therefore make the simplifying assumption that the quantity of labor of any given kind can be measured in hours. The total quantity of any given type of labor offered to employers then depends on two factors. One is the number of hours each worker is willing to work. The other is the number of workers. Thus the quantity of weaving offered for sale may increase because of a rise either in the number of hours worked by each weaver or in the number of weavers. To find out how the total number of hours of weaving offered will vary with the hourly wage of weavers, we must answer two further questions. The first is, "How does the hourly wage affect the number of hours per week which an individual weaver is willing to work?" The second is, "How does the wage affect the number of individuals willing to work at weaving?"

The Number of Workers and the Supply of Labor

If we can assume, as frequently we can, that the number of hours to be worked by each individual is fixed by custom or by contract, the problem of the supply of labor resolves itself into the second of the two questions above. In many industrial processes the hours of work are fixed either by law or by agreement with a trade union. The only way in which an employer can then obtain more labor is by taking on more men, and the only way in which the workers can offer more labor is through more men offering to work. In this case the relationship between the wage and the quantity of labor offered is a direct relationship. A rise in the wage offered to any particular occupation, other wages remaining the same, is bound to attract men into it out of other occupations, or perhaps even out of idleness. The higher the wage, therefore, the more labor will be offered, and the lower the wage, the less labor will be offered—labor, of course, of a particular kind. This is not to say that if wages are lowered in all occupations simultaneously there will be less labor offered. In this section we are discussing not the supply of labor as a whole but the supply of labor of a particular kind.

The Elasticity of the Supply of Labor

In the above circumstances the elasticity of the supply of labor will depend almost entirely on the *mobility* of labor into the occupation in question and out of other occupations. If the type of labor under consideration is mobile, and if the occupation is one which is easy to enter and which does not require much skill or unusual ability, then its supply will be elastic. A small rise in its wage will attract large numbers of workers away from other occupations, a small decline in wage will drive large numbers of workers away into other occupations. If, on the other hand, the occupation is difficult to enter or to leave, if it requires a great degree of skill which is not easily acquired or easily abandoned, or if it requires unusual ability, then the supply of labor will be inelastic. A high wage will not tempt many newcomers in; a low wage will not drive many old-timers out. Here is a phenomenon which is common to all supply curves. The longer the period which the curve represents, the more elastic it will be. A temporary rise in wages may attract few people into an occupation. The same rise in wages maintained over a number of years may attract large numbers into it. This is particularly true of occupations which require long training. In this case a rise or a fall in wages must be maintained perhaps for a generation or more before it produces its full effect on the quantity of labor supplied.

The Supply of Labor from the Individual Worker

It is not always true, of course, that the number of hours of work performed by an individual worker cannot be varied. In many cases considerable variation in individual effort is possible. Particularly is this so where the worker is himself employing his own labor. The labor of the artist, the writer, the independent craftsman, the farmer, and, above all, of the businessman himself falls into this category. Even the worker whose daily stint is fixed by agreement or custom has a certain ability to vary the number of days' work done in a year, as the wartime phenomenon of "absenteeism" clearly showed. Under these circumstances a peculiar phenomenon sometimes appears. At low wages it is probably true that an increase in the hourly wage will call for a greater number of hours' work per "week" from the individual. At higher wages this may not be true. The desire for leisure may then be so strong that an increase in the hourly wage will result in a decline in the number of hours which the individual is willing to work. Suppose, for instance, that an individual did not wish to earn more than a given money income. If his wage was such that he could obtain this money income without an unreasonable effort, any increase in the wage would result in a decline in the number of hours for which the worker would work. At the higher wage he could obtain the income of his heart's desire by working fewer hours than at a lower wage.

Graphic Illustration.   In this case we have what is called a "backward-sloping" supply curve, in which the relationship between the wage and the quantity of labor supplied is actually an inverse relationship. This is illustrated in Fig. 41. Here the hourly wage is plotted along OY, the number of hours which the individual will work along OX. SPS' is the individual supply curve for labor. Below wage OS he will not work at this particular occupation at all. As the wage rises above OS he will at first be encouraged to work longer hours to get a still larger income. But with the rising wage his demand for income in the form of money, or rather of the commodities to be bought with money, is gradually overshadowed by the pleasing prospects of slumber, relaxation, and recreation. At a wage ON the amount of labor which he will offer reaches a maximum, NP. At higher wages than ON the amount of labor offered declines. If OK is the wage at which the maximum income desired is obtained, the area $OKQH$ being the maximum income itself, then at higher wages the curve QS' will have an elasticity of supply of -1. An increase in the wage will then result in an equal proportionate decrease in the number of hours worked.

The Importance of "Backward-Sloping Supply Curves. These "backward-sloping" supply curves for the labor of individuals can result in a backward-sloping supply curve for all labor of a particular kind only when the number of individuals in the occupation cannot easily change. If the number of workers in a particular occupation can change easily and quickly, a rise in wages will nearly always result in an increase in the total quantity of labor supplied, even if the quantity supplied by each

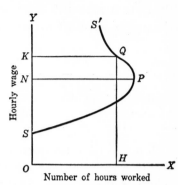

FIG. 41. The Backward-Sloping Supply Curve.

individual declines. The decline in the quantity supplied by each individual will be outweighed by the rise in the number of workers supplying the labor. Where, however, the number of workers in an occupation is relatively fixed, the individual backward-sloping supply curve may be reflected in the general supply curve. As the number of individuals in an occupation frequently cannot be changed in short periods of time, a general backward-sloping supply curve is often found in short periods, less often over long periods. The phenomenon is of considerable importance, therefore, in interpreting the short-period supply of some forms of labor. As we shall see in the next chapter, certain phenomena relating to the supply of agricultural produce can be interpreted only with the aid of this principle. Even more important, the supply of enterprise itself may be subject to this law. When times are good and the remuneration of the business man is high, he may take time out, pay frequent visits to the club and the golf course, and neglect his business. When times are bad and his remuneration is low, he may stick close to the office, pay scrupulous attention to detail, and work two or three times as hard as he does in more prosperous times.

Economic Rent

We should not leave our survey of the topic of distribution without a brief consideration of the concept known as "economic rent." Economic rent may be defined as any payment to a unit of a factor of production, in an industry in equilibrium, which is in excess of the minimum amount necessary to keep that factor in its present occupa-

212   DEMAND AND SUPPLY

tion. Although first worked out in connection with the services of land (hence the name—economic "rent"), this concept applies to any factor of production which does not have a perfectly elastic supply. We may illustrate it first in the case of labor. Table 16 shows a small portion of a supply schedule for weaving.

TABLE 16.   SUPPLY SCHEDULE FOR WEAVING

Wage ($ per week)	$50	$51	$52	$53	$54	$55
Number of Men Offering Labor	1000	1100	1200	1300	1400	1500

Here we have assumed that for every increase of a dollar in the weekly wage, 100 more men are willing to work at weaving. If the wage is $50 per week, 1000 men will offer their services. If the wage rises to $51 per week, the extra dollar will attract 100 new men to weaving. Therefore, $51 is the lowest wage which will make these 100 men offer their services. If the wage is $52 per week, another 100 men will offer their services. But the 100 who would work for $51 per week will now receive more than is necessary to keep them at the occupation of weaving. Each of these men would work for $51 per week, but in fact he receives $52 per week. Each therefore receives an "economic rent" of $1 per week, and the total economic rent received by the 100 men is $100. If the wage is $53 per week, the 100 men who would just be willing to work for $51 per week will get an economic rent of $2 each, or $200 in all, and the 100 men who would just be willing to work for $52 per week will receive an economic rent of $1 each, or $100 in all. The higher the wage, the greater will be the economic rent received by all those workers who would be willing to work at a lower wage, and the greater will be the economic rent received by all workers.

Graphic Illustration. This principle is illustrated graphically in Fig. 42. Here the wage is measured along *OY,* and the number of men who will offer their services at each wage along *OX.* The broken line *ABCDEFGHIJ* is the supply curve. We have assumed a discontinuous supply curve for the sake of exposition, but as we can make the "steps" as small as we like our conclusions also hold for a continuous curve. Below a wage *OA,* then, there will be no labor offered. At the wage *OA* a number of men measured by *AB* offer their services. These are the men who are most attracted by the occupation in question and who will therefore work in it at a low wage. At a higher wage, *OP,* an additional group of men, *CD,* will enter the occupation, bringing the total number to *AB + CD,* or *PD.* At a wage *OQ* a less eager group, *EF,* enters the occupation. At a wage *OR* a still less eager group, *GH,* and at a wage *OR'* an even less eager group, *IJ,* will be persuaded by the high wage to enter the occupation. If, now, the demand curve cuts this supply curve at *H* the wage will be *OR.* The first, most eager group, represented by *AB,* will receive this wage, *OR.* They would, however, have been willing to work for a wage *OA.* The total remuneration of the group at a wage *OR* is *OR* × *OK,* or the area *ORSK.* At a wage *OA* the total remuneration would have been *OA* × *OK,* or the area *OABK.* The "economic rent" of this first group, therefore, is the area of the rectangle *ARSB.* Similarly, at the wage *OR* the total economic rent received by the

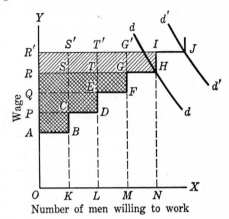

FIG. 42.   Economic Rent.

second group, *CD,* is the area *CSTD;* and that received by the third group, *EF,* is the area *ETGF.* No rent is received by the group *GH,* who are only just attracted into the occupation at the wage *OR.* The total economic rent received by all the workers at the wage *OR,* then, is the heavily shaded area *ARGFEDCB.*

Effect on Economic Rent of a Rise in Demand

Suppose, now, there is a rise in demand, the new demand curve passing through the point *J.* The wage will rise to *OR'.* The economic rent, therefore, received by the first group of men, *AB,* will increase, becoming the area *AR'S'B.* The economic rent received by all the workers together will also rise. It will now include the lightly shaded area *RR'IH* as well as the heavily shaded area, the total rent being represented by the area *AR'IHGFEDCB.*

Perfectly Elastic Supply Yields No Economic Rent

Thus we see that both economic rent and a less than perfectly elastic supply curve arise from the same cause—the *difference* in the eagerness with which the owners of various units of the factor in question will offer their services. If all the owners of a given factor are equally eager to sell all they own, there will be some price at which each will offer all the factor he possesses. A lower price than this will result in a complete absence of offers. Suppose that in the example in Table 16 a very large number of weavers are willing to offer eight hours of weaving per day at a wage of $50, and none below that wage. Then at any wage below $50 no weaving will be supplied. At a wage of $50 any amount of weaving may be obtained. The supply of weaving is perfectly elastic. No matter how great the demand for weavers, the equilibrium wage will be $50, which is the lowest wage that will persuade each weaver to offer his services. There is therefore no economic rent, no matter how great the demand for weaving.

To put the matter in another way. If the supply of any commodity is not perfectly elastic a higher price must be offered to induce a greater quantity of the commodity to come on to the market. The higher price is necessary to overcome the diffidence of those who are not eager to sell the commodity. At a high price, therefore, those who are more eager to sell will receive more than the least sum which will induce them to part with the commodity. This excess is economic rent. It should be noted that we have assumed in the above argument a fixed quantity supplied by each individual supplier. That is, in the case of weaving, we assumed that an increased offer of weaving could come only through more men offering to weave, and not through the existing weavers offering to work for longer hours. If this assumption is relaxed the problem of economic rent becomes more complicated.

QUESTIONS AND EXERCISES

1. Suppose that the following schedules represent the demand and supply schedules for a certain form of labor—say, weaving. Assume that the number of hours worked per day is fixed by technical considerations, so that variation in the quantity of labor employed can come about only through a variation in the number of men employed.

At a wage of:	35	40	45	50	55	60	65	$ per week
Employers will employ:	50	45	40	35	30	25	20	thousand men
Employment will be wanted by:	20	30	40	50	60	70	80	thousand men

a. If the market is perfectly competitive, what will be the equilibrium wage and the number employed at that wage?

b. Suppose that there is a strong Weavers' Union with a membership of 25,000 men. Suppose, furthermore, that the industry has a "closed shop" policy so that only union men can obtain employment. What wage should the union try to get? How many men outside the union would like to get employment at that wage? Why are they unable to do so?

c. Suppose the union had a membership of 40,000 men, and that it undertook to pay to its unemployed members an income equal to the weekly wage of its employed members. What wage would give the union members the highest weekly income, assuming that the employed members were taxed by the union to support the unemployed members, and that the expenses of administration were insignificant? How many members would be unemployed at that wage? (Note: Calculate the total payroll at each wage.)

2. Although the demand for houses is probably quite elastic, the demand for labor of various kinds and for raw materials in the building industry is probably very inelastic. How would you account for this? The supply of each kind of labor and raw material in the building industry is generally in the hands of a monopolistic organization. Because the demand for each of these things is inelastic, it is very difficult to reduce their prices. Why? If in a depression the prices of labor and materials in the building industry were reduced 25 per cent, there would probably be a spectacular increase in building which would more than compensate all the elements in the industry for their reduced prices. Why, then, does not this happen?

3. Agricultural wages are generally higher in neighborhoods which are near industrial centers. Is this because:

   a. Farmers are more kindhearted when near the civilizing influence of a city.

   b. Workers who can get to a movie once a week are more efficient.

   c. City people come out and buy up all the cottages for summer homes.

   d. The attraction of high wages in the city naturally pulls up agricultural wages.

   e. Agricultural workers are relatively more scarce when they can easily get city jobs.

4. A trade union official in a textile town once advised his men to ask for a 10 per cent cut in wages. Was he crazy? If not, why not?

5. Many people believe that there are "only so many jobs to go round" and that therefore if one man gets a job another must lose one. Do you agree? If not, how would you meet this argument?

6. Suppose a college suddenly decided to move to a small village in a rather remote part of the country. What do you think would be the effect of this move (a) immediately, (b) as time went by, on: (i) The wages of servants in the village. (ii) The rent of houses in the village. (iii) The price of building lots in the residential section. (iv) The rent of stores in the center of the village?

7. Illustrate with graphs the following propositions:

   a. If the supply of a particular kind of labor is perfectly inelastic, no change in demand for it will change the quantity of it which will be supplied.

   b. If the demand for a product rises, the price of those types of labor going to make it will also rise. The more inelastic the supply of any one of these types, the greater will be the rise in its price.

c. If the demand for a product rises, the demand for the types of labor going to make it will rise. The greater the part played by the labor in the process, the greater will be the rise in demand for it, and the greater will be the rise in the price of the labor.

8. An oil company in Mexico found that in order to get more hours of labor it had to *reduce* the hourly wage which it offered. How would you account for this?

9. Prove that in the case of a factor of production whose supply is perfectly inelastic at all prices the whole remuneration of the factor is "economic rent."

10. The concept of economic rent was first evolved in connection with the remuneration of land, hence the name "rent." Why should economic rent be regarded as peculiarly characteristic of the remuneration of land?

11. Class Exercise: to construct a supply schedule of books from a class. Let each person write down on a slip of paper the least price for which he would be willing to sell his copy of the text at the end of the course. (Some writers call this the "reservation price" of each person.) Let the instructor collect these slips and arrange them in order, the lowest price at the top of the pile. From these slips the supply curve can immediately be constructed. Suppose, for instance, that the first few slips showed figures of $0.25, $0.50, $0.75, $0.75, $1, $1, $1. Then if a buyer offered less than $0.25 for the books he would receive none. If he offered $0.25 he would receive one. At $0.50 per copy he would receive two; at $0.75, four; and at $1, seven; and so on. The supply schedule would be as follows:

Price ($)	0.25	0.50	0.75	1.00 ...
Amount offered	1	2	4	7 ...

If in this case the buyer wished to purchase seven books he would have to offer a price of $1.00 apiece. In that case the seller who cared so little for the book that he would sell it for $0.25 would receive an "economic rent" of $0.75. The one who would offer it for $0.50 would receive an economic rent of $0.50, and so on for the others.

The supply curve for the class should be plotted, and the total economic rent calculated for a series of possible prices.

CHAPTER 12

SOME FURTHER APPLICATIONS

FURTHER ANALYSIS OF A SHIFT IN DEMAND FROM ONE COMMODITY TO ANOTHER

Some of the specimens of analysis already given can now be carried considerably further. Take, for instance, the problem of the changes involved in a transfer of demand from silk to cotton, investigated in Chapter 9. We then saw that if there is a shift in demand from silk to cotton, the immediate effect will be a rise in the price of cotton and a fall in the price of silk. This will make the cotton industry unusually profitable and the silk industry unusually unprofitable. The cotton industry will therefore grow, the silk industry decline, until they are once more equally profitable. If the normal supply of these commodities were perfectly elastic, we should expect their prices to move to the original levels. If, however, the normal supply is less than perfectly elastic, we should expect the price of cotton to be a little higher and the price of silk a little lower, in the final adjustment, than they had been before.

Effect on Remuneration of Factors of Production

Now, what will be the effect of these changes on the prices of the factors of production employed in these two industries? The rise in demand for cotton will, as we have seen, by making cotton production more profitable bring about a rise in demand for all the factors of production which go into the making of cotton. If the prices of all these factors of production were previously at their equilibrium level, this rise in demand may cause a reaction upon both the price of each factor and the quantity of it which will be employed. The extent of the reaction will depend, of course, on the elasticity of supply of the factor concerned. We can apply the diagram in Fig. 38A, page 174, to

217

each factor employed. Suppose, for instance, that it referred to cotton pickers. Then along the axis oy in Fig. 43A we measure the wage of the pickers. Along ox we measure the amount of employment which they will be offered or will offer at each wage. Suppose that before the rise in demand for pickers a number equal to os_0 is employed at a wage s_0p_0. Now suppose the demand for pickers rises from dd' to ee'.

Impact Effect: Final Effect with Elastic Supply. If the supply of pickers is perfectly inelastic, i.e., if there are only a given number of pickers whose force cannot be augmented, the wage of pickers will rise

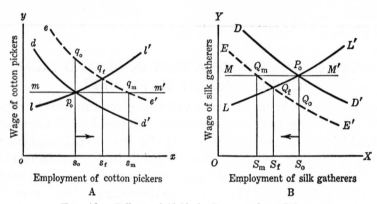

Employment of cotton pickers

A

Employment of silk gatherers

B

FIG. 43.   Effect of Shift in Demand on Wages.

to s_0q_0. This might be the immediate effect. However, any rise in the wage of cotton pickers will be sure to attract workers into that occupation, and in consequence the number of people offering to work at cotton picking will increase, and the wage will decline. If ll' is the normal supply curve of cotton picking, the wage will decline (and probably fairly rapidly) to the level s_fq_f, where the amount of employment given is os_f. If, now, the normal supply of pickers were perfectly elastic, represented by the line mm', the final result of the rise in the demand for picking would be an increase in the employment of pickers to os_m, without any increase in their wage, for $s_mq_m = s_0p_0$.

The effects of this change on the wages of silk gatherers are illustrated in Fig. 43B. If the supply curve of silk gathering, LL', is less than perfectly elastic, the result of a fall in the demand for silk gatherers will be a fall in their wage, from S_0P_0 to S_fQ_f. If, however, the supply of silk gathering is perfectly elastic, as represented by the line MM', the final result will be a decline in the number of silk gatherers employed from OS_0 to OS_m, but there will be no fall in the wage of the silk gatherers, as $S_mQ_m = S_0P_0$.

Elasticity of Supply a Result of Mobility of Factors

Now under what circumstances is the supply of cotton picking or of silk gathering likely to be perfectly elastic? Suppose that the cotton fields and the silk fields are adjacent, and that cotton picking and silk gathering require just about the same amount of skill and training and are about equally toilsome. That is to say, suppose that the nonmonetary advantages of these occupations are identical and that there are no hindrances to the free movement of workers between them. In that event it is clear that there cannot be any permanent divergence between the money wage of cotton pickers and of silk gatherers. Beginning with an equilibrium situation with the money wages of cotton pickers and silk gatherers equal, if the result of our shift in consumers' demand from silk to cotton is a rise in the demand for cotton pickers which just equals the fall in the demand for silk gatherers, we may suppose that the final result will be the transfer of a number of workers from cotton picking to silk gathering. There will be no change in the wage of either, for the supply of both kinds of workers will be perfectly elastic. Any rise in the wage of cotton pickers, any fall in the wage of silk gatherers, will bring about such a transfer of workers from one field to another that wages will soon return to their original levels.

Suppose now at the other extreme that we have a society in which silk gatherers and cotton pickers each form a hereditary caste, into and out of which nobody can move. Then the supply of both cotton picking and silk gathering will be perfectly inelastic, at least over considerable periods of time. A shift of demand from cotton to silk will result in a rise in the wage of silk gatherers and a fall in the wage of cotton pickers which will not be temporary but will persist. If we assume that the wage in this case does not influence the number of surviving children raised by the average family, this difference will persist indefinitely.

It is evident, then, that the elasticity of supply of a factor of production in any one use depends mainly on the ease with which similar factors of production can be *transferred*, either from other uses into the use in question or from the use in question into other uses. The more *mobile* is any factor of production between occupations, the more *elastic* will be its supply, and the more stable will be its price in any one occupation. It is because factors of production cannot be transferred easily from one occupation to another that their supply is less than perfectly elastic, and this fact also makes less than perfectly elastic the supply of the products which they produce, as we shall prove later.

THE INCIDENCE OF TAXATION

This analysis can be applied to the consideration of another very important problem—the "incidence" of taxation. By the problem of the incidence of taxation we mean, "Who really pays taxes?" That is to say, who is really worse off, and by how much, because of a given tax? We saw on pages 143–146 that a tax on a given commodity will generally raise the price to the consumer and lower the price to the producer. This, however, does not answer the question, "Who really pays the tax?" Let us return to our previous illustration of a specific tax on cigarettes. Because of this tax the consumer pays a higher price and smokes a smaller quantity. If his demand is inelastic, he will spend more on cigarettes than he did before; if it is elastic he will spend less. Everyone who is a smoker, however, is a little worse off because of the tax, for the price of cigarettes is raised.

Effect of a Tax on Industry: Falls on Immobile Factors

But that is not the whole story. What happens to the producers and to the factors of production employed in the making of cigarettes? The immediate result of the tax will be a decline in the output of the industry, and therefore a decline in the demand for all the factors of production involved in the industry. In the case of those factors which are mobile, i.e., which can get out of the industry, some will remove themselves, with more or less difficulty. The difficulties experienced by these factors in moving out of the industry must be written up to the tax. However, for any factor whose supply is perfectly elastic enough of the factor will move out of the industry to bring the price of that factor back to where it was before. Consequently, in the final result the burden of the tax will *not* be borne by the owners of those factors of production—be they the services of men or of things—which can move easily out of the industry. Their remuneration will finally be pretty much what it was before, either inside the industry or in some industry into which they have moved. But the immobile factors in the industry which cannot easily get out of it, i.e., which are inelastic in supply, will have to bear the brunt of the tax. If there are any factors in the industry whose supply is perfectly inelastic, no units of the factor will be able to escape the tax, for none can escape the industry. The demand for such a factor will fall, but as the quantity supplied cannot change, its price will fall in proportion to the fall in demand.

Suppose, for instance, that there is land which can be used only for tobacco growing. Then a tax on tobacco will reduce the demand for that land, and will reduce the price of its services. But the owners of the land will not be able to do anything about this fall in rent. They will have to be content with the decreased rent, and will continue to use their land for tobacco. However, if the reduced demand for tobacco pickers causes a reduction in their wage, they can do something about it—they can escape into other industries.

Effect of a Tax on Economic Rent

Wherever economic rent exists, the effect of a tax is always to reduce it. Even where the supply curve of a factor is not completely inelastic, a fall in the demand for the factor will lower its price, and will lower the economic rent on those units of the factor which would still be supplied at even lower prices. This is seen again in Fig. 42, page 213. If a fall in the demand from $d'd'$ to dd causes a fall in price from OR' to OR, the total economic rent of all units of the factor will fall from the triangular area $AR'I$ to the area ARG. The more inelastic the supply of the factor in the range between J and H, the greater will be the fall in the economic rent. Where the supply curve is neither perfectly elastic nor perfectly inelastic, then, as in Fig. 42, some units of the factor will escape into another industry, i.e., those units which are least satisfied with their lot, represented in the figure by IJ. The remaining units will suffer a loss in their remuneration. As, however, this is merely a loss in economic rent, they will not be able to escape the loss, for they will still receive more than the minimum sum required to keep them in the industry. If any factor is perfectly inelastic in supply over the whole range of the supply curve, i.e., if it will be supplied in a given quantity no matter what price it receives, the whole remuneration of the factor is "economic rent," for even at a zero price it will still be supplied in the same quantity as at all other prices. In that case the reduction in demand for the factor consequent upon a tax will be reflected wholly in a reduction in the economic rent, for no units of the factor will be able to escape from the industry.

On Which Factors Does a Tax Fall?

Thus, the more inelastic the supply of a factor, the more does it bear the burden of a tax. It is because land is reputed to be a factor which is inelastic in supply that the burden of a tax is frequently supposed to rest on the landowner. This will be the case, however, only where the tax is a general one on all the commodities which may be grown in a given area. If the tax is laid upon one only of a number of commodities which may be produced in a given area, the landowner may escape the tax as easily as the worker by turning his land over to another employment. At tax on corn alone, for instance, would result in a considerable turnover of land as well as labor to wheat and other crops. A tax on all agricultural products would be more difficult for the landowner to escape. Frequently, however, it is some form of labor rather than land which is most inelastic in supply to a given industry, and which therefore would have to bear the chief burden of a tax. A tobacco auctioneer, for instance, may be fastened down to the tobacco industry more firmly than any acre of tobacco land in the country, and consequently may suffer more than any landlord by a decline in the tobacco industry. Similarly, the services of highly specialized equipment may be very inelastic in supply, especially in short periods. The owners of a tobacco-curing plant may suffer by a tax on tobacco more than a landowner.

Elasticity of Supply Depends on Period of Time Taken

One general rule which we have noticed applies in this case also. It is that the longer the period of time taken into consideration, the more elastic will be most supply curves. Over long periods the supply of special skills or of special equipment may be almost perfectly elastic, and the owners of labor and of equipment will gradually be able to shift the burden of the tax. Over long periods also there is more justification for regarding land as peculiarly inelastic in supply, especially if it is specialized to the production of some commodity, for differences in the suitability of different acres of land for a particular employment may persist indefinitely. These differences are permanent, and lead to less than perfectly elastic supply curves for land even in long periods, whereas the differences which give rise to inelastic supply curves for labor and equipment may be only temporary.

Where All Factors Are Mobile, a Tax Falls on Consumers

If all the factors of production used in an industry are perfectly mobile, and if there are no difficulties of organization involved in using larger or smaller quantities of factors, then the supply of each of the factors and also the supply of the product will be perfectly elastic. In this case a tax will fall ultimately on consumers. It is true that the industry will decline and that some trouble will be given to factors thereby in getting out of the industry. However, once equilibrium is established again the price of each factor will be what it was before, and the price received by producers as a whole for the product will be the same as before—though of course the quantity of factors employed and the total output of the product will be smaller. But the price to the consumer will be higher by exactly the amount of the tax, as in Question 2, page 153.

We can therefore formulate the following proposition: The burden of any commodity tax will be shifted from the consumer to the factors of production engaged in making the commodity only in so far as the supply of these factors is less than perfectly elastic.

REGRESSIVE SUPPLY CURVES

Yet another problem may be interpreted with the help of the analysis of the preceding chapter. It is frequently observed that in agricultural production particularly, a fall in the price of the product —e.g., wheat—does not seem to have the effect of choking off production, as we might expect, but actually seems to encourage more production. That is to say, the supply curve of some commodities, instead of being positively sloped so that a rise in price encourages production and a fall in price discourages production, is sloped negatively, so that a rise in price discourages production and a fall in price encourages it. The explanation is to be found in the "backward-sloping" supply curve of an individual worker, shown in the preceding chapter. Agriculture is an occupation in which labor plays a large part. The worker is often his own boss; i.e., the farmer himself, on a small farm especially, not only is an employer and organizer but also performs the necessary acts of physical labor himself. This fact, however, does not materially alter his status as a "worker." Consequently, when the price of farm products falls the individual farmer, who does not contemplate abandoning his occupation, may think, "The price of wheat is bad this year; I will have to plant more and work harder to make a living." When the price of wheat is low he therefore puts forth all his energies and produces a large crop. On the other hand, when the price is high he may say to himself, "Prices are pretty good this year; I guess I can get along with a smaller crop than usual and I won't have to work so hard." So when prices are high, he is lazier and does not produce so big a crop.

Unstable Equilibrium

If the supply curve slopes backward so far that its slope is actually less than that of the demand curve, as in Fig. 44, the equilibrium represented by the intersection of the two curves at the point P is *unstable;* although at that point the quantity demanded is equal to the quantity supplied, if there is a slight disturbance resulting in either excess supply or excess demand, the economic forces operate to pull the price and the quantity *away from* the point of equilibrium, instead of toward it. Thus suppose that a year of short crop resulted in a total output equal to ON_1. The higher price, N_1D_1, now *discourages* production instead of encouraging it, so that the next year there is likely to be a still smaller production, ON_2 ($= M_1S_2$). This brings a still higher price, N_2D_2, which results in a still smaller crop, ON_3,

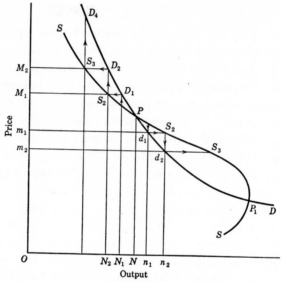

FIG. 44.   Unstable Equilibrium.

and so the industry moves away from the equilibrium point P, following the path $D_1S_2D_2S_3 \cdots$. Similarly, if there is a production slightly above the equilibrium level, say On_1, the price will be n_1d_1, which will call forth a *larger* output in the next year, On_2, with a resulting lower price, n_2d_2, which in turn produces a large output, m_2s_3. This process will go on until either a fall in prices loses its power to expand production, in which case the supply curve will bend around to intersect the demand curve at a point of stable equilibrium P_1, or else a disturbance of the underlying conditions of supply or of demand will shift the whole supply curve or the whole demand curve to a new position.

Example from Agriculture

Something of the peculiar instability of certain branches of agriculture may be explained along the lines of this analysis. The supply

curve in Fig. 44 is essentially a short-run supply curve, representing
the output which a given *number* of producers will produce in response to various prices. It may well be that if the number of producers is large, the position of stable short-run equilibrium, P_1, is at so
low a price that the whole industry is highly unprofitable. Such a condition cannot endure for very long, for producers will leave the industry. When that happens the short-run supply curve will shift to the
left, to a position something like that in Fig. 45, where there is a stable
equilibrium at a very high price, P_2N_2, and the industry will move

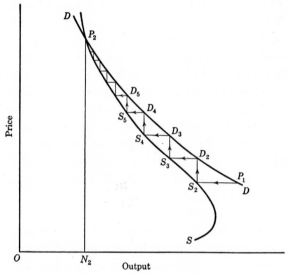

FIG. 45.   Short-Run Instability.

from the point P_1 toward P_2, following the path $P_1S_2D_2S_3D_3S_4D_4$ · · ·
etc., until the conditions of short-run supply or demand change again.
At P_2 the industry might be unusually profitable, which would attract
new producers who would shift the short-run supply back to a position
more like Fig. 44, with subsequent expansion of output and fall in
price. It is evident that with a backward-sloping short-run supply
curve, slight shifts in either supply or demand curves will cause large
shifts in the position of stable equilibrium.[1]

[1] It should be observed that the backward-sloping supply curve in this case is a purely
short-run phenomenon, depending on the assumption that the variation in output comes
from changes in the output from each producer, and not from a change in the number
of producers. A case will be considered later in which a very long-run supply curve can
have a downward slope due to the economies of industrial growth, but this phenomenon
has nothing to do with the backward-sloping short-run curve.

INTERRELATIONSHIPS AMONG DEMANDS AND SUPPLIES

In all our previous analysis we have tacitly assumed that the demand curves and the supply curves for various commodities are independent In fact this is not usually the case, and we must now extend our analysis to include some important cases where the demand or supply curves for various commodities are interdependent.

Complementary, Independent, and Competitive Relationships

Two commodities may be related in demand or supply in any of three ways. They may stand in a *complementary* relationship, they may be *independent*, or they may stand in a *competitive* relationship. They are complementary in demand, or in "joint demand," when a rise in the consumption or purchases of one causes a rise in the demand for the other; that is, a rise in the quantity of the other which would be purchased at each hypothetical price. They are independent in demand when a rise in the purchases of one has no effect on the demand for the other. They are competitive in demand when a rise in the purchases of one brings about a fall in the demand for the other.

Knives and forks, razors and razor blades, pipes and tobacco, right shoes and left shoes, pens and ink, are all examples of joint (complementary) demand. These are commodities which must be consumed in certain more or less definite proportions. Each pair is consumed as a single commodity, for each is useless, or at least of much less use, without its counterpart. At the other extreme are pairs or groups of commodities which are good substitutes for each other—beef and lamb, cotton and silk, oranges and grapefruit, oatmeal and corn flakes. These are competitive in demand, for any one of a group can be used as a substitute for any other in the fulfillment of a want. The more easily two commodities can be substituted one for another, the more competitive will be their demands. Two commodities have independent demands if they cannot be substituted one for another in consumption—cheese and spark plugs, molasses and taffeta, pussy cats and powerhouses.[2] If two commodities are complementary in consumption then we may say that they are "negatively substitutable."

[2] This statement is true only as a first approximation. The true test of independence in demand is that a rise in consumption of one commodity (A) will not affect the demand for the other commodity (B). If the demand for commodity A is relatively elastic, a fall in the price of A will raise its consumption and also the amount spent on it. Consequently, there will be less to spend on all other commodities, and for this reason demand for all of them—including B—will fall. In this case even if the commodities have zero substitutability, they will be slightly competitive. If the demand for A is relatively inelastic, commodities with zero substitutabiliy will be slightly complementary in demand. Only if the elasticity of demand for both commodities is unity is the above statement wholly true. Nevertheless, for most commodities the inaccuracy is inconsiderable.

Dependence in Supply

As in demand, so in supply we can distinguish three cases. Two commodities are complementary in supply, or in "joint supply," if a rise in the output of one must necessarily be accompanied by a rise in the supply curve of the other. They are independent in supply if a rise in the output of one does not affect the supply curve of the other. They are competitive in supply if a rise in the output of one must necessarily be accompanied by a fall in the supply curve of the other. Complementarity in supply arises from the fact that many processes of production have multiple end products. Beef and hides are both obtained from cattle, wool and mutton from sheep, grain and straw

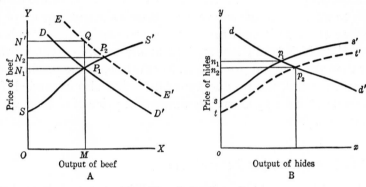

FIG. 46.   Joint Supply.

from wheat, and steel and slag from blast furnaces. In these cases and in many others if we want one commodity, we must also produce the other; just as if we want a wife to come to a dinner party we must usually take the husband also.

Competitiveness in supply arises because many groups of products are produced with the same factors of production. Consequently, if the production of one commodity increases, resources which are necessary for the production of the competing commodity are withdrawn. Various agricultural crops, for instance, compete for land. If there is an increase in the production of wheat, there is likely to be a decrease in the supply of oats and barley, particularly if wheat, oats, and barley can all play the same part in the crop rotation.

Example: A Rise in Demand for Beef May Cause a Fall in the Price of Hides.   The problems created by dependent supplies or demands can best be illustrated by an example. Consider, for instance, two commodities produced under conditions of joint (complementary) supply. Beef and hides are both produced by the cattle industry. Suppose, then, that there is a rise in the demand for beef. The immediate result, as we have seen, will be a rise in the price of beef. The rise in the price of beef will make the cattle industry more prosperous than before, and it will expand. The rate of production of cattle will increase, and therefore the rate of production of both beef and hides will increase. The price of beef will then fall to some point a little above its old level, and the price of hides will fall below its old level. The net result of a rise in demand for beef, therefore, is a rise in the price of beef and a fall in the price of hides—assuming, of course, that the demand for hides does not change. This situation is illustrated graphically in Fig. 46. DD' is the old demand for beef, SS' the long-run supply curve for beef. In Fig. 46B, dd' is the demand curve for hides, ss' the original long-run supply curve for hides.[3] Now if there is a rise in the demand for beef to EE', the immediate result will be a rise in the price of beef to MQ, or ON'. This high price encourages production, which rises from N_1P_1 to N_2P_2 and the price falls finally to ON_2—still, however, higher than the original price, ON_1. Meanwhile, as the production of beef has expanded, the production of hides has also expanded, from an original n_1p_1 to n_2p_2. Correspondingly, the price of hides has fallen from on_1 to on_2.

Extent of These Changes Depends on:

1. *Elasticities of Supply and Demand.* The extent of these changes depends on two things. First, as always, it depends on the elasticities of supply and demand in question. If the cattle industry as a whole is elastic in supply, i.e., if a small rise in its profitability causes a large influx of resources into it, then a rise in demand for beef will produce but little effect on the price of beef. It may, however, produce an appreciable effect on the price of hides. If the supply of cattle is inelastic, then a rise in demand for beef will produce a considerable effect on the price of beef, but it will not cause much expansion of the cattle industry, and will therefore not affect greatly either the output or the

[3] The nature of the supply curves drawn in this example requires some explanation. The profitability of cattle production depends on the price of both beef and hides. The total quantity of beef, therefore, which will be produced at each price of beef depends in part on the price of hides. The greater the price of hides, the more beef will be produced at each price of beef. That is to say, instead of having a single supply curve for beef we have a series of supply curves, each corresponding to a certain price for hides. The greater the price of hides, the farther toward the right will the supply curve for beef lie. Similarly, for each price of beef there is a different supply curve for hides. Fig. 46, then, assumes that the supply curve SS' is that supply curve for beef which is consistent with a price of hides equal to on_2, and that the supply curve for hides, ss', is consistent with the price of beef ON_1, and the supply curve tt' is consistent with the price of beef ON_2.

price of hides. If the demand for hides is elastic, a greater output of hides will, of course, produce less effect on the price than if the demand were inelastic.

2. *Possibility of Substitution.* In the second place, the extent of these changes depends on the degree to which beef and hides can be substituted in the productive process. If the proportions of beef and hide produced are absolutely inflexible, any increase in the output of beef must also produce the same proportionate increase in the output of hides. If cattle always yielded beef and hides in the same proportion, an increase of 1 per cent in the output of beef could only be brought about by an increase of 1 per cent in the output of cattle, which would also bring about an increase of 1 per cent in the output of hides. If, at the other extreme, it were possible to breed cattle without skins, then an increase in the output of beef might be obtained without any change in the output of hides. In practice the truth generally lies between these two extremes. There are some processes in which the proportions of the products are absolutely fixed—some chemical processes, for instance. But in most cases some variation is possible in the emphasis on the different products of the same process. Although we cannot breed cattle without skins, we can at least breed them specially for beef—we may be able to get more and better beef inside each hide. We could conceivably breed specially for hides, though this is not in fact the case in the cattle industry, the hide being a relatively small part of the total value of a beast. In the sheep industry, however, we find this specialization carried to considerable degree. Some sheep are bred specially for their wool, such as Merinos, and in this case the mutton or lamb is merely a by-product. Some sheep, on the other hand, are bred for their meat, and in this case it is the wool which is the by-product. A by-product may be defined as one of two or more joint products whose total value is small compared with that of its fellow products.

If we suppose that the proportion of beef to hide in a beast can be changed easily, then the result of our increase in demand for beef will be to shift the proportion in the favor of beef. That is, the fact that the price of beef has risen while the price of hides has fallen will make it profitable to breed cattle which contain more and better beef inside each hide. Consequently, there will not be so much of a rise in the output of hides as there might be if the proportion of beef to hide produced by a single beast were absolutely inflexible. If, therefore, beef and hides are substitutable in production, a change in the demand for beef will bring about a smaller change in the price of hides than it would if beef and hides could not be substituted one for another.

Competitive Supply

The analysis of competitive supply follows the same lines. Suppose, for instance, that cotton and tobacco are in competitive supply, for both are grown in the same region on the same kind of land. Then a fall in demand for tobacco will lower the price of tobacco, drive resources out of the tobacco industry, make the rent of the tobacco-cotton land cheaper, lower the costs of production of cotton, raise the supply of cotton, and therefore lower the price of cotton.

Complementary (Joint) Demand

Similar propositions can be derived from the study of complementary and competitive demands. Consider first the case of a rise in the supply curve of a commodity which is jointly demanded with another. For instance, if an improved pig is discovered which will produce bacon much more quickly and cheaply than previous pigs, there will be a rise in the supply of pigs, for at each price, now, more will come on to the market than before. This will cause a fall in the price of pigs and of bacon, and a rise in the consumption of pigs and bacon. A rise in the consumption of bacon, however, may well cause a rise in the demand for eggs, for more people will now have bacon and eggs for breakfast or lunch than before. A rise in the demand for eggs will usually bring about a rise in the price of eggs. Thus an improvement in pigs may raise the price of eggs. This can be illustrated with supply and demand curves, just as in the last case. The extent of these movements again depends upon two things. The first is the elasticity of demand and of supply—especially the elasticity of demand for bacon and the elasticity of supply of eggs. Second, it depends on how much the proportions in which the two commodities are bought can be varied. If we imagine that there is a law which makes it obligatory for each housewife to drop one egg in the pan for every three rashers of bacon, and if eggs were used only for frying with bacon, then any increase in the consumption of bacon will be accompanied by an exactly proportionate increase in the consumption of eggs. If at the other extreme eggs and bacon were not used together at all, then of course an increase in the consumption of bacon would cause no appreciable change in the consumption of eggs.

Competitive Demand

The case of competitive demands can be analyzed in the same way. Suppose, for instance, that beef and pork are competitive in consumption. Then the improved pig, which we saw might result in a rise in the price of eggs, will cause a fall in the price of beef. The increased supply of pork will lower its price and increase its consumption. Consumers will turn away from the dearer commodity, beef, toward the cheaper pork. The demand for beef will decline, and the price and output of beef will also decline, except in the unlikely circumstance of a perfectly elastic supply of beef.

Application to Factors of Production

The interrelationships of demand are of great importance in interpreting the demand for factors of production. Where two factors of production are substitutable in production their demands will be competitive. A rise in the price of one without any change in the price of the other will cause a fall in the employment of the first but a rise in the employment of the second. Land and labor are frequently in this relationship. Where land is cheap and labor is dear, "extensive" farming is the rule, using much land and little labor. Where land is dear and labor is cheap, we have intensive farming, using little land and much labor.

Two factors of production may, however, stand in a relation of complementary demand. A good example is the demand for machines and for skilled machinists. In this case a scarcity of one factor will cause a fall in the demand for the other. If there are few machinists there will be little demand for machines. If there are few machines there will be little demand for machinists. A fall either in the wages of machinists or in the price of their machines will bring about a rise in the employment of *both* machinists *and* machines. A fall in the price of machines, therefore, may cause a decline in the demand for unskilled labor and a rise in the demand for skilled labor. This example should warn us against the fallacies which result from treating factors of production in too broad categories. From the point of view of economic analysis it is hardly too much to say that there is no such thing as "labor as a whole," and the movement of such a "whole" must always be analyzed in terms of movements in its component parts.

Questions Reserved for Part III

We have now reached the end of this part of our inquiry. We have asked ourselves, "Why are particular prices what they are?" We have given an answer to this question in terms of two powerful weapons of analysis—supply and demand. We have not as yet delved deeply into the question of *why* supply and demand are what they are, although we have gained some ground on that point. This question, however, is taken up in Part III. There we shall go into the theory of production and of the individual firm to seek for the underlying forces which determine the position of supply curves. We shall also go into the theory of consumption and of individual choice to seek for the underlying forces which determine the position of demand curves. Another topic which we have mentioned only in passing is that of monopoly and the effects of monopolistic elements in the competitive system. This also must be postponed. For all the importance of these topics they are, in a sense, secondary to the purpose of this part, which was to get a broad picture of how the system of economic life works and by what devious paths economic change operates. Consequently, we shall leave the problems of particular prices now and go on to enter another broad province of our subject—the province usually known as the theory of money, which might perhaps be better known as the theory of general prices and outputs, or macroeconomics.

QUESTIONS AND EXERCISES

1. Suppose that (a) lemons can be grown only on a certain very limited area of land in California; (b) imports of lemons into the United States have been prohibited for some time past. Suppose now that doctors discover that a sure way to avoid colds is to eat two lemons a day. What do you think would be the effect of this discovery on the following?
   a. The normal demand for lemons.
   b. The normal supply of lemons.
   c. The price of lemons (i) immediately and (ii) eventually.
   d. The output of lemons (i) immediately and (ii) eventually.
   e. The wages of lemon pickers (i) immediately and (ii) eventually.
   f. The profits of lemon growers (i) immediately and (ii) eventually.
   g. The rent of lemon-growing farms (i) immediately and (ii) eventually.
   h. The orange industry (i) immediately and (ii) eventually.
2. Suppose in the above case that coincident with the doctor's discovery the prohibition on the import of lemons is removed. Compare the effects of the discovery in this case with the effects in the last case.
3. Discuss the probable effects of a tax on sugar refined in the United States.
4. The government of Northern Ireland placed a tax on *all* butter sold in Northern Ireland, whether produced at home or imported. The proceeds of this tax were given as a subsidy to the Northern Ireland butter producers. Discuss the probable effects of this policy.
5. It has been claimed that government assistance to agriculture is useless, as all subsidies eventually find their way into the pockets of the landowner in the form of higher rents. Discuss this criticism.

6. What will be the effect of a tariff on the remuneration of factors of production employed in the protected industry? Who really benefits from a tariff? Who suffers?

7. (a) Suppose that the supply curve in Figs. 44 and 45 *coincided* with the demand curve over a certain range of output. What would be the economic significance of such a demand and supply? (b) Discuss the case in which the demand curve lies wholly above or below the supply curve.

8. Under certain agricultural marketing schemes (e.g. hops in Britain, tobacco in the United States) each producer is allotted a marketing quota, and is penalized if he sells more than his quota. Discuss the probable effects of such a scheme on the remuneration of the various factors of production involved and on the price of the product. Who gets most of the benefit from such a scheme?

PART II

MACROECONOMICS

CHAPTER 13

ECONOMIC AGGREGATES AND AVERAGES

"Macro-" and "Micro-" Economics

There are two main branches of modern economic analysis, to which the names "microeconomics" and "macroeconomics" may conveniently be given. Microeconomics is the study of particular firms, particular households, individual prices, wages, incomes; individual industries, particular commodities. It is in this part of the subject that the tools of demand and supply, the marginal analysis, and the theory of the individual firm and industry are particularly useful. Many economic problems and policies, however, are concerned not so much with individual prices, commodities, and firms, but with *aggregates;* not with the price of cheese, but with the price of everything, or the "general level" of prices; not with the output of butter but with the general level of output as a whole; not with individual firms but with the whole economic system. Macroeconomics, then, is that part of the subject which deals with the great aggregates and averages of the system rather than with particular items in it, and attempts to define these aggregates in a useful manner and to examine how they are related and determined.

Policy Significance of Macroeconomics

From the point of view of economic policy macroeconomics is extremely important. This is because the economic policies of governments concern themselves of necessity not with individuals, but with large groups and aggregates of individuals. Indeed, from an economic point of view the national state itself is an aggregate of individuals, and must therefore be treated in macroeconomic terms. It is true, of course, that governments may have to concern themselves with the detailed regulation of particular prices and particular firms or households. Unless it is an arbitrary and tyrannical government, however, it

237

must deal with individuals not *as* individuals but as members of some group or aggregate of individuals; this is what is meant by the "rule of law." It can be said also that the main economic responsibilities of government lie in the regulation of the aggregates of the system—general prices, general outputs, the general volume of trade, and so on—and that the more it intrudes itself into the detailed regulation of particular prices, wages, and the like, the less successful is its policy likely to be.

Difficulties in Macroeconomic Analysis

There are certain difficulties and dangers in macroeconomic thinking which should command attention. In the first place, many propositions which are true of individuals or of small groups turn out to be untrue when we are considering the system as a whole. There are many things also which an individual can do only because most other individuals refrain from doing it. Most of us, having money in our wallet, feel able to go to a movie or take a train ride. Yet, clearly, if everyone tried to do these things at once, there would be no seats available for most people either at the movies or on the train. Similarly, in normal times anyone who has a bank deposit is free, and able, to go to the bank and exchange it for cash; but if every depositor did this at once, the bank would have to close. Any individual can increase the amount of money he has by simply not spending as much money as he receives. Unless there is actual creation of new money, however, it is impossible for all people to spend less than they receive; for every expenditure is at the same time a receipt to the person to whom it is made. In macroeconomics, therefore, we must be on our guard against generalizing from our individual experience; just because we ourselves can do something is no reason for supposing that everybody can do it at the same time. Generalizing from our own experience is such a common habit that we constantly fall into it; it is, however, one of the greatest sources of error in social thinking.

Dangers in "Aggregative" Thinking

The second danger in macroeconomic thinking is of a quite different kind; it is that we may think too easily in terms of aggregates as if they were homogeneous, without realizing the significance of their internal composition and structure. We see many examples of this in political thinking. Constantly in discussion we speak of "France," "Russia," or "The United States," as if these aggregates of people were single entities. For some purposes they can, indeed, be so regarded, and unless they are so regarded discussion becomes almost impossible. We cannot, every time we mention "The United States," substitute "The people living on North American between Canada and Mexico, their separate habits, characters, divisions, groups, classes, parties, institutions, and organizations." Nevertheless, it is easy in discussion of any kind to forget that shorthand symbols like "The United States" in fact stand for a great, complex diversity of men and institutions, which for some purposes, but not for others, can be regarded as a single entity. In macroeconomic discussion likewise it is easy to forget that the aggregates or averages under discussion are in fact made up of innumerable individual items, and that changes in their internal structure or composition may be more significant in the interpretation of some particular problem than changes in the aggregate itself. To take but a single example: Many economists have tried to postulate a relationship between the average wage and the volume of employment, on the analogy of the "demand for labor" of a particular kind. The "average wage," however, is derived from a very large number of particular wages—e.g., wages of carpenters, machinists, nurses; and the volume of aggregate employment, in so far as it depends upon wages at all, may depend much more on the relative structure of wages than on the average level. If, for instance, wages of carpenters rose but wages of nurses fell, the average might remain unchanged; but if the employment of carpenters fell only a little, whereas the employment of nurses rose a great deal, aggregate employment would rise.

Aggregates Must Be "Interesting"

A third danger in aggregative analysis is that the aggregates which compose our system may not be significant or "interesting." An aggregate consists of all the items in a given universe which conform to some *definition*. A definition is a kind of verbal hedge or wall—it sets up an enclosure inside of which stand all the things which conform to the definition and outside of which stand all things which do not so conform. There is no limit to the number of such enclosures which can be made. Some of them however are interesting and some are not. Thus we might define a *gazoola* as a left-handed person with red hair. There will be some argument of course as to how left-handed and how red-headed a person has to be before he can qualify as a gazoola, as practically all definitions are a little vague—the enclosure is divided off from the outside world by a fog rather than by a fence. One might even imagine learned disputes among the gazoolologists as to what constitutes a "real" gazoola. Gazoolas of course, once we agreed on a definition, could be counted, and statistics, even time series, of the number of gazoolas compiled. Studies could be made of their geographical distribution, their heredity, their marital histories, their aggregate and per capita income, their wealth. Doctoral dissertations and textbooks could be written about them, professors of gazoolology established, even interdisciplinary research developed between gazoolologists and related disciplines. In fact this does not happen, even though some things which happen in academic circles are only slightly less ridiculous. It is important to ask why the gazoola is so neglected, if only to throw light on why certain other definitions, concepts, and fields of study are pursued. The answer is simple: the gazoola is neglected, indeed was not even named until I named him, because he is not interesting.

Aggregates Are Interesting Only if They Can Be Functionally Related

Interest is the nutrition of science, and no concept or study will live in the minds of men unless *somebody* finds it interesting. The gazoola is not interesting in spite of the fact that he exists, and that a whole potential field of study waits to be erected around him. The gazoola is just as "real" as the plumber, the Seventh-Day Adventist, the American, the Jew, the Negro, the economist. Like these he could be identified, seen, touched, smelt, heard, and perhaps even, in some cultures, tasted. He is not interesting because he has no *function*. Gazoolas do not do anything, and do not have anything done to them, *as such*. They are not perceived by others as constituting a group, nor do they perceive themselves as a unity. Their behavior as an aggregate is simply the sum total of the individual behavior of particular gazoolas: it cannot be assumed to depend on the behavior of any other aggregate. In mathematical language, if G is some quantity descriptive of the aggregate of gazoolas—their number, weight, income, I.Q., or any other quantity—it makes no sense to write that G is a function of H ($G = F(H)$) where H is any other quantity in the universe. If it was discovered that such functions or relationships existed in any society, even if the gazoola were not perceived as such in the society, the concept would immediately have scientific interest. Suppose for instance that all or most gazoolas were more inventive, or stupider, or more prejudiced than people who are not gazoolas. Immediately the concept would become interesting, for the percentage of gazoolas in any group would be directly related to the inventiveness, stupidity, or prejudice of the whole group. The gazoola index might become almost as use-ful, and even more meaningful, than the intelligence quotient.

Difficulties of Definition

I have used what may seem to be an absurd or even frivolous example above because so many grave discussions in economics as in other sciences are almost as absurd. A great deal of breath and ink have been wasted in economics, for instance, on the question of the "correct" definition of concepts associated with words like "capital," "income," "value," and so on. For a long time it was customary in textbooks of economics to begin with a chapter of definitions and concepts. The definitions given in Chapter One were usually forgotten by the middle of Chapter Two, but at least the author had paid homage to the great principle of linguistic monogamy—one meaning wedded to one word. Unfortunately this is a principle quite inadequate to take care of the number of meanings wanting words, and some form of linguistic polygamy, or at least Hollywood marriage, seems to be in order.

Economic Dimensions

About the only distinctions which are quite clear, and about which there can be no argument or shadow of doubt, are those based on differences in *dimensions*. In Newtonian physics, for instance, all quantities can be reduced to some combination of powers of the three basic dimensions: Length (L) Mass (M) and Time (T). Thus distance is simple length (L), or so many feet. Velocity is measured as a length per unit of time $\left(\dfrac{L}{T}\right)$, or as so many feet per second. Acceleration is the change in *velocity* per unit of time, and is measured therefore as a length per unit of time per unit of time $\left(\dfrac{L}{T^2}\right)$ or as so many feet per second per second. Distance should never be confused with velocity, or velocity with acceleration; the difference in dimensions between these concepts constitutes a clear and unscalable barrier between them. Similarly in economics there are three basic dimensions: Commodity (C), Money (M) and Time (T). The commodity dimension is in fact multiple: it should really be written $C_1, C_2 \ldots C_n$, each symbol standing for the different physical measure of different commodities—tons of steels, bushels of wheat, bars of soap, units of Chevrolets. The money dimension likewise may be multiple: it may stand for dollars, pounds, francs, etc.

All economic quantities can be expressed in terms of some combination of these dimensions.[1] Thus capital in physical terms has the dimensions C: it is always a stock of some physical objects, defined at some instant of time. Income on the other hand has the dimensions $\frac{C}{T}$. Capital is a number of bushels or tons of something; income is bushels or tons per day or per week or per year. The capital and income concepts are therefore quite distinct, and should never be confused. It is no exaggeration to say that the major source of confusion and error in the classical economics is the constant confusion between the "capital" (stock, fund) concepts and the "income" (flow) concepts. The wage-fund theory in its crude form exhibits this confusion, as it identifies a stock (a portion of capital) with a flow (the wages bill)—two things which cannot from their very nature be identified, though they may be related.[2]

Definition Within a Single Dimension Depends on Its Purposes

I have emphasized the necessity of maintaining clear and precise distinctions between quantities having different dimensions, both in thought and language. The boundary between capital and income is a "natural" boundary, like an ocean which separates two continents. The boundaries *within* the capital or the income concepts however

[1] For some purposes an additional dimension, utility or satisfaction (U), is necessary. Most economic theory, however, can be developed without it. See Chapter 32 for a discussion of this dimension.

[2] Some other dimensions of economic quantities are of interest, and may briefly be noted here. A ratio of exchange or "value" is the ratio of two quantities of commodity, or $\frac{C_1}{C_2}$. The special case of a price is a ratio of a quantity of money to a quantity of commodity, or $\frac{M}{C_1}$. We can if we like regard money as simply a special case of commodity, in which case it would be included in the commodity dimension. Its peculiarities, however, perhaps make it worthy of a special symbol. The concept of commodity here includes any asset whatever which can be exchanged; it includes therefore such things as securities, bonds, futures contracts, mortgages, and any other exchangeable financial instrument. The dimensions of the rate of interest are perhaps a little surprising at first sight. The rate of interest is measured as a per cent per annum. The "per cent" has no dimensions at all, as it is a ratio of two quantities which have the same dimensions. Thus "5 per cent" is simply five "dollars" divided by a hundred "dollars," or one twentieth. The dimensions of a per cent per annum therefore are $\frac{1}{T}$. Thus the reciprocal of the rate of interest is a period of years (the period of purchase): 5 per cent per annum is exactly equivalent to twenty years purchase. The dimensions of the rate of interest can also be visualized as the ratio of a constant income to its capital value—say 5 dollars per year per hundred dollars. This would be symbolized as $\frac{\frac{M}{T}}{M}$, or again, $\frac{1}{T}$. The dimensions of the velocity of circulation of money are likewise $\frac{1}{T}$; its reciprocal is the period of turnover—also a length of time (see page 314).

are to a large extent artificial, like the boundaries of states. Definitions within the broad continent of "stocks of things" or the other great continent of "flows of things" are to some extent arbitrary, are matters of convenience, imposed on us in the last resort because of the limitations of language. There is no point therefore in discussing what is the "right" concept of capital or of income, if we mean by the "right" concept some particular section or area within the broad field of "stocks of things" or of "flows of things." There are a great many useful concepts within each field, and likewise a great many useless ones. The usefulness of a concept depends mainly on the extent to which the aggregate defined by it can be related to others, as we have seen. The problem is in many ways analogous to the problem of the geographer in defining a "region." Everyone would agree that the "Middle West" is a useful concept in geography, even though it might be difficult or even impossible to reach agreement as to where its exact boundaries lie. Similarly within the broad field of "stocks of goods" we might define a "region" of, say, "circulating capital," or "goods in process," even though it would be impossible to draw the boundaries of this region in a way that would please everybody.

Overlapping Regions

Just as the "regions" of a geographer may overlap, depending on the purpose for which they are constructed, so may the concepts of the economist. Thus for some purposes "Michigan" is a significant geographical entity, because it shares a common state government and state law. For other purposes it is useful to run a boundary right through Michigan, joining its southern part to the "Middle West" region and its northern part to the "cutover forest" region. Similarly within the broad field of "capital," or stocks of goods, we may define overlapping "regions." Thus for some purposes a distinction between "household goods" and "business goods" may be valuable, in so far as businesses and households behave differently. Cutting across this distinction altogether is a distinction between "durable" and "nondurable" goods. Households possess both durable goods like refrigerators and nondurable goods like sugar. Businesses likewise possess durable goods (factories and machines) and nondurable goods (machine oil, gasoline). The essentially arbitrary nature of these distinctions, and also the fact that their arbitrary nature in no way detracts from their usefulness, is admirably illustrated by this last distinction. It is clearly impossible to draw any clear line between "durable" and "nondurable" goods. There is a continuous, or nearly continuous, scale of durability of goods, and any line that we draw is arbitrary. For some purposes we may want to draw several lines—for instance, we may wish to divide the stock of goods into durable, semidurable, and nondurable. The United States Department of Commerce does this. We draw these lines, however, mainly because the continuum of the durable-nondurable scale is too complex to talk about. No matter where we draw the line between durable and nondurable, within reason, the study of the changes in the composition of the stock of goods from the standpoint of durability will probably be reflected in changes in the proportion of nondurable to durable goods according to our arbitrary definition.

Dangers in Arbitrary Definitions

The above example will also serve to illustrate the dangers as well as the uses of arbitrary definition. Suppose for instance that we draw the line between durable and nondurable goods at a length of useful life of one year, so that all goods with a length of life of less than a year are classified as "nondurable" and all goods with a length of life of a year or more are classified as "durable." Suppose now that there is a large increase in goods lasting thirteen months and a large decline in goods lasting eleven months. This change in the composition of the total stock of goods will be reflected in a sharp rise in the quantity of "durable" goods according to our definition, and a sharp fall in the quantity of "nondurable" goods. It will look as if there has been an important change in the durability of the stock of goods, in the direction of a rise in durability. In fact the change may be quite insignificant; it is merely the accident that the change occurred across the arbitrary boundary which made it look significant. The measurement of changes therefore at arbitrary boundaries is always open to some question. Changes across these definitional boundaries are accurate measures of the total changes in the composition of an aggregate if the actual changes are uniformly distributed through the total field. Thus if all items in the capital stock increased in durability, then no matter where we drew the line between durable and nondurable goods there would be a rise in the proportion of durable goods as defined, which would have some significance as a measure of the general rise in durability.

Classifications of Goods: Instruments and Goods in Process

Many other classifications of the total stock of goods are possible, based on more or less continuous arrangements of properties of these goods. Thus we may make a distinction between "instruments" and "goods in process." "Instruments" are those goods which are complete in themselves and which render a succession of services over a period of time. Houses, factories, machines, automobiles, domestic animals are all examples. These things are frequently called "fixed capital," not so much because they are fixed in position as because their physical form does not change significantly in the course of their service. Such things depreciate in value as they are used, even apart from any minor changes in their physical form. Even the celebrated one-hoss shay, whose physical form remained unchanged for a hundred years, would have depreciated in value between the time of its creation and the dramatic moment of its dissolution.

"Goods in process" are those things which are not complete in themselves and which must undergo a complete transformation of form before they render services. Raw materials of all kinds, such as wheat, flour, coal, or iron, are good examples of this category. These are frequently called "circulating capital" as they must be completely transformed physically before they yield services. Wheat must be turned into flour, flour into bread, before they can yield satisfaction. The distinction between "fixed" and "circulating" capital, like other classifications of capital, is not absolutely clear, nor is it important that it should be so. Taken over a hundred miles, the gasoline in the tank of a car is clearly circulating capital and the tires are fixed capital, for although they wear a little their form is essentially unchanged. Over twenty thousand miles, however, the tires are as much circulating capital as the gasoline, for they have yielded up their form entirely. The tires as well as the gasoline have been transformed into "miles."

"Original Goods" and "Produced Goods"

Another distinction frequently made is that which involves the division of the total stock of goods into "original goods" and "produced goods." Original goods are those which have value but which have not been produced by man. Land is usually regarded as the main example. Minerals, coal, and other minable deposits may also be included. Produced goods, on the other hand, include such things as buildings, raw materials in storage, and equipment of all kinds, which have been created by the activity of man. This distinction is perhaps the most difficult of all to maintain clearly, yet it has played an important part in economic thought. According to Ricardo, for instance, "land" is the "original and indestructible properties of the soil." But in any given case it is difficult, and often impossible, to distinguish between what is "original and indestructible" and what is produced and mortal. It may be questioned, in view of what neglect and erosion can do, whether there are any properties of the soil which are indestructible, except perhaps in the ever-fertile river bottoms. It may be questioned also whether land is indeed not "produced." Is not the labor and investment of the pioneer whose sole reward is the ownership of land an act of "production" of land? It will not do to assume too hastily that there is a vital and clear distinction between "land" and "produced goods."

Nevertheless, the distinction has some foundation in reality. There is a difference between those goods which come into being as a result of conscious effort and those goods which are "windfalls," which are discovered accidentally. The prospector who finds a gold mine after twenty years of heartbreaking search has perhaps "produced" the gold mine as a result of his activity. The man who finds a gold mine by accident in his back yard has not "produced" it, for it has not come into being as a result of purposeful activity. The importance of this distinction rests in the fact that the supply of genuinely original goods is perfectly inelastic. The quantity of them which will be forthcoming depends in no way on their price. The probability of discovering the gold mine in the back yard, for instance, depends not at all on the price of gold. But the supply of "produced" goods will always have some degree of elasticity, over a sufficiently long period of time. If the price of gold is high, presumably more prospectors will be encouraged to pursue their labors, and therefore the probability of discovering gold is greater than it would be if the price were low.

A Classification Diagram

It will perhaps be helpful if these distinctions are shown in diagrammatic form, as in Fig. 47. We suppose first that all things in existence at a moment of time are spread out in the "field" of the paper. The thick black line then represents the "definition" of capital in the broadest sense as the total stock of things at a given moment having economic significance. The shape of the figure is of no importance; I have drawn it as a closed figure, however, to show that the number of things having economic significance is limited, whether the total universe is infinite or not. It is not always perfectly clear exactly where this boundary lies, but there will be agreement as to its general location. Things which are priced, are actually exchanged, or are offered for exchange are clearly within the boundary. Things which are potentially priceable or exchangeable probably should be in it. Things which may influence things which are exchangeable are more doubtfully included or excluded. Argument about the exact position of the boundary, however, does not invalidate the concept of a region. Within the region, therefore, we can distinguish subregions by drawing further boundaries. In the figure I have drawn four such subboundaries, each dividing the total region into two parts. The line *aa* separates the region into durable and nondurable goods, *bb* into business and household goods, *cc* into original and produced goods, *dd* into instru-

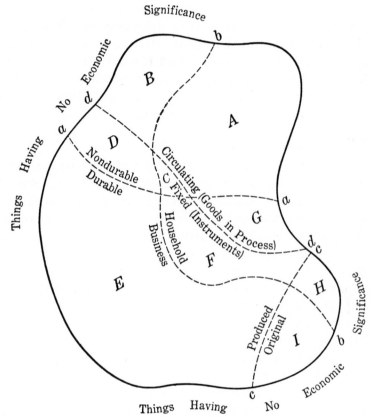

FIG. 47.   Classifications of Goods.

ments and goods in process. Clearly many other divisions could be made. With four such divisions the maximum number of classifications or "cells" in the figure would be 16, or 2^n where n is the number of twofold divisions. Thus all goods in the area "*A*" are nondurable, household, in process, and produced. Only nine of these cells are represented in the figure because of the way in which the dividing lines have been drawn. Thus *dd* and *aa* do not intersect *cc*. This reflects an assumption that all original goods are both durable and are instruments. The figure, however, is not intended to express the exact empirical relationships among these divisions, but merely to illustrate a principle.

THE INCOME CONCEPTS

The problems of classification and definition which we have examined briefly in the case of the capital concepts are present to an even greater extent in the case of the income concepts. The general distinction between the capital and income concepts is, of course, a very clear one, based as it is on a difference in dimensions. Any quantity which is measured without reference to a period or length of time, but only with reference to a date or instant of time, is a "stock" or capital quantity. Any quantity which is measured as so many units *per unit of time*—dollars per year, bushels per day, gallons per second—is a flow or income quantity.

Production, Consumption, Accumulation

Corresponding to the broad concept of physical capital as the total inventory of economically significant objects we have three "flow" concepts—production, consumption, and accumulation. The total inventory of stock may be compared to a gigantic "pool" of things. Into this pool new things are constantly pouring from the productive process. Bushels of wheat are added to it as they are grown, piglings are added to it as they are farrowed, pigs are added to it as piglings grow up, buildings are added to it as they are built, and so on. Out of this pool things are constantly draining away into consumption. Food is eaten; clothes are worn out; coal is burned up; machines grow obsolete, depreciate, and are scrapped. Production, therefore, is the process of adding to the total inventory of stock. Consumption is the process of subtracting from this total inventory. The difference between the rate of production and the rate of consumption may be called the rate of real accumulation; it is the rate at which the stock is increasing. If wheat is being produced at a rate of 100 million bushels a year and consumed at the rate of 90 million bushels a year, then the stocks of wheat are increasing at a rate of 10 million bushels a year.

The Problem of "Netness"

In the case of a single commodity there is not much difficulty in identifying production as the gross rate of addition to the total stock of the commodity, consumption as the gross subtraction from the total stock, and accumulation as the net additions. Even in this case, however, a certain difficulty may arise where some of the stock is used in the production of further stock. Thus scrap iron is used in the production of further iron—should the consumption of scrap iron in the furnaces be counted in the total of consumption, and the iron produced from these same furnaces be counted as production, or should the iron used in the furnaces be deducted from the iron produced by the furnaces to obtain a figure for "net" production? This problem of what constitute "netness" in production is one of the most troublesome in the theory of income. If the definitions are consistent the measure of *accumulation* is not affected, but the more "gross" our concept of production the larger will be the totals of both production and consumption. Thus in the case of iron, suppose that 100 million tons are produced at the furnaces, 25 million tons of scrap are consumed in the furnaces, and 10 million tons are lost or consumed by rust. We can if we like say that 100 million tons have been produced and 35 consumed, with a consequent addition of 65 to the total stock of iron, or we can say that *net* production was 75 million tons, net consumption 10 million, again with an accumulation of 65 million tons.

Depreciation and "User Cost"

In considering the problem of what should be included in the aggregate of all production and consumption, the problem of how "gross" our measures should be becomes an acute one. Wheat is made into flour, flour into bread; should we count the wheat and the flour and the bread, or should we count only the bread in the total of production, on the grounds that to include the wheat and the flour would result in "double counting," since the wheat is simply transformed into the flour and the flour into the bread? We may feel fairly sure of the answer in the above case, as the "net" concept here seems to be clearly more interesting and significant than the "gross" concept. The problem does not end at this point, however. Some machinery will have depreciated in the course of producing the flour and the bread. This depreciation is clearly part of total consumption, yet should it be deducted from the production of bread in order to arrive at an aggregate of *net* production? It would seem that if we deduct the flour we should also deduct the wear and tear on the machinery, for both are equally "real costs" of producing the bread—both represent a diminution in the stock of flour or machinery in order to increase the stock of bread. There is, however, a possible difference. If the bread were not made, the flour would presumably remain intact, short of damage in storage. If the bread were not made and the bakery stood idle, however, it would still depreciate, perhaps less—or perhaps even more—than it would if it were used, through the inexorable processes of physical and chemical decay, the "iron law" of moth and rust. Perhaps therefore we should deduct only that part of depreciation which can be clearly attributed to the production (called by Keynes "user cost") in defining our "net" product.

Subsistence as a "Cost"

The difficulty, however, does not even rest at this point. Production almost inevitably involves labor, and labor cannot be performed unless the worker is fed and clothed. Should therefore the "subsistence" of the worker be deducted from the total of production in order to arrive at a "net product"? Ricardo and the other classical economists certainly thought so. We do not count the food of the cow in the total net product, only the milk which that food produced by being, as it were, passed through the cow. Why, then, should we not also deduct the food of the stockman and the milker from the gross product, as this equally goes to produce the energy which is just as necessary as the feed in the production of the final product? At this point, however, the modern economist generally revolts: in a democratic society we cannot lump together the "laboring poor and the laboring cattle" as Adam Smith did, and regard the subsistence of both as simply a "real cost" which must be deducted from the final product in order to arrive at the true net product. Sentiment apart, however, there is much to be said in logic for the classical point of view.

Accumulation Concept Not Affected by "Netness" of Income

The above concepts are illustrated in Fig. 48. Suppose that the vertical distance AC measures the *gross production* of a commodity, say flour—that is, the total number of units of flour created during a given period of time, say a year. AD represents the gross consumption of flour—that is, the total number of units of flour destroyed, by any method and for any purpose, during the same period of time. DC then represents the accumulation of flour, or the net increase in the stock of flour during the same period. If consumption exceeds production DC will, of course, be negative, indicating a decumulation or diminution in the total stock of flour. Now we suppose that a certain amount of the consumption of flour, AE, is consumed in the production of other things (or of flour itself). EC is then the net production of flour, ED the net consumption. DC still represents the amount of flour accumulated. It is clear that DC is equal to the difference between net production and net consumption, no matter where we place the point E. For different purposes we may wish to place the point E at different levels, say E_1, E_2, etc.

Goods of Zero Length of Life

If now we wish to get a picture of the aggregate production-consumption-accumulation patterns, in real terms, we need to visualize a figure like Fig. 48 for *every* commodity. For every commodity we can postulate a gross addition to stocks (gross production), a gross subtraction (gross consumption), and various definitions of net production and consumption, depending on our definition of "consumption for further production." We may find some items which seem at first sight difficult to fit into this picture, but we shall find nothing in economic

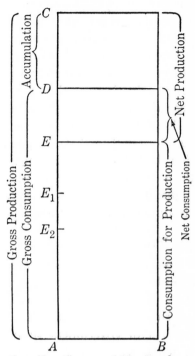

FIG. 48.   Gross and Net Product.

life which is basically inconsistent with it. Thus there are some commodities (services) which have so short a length of life that we can hardly regard them as having any "stocks" at all. Production and consumption in this case occur simultaneously, and it seems a little odd to regard production as the act of adding to zero stocks, an addition which is immediately subtracted in consumption. Nevertheless by so regarding the production of services we can fit the concept into the general pattern without any distortion of reality.

Services and "Psychic Capital"

From one point of view, indeed, it can be argued that all things which we regard as services involve the creation of capital. Thus a haircut involves the creation of a capital good—the barbered head—which inexorably depreciates as the days go by and must be replaced after a period suitable to the profession of the subject. The growth of a discommodity, whether it is unwanted hair or unwanted grass, is as much depreciation as the decline of a commodity. Even in the case of services where the embodiment is not apparent to the senses we can suppose that "psychic capital" is created which also depreciates and eventually has to be replaced by another act of production. Thus attendance at an opera produces a "psychic good" which might be called "just having heard an opera." As long as this psychological state is in good repair we feel no urge to go to another opera. The state, however, decays, and after a period we find ourselves in the state of "not having been to the opera for a long time," whereupon we go to hear another opera and restore the original state of agreeable musical fullness. It is pleasant to speculate whether the memory of a bad opera lasts longer than that of a good one; however that may be, it is clear that the rate of depreciation varies greatly from person to person. For the ardent fan the state of "just having been to the opera" decays overnight; in another the state may be kept in repair quite adequately by an annual visit to the Metropolitan.

The "Product" of Government

Some difficult problems are presented in the field of income concepts by government activity, mainly because the "product" of government activity in real terms is difficult to measure, and cannot be measured directly, and also because it is difficult to say how the product of government should be apportioned among the various beneficiaries. At one extreme the cost of government might be regarded as a sort of "overhead" of society at large, providing something of the framework within which the productive process is carried on, but not in itself constituting a product. On this assumption the whole cost of government would be deducted from the gross product in order to calculate a net product. At the other extreme one might assume that government produced an intangible but real product which was apportioned among the people in proportion to the taxes paid. This assumed that corresponding to the flow of taxes to government there is a flow of some invisible real product for which the taxes are payment. Neither of these extreme assumptions is at all satisfactory, and in the practice of national income accounting uneasy compromises must be made between them.

AGGREGATES OF CIRCULATION AND EXCHANGE

The concepts of production, consumption, and accumulation are "flow" or income concepts in the sense that they are measured in units per unit of time. There are however other important "flow" concepts in economics which correspond more closely perhaps to the physical analogy of a stream. These are the flows of circulation or exchange, and also of geographical movement. So many "bushels of wheat per year" might refer not only to quantities produced, consumed, or accumulated; it might also refer to quantities flowing across a boundary, or between two points, or between two owners or sets of owners, or from farms to warehouses. Literal streams of wheat flow from the wheat fields to the cities; streams of automobiles flow from Detroit to the ends of the earth. These flows constitute the total volume of physical *trade*. Against them flow corresponding "streams" of means of payment (money). Even though the money flows may not correspond geographically to the flows of commodities, they always consist of transfers of money per unit of time between economic organisms, opposite in direction to the flows of the things for which money is paid.

Distinction Between Income and Exchange Concepts

For all that they have the same economic dimensions there is a clear and vital distinction between the production, consumption, and accumulation concepts on the one hand and the trade and money flows concepts on the other, and much confusion has been caused in economics by a failure to keep this distinction in mind. Production and consumption measure the creation and destruction of things; trade and exchange measure the extent to which existing things are shuffled around among owners or among regions. In exchange no physical asset is either produced or consumed, but assets shift owners. A *transfer* is a simple shift of ownership from one economic organism to another, such as a gift. An exchange is two transfers in opposite directions between the same two parties. Likewise a money transfer, or *payment,* involves no creation or destruction of money, but simply a shift in its ownership. Every payment therefore is both an expenditure and a receipt—an expenditure to the account out of which money is transferred, and at the same time a receipt to the account into which the money is transferred.

Confusion arises among these concepts because a money payment in purchase of a household good measures three things: the amount of the money payment itself, the *value* of the goods for which the money was paid, and the value of the consumption of these goods when they are consumed. For purposes of analysis, however, these three things must be kept distinct. Thus even when somebody buys and eats a ten-cent ice cream three things have happened: (1) a transfer of money (ten cents) from the buyer to the seller, (2) a transfer of ten cents' worth of ice cream from the seller to the buyer, (3) the consumption of ten cents' worth of his assets (ice cream) by the buyer. The first two items constitute an exchange. If they are included in aggregates they will be in aggregates of trade or of money flows. The last item is part of consumption, and will be included in the aggregate of consumption.

Exactly similar considerations apply to the important distinction between the *earning* of income and the *receipt* of money. The receipt of a pay check is not the earning of income, but is again an exchange, though not such an obvious one as the exchanges involved in the purchase of consumer goods. We go to the pay office possessed of a claim on our employer for, say, $100. We return with a check which is essentially a claim on a bank for $100. In the earning and receipt of wages, therefore, three distinct items or operations are again present. The *earning* of income is the accumulation of a claim against the employer as labor is performed. When wages are paid this wage claim is given up to the employer. Even though nothing physical changes hands it is generally understood that the payment of wages constitutes a relinquishment of the wage claim. Then in return for the relinquishment of the wage claim the employer pays the worker an equivalent sum in money. These distinctions may seem almost trivial; their importance, however, especially when the individual items are aggregated, will become clearer in later chapters.

Aggregates of Prices and Valuation Coefficients

Just as there is a problem of the definition and classification of aggregates of stocks or of flows of goods, so there is also a problem—fortunately fairly simple—in defining and classifying aggregates of prices. A price is the ratio of a number of monetary units (e.g., dollars) to a related quantity of some physical good. There are two kinds of price ratios which are significant in economics. The most obvious is the ratio of exchange—i.e., the ratio of the amount of money paid for something in an actual transaction to the amount of goods or other assets paid for by the money. Thus if somebody buys 20 tons of wheat for $40, the price of wheat in the transaction is $\dfrac{\$40}{20 \text{ tons}}$, or $2 per ton. Prices as quoted and recorded in statistics frequently represent not ratios of exchange in actual exchanges but *offers* to sell or to buy at the ratios quoted. Thus a price tag in a store is equivalent to an offer to exchange the goods in question at the ratio quoted. Price ratios also exist, however, which are neither descriptive of actual exchanges nor of offers to trade. These ratios may be described as *valua-*

tion coefficients. Valuation is the process whereby we calculate the *equivalent* in some measure of value of a physical quantity of the valued objects. The valuation coefficient then is the ratio between the *value* of something, expressed in units of the measure of value— "dollars" again are an example—and the *quantity,* expressed in some physical terms, of the thing which is valued. Thus in compiling a list of personal assets we might value two carpets at $400. The $400 is simply a figure expressing the equivalent of the carpets in the measure of value. It does not represent an offer to sell, or a ratio of actual exchange. The valuation coefficient would be $200 per carpet.

The problem of defining and measuring price *levels* will be discussed in the following chapter. Here, however, it should be observed that every price level refers to some specific aggregate of prices or valuation coefficients. Within the total universe of prices various significant classifications can be made, some of which may overlap, just as in the case of the classification of the stock of goods. One important classification, for instance, is into wholesale and retail prices—i.e., according to the stage in the process of production at which the prices are measured.

It should be observed that exchange ratios, actual or potential, always refer to actual or potential *flows;* valuation coefficients generally refer to *stocks.* In general valuation coefficients are based in some way or another on exchange ratios, past, present, or future. Thus a valuation may be made by recording the original exchange ratio when the valued article last participated in an exchange (was bought) and making some allowance for depreciation (or even appreciation) since that exchange. Or it may be made by observing the actual exchange ratios of similar objects which are being exchanged at the moment. Or it may be made by noting the ratio at which the object will be exchanged at a future date (say, in the case of a bond) and making some allowance (discounting) for the futurity of the exchange. In any case it is clear that no basis would be present for valuation unless there was in continuing existence a system of actual exchanges. This gives the price aggregates of actual exchanges a peculiar importance.

QUESTIONS AND EXERCISES

1. Each of the "cells" of Fig. 47 represents a fourfold classification of capital. Write out the exact classification corresponding to each cell. How many possible classifications are missing from the figure? What are they? Draw a figure in which all the possible classifications based on the divisions of Fig. 47 are included. Draw a figure which shows all possible classifications based on *five* twofold divisions.

2. What are the dimensions, in terms of the length-mass-time system, of the following physical quantities: (a) atmospheric pressure, (b) rainfall, (c) stream flow, (d) density.

3. What are the dimensions, in terms of the commodity-money-time-length system, of the following economic quantities: (a) gold reserves, (b) depreciation of capital, (c) yield of crops per acre, (d) density of population, (e) elasticity of demand, (f) a specific tax, (g) an ad valorem tax. (Note: in determining the dimensions of any quantity, always start by investigating the nature of the unit in which it is measured.)

4. List the economic quantities which have the following dimensions:

(a) $\dfrac{\text{Commodity I}}{\text{Commodity II}}$ (b) $\dfrac{\text{Money}}{\text{Length}}$ (c) $\dfrac{\text{Money}}{\text{Time}}$

5. Suppose that it takes 10 bushels of wheat to produce 8 bags of flour, and that 1 bag of flour produces 30 loaves of bread. Suppose that in a given time period gross production is 120 bushels of wheat, 88 bags of flour, and 2100 loaves of bread. Net consumption (that is, consumption not resulting in further production) is 5 bushels of wheat, no flour, and 2100 loaves of bread. What is the net production, the gross consumption, and the total accumulation of each of the three commodities? Show that the accumulation can be expressed either as the difference between gross production and gross consumption, or as the difference between net production and net consumption in each case.

CHAPTER 14

THE MEASUREMENT OF ECONOMIC AGGREGATES

In the previous chapter we discussed the definition and classification of economic aggregates. We did not attempt to reduce them to any common measure, but thought of them essentially as "lists" or inventories of many different heterogeneous items, conforming to some definition but not otherwise having much in common. The problem of the measurement of aggregates resolves itself mainly into the question of how to express a heterogeneous list of items as a single number or quantity.

In ordinary accounting this is done by valuing each item of the heterogeneous list in terms of a monetary unit such as the dollar. The concepts and procedures of accounting are of such importance in understanding the measurement of economic aggregates, especially in what is called "national income accounting" (see the appendix to this chapter), that it will be advisable at this point to devote some space to the elementary concepts. Readers who are familiar with accounting principles may wish therefore to continue the argument at page 270; for the sake of completeness, however, some exposition of the basic accounting concepts is necessary.

The Balance Sheet

At the heart of accounting procedures is the statement known as the "balance sheet" or "position statement." In its primary form this is simply an aggregate or inventory of items of value (assets) pertaining to some specific organization or group of organizations. It is an aggregate of assets defined by their relevance to the organization for which the accounts are made. These assets may be both positive or negative: positive assets are items of value over which the organization has certain rights of use, control, and exchange; negative assets (liabilities) represent claims which others have against the organization, or which represent deductions of some kind from the positive assets.

Net Worth

If now a sum of the positive and negative items is to be calculated, in order to express the total net position of the organization, the various items must be capable of measurement in some common unit of value, such as the dollar. If all the items can be so valued the value of the positive and negative assets can be summed, and the algebraic sum is called the *net worth*. The net worth, that is to say, is the sum of the positive assets, less the sum of the negative assets or liabilities; it is the net value of all the assets which can be related to the organization. Ordinarily these aggregates are expressed in the form of a balance sheet, in which the positive assets are listed on one side (the left-hand side in American convention) and the liabilities and the net worth are listed on the other side. As the net worth (N) by definition is the sum of the positive assets (A) less the sum of the liabilities (L), or $N = A - L$, the sum of the positive assets must be equal to the sum of the liabilities plus the net worth, or $A = N + L$. The two sides of the table therefore have an equal sum—that is, the balance sheet "balances."

Equities

In American practice the liabilities and net worth are called "equities." They represent the distribution of claims on the total of positive assets between those claimants who are in some sense "outside" the organization, whose claims are liabilities, and those claimaints who are "inside" the organization, whose claims are net worth. The distinction between liabilities and net worth is not always perfectly clear, as claimants which for some purposes might be regarded as "outside" the organization, such as bondholders, for other purposes (for example, in financial reorganization) might well be regarded as "insiders." By this time, however, we should have realized that lack of clarity in a distinction in no way detracts from its importance.

The Personal Balance Sheet

We may illustrate these concepts first with reference to a personal balance sheet. Suppose, for instance, that John Doe owns houses and land worth $10,000, a car worth $500, personal effects (furniture, clothes, etc.) worth $1000, corporation bonds worth $5000, a promissory note from Mr. Smith worth $500, an account receivable for $100 for services rendered to Mr. Robinson, and cash worth $400. These things are his *assets*. He may also, however, have certain claims against him called *liabilities*. Suppose he has debts consisting of a mortgage with $6000 outstanding, accounts payable to various companies amounting to $300, a promissory note to Mr. Brown for $100, and a tax bill for $200. With this information we can calculate his "net worth" by the process of adding up the values of all his assets and subtracting from this total the sum of the liabilities or claims against him. In this case the total of his assets is $17,500. The total of his liabilities is $6600. His "net worth," therefore, is $17,500 − $6600, or $10,900. The net worth may be visualized as the sum which would be left to his estate if it were liquidated—i.e., if all his assets were turned into cash and all the claims against him settled.

Claims

The balance sheet in Table 17 gives a classification of these assets and equities together into five groups. These are not necessarily the

TABLE 17. Balance Sheet

John Doe

Assets		*Equities*	
(a) Things		(d) Liabilities (claims)	
Houses and land	$10,000	Mortgage	$ 6,000
Car	500	Accounts payable	300
Personal effects	1,000	Notes payable	100
		Taxes payable	200
(b) Claims			
Bonds	5,000	(e) Net Worth	10,900
Promissory note	500		
Account receivable	100		
(c) Cash	400		
Total	17,500	Total	17,500

classifications usually made by the accountant, for we are here discussing economic principle rather than accounting practice. We divide assets into three groups: (a) things, (b) claims, and (c) cash. "Things" are those items of property the value of which enters into no other balance sheet than the one in which they figure. Cash (from which we exclude bank notes and deposits) also enters into no other balance sheet than the one in which it figures. Claims, however, have the property of appearing on two balance sheets. They appear as an asset on the balance sheet of the person who makes the claim and as a liability on the balance sheet of the person against whom the claim is made.

In the example, for instance, one of John Doe's assets is a $500 promissory note receivable from Mr. Smith. This promissory note, therefore, represents a $500 liability—a note payable to John Doe—on the balance sheet of Mr. Smith. Similarly, the account receivable from Mr. Robinson becomes an account payable to John Doe on the balance sheet of Mr. Robinson. All the items under (b) on the assets side of Table 17 will therefore be found on the liabilities side of other balance sheets, and all the items under (d) on the liabilities side will be found on the assets side of other balance sheets.

The Summation of Balance Sheets

Imagine a society in which all property is held by individuals, and all balance sheets are individual balance sheets. If *all* the balance sheets of this society were collected and all the asset items were listed on one side of an enormous sheet and all the equity items on the other side, the "claims" on the asset side and the "claims" (liabilities) on the equities side would exactly cancel out. Each claim would be represented in two places on this "total balance sheet"—once on the assets side and once on the liabilities side—for each claim is the asset of one person and the liability of another. The sum of the (a) and (c) items on the assets side would therefore be equal to the sum of the (e) items on the equities side. That is, the total value of the things and cash held by the society would be equal to the total of all individual capital —i.e., to the total net worth of the society.

The Balance Sheet of a Firm

The existence of firms does not change this conclusion. The balance sheet of a firm does not differ essentially from the balance sheet of an individual. Its assets consist of "things," "claims," and "cash." Its equities likewise consist of two parts, one corresponding to the liabilities, called the "contractual claims," and the other corresponding to the "net worth," called the "residual claim." Such things as bonds, accounts payable, notes payable, interest due, wage claims, and so on, are "contractual" claims, as they represent claims for *definite* sums. The amount by which the total value of the assets exceeds the total value of the contractual claims is the total of "residual claims." In the case of a private business the residual claim is the value of the business to the owner. It will appear as an asset in the owner's personal balance sheet. In the case of a partnership the residual claim is divided among the partners according to some prearranged plan. If, for instance, a firm has two equal partners and a total residual claim of $100,000, each partner will count his property in the business as a $50,000 asset in his personal balance sheet.

In the case of a corporation the residual claim represents the total book value of the stock of the corporation.[1] Suppose a corporation has 1000 shares of stock and a total residual claim of $1,200,000. The book value of each share is one-thousandth part of the total residual claim, or $1200. Corresponding to this claim against the corporation there are $1,200,000 in assets in the personal balance sheets of all the stockholders. In each case it is seen, then, that *all* the items on the equities side of the balance sheet of a firm are represented as assets in the balance sheets of other firms or individuals. This is what we should expect, as a firm is only a vehicle of ownership. Ultimately, the real ownership of all the "things" possessed by a society must be found in individual persons. So the existence of firms does not invalidate our conclusion that the total value of the goods and cash held by a society should be equal to the total value of the capitals of the individuals of that society.

Insolvency and Bankruptcy

When the total of liabilities, or contractual claims against a firm, is greater than the total of assets of all kinds the firm is said to be "insolvent." The "net worth" in this case is zero, or may even be considered negative if the net worth is defined as the difference between assets and liabilities. A firm may be insolvent for a considerable period, however, without going out of existence, as long as all its creditors do not demand payment. It is possible for a firm to meet its *current* obligations for a time, although it could not possibly meet all its obligations. When the insolvency of a firm is so manifest, however, that its creditors have given up hope of ever seeing it restored to solvency, the firm is *bankrupted.* Its existence as an entity ceases, al-

[1] In a corporation the "residual claim" is usually divided into three parts. One part is called the "capital stock" and represents the *nominal* value of the stock of the corporation. Another part is called the "surplus" and represents that part of the excess of the total residual claim over the nominal value of the stock which may be regarded as permanent. The third part is called "undivided profits" and represents that part of the excess of the total residual claim over the nominal value of the stock which is *not* regarded as permanent. Suppose that in the example in the text the total residual claim of $1,200,000 were divided as follows: capital stock, $1,000,000; surplus, $150,000; undivided profits, $50,000. This would mean that the total equity of the shareholders was $1,200,000. The corporation would expect to reduce this by $50,000 in the near future by declaring a dividend—i.e., by taking $50,000 in cash from its assets and distributing it among the shareholders, thus reducing the assets by $50,000 and also therefore reducing the residual claim by $50,000. The "permanent" equity of the stockholders is then divided, in the accounts though not in any "real" sense, into two parts: one representing the nominal value of the capital stock, the other the "increase" or "surplus" of the permanent equity over this nominal value.

though it may be resurrected in a new form by the process known as "reorganization." In a complete bankruptcy the assets are liquidated, i.e., sold and converted into cash, and the creditors receive a portion of their claims according to some principle of distribution. Usually some claims—e.g., taxes—have to be paid in full. Then the remainder is distributed in proportion to the original claim of each creditor.

Suppose, in the case of John Doe, whose balance sheet appears on page 259, that a fire destroys his uninsured property to the value of $11,700. He will then be insolvent, as his assets have declined in total value by a sum greater than his net worth ($10,900). His creditors may not, in that case, bankrupt him, for he still has an asset not reckoned in the account—his body—and they may hope that in time he will be able to recover his financial solvency once more. If, however, he is bankrupted, his assets will be liquidated—realizing, if their valuations on the balance sheet are correct, a sum of $5800 ($17,500 − $11,700). Out of this we may suppose that $200 must be paid for taxes, which have a prior claim. The remaining $5600 will then be divided among his creditors in proportion to their claims. The total of such claims is $6400. Each creditor, therefore, will get $56/64$, or $7/8$, of his claim.

The Difficulties of Valuation

It must not be thought that the valuation of the "things" possessed by a society is a simple, easy, or even certain process. There are many undoubtedly valuable things that are not ordinarily valued at all. The human body is the prime example. In a slave society it is evident that the human body is as much part of the "inventory of stock" as, shall we say, domestic cattle, and the value of human bodies is entered into the balance sheets of their owners. In a free society where each man possesses his own body it is not customary to put a valuation on it or to enter such a valuation on the balance sheet. In strict logic, however, our accounting will not be satisfactory without this, and indeed some of the ills of our present society can be attributed to the fact that our system of accounting makes no allowances for the changing value of our bodies. Perhaps the reason for our careless personal accounting is that the only time we are compelled to make an exact reckoning of a personal estate is immediately following its owner's demise, in which case his person is a liability to the estate rather than an asset. There is, however, a slowly growing recognition that a value should be placed on the human body in accounting. When a concern insures the lives of important members of its personnel, it is making a partial valuation of their "bodies." There are also many other things which are valuable but on which we do not easily place dollar valuation. These "things" do not have to be material and tangible. A patent or a copyright, for instance, is an asset of its owner, but is not a liability of any other person.

All Valuations a Matter of Estimate

The difficulties of valuation, however, extend far beyond the case of things which are not usually valued. Even those values which normally figure on balance sheets are calculated by a process of estimate according to certain rather arbitrary principles. We cannot at this point go into the theoretical and practical problems connected with valuation, for these would require a volume in themselves. We have noted in the previous chapter that dollar values are derived from physical quantities of assets by multiplying the physical quantity by a price or valuation coefficient. Thus the value of 100 bushels of wheat at $2 per bushel is 100 × $2, or $200. In balance sheet valuations the values are all strictly derived from valuation coefficients rather than from exchange ratios, though as we have seen (page 255) all valuation coefficients are ultimately derived from the exchange ratios, past, present, or future.

It should be observed that in spite of the uncertainty which surrounds many estimations of the dollar value of assets, the principle of the cancellation of claims still holds. No matter how inaccurate the estimates of the value of assets, the total capital of a society will always be equal to the estimated value of the things and the cash which it possesses. Any error in valuing assets will be reflected in a like error in the net worth. If, for instance, in Table 17 the "true value" of John Doe's houses and land were $8000 instead of $10,000, his net worth would have a true value of $8900 instead of $10,900. Whatever change is made in any of the asset items is reflected in an equal change in the net worth.

Income Accounts and Asset Transfers

The balance sheet is essentially an aggregate of capital, or "stock." It is also necessary, however, both for purposes of the individual business and for society as a whole, to aggregate incomes. The income concept developed in the previous chapter can be applied here to the interpretation of the profit-and-loss statement, or income account, in which is calculated the net income of an organization in a given time period—a year or a quarter.

All the *events* of which an accounting system takes cognizance can be recorded as *changes* in the balance sheet. These changes are of several kinds. First there are *asset transfers*—a diminution in one asset with a corresponding increase in another. Asset transfers can result from sales, purchases, miscellaneous exchanges, or production transformations. Thus a sale of goods results in a decline in the inventory of goods item and an increase in the cash item. Purchase of goods similarly results in a decline in cash and a rise in inventory. Exchanges need not involve money—there may be barter exchanges of goods for goods, or securities for securities. Finally assets are transformed in the process of production. When the baker bakes bread his stock of flour and other ingredients diminishes and his stock of bread rises.

A second type of balance sheet change recording an event is a simultaneous change in both assets and liabilities. When labor is employed the product of the work usually appears as an asset somewhere, and the wage claim appears as a liability. When wages are paid the wage claim is extinguished, and cash diminishes in equal amount on the other side of the balance sheet. The combined activity of employing a man and paying him a wage therefore resolves itself into an asset transfer, or a set of asset transfers. In the employer's balance sheet it shows itself in a diminution of cash, also in a diminution in raw materials or other items, and an increase in the goods which are the product of the work. Thus suppose a man is paid $60 a week to turn yarn into cloth. Suppose that he uses up $100 worth of yarn and $20 worth of miscellaneous assets (machines, etc.). The *cost* of the cloth produced is then the sum of all the diminutions in assets which its production entailed, or $180. If the cloth is valued in the balance sheet at cost, the result of the week's activity is a simple asset transfer —an increase of $180 in the "cloth" item and a diminution of $180 in the cash, yarn, and other items taken together.

If we regard liabilities as negative assets, then simultaneous increases or decreases in assets and liabilities together can also be regarded as asset transfers, and the concept of an asset transfer extended to include all those changes in the balance sheet which do not change the net worth, and which consist either of equal positive and negative changes in assets, equal positive and negative changes in liabilities, or equal positive *or* negative changes in assets *and* liabilities. Thus if some assets increase by $1000 while other assets decrease by $1000, *or* if some liabilities increase by $1000 while other liabilities decrease by $1000, *or* if some assets increase by $1000 and some liabilities increase by $1000, *or* if some assets decrease by $1000 and some liabilities decrease by $1000, no change has taken place in the net total of assets and liabilities, or net worth.

Revaluations of Assets

There is, however, another kind of change possible in the balance sheet which involves *changes* in net worth. For net worth to change there must be a *revaluation* of assets. Suppose, for instance, in the above example, that the cloth, which is valued in the books at its "cost" of $180, were sold for $200. This transaction would be reflected in the balance sheet of the firm by a diminution of the inventory item to the extent of $180, and an increase in the cash item by $200. The transaction results therefore not only in a *transfer* of assets from one category to another, but an increase in the net worth. We can regard the transaction as consisting of two parts—a *revaluation* of the assets at the moment of sale, increasing the value of the inventory of cloth from $180 to $200, and an asset transfer consisting of the shifting of $200 worth of assets from cloth into cash. The distinction is an important one, even though in practice the asset transfer and the revaluation seem to be almost indistinguishably part of a single operation, because it is only by asset (or liability) *revaluations* that net worth can be increased. Although sales in ordinary accounting practice are probably the most important source of these revaluations, they can take place in other ways. Thus depreciation represents a revaluation of fixed capital to make allowance for its physical decay, or perhaps obsolescence. Depreciation therefore represents a decline in the value placed in certain assets, with a corresponding decline in net worth.

Net Income as the Increase in Net Worth, Plus Withdrawals

We now have a clue to the essential nature of the making of profit, or net income. Net income is the increase in net worth in the given period, not counting withdrawals from net worth such as dividends. Net income can be defined therefore as the amount by which net worth would have been increased had there been no withdrawals from it, or as the sum of the actual increase in net worth and actual withdrawals from it. The process of earning income, therefore, is the process of increasing net worth by manipulating the asset structure through exchange and production in such a way that upward revaluations of assets are justified. The commonest source of such justifiable revaluations is in the sale of assets above cost, as we have noted above. The "profit and loss" or income statement, then, can be interpreted essentially as a statement, first, of the value of the revalued assets (sales or revenues); second, of the cost or expense of producing these assets, that is, the sum of the *diminutions* in assets which were involved in obtaining the sales or revenues recorded; and third, the difference between these two quantities, which is the net income. Thus our example of cloth weaving might be placed in tabular form as follows:

TABLE 18. Income Statement

Sales (Revenues)	$200	Expenses (Cost)	
		Labor	$ 60
		Materials	100
		Other	20
		Total expenses	180
		Net income	20
Total	$200	Total	$200

Revaluation of Assets Produces Income

Under usual accounting procedures any *revaluation* of assets will be reflected in income. A rise in the value of existing assets will be recorded as positive income; a fall as negative income—that is, as a subtraction from income. Many difficult questions in accounting and in economic theory arise because of this identity between revaluation and income, for there are some items of revaluation which do not seem properly to fall in the same classification as others.

Inventory Valuation

A good example of this problem is the controversy between two systems of inventory valuation, known as the "Last in, first out" method (LIFO) and the "First in, first out" method (FIFO) (See page 857). Inventory valuation is necessary for two purposes—for showing the value of goods in stock in the balance sheet, and for showing the change in the value of inventory between the opening and closing dates of the income period. Thus suppose that in the previous example $150 worth of the cloth produced was sold, and the remainder remained in stock, this being an addition to the total inventory of cloth. It would clearly be misleading to record in the income statement only sales, for against the expenses recorded there is not only the increase in cash of $150 but also an increase in cloth. The question is how should this increase in cloth be valued? It might, of course, be valued at the current selling price of cloth, in which case the value of the sold cloth and of the unsold cloth would still be $200, and it would make no difference to the net income whether the cloth was sold or not. Current accounting practice does not favor this procedure. Generally inventories are valued at cost, or at "cost or market, whichever is the lower." If the price structure and the techniques of production do not change there is no ambiguity in cost. Thus in the above example the cost of the cloth was $180, so that the cost of a quarter of it would be $45, and the income statement would look like Table 19.

TABLE 19. Income Statement (with Inventory)

Sales	$150	Expenses	$180
Increase in stock	45	Net income	15
	$195		$195

"FIFO." Suppose, however, that wages and the price of yarn have risen during the income period, so that the cost of cloth has been rising. The inventory consists of cloth of different ages, and therefore of different costs. The most obvious procedure is to take the cost of the most recently completed items of stock. This assumes in effect that those items which were sold were the oldest items in the existing stock. This is the FIFO method. This method has many advantages. It has one important disadvantage, however, that in times of rising prices the rise in the value of the stock of goods is reflected in an increased net income figure, and falling prices likewise lead to a decrease in the net income figure. These changes in recorded income are in some sense spurious, or at least are a different kind of income from that which is generated by production. Thus suppose that in the previous example the cost of cloth has risen so rapidly that at the end of the income period it was double the average value during the period. The value of the increase in stock would then be $90, and the statement would look like Table 20. The increase in the value of the existing

TABLE 20. Income Statement in a Period of Rising Prices and Costs

Sales	$150	Expense	$180
Increase in stock	90	Net income	60
	$240		$240

stock has inflated the net income figure considerably. On the other hand, suppose that the cost of cloth had fallen so sharply that at the end of the period it was only half what it had averaged during the period. The income statement would look like Table 21. In this case the net income has been wiped out altogether and turned into a loss.

"LIFO." In all three cases (Tables 20, 21, and 22) the *physical* events are identical; the changes in the physical items in the balance

sheet are identical. The difference in results arises from differences in methods of valuation. It is the feeling that accounting should in some sense give a single measure of the results of these complex changes in the *physical* balance sheet that has led to the introduction of the LIFO method of inventory valuation. By this method the stock is valued at the prices of the *earliest* items recorded. This means in effect

TABLE 21.   Income Statement in a Period of Falling Prices and Costs

Sales	$150	Expense	$180
Increase in stock	22.50	Net income	−7.50
	$172.50		$172.50

that the inventory is valued at constant prices, and hence its value does not reflect the shifts in the price structure. Thus suppose in the above example the increase in stock was 50 yards, and that the cost of the first cloth made by the enterprise was 80 cents per yard. The change in inventory would be recorded as $40, no matter what the current cost or price. This method has the disadvantage that the value of inventory as recorded in the balance sheet is unrelated to current values, and especially in times of inflation or deflation becomes a quite misleading figure. It does, however, get rid of the distortions in the income statement which are the result of fluctuating price and cost levels.

Capital Gains from Inflation

Similar problems arise in the valuation of all assets. Thus suppose a man buys a house for $10,000 and sells it some years later for $15,000. Does the $5000 difference represent "income"—neglecting maintenance and carrying costs? In terms of conventional accounting it does: if the house is carried on his books at $10,000 and he gets $15,000 for it, there is a rise in his net worth of $5000 as a result of the transaction; as we have seen, it is this rise in net worth which constitutes income. If, however, he has to buy another house with the money he may find—as a good many people in the 1940's did find—that the "income" is somewhat illusory; if all houses have risen in about the same proportion, he will have to spend the $15,000 in buying a house just about as good as the one he sold. Measured in terms of houses, then, his net worth has not increased at all—the increase in dollars is merely a reflection of the fact that the value of the dollar has declined, and that $15,000 at the later date represents the same quantity of "house" or real purchasing power as $10,000 at the earlier date. The apparent $5000 income is not all illusion, however, as the man is clearly better off than he would have been had he *not* bought his first house, but had held on to his $10,000 in the form of cash or bonds. If he had done this his net worth in terms of houses would have been only two-thirds as great at the later date than it would have been had he bought the house.

Are Capital Gains Income?

The rise or fall in the value of existing assets because of changes in their price, or valuation ratio, may best be called capital gains and losses, following the terminology of the United States income tax. From the point of view of society as a whole they should clearly not be included in income, as they do not represent any value of physical or "real" production. From the point of view of individuals, however, they represent *relative* shifts in the distribution of income: a rise in prices makes those who hold real goods better off at the expense of those who hold money and bonds, and a fall in prices does the opposite. In individual accounting, therefore, there is something to be said for retaining capital gains and losses, if not directly in the income category, at least as a kind of porch or appendix. The United States income tax recognizes the anomalous position of capital gains and losses by taxing them at a different rate from "ordinary" income.

"Real" Capital Gains and Losses

Capital gains and losses which are due to price changes should be distinguished sharply from those gains and losses which are due to unexpected additions to, or subtractions from, the stock of physical capital. If an uninsured house burns down there is a loss to the owner, reflected in a decline in his net worth, which should probably be treated in a different category from items of ordinary cost or consumption. Even if the house is insured there is a loss to society, represented by a decline in the net worth of the insurance company. If there were no fires, however, there would be no insurance companies, so we face the paradox that over society at large losses by fire look much more like items of regular cost or consumption than they do for the individual. Similar problems arise on the other side of the ledger; for instance, when oil fields are discovered, should the value of the discoveries count as income, or should it be placed in a special category? There is no clear answer to these questions; it is evident that we are dealing here, as usual, with an aggregate ("income") which does not have perfectly clear edges.

Accounting and Statistics

Just as accounting runs into acute difficulties when the value of its basic unit (e.g., the dollar) changes, so do all statistical measurements of aggregate quantities. The basic problem of accounting is that of reducing a heterogeneous mass of data to a single figure or quantity. The problem in itself is theoretically insoluble, as a heterogeneous mass of data cannot be completely represented by a single figure. Nevertheless the procedures of the accountant do produce *information*—that is, we seem to know more about the data after we have performed these operations than we did before. Basically, therefore, accounting and statistics have the same broad end—to simplify a complex mass of data to the point where more information is obtained about it than could be obtained by the presentation of the data itself. It may be that the time is almost ripe for a thorough overhauling of both accounting and statistical procedures, perhaps even for a marriage of accounting and statistics by a theory of information. Both accounting and statistical procedures grow up by accretion and tradition, and a thorough review based on the question, What is it we really want to *know*, and why? might have startling results. Such, however, is not the task of this work, and this chapter may profitably be concluded by a brief survey of the attempts made by statisticians to come to grips with the problem of the measurement and description of aggregates.

Measurement of Aggregates of Goods

The first problem is how to measure the physical quantity of some heterogeneous aggregate—which may be an aggregate of stocks, as in the balance sheet, or an aggregate of flows, as in the income statement. We cannot obtain such a measure by simply adding the various quantities in the inventory, for the numbers representing these quantities are quite arbitrary, depending on the size of the unit of measurement. Thus an identical quantity of wheat may be represented by the number 1 if measured in short tons, 2000 if measured in pounds, 32,000 if measured in ounces, and so on. The incommensurability of a stock of various goods may be seen clearly if we ask ourselves the question, "Add a grand piano to the total stock and take away a cow; has the total stock increased or decreased?" There is clearly no way of answering this question unless we have some measure of assessing the *significance* or "value" of the various items in the inventory. If a grand piano is "equivalent" in some way to three cows, then adding a grand piano and subtracting a cow is clearly equivalent to adding two cows,

or two-thirds of a piano. If, however, a grand piano is only equivalent
to half a cow, then adding a grand piano and subtracting a cow is
equivalent to subtracting half a cow or one piano. It is evident that
a "list" or inventory of things can only be summed if each quantity
can be converted into some common "equivalent" by multiplying it
by some valuation coefficient, or "ratio of equivalence." This "ratio
of equivalence" is called in statistics the "weight" of the quantity in
question. This commonest "weight" is of course the money price of
the commodity. If the physical quantity of each commodity is multiplied by its price a "dollar value" is obtained; these dollar values can
be added together, as in Table 22, to get the total value of the in-

TABLE 22. Aggregates of Goods

Commodity	Quantity	Price	Value
Wheat	50 bushels	$ 1.80 per bushel	$90
Eggs	8 dozen	.50 per dozen	4
Shirts	30 shirts	4.00 per shirt	120
Drills	3 drills	100.00 per drill	300
			$514

ventory. It is clear in this example that adding "bushels, dozens, shirts
and drills" makes no kind of sense. Multiplying each quantity, however, by its price gives us a list of values, each of which is expressed
in the same unit—the dollar—and which can be added to get a sum
of dollar values, or *dollars' worth.*

Ambiguity in Indices

This is essentially the procedure by which balance sheets and income accounts are constructed, as we have seen. It must be emphasized,
however, that the dollar value of an inventory of stock, or of those
changes in stock which constitute income in a physical sense, are only
significant as measures of physical volume if the prices at which the
items are valued are constant and in some sense significant. If relative
prices are not constant there is an unavoidable ambiguity in the very
concept of a change in the quantity of goods, for the result will depend
on whether we take prices prevailing at the beginning or at the end
of the period under consideration. The point can perhaps best be illustrated by an example, as in Table 23. Here we take two commodities only for the sake of simplicity—wheat and shirts. The quantity at
the beginning of the change (the "base date") is indicated by the
column q_0, the quantity at the end of the change (the "end date") by
the column q_1; the corresponding prices are p_0 and p_1.

On the base date the total value of wheat and shirts together (V_0) is $210; on the end date the total value (V_1) is $310. This change, though it is significant for many purposes, does not measure in any sense the change in the physical quantity of wheat and shirts; for the "weights" (i.e., the prices) have changed. It is possible, for instance, for the total

TABLE 23.   Price and Quantity Indices

	q_0	p_0	$q_0 p_0$		q_0	p_1	$q_0 p_1$
Wheat	50	$1.80	$ 90	Wheat	50	$3.00	$150
Shirts	30	4.00	120	Shirts	30	2.00	60
Total (V_0)			$210	Total (W_0)			$210

	q_1	p_0	$q_1 p_0$		q_1	p_1	$q_1 p_1$
Wheat	100	$1.80	$180	Wheat	100	$3.00	$300
Shirts	5	4.00	20	Shirts	5	2.00	10
Total (W_1)			$200	Total (V_1)			$310

value of a stock of goods to increase merely because of increase in prices without any change whatever in the composition of the stock. To obtain any measure of the change in physical quantity we must compute either what would be the value of the stock on the end-date at base-date prices (W_1), and compare this figure with the value of the stock at the base date at base-date prices (V_0); or we must calculate what would have been the value of the stock on the base date at end-date prices (W_0), and compare this with the actual value at the end date at end-date prices (V_1). In the example the figures have been chosen for convenience to make the base-date values the same both at base-date and at end-date prices $(V_0 = W_0 = $210)$. In this case, however, we find that valued at base-date prices the total stock has fallen from $210 to $200, whereas valued at end-date prices the same stock has risen from $210 to $310!

In this particular case we emerge with the paradoxical result that measured in one way the total quantity of goods has fallen, and measured in another way the total quantity has risen—the detailed changes in both cases being identical! There is no escape from this dilemma; there can be no single definition of a "total quantity of goods," because the total quantity can only be defined on the assumption of some system of "prices" or "ratios of equivalence," and the system of prices which may be relevant for one purpose may not be relevant for another.

It must not be thought, however, that because of this difficulty the concept of a total physical stock of goods is without meaning. In any particular discussion the concept can be defined as accurately as we wish by defining the relevant system of prices. Moreover, in fact, relative quantities or prices do not usually shift radically, especially over fairly short periods, so that fairly similar results are obtained no matter whether base-date, end-date, or any other reasonable prices are used as weights. If the relative quantities are unchanged (that is, if all quantities change in the same proportion) the quantity index is independent of the price weights used. Thus if all quantities double the index will double, no matter what prices are used.[2]

Measurement of Price Levels

The problems which are involved in measuring price levels are essentially similar to those involved in measuring quantity aggregates. The problem is to get some single figure which is descriptive of change in a given aggregate or list of prices. If all prices change in the same ratio there is no problem—any measure of the average of all the prices, or the price level, will change in the same ratio. If prices change in different ratios, however, the problem of how to "weight" the various changes arises, just as in the case of quantity aggregates.

Price Levels and Quantity Levels

The close relationship between the measurement of price levels and of quantity aggregates can be seen if we define the price level in the same way as we define a price—as a ratio of a quantity of money to the quantity of goods which is exchanged for the money. Thus the price

[2] Suppose that for any commodity $q_1 = kq_0$, k being a constant.
Then

$$V_0 = \Sigma p_0 q_0 \qquad\qquad W_0 = \Sigma p_1 q_0$$
$$W_1 = \Sigma p_0 q_1 = k\Sigma p_0 q_0 \qquad V_1 = \Sigma p_1 q_1 = k\Sigma p_1 q_0$$

Then the quantity index at base-date prices, $Q_b = \dfrac{W_1}{V_0} = k$, and the quantity index at end-date prices, $Q_e = \dfrac{V_1}{W_0} = k$. The quantity index is always k no matter what the prices used.

Similarly, if relative prices are constant, for any commodity $p_1 = Kp_0$.
Then

$$W_0 = K\Sigma p_0 q_0 = KV_0$$

and

$$V_1 = K\Sigma p_0 q_1 = KW_1$$

and

$$Q_1 = \frac{V_1}{W_0} = \frac{KW_1}{KV_0} = \frac{W_1}{V_0} = Q_0$$

The quantity index is independent of the actual *level* of prices but depends only on their relative structure.

of cheese is the ratio of the quantity of money paid for cheese to the quantity of cheese bought. If $100 are paid for 200 pounds of cheese, the price is 50 cents per pound.

Similarly, a "price level" of a given list of commodities is the ratio of the total money value of the commodities to their total quantity; that is;

$$\text{Price Level} = \frac{\text{Total money value of commodities}}{\text{Total physical quantity of commodities}}$$

All the difficulties and ambiguities, therefore, which we noted in considering the concept of the total quantity of a list of heterogeneous commodities apply equally to the concept of a price level. Just as the way to measure a change in a "quantity level" is to calculate the value of the list of commodities at different dates on the assumption of constant prices, so the way to measure a change in the price level is to calculate the change in the value of a constant list or "basketful" of commodities. Thus, in Table 23 the change in price level between the two dates may be measured either by comparing the value of the base-date quantities first at base-date and then at end-date prices—i.e., by comparing W_0 with V_0; or by comparing the value of end-date quantities, first at base-date and then at end-date prices—i.e., by comparing V_1 with W_1. Again the ambiguity shows up. The value of the base-date quantities, 50 bushels of wheat plus 30 shirts, has not changed at all between the two dates; the value of the end-date quantities (100 bushels of wheat plus 5 shirts) has increased from $210 to $310. On the first criterion there has been no change in the price level. If the index of the base date is 100, the index of the end date will also be 100. In the second case, however, there has been apparently a substantial increase. If the index of the base date is 100, that of the end date is $\frac{310}{210}$ (100) or 147.6.

The Index as a "Range"

There is no particular sense in asking which of these two apparently contradictory results is "right." Each of them is meaningful, in the sense that it has a simple physical interpretation. In some sense these values constitute the extreme limits of the meaningful range of values. There is much to be said for quoting the extreme range in using these indices. Thus we might say in the above case that the price level has moved from 100 to between 100 and 147.6. This statement gives us as much information as the nature of the problem entitles us to have. It is important information: we know that the price level has not doubled, and has not fallen. It would no doubt be agreeable to know that it has risen to exactly, let us say, 125, but in the nature of the problem such a figure would be meaningless. It should be observed that this problem of the "range" is present in all measurement. When we say that something is 10 inches long, we mean strictly that measured with instruments capable of distinguishing hundredths of an inch it is between 9.99 and 10.01 inches. If the ranges are broader in the case of economic aggregates, the apparent inaccuracy is merely a matter of degree, and is inherent in the nature of the problem.[3]

How Significant Are Indices?

It is evident that the significance of a price index depends on the retention of significance of the list of commodities comprised in it. For this reason comparisons of price levels are more and more difficult the longer the period of time over which the comparisons are made. Even over fifty years the composition both of the stock of goods and of the flows of production and consumption change enormously. How can we compare, for instance, the automobiles and washing machines of today with the "horseless carriages" and washtubs of 1900? Still more difficult is it to make any meaningful comparison between the goods of today and the chariots and fibulas of ancient Rome. It is for this reason that the measurement of price levels over long periods is confined for the most part to the staple wholesale commodities— grains, metals, and so on—which remain much the same from century to century. Even cost of living indices (that is, price levels of consumers' goods) become almost meaningless in a few decades.

Consistency of Indices

For all their unsatisfactory nature, the price-level, quantity-level concepts cannot be dispensed with, and the temptation to deal only with measurable dollar-values must be resisted. The dollar value of

---

[3] This basic conceptual difficulty vitiates the various attempts which have been made (notably that of Irving Fisher in *The Making of Index Numbers*, New York, 1923) to construct an "ideal" index number which would give an unequivocal figure for a price level. There are indices (e.g., the weighted geometrical means) which are superior to the weighted arithmetic indices used above as judged by certain statistical tests, such as "reversibility." (Reversibility means giving the same result whether calculated forward or backward in time.) There are no other indices which have such a simple and obvious economic meaning, however, as the weighted arithmetical indices which measure the change in the value of a given "basketful" of goods. There are no other indices, either, which are so easy to compute. For these reasons the weighted arithmetical index is predominant. It is usually weighted by base dates, as the evaluation of the weights is a difficult and expensive task and is not repeated annually. Cost of living indices are almost universally arithmetic averages weighted by quantities derived from budget studies at the base date.

any commodity is a product of a "price" and a "quantity," and similarly the dollar value of a group of commodities is in some sense a product of a price level multiplied by a quantity level. The exact division of any given dollar value into its two factors may be in some degree arbitrary, but this arbitrariness is implicit in the very nature of the problem. As long as our concepts of price level and quantity level are consistent, the element of arbitrariness need not cause any confusion of thought. The test of consistency is that the product of the price-level index and the quantity-level index should be equal to the index of the change in dollar value.

Following the notation of Table 23, we have:

$V_0 = \Sigma p_0 q_0 =$ The value of base-date quantities at base-date prices
$W_0 = \Sigma p_1 q_0 =$ The value of base-date quantities at end-date prices
$W_1 = \Sigma p_0 q_1 =$ The value of end-date quantities at base-date prices
$V_1 = \Sigma p_1 q_1 =$ The value of end-date quantities at end-date prices

V_0 and V_1 are actual dollar values; W_0 and W_1 are fictitious. From these we derive four possible concepts of price and quantity indices, or relatives, for the end-date with the base-date index $= 1$.

$$P_b = \frac{W_0}{V_0} = \text{Price level with base-date quantity weights}$$

$$P_e = \frac{V_1}{W_1} = \text{Price level with end-date quantity weights}$$

$$Q_b = \frac{W_1}{V_0} = \text{Quantity level with base-date price weights}$$

$$Q_e = \frac{V_1}{W_0} = \text{Quantity level with end-date price weights}$$

It is evident immediately that P_e and Q_b are consistent measures, for $P_e Q_b = \frac{V_1}{V_0}$, the index of the change of real values. Similarly, P_b and Q_e are consistent measures. P_b and Q_b, or P_e and Q_e would not be consistent. The rule, therefore, emerges that if end-date price weights are used in calculating the quantity index, base-date quantity weights must be used in calculating the price index, and vice versa.

Graphic Analysis

The principles underlying the use of index numbers can perhaps be made clearer with the aid of the following graphical analysis. For simplicity we assume two commodities, one of which is money. In Fig. 49, then, we measure the quantity of money along the vertical axis, and the quantity of some commodity, say wheat, along the horizontal axis. Any point in this field then represents a combination of quantities of money and wheat. These quantities can be regarded as stocks or as flows—it makes no difference to the argument. Suppose then that we have two money-wheat combinations, A_0 with OH_0 wheat and H_0A_0 money, and A_1 with OH_1 wheat and H_1A_1 money. The problem is which of these two combinations is the "larger," and by how much. The question cannot be answered, as we have seen, unless we have a system of valuation ratios—i.e., unless we can express any

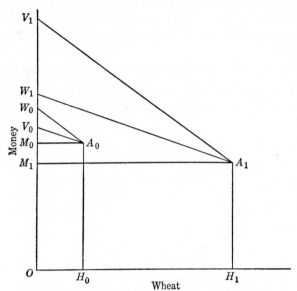

FIG. 49.   Price and Quantity Indices.

quantity of the one asset as an equivalent quantity of the other. In this example this means we must know the price of wheat, as the "price of money" is 1. The price of wheat can be expressed by the slope of a line drawn from any point such as A_0 or A_1. Thus suppose we draw a line A_0V_0 to the vertical axis, and drop a perpendicular to the same axis A_0M_0. Then if M_0V_0 is the money value of the amount of wheat M_0A_0 ($= OH_0$), the price, or more strictly the valuation coefficient, of wheat is $\dfrac{M_0V_0}{M_0A_0}$, which is the slope of the line A_0V_0, or the tangent of the angle $V_0A_0M_0$. Thus if M_0V_0 represented \$100 and M_0A_0 50 bushels, the price of wheat would be $\dfrac{100}{50}$, or \$2 per bushel. The line A_0W_0 represents a higher price of wheat, giving a higher money value (M_0W_0) for the same quantity, M_0A_0. Suppose now that the slope of the line A_0V_0 shows the base-date price of wheat, at the date when the quantity combination is at A_0, and that the slope of A_0W_0 shows the end-date price of wheat, at the date when the quantity combination is at A_1. OV_0 is the total money value of the money and wheat together at A_0, at base-date prices (OM_0 is the value of the money, M_0V_0 the value of the wheat). Similarly OW_0 is the total money value of the A_0 combination at end-date prices. If we draw A_1W_1 parallel to A_0V_0, the slope of A_1W_1, being the same as the slope of A_0V_0, measures the base-date price of wheat, and OW_1 is the total money value of the A_1 combination at base-date prices. Similarly drawing A_1V_1 parallel to A_0W_0 gives us the end-date or actual value of the A_1 combination, OV_1.

Value Change as a Combination of Price and Quantity Changes

The movement from OV_0 to OV_1 represents the increase in the total money value, at current prices, represented by moving from A_0

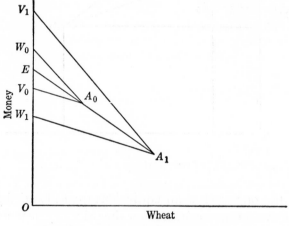

Fig. 50.   Price and Quantity Indices.

to A_1. The movement is partly an increase in quantity, partly an increase in price. The breakdown between the quantity and the price movement can be made either at W_0 or at W_1. If it is made at W_0, then V_0W_0 measured the price change, at base-date (A_0) quantities. This is the change in the value of the "basketful" represented by A_0. W_0V_1 measures the quantity change, at end-date prices. These are consistent indices, as V_0W_0 and W_0V_1 together give the total change in value, V_0V_1. Similarly we may make the break at W_1, in which case V_0W_1 shows the quantity change at base-date prices, and W_1V_1 shows the price change at end-date quantities. It is not consistent, however, to take, say, V_0W_0 as the measure of price change and V_0W_1 as the measure of quantity change, as these do not exhaust the total movement in current value.

Some valuation coefficient, or set of valuation coefficients, can always be found which will make the values of any two sets of physical quantities equal. Thus, in Fig. 50, if the price of wheat is measured by the slope of A_0A_1, the value of both combinations is the same, OE. If the price of wheat is higher than this, A_1 will be the "larger" combination—OV_1 is greater than OW_0. If the price of wheat is lower, A_0 will be the "larger" combination—OV_0 is greater than OW_1. We see clearly how with different price weights the same physical change can appear either as an increase or as a decrease in physical quantity.

QUESTIONS AND EXERCISES

1. What do you understand by "measurement." Are the problems of measurement essentially different in the social sciences from what they are in the physical sciences? Measurement in the social sciences is often regarded as more difficult than in the physical sciences. Why?
2. "It is impossible to measure the total quantity of capital. We cannot even be sure when it is increasing and when it is decreasing." Discuss.
3. Draw up your own personal balance sheet, as far as you can, and calculate your "net worth."
   a. Arrange the items roughly in order of the *certainty* of their valuation.
   b. Arrange the items roughly in order of their *liquidity*. These two arrangements will be fairly similar. Why?
   c. How would you express, if at all, the value of an education in the balance sheet?
   d. Discuss the effect on your personal balance sheet of the following events: (i) the purchase of a suit of clothes; (ii) a gambling loss of $100; (iii) borrowing $1000 from a bank; (iv) the purchase of $1000 worth of bonds.
4. Discuss the immediate effect on the *composition* of your personal assets of (a) the purchase of a candy bar; (b) the payment of a grocery bill by a check; (c) the purchase of a house by taking out a mortgage. What light if any do your answers throw on the nature of liquidity?
5. The following are the items in the balance sheet of a partnership which has three equal partners: buildings, $50,000; equipment and plant, $80,-000; accounts payable, $4000; accounts receivable, $5000; taxes payable, $1000; debt to bank, $10,000; unpaid wages, $500; cash, $1000; United States bonds, $5000; mortgage on buildings, $10,000. Draw up the balance sheet, and calculate the net worth of the business and the equity belonging to each of the three partners.
6. A firm is *insolvent* when its total net worth, or the residual claim in the

case of a corporation, is zero or negative. Suppose that in the above case a fire destroyed buildings and plant worth $120,000, which were not insured. Would the firm then be insolvent? Would the firm be insolvent if the damage had amounted to $110,000?

7. The following tables represent, in simplified form, the balance sheets of four firms.

FIRM A

Assets		Equities	
Goods and cash	$100,000	Due to other firms	$ 80,000
Due from Firm B	20,000	Net worth	90,000
Due from Firm C	40,000		
Due from Firm D	10,000		
Total	$170,000		$170,000

FIRM B

Assets		Equities	
Goods and cash	$ 72,000	Due to other firms	$ 70,000
Due from Firm C	20,000	Due to Firm A	20,000
Due from Firm D	18,000	Net worth	20,000
Total	$110,000		$110,000

FIRM C

Assets		Equities	
Goods and cash	$ 38,000	Due to Firm B	$ 20,000
Due from Firm D	32,000	Due to Firm A	40,000
		Net worth	10,000
Total	$ 70,000		$ 70,000

FIRM D

Assets		Equities	
Goods and cash	$ 50,000	Due to Firm C	$ 32,000
Due from others	20,000	Due to Firm B	18,000
		Due to Firm A	10,000
		Net worth	10,000
Total	$ 70,000		$ 70,000

a. Calculate the total value of goods and cash owned by these four firms. Show that this total is equal to the sum of the net worths of the four firms, plus the net amount due to other firms outside the four. Prove from this that in a closed society the total value of goods and cash must be equal to the total of net worths.

b. Suppose that a hurricane destroyed $40,000 worth of the goods belonging to Firm D. Suppose further that in bankruptcy the assets of a firm are liquidated (turned into cash) and then divided among the creditors in proportion to each creditor's claim. What will be the effect of the hurricane on the balance sheets of the four firms? Which firms will be insolvent? (Assume that all insolvent firms are bankrupted.) Show that the total loss of net worth in the four firms is equal to the $40,000 of value destroyed by the hurricane.

8. Figure 50 shows how different price weights can measure a given change in quantities either as an increase or as a decrease. Construct a figure to

show how different quantity weights can measure a given change in prices either as an increase or as a decrease in the price level.

9. The following table shows the prices and sales of three commodities at two different localities, X and Y.

Commodities	Locality X		Locality Y	
	Price	Quantity	Price	Quantity
A	100	50	80	5
B	5	1000	10	10
C	20	30	15	2

Calculate (a) an index of the physical volume of sales in the two localities for each set of prices; (b) an index of the price level of the sales in the two localities for each set of quantities; (c) an index of the total value of sales in each locality.

In calculating all the indices make the value in locality Y = 100. Which of these sets of indices are consistent, and which are not? Comment on the results.

APPENDIX TO CHAPTER 14

NATIONAL INCOME ACCOUNTING

One of the most important developments in economics since the 1920's has been the rise of national income accounting by governments. Before 1929 there was no good information about the gross aggregative structure of any economy. The collection and publication of information regarding national income and product, its sources and its distribution, have resulted in an impressive cumulation of knowledge about the most important economies of the world. The facts so revealed are not only vital to the intelligent pursuit of economic policy but have also forced economists to clarify concepts and to fit their theories into a form which is consistent with the collection of aggregate information. The collection of this information has also led to the "debunking" of many economic myths, which could be held without possibility of contradiction only so long as no adequate information was available by which they might be tested. Thus the Marxist theory of increasing misery of the workers looks foolish in the presence of national income statistics which show the labor force receiving a rather constant share of a rapidly increasing "pie" of national income. Henry George's idea of the "single tax" fares ill when we compare what is absorbed by government with the small fraction of national income which goes to rents and royalties.

Income as Product

The key to the understanding of national income and product figures, as published, for instance, by the United States Department of Commerce, is the realization that they start with *product,* and that income is derivative from the more basic notion of product. Product, of course, can only be measured in value terms, which means that the various physical items must be reduced to dollars worth. What we are measuring, however, is dollars worth of physical product rather than dollars paid for physical product. Not all product is sold, but what is not sold is still part of the product and must be valued in dollar terms, even though there is no flow of money which corresponds to it. The gross national product, then, or GNP, is the dollar value of goods and services produced by a defined section of the world's population, double counting being eliminated with the exception of the depreciation of fixed capital.

Breakdowns of the GNP

The GNP can be broken down into segments in many ways, of which the three most interesting are (1) The various ways of *disposing* of the product, (2) the allocation of the product among those factors of production which have contributed, and (3) the allocation of the product among those industries which have contributed.

Disposal of the GNP

Four main categories of disposal of the GNP are usually recognized: (D_1) personal (household) purchases, (D_2) gross private domestic investment, (D_3) net foreign investment, and (D_4) government purchases. If we think of the GNP as goods and services originating first in the hands of "businesses" (a business being by definition any person or organization where goods and services originate), then it is clear that the goods and services produced in a given period must either be taken off the hands of businesses by households (D_1), by foreigners (D_3), and by government (D_4), or they must still be in the hands of businesses— that is, they have been added to the stock of goods held by businesses (D_2). Household "purchases" include receipts in kind. Net foreign investment consists of goods shipped to foreigners less goods received from foreigners, plus production abroad credited to domestic owners, minus production at home credited to foreign owners. In the United States accounts an item of net cash gifts and contributions from abroad is included, somewhat illogically, as this would better be regarded as a transfer item rather than a product item. Government purchases include the purchases of labor services from government employees, and the net purchase of goods from the rest of the economy. In the United States accounts, government sales of goods abroad are deducted from D_4 and included in D_3.

The Net National Product

The net national product (NNP) is the GNP less the allowance made by businesses for depreciation (consumption) of fixed capital (D_c). The four main categories of disposal apply also to the NNP, with the exception that instead of gross private domestic investment we now have *net* private domestic investment (D_{2n}), equal to gross investment (D_2) minus depreciation (D_c). In the United States accounts D_c includes accidental damage to private fixed capital, and capital outlays charged to current expense.

The National Income

In the United States accounts certain items are deducted from the net national product in order to arrive at the concept described as the national income (N). These deductions are (N_1) indirect business taxes, including some taxlike charges (fines, rents, etc.); (N_2) business transfer payments; (N_3) "profits" of government enterprises, less government subsidies; and (N_4) statistical discrepancy. Indirect taxes (N_1) are deducted because it is assumed that the prices of final products include these indirect taxes, and therefore of the total value of final product part has to be allocated to indirect taxes. This is by far the largest of these items. Business transfer payments (N_2) is a small miscellaneous item (bad debts, business gifts to charities, etc.) which consists of things which are deducted from gross receipts as costs in calculating profits but which do not find their way into the earnings of factors of production. The "profits" (surpluses) of government agencies (N_3) again are deductions from the total product which do not accrue to any private individual or factor. In the United States, government subsidies are included in this item largely to avoid the difficult task of revaluing the product of private industry to account for the distribution of these subsidies. As national income is calculated directly from the earnings of factors, there is usually a slight discrepancy between the sum as so calculated and the sum as calculated by making these various deductions from the value of the GNP (N_4).

Allocation of the National Income

The national income as defined above can then be allocated among the claims of the various factors of production. (L_1) is wages and salaries, which equal wage payments (L_{1p}), wages accrued but not paid (L_{1a}), and various supplements (L_{1s}), such as employers' contribution to social security, pension funds, etc. (L_2) is income of unincorporated business. This is one of the least accurate items in the accounts; much estimation must be used, and data are not adequate. (L_3) is rental and royalty income of persons from individually owned property. This does not include rents received by a "business," which if the business is unincorporated appear in (L_2) and if incorporated appear in (L_4). (L_4) is corporate profits before tax. This includes (L_{4t}) corporate tax liability, (L_{4d}) dividends, (L_{4u}) undistributed profits, and (L_{4v}) inventory valuation adjustment. The last item (L_{4v}) is necessary in the United States accounts because in business accounts inventories are valued by methods (cost or market, LIFO or FIFO) different from those in the national income accounts, where the valuation is made at weighted *average* prices. This difference is reflected in the book value of profits, which depend, as we have seen (page 266), on the methods of inventory valuation. Inventory valuation adjustments are also made in the unincorporated business item, (L_2). The last item is (L_5) net interest. This includes not only interest actually paid but also certain imputed interest. Thus when a mutual insurance company accumulates reserves, these "belong" to the policyholders but are not paid out to them. Similarly when bank charges do not cover the actual cost of carrying the account, the depositor is receiving "virtual interest" equal to the difference between the cost and the charge. It should be noted that this item (L_5) does *not* include interest on government debt, which is regarded in the United States accounts as a transfer payment.

Personal Income and Saving

In addition to the above concepts the United States Department of Commerce calculates an aggregate of *personal income* (I_p). Part of the national income is not available to persons. These deductions are (L_{4u}) undistributed corporate profits, (L_{4t}) reserves for corporate tax liability, (L_{4v}) corporate inventory valuation adjustment, (L_{1s}) employers' contributions to social security and pension funds, (L_{1a}) the excess of wage accruals over wage disbursements—only wage *payments* are assumed to be personal income, not wage accruals. There are other items, however, which are not in the national income, not being earned by current services of factors of production, but which are included in personal income. These are interest (T_1) paid on government debt, (T_2) government transfer payments (i.e., payments by government to individuals which are *not* for current services rendered, but are "gifts" —pensions, GI benefits, etc.), and (N_2) business transfer payments.

Disposable Personal Income

Personal income less direct taxes (T_d) is *disposable personal income* (I_d), and disposable personal income less household purchases (D_1) is *personal saving* (S_p). We have then $S_p = I_p - D_1 - T_d$. $\qquad$ (1) The basic identity is that the sum of the allocations of the net national product to sources is equal to the sum of methods of disposition; that is,

$$L_{1p} + L_{1a} + L_{1s} + L_2 + L_{2v} + L_3 + L_{4t} + L_{4d} + L_{4u} + L_{4v} + L_5 + N_1 + \\ N_2 + N_3 + N_4 = D_1 + D_{2n} + D_3 + D_4 \quad (2)$$

Then we have:

$$I_p = L_1 + L_2 + L_3 + L_{4d} + L_5 + N_2 + T_1 + T_2 \qquad (3)$$

whence

$$S_p + L_{1a} + L_{2v} + L_{4v} + L_{4u} + N_4 = \\ D_{2n} + (D_4 + T_1 + T_2 - L_{4t} - N_1 - N_3 - T_d) + D_4 \quad (4)$$

This is the "sources and uses of net saving" identity. The sources of net saving are identified on the left-hand side as personal saving, net wage accruals, inventory valuation adjustments, undistributed profits, and the statistical discrepancy. The uses of net saving are identified on the right-hand side as net business investment (D_{2n}), net foreign investment (D_4), and the item in the bracket, which is the *government deficit*, G, equal to government purchases (D_4), plus government transfers $(T_1$ and $T_2)$ minus tax receipts and accruals (L_{4t}, N_1, T_d) and net government "profit" receipts (N_3). Looking at the same identity in another way, the left-hand side is the *disposition* of the total increase in net worths as between personal and nonpersonal balance sheets; the right-hand side is the sources of this increase in net worths—private investment appearing as an increase in net assets, and government deficit appearing as an increase in private money or government security holdings.

Criticism of the National Accounts

There are some valid criticisms of the above concepts from an ideal theoretical point of view, although the difficulties of acquiring certain information may justify a practice which is short of a theoretical ideal. Perhaps the most serious deficiency is the omission of the services of housewives—mainly on the grounds of difficulty of estimation. This, however, leads to the paradox that if a man marries his housekeeper the national income falls, whereas one would think in reality it should rise! The other great difficulty lies in assessing the contribution of government. The assumption of the national accounts is that the government produces goods and services which can be valued according to their cost. This may well overestimate the contribution of government; on the other hand, to leave government out altogether would certainly underestimate its role. For this reason the significant measure of national economic welfare may lie somewhere between the national income of the accounts and the disposable personal income.

The student should study the annual National Income Supplement of the *Survey of Current Business,* issued by the United States Department of Commerce. The 1951 edition gave an unusually full account of the procedures involved in the calculations.

QUESTIONS AND EXERCISES

1. Take the latest national income accounts for the United States as given in the *Survey of Current Business* and tabulate them in the form of equation (2), page 285. Show that identity (4) also holds.
2. Discuss the effect on the various items in equation (2) and on the GNP, the NNP, personal income, and personal savings of the following events:
   a. A corporation makes $1000 worth of shirts with a labor cost of $300, a materials cost of $500, and a profit of $200; $800 worth are sold at home, $100 worth abroad.
   b. The government spends $10,000,000 in building a dam; $3,000,000 is spent for labor, $6,000,000 for materials, $1,000,000 for land.
   c. An exporter buys $10,000 worth of cloth from a manufacturer and ships it abroad.
   d. The government increases its tax collections by $1,000,000 and increases its expenditures by the same amount.
   (Note: Where further assumptions are necessary to obtain specific answers, make these assumptions explicit.)
3. What is the significance of the various national income concepts (GNP, NNP, etc.) for employment theory?
4. In calculating the amount of GNP originating in the banking system it is necessary to debit depositors with the actual cost of maintaining their account, rather than with the bank's service charges. Why?

CHAPTER 15

MACROECONOMIC MODELS: MODELS OF PRODUCTION AND CONSUMPTION

The previous three chapters have been devoted essentially to the problems involved in the classification, definition, and measurement of economic aggregates. Mere classification, however, is not enough. We want to know not only "what" but "why" and "how." It is not enough to have a good system of definitions, even a good system of accounts and measurements. We also want to know something about the causal factors involved in economic systems. It is not enough to measure the national income and its distribution, for instance. We are also interested in why the national income and its various components are what they are, and why they exhibit their various changes and fluctuations. The construction of economic "models" is an attempt to give some answers to the question of the determinants of the economic system—some answer, that is, to the "why and how" questions.

Economic Models

What, then, do we mean when we ask "why is the national income what it is"? We may mean many things, depending on the level of argument. In economic analysis, however, we feel that we have a satisfactory answer to the above question if we can show that there is a system of relationships among the various variables of the system *which are satisfied* if these variables are what they are. Such a system of relationships is called a "model." There are two main kinds of these models: equilibrium models and dynamic models. In equilibrium models the system of relationships can be expressed as a set of equations or identities which can only be satisfied by one (or at most a limited number) of values of the various variables which the equations relate. In order to obtain these conditions there must be an equal number of equations and "unknowns," or variables, to be determined.

287

In dynamic models the values of present variables are related in definite ways to values of these and other variables in the past, which in turn are related to variables in the more remote past, and so on in an infinite regression. The next two chapters will deal mainly with equilibrium models; dynamic models are discussed in Chapter 20.

Identities

The concept of a model will become clear as we proceed to examples. The relationships which constitute a model are of two kinds, *identities* and *behavior equations*. All models seem to possess them both. *Identities* are true by definition. They are derived generally by taking some aggregate and expressing it as a sum of parts, or as a product of components. If then we put a whole aggregate equal to the sum of its parts, or if we equate two different breakdowns of the same aggregate, we shall have an identity. Thus any human population (N) can be divided into people called Smith (S) and people not called Smith (T), and we can write[1]

$$N \equiv S + T \tag{1}$$

The same population can also be divided into people called Jones (J) and people not called Jones (K), so that we have

$$N \equiv J + K \tag{2}$$

from which we might derive other identities, such as

$$S + T \equiv J + K, \text{ or } S - J \equiv K - T \tag{3}$$

We seem even to have derived a theorem, that the excess of Smiths over Joneses in any population must be equal to the excess of non-Joneses over non-Smiths. These particular identities are not very interesting, though nobody can deny their truth. They are not interesting because the aggregates which they relate are not particularly interesting—to the economist, at least—and, as we have seen (page 240), aggregates are not interesting if they are not *related* to anything else. If it were true, for instance, that the number of Smiths and Joneses were causally or empirically related, the above identities might become part of a model and would become interesting.

Suppose, for instance, that the Smiths formed a tight ruling class, and had an inflexible rule (enforced by execution) that the number of non-Smiths should always equal the number of Smiths, and further kept their own numbers always at 1000, we would have a "model"

---

[1] Identities are generally indicated by the sign $\equiv$, which should be read "is identical with."

from the conditions of which the equilibrium value of all the variables could be deduced. It would be expressed in three relationships: the identity $N \equiv S + T$, and two behavior equations, $S = T$ and $S = 1000$. As there are three unknowns, N, S, and T, these three equations can be solved—that is, values of N, S, and T which satisfy all three relationships simultaneously can be discovered. In this case there is only one solution: $N = 2000$, $S = 1000$, $T = 1000$.

Behavior Equations

Behavior equations, then, are relationships which express certain empirical facts about the behavior of the individuals of the system. They are not *necessarily* true, as identities must be; they derive their validity from the empirical observation that if they are *not* satisfied, behavior, and therefore change, will take place which will not cease until they *are* satisfied. Thus suppose in the above slightly absurd example that the total population was 2500, with 1000 Smiths and 1500 non-Smiths. Following their rule of behavior the Smiths would have to kill off 500 non-Smiths in order to bring their numbers to equality, which would reduce the population to 2000. If the population were 2500 divided between 1250 Smiths and 1250 non-Smiths, both rules would come into play: 250 Smiths would be killed off to reduce the Smith population to the legal 1000, and 250 non-Smiths killed off to bring the numbers of the two groups to equality. If the total population were 1500, say 750 Smiths and 750 non-Smiths, the Smith population would be allowed to grow until it reached 1000, and the non-Smith population would be allowed to grow equally, bringing the total population again to 2000. It is evident that the equilibrium is a stable one. If N is *not* 2000, forces are brought into play to restore that figure. What the population will be on any given date, of course, depends on the dynamic relationships involved—on whether, for instance, the movement toward equilibrium takes place quickly or slowly. In equilibrium models, however, we consider only the equilibrium position itself. The problem of the movements toward (or away from) equilibrium will be discussed in Chapter 20.

Adding New Variables

The models can be made as complicated as we wish by adding new variables and new relationships, as long as we add one independent equation or identity (that is, one that cannot be derived from the existing relationships) for each new variable. Thus suppose we add a new variable to our previous model—say, the number of Joneses, J.

In order to make the model determinate we must find a relationship of some kind between J and the other variables. Suppose for instance that the only function of the Joneses was to cut hair for the Smiths, and that each Jones could handle 20 Smiths. Then in equilibrum we would have an additional relationship, $20 J = S$. As we know that in equilibrium $S = 1000$, $J = 50$. If now we wish to determine the number of non-Joneses, K, this new variable can be taken care of with the identity (2), so that $K = 1950$.

The above illustration is, of course, far-fetched in the extreme, in that the behavior equations postulated are most unlikely to be found in any real society. An absurd case, however, illustrates the generality of a principle better than a realistic one, and it is not difficult now to go on to more realistic models involving economic variables.

The "Basic Model" of Macroeconomics

The simplest, and perhaps the most important macroeconomic model is one of three relationships and three variables. Let P be the total physical output of a society in a given period. Its exact definition, and the exact degree of "netness" involved in its definition is not particularly important. Let C be the amount of this physical output consumed during the period, and A be the amount accumulated— that is, added to stocks. Then we have an identity:

$$P \equiv C + A \qquad (4)$$

The concepts, of course, must be defined in such a way as to make this identity necessary. What it states in effect is that whatever has been produced in a given period must either have been consumed in that period or must be still around somewhere. Production is conceived, as we have seen, as a gross addition to total stock; consumption as a subtraction from total stock; and accumulation, therefore, is the difference between what has been added and what has been subtracted.

Consumption and Investment Functions

In addition to the identity (4) we need two behavior equations. These are

$$C = F_c(P) \qquad (5)$$

$$A = F_a(P) \qquad (6)$$

We do not postulate an exact algebraic relationship, but a general function. Equation (5) is read "C is a function of P." It means simply that the amount of consumption *depends on* the amount of production in a definite way, so that for each amount of production there is only[2] one amount of consumption which is consistent with it. A behavior equation is not much use, of course, unless there is some assumed behavior behind it. The link here is that decisions to consume on the part of individuals, in so far as they have freedom to choose, are very closely related to their individual incomes. Generally speaking, the larger a person's income, the larger his consumption. Personal incomes, however, are very closely related to total output, P. For any given value of P, therefore, there is likely to be a given value of personal incomes, and for each value of personal incomes there will be a given amount of consumption. It is not unreasonable, then, to assume that with a given distribution of income and stable patterns of individual consuming behavior there is a fairly definite relationship between total output and the decisions which result in consumption, and hence the volume of consumption itself.

The behavior patterns which underly the accumulation equation (6) are more complex, and more dubious. What the equation states is that for any given level of output there is only one value of total accumulation which is *consistent with* the given level of output. This assumes that at each level of output there is some level of accumulation which is satisfactory to the people who are holding the additions to stocks of goods—call it Ā. If the *actual* level of accumulation is greater than the "satisfactory" level, the people who hold goods will feel that they are holding too much—they will feel "overstocked." Manufacturers, wholesalers, retailers, and householders may feel that they are holding too large stocks of goods and will try to reduce these stocks. *How* they try to reduce stocks is a critical question in the dynamics of the system. For the moment, however, we will assume that the simplest way to reduce stocks is to cut back production. We have supposed that consumption is given (for each value of P) so that there is not much opportunity to reduce stocks by expanding consumption. Similarly, if the actual level of accumulation is less than the satisfactory level, people will feel "understocked" and will try to increase these stocks. We assume for purposes of this model that they can increase stocks only by increased production. Thus in the first case if householders feel overstocked, say with shirts, they reduce purchases of shirts until some of those they have wear out. The reduced pur-

---

[2] In strict mathematical terms, the existence of a general function relating two (or more) variables means only that there is a *limited number* of possible combinations of values of the variables. In the present case it is reasonable to assume that there is in fact only one value of consumption corresponding to each value of output. When this limitation is placed on the nature of the function, it is said to be *monotonic*.

chases result in an overstock on the part of the retailer, who reduces purchases from the wholesaler; reduced purchases from the retailers lead to overstock at the wholesaler, who reduces purchases from the manufacturer. The manufacturer responds to his resulting overstock by laying off men and decreasing the output of shirts. By a similar chain an understock anywhere in the system will lead to increased production.

We see, therefore, that if the behavior equations are *not* satisfied certain *changes* in behavior will take place, and if the equilibrium is a stable one these changes will operate to adjust the values of all the variables of the system in a direction which makes the equations more nearly satisfied. This process will presumably go on until the equations are satisfied, at which point there will be no further changes in behavior and the system will reproduce itself indefinitely in equilibrium until the equations change.

Arithmetical Example of Macroeconomic Equilibrium

This simple model can be illustrated by arithmetical and graphical examples. Suppose that Table 24 shows the relationship in some society between total output (P) and those levels of consumption (C) and accumulation $(\bar{A})$ which are consistent with each level of output.

TABLE 24. Output Equilibrium

1. Output (P)	0	20	40	60	80	100	120	140	160	180	200
2. Consumption (C)	60	73	87	97	106	113	120	126	130	134	137
3. Willing accumulation (investment) $(\bar{A})$	−30	−13	0	7	15	21	24	27	30	32	34
4. Total absorption $(\bar{A} + C)$	30	60	87	104	121	134	144	153	160	166	171
5. Actual accumulation $(P - C)$	−60	−53	−47	−37	−27	−13	0	14	30	46	63
6. Surplus (+) or deficit (−) accumulation $(P - (\bar{A} + C))$ or $((P - C) - \bar{A})$	−30	−40	−47	−44	−41	−34	−24	−13	0	+14	+29

The relationship between output and consumption, $C = F_c\ (P)$, is known as the *consumption function*. The relationship between output and "willing" accumulation, $\bar{A} = F_a\ (P)$, is often called the *"investment function,"* investment being defined as the amount of "voluntary" or "willing" accumulation which is consistent with a given level of output.[3] Thus the table should be read: if the output were 0, the society would be willing and able to consume 60, and would be will-

---

[3] In the Keynesian system investment is not generally regarded as a function of output, but of other things, such as the rate of interest. These complications will be introduced later.

ing and able to invest −30 (that is, to disinvest, or decumulate 30); if the output were 20, the society would be willing and able to consume 73, and invest −13; and so on. The fourth line of the table shows the algebraic sum of consumption and investment. It is useful to have a name for this quantity, so I have called it "total absorption." If we think of consumption and investment (willing accumulation) as the only two ways in which the product can be absorbed or disposed of willingly, the total of consumption and investment together shows the total amount of product which will be voluntarily "absorbed" by the system. If the actual output is greater than the total (willing) absorption, there will be *unwanted* accumulations; if actual output is less than total (willing) absorption, there will be unwanted decumulations, and, as we have seen, these will produce changes in behavior which will change output itself.

Assumptions of the Model

In constructing Table 24 we made certain assumptions about the *nature* of the consumption and investment functions. These assumptions are plausible, but not absolutely necessary. The actual shape of the function is a matter of fact in each case which can only be determined by empirical research. Thus we assumed that at zero output, should such a state of affairs be even possible, there would still be some consumption (60), as existing capital depreciates and people must eat even if they are not producing. In a state of such extreme depression, however, it is most unlikely that anyone would be willing to accumulate. Indeed, the reverse is assumed—that at very low levels of output the society is only willing to *decumulate*, i.e., to live on its existing stocks. As we advance (hypothetically) to higher levels of output we assume that both consumption and investment rise. In the example we have assumed further that they both rise at a decreasing rate, so that a unit rise in output at high levels of output produces a smaller increase in C and A than does a unit rise in output at low levels. This assumption, though plausible, is in no way necessary for the argument, as we shall see later.

Surplus or Deficiency in Accumulation

If now we subtract the total (willing) absorption figure from the output figure we get a measure of "surplus" or "deficiency" in actual accumulation (item 6, Table 24). If there is an accumulation surplus (as there is in the table at levels of output above 160), this means that at these levels of output actual accumulation is greater than the amount of accumulation which the people of the society are willing to accept voluntarily. If there is an accumulation deficit, as there is below an output of 160, then actual accumulation is less than the desired level of accumulation. We can suppose that actual accumulation (item 5) is the difference between output and consumption at each level of output. Then the accumulation surplus or deficit can also be obtained by subtracting the figures of item 3 (willing accumulation) from the corresponding figures of item 5 (actual accumulation).

Equilibrium of the Model

We can now see clearly that there is only one output figure at which the system is in equilibrium. At an output of 160 total absorption is also 160; willing accumulation is equal to actual accumulation (30) and there is no surplus or deficit accumulation. At all outputs lower than 160 total absorption exceeds output; the amount that the society is willing to accumulate exceeds what it actually succeeds in accumulating and there is deficit accumulation. Thus at an output of 140, consumption is 126, so that actual accumulation is 14. The amount that people wish to accumulate, however, is 27. The society is "understocked" and output will increase. Similarly if output is 180, consumption is 134, so that actual accumulation will be 46. People only wish to accumulate 32, so that there will be a surplus accumulation of 14, and output will be reduced to try to get rid of the surplus.

Graphic Illustration. This model can also be illustrated graphically. In Fig. 51 output is measured on the horizontal axis, and consumption and accumulation on the vertical axes. It should be remembered that these measurements are indices of *real* output or consumption, and that the indices chosen must be consistent. This means that the relative price structure used in computing an index must be the same for all the indices. CC' is then the consumption curve, corresponding to the consumption function of items 1 and 2, Table 24. II' is the investment curve, or willing accumulation curve. BB' is the vertical sum of these two curves, or the total absorption curve (items 1 and 4 of the table). We now draw a line OB_e from the origin at an angle of 45° to each axis, cutting the curve BB' at B_e. The 45° line represents the identity $P \equiv C + A$. The point B_e then gives the equilibrium output, OO_e, for at this point output, $OO_e = O_eB_e = O_eC_e + C_eB_e = O_eC_e + O_eA_e = C + A$. The equilibrium point can also be found in two other ways (i) by drawing the actual accumulation curve AA' (items 1 and 5 of Table 24). This is given by the vertical distance between the line CC' and the 45° line OB_e. Where the curve AA' intersects the curve II'—i.e., where actual accumulation is equal to desired accumulation, is the point of equilibrium. Another method is to draw the surplus-deficit accumulation curve SS' (items 1–6 of the table). Where this cuts the horizontal axis—that is, where the surplus or deficit accumulation is zero—is the point of equilibrium.

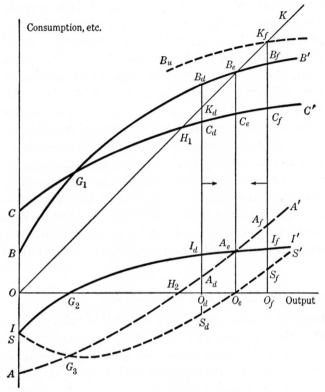

FIG. 51.   Output Equilibrium.

This diagram also illustrates the stability of the equilibrium. Thus suppose output were below the equilibrium output, say at OO_d. Consumption would be O_dC_d. Actual accumulation therefore would be C_dK_d, where K_d is on the 45° line, as $O_dK_d = OO_d$. Desired accumulation is $C_dB_d(= O_dI_d)$. There is therefore a deficit of actual accumulation below the desired level amounting to B_dK_d ($= I_dA_d = O_dS_d$). This deficit will cause an increase in output, and the whole system will therefore move toward the equilibrium. Similarly, if output is above the equilibrium, say OO_f, there will be a surplus accumulation ($B_fK_f = I_fA_f = O_fS_f$) which will cause cutbacks in output and again return it to the equilibrium value OO_e.

Effect of a Rise in the Absorption Curve

This model, simple as it is, is so powerful in the explanation of movements in aggregate incomes, even in the explanation of business cycles, that it is worth examining some of its properties in greater detail. We see first that a rise in either the consumption or the investment curves, or in both, will raise the equilibrium output. Thus in Fig. 52 we suppose a total absorption curve b_1B_1, with the point of equilibrium at B_1, OB_1 being the 45° line. If the total absorption curve rises to b_2B_b, that is, if the total of consumption and willing accumulation is larger, *at each level of output,* than it was before, the equilibrium output will rise from OE_1 to OE_2. Similarly, a fall in the absorption curve results in a fall in the equilibrium output. These changes in the total absorption curve may have several origins. There may be a spontaneous rise in the consumption function itself—that is, the people of the society may decide to consume more at each level of income than they did before. There may likewise be a spontaneous increase in the investment function—that is, people may become willing to accumulate more goods at each level of income than they did before. There may also, as we shall see later, be an increase in absorption by government without an offsetting decline in absorption by private persons.

The Propensity to Absorb and the Multiplier

Whatever the causes, there is an interesting relationship between the *extent* of the increase in the willing absorption of product and the increase in the equilibrium output which is called forth. In Fig. 52 we have supposed that the total absorption curve is a straight line. Modifying the Keynesian terminology somewhat, we may call the slope of this line the *propensity to absorb.* The propensity to absorb, then, is the increase in total willing absorption of output which results from a *unit* increase in output. Thus if an increase in output of 10 units resulted in an increase in willing absorption in consumption and investment of 8 units, the propensity to absorb in this range would be $\frac{8}{10}$, or 0.8. In the figure, if a perpendicular is dropped from B_1 to E_2B_2 at L_2, the propensity to absorb, a, is $\frac{L_2M_2}{B_1L_2}$. The ratio of the "vertical" increase in the absorption function to the resultant increase in the equilibrium output is called the "multiplier." The historic reason for this term is that it was first used in connection with the increase in income (output) which would result from a unit in-

crease in *investment,* investment being assumed to be independent
of output, so that the multiplier is the amount by which the initial

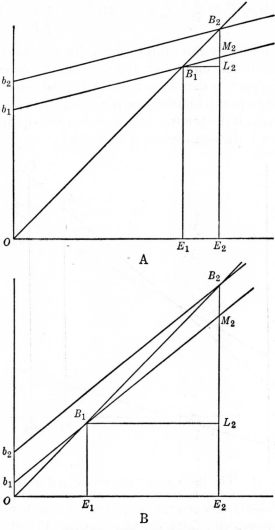

FIG. 52.   The Multiplier.

increase of investment multiplies itself in producing income. In the
figure, then, the multiplier, m, is the ratio $\dfrac{B_1 L_2}{M_2 B_2}$; that is, it is the
amount by which output increases for a unit vertical rise in the ab-
sorption function.

There is a relatively simple mathematical relationship between the
multiplier, m, and the propensity to absorb, a. Thus we have in the

figure $B_1L_2 = L_2B_2$, by construction. It follows then that

$$m = \frac{B_1L_2}{M_2B_2} = \frac{L_2B_2}{M_2B_2} = \frac{L_2B_2}{L_2B_2 - L_2M_2} = \frac{1}{1 - \dfrac{L_2M_2}{L_2B_2}} = \frac{1}{1 - \alpha} \quad (7)$$

It follows immediately from this formula that the closer a lies to 1, the larger will be the multiplier. If $a = 1$ the multiplier is infinite; the absorption curve is then at an angle of 45° and coincides with the 45° identity line. In this limiting case the equilibrium itself, of course, is indeterminate. If the propensity to absorb at the equilibrium point is greater than 1, the equilibrium is unstable.

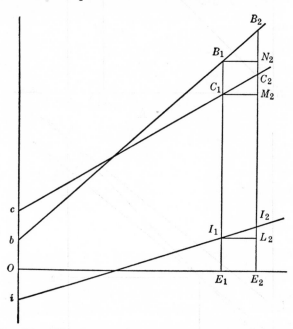

FIG. 53.   The Propensity to Consume and to Invest.

The relationship between the propensity to absorb and the multiplier can be visualized graphically by comparing Fig. 52A, where the propensity to absorb is small (about 0.25) and where the multiplier is also small (about 1.33), with Fig. 52B, where the propensity to absorb is large (about 0.8) and the multiplier therefore is also large (about 5). The same upward shift in the absorption curve in both figures, b_1b_2, produces a much larger change in output (B_1L_2) in Fig. 52B than it does in 52A.

The Propensities to Consume and Invest. The propensity to absorb is the sum of two similar quantities—the propensity to consume and the propensity to invest. This is shown in Fig. 53. I_1I_2, C_1C_2, and B_1B_2 are segments (assumed to be straight lines) of an investment curve, a consumption curve, and the derived total absorption curve. From the method of construction we know that $E_1I_1 + E_1C_1 = E_1B_1$ and $E_2I_2 + E_2C_2 = E_2B_2$. It follows that $E_2I_2 - E_1I_1 + E_2C_2 - E_1C_1 = E_2B_2 - E_1B_1$, or $L_2I_2 + M_2C_2 = N_2B_2$. Dividing through by E_1E_2 or its equivalent we have: $\dfrac{L_2I_2}{I_1L_2} + \dfrac{M_2C_2}{C_1M_2} = \dfrac{N_2B_2}{B_1N_2}$. $\dfrac{L_2I_2}{I_1L_2}$ is the propensity to invest a_i—that is, the increase in willing accumulation for a unit increase in output. $\dfrac{M_2C_2}{C_1M_2}$ is the propensity to consume (a_c)—the increase in consumption per unit increase in output. $\dfrac{N_2B_2}{B_1N_2}$ is the propensity to absorb, a. We have therefore $a = a_i + a_c$. In the Keynesian system proper the propensity to invest is generally taken to be zero unless there is "induced investment," of which the propensity to invest is a measure. If the propensity to invest is zero we have $a = a_c$, and

$$m = \frac{1}{1 - \alpha} \tag{8}$$

In fact it seems probable that the propensity to invest is at least a small positive figure, and under some circumstances it may be quite important. The larger it is, of course, the larger also will be the propensity to absorb and hence the multiplier.

The "Shiftability" of Equilibrium

The multiplier concept was developed, as noted earlier, in the attempt to determine the increase in national output, income, or employment which would result from a given spontaneous increase in investment or in government expenditure. The limitations which have to be placed on the model in order to make it meaningful are so restrictive that in its original meaning it does not seem to be particularly useful. Thus we would have to assume that the consumption function was unchanged in the face of investment changes, and that there was no induced investment before the formula (8) takes on much meaning. Nevertheless the multiplier, or what is practically the same thing in a different measure, the propensity to absorb, is an extremely important property of the model, for it measures the degree of "shiftability" of the equilibrium position. If the multiplier is small, as in Fig. 52A, a given shift in the underlying determinants of the system, as reflected in a change in the position of the absorption curve, will not produce a very large change in the position of equilibrium itself. By contrast, when the multiplier or the propensity to absorb are large, as in Fig. 52B, quite small disturbances in the underlying conditions will produce large changes in the national income or output.

This fact is of great importance for highly industrialized modern economies like that of the United States, as it is a possible explanation of the great instability of these economies. The propensity to absorb in America, for instance, seems to be at least of the order of 0.8. Quite slight changes in the underlying behavior patterns therefore may give rise to very large changes in the position of equilibrium; a slight fall in the level of the absorption function may give rise to devastating depression and unemployment, and an equally slight rise may result in full employment, prosperity, and even inflation.

APPLICATIONS OF THE BASIC MODEL

Perhaps the most important application of the basic model is in giving at least a rough explanation of the phenomenon of depression and unemployment. There is nothing in the equilibrium of the model as we have described it which says that the equilibrium position of output is at "capacity" output. The equilibrium may therefore be at a level which is below what the society is capable of reaching, even with the resources which it has available at the moment. If the equilibrium output is below capacity, then, some resources will be unemployed. A measure of unemployment is the difference between capacity output and the actual or equilibrium output. Thus, returning to Fig. 51, page 295, suppose that OO_f represents capacity output. Equilibrium output is OO_e. The difference, O_eO_f represents that output which could be produced but which it not being produced because certain resources are unemployed. It is therefore a measure of the amount of unemployed resources in the system.

Unemployment Equilibrium

If now we inquire *why* there is unemployment, the answer is to be found in a study of what would happen if in fact the system were operating at capacity, i.e., at OO_f. At this level of output we see that consumption and investment (willing accumulation) are insufficient to absorb the whole product. In other words, there is a deficiency in "effective demand." This reflects itself, as we have seen, in unwanted accumulations amounting to B_fK_f (O_fS_f). These unwanted accumulations produce a downward pressure on output, so the economy cannot remain at full employment. At full employment it will be accumulating stocks of goods at a rate faster than its people are willing to take. We see unemployment, therefore, as an attempt on the part of the system to cut down its rate of accumulation to a level that its people are willing to absorb. Output has to be cut back by *more* than the excess accumulation, because cutting output back itself reduces consumption, and the reduction in consumption to some extent offsets the decline in production. Because, however, consumption does not decline as much as production, the reduction in production does bring about a decline in the surplus accumulation, and will go on until this surplus is reduced to zero. If the propensity to absorb is high, consumption and investment decline sharply as output declines, which reduces the effect of the decline in production on accumulation; the decline may therefore have to go a long way before the surplus accumulation is eliminated. Suppose, for instance, that with an output of 200, willing absorption is 180, leaving a surplus accumulation of 20. If now the society cuts back its production to 180, it will still have a surplus accumulation, because willing absorption will also have declined, say to 165, still leaving a surplus of 15, and production must be cut back further.

A Full-Employment Model

A very important question must now be raised regarding the relevance of this model to the actual world. Underemployment equilibrium can only exist if the consumption and investment functions are stable and, in particular, are unaffected by the level of unemployment. It is not difficult to expand the basic model by adding another variable, let us say, "unused capacity," U, and then postulating that both consumption and investment are themselves related to unused capacity as well as to output. We can then postulate an equilibrium value for unused capacity—say zero—and we have added another equation which is sufficient to determine the system. Thus we have four unknowns, P, C, A and U, and four relationships, the identity $P \equiv C + A$ as before, and three new behavior equations:

$$C = F_c(P,U) \tag{9A}$$
$$A = F_a(P,U) \tag{9B}$$
$$U = U_e \tag{9C}$$

If $U_e = O$ we have essentially the "classical" employment theory which assumed that unemployed resources would always be zero in equilibrium. In order to assure a stable equilibrium we must make an additional stability assumption: that the existence of unemployed resources produces an *upward* shift in the total amount absorbed at each level of output. In terms of the graphic analysis this means that in Fig. 51, page 295, for instance, if there is unused capacity the total absorption curve will move upward until it reaches a position such as B_uK_f, where it intersects the 45° line at K_f. The surplus accumulation is reduced to zero in this case not by a decline in output, but by a rise in the whole level of the absorption curve.

The Keynesian Controversy

Much of the dispute between the Keynesian and the "classical" school of employment theorists (as represented, say, by Pigou) rests on the question of the extent to which there is anything in reality to correspond to the behavior equations outlined above. The full discussion of the behavior patterns involved must wait until we have discussed the operations of the monetary and price systems, but at least an outline can be given here. The Keynesian model assumes that there is no "natural" tendency in the system tending to raise the level of the absorption curve as output falls below capacity, and that if full employment is to be maintained there must be active intervention on the part of government to raise the level of the absorption curve to the point where capacity output will not result in surplus accumulations. We can, of course, if we like regard this governmental intervention as itself part of an equilibrium system, and assume that a rise in U above a certain critical level will call forth expansionary activity on the part of government, and vice versa. In that case U_e would be a true equilibrium, though the behavior equations which determine it rest on political rather than on strictly economic behavior.

The "Classical" System: Deflation of Prices Rather Than of Outputs

The classical assumption regarding the behavior which underlies the equations is that the development of surplus accumulation, or overstocking, will produce a downward pressure on *prices* rather than on outputs. If all markets are competitive and therefore all prices flexible, this assumption is not implausible. Unwanted stocks of commodities produce deflations in the prices of these commodities, as the owners of these unwanted stocks try to get rid of them by selling them. Similarly, if labor markets were competitive, unemployment would produce a downward pressure on *money* wages (not necessarily on real wages) which would supplement and encourage the general price decline. Thus we see the major consequence of a surplus accumulation, on these assumptions, is a general and widespread decline in the whole price-wage level.

Effects of Deflation

On Consumption. The economic consequences of general *deflation,* which is the name given to a general decline in the level of money prices and wages, are complex in the extreme. Nevertheless two major sets of consequences may be expected to affect the consumption and investment functions. In the first place deflation produces a marked redistribution of income and of wealth among different groups and classes of people in the society. People who have incomes which are fixed, or which are relatively inflexible in money terms (i.e., in "dollars"), gain at the expense of those whose dollar incomes are flexible. Thus there are gains to bondholders, debt holders in general, pensioners, people living on annuities, and people with salaries and wages which are set by contract or by convention and changed only under severe pressures or at infrequent intervals. These gains are obtained at the expense of businessmen, farmers, people who live from profits in general, people whose incomes depend on flexible prices or wages. These shifts in the distribution of income on the whole are likely to raise the consumption function, as the people who gain are for the most part the "low savers"—people who consume nearly as much as, or more than, they produce. The people who lose are on the whole the "high savers," businessmen and farmers, people in the prime of life who are building up an estate and who therefore consume much less than they produce. Deflation, therefore, is likely to shift income from the "high savers" to the "low savers," and therefore will encourage the consumption of the people who gain more than it discourages the consumption of the people who lose. The net result therefore is likely to be a rise in the amount that will be consumed at each level of income—i.e., a rise in the consumption curve.

On Investment. The effects of the redistribution of income on the investment curve are perhaps more difficult to estimate, but it is probable that the effects will be *unfavorable* to investment. On the whole it is the businessmen and farmers who make the major investment decisions, and whose willingness to hold increased stocks of goods, new buildings, and so on is the main factor influencing the level of the investment function. It is precisely these people who are injured by deflation. The profit maker obtains his income by selling dearer than he buys, usually after some interval of time. If during the interval between purchase and sale all prices have fallen, the chance that the value of sales exceeds the value of purchases is so much the less. In extreme deflation profits may even disappear altogether, and become losses. Under these circumstances it is extremely unlikely that there will be much desire to increase holdings of goods, for it is precisely the holding of these goods, which are declining in price, that is the source of loss. We may reasonably expect, therefore, that deflation will have an adverse effect, at least in the short run, on the investment function. The net effect of the redistribution of income and wealth effected by deflation, then, depends on the relative magnitudes of the effects on consumption and on investment, which are likely to be in opposite directions and so serve to offset each other. If the rise in consumption is larger than the fall in investment at each level of output, the net effect will be a rise in the total absorption curve, and hence a rise in output toward full employment. If, however, the fall in investment at each level of output exceeds the rise in consumption, the system is in a sad plight. The result of surplus accumulation will be a *decline* in the total absorption curve, an *increase* in the surplus, and a further decline in output. Output will decline in this case until a "floor" is reached, imposed by the necessity for maintaining at least a subsistence level of consumption, and the impossibility of disinvesting at more than the rate set by physical decay. In terms of Fig. 51, if the effect of deflation is to lower investment by more than it raises consumption, instead of the total absorption curve moving upward from $B_d B_f$ to $B_u K_f$ under the impact of unused capacity, the curve will move downward, thus *increasing* the unused capacity, and will continue to move downward until the favorable effect on consumption just outweighs the unfavorable effect on investment.

The "Liquidity Effect"

The distribution effect of deflation is not the only one which may be relevant to the absorption function. There is also a "liquidity effect." If the quantity of money is constant the fall in the price-wage level increases the purchasing power of the existing stocks of money. People therefore find themselves more "liquid" than before, with a larger proportion of money in their total asset structure, as the money value of other assets has declined. This increased liquidity should encourage both consumption and investment. It is reasonable to suppose that increased money stocks with constant prices will encourage consumption and investment, as the increased stocks of money give people a greater feeling of *power* to consume and invest. A fall in prices with constant money stocks should have the same result. The liquidity effect therefore may reasonably be supposed to augment the favorable effect on consumption, and to offset at least in part the unfavorable effect on investment of the distribution effect. It increases the probability that the existence of unused resources will tend to raise rather than lower the total absorption curve, and therefore makes a full employment equilibrium more plausible. We shall return to this topic in a later chapter, when we have developed some further analytical tools. It is sufficient to notice now that the difference between the two systems rests mainly on whether the development of surplus stocks will produce cutbacks in *output* or in *prices*. This is a matter of fact, and the facts may differ from place to place and time to time, so that the Keynesian model may be relevant in one society and the classical model in another.

Inflation in the Basic Model

The basic model throws some light also on the problem of inflation, though here again a full treatment must be delayed until further tools have been developed. Inflation results when the equilibrium output of the basic model is *greater* than capacity output. Obviously output itself cannot expand beyond capacity, and hence if *at* capacity output there is still a deficit in accumulation, and the society is still wishing to consume and accumulate more than it is in fact producing, changes must take place in the society which will tend to get rid of the deficit accumulation in other ways than by an expansion of output. Thus suppose in Fig. 51, page 295, again that capacity output were OO_d. At this output there is a deficit in accumulation of $K_d B_d$, indicating that people would like to accumulate more than they are succeeding in doing, and there is therefore a deficiency or shortage in stocks. In this case, of course, the output adjustments are manifestly impossible, except in so far as it is possible, especially under conditions of stress such as a war, for a society to expand its capacity beyond what it formerly believed it to be. If there is still a deficit in accumulation where the limits even of extreme capacity have been reached, the result will be either inflation or government controls designed to lower the consumption and accumulation curves.

The Mechanism of Inflation

The mechanism of inflation will be described in more detail in Chapter 16. Its impact on the consumption and investment functions is all that concerns us here. This impact, as in the case of deflation, is likely to operate through two main mechanisms—the redistribution of income on the one hand, and a liquidity effect on the other. Both operate in an opposite direction to the way they operate in deflation.

Thus inflation redistributes income *toward* the profit makers and the holders of goods, and away from the *rentiers*—the debt holders, pensioners, annuitants, and people with relatively fixed money incomes. In this case, therefore, the gainers are likely to be the "high savers" and the losers the "low savers." The effect of the redistribution therefore is likely to be a decline in consumption at each level of output. The effect on investment, however, is likely to be in the opposite direction: the high profits of inflation encourage investment; the holding of goods becomes profitable and so the willingness to hold *more* goods—i.e., to accumulate—increases.

Again the net effect of the redistribution depends on the magnitude of these changes: if the effect on consumption is large and on investment is small, the net effect will be a decline in the total absorption curve and the inflation will therefore be effective in lowering the deficit accumulation and in moving toward an equilibrium. If, however, the effect on consumption is small and on investment is large, the inflation adds fuel to its own flames—the more it proceeds, the greater the deficit in accumulation and the greater the inflationary pressure. In such a case an inflation may lapse into "hyperinflation," in which the rate of rise in the price level approaches a limit set by physical circumstances. This limit, if we may judge from the experience of hyperinflations, seems to be about 100 per cent per week.

Liquidity Effect in Inflation

Inflation also may have a "liquidity effect." If the rise in prices proceeds faster than the increase in the money stock (which is frequently the case), then even if the money stock is increasing people find themselves "less liquid" because the purchasing power of their money stock declines. This may make them less willing to consume and to invest at each level of income, as they feel their power of consuming and investing is less. The liquidity effect therefore operates to lower both the consumption and investment functions, and hence has a doubly restraining effect on total absorption. It is an effect which lessens the deficit accumulation and helps to restore equilibrium. We may find, therefore, that there is some constant rate of inflation at which the total absorption curve is pulled down to the point where there is no deficit or surplus in accumulation.

QUESTIONS AND EXERCISES

1. Construct identities relating the following sets of variables:
   a. The average yield of wheat per acre (y), the total number of acres harvested (A), and the total production of wheat (W).

b. The average number of vehicles per mile of highway (n), the average speed of the vehicles (v), and the density of traffic (number passing a given point per hour) (D).

2. Express the variables of a balance sheet as an identity. Can the balance sheet identities of various individuals be summed to produce a consolidated balance sheet identity? If so, what variables will it contain?

3. What is the interpretation of the points of intersection G_1, G_2, G_3 and H_1, H_2 in Fig. 51, page 295.

4. In Table 24, page 292, suppose that government is able to absorb 14 units of product from the economy without causing any decline in consumption or investment. Calculate and tabulate the total absorption, the actual accumulation, and the surplus or deficit accumulation at each level of output. What now will be the equilibrium output?

5. In the model of Table 24, page 292, suppose that government absorbs 20 units of output, but that this absorption is financed in such a way that it causes a drop of 7 units of consumption and 3 units of investment at each level of output. Using the graphical technique of Fig. 51, page 295, find the equilibrium output.

6. Suppose that the total absorption curve BB' of Fig. 51, page 295, was moved vertically downward until it was tangent to the line OK. Discuss the nature of the equilibrium at the point of tangency. How would you interpret the model if the curve BB' lay wholly below the line OK?

7. Suppose that a rate of inflation of x per cent per annum will lower the total absorption at each level of output by $\dfrac{x\%}{2}$. Suppose now that in the conditions of the model of Fig. 51 (page 295) and Table 24 (page 292), the capacity output of the system was 140 units. What rate of inflation would be necessary in order to equate total absorption with output? Draw the family of curves of Fig. 51 under these new conditions.

CHAPTER 16

MACROECONOMIC MODELS: MODELS OF MONETARY CIRCULATION AND EXCHANGE

The Exchange System

The economic models of the previous chapter were *nonmonetary*, in the sense that all the variables in them were aggregates of goods. Production, consumption, investment, were defined as aggregates of goods created, destroyed, or accumulated. Income was identified with output as an aggregate of real goods produced.[1] In expanding the model we must now turn to the aspects of the system which are involved in the circulation of money and the exchange of goods. The "basic model" of Chapter 15 makes no explicit mention of exchange, which is the process whereby the *ownership* of goods and of money and other assets is transferred and circulated among the various individuals of the society. In exchange no physical, identifiable asset is created or destroyed, even though utilities are generally created, but the previously produced assets change owners in the course of their life history from their birth in production to their death in consumption.

Money as a Measure of Value

In this process of exchange money plays an essential role in any developed economy. Barter—that is, the exchange of goods for goods, or of any nonmoney asset for any other—is important in primitive societies and is never wholly absent even in the most advanced economies. A pure barter system, however, is rare even among primitive societies. In the course of the development of economic institutions

[1] It is curious that what is really the basic model of the Keynesian economics should be essentially nonmonetary, when even Keynes himself, at least for a long period in the development of his thought, regarded his main contribution as the development of a "monetary" economics as opposed to the "real goods" economics of the classical school. In fact, however, the monetary elements in the Keynesian system are essentially subordinate to the "real" elements.

the evolution of a standard and measure of value takes place at a very early date. A pure barter economy only seems to be possible where exchanges are rare and the commodities exchanged are highly diverse. As soon as anything like a "market" develops—that is, frequent and repeated exchanges of more or less standardized commodities—the principle of arbitrage will operate (see pages 73–76) to bring the exchange ratios of various commodities into rough consistency with each other. When this happens it becomes possible to use one commodity as a measure of value, and a convention arises whereby "prices" are quoted in terms of the standard commodity, even though this may not participate in all exchanges. A great variety of such standard commodities have been used in different societies—cattle ("pecuniary" comes from the latin *Pecus,* cow), seashells, beads, stones, tobacco, cloth, grain, and all the common metals.

All Measurement as Valuation

The same process takes place in the development of almost any kind of measurement. Measurement is the expression of *equivalence* in some quality between different objects. Thus we might say that a house was "ten pianos long" or "seventeen sheep long" or "800 thimbles long," meaning that we had established a ratio of equivalence in length between the house and ten pianos, or seventeen sheep or 800 thimbles. It is very convenient, however, to have a single measure, and in the case of length some common object, such as a foot or a hand, generally first serves this purpose. Similarly in the case of "value" we might say that the house was "worth" 5000 yards of cloth or 10,000 bushels of wheat or 25 horses, expressing here an equivalence in exchange. In this case also it is convenient to have a single measure, and a society soon comes to adopt a convention to use one commodity to measure all values. If then we know the equivalence of two objects in terms of the measure, we know their equivalence in terms of one another. If a house is 50 feet and a table is 5 feet long, we know immediately that the house is as long as 10 tables. Similarly, if a house is worth 30 cows and a horse is worth 2 cows, we know that a house is worth 15 horses.

The Abstract, Standard Measure

As measurement is essentially an abstract process and is not necessarily tied to any physical object as a measure, it is not surprising to find in the course of development that concrete measures give way to abstract units of measurement. This is mainly because all concrete measures are apt themselves to vary in the quality measured. If we measure lengths by actual feet or paces, we run up against the problem that one person's foot or pace is different from another's. Consequently the idea of a "standard" foot emerges, which may not be the length of any actual foot. Similarly an abstract measure of value emerges in the shape of a monetary unit, the "dollar" or "pound" or "franc." The "dollar" as a unit of measurement is not a commodity, not even a certain weight of gold. It is essentially an abstract unit by which the values, or exchange equivalences, of assets are compared.

Money as a Medium of Exchange

It is quite possible for a society to have a unit of account, or a measure of value, which is purely abstract and is not represented in any physical form. In England, for instance, the price of luxury articles is often quoted in "guineas," although the guinea coin (worth 21 shillings) disappeared many generations ago. Usually, however, the unit of account is embodied in some physical object or asset, in which case it is said to be a *medium of exchange* or a *store of value*. In societies where a commodity is used as a unit of account, such as gold or tobacco, the same commodity in its physical form also generally becomes a medium of exchange, that is, an *intermediary* between final exchanges. The worker exchanges his labor for the "money," whatever it is, not because he wants it for its own sake, but because he can buy other things with it. His final exchange is labor for goods. This, however, is broken down into two sets of exchanges, labor for money and money for goods. The medium of exchange in a society, then, is that asset or group of assets which is wanted primarily because it is readily exchangeable. This attribute of ready exchangeability is called "liquidity."

Liquidity

It is important to realize that "liquidity" is a *quality* of assets which they may possess in greater or less degree. Liquidity is not a very clear or easily measurable concept; yet it is of the utmost importance in understanding the nature of money.

Consider, for instance, the difference between an automobile worth $2000 and a roll of twenty hundred-dollar bills. Both objects are "worth" $2000. What this means is that each of these objects *could be exchanged* directly or indirectly for $2000 worth of any other commodity or group of commodities which are offered on the market. The amount in both cases represents a "claim" on the other goods and services of society. In both cases there is an understanding, implicit in the whole system of exchange relationships and valuations, that I can find someone who will give me $2000 dollars' worth of something else in return for what I have. The difference, however, lies in the fact that the twenty hundred-dollar bills could quickly and easily be exchanged for anything that is offered for sale in the United States, whereas the automobile could not easily be exchanged for anything except money. That is to say, the twenty hundred-dollar bills possess a certain quality of *convenience and ease* in exchangeability which the car does not possess. We might illustrate this again by an analogy from length. If we knew that an automobile was exactly ten feet long we *could,* of course, measure the length of a house by taking the automobile and "pacing" the house with it; thus we might find that the house was 5½ automobiles, or 55 feet, long. But this would be very inconvenient. To measure the length of the house we use a foot rule or, even better, a tape measure. So if we want to buy $2000 worth of cheese we do not take an automobile and say, "Give me $2000 worth of cheese for this." We take twenty hundred-dollar bills or, even better, the monetary equivalent of the tape measure, a check for $2000.

The "Order of Liquidity"

Just as *long* objects can be arranged in an order showing their convenience for use in the measurement of length—with mules, perhaps, at the bottom and tape measures at the top—so *valuable* objects can be arranged in an order showing their convenience for use in exchange, with things like real estate, buildings, furniture, and personal effects at the bottom, ranging up through stocks of standard commodities, ordinary shares, long-term bonds, short-term bonds, call money, and so on through to bank deposits and cash at the top. This is the *order of liquidity.*

The Arbitrary Definition of Money

Things at the top of this scale are called "money"; things at the bottom of the scale, i.e., illiquid things, are what may be bought with money. But just where to draw the line—just what is money and what is not—is difficult to define. Some writers, for instance, include bank deposits on current account in "money" and some do not. Some writers would confine the term "money" to mean cash plus bank notes, and some would include even savings deposits. However, strange though it may seem, where the line is drawn does not matter very much. The quality of being "money" is a matter of degree rather

than of kind, and under certain circumstances even things like diamonds or cigarettes behave like money. For purposes of exposition
it is often convenient to draw a sharp line at some point in the scale
of liquidity and say, "everything more liquid than this is money, and
everything less liquid than this is not money." It is important to
realize, however, that wherever this line is drawn will be a more or
less arbitrary point. Consequently, arguments as to whether a certain
thing is or is not money are usually a waste of breath. If we are clear
about our definition, whatever it is, we shall not go far astray.

False Definitions of Money

With the above analysis it is at least possible to criticize some attempted definitions of money as not being significant. It is clear, for
instance, that in our society gold and silver for most purposes are not
money at all, though they were in California around 1850 and still
are in North Africa. But most people who are likely to read this book
would never think of going down to the store with a bag of gold dust,
and it would be most doubtful whether they could buy anything with
it if they did—the storekeeper would be more likely to call for the
police! Similarly, it is not the "redeemability" of paper money which
gives it liquidity, for most paper money is not redeemable (i.e., exchangeable into gold or silver at a fixed legal rate); and yet we find
no difficulty in buying groceries with it and redeemability in groceries
is much more important than redeemability in gold! Nor does the
right of legal tender necessarily characterize money—i.e., the legal
obligation on the part of creditors to receive the money in settlement
of a debt. Most paper money, it is true, is legal tender, but some paper
money (e.g., Scottish bank notes) is not, nor are bank deposits; yet the
absence of this privilege does not make these assets any less useful as
money. Under certain circumstances commodities may become more
"liquid" than "official" money—as were cigarettes in many parts of
postwar Europe. We may perhaps therefore venture on a rough definition of money as "those assets which are customarily exchanged for a
wide variety of other assets, and which are wanted mainly because of
a belief in their continuing ability so to be exchanged."

Money as a Store of Value

The attribute of money as a "store of value" is closely related to its
use as a medium of exchange, yet has certain peculiarities. The need
for a store of value arises because of a desire to postpone the consump-

tion of assets to a future date, usually because of some irregularities in the flow of production or income, or in anticipated needs. Consumption can be postponed, however, only if assets are held in a form which does not depreciate or decay, or at least decays slowly. The property of durability in purchasing power therefore has been an important element in determining the selection of various commodities or assets as money. The popularity of metals, and especially of the precious metals (those with high value per unit weight), for use as money is closely related with their convenience as a store of value. They are easy to store, do not decay or corrode, and seem to have had a fairly stable purchasing power at least over short periods. No commodity or financial instrument has ever proved completely satisfactory as a store of value, as even those assets which do not decay in a physical sense are almost universally subject to changes in purchasing power. About the closest we could get to a perfect store of value would be a bond or financial obligation with a price-index clause, which would have a constant purchasing power in terms of some price index. Even an instrument of this kind, however, would be no safer than its issuer, and no price index can give a completely satisfactory measure of changes in purchasing power.

Change in Price Level as a Rate of Interest on Money Stocks

The "store of value" aspect of money takes on peculiar importance in times of inflation and deflation when price levels are changing rapidly. When prices are rising, money, along with any other asset which is measured as a constant sum of "dollars," declines in purchasing power. Thus if the price level doubles during a year, $100 will only buy half as much at the end of the year as it would at the beginning. A rise in the price level is therefore equivalent to a *negative* rate of interest, in terms of purchasing power, on all assets whose value is fixed in terms of the monetary unit. Similarly a fall in the price level *raises* the purchasing power of these assets, and is equivalent to a positive real rate of interest. If the price level halves during a year, $100 is worth twice as much in terms of its command over commodities at the end of the year than it was at the beginning. Putting the same thing in another way, the owner could spend and consume $50, and still have as much purchasing power at the end of the year as he had at the beginning. It is clear that the expectation of rising prices will lower the willingness to hold money, and that the expectation of a fall in prices will make people more eager to hold money.

The Velocity of Circulation

If therefore we wish to analyze the forces which underly the circulation of money and the volume of exchanges, some method must be devised for describing and defining not only the quantity of money and of other relevant assets but also for measuring the willingness or "eagerness" to hold money. There are several methods for doing this. A crude but very useful method is through the concept of the *velocity of circulation*. Suppose that we define the money stock of a society, M, in some arbitrary manner. The total volume of *payments* in the society, E, is then defined as the sum of all the quantities of money which change owners in a unit time period. A single payment is a transference of ownership of money from account A to account B. It is recorded as an *expenditure* to A and as a *receipt* to B; the expenditure and the receipt, however, are merely the two "ends" of the same payment. The total of all such payments (which can be reckoned as the total of all expenditures, or as the total of all receipts) is the total volume of payments, E. The velocity of circulation, V, or more accurately the *payments velocity* of circulation, is the ratio of the total volume of payments to the total money stock. That is,

$$V \equiv \frac{E}{M} \text{ or } E \equiv MV \tag{1}$$

What Does the Velocity of Circulation Measure?

Identities, as we have seen, only have significance if the variables which they contain have a certain independent validity as "parameters of behavior"—that is, as quantities which vary in a regular way with certain aspects of human behavior. The velocity of circulation is such a quantity. It is a rough measure of the willingness to hold money; an increase in the willingness to hold money will diminish the velocity of circulation. It may be thought of as the average number of times in a year that a dollar of the money stock changes hands in a payment. Thus if the "average dollar" changes hands (makes a payment) 20 times a year, and if the total money stock is a million dollars, the total volume of payments will be $20,000,000 per annum. The reciprocal of the velocity of circulation may be called the "period of turnover"; it is the average period of time which elapses between the successive payments of a single dollar. Thus if the velocity of circulation is 20 times a year, the period of turnover will be $\frac{365}{20}$, or $18\frac{1}{4}$ days.

Illustration. In order to perceive the truth of this proposition, imagine a society consisting of thirty people in a classroom, each possessing a one-dollar bill. The total quantity of money in the society is $30. Every time a bell rings, each person passes his dollar bill on to another, and receives in turn a dollar bill from another. The acceptance of the dollar bill represents receipts; the giving out of the dollar bill represents expenditure. Suppose the bell rings every minute. The receipts (and the expenditure) of each person are $1 a minute, or $60 an hour; the total receipts of the society are $30 a minute, or $1800 an hour, although there are only thirty dollar bills in the room.

Now if the velocity of circulation doubles—that is to say, if the bell rings every thirty seconds instead of every sixty seconds—the period of time for which each individual holds his dollar bill is cut in half. The receipts (and expenditure) of each individual are now $2 a minute; the receipts of the society are $60 a minute, or $3600 an hour. The receipts of the society have doubled, although there is just the same quantity of money in the room, merely because the velocity of circulation has doubled, or, what is the same thing, because people hold on to their money only half as long as they did before!

Suppose again that the bell rings only once a minute, so that the velocity of circulation is again "once a minute." Let each individual have two dollar bills instead of one. The receipts of each individual will now be $2 a minute. The quantity of money has doubled, the velocity of circulation has stayed the same, and consequently the receipts of the society have doubled. Or suppose that the quantity of money doubles—to two dollar bills per head—but that the velocity of circulation is cut in half—to once every two minutes. Then the receipts will be the same as before—$30 an hour. Evidently, in this very simple case, our formula is correct.

Velocity of Circulation as an Aspect of Human Behavior

The significance of the velocity of circulation concept lies in the fact that it is something more than a convenient statistical ratio; it is a true average of *individual* velocities of circulation, each of which is a figure representing a definite aspect of individual behavior. The average velocity of circulation represents, therefore, a kind of "social average" of individual patterns of behavior.

In the case of a single individual the ratio $\dfrac{\text{Money Receipts}}{\text{Money Stock}}$ may be

called his individual velocity of circulation; the ratio $\dfrac{\text{Money Stock}}{\text{Money Receipts}}$

is his individual period of turnover. Thus, if an individual with annual receipts of $10,000 holds a money stock of $500, his velocity of circulation is twenty times a year. This may be visualized as the number of times a year the reservoir of his money stock would have to be emptied and refilled in making his money payments. His period of turnover is $18\frac{1}{4}$ days—this may be visualized as the average length of time that a dollar stays in his money stock, or the average interval between receipts and expenditures. The velocity of circulation of the whole system is simply the weighted average (weighted by the amounts of money held by each individual) of all the individual velocities of circulation.[1]

Effect of a Change in Velocities

The average velocity of circulation is therefore a figure which is determined by individual decisions. Each individual is free to decide how large he wants his money stock to be in proportion to his total receipts; the result of all these decisions is the total volume of receipts. It should be observed that the effect of a change in the individual velocity of circulation is different in the case of an individual from that of society at large. An individual who wants to decrease his velocity or increase his period of turnover does so by increasing the amount of money that he holds, usually—as he regards his receipts as for the moment a given factor—by reducing his expenditures. The effect of his decision on the whole society, however, is not of itself to increase the quantity of money, though that may happen as a secondary effect, but rather to diminish the total of receipts through the diminution of what is the same thing, the total of expenditures. Thus the individual is mainly conscious of his ability to regulate his individual velocity by changing the quantity of money which he holds. The effect of his decision on society, however, will be a change in the total volume of payments, unless there are secondary effects on the quantity of money. Money cannot be destroyed by spending it, for

[1] Let $m_1, m_2, \ldots m_n$ represent the money stocks of the individuals 1, 2, ... N of a society, and $v_1, v_2, \ldots v_n$ represent their individual velocities of circulation. Let M be the total quantity of money in the society, E the total of receipts (expenditures), and V the average velocity of circulation. Then if $e_1, e_2, \ldots e_n$ represent the individual receipts (expenditures) we have:

$$e_1 = m_1 v_1, \quad e_2 = m_2 v_2, \quad \cdots e_n = m_n v_n, \quad \text{whence}$$

$$V = \frac{E}{M} = \frac{e_1 + e_2 + \cdots + e_n}{m_1 + m_2 + \cdots + m_n} = \frac{m_1 v_1 + m_2 v_2 + \cdots + m_n v_n}{m_1 + m_2 + \cdots + m_n}$$

That is, V is the weighted arithmetic mean of $v_1, v_2, \ldots v_n$, weighted by the respective m's. Similarly, it can be shown that the average period of turnover is the weighted *harmonic* mean of the individual periods.

what one spends another gets. This principle will be developed in more detail in pages 321–329.

The "Fisher Identity"

We can now proceed to the consideration of a useful equation or identity known sometimes as the "equation of exchange," or from its author as the "Fisher identity."[2] The Fisher identity is based on the assumption that every payment is payment *for* something and that the dollar value of what is bought and sold with, or for, a payment must be equal to the payment itself. The dollar value of anything bought or sold, however, is equal to the price of the thing multiplied by the quantity. Thus, consider a transaction in which 1000 bushels of wheat change hands at $2 per bushel. The *value* of the wheat is $2000; the payment which is made for the wheat is two thousand dollars. If, therefore, we represent the price of anything by p, the quantity traded by q, and the amount of money paid by e, we have:

$$pq \equiv e, \text{ or } p \equiv \frac{e}{q} \tag{2}$$

This identity is really the definition of price as the ratio of the money paid for anything to the quantity of the thing bought. If now we define indices for the price level P and the quantity level Q of all things for which payments are made, so defined (as we have seen on page 276) that PQ represents the total value of all things for which payments are made, then we must have

$$PQ \equiv E \tag{3}$$

E being the total volume of payments. All that this identity states is that the price of everything exchanged, multiplied by the quantity of everything exchanged, must be equal to the total amount paid for (or received for) everything exchanged. Now putting equations (3) and (1) (page 314) together, we have:

$$PQ \equiv MV \tag{4}$$

This is the "equation of exchange," or the Fisher identity.

The Fisher identity can also be used in another form known as the "income form." If P' represents the price level of output, and Q' represents its volume, $P'Q'$ is the total value of output or the national money *income*. If now we define V', the "income velocity," as the average ratio of individual incomes to the quantity of money, the na-

[2] Irving Fisher, *The Purchasing Power of Money*, New York, 1911.

tional income must also be equal to MV'. The income velocity may also be regarded as an expression of the average individual behavior toward money, though it is a concept open to certain objections and must be used carefully. We can, however, write an "income identity."

$$P'Q' \equiv MV' \qquad (5)$$

Fisher Identity Models

The Fisher identity is a powerful tool in the analysis of monetary problems—more powerful, probably, than many modern theorists are willing to recognize. It must, however, be used carefully. It separates out the three main elements which affect the general level of prices, but it does not tell us what determines the magnitude of these elements or how they react on one another. Nevertheless, it forms the basis of a number of interesting models. The simplest model is that which assumes that M is given $(= M_1)$ at any particular time by the processes of historical accumulation of the money stock, V is given $(= V_1)$ by the psychological propensities of the people, and Q is given $(= Q_1)$ by the historical development of productive capacity. This gives us three very simple equations, which when combined with the identity gives an immediate solution for the price level, $P = \dfrac{M_1 V_1}{Q_1}$.

The Quantity Theory

This model, simple as it is, illustrates the conditions under which the "crude" quantity theory of money is true. The quantity theory in its simplest form states that the price level varies in direct proportion to the quantity of money, or $P = KM$. We see immediately from the Fisher identity that this relationship only holds if the ratio $\dfrac{V}{Q}$ is constant. A rise in the quantity of money will not cause a rise in prices if it is offset either by a decline in V or an increase in Q. The usefulness of the quantity theory as a rough explanation of large changes in the price level lies in the fact that over short periods, at any rate, the possibilities of variation in V and Q are much less than the possibility of variation in M.

An Extended Fisher Model

The Fisher model can be extended by assuming various empirical relationships among the variables. Thus suppose we assume that the quantity of money is itself a function of the price level, and that a rise in prices to a new level will call forth an additional quantity of money, either from the banking system or from the government. Thus we replace the equation $M = M_1$ in the first model by the equation $M = F_m(P)$. Fig. 54 shows a graphic solution for this model. The quantity of money, M, is measured on the vertical axis, the price level on the horizontal axis. The curve AB shows the relation between the

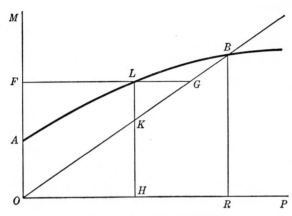

FIG. 54.   A Fisher Model.

price level and the quantity of money which each price level calls forth, $M = F_m(P)$. The straight line OB represents the basic identity, $M = \frac{Q}{V} P$. Q and V are assumed to be given. The slope of this line is $\frac{Q}{V}$; it should be observed that it does not necessarily have a 45° slope, as in the somewhat analogous figure in the basic employment model, Fig. 51, page 295. The point of intersection of AB and OB is the position of equilibrium. OR is the equilibrium price level; RB is the equilibrium stock of money. If the price level is below the equilibrium level, say at OH, it will call forth a quantity of money HL, which will force the price level up to LG, and so on. Similarly, if the price level is above the equilibrium it will call forth a stock of money which will force the price level down. The equilibrium therefore is stable, as long as AB cuts OB from above; that is, the increase in money stock called forth by a unit increase in the price level must be less than $\frac{Q}{V}$.

Instability of the Model

This model, simple as it is, throws some light on the mechanics of inflation and hyperinflation. If the money stock is very elastic with respect to the price level, equilibrium will only be established at a high level of prices, if at all. If the elasticity of the money stock with respect to price level is greater than the ratio $\frac{Q}{V}$ no equilibrium is possible, as the lines AB and OB will not intersect. We are not in a position yet to examine in detail the dynamics of this model. It should be observed, however, that the process of inflation (that is, a positive rate of increase in the price level) is likely to increase the velocity of circulation, as money loses its ability to be a store of value and people hence try to hold as little as possible. Inflation itself, then, assuming full employment and no increase in Q, will increase V and lower the ratio $\frac{Q}{V}$. The line OB will rotate toward the P axis, and the position of equilibrium will move out to higher price levels. The movement toward the equilibrium therefore pushes the point of equilibrium away from the present position, like a man chasing a burglar. Similarly deflation tends to rotate the line OB toward the M axis, and the equilibrium position will fall. It is evident that if equilibrium is to be reached the rotation of the line OB (that is, the fall or the rise in V) must eventually slow down. Once equilibrium is reached, however, the line OB will swing back again to its original position and the chase starts all over again! Such a system will obviously be subject to cyclical fluctuations.

Reciprocal Relation of P and Q

An important feature of the economic system to which the Fisher identity calls attention is the reciprocal relation between P and Q. If the total *value* of transactions falls, as a result of a change in M or in V, or in both, this fall in value must be reflected *either* in a decline in P *or* in a decline in Q. The more P declines the less Q will decline, and vice versa. This proposition is important in interpreting the behavior of different sectors of the economy in the course of the business cycle. Thus a depression generally results in a fall in the total *value* of the output of all industries. In some industries, however, this fall in the value of output is achieved mainly by a fall in prices, in which case output will not be much changed, as in agriculture. In other industries the fall in the value of output is achieved mainly by a fall in *output,* in which case prices are not much changed.

The "Market Identity"

The Fisher identity is essentially a relationship among the "flows" of the system. An identity can also be developed which expresses a price level in a relationship among "stocks." This is the "market identity" which we have already noted in the case of particular prices on page 59; it remains to be observed that the identity also holds for any group of commodities or exchangeables, or for all of them. Thus suppose P_a is the price level of all nonmonetary assets, and Q_a is the total physical quantity of nonmonetary assets. These quantities have to be defined, of course, as index numbers, and must be so defined as to make the product $P_a Q_a$ equal to the total value of nonmoney assets, V_a. Then if M is the total stock of money, and r is the preferred liquidity ratio—i.e., the proportion of the total value of assets which people as a whole wish to hold in the form of money—we must have:

$$r \equiv \frac{M}{M + P_a Q_a}$$

i.e.,

$$P_a \equiv \frac{M(1 - r)}{Q_a r} \tag{6}$$

This is an extremely useful identity in interpreting movements of price levels, as both M and Q_a can be regarded as historically determined at any one moment and P_a then becomes a simple function of the preferred liquidity ratio or "liquidity preference," r. If r rises, people feel that at existing prices they are holding too little money; they will individually endeavor to increase their money holdings by selling nonmoney assets. A general attempt to sell nonmoney assets, however, will result in a fall in their price level. As the price level falls, the total value of assets falls, and the proportion which the quantity of money bears to this total rises, as the dollar value of the money stock is constant. The fall in prices will go on until people on the whole are satisfied with the higher proportion of money to total assets. Similarly, if r falls, people try to get rid of money by buying other assets. prices rise, and the total value of assets rises until people are once more satisfied with the amount of money in existence.

THE PAYMENTS MATRIX

In the Fisher identity and the models based on it we consider the payments system as an aggregate. For many purposes, however, it is necessary to break down this aggregate, and to consider the individual payments, or a smaller aggregate. These can be conveniently expressed in the form of a payments table, or *matrix,* as in Table 25. The various individuals of the society are A, B, C, D. In the table we have considered a society of only four individuals, but the argument can clearly be extended to any number. The individuals are ranged both horizontally and vertically, so that the table has N^2 compartments, where N is the number of individuals. In each compartment we write the total payment *from* the individual in whose row the compartment lies

TABLE 25.   The Payments Matrix

	A	B	C	D	Expenditures
A		20	8	15	43
B	5		15	10	30
C	16	9		11	36
D	10	8	15		33
Receipts	31	37	38	36	142

to the individual in whose column it lies. Thus in Table 25, 20 represents the payment from A to B, 8 the payment from A to C, and so on. Each payment therefore is a receipt to the individual of its "column" and an expenditure to the individual of its "row." The total expenditure of each individual is then obtained by adding up the figures in the rows, and the total receipts of each individual is obtained by adding up the figures in the columns. Thus in the example the total expenditure of A is 43 and the total receipts of A is 31.

Total Expenditures = Total Receipts — Money Created

It follows immediately from this figure that the total of expenditures in a closed society is equal to the total of receipts. Whether we add the column of total expenditures or the row of total receipts the result must be the same (142), because these represent simply two different ways of adding up the same list of individual figures. This proposition is only true, however, as long as every receipt and every expenditure is a "payment." If money is either created or destroyed by any individual, and if we count the creation of money as a "receipt" and its destruction as an "expenditure," then the above proposition must be modified; its general form is that the excess of all receipts over all expenditures must be equal to the total money created during the period. If money is destroyed, of course, there will be an equal excess of total expenditures over total receipts. Suppose, for instance, in Table 25, that A destroyed 10 units of money. His expenditure would now be 53, but no receipts would be altered; the total of receipts as before would be 142, but the total of expenditures 152.

Hoarding = "Dishoarding" + Money Created

From Table 25 we can immediately deduce the change during the period in the money holdings of each individual—i.e., his hoarding or "dishoarding," as in Table 26.

It will be observed that the total amount of hoarding is exactly equal to the total amount of dishoarding. This necessarily follows if

TABLE 26.   Hoarding and Dishoarding

	Receipts	Ex-penditures	Hoarding	Dis-hoarding
A	31	43		12
B	37	30	7	
C	38	36	2	
D	36	33	3	
Total	142	142	12	12

there is no creation or destruction of money, and is a corollary of the proposition that total receipts equal total expenditures. No matter how the receipts and expenditures change, if the total quantity of money in the society is constant, money is merely shifted around from pocket to pocket; and the increase in the pockets of some people must be exactly balanced by the decrease in the pockets of others. This proposition may be generalized in the form that the net hoarding of all individuals in a closed society must be equal to the total amount of money created. If money is destroyed, there will of course be net "dishoarding." This simply amounts to the proposition that the net change in the sum of the total money stocks of all individuals must be equal to the net change in the stock of money.

Total Hoarding Not Determined by Decisions to Hoard

The proposition is so obvious once stated that it seems almost trivial. Nevertheless, it is astonishing how many people—even bankers—fail to understand it. Thus during World War II there was a large increase in the quantity of money, mainly because the money expenditures of the government were much greater than its money receipts (i.e., there was a deficit in the cash budget). This increase in the quantity of money must, of course, be reflected in the money stocks (balances) of individuals—somebody must hold all the newly created money! The mere fact of the creation of money therefore necessitated "hoarding" —i.e., an excess of money receipts over expenditures—on the part of individuals. Nevertheless, we continually found distinguished members of the financial community making speeches in which they praised the public for the immense amount of "money saved" during the war, apparently oblivious of the fact that these "savings" (i.e., the increase in money holdings) were not the result of financial virtue on the part of individuals but the result of financial vice on the part of government! No matter what individuals had decided to do about their expenditures and receipts they could not have helped "hoarding" during this period while money was being created. This is a truth which we are somewhat unwilling to accept, for we see so clearly that the amount of money that we, as an individual, hoard or dishoard is within limits under our control that it seems absurd until we look into the matter further to suppose that the sum of the decisions of individuals in regard to hoarding do not determine the total hoarding of society. Yet such is indeed the case, as can be seen by returning to Table 25.

Decisions to Hoard Decrease Total Payments

We see in Table 25 that A is quite a spendthrift, and that he is "dishoarding" (i.e., diminishing his money stock) by 12 units in this period. Obviously, he cannot go on doing this indefinitely, so let us suppose that he decides to cut down his expenditure in the endeavor to make ends meet. Let us suppose initially that there is no change in the expenditure patterns of the other individuals. We might suppose at first glance that as A has stopped "dishoarding," and the others have not changed their behavior, that there will be net hoarding in the society. But Tables 27 and 28 show what happens.

TABLE 27.   Effect of Hoarding

	A	B	C	D	Expenditures
A		16	4	11	31
B	5		15	10	30
C	16	9		11	36
D	10	8	15		33
Receipts	31	33	34	32	130

Two things should be observed—one is that as a result of A's decision to curtail his expenditures he has, indeed, "balanced his budget," but his decision to do this has resulted in a decline in the total receipts of the society by an amount exactly equal to his contraction in expenditures. This follows inevitably from the proposition that total receipts and expenditures are equal. In the second place, it will be observed that there is still no net hoarding; hoarding and "dishoarding" are still equal, the decline in A's "dishoarding"

TABLE 28.   Effect of Hoarding

	Receipts	Ex-penditures	Hoarding	"Dis-hoarding"
A	31	31	0	
B	33	30	3	
C	34	36		2
D	32	33		1
Total	130	130	3	3

from 12 to 0 being just counterbalanced by a decline in the hoarding of the others due to the reduction in their receipts which A's decisions involve. Thus we see again that a net decision to increase money stocks (hoard) on the part of individuals does not result in an increase of money stocks unless there is creation of money; it results merely in a decline in money receipts (expenditures). Similarly, a net decision to "dishoard" (decrease money stocks) on the part of individuals does not result in a decline of money stocks unless there is destruction of money, but results rather in an increase in money receipts (expenditures).

Balance of Payments = Hoarding, for an Individual

The excess of receipts over expenditure of an individual is frequently called his "balance of payments"; if this is positive, the balance is said to be "favorable"; if negative, the balance is said to be "unfavorable." The terminology dates from the days of the Mercantilists, and the terms "positive" and "negative" are more accurate than "favorable" and "unfavorable": It is not necessarily advantageous to have a positive (favorable) balance of payments, nor is it necessarily disadvantageous to have a negative (unfavorable) balance of payments in any given period. It is clear that for any individual a positive balance of payments is equal to the amount of his "hoarding"—i.e., the amount by which his money stocks have increased—and a negative balance is similarly equal to his "dishoarding."

And for a Group

From Table 25 an important proposition relating to any *group* of individuals can be derived—that the difference between the receipts of any group from nonmembers, and the expenditures of the group toward nonmembers, i.e., the balance of payments of the group, must equal the total net gain in money stocks of the individuals of the group. This is again illustrated in Table 29. A and B are regarded as a group ("nation"). Their total receipts from "outsiders" (C and D) amount to 43; their total expenditures to outsiders, to 48. The difference (−5) is the net loss of money from A and B together (A losing 12 but B gaining 7). The reason for this is clear; the payments which are internal to the group (A's to B and B's to A) are common to the group's total expenditures and to the group's total receipts.

TABLE 29.   The Balance of Payments

	A + B	C	D	Expenditures
A + B		23	25	48
C	25		11	36
D	18	15		33
Receipts	43	38	36	117

Thus we have:

A's total receipts + B's total receipts − A's total expenditures − B's total expenditures = A's hoarding + B's hoarding

Subtracting A's receipts from B and B's receipts from A from the right-hand side, and the identical quantities, B's expenditures to A and A's expenditures to B from the left-hand side, we have:

(A + B)'s receipts from outsiders = (A + B)'s expenditures to outsiders + the increase in (A + B)'s money stock

The same reasoning can clearly be applied no matter how many individuals are in the group. The important result follows that the individuals of Table 25 can be replaced by *groups* (e.g., nations) and the properties of the table remain unchanged, the total of receipts (expenditures) now, however, representing the total of intergroup (international) payments.

Partial Velocities

The question now arises, Can any useful models be set up which will determine the various magnitudes of the payments matrix? The complete determination of the payments matrix of course would involve the determination of all the variables of the whole economic system— prices and quantities of goods exchanged as well as payments or values. Nevertheless it is possible to set up a simple model for the payments system as such by employing the concept of particular or partial velocities of circulation. The partial velocity of circulation from A to B, v_{ab}, is defined as the ratio of A's expenditure to B (or what is the same thing, B's receipts from A) in a given period to A's money stock at the beginning of the period. That is,

$$v_{ab} = \frac{\text{A's expenditure toward B in a given period}}{\text{A's money stock at the beginning of the period}}$$

Each partial velocity then is an expression of two aspects of economic behavior. It reflects the attitude of the spender toward money in general, and it reflects his attitude toward the commodity which he is purchasing from the receiver. Thus v_{ab} will probably rise if A decides that he is holding too much money, and adopts a more liberal spending policy in general. In this case v_{ac}, v_{ad}, etc., will also probably rise. A rise in v_{ab} may also reflect a shift in A's demand structure toward the things which B is selling and away from the things which C, D, etc., are selling. In this case a rise in v_{ab} may be accompanied by a fall in v_{ac}, v_{ad}, etc. The whole system of partial velocities therefore presents a rough picture of the over-all structure of demand in a system. It is not, of course, a complete picture, as it takes no explicit account of the relation between purchases and prices. Nevertheless it gives us a useful halfway house in the development of a model of general economic equilibrium.

Partial Velocities Determine the Payments Matrix

If now the partial velocities corresponding to each expenditure of the system are given, and the total quantity of money in the system is also given, the whole payments matrix can be calculated, on the assumption that all individual balances of payments are zero. Thus suppose, to take the simplest case, that we have a system with only two individuals, A and B. Let a_b be the payment from A to B and b_a the payment from B to A. The payments matrix is shown in Table 30A.

TABLE 30.   Determination of Payments Matrix

	A				B	
	A	B	Exp.		A	B
A		a_b	a_b	A		v_{ab}
B	b_a		b_a	B	v_{ba}	
Rec.	b_a	a_b	$a_b + b_a$			

Suppose now that we are given, as parameters of behavior, the partial velocities v_{ab} and v_{ba}, as shown in Table 30B, and the total quantity of money in the system, M. Suppose this is divided between the two parties, M_a in A's possession and M_b in B's. Then in equilibrium we have:

$$a_b = b_a \tag{7}$$
$$a_b = M_a v_{ab} \tag{8a}$$
$$b_a = M_b v_{ba} \tag{8b}$$

whence
$$M_a v_{ab} = M_b v_{ba} \tag{9}$$

we also have
$$M_a + M_b = M \tag{10}$$

Equations (9) and (10) can be solved to give values of M_a and M_b:

$$M_a = \frac{M v_{ba}}{v_{ab} + v_{ba}} \qquad M_b = \frac{M v_{ab}}{v_{ab} + v_{ba}} \tag{11}$$

Then inserting these values in equations (8) we get values for the payments themselves,

$$a_b = b_a = \frac{M v_{ab} v_{ba}}{v_{ab} + v_{ba}} \tag{12}$$

Distribution of Money Stock Determined by Relative Partial Velocities

Some interesting features emerge even from this very simple model. The distribution of the money stock of the society between its two parts in equilibrium is seen to be determined by the *relative* partial velocities. If both partial velocities change in the same proportion, there is no change in the distribution of the money stock. If one rises relative to the other, the money stock shifts toward the individual whose partial velocity has risen least.

No matter how many individuals there are in the society, there is normally only one set of payments which will be consistent with any given system of partial velocities, given the quantity of money in the system and assuming that all balances of payments are zero.[3] The

[3] Suppose we have n individuals, A, B, . . . N. If M_a, M_b, . . . M_n are the equilibrium money stocks of these individuals, the payments matrix is as follows:

	A	B	C	⋯	N
A		$M_a v_{ab}$	$M_a v_{ac}$		$M_a v_{an}$
B	$M_b v_{ba}$		$M_b v_{bc}$		$M_b v_{bn}$
C	$M_c v_{ca}$	$M_c v_{cb}$			$M_c v_{cn}$
⋮					
N	$M_n v_{na}$	$M_n v_{nb}$	$M_n v_{nc}$		

As for each individual we assume the sum of receipts to be equal to the sum of expenditures, we have n equations of the form

$$M_a v_{ab} + M_a v_{ac} + \cdots + M_a v_{an} = M_b v_{ba} + M_c v_{ca} + \cdots + M_n v_{na}$$

actual solutions become more and more complicated as we increase the number of individuals. Nevertheless certain general principles emerge. An increase in the partial velocities of one set of individuals relative to another set is always likely to push the money stock into the hands of those with the smaller velocities. The money stock must be thought of as a sort of shifting cargo, the distribution of which among its various owners is the result of a complex game of pushball. Individuals, or groups of individuals, will only be successful in diminishing their money stocks if their "push" is *relatively* stronger than others, and will only succeed in increasing their money stocks if their "push" is relatively weaker than others. It can hardly be overemphasized that the distribution of the money stock and of payments is the result of *all* the decisions of *all* the people, and that no one individual can determine the results apart from the decisions of all the others.

QUESTIONS AND EXERCISES

1. After World War II cigarettes came to be used as a kind of "money" in many parts of Europe. Why do you suppose this happened? Discuss the advantages and disadvantages of cigarettes in the performance of the various functions of money.
2. Money is sometimes defined as that which is not wanted for its own sake but is wanted only for its power of exchanging for other things. On the other hand it is also said that money is wanted because it possesses the property of "liquidity," just as water is wanted because it possesses the property of "drinkability." Can these two views be reconciled?
3. What other things besides money can serve as (a) a measure of value, (b) a store of value, (c) a medium of exchange?
4. Suppose the relationship between the stock of money M and the price level P is given by the equation $M = 500 + 10P$. Suppose the velocity of circulation is constant at 20 times a year, and the volume of transactions is constant at 1000 units. What are the equilibrium values of P and M? Solve both algebraically and graphically. Suppose the velocity of circulation rises to 40 times a year. What are now the equilibrium values of P and M? Repeat with $V = 10$ times a year. Illustrate the three solutions on a single graph.
5. Imagine a closed economic system in which the quantity of money was

---

Any one of these however can be derived from all the others, so that we have only $n - 1$ independent equations. We have, however, a further equation

$$Ma + Mb + \cdots + Mn = M$$

where M is the total stock of money. We have, therefore n independent equations, sufficient to determine the n unknowns M_a, M_b, . . . M_n. Once the distribution of the money stock is determined each individual payment can be derived by multiplying the given partial velocity by the appropriate money stock.

$100,000,000. Suppose that in one year the total volume of payments was $7,300,000,000. Calculate: (a) the payments-velocity of circulation, (b) the period of (payments) turnover.

Suppose that the quantity of money is constant, and the payments velocity of circulation falls to 50 times a year. What would be the period of turnover? What would then be the volume of payments? Suppose that the quantity of money rose to $120,000,000 and the period of turnover rose to 10 days. What would be the total volume of payments?

6. The following table represents the expenditures and receipts of a closed society of three individuals, each figure representing a payment from the individual in whose row it stands to the individual in whose column it stands.

	A	B	C
A		100	150
B	166		58
C	100	156	

Calculate and tabulate:

a. The total expenditure, total receipts, and the net addition to or subtraction from the money holdings for each individual (i.e., hoarding or dishoarding).

b. Calculate the total of all receipts, and show that this is equal to the total of all expenditures.

c. Suppose that the above table shows the condition in a certain "week," week 0. In the next week, week 1, suppose that each individual attempts to "balance his budget" by reducing or expanding his expenditures in order to make them equal to his receipts of week 0. Suppose that the change in expenditures is divided equally between the other two individuals in each case. (Thus, if A diminishes his expenditure by an amount x, take $\frac{x}{2}$ from his expenditure toward B and $\frac{x}{2}$ from his expenditure toward C.) Draw up the payments table for week 1, and repeat the calculations (a) and (b). It will be found that the individuals have failed to "balance their budgets," as their receipts have changed. Continue now to weeks 2, 3, 4, etc., on the same assumptions by which we proceeded from week 0 to week 1. Can you formulate any law governing the movement of the payments, hoardings and dishoardings, and balances? Does the system move toward an equilibrium?

7. a. Repeat Exercise 6c on the assumption that only those individuals who are "dishoarding" (i.e., have an unfavorable balance of payments) make any adjustments in their expenditure.

b. Repeat Exercise 6c on the assumption that only those individuals who are *hoarding* make any adjustments in their expenditures. In what way do the results of Exercise 7 differ from the results of Exercise 6?

8. The following represents another payments table in a society of three individuals:

	A	B	C
A		64	128
B	64		96
C	128	96	

Calculate as before the total receipts, expenditures, and balances of payments. Suppose now that C cuts his expenditure in half, paying 64 to A and 48 to B; suppose that he keeps these rates constant. Assume that A and B react to the situation thus created by trying to balance their budgets as in Exercises 6 and 7, making their total expenditures in each week equal to their total receipts of the previous week, and distributing the decline in expenditures equally between the two recipients. Follow the course of the payments table for 5 weeks.

Make a table showing the total change in money stocks of each individual, week by week. Is the system moving toward equilibrium?

9. What will be the equilibrium position of the receipts table of Question 8 after an indefinitely large number of weeks? (Note: Question 9 cannot be answered without knowledge of the summation of infinite geometric series.)

10. If the preferred liquidity ratio is 10 per cent and the total quantity of money is $100,000,000, what is the total dollar value of nonmoney assets?

CHAPTER 17

THE FINANCIAL SYSTEM

The analysis of the preceding chapters can be applied fruitfully to the understanding of the financial system, and more especially to the interpretation of the effect of banking on the economic system. What we know as the "financial system" consists of those institutions which are mainly concerned with the creation, destruction, and exchange of "claims." Claims may perhaps be defined as those balance-sheet items which appear on two different balance sheets at the same time, being an "asset" on one and a "liability" on another. Thus loans, bank deposits, securities of all kinds, annuities, insurance policies, and the like, all fall in this category, and the institutions which deal in them—moneylenders, banks of various kinds, discount houses, investment trusts, insurance companies, stockbroking and jobbing firms, stock and bond markets, and so on are all "financial" institutions, the greatest of these being of course the government.

At the basis of the whole financial system lies a principle which we may call the principle of the creation of claims. Assets, as we have seen, can be divided into two great divisions—"things" (including cash) and "claims." Every item which features as a claim in the assets of one balance sheet also figures as a liability in the equities of another balance sheet. It follows that when all the balance sheets of a closed society are added together, the total of "claim" assets is equal to the total of "claim" liabilities. The total value of the "things" possessed in a society, and therefore the total value of its individual capitals, is not necessarily connected with the total value of claims. In other words, claims which are assets to one person and liabilities to another may be created without affecting the total value of the capital of a society. When, for instance, a corporation issues bonds, when a building and loan society writes a mortgage, when an individual makes a deposit with a savings bank, when a commercial bank grants a loan or accepts a deposit, "claims" are created which figure as an asset in one balance sheet and as a liability in another. The total of all assets is increased, but in the immediate act of the creation of a claim the total value of "things" or of capital is not necessarily increased. Of course, as a subsequent result of the creation of claims the value of "things" may be increased. If, for instance, a corporation uses the money raised by the sale of bonds to build a factory, the building of the factory will increase the value of the "things" on the balance sheets and will also result in a net increase in the total of personal capitals (net worths). But the mere creation of claims, in and of itself, does not increase the total of personal capitals.

Why Do We Have "Claims"?

Why, then, are claims created? Why bother with this complicated structure of debit and credit, which is built up so assiduously and which so often collapses in partial ruin? Obviously because claims (debts and credits) fill a need. In the first place the existence of claims makes it possible to divorce the "real" ownership or "equity" in capital goods from the control of these goods. A man who has a mortgage on his house does not possess in his "net worth" the full value of the house, but within certain limits he is responsible for the house and controls it. A corporation bondholder possesses a certain equity in the general assets of a corporation; but unless the corporation is bankrupted, he has no control over these assets. If there were no claims each capital good would have to be owned by some individual person, and the great aggregations of goods necessary in the organization of modern industry would be impossible.

Liquid Assets and Commercial Banks

The other need fulfilled by the existence of claims is the need for *liquid* assets, that is, for assets which may be used in the purchase of goods or in the settlement of debt. Generally speaking, there is only one type of financial institution which can create claims of this kind, claims which are not merely assets to their possessors, but *liquid* assets. This type is the *commercial bank*. When we speak of a "bank" in the following pages, then, we mean a commercial bank, not a savings bank or an investment bank.

Creation and Circulation of Claims

In order to understand the role played by claims in the economic system it is important to distinguish between two distinct but related processes. Just as we have on the one hand the production and consumption of goods and on the other their circulation and exchange, so also we have two distinct operations in regard to claims—their creation and destruction on the one hand, and their circulation and exchange on the other. These processes are often confused in the case of claims because in many instances the production and the exchange of a claim are bound up into a single operation. For the sake of conceptual clarity, however, it is vitally important that these two processes be distinguished.

Creation of Securities

It is not the function of a theoretical work to give an exhaustive list of various types of claims or securities with a description of how they are created and exchanged. Some examples, however, will illustrate the importance of a concept. One of the simplest forms of creation of claims is the issuance of securities, whether bonds or stock by a corporation. These securities represent an *obligation to grant* certain benefits on the part of the issuer and a *right to receive* these benefits on the part of the owner. At the moment of their creation, before the securities are sold, we may think of their creation as representing a simultaneous addition to both the assets and the liabilities of the issuing corporation. As a right to receive something, the security is an asset; as an obligation to grant something, it is a liability. The creation of securities always involves a simultaneous creation, therefore, of an asset and an equal liability. The securities do not, of course, usually remain in the possession of the issuing corporation, or there would be very little use in creating them. There is no point in the creation of securities which are not exchangeable, which is one reason why their creation and exchange are so often confused. Any individual could write himself out a promissory note for a million dollars, and so inflate his assets and liabilities by that amount, but the action would not be very significant unless he could find a buyer for the note! Similarly, corporate securities are issued in the hope that they will be exchangeable for other assets, and ultimately for goods.

Exchange of Securities

Once securities are "born," then, they almost always enter some kind of a market. In the case of the stocks or bonds of recognized companies this market is highly organized, competitive, and speculative. A security once launched may change hands many times before it disappears. The prices of securities are determined, as we have seen (pages 93–99) much as any prices are determined—by the relative quantities of the different kinds and by the relative preferences for them. If the preference for any particular kind of asset declines relative to others, if people become, that is to say, relatively less willing to hold it, its price will fall and its value decline relative to others until people can be found who are willing to hold the quantity that exists in the market. Similarly, if the quantity of any particular kind of asset rises, in the absence of any change in preferences, the price will have to fall until enough people can be found who are willing to hold this increased quantity.

THE BANKING AND FINANCIAL SYSTEM

Savings Banks

The banking system is so important as an instrument for the creation of claims, and especially of liquid assets, that it is necessary to examine its operations in some detail. We may dismiss fairly briefly those elements of the banking system outside the commercial banks, as not presenting any difficult theoretical problems. Savings banks create claims in the form of savings deposits, which are liabilities to the bank and assets to the depositor. When a savings bank "sells" $100 of these deposits to the depositors for cash (or, say, for commercial bank deposits), in the first instance the savings bank increases its assets by $100 in cash or commercial bank deposits and increases its liabilities by $100 in deposits. The savings banks, however, will normally exchange most of this cash for earning assets of some kind, such as bonds. If no new bonds are being issued, the operations of savings banks may force up the price of bonds, thus, as we will see more clearly later, lowering the rate of interest. If the creation of new bonds is elastic with respect to the interest rate, the operations may increase the quantity of bonds rather than affect their prices.

Investment Trusts

Investment trusts and holding companies are a significant element in the financial system, but again present few problems of a general theoretical nature. The device of incorporation permits the "pyramiding" of claims through the development of intermediary corporations whose assets consist of the claims of other corporations and which themselves issue securities. Thus an investment trust may hold as assets the securities of a great variety of other corporations, and will itself issue shares which it can persuade individuals, or other corporations, to hold. By this means the risks of the individual holder are spread, and people may be persuaded to hold a greater volume of securities than otherwise would be the case. Abuse of the holding company device, especially in the 1920's, led to fairly severe legal restrictions on its use.

Insurance Companies

Insurance companies, especially life insurance companies, have become an increasingly important element in the financial system. Here we must distinguish between two forms of insurance. On the one hand "term," or pure service, insurance consists essentially of the purchase of "protection" against certain possible losses or calamities by making a "bet" with the insurance company to be paid off if the feared calamity occurs. In this type of insurance no equity is created for the insuree, except in so far as premiums are paid in advance and have unexpired value; the insurance transaction does not involve "saving." Most life insurance policies, however, are not of this kind, but involve the payment of larger premiums than would be necessary to buy pure protection, and so build up the net worth of the insured persons. Insurance companies thereby become important financial intermediaries, holding as assets large amounts of securities of other institutions, and showing as liabilities the net worth or equities accrued to their policyholders.

Commercial Banks

None of these institutions, however, have the impact on the economic system of the commercial banking system, and to this we must now turn.

Our first task is to clear away any possible illusions concerning the nature of a commercial bank. A bank is not, primarily, an institution for keeping money locked up in a safe place. It is true that the first bankers were goldsmiths, to whose care people entrusted their surplus stocks of gold, and it is true that to this day most banks have safety deposit boxes in which valuables can be deposited for safekeeping. But this is only a minor part of a bank's business, and a "bank deposit" does not mean a sum of money locked up in a bank's strong room. Another illusion concerning banks is that a bank is an institution which "lends your money to other people." It is true that the primary function of a bank is to grant and to receive loans, and that when one person lends money to a bank, the bank is thereby enabled to make loans to others. But a bank is much more than a "loan broker," and it does more than act as an intermediary between those who wish to lend and those who wish to borrow.

Deposits

The loans which are made to a bank are called "deposits." The name is an unfortunate one, for it calls up a picture of a little pile of money resting in the bank's vault. But a deposit is not money given to the banker for safekeeping; it is a *loan* to the banker, given to him under certain peculiar conditions. Chief among these conditions is that the loan shall be repayable *on demand,* i.e., at any time the depositor wishes to have it repaid. A bank deposit, that is to say, is a peculiar kind of "security." It represents a promise made by the banker to pay the owner of the deposit any sum, in legal money, up to the amount of the deposit, at any time when the depositor may walk into the bank and demand it. There are two principal forms of bank deposit. Demand deposits, or current deposits, represent an obligation of the bank to pay the sum in question immediately on the demand of the owner. Time deposits, or savings deposits, represent an obligation of the bank to pay the sum in question a certain time (usually three days) after notice has been given. We shall not be concerned with the specific consequences of this distinction, as these are matters of detail rather than of principle.

Purchase and Sale of Deposits for Cash

One of the things a bank does, then, is to receive cash in return for deposits and to pay out cash in settlement of deposits. If I take $100 to the bank in cash (legal tender) and pay it into my deposit, this is in a sense a "purchase" of a bank deposit worth $100. The result of the transaction is that the bank now has $100 in cash which it did not have before, and it also has an obligation to pay me $100 which it did not have before. On the other hand, I have $100 less cash than I had before, but I possess a promise by the bank to pay me $100. In effect, I now possess a kind of "security" worth $100, in the form of a bank deposit. Similarly, when I withdraw $100 of my deposit in cash, the bank as a result has $100 *less* cash than it had before, and I have $100 *more* cash. But the bank no longer owes me $100, as I have given up my deposit.

Bank Notes: Similar to Deposits

Another thing a bank may do is to issue *notes.* This privilege is by now largely of historic interest, as far as the ordinary banks of England

and the United States are concerned, for the privilege of note issue has been gradually confined to the Bank of England in the one case and the Federal Reserve banks in the other. In the nineteenth century, however, nearly all banks issued notes, and even now in many countries— e.g., Scotland and France—note issue is still an important part of a bank's business. A bank note is an obligation much like a deposit. A deposit, however, is an obligation of the bank to a particular person, whereas a note is an obligation of the bank to anyone who possesses the note. That is to say, a bank deposit of $100 is a promise, made by the bank, to pay a specific person—Mr. Jones—$100 on request. A bank note of $100 is likewise a promise on the part of the bank to pay $100—to the person who owns the note and presents it to the bank. When a bank pays out legal tender money for a bank note, the process is called "redemption," for when that is done the bank "redeems" its promise.

Other Methods of Acquiring Deposits

An individual may acquire a deposit in ways other than purchase with cash. Indeed, the commonest way for an individual to acquire a deposit is by paying in a check. Another common way is by selling something to a bank, such as a bond or a promissory note. Indeed, the key to understanding the banking process lies in the analysis of what happens when a bank buys something, whether it is a bond, a mortgage, or a promissory note. It should be observed that "making a loan" on the part of a bank is essentially similar to "buying a security." What happens when a bank makes a loan is that it "buys" from the borrower a promissory note, promising to pay the bank a certain sum on a certain date. The only difference between a bond and a promissory note is that a bond generally represents a promise to pay a series of sums at a series of dates, whereas a promissory note generally, though not always, consists of a promise to pay a single sum on a single date.

How the Purchase of Assets Creates Deposits

Now, what happens when a bank buys anything—say, a bond from Mr. Smith? The ownership of the bond is transferred from Mr. Smith to the bank *and in the first instance the bank gives Mr. Smith a deposit equal to the value of the bond which has been purchased.* That is, Mr. Smith gives the bank a bond, and receives in return a "promise to pay"—a deposit—equal to the value of the bond. This may seem a little strange until we recall that a bond is also a promise, so that the exchange of one promise for another is not unreasonable. Notice, however, what has happened in this transaction. The number, and value, of assets has increased, for a promise to pay is an asset whose value can be measured in dollars. It is almost as if Mr. Smith said to Mr. Jones, "You lend me a million dollars and I'll lend you a million dollars." In that event Mr. Jones and Mr. Smith might each give to the other an I.O.U. for $1,000,000. Each would have a piece of paper worth, nominally, a million dollars. Two million dollars' worth of securities would have been created, apparently by the mere stroke of a pen. Something of this kind happens when a bank grants a loan. By that act securities (promises to pay) are immediately created to the value of twice the amount of the loan. Suppose, for instance, that a bank makes a loan of $5000 to Mr. Robinson for six months. The moment after the loan has been made, the bank owns a security worth $5000—Mr. Robinson's promise to pay the bank $5000, or rather more if we take interest into account, in six months. Mr. Robinson now owns a security also worth $5000—a deposit at the bank, or a promise on the part of the bank to pay Mr. Robinson $5000 on demand.

Why Deposits Are Regarded as Liquid Assets by Their Owners

However, there seems to be a difference between this case and the case of the two friends who lent each other a million dollars each. The transactions of Mr. Jones and Mr. Smith are purely fictitious, for neither could fulfill his promise alone. They could cancel out their obligations, but one could not, presumably, pay off his obligation without the other at the same time paying off his. In the case of the banker this is not so. The banker can fulfill his promise to pay Mr. Robinson $5000 long before Mr. Robinson fulfills his promise to pay $5000 to the banker. If Mr. Robinson wishes, the banker will carry out his promise immediately the loan has been made, and give Mr. Robinson $5000 in cash. This will extinguish Mr. Robinson's deposit, for the result of this transaction is that $5000 in cash is transferred from the banker to Mr. Robinson, and a $5000 "security"—the bank deposit—has been destroyed. Suppose Mr. Robinson takes his $5000 *in cash* as soon as he has made his promise to pay this sum back to the banker, with interest, in six months. Then the net result of these transactions is that $5000 in cash has changed owners, and a "security" of $5000 (Mr. Robinson's debt to the bank) has been created. This is what happens when anyone makes a loan. I do not have to be a banker to lend $5000 in cash to Mr. Robinson, and he might as well have obtained it from me, a private individual, as from a banker—if he could have done so. By a private loan of cash a security is also created—the promise to pay back the cash in a given time. The thing to be explained, which is peculiar to bankers, is how a banker, in making a loan, contrives to create not one security but two—one, the loan itself, and the other, a bank deposit which is not immediately redeemed. For normally Mr. Robinson will not transform his $5000 deposit into cash immediately. He may transform some of it into cash, but most of it he will probably transfer to other people by means of the instrument known as a *check*.

The Transferability of Claims

How can deposits be *transferred* from one person to another? The transfer of deposits is a special case of an important general principle, which we may call the principle of the transferability of claims. If A owes a debt to B, he can extinguish it by passing on to B a claim which A has against a third party, C, provided B is willing to accept this claim. Thus suppose A owes B $100 and C owes A $100. This situation is reflected in the balance sheets in item 1 of Table 31. Now if A can

TABLE 31.   The Transference of Claims

A		B		C	
Assets	Liabilities	Assets	Liabilities	Assets	Liabilities
1. From C $100	to B $100	From A $100			to A $100
2.		From C $100			to B $100

persuade B that a debt from C is just as good as one from A, he can "pay his debts" (i.e., cancel out his assets against his liabilities) by giving B C's note. The situation then is shown in line 2. It may be observed that if in the above situation C had owed $100 to B, all the debts could have been cancelled out against each other.

Bills of Exchange

A bill of exchange is an order written by one person, A, ordering another person, B, to pay a given sum to a third person, or to the holder of the document, C. Suppose that B owes a debt to A—i.e., that A has a claim on B for, let us say, $100—and A owes $100 to C. A then writes what is in effect a "letter" to B, or, as we say, he "draws" a "bill of exchange" on B, ordering B to pay C a sum of $100, usually in two or three months' time. A then sends this document to C. Its possession gives C a claim on B for the sum stated. If, therefore, C has a debt to pay to another person, D, he can pay his debt by "indorsing" the bill and passing it on to D. The "indorsement" consists now of C's signa-

ture on the back of the bill. The signature, however, really sym-
bolizes another "letter" to B, saying in effect: "Dear B. Please pay to
D the $100 which you are ordered to pay to me. Yours sincerely, C."
D now owns a claim on B for $100, which he can pass on to E if he
wishes, and so on, until finally the time comes when the initial order
has to be fulfilled. B then pays $100 to the person who owns the bill,
and the bill disappears from circulation. This method of settling debts
is but little used now, except in international trade. At certain stages
of economic development, however, it is common in internal transactions. Everywhere, in fact, it tends to be a stage in the development of
banking.

The Checking System

The commonest method now of settling debts in the more advanced
systems is by *check*. The inconvenience of a bill of exchange is that it
gives the owner a claim for the sum stated *only at a specific date* in the
future. Obviously one would normally be more willing to accept in
settlement of a debt a document which entitled the owner to receive
the sum stated *at any time,* i.e., on demand. But this is precisely the
nature of a check. A check, in fact, is a "bill of exchange" drawn on a
banker. A bank deposit is a debt, payable by the banker on the demand of the depositor, who is the creditor. If A owns a bank deposit,
he owns a promise, made by the banker, to pay him a sum on demand
equal to that deposit. If, therefore, A owes C a sum of $100, and has
a deposit with Banker B of an amount not less than $100, he can send
a letter to the banker which might perhaps read: "Dear Banker, Please
pay Mr. C the sum of $100, whenever he wants it. Yours sincerely, A."
This letter is a check. In practice it has been formalized a little, but if
a check is examined it will be seen to follow closely the form of a
letter to the banker. It would be possible for C to indorse this check
and pass it on as it stands to D, and for the check to circulate just as
bills of exchange have occasionally circulated. This may happen sometimes, but it is rare. Most people, on the receipt of a check, take it to a
bank. They may compel the banker to fulfill immediately the obligation which the check implies, that is, to exchange the check for cash.
Or they may prefer to exchange the check for a bank deposit of the
same value.

Bank Deposits as "Money"

This fact—that a bank deposit can be transferred easily from one
person to another by means of a check—explains why bank deposits

exist at all. A bank deposit is a promise, made by the banker, to pay cash to the owner of the deposit any time he wants. Why, then, does not everyone call on the bankers to fulfill this promise; why does not everyone substitute cash for the sum of his bank deposit? In answering this question we must first ask, "Why do people want cash?" The answer is, "To pay for things," or, what is practically the same thing, "To settle their bills," i.e., to fulfill their own promises to pay. But, as we have seen, Mr. Jones can fulfill a promise to pay, say, $100 to Mr. Robinson by writing him a check. Indeed, this may be a more convenient way of paying Mr. Robinson than paying him in cash, for cash may be lost or stolen on the way, while the check is no use to any-one but the person for whom it is intended. For making many pay-ments, therefore, checks are a more convenient form of payment than cash. This is not true of all payments; generally speaking, small ir-regular payments to persons with whom we are not very well ac-quainted are best made in cash, and large regular payments to persons with whom we are acquainted are most conveniently made by check. Most people who have payments of this latter kind to make will wish to have some proportion of their resources in the form of bank de-posits and some proportion in the form of cash. Bank deposits, that is to say, are a liquid form of property, like cash. Indeed, for certain pur-poses they are actually more liquid than cash, and therefore more en-titled to be called "money." We should not be surprised at this if we remember that all money, even cash, is essentially a "promise to pay" goods and services to the appropriate value. If I own $100 in cash it signifies that I have a right to receive, on demand, $100 worth of goods and services. If I own a $100 bank deposit, that signifies that I have a right to receive, on demand, $100 in cash—which is the same thing as a right to receive $100 in goods and services. It is little wonder, then, that cash and bank deposits are such close substitutes for each other.

The Balance Sheet of a Single Bank

Perhaps the simplest way to illustrate these principles is by arith-metical examples. Imagine a system in which there is only a single bank —let us call it The Bank, with capital letters. In drawing up a balance sheet for The Bank we shall neglect the fact that a bank has capital and buildings and equipment; we shall consider only its rights to re-ceive money from outsiders and its obligations to pay money to out-siders.

1. *Effect of Depositing Cash.* Suppose that The Bank opens for business, and the people of the society bring $1000 in cash, and give

it to The Bank in exchange for deposits. The balance sheet will now look like Table 32A.

TABLE 32A

Assets		Liabilities	
Cash	$1000	Deposits	$1000

2. *Effect of Granting a Loan.* Now suppose The Bank grants a loan of $500 to Mr. Smith. The balance sheet will in the first instance look like Table 32B.

TABLE 32B

Assets		Liabilities	
Cash	$1000	Deposits	$1500
Loans	500		

The loan has added $500 to both assets and liabilities.

3. *Effect of Withdrawing Cash.* But if Mr. Smith draws out $500 in cash—that is, if he exchanges his $500 deposit for $500 cash—the balance sheet will look like Table 32C.

TABLE 32C

Assets		Liabilities	
Cash	$500	Deposits	$1000
Loans	500		

4. *Effect of Paying Out Checks.* Suppose, however, that instead of drawing out his $500 in cash, Mr. Smith pays it out in checks to Jones, Robinson, etc., who pay them into their own accounts at the bank. The result of this may be seen in Table 32D.

TABLE 32D

Assets		Liabilities	
Cash	$1000	Deposits	$1500
Loans	500		

Smith's deposits have merely been transferred to Jones, Robinson, etc., and the total of deposits has not changed. Now if, as a result of this increase in deposits, people feel that they would like to hold a little more cash, and transfer, let us say, 10 per cent of these new deposits, or $50, into cash, the result will be as in Table 32E.

TABLE 32E

Assets		Liabilities	
Cash	$950	Deposits	$1450
Loans	500		

This table represents the final result of making a loan. There will be an increase in deposits almost, but not quite, equal to the amount of the loan, and a decrease in cash equal to the difference between the amount of the loan and the increase in deposits. In this case, with a loan of $500, we assumed that there was an increase in deposits amounting to $450, and a decrease in cash held by the bank amounting to $50.

Limitations on the Expansion of Loans

As The Bank went on increasing its loans it would find that its deposits increased, but not quite in proportion to loans, the difference being reflected in a decline in cash. A physical limit to the amount of loans The Bank could issue would be reached when the cash touched zero, but long before this limit was reached, The Bank would cease expanding loans, for no bank likes to be denuded of cash completely.

Usually banks have tried to maintain a relatively constant ratio between total deposits and liquid reserves (the "cash" of this illustration). Suppose this ratio (called the "reserve ratio") were fixed at 10 per cent, by law or by custom. Then if the conditions in Table 32E were operating, loans could be expanded until they reached the total of $4737. The deposits created by these loans would amount to $\frac{9}{10}$ of this, or $4263. Total deposits then would be $4263 plus the original $1000, or $5263. The cash lost to the public would be $\frac{1}{10}$ of $4737, or $473.70; the total cash in the hands of The Bank would therefore be ($1000 − $473.70), or $526.30. The reserve ratio is then $\frac{526.3}{5263}$, or 10 per cent. If loans were expanded beyond $4737, the reserve ratio would fall below 10 per cent.[1]

[1] The algebraic formula for finding the amount of loans, L, possible with an initial cash deposit, C, when the reserve ratio is r and the public withdraw a proportion of their new deposits, k, is as follows:
The amount of deposits created is finally $L(1 - k)$.
The total of deposits is then $C + L(1 - k)$.
The total of cash finally, after Lk has been withdrawn, is $C - Lk$.
We have therefore:

$$r = \frac{C - Lk}{C + L(1 - k)},$$

or

$$L = \frac{C(1 - r)}{r + k(1 - r)}.$$

The student may profitably apply this formula to the example in the text.
This formula, and the example, assume that the bank derives its cash initially from people who "purchase" deposits from it. In fact, a bank also derives a certain amount of cash from the sale of capital stock or from the capital of its proprietor. If this amount of

A System with More Than One Bank

Now if instead of one bank our system has a number of banks, what will be the effect of an expansion of loans by a *single bank*—let us call it the Podunk Bank? The effect will be similar in kind to the case of the one-bank system which has just been discussed. If the Podunk Bank increases its loans by $500, it may expect to have some increase in its deposits, coupled with some loss of its cash. The loss of cash, however, can take place for a reason additional to the one already given. The Podunk Bank will lose cash not only because some of the people whose deposits have been increased as a result of the loan will want to exchange part of their increased deposits for cash, but also because some of them will transfer these deposits, by check, to people who have deposits *with other banks.*

Effect of a Check on Another Bank. What happens, then, when Mr. Smith, who banks with the Podunk Bank, gives Mr. Robinson, who banks with the Toonerville Trust, a check for $100? This check is a "letter" to the Podunk Bank requesting it to pay Mr. Robinson $100 cash on demand. Suppose that Mr. Robinson does not want $100 cash, but wants to add $100 to his deposit with the Toonerville Trust. He gives this check to the Toonerville Trust, with his signature upon it, i.e., his "indorsement." His indorsement, as we have seen, is an abbreviated form of another letter, also to the Podunk Bank, saying, "Will you please pay this $100 to the holder of the check. Yours sincerely, J. Robinson." That is to say, as he has given it to the Toonerville Trust, the check with his indorsement is now an obligation of the Podunk Bank to pay $100 to the Toonerville Trust. Now, the Toonerville Trust will not be content to hold this promise in its hand; it will go to the Podunk Bank and collect the $100 in cash, and the deposit will finally disappear.

Loss of Cash to Other Banks Prevents Unilateral Expansion. If, then, these two banks are the only two banks in the system, and if the Podunk Bank increases its loans to Mr. Smith by $500, the results will be something like the following: The Podunk Bank will gain some deposits—say, $200—in so far as Mr. Smith retains his new deposit or pays it out in checks to people who bank with the Podunk Bank, and who also retain their new deposits. The Toonerville Trust will also

---

cash is P, the student should not find it difficult to prove that the above formula must be amended to read:

$$L = \frac{P + C(1 - r)}{r + k(1 - r)}.$$

gain deposits—say, by $250—for Mr. Smith will pay some of his $500 to people who bank in Toonerville, and who will also wish to retain some of their deposits. The Podunk Bank will lose a certain amount of cash to its depositors—say, $50—if Mr. Smith and his debtors do not wish to retain all their new deposits in that form. The Podunk Bank will also pay out cash to the extent of $250 to the Toonerville Trust, corresponding to the increase in the Toonerville Trust's deposits, for that has been due to the paying in of checks on the Podunk Bank which the Toonerville Trust will collect. By making a loan of $500, then, the Podunk Bank will gain $200 in deposits and lose $300 in cash. It is evident that in this case the ability of the Podunk Bank to increase its loans *all by itself* is very limited; much more limited than in the case of The Bank of our one-bank system, for there a loan of $500 might only result in a $50 loss of cash.

But All Banks May Expand Loans Together. Now, what happens in our two-bank system when *both* banks increase their loans? In the absence of any loans by the Podunk Bank, a $500 loan by the Toonerville Trust may be expected to increase its deposits by $200, decrease its cash by $300, and increase the deposits of the Podunk Bank by $250. Suppose, however, that *both* the Podunk Bank *and* the Toonerville Trust increase their loans by $500. The Podunk Bank will gain $200 in deposits from its own loan, plus $250 in deposits from the Toonerville Trust loan, or $450 in all, while it will lose $50 cash to the public. Likewise, the Toonerville Trust will gain $450 in deposits and lose $50 to the public. Neither bank will pay cash to the other for each will have a claim of $250 on the other, which can be "cleared." In this example we have assumed that the banks are the same size and are symmetrical in their relations. If the Podunk Bank is a large one and the Toonerville Trust a small one, then a given loan by the Toonerville Trust would bring about a large transfer of cash to the Podunk Bank, whereas the same loan by the Podunk Bank would bring about only a small transfer of cash to the Toonerville Trust.

It is clear, then, that while the lending ability of a single bank, in a two-bank or a many-bank system, is very limited, the ability of the system as a whole to expand its loans is considerable, provided that all the banks do it together. A many-bank system is rather like a number of balloons tied together with string; if one balloon tries to get away from the others the strings will bring it back, but all the balloons can rise together without difficulty. The "string" in the case of a banking system is the loss of cash reserves. One bank expanding loans disproportionately will lose reserves to the other banks, but if all banks expand together they will all lose reserves to each other, which means of course that no bank loses reserves on balance except to the public.

Effect of Decrease in Loans. An exactly similar process, in reverse, happens when a bank decreases its loans. If the Podunk Bank decreases its loans by $500 it will lose some deposits, and the other banks will also lose some deposits; but it will gain cash both from the public and from the other banks. Its reserve ratio will therefore rise. If its reserve ratio is persistently above the limit which it wishes to set, it will try to expand the volume of its investments, by granting loans or buying securities. If it finds its reserve ratio falling below the limit, it will contract the volume of its investments by not renewing loans as they fall in, or by selling securities, and so will increase its holdings of cash.

The Central Bank

In the foregoing argument we have assumed that the individual banks of a system hold their reserves in the form of cash. In a developed system this is not usually the case, for the individual banks will hold their reserves in the form of deposits at a *central bank*. A central bank, such as the Federal Reserve banks, the Bank of England, the Bank of France, or the Bank Deutscher Länder, has several tasks to perform. It is a bankers' bank; it makes promises to pay money to bankers (deposits) and also receives from bankers promises to pay money to it. It is the government's bank; it holds the government's deposit, and may make the government loans. It is usually entrusted by the government with a certain responsibility for the management of the monetary and banking system of the country. It frequently holds the national stock of gold, and usually issues notes which form part of the stock of legal tender.

Member Bank Reserves Are Deposits at the Central Bank

When individual banks find that they have claims on each other, which in the absence of a central bank would have to be paid in cash, they can pay them by transferring deposits at the central bank. If, for instance, the Toonerville Trust found that at the end of a week it possessed checks on the Podunk Bank for $5000, and the Podunk Bank possessed checks on the Toonerville Trust for $6000, these claims could be settled by a transfer from the Toonerville Trust to the Podunk Bank of a $1000 deposit at the Federal Reserve bank.[2]

[2] In the English banking system the Bank of England is the only "bankers' bank," and virtually all transfers of reserves among the member banks are carried out by transferring the ownership of deposits at the Bank of England. In America the Federal Reserve

A Central Bank Can Create Bank Reserves

The significance of a central bank lies mainly in the fact that it can create *bank reserves,* much as an individual bank can create deposits, by the process of making loans to the individual member banks, or by the purchase of other securities.

1. *Rediscounting.* It can make loans by the process known as "rediscounting." A banker will go to his Federal Reserve bank with "commercial paper" of a special kind—that is to say, with a document which gives the holder a right to receive a certain sum on a certain date from some firm or individual. He then hands over this paper and receives in return an equivalent deposit with the Federal Reserve bank. This commercial paper is supposed to be the result of some genuine commercial transaction. Mr. Smith, for instance, may buy wheat for shipment to Europe and know that he will be paid for the wheat within 60 days. He has to pay for the wheat he has bought, we will suppose, on the day when he buys it, and may not have the cash in hand. So he borrows from a bank for 60 days. That is, he gives the banker a document stating that he, Mr. Smith, promises to pay the banker, say, $5000, in 60 days from today. In return the banker gives him a deposit for a little less than $5000, say, $4950. If now the banker is running short of reserves he may take this document to the Federal Reserve bank and "rediscount" it—give it to the Federal Reserve bank in return for a deposit which is just as good as a cash reserve.

2. *Advances.* A Federal Reserve bank can also increase a bank's reserves by making "advances" to it; i.e., by giving it a deposit in exchange for a promise on the part of the member bank to pay the Federal Reserve bank an equivalent sum on a given future date.

3. *Open Market Operations.* Commercial bank reserves are also changed, as explained below, by purchases and sales of securities by a central bank in the open market.

How the Central Bank Controls Credit

The Rediscount Rate. It is evident, then, that the central bank can have a great deal of influence on the conduct of the member banks (and therefore on the whole volume of loans and deposits), and through these on the whole structure of incomes, prices, and interest rates. It exerts this control in a number of ways. First, it may change the rate of interest at which it is prepared to lend. This is the "bank

System has not yet achieved this position, for a number of private banks, in New York City especially, hold deposits which belong to the smaller banks, and so act as "bankers' banks."

rate" of the Bank of England, the rediscount rate of the Federal Reserve banks. In the case of the Bank of England this power was very important, for the "bank rate" was an effective weapon in changing the rates of interest at which the *member* banks were prepared to lend. This was so partly because the Bank of England at one time acted not only as a central bank but also as a private bank; i.e., it competed to some extent in the market with the other banks in granting loans to private firms and individuals. Consequently, the rate at which the Bank of England lent "led the market," and the custom grew among the other banks of lending at this rate, less a fixed amount. This habit persisted even after the Bank of England ceased to compete with the private banks. When the Bank of England raised the bank rate, the other English banks also raised their rates of interest, and this helped to choke off loans. Similarly, when the Bank of England lowered the bank rate this helped to raise the volume of loans.

In the Federal Reserve System the rediscount rate is not such an important instrument of policy. It does have an effect, however, in encouraging or restraining borrowing by the member banks. If, now, the central bank can raise or lower the rate of interest at which people can borrow from the banks, it will clearly be able to affect the volume of bank deposits. If it raises the rate of interest, borrowing will be discouraged. Loans that fall in will not be renewed, loans that might have been made will not be made, and the volume of both loans and deposits will shrink. Similarly, if it lowers the rate of interest, borrowing will be encouraged, and both loans and deposits will increase.

Open Market Policy. Another weapon of the central bank, of great importance nowadays, is what is known as "open market policy." This means the direct manipulation of the securities market by buying and selling securities on the open market, in order to raise or lower the price of securities and in order to raise or lower the volume of central bank deposits (i.e., bank reserves). Thus when a central bank buys securities it pays for them by creating central bank deposits; that is, it writes up in its balance sheet an asset (the security bought) and a liability (a deposit owned in the first instance by the previous owner of the security). If the seller was a bank the total of bank reserves is immediately increased by the amount of the reserve bank deposit. If the seller was not a bank (say a private individual) he is likely to "sell" his central bank deposit to a commercial bank for a commercial bank deposit, as private individuals do not normally bank with a central bank. When this happens the reserves (central bank deposits) of the commercial banks and commercial bank deposits are increased by the amount of the purchase. The reserve ratio of the commercial banks, however, has risen, and they are now in a position to expand their asset holdings and deposits up to the point where the reserve ratio once more is at the minimum level.

Regulation of Member Bank Reserve Ratios. Another possible weapon of central bank policy is the regulation of the reserve ratio of the member banks. A rise in the legal reserve ratio automatically curtails the maximum amount which member banks can lend and a fall automatically raises that amount.

Banks Have More Control Over Their Assets Than Over Their Liabilities

It should now be clear that the *active* part of banking is making loans. A banker does not have much control over the amount of deposits which he gets, although theoretically he could encourage depositors by offering higher rates of interest or greater conveniences, or by advertising. This is done to some extent, but on the whole banks do not go in for the competitive attraction of depositors. The rates of interest on deposits, even on savings deposits, are generally fixed by custom or agreement, as are the charges for checks, etc. In the making of loans, however, a banker has a good deal of discretion. He can attract or discourage loans in two ways: either by manipulating the rate of interest which he charges or by manipulating the other conditions of a loan. Generally speaking, the lower the rate of interest, the more *applications* for a loan will the banker receive, and the higher the rate of interest, the fewer applications will he receive. A banker is not obliged to grant a loan to anyone who applies, however; in this he differs sharply from a shopkeeper, who usually sells to anyone who comes to buy. A banker has to look to the repayment of the loan; and if he feels that the risk of nonpayment is too great, he will not grant the loan. Or if he feels that he does not wish to expand his loans, he can still refuse to grant the loan, even if the person seeking the loan is in sound financial standing.

The "Rationing" of Loans

This power of the banker to make loans or not, as he sees fit, is of great importance. We may call it his power of "rationing" loans. As we saw in an earlier chapter, the price of any commodity can be kept permanently below its equilibrium price only if there is "rationing" of some kind. If a price is below its equilibrium level, buyers will wish to buy more than sellers wish to sell. If buyers are to be prevented from raising their bids, then, there must be some way of apportioning among them the small quantity which is available. If a rise in price to choke off the buyers is not allowed, some other way of choking them off must be found. This other way is "rationing." In the case of loans, then, the rate of interest is an index of the "price" of loans. If at a given rate of interest borrowers wish to borrow more than the banker wishes to lend, in a competitive market the result will be a rise in the rate of interest. The market for bank loans, however, is not a competitive market. If at a given rate of interest borrowers wish to borrow more than a banker wishes to lend, the banker does not have to raise the rate of interest in order to choke off the too-eager borrowers. All he needs to do is put on a stern face and refuse the borrower the loan when he applies. This fact is of great importance, especially in interpreting recent banking history.

Central Bank Policy

The degree of control which a central bank is able to exercise over the monetary system depends on the nature of the reactions of commercial banks and other institutions to its policies, and also on the objectives of these policies themselves. Central banks operate directly by withdrawing or releasing securities of various kinds, thus affecting the holdings of these securities in the hands of other persons or institutions, and also by creating or withdrawing central bank deposits. The effects of these operations depend of course on the stability of the reactions of money market agencies and organizations. If the central bank contracts its deposits by selling securities, the commercial banks may be able to offset this contraction in their reserves by lowering their reserve ratios, or by other devices designed to economize reserves. In the depression of the 1930's the expansionary policy of the Federal Reserve System was in part offset by a rise in the "voluntary" reserve ratio of the commercial banks—i.e., a rise in their reserve ratio above the legal minimum. In the inflation of the 1940's the ability of the Federal Reserve System to offset the inflationary effects of war finance and its aftermath was largely destroyed because of the policy of supporting the price of government bonds. Between about 1942 and March, 1951, the Federal Reserve System virtually established a "government bond standard," standing ready at all times to buy government bonds if their prices fell below a level which would yield an appropriate rate of interest. This meant that all government bonds which the market did not want to hold at the established rates of interest found their way into the portfolios of the federal reserve banks, with consequent enlargement of federal reserve deposits and hence of member bank reserves.

Effects of a Banking System

It is clear that the development of a banking system produces great effects on the economy, both on the volume of securities of various kinds, the volume of liquid assets, and also on the price level and on the volume of payments and of incomes. It is impossible at this stage to follow all these ramifications. Simple models of the effect of the introduction of a banking system can be developed with the aid of an extended form of the "Fisher identity" (page 317).

Let us suppose, for instance, a system in which there is no central bank, in which there is only one form of "legal money" (say gold coin), and in which bank reserves are all in the form of legal money. Then if M is the quantity of legal tender money in the possession of the public, and V is its velocity of circulation, the product MV is the total flow of money directed toward the purchase of commodities which are bought with legal money. Similarly, if M' is the total quantity of bank deposits in the possession of the public, and V' is the velocity of circulation of these deposits, the product $M'V'$ is the total flow of money directed toward the purchase of those things which are bought with bank deposits. As practically all commodities are bought either with legal money or with bank deposits, the total flow of money directed toward the purchase of commodities must be $MV + M'V'$. This, as we saw in the previous chapter, is equal to the value of the commodities bought, or PQ. We can therefore rewrite the Fisher equation:

$$PQ \equiv MV + M'V' \tag{1}$$

If there were other forms of money in the system, say, private bank notes, these could be brought into the equation in the same way. If the quantity of this form of money were M'' and its velocity of circulation were V'', then the flow of money directed toward the purchases of goods bought with this kind of money would be $M''V''$, and the equation would become:

$$PQ \equiv MV + M'V' + M''V'' \tag{2}$$

In a similar way it could be extended to include any number of kinds of money used in the purchase of commodities.

How Banking Increases Payments

1. *Relations Between* M *and* M'. We can now see how the banking system increases payments. Suppose that the reserve ratio is 10 per

cent. Then a banking system can create a sum of deposits ten times as great as the sum of its reserves. If a depositor brings, say, $1000 in legal money to a bank and "buys" a deposit with it, the total quantity of legal money in the possession of the public (M) falls by $1000. The bank's reserves, however, increase by $1000, and therefore the banking system will be able to expand its loans until deposits have increased by about $10,000. Now we may assume that each individual wishes to maintain some average proportion between the amount of legal money which he holds and the amount of his bank deposits. Similarly, in a society as a whole there will be some average proportion which people wish to maintain between their holdings of legal money and of bank deposits. Suppose that this proportion was one dollar of legal money to every five dollars of bank deposits. If under these circumstances the total of bank deposits were only, say, four times as great as the total of legal money in the pockets of the people, people would deposit some of their legal money with banks. This would decrease the people's holdings of legal money, and increase bank reserves and bank deposits, until the one-to-five ratio was established.

Example. Suppose that we had a system which contained 300 million dollars in legal money before the introduction of banking. Now let banking be introduced. If the reserve ratio is 10 per cent, then after 100 million dollars has been transferred from the public to the banks, the public holds 200 million dollars, the banks have 100 million dollars as reserves, deposits amount to ten times this amount—1000 million dollars—and the desired ratio of legal money to deposits, 1 to 5, is attained.[3]

2. *Velocities of Circulation.* The velocity of circulation of bank deposits is actually greater than the velocity of circulation of legal money. The introduction of banking, therefore, must lead to a rise

[3] Let S be the total amount of legal money possessed by the system, r be the reserve ratio, and h be the desired ratio of legal money to deposits. Let x be the amount of legal money transferred from the public to the banks. Then we have, when the ratio h is satisfied:

$$M = S - x,$$
$$M' = \frac{x}{r}.$$

Therefore,

$$h = \frac{M}{M'} = \frac{r(S-x)}{x},$$

or

$$x = \frac{rS}{h+r}.$$

in the total flow of money transactions $(MV + M'V')$. Suppose, for instance, that the velocity of circulation of legal money was 20 times a year, and the velocity of circulation of bank deposits was 60 times a year. If the introduction of banking did not change these figures, then before the introduction of banking the flow of money transactions of the society in our previous example would be 300 × 20, or 6000 million dollars a year. After the introduction of banking we have $M = 200$, $M' = 1000$, and the total flow of money transactions is $(200 \times 20) + (1000 \times 60)$, or 64,000 million dollars a year. In this case the introduction of banking results in a more than tenfold increase in the total money flow.[4]

3. *Effect of Central Banking.* The introduction of central banking changes the model somewhat. The reserves of the member banks are now determined mainly by the volume of assets held by the central bank. If, for instance, previously the reserves of the commercial banks were in the form of gold, the introduction of a central bank and the centralization of the gold stock into the possession of the central bank may increase the total of the commercial bank reserves, as the central bank may hold other assets besides gold. In a central banking system also the decisions of the public as to the desired proportion of bank deposits to other forms of money can largely be neutralized by appropriate central bank action. Thus if the American public suddenly decides to hold a larger proportion of "folding money" (federal reserve notes, for the most part) to bank deposits, the Federal Reserve System stands ready to expand its note issue to accommodate the new demand, and at the same time to expand its holdings of securities enough to prevent a serious decline in member bank reserves and deposits.

[4] If the velocity of circulation of bank deposits were very small, the introduction of banking might theoretically cause no change in the total flow of money transactions. If in the above example the velocity of circulation of bank deposits were 2 times a year, the money transactions after the introduction of banking would be $(200 \times 20) + (1000 \times 2)$, or 6000 million dollars a year—the same as before. If there is to be no change in total money transactions due to the introduction of banking we must have, using the notation in footnote 3:

i.e.,
$$MV + M'V' = SV,$$
$$M'V' = V(S - M) = Vx,$$

i.e.,
$$\frac{x}{r}V' = Vx, \quad \text{or } V' = Vr.$$

That is, if the ratio of the velocity of circulation of bank deposits to the velocity of circulation of legal money were equal to the reserve ratio of banks, there would be no change in the flow of money transactions due to the introduction or extension of banking. In fact, with $r = \frac{1}{10}$ and $V' = 3V$ (approximately), the extension of banking causes a large increase in incomes. Even a reserve ratio of 100 per cent would not destroy the influence of the banking system on total money income if the velocity of circulation of deposits were greater than the velocity of circulation of legal money.

A simple model of such a system is illustrated in Table 33. The columns of the table show the simplified balance sheet of the central bank and of the aggregate of member banks. In column 1 we show the

TABLE 33.   Model of a Central Banking System

			1	2	3	3A	4	4A
Central Bank Assets	Gold	(g_f)		200	300		200	
	Securities	(s_f)			100		135.7	
	Total			200	300		335.7	
Liabilities	Notes	(n_f)	50^a	50	75	(1500)	111.9	(2238)
	Deposits	(d_f)		150	225		223.8	
Member Banks Assets	Reserves	(d_f)	150^b	150	225		223.8	
	Securities	(s_m)	1350	1350	2025		2014.0	
	Total		1500	1500	2250		2237.7	
Liabilities	Deposits	(d_m)	1500	1500	1500	(135,000)	2237.7	(134,262)
Total Payments		(E)				(136,500)		(136,500)

^{a} Gold in hands of public.
^{b} Gold in hands of banks.

condition before the establishment of the central bank. We suppose 50 "dollars" of gold in monetary uses in the hands of the public, 150 in the vaults of the commercial banks. We suppose a reserve ratio of commercial banks of 10 per cent, and a preferred ratio of 1 dollar of "cash" (gold coin, say) to 30 dollars of bank deposits on the part of the public. That is, $r = \dfrac{d_f}{d_m} = 0.1$, and $h = \dfrac{n_f}{d_m} = \dfrac{1}{30}$. Now let us suppose the establishment of a central bank in which all gold is centralized. The first impact is shown in column 2; the n_f and d_f of column 1 become the initial 200 (g_f) in column 2. The $50 gold in the hands of the public is replaced by $50 central bank notes, and the $150 of gold reserves in the vaults of the commercial banks is replaced by $150 of central bank deposits. There is no change in the system otherwise, as we suppose that r and h are unchanged. Now, however, suppose the central bank buys securities ($100) by creating central bank deposits. These deposits as we have seen will come into the possession of the member banks and appear in their reserves. This situation is shown in column 3. Member banks are now able to expand their loans and investments to 2025, their deposits to 2250, and central bank notes expand to 75. If $V = 20$ and $V' = 60$ the total volume of payments will have increased from 91000 ($50 \times 20 + 1500 \times 60$) to 136500 (column 3A).

Now suppose that the objective of central bank policy is to stabilize the volume of payments, and that there is a shift in the ratio h from $\frac{1}{30}$ to $\frac{1}{20}$. That is, people decide they want to hold a larger proportion of central bank notes and a smaller proportion of bank deposits. This result is achieved in column 4. The ratio $\frac{n_f}{d_m}$ is now $\frac{111.9}{2237.7}$, or $\frac{1}{20}$. E is still 136500, but in order to achieve this result it has been necessary for the central bank to expand its holdings of securities to 135.7. The note circulation has expanded from 75 to 111.9, and the member bank reserves, loans and investments, and deposits have undergone a small contraction to offset the increase in notes.[5]

4. *Volume of Transactions and Output*. If the output of goods in a society remained the same we should expect the introduction or extension of banking to result in a large rise in prices. Historically, however, the development of banking has gone hand in hand with a large increase in the total output of society, an increase due partly to increasing population, partly to improved techniques of production. It is true that the price level has increased considerably since the seventeenth century, which saw the beginnings of large-scale banking in the western world. Nevertheless, the main result of the development of banking has been to prevent the great *fall* in prices which would otherwise have resulted from the expansion in population and output. How far the absence of banking would have prevented this expansion of output is an interesting problem to which there seems to be no definite answer. It is true that a rising price level encourages enterprise, even while it may often guide it into wrong channels. It is true also that an expansion of bank loans implies that there is an increased quantity of capital goods, for loans are issued mainly for the purpose of enabling entrepreneurs to create goods. An expansion of

---

[5] In algebraic terms the model has two basic identities, representing the balance sheet identities of the central bank and of the member banks:

$$g_f + s_f = n_f + d_f \tag{i}$$
$$d_f + s_m = d_m \tag{ii}$$

Various behavior equations may be postulated. Thus in the above table we have suppose two equations:

$$d_f = r d_m \tag{iii}$$
$$n_f = h d_m \tag{iv}$$

Equation (iii) supposes that bankers keep a constant ratio of reserves to deposits; equation (iv) that the public keeps a constant ratio of cash (notes) to deposits. Column 3 of Table 33 simply assumes g_f and s_f given; the four equations above are then used to solve for the four unknowns, n_f, d_f, s_m, d_m. We can if we like assume a fixed reserve ratio for the central bank, $r_c = \frac{d_f}{g_f}$. Then given g_f, the other five unknowns can be derived. In column 4 of Table 33, the fifth equation is $E = n_f V + d_m V'$, E, V, and V' being given. Many other models corresponding to various types of policy can be constructed.

bank loans, therefore, unless the loans are sadly misapplied, should result from an expansion of the volume of transactions and of output. This will have the effect of moderating the fall in prices which would otherwise occur, as will be seen from the Fisher identity. It can be argued that there is some rate of expansion of the banking structure which will just enable the flow of money to keep pace with the rising volume of transactions, thereby keeping the price level constant. Some writers believe this to be an ideal of banking policy. This question, however, must be reserved for a later discussion.

QUESTIONS AND EXERCISES

1. Suppose we have a system with a single bank. What will be the immediate and ultimate effects on (a) the assets, liabilities, and reserves of The Bank, and (b) the assets and liabilities of private persons, of the following actions?

    a. Mr. Smith takes $100 in cash and "pays it in" to The Bank.

    b. Mr. Smith pays in a check for $50, received from Mr. Jones.

    c. The Bank discounts a three-months' bill for $5000 for Mr. Robinson.

    d. Mr. Smith asks for, and receives, $100 of his deposit in the form of bank notes.

2. Suppose we have a system with two banks, one of which has ten times the volume of deposits, and ten times the number of depositors, as the other. What will be the probable effect on both banks (assets, liabilities, and reserves) of the repayment by Mr. Jones, in cash, of a loan of $5000 at the larger bank? Be clear as to your assumptions.

3. Define carefully, in your own words, the following terms: (a) A bank. (b) A bank deposit. (c) Commercial paper. (d) A Central Bank. (e) The reserve ratio. (f) Rediscounting.

4. It has been proposed that banks should be compelled by law to have a 100 per cent reserve ratio. Discuss the possible effects of such a law on the practices of banks and on the power of the banking system to affect prices.

5. Suppose there was a system which possessed 600 million dollars of legal money, in which the income velocity of circulation of legal money was 25 times a year, and of bank deposits 50 times a year. Suppose the banks kept a reserve ratio of 20 per cent, and that people wished to have 7 dollars of bank deposits for each dollar of legal money. What would be the total money receipts of such a society, assuming that all bank reserves consist of legal money?

6. In Table 33, page 355, suppose that the central bank followed the policy of holding a constant ratio of its deposits plus notes to its gold holdings, so that $n_f + d_f = 2g_f$. What will be the equilibrium position

of the system, the other assumptions being held constant as in column 3?

7. Suppose that in Table 33, column 3, we retain the assumption that the object of central bank policy is to keep the total payments constant at 135,000. Suppose now that the velocity of circulation of notes falls from 20 to 15 times a year, and of deposits falls from 60 to 50 times a year. What will be the new equilibrium position of the system?

8. Suppose that in order to finance a war the member banks were obliged to increase their holdings of securities to 10,000 from the position of Table 33, column 3. What will then be the total volume of securities held by the central bank?

9. At present the banks of the United States hold a considerable proportion of their assets in the form of government securities. What would be the effect of a sharp fall in the price of government securities on the solvency of banks? Might this effect be expected to hamper the Federal Reserve System in its open market policy? If so, how?

10. Suppose the government raised the rate of interest on Post Office Savings certificates from 2 to 3 per cent. What effect might this have on the banking system?

11. "Banks do not create money; they merely increase its velocity of circulation." Discuss critically.

12. Explain, by means of the Fisher identity, how speculation may affect prices.

CHAPTER 18

SAVING AND INTEREST

With the tools of analysis developed so far we can throw a good deal of light on two dark areas of economic theory—the concept of saving and the theory of interest.

Difficulties in the Concept of Saving

The concept of saving has caused a great deal of trouble in economic theory, and even though it can be dispensed with almost entirely in modern economics, its traditional importance is such that it may be well to relate it to the concepts of the preceding chapters. The difficulties created by the concept have been of two kinds. One has arisen because saving is equated in some sense with the idea of "not consuming," and negative concepts of this kind always cause difficulty: the realm of the might-have-beens is always difficult to define. Thus it is much easier to say what one had for dinner last night than to say what one did not have for dinner; and if saving is "not consuming," the question "What did you not consume?" becomes almost meaningless. For this reason it is generally much safer to use the consumption concept than the saving concept; consumption as an *activity* is much more positive and easy to define than saving. The other difficulty has arisen because of the confusion between saving in the sense of "hoarding" (accumulating liquid assets) and saving in the more proper sense as the accumulation of net worth, or assets in general. This is an example of a common confusion (see page 253) between the process of production, consumption, and accumulation on the one hand and the process of the circulation of money by means of "payments" on the other.

The Savings-Investment Controversy

A good example of the difficulties involved in the concept of saving is to be found in the so-called "savings-investment controversy" which is associated with the work of J. M. Keynes. As early as 1924, Keynes[1] hinted that economic fluctuations might be a result of the fact that investment was performed by one set of people and saving by another set, and that there was no direct relationship between these two sets of activities. In his *Treatise on Money* in 1931 Keynes tried to define saving and investment in such a way that the divergence between them could be used in the explanation of monetary changes. This attempt, however, was unsuccessful, and in his *General Theory of Employment, Interest and Money* (1936) Keynes finally formulated the *identity* between savings and investment which is the basic identity of modern macroeconomics. This identity in real terms is nothing more or less than the basic identity (iv on page 290):[2]

Accumulation = Production minus Consumption = (Saving)

or

$$A = P - C \tag{1}$$

Production means adding to the total stock; consumption means subtracting from the total stock; "investment," in real terms, is the net amount added to the total stock of real capital. Production is real income; consumption is real "outgo." "Saving" in real terms is the excess of real income over consumption. In real terms, therefore, investment and saving are identical, in the sense that they are simply different ways of looking at the same phenomenon.

Effect of Price Changes on Saving

A difficulty arises when we are considering saving and investment in their financial, or "dollar value," aspect. Investment in this sense means the growth in the value of real assets. The value of real assets, however, can grow not merely because additions to real assets (production) exceed subtractions (consumption) but also because the prices of existing assets rise. Suppose, to take a simple example, that there is only one real asset, wheat. Suppose, now, that the stock of wheat at the beginning of a year is 500 million bushels, and that 800 million bushels are produced and 700 million bushels consumed during the year. Evidently, the stock of wheat will rise by 100 million bushels to 600 million bushels during the year. If the price of wheat were constant at $2 per bushel, the value of the wheat at the begin-

---

[1] J. M. Keynes, *A Tract on Monetary Reform*, London, 1924.

[2] This is the proposition which in a somewhat frivolous mood I have labeled the "bathtub theorem"—the total stock being the water in the tub, production the flow from the faucet, consumption the flow down the drain; the difference between production and consumption being the rate of accumulation of water in the tub. This is positive if the inflow (production) exceeds outflow (consumption)—negative if outflow exceeds inflow.

ning would be $1000 million, and at the end would be $1200 million, the rise of $200 million (investment), representing exactly the difference between income ($1600 million per annum) and outgo ($1400 million per annum). If, however, the price of wheat changes during the year, the situation is more complicated. Suppose, for instance (to avoid difficulties in the valuation of income and outgo), the price remains at $2 per bushel all through the year and jumps suddenly to $3 on the last day of the year. The value of the 600 million bushel stock is now not $1200 but $1800 million—the value of the stock has risen during the year not by $200 but by $800, whereas the difference between income and outgo remains at $200. What are we to do in such a case? Two alternatives are open—we can either redefine income to include changes in the value of an existing stock due to a change in its price ("capital gains") or we can restate our original proposition in the form,

$$\text{Investment} = \text{Saving} + \text{Capital Gains}$$

These alternatives are of course merely verbal; in both cases the full equation reads:

$$\begin{array}{c} \text{Increase in Value} \\ \text{of Stock} \end{array} = \begin{array}{l} \text{Value of Production} \\ - \text{Value of Consumption} \\ + \text{Capital Gains} \, (- \text{Capital Losses}) \end{array}$$

In the first alternative we define "income" as the value of production plus capital gains; in the second, we leave the definition of income as the value of production alone. The ambiguity in the concept of income revealed by this analysis shows up in the United States income tax, according to which some capital gains are recognized as "income" but are taxed at a different rate from other income, thus paying tribute to the fact that capital gains are in some sense income but of a peculiar kind!

Hoarding

In the case of an individual the term "saving" sometimes carries the meaning of the excess of *receipts* (money payments in) over *expenditures* (money payments out). The term "hoarding" is sometimes used to express this quantity; it is of necessity equal to the increase in money assets. The difference between "saving" (the increase in total assets) and "hoarding" (the increase in money assets) may be seen most clearly perhaps from an example. Suppose a man has at the beginning of a year a total net worth of $20,000, of which $2000 is in the form of money and $18,000 in the form of goods. Suppose during the year he produces (earns) $10,000—i.e., he adds $10,000 worth to his total assets—and suppose that $8000 worth of assets are consumed. Clearly, his total assets (neglecting capital gains) are now $22,000, and he has "saved" $2000. While he has been saving $2000 in total assets, suppose that his total money receipts have been $12,000. His receipts exceed his income, indicating that he has received money not only from the sale of his current production or labor but also from the sale of some previously possessed asset—say, a piece of land. His money expenditures, we suppose, have been $11,000. These exceed his consumption, indicating that his purchases were not all immediately consumed but that some of his purchases were in the form of durable goods—say, a house or an automobile. We can immediately deduce that his money assets will have increased by the difference between money paid in and money paid out—i.e., $12,000 − $11,000, or $1000. At the end of the year, therefore, his money assets must be $3000 and his nonmoney assets $19,000. He has "saved" $2000, but has only "hoarded" $1000. It is evident from this example that it is quite possible for an individual to be saving and "dishoarding"—i.e., increasing his total assets but diminishing his money assets—in the same period. It is equally possible to hoard and "dissave" simultaneously.

Keynes' Concept of Saving and Investment

It should be pointed out that the concepts of saving and investment in Keynes' *General Theory* are not quite the same as the concepts developed above. Keynes defines saving as the excess of income over *consumers' expenditure,* not as the excess of income (production) over consumption. Consumers' expenditure is equal to the value of consumer (i.e., household) purchases. It differs from consumption because many household purchases are of durable goods which are not immediately consumed, and consumption, both of consumer durables and of goods held by businesses, takes place quite independent of the processes of purchase and sale. Suppose now that we divide the economy into two sectors, businesses and households. Suppose further that all product originates in the hands of businesses, by the definition of a business. It follows that the total product (P) must be equal to household purchases (H) plus business accumulations (A_b), for everything that is produced during a given period must either have been taken off the hands of businesses by households (consumer purchases) or it must still be in the hands of businesses (business accumulations). Putting the identity the other way round, it follows that business accumulations must be equal to total income (product) minus household purchases, or

$$A_b = P - H \tag{2}$$

The expression $P - H$ is Keynes' 1936 definition of saving. A_b is the "real" equivalent of his definition of investment, though Keynes himself obscures this concept by trying to define it in terms of business *purchases* of investment goods.

We have, then,

Production $(P) =$ Household accumulation (A_c)
$\qquad$ + Business accumulation (A_b) + Household consumption (C_h)
$\qquad\qquad\qquad\qquad$ + Business consumption (C_b) $\quad$ (3)

Household purchases represent goods which are added to stocks in the possession of households, however briefly. Household consumption is the destruction of stocks which are in the possession of households. In any period, then, household accumulation (i.e., the net addition to stocks of goods in the possession of households) must be equal to household purchases less household consumption; that is,

$$A_h = H - C_h, \quad \text{or} \quad H = A_h + C_h \tag{4}$$

Identity (3) therefore can be written either in the form

$$P = A + C, \tag{5}$$

where $A = A_c + A_b$, and $C = C_h + C_b$, or it may be written in the form

$$P = H + A_b + C_b \tag{6}$$

Either of these forms may be useful in different models. It should be observed that the C_b item depends on the "netness" of the definition of production. If P is the gross national product, C_b represents depreciation of durable goods in the hands of business. If $P = P_n$, the net national product, C_b is zero, so that

$$P_n = H_p + A_b \tag{7}$$

This is the "Keynesian" form of the identity.

Saving Not "Postponed Consumption": Satisfaction Derived from Use Not Consumption

It is now necessary to discuss yet another aspect of the saving concept, the notion of saving as "postponed consumption." This is common in economic literature, yet it seems to embody a profound misconception of the nature both of saving and of consumption. The difficulty seems to arise because of a confusion between the idea of consumption as we have used it in this work, and as it is also used by the classical economists, as the "using up" or the destruction of stocks of goods, and the idea of consumption as the source of satisfactions or enjoyments. In fact these are two quite distinct ideas. Enjoyment or satisfaction is normally derived not from the *using up* but from the *use* of a good. This is obvious in the case of durable goods. When I go for a ride in my car the fact that the car is being consumed—i.e., is wearing out—in no way contributes to my satisfactions; indeed, quite the reverse. What I get satisfaction from is the *use* of the car, not the fact that rust, wear, and grit are nibbling away at it. If I had an indestructible car my satisfaction in the ride would in no sense be diminished. Similarly, if we had unbreakable china, clothes that never got soiled or worn, houses that never decayed, and machines that never wore out, consumption would be much diminished, but we would be all the richer for that. Satisfactions, therefore, must be regarded as proceeding from the *stock* of goods, not from their consumption. It is the size of the house we live in, the elegance of the clothes we wear, that give us satisfactions, not the incidental and regrettable fact that in the course of yielding these satisfactions, or even when they are not yielding satisfactions, they happen to be afflicted by decay and consumption.

Economy in Consumption Always Desirable

The reader may object that this argument does not apply to non-durables, or "one-use goods," such as food, which are destroyed in the very act of enjoying them. It is only because consumption and satisfaction are close together in time, however, that we tend to identify them; analytically they must be kept separate. Even in the case of one-use goods *economy* in consumption is always desirable, and if we examine the use of these goods closely we will always find that they are consumed in the *maintenance* of some desired but *depreciating* state. Thus we burn fuel because the warmth of our houses "depreciates" in a cold climate. The *less* fuel we can burn to maintain a given temperature, the better off we are. We need food similarly to maintain certain bodily states which likewise depreciate. The less food we need to keep us from being hungry and to maintain our bodily temperature and energy, the better off we are. Similarly we need entertainment to maintain certain mental or emotional states (see p. 252). It should be observed that the depreciation of goods (i.e., of desirable states) frequently involves their *physical* growth. Thus a shaved chin, a clipped head, or a mowed lawn depreciates by the process of growth of a "discommodity" (whiskers, hair, grass) and needs to be restored by periodic shaving, haircutting, or mowing. In this case it is the growth of the discommodity which constitutes "consumption" in the economic sense, and its removal which constitutes production.

Saving as Accumulation and as the Sacrifice of Consumption

In the light of these considerations, then, what is the significance of "saving"? Saving is the process by which goods are accumulated— i.e., by which the total stock of goods is increased. This can only be done by producing more than is consumed. If society is producing at capacity, saving does imply a certain "sacrifice" of consumption, in the sense that consumption would be greater if there were no saving. The sacrifice of consumption is also likely to lead to a sacrifice of satisfactions, unless there is at the same time an economizing of con-sumption—i.e., a decline in the amount of consumption which is necessary to maintain given states of satisfaction. Because of these sacrifices, however, the total stock of goods (desirable states) is in-creased, and the total *future* flow of satisfactions is presumably in-creased also. In this sense saving does involve the sacrifice of present satisfaction in order to increase satisfaction in the future. It does not, however, necessarily involve the sacrifice of present consumption in order to increase future consumption. It is true that future consump-tion may be increased as a result of saving, both because a larger stock of goods in itself implies a higher rate of consumption and because the accumulation of the larger stock may permit higher rates of pro-duction. We do not generally, however, accumulate now *in order that* we may decumulate in the future; we do not build up a stock of goods in order to tear it down in the future, but in order to be able to *main-tain* and *increase* this stock in the future. We have not built up all this apparatus of houses, farms, roads, machines, harbors, and factories in order that some day we may allow them to fall down and so return to living in holes in the ground and to grubbing our food from berry bushes!

Saving in a Subsistence Society

An illustration may clarify these principles. Suppose that we have a society which is living just above the edge of subsistence, with its productive activities just sufficient to maintain the bodily strength of its people, to reproduce the generations as they die off, and to main-tain the miserable huts in which the people live and the scanty clothes which they wear. How does such a society ever progress to a better state? If it is to improve, it is clear that it must build up its stock of capital: it must have more implements, more machines, more livestock, better houses, and so on. In order to do this (without aid from outside) it must withdraw resources from maintaining the existing fabric of the society in order to devote them to making the increased stock of implements, etc. This means that some of its existing states cannot be maintained as well as before; people may have to go a little hungry in order that the implement makers can be spared from food-production, leisure time and ceremonial activities may have to be skimped in order to release time for building, and so on. All this involves curtailment of satisfactions as well as of consumption. If, now, the result of this process is simply a larger stock of things—bigger houses, better clothes, and so on—without any improvement in the productivity of the society, as measured in some sense by output per man-hour, the society may be no better off than before. In order to maintain its bigger houses and finer clothes the society may still have to withdraw resources from previously enjoyed occupations, though not so much as in the period of building up the stock. If, however, the increased stock is at least partly in the form of instruments and implements which increase output per man-hour, the society is *permanently* richer as a result of the accumulation; and if the improvement is sufficient it will not only be able to maintain its increased stock with no more effort than it previously took to maintain its smaller stock, but may even be able to maintain the larger stock with less effort than it took to maintain the smaller one. In that happy event the society will not only be richer, but will find it easier to get still richer, as it will be able to devote to further accumulation the resources released from maintenance by its increased productivity.

Individual and Aggregate Saving

Up to this point we have discussed saving in the aggregate; we have not examined adequately the relation between *individual* saving and aggregate saving. An individual saves, as we have seen, when he increases his net worth. The sum of individual net worths is equal to the total value of the real capital of society, so that when a society "saves" (increases the value of its real capital) individuals also must have saved (increased their net worths). Thus if the real capital of society increases in value by a million dollars, this million dollars must show up as an increase in individual net worths. We may say perhaps that an increase in physical capital represents "real" saving, whereas an increase in the value of a constant physical capital because of price increases, or an increase in government debt, is "false" saving. Real or false, however, any increase in the dollar value of real assets will show up as individual dollar saving, assuming, of course, that all debts cancel out when balance sheets are aggregated. It does not follow, however, that action on the part of a single individual to increase his own net worth, even successful action, will necessarily increase aggregate saving by an equal amount, because an individual may increase his own net worth at the expense of others, or even to the benefit of others. The most obvious case of this phenomenon is plain theft, where ownership of physical capital (say a diamond ring!) is simply transferred from the robbed to the robber. There are many other cases of such transfer, however, many of them legal. In any speculative boom and crash, for instance, there are widespread redistributions of net worth, and the gains of one may be offset by the losses of another. An even more significant case is where the attempt on the part of many or most individuals in a society to increase their net worths by restricting their personal consumption results not in accumulation at all, but in a diminution of production through unemployment.

The "Paradox of Thrift"

This is the famous "paradox of thrift" which has haunted economics in the underworld of Mandeville and Malthus,[3] and finally achieved respectability in Keynes. The restriction of consumption only leads to a corresponding amount of accumulation if production remains unchanged. Thus if production remains at 100, and consumption falls from 80 to 70, accumulation rises from 20 to 30. But if the decline in consumption from 80 to 70 results in a decline in production from 100 to 90, the decline in consumption produces no increase in accumulation. The "abstinence" in this case is not transmuted into "saving." And as we have seen in the "basic model" (pages 290–300), a fall in the consumption *function,* other things being equal—that is, a decline in the amount that will be consumed at all potential levels of income—will have the effect of decreasing the equilibrium level of output at which there is no excess of accumulation.

Saving and Age

Another factor of great importance in considering the relation between individual and aggregate saving is the age distribution of the population. There is a fairly regular pattern of accumulation and decumulation in the course of a single human life. In childhood and

[3] B. de Mandeville, *The Fable of the Bees* (London, 1714); T. R. Malthus, *Principles of Political Economy* (2nd ed., 1836).

youth the individual generally consumes more than he produces. We do not, of course, carry the concepts of accounting in any exact way into the economic life of the family, but it is clear that in a sense the growth of children and young people represents a great deal of consumption which is not offset by any production of goods by them, but is offset in part by the growth of "human capital." Thus the young person entering his first job represents a substantial investment on the part of society. In the middle years the individual generally produces much more than he individually consumes. Part of the excess of his income over his personal consumption may be consumed in raising a family; part of it may be represented by a growth in his net worth— i.e., by saving. In old age the individual again returns to a condition where he is decumulating—i.e., where he is consuming more than he produces and his net worth is diminishing.

"Rainy Day" Saving Does Not Result in Aggregate Saving

If the object of individual saving is simply to save for old age or for a rainy day, the individual over his whole life will not make any con-tribution to *aggregate* saving, as what he saves in his productive years; will all be used up in his unproductive years. Similarly a society in which all saving is of this nature will not achieve any net accumulation: the excess of income over consumption of those in middle life will just be offset by the excess of consumption over production of the young and the old.

Aggregate Saving and the Age Distribution

It should be observed, however, that the *age distribution* of the population has an important effect on the net result of "rainy day" saving. If the population is heavily concentrated in the middle age groups it is quite likely to have an excess of attempted saving, or an "underconsumption problem," because it is these age groups which consume less than they produce. If on the other hand the population is heavily concentrated in the young and the old age groups, it may run into an "overconsumption" problem—the consumption of the un-productive young and old constantly eats up all the excess production of the middle age groups. These find it difficult to produce enough to support their dependents and so the society finds net accumulation difficult. The difficulties of the United States in the 1930's were closely related to the fact that at that time an abnormally large proportion of its population was of working age. The immigrants of the great wave of 1900–1914 were still largely in the labor force, declining birth rates;

had strikingly reduced the proportion of children in the population, and the rising expectation of life had not yet had its full impact in increasing the numbers of old people. It is little wonder that the consumption function was low and that the economy was subject to violent depression. By the 1950's, however, the situation had changed. The proportion of old people was increasing rapidly, and also the remarkable rise in the birth rate from 1940 on had greatly increased the numbers of children and young dependents. The rise in the level of the consumption function since 1930, which has contributed in no small degree to the resiliency of the American economy since 1945, is in large part due to the change in the age composition of the population.

Saving and the Expectation of Life

The proportion of a population of working age depends in considerable degree on the average age at death. Where the average age at death is low a large proportion of the resources of the society must be devoted to the simple replacement of its human capital, and a large proportion of the population will consist of children. Such a society consequently finds accumulation difficult—the consumption of its product by children is always pressing on the meager productive powers of the adults. The difference in this regard is striking between the "underdeveloped" areas, where the expectation of life generally is about 30 to 35, and the "developed," where the expectation of life is generally about 60–65. For this reason investment in longevity (health services, better food production, and so on) may be of outstanding importance for an underdeveloped culture.

THE THEORY OF INTEREST

We have now come to the point in the analysis where we may profitably take up another problem of great importance to economics —the theory of the rate of interest. Many of the details of this theory must wait until we have developed more refined analytical tools, but the equipment available at this point will at least enable us to block out its main lines.

The Rate of Interest as a Rate of Growth

We must first consider what are the dimensions of a rate of interest —that is, what kind of a quantity it is. A rate of interest is not a price, nor a simple exchange ratio, but a *rate of growth*. Thus if something grows at a rate of 5 per cent per annum, this means that it increases during a year by one-twentieth of its size at the beginning of the year. A rate of growth of 5 per cent per annum is the same as a rate of $\frac{5}{1200}$, or $\frac{1}{240}$ per month. The dimensions of a rate of growth, that is to say, are $\frac{1}{\text{Time}}$; the reciprocal of a rate of growth is a length of time. Thus we may express the same fact about an investment by saying that it yields 5 per cent (that is, one-twentieth) per annum, or that it can be capitalized at twenty years' purchase. The rate of interest is commonly defined as the ratio of a steady and perpetual income to the capital sum which will purchase it. Thus if $100 will buy an income of $3 per year for ever, the rate of interest is then 3 per cent per annum. This, however, is merely a special case of the more general definition. If $100 grows at 3 per cent per annum for a year, it will amount to $103. Three dollars can then be taken from it as "income," and the process can be repeated indefinitely.

The Rate of Profit as a Rate of Growth

There are two aspects of the rate of growth of capital which are significant in economics. One is the gross rate at which the value of the total assets of firms grows through the processes of purchase, production, and sale. This may properly be called the *rate of profit*. The other is the gross rate at which the value of contractual obligations such as bonds grows. This is properly called the *rate of interest*. Thus suppose I have $100 in a savings deposit at 2 per cent per annum. This begins as an asset of $100 in my balance sheet, as a liability of $100 in the balance sheet of the bank. In a year's time it will be $100 (1.02), or $102; in two years' time, $100(1.02)^2$, or $104.04; in n years' time it will be $100(1.02)^n$.

Growth and Withdrawals

We have defined both the rate of profit and the rate of interest as a *gross* rate of growth because the net rate of growth of a capital sum depends on the sums withdrawn from the account for dividend or interest *payments*. Thus suppose we have a firm, the total value of assets of which is $1,000,000 at the beginning of a year. Suppose that during the year by the process of buying things, transforming things, and selling things the asset total rises to $1,040,000 without any withdrawals for dividends or their equivalent. The rate of profit is clearly 4 per cent per annum. If now the firm declares a dividend of $30,000 —or, if this is a single proprietorship or partnership, if the owner or owners withdraw $30,000 for their own use—the asset total falls to $1,010,000, as $30,000 in cash will be withdrawn from it without any substitute. The rate of profit is not therefore the actual rate at which asset totals are growing, but the rate at which these totals would grow in the absence of withdrawals on the owner's account. Similarly the rate of interest in a contractual investment is not the rate at which the asset-liability actually grows, but the rate at which it would grow if there were no interest *payments*. Thus, if I own a security which pays me $3 per annum and which cost $100, if the payments were not made to me but added to the value of the account, the capital sum would grow at a rate of 3 per cent per annum.

Growth of Net Worth

When a firm has contractual liabilities (e.g., bonds or promissory notes), the *net worth* of the firm grows at a rate which is greater the greater is the excess of the rate of profit over the rate of interest. Thus suppose a firm starts at the beginning of a year with assets totaling $1000, liabilities of $600, and a net worth of $400. Suppose that during the year assets rise to $1100 in the course of the firm's business, the rate of profit being 10 per cent per annum. Suppose the firm incurs a 5 per cent per annum interest charge on its liabilities. Before making the interest payment the liabilities at the end of the year will amount to $600 (1.05), or $630, and the net worth will therefore be $1100 − 630, or $470. The net worth has grown at a rate of $\frac{70}{400}$, or 17.5 per cent per annum.[4] If the rate of interest had been, say, 3 per cent the liabilities would have grown to $618 and the net worth to $482, at a rate of $\frac{82}{400}$, or 20.5 per cent per annum. It should be observed that the actual payment, as opposed to the mere accrual of interest, makes no difference to this result. If, in the first example, the firm paid $30 interest at the end of the year, this would reduce the assets to $1070

---

[4] If the rate of profit is r_a, the rate of interest r_e, the rate of return on net worth (i.e., the rate of growth of net worth) is r_n, A is the total value of assets at the beginning of the year, L the total value of liabilities, and N the net worth, then at the end of the year we have as the balance sheet identity:

$$N(1 + r_n) \equiv A(1 + r_a) + L(1 + r_e),$$

that is, as

$$N \equiv A - L,$$

$$r_n \equiv \frac{Ar_a - Lr_e}{A - L} \equiv \frac{A}{N}(r_a - r_e) + r_e$$

It should be observed that when $r_a = r_e$, $r_n = r_a = r_e$—that is, when the rate of interest is equal to the rate of profit, both rates are also equal to the rate of return on net worth. r_n will be zero when $r_e = \frac{A}{L} r_a$.

through a diminution of cash, and would reduce the liabilities to $600; the net worth would remain at $470. It is only the *accrual,* not the *payment* of interest, which reduces the net worth.

Rate of Interest Determined by the Price of "Bonds"

We must now prove an important proposition: that the rate of interest in any *given* set of contractual obligations is inversely related to, and is *determined by,* the present price of these obligations. A set of contractual obligations may be called a "bond," for want of a more general term, as we have already seen (page 91). On the part of the issuer it consists of an obligation to pay certain benefits at definite dates in the future. From the point of view of the owner of the bond it is a right to receive these benefits. The benefits, and the dates, are specified or are understood in the contract. The rate of interest on the bond is that rate of growth or accrual of the initial value of the bond which will just permit all the designated benefits to be paid without there being any deficiency or excess of value at the end of the period. It is clear that the smaller the initial value, or price, of the bond the greater must be the rate of interest accrual if any *given* set of benefits is to be paid. That is, the smaller the present price of a given expectation, the greater the rate of interest in the investment.

This principle can be illustrated in a simple case: a promissory note in which John Doe promises to pay $105 to the holder at a date one year from the present. Whoever owns this document now owns an "expectation" of receiving $105 in one year. We shall suppose that there is no doubt about the fulfillment of the promise, so that the element of risk can be neglected. The rate of interest on such a security would be equal to the ratio of the *increase* in its value to the original value. If, for instance, Richard Roe pays $100 for this note, he will in effect exchange $100 of "present money" for $105 in one year's time. The total *amount* of interest he will receive is ($105 − 100), or $5. The *rate* of interest his capital will earn is $\frac{5}{100}$ per annum, i.e., 5 per cent per annum. If he paid $95 for the note, he would be exchanging $95 now for $105 in one year's time. The amount of interest would be $10 and the rate of interest would be $\frac{10}{95}$ per annum, or 10.5 per cent per annum. Similarly, if he paid $102 for the note, the rate of interest would be $\frac{3}{102}$, or 2.94 per cent. If he paid $105 for the note, the rate of interest would be 0 per cent per annum. It is evident from these examples that the greater the price paid for a security representing a *given* expectation of future payments, the *smaller* is the rate of interest in the purchaser's investment. The principle is true no matter how many, or how frequent, the expected payments may be.

Consider another simple case—that of a "perpetuity," such as British Consols. The possession of one of these bonds entitles the owner to receive a stated sum, once every year, in perpetuity. Suppose we have a bond, for instance, which entitles us to receive $50 on the first of January every year. If we paid $1000 for this bond, the rate of interest on our perpetual investment is $\frac{50}{1000}$, or 5 per cent per annum. If we had paid $2000 for the bond, the rate of interest would be $\frac{50}{2000}$, or 2½ per cent per annum. If we had paid $500 for the bond, the rate of interest would be $\frac{50}{500}$, or 10 per cent per annum. It is evident in this case also that the greater the price paid for the security, the smaller will be the rate of interest earned.

What Determines the Rates of Interest?

It is evident from the above that what determines the price of a *given* expectation also determines the rate of interest in that particular form of investment. As we saw in Chapter 6, however, the price of any given expectation in a competitive market will be that price at which the amount offered is equal to the amount demanded. For each class of security we can draw supply and demand curves and find the equilibrium price and quantity as in Fig. 4, page 58. Or we could determine the equilibrium price of any security by constructing its "total market curve," as in Fig. 6, page 67, and finding where the excess demand or supply amounted to zero. The price of any class of security is determined by the "height" of its total market curve, which again is a measure of the general eagerness to buy it. "Why is there a rate of interest?" then, is exactly the same question as "Why is the price of a security less than the total of future payments which are expected from it?" Why are not people so eager to buy securities that their price rises to the point where they bear no interest? Why, for instance, does not the price of promissory notes which promise to pay $105 next year stand at $105 now, instead of, say, $100?

The Principle of Equal Advantage Applied to Securities

To answer the above questions we must invoke a principle with which we are already familiar—the principle of equal advantage. If capital is mobile, the *total advantages* which result from holding it in all its various forms must tend to be equal. The enjoyment of interest on capital is not the only advantage, however, accruing to its owner. The various forms of capital differ in many ways, and these differences account for the varying rates of interest to be obtained among them. Just as differences in money wages in various occupations of labor may exist permanently, so differences in rates of interest in various occupations of capital may continue. Pleasant and convenient occupations, like teaching, which possess large nonmonetary advantages, receive relatively small money wages. Similarly, convenient and desirable occupations of capital receive small rates of interest. Generally speaking, the most desirable attributes of capital are first, safety, and second, what is called *liquidity*—i.e., easy exchangeability for other things. Suppose we had to choose among three ways of holding $1000 worth of capital. We might hold it in the form of cash, in the form of a United States government bond, or in the form of a share in a Ruritanian oil company. If, now, the rates of interest we expected to receive were equal in all these cases, it is probable that we should prefer to hold our $1000 in the form of cash, for cash possesses greater liquidity than United States bonds, and certainly greater safety than a Ruritanian oil share. The price of United States government bonds would have to be low enough to afford us a certain small rate of interest before we should be likely to prefer holding our capital in that form. The price of Ruritanian oil shares would probably have to be very low indeed before we should be tempted to hold our capital in that form. They would have to be still lower in order to persuade us to hold them if there were any other disadvantages, such as disreputability, attached to their possession. We might indeed add a third attribute of capital to the two mentioned above—respectability, and say that the more respectable is any form of capital, the lower will be its monetary yield.

Liquidity Preference

It is evident that the rate of interest which capital enjoys when it is held in a form not wholly liquid or perhaps wholly safe is something in the nature of a "bribe" to induce capital to remain in that form. In the same way, the high wages of a steeple jack are a "bribe" to induce people to enter a dangerous and rather unpleasant occupation. If people are to hold capital in an "illiquid" form, i.e., in the form of securities or of real property, the price of these things must be low enough to enable the holder to obtain a certain rate of interest. If this were not so—if, for instance, the price of securities were so high that they yielded a zero rate of interest—most people would not be willing to hold their capital in this form. That is, they would try to sell their securities—to exchange them for cash, which also bears a zero rate of interest but has advantages in the form of liquidity and safety which securities do not have. The result of this rush to sell would be, of course, a fall in the price of securities, which is the same thing as a rise in the rate of interest if the expectations which the securities represent do not change. The rise in the rate of interest would go on until on balance there was no desire to transfer capital holdings from the form of securities to the form of cash. At this point the price of securities would be that at which the quantity offered was equal to the quantity demanded.

A Change in Liquidity Preference

If there is a change in liquidity preference in the market—i.e., a change in the general estimate of the desirability of holding capital in the form of money—this will be reflected in a change in the price of securities and in the rates of interest which they bear. Suppose that for some reason—let us say, a war scare—the holding of money suddenly becomes more desirable. That is to say, there is an increase in liquidity preference. People as a whole wish to hold more of their capital in the form of cash, less in the form of securities. The result is greater eagerness to sell securities coupled with less eagerness to buy them. The demand curve for most securities will fall (shift to the left). The supply curve will rise (shift to the right). The result will be a fall in the price of the security. This means, however, a rise in the rate of interest. That is, when holding money becomes more desirable and holding securities less desirable, a greater "bribe" must be paid to induce people to hold securities instead of money.

The "Market Identity" and Liquidity Preference

This phenomenon can be expressed very conveniently in the form of the "market identity" of page 59. If P_b is the price of a given kind of bond (i.e., a given set of future obligations), M is the quantity of money in the market, B the quantity of these bonds in the market, r_m

the proportion of total asset values which people wish to hold in the form of money, and r_b the proportion which they wish to hold in the form of bonds, then

$$P_b = \frac{Mr_b}{Br_m}$$

Other things being equal, then, the greater the quantity of money in the market, and the greater the preference for the bonds, the higher will be their price and the lower will be the rate of interest on them. The greater the quantity of the bonds on the market and the greater the preference for money, the lower will be the price of the bonds and the greater will be the rate of interest. This, in essence, is the "liquidity preference" theory of interest, which is nothing more or less than an application of price theory to the price of bonds.

Models of Liquidity Preference

The market identity also points up some of the weaknesses of the liquidity preference theory of interest. The market identity by itself is not a "model" of the bond market. We must assume at least four other behavior equations or assumed constants in order to determine the five quantities of the market identity. In its least sophisticated form the liquidity preference theory assumes that B is given, r_b and r_m are likewise given by the psychology of the market, and that hence P_b, and therefore the rate of interest, is a simple function of M—i.e., increasing the quantity of money will result in a decline in the rate of interest. This is assumed in the model which underlies Keynes' *General Theory*, in which *investment* is assumed to be a function of the rate of interest, and the rate of interest is a function of the stock of money.[5]

Weakness of Liquidity Preference Models

The weakness of this model of the bond market is that it wholly neglects possible repercussions of an increase in the money stock on the other variables. In short-run dynamic considerations the impact of changes in price on the preference parameters, r_b and r_m, is very important (see page 97). Thus *rising* prices of bonds may increase

[5] The model consists then of the following equations:
1. The basic identity, $P = A + C$
2. The consumption function, $C = F_c(P,i)$
3. The investment function, $A = F_a(i)$
4. The liquidity function, $i = F_i(M)$,
The stock of money, M, being given, we have a system with four equations and four unknowns, $P, A, C,$ and i.

r_b and diminish r_m and so contribute to the rising price itself. Even more important, however, from the point of view of long-run equilibrium, is the possibility of changes in B—i.e., in the total volume of debt outstanding. We can postulate a "normal" equilibrium rate of interest in any particular kind of security, r_e. If the market rate of interest, as defined by the market price of the security, is above r_e we may suppose that the quantity of the security in the market will fall, since it will not be profitable to create new securities of this type, because as old securities mature and disappear from the market they will not be replaced, so that the total stock of the securities will continually decline. As this stock declines, however, the price will tend to rise, and the market rate of interest to fall. When the market rate comes down to the normal rate it will be found profitable to create enough new securities just to replace those which are maturing, and the stock of the securities—and therefore their price—will remain constant. We are assuming here of course that the quantity of money and the asset preferences do not change. Similarly, if the market rate of interest on any particular kind of security is *below* r_e, more will be created than are destroyed, and the total stock will rise; as it rises the price falls, and the rate of interest rises until once again it is just sufficient to maintain the stock constant.

The Normal Rate of Interest

It will be observed that the process described above is exactly analogous to the equilibrium of normal price of a commodity, as described on pages 107–114. If the market price of a commodity is "too low" its stocks will decline, which will raise the market price; if the market price is "too high" stocks will increase, which will lower the market price. The normal price is that which adjusts production and consumption to the point where stocks are constant, or rather where they grow at a rate appropriate to the whole growth of the economy. Similarly the normal rate of interest on any kind of security may be defined as that which will adjust the creation and destruction of these securities to the point where the rate of growth of the total stock of the security—that is, the excess of creation over destruction—is appropriate.

The Supply of Securities

The next question which arises is "What determines the net amount of securities created?" as this question must be answered before we can give a satisfactory answer to the question "What determines the normal rate of interest?" Unfortunately satisfactory answers to these questions cannot be given until we have gone further into the theory of the individual enterprise. Even at this stage, however, it is clear that the willingness of people to create and to hold debt depends in large measure on the rate of profit on "real" asset combinations. If the rate of profit is high the normal rate of interest on various types of securities is also likely to be high, for if it is not it will pay to issue securities in order to obtain control of more real assets.

Thus in the previous example we saw that if the rate of profit was 10 per cent and the rate of interest was 5 per cent per annum, a firm which started with assets of $1000 and liabilities of $600 would find its net worth growing at a rate of 17.5 per cent. Suppose now that the firm borrowed $1000, without change in the rates of profit or interest. Assets would now start at $2000, liabilities at $1600, net worth still remaining at $400. In a year assets would grow to $2200, liabilities to 1680, net worth to $2200 − 1680, or $580. The rate of growth of net worth is $\frac{180}{400}$, or 45 per cent per annum. It is clear from the equation in footnote 4 (page 371) that the more we borrow, the greater the rate of return on our net worth as long as the rate of profit is greater than the rate of interest. Indeed, if there were no uncertainty it would be impossible for the rate of profit and the rate of interest to diverge for long; if the rate of profit under these circumstances were to exceed the rate of interest even slightly, there would be a strong incentive to borrow (i.e., to create and sell securities) and the new securities coming on to the market would depress the price of all similar securities and would raise the rate of interest until it was equal to the rate of profit. The expansion of assets might also have an effect in reducing the rate of profit, so that the divergence between the rates of profit and of interest would be eaten away from both ends.

Effect of Uncertainty

Because of the presence of uncertainty in all economic affairs, however, rates of profit and rates of interest may diverge even in equilibrium under perfectly competitive markets. The more we borrow, the greater the risk of losing our net worth if things turn against us and the rate of profit actually turns out to be negative. Thus suppose in the above example the rate of profit actually turned out to be minus 20 per cent. With initial assets at $1000 and liabilities at $600, assets would decline in a year to 800, liabilities grow to 630, so that net worth would decline from 400 to 170—a serious matter enough! If, however, the firm borrowed an additional $1000, so that it started with assets of $2000 and liabilities of $1600, assets would decline to $1600, and liabilities grow to $1680; the net worth would be −$80, that is, the firm would be insolvent. It is clear that the larger the proportion of liabilities to net worth, the greater is the chance of insolvency if things do not go well. Consequently even if the most likely expectation of the rate of profit is greater than the rate of interest, the businessman may still hesitate to expand his loans and his assets because of the increasing risk of insolvency, or of irrecoverable loss.[6]

Loan Rationing

Another important reason for divergence, even in equilibrium, between profit rates and interest rates is the existence of *rationing* in the loan market, especially in the market for bank loans (see page 350). Conditions which in a more competitive market would be reflected in a rise in the rate of interest (that is, conditions which necessitate a contraction in the creation of new debt) may in fact simply be reflected in more severe collateral[7] requirements or by a stiffening in the requirements for the granting of loans.

Normal Rate of Interest and the Rate of Profit

Even though there is likely to be a divergence, in equilibrium, between the rate of profit and the rate of interest, it is clear that if this divergence is fairly stable then the main force determining the rate of interest in the long run is the rate of profit. This, indeed, is the core of Adam Smith's criticism of the liquidity preference theory of the mercantilists. Nevertheless the short run may be a long time in the affairs of men, and we cannot afford to neglect it. The short-run, liquidity preference theory of the capital market and the long-run theory are not, therefore, competitors, but complement each other.

Interest and the Banking System

With the analysis developed to this point we can now proceed to examine an extremely important aspect of the theory of the securities market, which is the impact of the banking system on the rate of interest and on the creation of securities. Commercial banks differ from other economic organizations in that their deposit liabilities constitute liquid assets, or money, for those who hold them as assets. We have

[6] This is the principle known as the *principle of increasing risk*. See M. Kalecki, "The Principle of Increasing Risk," *Economica*, November, 1937, p. 440.

[7] "Collateral" consists of borrower's assets which are pledged to the lender and which become the property of the lender if the borrower fails to meet the conditions of the loan contract.

380   MACROECONOMICS

seen also (page 338) that when securities are sold to banks the total of bank deposits increases, by an amount roughly equal to the increase in the bank's holdings of securities, less any losses of reserves or other assets. Consequently when a bank makes a loan, not only is a security created (the promissory note) and put on to the market, but a deposit (money) is also created. When a nonbank institution or an individual makes a loan, a security is created (the promissory note, or bond of the borrower) but no money is created directly; money is merely transferred from the lender to the borrower. An expansion of bank loans, therefore, may have an effect on the price of securities in general very different from that of the expansion of other securities. The creation of securities and their absorption into the market (i.e., the finding of people to hold them other than their original issuers) will generally depress the price of securities and so raise rates of interest. The sale of securities to banks, however, also results in the creation of money, which will in large part offset, or will more than offset, the tendency to lower the price of securities.[8] A good illustration of the above principles is found in the discussion of war finance (pages 479–485).

The Wicksellian Model

The simultaneous creation of securities and of money through the banking system leads to the possibility that a divergence between the

[8] Let M be the quantity of money, B the stock of securities, r_b the preferred security ratio, and r_m the preferred liquidity ratio. The price of securities, P_b, is given by the market identity,

$$P_b = \frac{Mr_b}{Br_m}$$

Now suppose that securities increase by dB, and that as a result of these being sold to banks the money stock (deposits) increases by dM. Suppose preference ratios do not change; then the new price of securities, P'_b, is given by

$$P'_b = \frac{(M + dM)r_b}{(B + dB)r_m}$$

It follows that

$$\frac{P'_b}{P_b} = \frac{(M + dM)B}{(B + dB)M} = \frac{1 + \frac{dM}{M}}{1 + \frac{dB}{B}}$$

We have therefore:

$$P'_b \underset{<}{\overset{>}{=}} P_b, \text{ according as } \frac{dM}{M} \underset{<}{\overset{>}{=}} \frac{dB}{B}$$

That is, if the proportionate increase in money is greater than the proportionate increase in securities, the price of securities will rise and the rate of interest fall. If now we have, as will be approximately the case where the new securities are sold to banks, $dM = dB$, the issue of the securities will cause a fall in the rate of interest if M is smaller than B.

market rate and the normal rate of interest might lead, not to a change in the stock of securities which will bring the market rate back to the normal rate again, but to simultaneous changes in the stock both of securities and of money which will lead to general inflation or deflation. This is a view held by the great Swedish economist, Knut Wicksell. If the market rate is below the natural rate, there will be net creation both of securities and of bank deposits. If now commodity prices are flexible, there will be an increase in commodity prices and, indeed, a rise in the whole wage-price level, but there may not be a movement of the market rate of interest up toward the normal rate. Indeed, the movements may even tend to *widen* the divergence between the market and the normal rate. The price inflation will raise rates of profit on real investment, and so will increase the normal rate; the increase in bank deposits may outweigh the influence of the increase in securities, so that the price of securities themselves may rise and the market rate fall. Similarly, if the market rate is above the normal rate, the result may be a shrinkage in securities and in bank deposits and general deflation without any tendency for the gap to be filled—the normal rate declining with the price deflation, and the market rate rising with a falling price of securities. It must be emphasized that these perverse dynamics are not *necessary*, in the sense that models can easily be constructed which possess much greater dynamic stability. Nevertheless there is a great deal of historical evidence to suggest that processes like those outlined above do go on, at least for short periods. The inflationary process may be brought to an end by the banking system bumping up against legal or conventional reserve requirements and inelastic reserves, for as the expansion proceeds of course reserve ratios fall. The deflationary process may be more difficult to stop, especially if the price-wage level is sticky and the deflation consequently takes the form of a reduction in output and employment. Profit levels in a sharp deflation fall even below zero, and there is no sharp upper limit on the growth of reserve ratios, or of liquidity ratios in general, in the way that legal or conventional requirements impose a sharp lower limit.

SAVING AND INTEREST

We are now in a position to bring together the two parts of this chapter and to ask ourselves what are the relationships between saving, investment, output, and interest rates. Some misconceptions must first be cleared out of the way. If we define saving, in real terms, as the difference between real income (or output) and consumption, and in·

vestment as real accumulation, it is clear that there cannot be any "divergence" between saving and investment, as they are identically equal. The theories therefore which regard the rate of interest as that quantity in the system which makes saving and investment equal must, to say the least of it, be very carefully interpreted. It does not make much sense, for instance, to draw supply and demand curves for "savings," the supply curve relating saving to the rate of interest, the demand curve relating investment to the rate of interest, and then to suppose that the equilibrium rate of interest is where these curves intersect. Such curves imply that income is independent of the volume of investment and consumption, which we know cannot be the case. Similarly we must beware of theories which conceive saving as the process of piling up liquid assets (money) which is then "invested" by being spent on investment goods. Money, as we have seen (page 323), is not accumulated by "hoarding" (i.e., not spending) and it cannot be got rid of by spending it! The surge of money stocks from household into business balances and out again is an important phenomenon, but it may be doubted whether it has anything much to do with the problems of interest or of investment except by its indirect effects.

The Rate of Interest Affects Consumption and Investment Functions

Nevertheless the rate of interest—which we take as a symbol of the whole condition of affairs in the market for securities—may have substantial effects on the major components of the system, through its possible effects on the consumption and investment *functions*. We may suppose, for instance, that the lower the rate of interest (i.e., the easier are the terms on which new securities can be created), the greater will be the amount of willing accumulation at each level of income—i.e., the higher the level of the investment curve.

We may if we wish also postulate an interest component of the consumption function, though there is not much empirical evidence for such, except perhaps in the case of farmers and small businessmen who have opportunities for investment at high rates of return in their own enterprises. Whether we do this or not, we can combine these functions, as in Fig. 51, page 295, into an excess accumulation function, and suppose that the excess accumulation at each level of income (output) is also a function of the rate of interest. This is illustrated in Fig. 55. Here we suppose that I_1 is the excess accumulation curve at a low rate of interest, I_2 at a higher rate, I_3 at a still higher rate. We postulate intermediate curves, of course, at each possible rate of interest. Then at a rate of interest corresponding to the curve I_1 total equilibrium output is OY_1; at the higher rates output is smaller (OY_2, OY_3). The critical question here is a factual one: whether the interest effect is large enough to make the interest rate important as an instrument of policy. If by lowering interest rates we could push equilibrium output from OY_2 to OY_1 in the figure, clearly interest and monetary policy would be very important in establishing full employment. If, however,

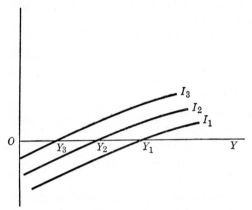

FIG. 55.   Interest and Employment.

a fall in the interest rate produces little impact on the excess accumulation curve, as in highly developed economies seems to be the case, the possibilities of interest rate manipulations seem rather meager, and we must fall back on the cruder but more powerful weapons of public finance.

QUESTIONS AND EXERCISES

1. How, in terms of the analysis of the basic model (page 290), could you interpret the suggestion that unemployment arises because saving is done by one set of people and investment by another set?

2. Suppose an economy with two sectors only, households and businesses. Suppose now that households on the whole exhibit a sudden desire to hold more money, and to that end they cut down their purchases from businesses. Trace the immediate effects of this set of decisions: (a) on the balance sheets of households and of businesses, (b) on the demand for bank loans on the part of businesses. Trace the possible effects on output and employment on the assumptions (a) that the supply of bank loans is very inelastic (bankers are reluctant to expand their loans), (b) that the supply of bank loans is highly elastic. Make clear the various assumptions involved. Repeat the exercise, starting from the assumption that households suddenly desire to hold less money. Repeat

the exercise again, on the assumption that this time the initial impulse comes from an increased desire to hold money on the part of *businesses*.

3. What is meant by saying that the money supply is "elastic" or "inelastic"? What are some arguments in favor of, or against, an elastic supply of money?

4. "The ability of people to hoard depends entirely on the elasticity of the money supply; the ability of people to save depends entirely on the amount of real capital which is being accumulated." Discuss the truth of this statement.

5. "Income (production) is only necessary because of consumption; the more we can economize consumption the better off we are; hence the less income we have the better off we are." Can you resolve this paradox?

6. What is the distinction between *depreciation* and *consumption?* Is this distinction (a) clear, (b) important? If it is important, for what purposes is it important?

7. Is it possible to reconcile the view that we "save in order to consume later" with the view that we save in order to build up a permanent stock of capital?

8. Under what circumstance may the increase in the total of individual net worths *not* be equal to the total value of the increase in real capital of a society?

9. What are the possible ethical implications of the proposition that the increase in the net worth of an individual is not always equivalent to an increase in the total net worth of all individuals?

10. Why do you suppose that Adam Smith and Ricardo rejected so vehemently the notion of the "paradox of thrift"?

11. Explain carefully why the age *distribution* of a population might affect (a) its actual output, (b) its capacity output.

12. "The *existence* of a rate of interest can be explained in the same way that we explain *differences* in wages." Explain, and discuss critically.

13. "The 'liquidity preference' theory is not a theory of interest, but a general theory of prices." Discuss.

14. What similarities and differences are there between the creation and destruction of securities and the production and consumption of commodities?

15. What elements in the economic system give rise to the suggestion that a divergence between the market and the normal rate of interest gives rise to changes in the *general* price level rather than to changes in the rate of interest itself? Why cannot the same argument be applied to a divergence between the market and the normal price of commodities?

16. What is the relation of the theory of saving to the theory of interest?

Is it true to say that they are related mainly through the theory of employment?

17. "The problem of the rate of interest is exactly the same problem as that of the present value of a source of income." Discuss critically.

18. During a year Mr. Smith earned $5000 salary, and received $4500 of this in cash and $500 in the form of retirement premiums. He spent $4000 on personal goods and services, and received $1000 from the sale of his automobile. He consumed $3800 worth of personal goods and services during the year, including $100 worth of garden produce which he raised himself. He purchased in addition $1600 worth of government bonds. Calculate the following:
   a. His money income
   b. His money outgo
   c. The total addition to his net worth during the year (saving)
   d. His total money receipts
   e. His total money expenditures
   f. The addition to (or subtraction from) his money assets (hoarding or dishoarding)
   g. The total addition to his other (nonmoney) assets
   Are there any other changes in his balance-sheet items during the year which may be deduced from the above information?
   Suppose that his balance sheet at the beginning of the year consisted of the following items: cash, 900; car, 1000; retirement equity, 5000; bonds, 1000; other goods, 5000. Construct his balance sheet at the end of the year, and show that (a) his net worth has increased by the amount saved, (b) his cash holdings have diminished by the amount dishoarded.

19. Suppose a firm in which the net worth is 100. Suppose that the firm can borrow in unlimited amounts at 5 per cent per annum. On a graph with r_n (the rate of return on net worth) measured on the vertical axis, and r_a (the rate of profit on total assets) measured on the horizontal axis, draw a series of lines showing the relationship between r_n and r_a for various values of total liabilities, L, say for $L = 50$, 100, 200, 300, 500, 1000, 2000. (Note: the r_n axis should run from about $r_n = .1$ to $r_n = -1$; the r_a axis from $r_a = .1$ to $r_a = -0.7$.) What is the significance of this family of lines? Why do they all go through the point $r_n = .05$, $r_a = .05$? What is the significance of the points of intersection of these lines with the line $r_n = -1$? Suppose now that the firm feels that it cannot possibly stand a value of r_n less than -0.3, and that it fears that the *worst* possibility during the coming year is $r_a = -0.2$. What is the maximum amount it can borrow, assuming that it cannot possibly risk an r_n of less than -0.3? Does this mean that borrowing is limited only by the fear of loss, and not by the hope of gain?

CHAPTER 19

INTERNATIONAL ECONOMIC RELATIONS

The topics which are usually grouped under the heading of the "theory of international trade" are in fact merely special cases of general economic analysis. Some of these cases have already been examined in Part I—e.g., the theory of comparative advantage, the theory of the foreign exchanges and the gold standard, and the "microeconomic" theory of tariffs.[1] It will be convenient, however, to group together a number of "macroeconomic" problems which arise either because of the fact that all economic activities are located at definite points on the earth's surface, or because of the existence of independent national states.

"International Trade" as a Sample

Let us examine first, then, the nature of the economic aggregates which constitute the subject matter of the macroeconomic part of the theory of international trade. By international trade we generally mean that part of the total geographical flow of goods and services which happens to cross national boundaries. It must be regarded therefore as a sample, and by no means a random sample, of the total volume of trade. It is a sample which acquires significance, in spite of its biased and unrepresentative nature, for two reasons. One is that the almost universal imposition of customs barriers at national frontiers leads to the collection of *information* about the movement of goods across these lines. The other is that different nations have different monetary, financial, and organizational systems and that hence the movement of goods across international boundaries has peculiar effects which are not noticed in the case of movements within a country.

[1] Pages 39–43, 81–91, 147–151.

Peculiarities of International Trade

Consider, for instance, the difference between a shipment of goods from Detroit across the river to Windsor, Ontario, and a shipment from Detroit to California. The first is "international trade," no matter how trivial or local in importance. The second is not international trade, although its magnitude and its consequences may be much more important. Nevertheless the shipment from Detroit to Windsor has consequences which are not involved in the other shipment. In the first place it is recorded at the customs office, and will appear in statistical compilations. The movements of internal trade are not so recorded, and are in consequence much more difficult to trace. Then customs duties may be collected on it, with consequences for the fiscal system of the importing country. This peculiarity is not perhaps as fundamental as might be thought, for as we have seen (page 149) customs duties may be regarded as an increase in the cost of transport, and as costs of transport have to be paid anyway, even in the case of internal trade, no new principle is introduced into the problem if we except certain difficulties which arise because the cost of transport is only charged in one direction. Thus customs duties may be thought of as simply increasing the distance between nations, and the duty itself is what has to be paid to the government to transport goods over this artificial barrier.

More important perhaps is the fact that the movement of goods across the boundary will have certain monetary consequences: it may leave Americans, for instance, in the possession of more Canadian dollars than they wish to hold, and so will have an effect on the rate of exchange of the two currencies. If this rate of exchange is "pegged" by a gold standard or by an exchange equalization fund, there may be secondary consequences in the form of transfers of gold or securities between different national accounts, which may have various consequences depending on the various national monetary and financial policies and institutions.

"International" Trade Problems as Distortions

The peculiarities of international trade, important as they are, should not, however, blind us to the importance of looking at the total network of trade, internal as well as international, and not merely at that sample of the total network which happens to cross the national frontiers. The problems of international trade in the narrow sense are problems of *distortion:* frontiers, tariffs, and national economies create distortions in the total network of trade, but do not create the network itself. It is not implied that these distortions are necessarily "bad." In thinking about this field, however, we must rid ourselves of the habit of regarding nations as homogenous "persons" called "France," "England," and so on trading around a table! It is true, of course, that with the increased socialization of trade the picture of a nation as a trading body becomes more true to life. Even here, however, unless socialization is complete, the nation as a trading body must be regarded simply as one trader among many participating in the total volume of trade. In fact, the "international trade" of any particular nation is usually a collection of completely heterogeneous flows, the aggregates of which may not only lack significance but may be quite misleading. To give but a single example. From the appearance of the aggregates, France is virtually self-sufficient in foodstuffs, exporting in normal years just about as much as she imports. The aggregate, however, covers up a great regional diversity. Most of the French import of food is from North Africa into the south of France; most of the export is from the north of France to the rest of northern Europe. Communications between the north and south of France are poor, and trade is not great. Hence when World War II disrupted communications, the south of France starved, being cut off from North Africa, its economic partner. Normandy had food enough, being cut off from its normal export markets, but the food of Normandy could not be applied to the starvation of Provence.

Foreign Investment

Another important aggregate, or set of aggregates, encountered in international trade theory is "foreign investment." By this is meant, in general, the increase in that part of the net worth of the inhabitants of a country which is represented by goods situated outside its borders. The gross foreign capital of a country may be defined as the total equity of its inhabitants in real capital (goods) located outside its borders. This is offset by the *gross foreign liabilities* of the country, this being the total equity of foreigners in the real capital located *within* its borders. The net foreign capital is the gross foreign capital minus the gross foreign liabilities. This is likely to be positive in the case of an "old" country which has been engaged in exporting capital for a while; it will be negative in the case of a country which has been importing capital. Foreign investment is the process by which the net foreign capital of the capital-exporter increases and of the capital-importer declines. This process takes place in many ways, both voluntary and involuntary. Thus an American corporation owned by Americans may build a factory in Brazil; a Brazilian corporation may sell shares or bonds on the New York stock market to Americans; a Brazilian importer may finance his stocks of goods in Brazilian warehouses by discounting bills in New York. All these operations represent voluntary foreign investment by Americans in Brazil; there is an increase in the equity of Americans (stockholders, bondholders, discount houses, etc.) in goods located in Brazil. A revaluation of a currency represents considerable involuntary international redistributions of equity, just as an inflation redistributes equity internally—the owners of the depreciated money, or claims in the depreciated money, suffering for the benefit of the owners of real goods.

International Claims on "Assets in General"

Not infrequently foreign investment results not in claims to *particular* foreign assets but on the assets of a country in general. Intergovernment debt is usually of this character. Thus if the United States makes a loan to Britain, this must be regarded as a vague kind of claim to British assets in general. The vagueness of these claims is reflected in their uncollectability, but as long as they are recognized they represent redistributions of equity in the international accounts. More important, liquid assets (money) must also be regarded as a claim on assets in general of the issuing country. Thus whoever has "dollars," whether bills or bank balances, has a claim on any American assets (goods) which are in the market, and he can exercise (and extinguish) that claim at any time by purchasing American assets with his dollars.

Trade and Investment

With this concept of foreign investment in mind, the relation between trade and investment becomes clearer. Suppose, for instance, that an American manufacturer exports automobiles to France. As long as he retains title to the automobiles on French soil the exports are clearly also foreign investment—i.e., their value represents an increase in American equity in goods located in France. If now he sells the automobiles and receives a deposit at a French bank in francs, no change is made in the foreign investment position apart from some possible revaluations, for, as we have seen, francs represent a claim in general on French assets. If now he exchanges the francs for dollars previously held by a Frenchman, the American's claim in general on French assets is extinguished, but at the same time a Frenchman's claim in general on American assets is also extinguished, so that the international investment position remains unchanged. Trade, therefore, always represents an export of capital from the exporting country to the importing country. It follows that the net export of capital from a country is equal to its "balance of trade"—i.e., the excess of exports over imports. An excess of imports over exports likewise represents a capital import.

The Balance of Trade

In equating the balance of trade with foreign investment it must be remembered that not only imports and exports of more or less durable goods are to be counted, but imports and exports of services. Thus when an American renders, say, a shipping service to a Frenchman he receives in the first instance French money in payment, which, as we have seen, constitutes a general claim on French assets. The effect is no different, from the point of view of the volume of international capital movements, from that of the sale of a durable good. Durable goods themselves depreciate, and their value is transferred, if they are part of a profitable complex, to other assets. Services differ from durable goods only in that they depreciate more rapidly.

The Balance of Payments

The balance of trade concept must be distinguished carefully from that of the balance of *payments*. The difference is roughly similar to the distinction we have made in the case of an individual between "saving" (increase in total assets) and "hoarding" (increase in liquid assets). Thus if a nation has a positive balance of trade, this means that its nationals are on balance increasing their total assets held abroad. If it has a positive balance of payments, it means that its nationals are increasing net *liquid* foreign assets. The situation is complicated of course by the existence of many forms of liquid assets—for example, different national currencies and even different forms of a single national currency. The existence of these forms makes it necessary to have a foreign exchange market, in which these various forms of liquid assets can be exchanged one for another. The theory of the determination of foreign exchange rates has already been outlined (pages 81–91). In so far as there are competitive markets the rates will be determined at the level at which the market is cleared—i.e., at which the holders on balance are content to hold the amount of each currency in existence. The situation is somewhat complicated—and made potentially rather unstable—in the foreign exchange market by the fact that only a small proportion of national liquid assets at any one time (that is, those balances which the owners expect to change into other currencies) can be regarded as relevant to the foreign exchange market. In times of unstable exchange rates speculative movements can often bring into the market funds from these reservoirs of "domestic" currency, and can so distort the exchange rates away from the values which the conditions of international trade as such might determine.

The "Payments Par" of Exchange Rates

We can define the "payments par" system of exchange rates as that system at which there will be no *unwanted* changes in the net liquid assets of all countries. The "payments matrix" analysis of Chapter 17, pages 321–329, helps to clarify this problem.

Let us suppose first that there are only two countries, America (A) and Britain (B). Suppose Table 34 shows the payments table of this two-part system for a given "week," the figures being in millions.

TABLE 34.   Payments Par in Foreign Exchange

	A	B	Total Exp.
A		$40	$40
B	£10		£10
Total Receipts	£10	$40	

We observe immediately that this table differs from those of Chapter 16 because the expenditures and receipts are not in the same currency. As a result of the week's transactions, Americans have paid out $40 and have received £10; Britons have paid out £10 and have received $40. Americans have increased their holdings of sterling and diminished their holdings of dollars; Britons have increased their holdings of dollars and diminished their holdings of sterling. If the status quo is to be restored, Americans must exchange their accumulated sterling for the dollars accumulated by Britons. It is evident in the example that the only exchange rate which will enable both parties to restore their previous asset structure will be $4 = £1, at which rate Americans will get back the $40 they have lost by giving their £10 for it, and Britons will get back the £10 they have lost by giving their $40 for it. It is shown in Appendix 1 to this chapter that no matter how many countries are involved there will always be some system of foreign exchange ratios at which the status quo, as far as money holdings are concerned, can continually be restored. These may be called the "payments par" ratios.

Equilibrating Forces in Foreign Exchanges

If the foreign exchange rates are not at the "payments par" levels, there will be an accumulation of foreign currency in the hands of nationals of one country or another. Thus, if in the preceding example the exchange rate had been $5 = £1, by the time Britons had exchanged all their surplus dollars ($40) they would only have received £8 for them from the Americans: hence, Americans would be left with a £2 increase in their sterling holdings, and Britons with a £2 decrease in their sterling holdings. Similarly, if the rate had been $3 = £1 there would have been a net transfer of $10 from American to British holdings by the time all the sterling had been exchanged. Obviously, these transfers will not go on indefinitely, though they might persist for short periods if individuals were willing to increase their holdings of foreign currencies. Eventually, however, there must be a change. This may take two forms. There may be an attempt on the part of the holders of the accumulating foreign currency to buy their domestic currency in the foreign exchange market. This will depress the price of foreign and raise the price of domestic currency and so bring the exchange rates back towards the "payments par." It is possible, however, that the payments themselves may be adjusted. This is the way in which purely domestic balances of payments are adjusted, as we have already seen. The people who are accumulating money will eventually stop this accumulation by increasing their expenditures; the people who are "decumulating" will stop the drain by decreasing expenditures. This method of attaining a payments equilibrium may be found to some extent in international trade even under a free foreign exchange market; the Americans, for instance, who are accumulating pounds may increase their purchases of British goods simply on that account.

The Gold Standard

Under a gold-standard system the method of attaining equilibrium in international trade approximates that in domestic trade, as exchange rates are fixed within narrow limits by the fact that the various national currencies are freely exchangeable for gold at fixed legal prices. Hence, under a gold-standard system, if Americans are accumulating sterling they will simply exchange it for gold at the Bank of England and bring the gold to America to be exchanged for dollars there. Similarly, if Britons are accumulating dollars they will take them to the United States Treasury and exchange them for gold, then take the gold to England and exchange it there for sterling. This operates through the "gold point mechanism" discussed in Chapter 6.

Self-Correcting Tendencies

Under the free-gold standard of the nineteenth century the movement of gold from one country to another tended to correct the conditions which gave rise to it. This is particularly true in a system with no central bank, where the reserves of all the private banks are kept in the form of gold. In such a case, when gold flows into the country from abroad, the reserves of the banks will increase. Consequently, if they normally keep a constant reserve ratio, each bank will find itself in a better position to expand its loans. There will therefore be an "expansion of credit"—i.e., the banks will increase the amount of their loans and investments, and the total volume of deposits will increase. If the velocity of circulation does not fall, the new deposits will increase the money incomes of the country. This in turn may increase the volume of output or it may increase prices.

Effect on the Flow of Gold

In any case the increase in the money incomes will cause people to buy more from abroad. Imports will increase. If there is a rise in internal prices, exports may be discouraged, for the things exported will have higher prices and will not sell so readily. But the increase in imports and decrease in exports will itself act to stop the flow of gold into a country. We can see this from the previous example. If Americans, for instance, are accumulating gold it is because they are buying "too little" from abroad and selling "too much," and hence paying out less than they receive. The internal inflation, whether of prices or incomes, which the gold inflow causes will, however, make Americans more eager buyers from abroad, and America will become a good place to sell both goods and securities. Similarly, the rise in American costs and prices will hamper American exports. Americans will therefore buy more and sell less abroad, and the gap in the balance of payments which caused the gold flows will close.

The Abandonment of the Gold Standard

Since 1931—and indeed, with a brief, unsuccessful intermission in the twenties, since 1914—the gold standard has been abandoned as an effective international standard. It is interesting to inquire why this has happened, for there seem to be many advantages in an international gold standard. International trade becomes much more difficult when the trader has to contend with fluctuating exchange rates, for then a trader must reckon on changes not only in the price at which he buys or sells, but also in the rate of exchange between the currency in which he has to buy and sell and his own. If an American sells a machine in England for £20 and the rate of exchange is £1 = $5, that means $100 to him; if the rate is £1 = $4 it means only $80 to him. A small shift in the exchange rates, therefore, may easily wipe out a trader's profit. Nevertheless, in spite of the advantage of stable exchange rates which it affords, the gold standard has broken down and will probably never be re-established, at least in its old form.

The Insulation of National Economies

In a somewhat narrow technical sense we can say that the inability of the western world to restore the international gold standard was due to the development of central banking and the increasing control of central banks over their respective national banking systems. Thus in a country in which all gold movements are centralized in the central bank, that bank can "sterilize" gold movements into or out of the country by substituting securities for gold, or gold for securities, in its asset total, thus keeping unaltered the total of its deposits (which, we recall, constitute the reserves of the member banks) in the face of quite large changes in the gold stock.

A much more fundamental reason for the breakdown of the international monetary system lies in the desire of individual nations to insulate themselves from depressions originating in other countries. In order to understand this phenomenon we must now examine some macroeconomic models for an "open" economy—that is, one in which trade and investment take place across the boundary of the system.

MACROECONOMIC MODELS OF INTERNATIONAL TRADE

The One-Country Model

It is not difficult first to extend the "basic model" of Chapter 15 to take account of imports and exports. It is clear that imports in the first instance add to total stocks of goods within the country, and that exports subtract from this stock. In this sense, therefore, imports have the same effect as production and exports as consumption. We can therefore extend the basic identity as follows:

$$A \equiv P + M - C - X \tag{1A}$$

where A is total accumulation, or additions to stocks, P is production, C is consumption, M is imports, and X is exports. For the purposes of the present model it will be convenient to rearrange this identity into an "exports identity":

$$X \equiv P - (C + A) + M \qquad (1B)$$

We can now construct an equilibrium model if we can postulate four behavior equations. Let us suppose the following:

    i. a consumption function, $C = F_c(P)$ (2)
    ii. an imports function, $M = F_m(P)$ (3)
    iii. an exports function, $X = F_x(P)$ (4)
    iv. a "desired accumulation" or investment function, $A = F_a(P)$ (5)

The assumptions involved are not necessarily very realistic; however, we will start from them as the simplest possible case. The first three behavior equations postulate that for every level of output (real income) there are unique levels of consumption, imports, and exports respectively, given by the consumption, imports, and exports functions. The exports function is not strictly necessary, but is put in for completeness. The fourth equation postulates that at every level of real output there is some desired level of internal accumulation of real goods, given by the investment function. To establish the dynamics of the system we must further assume that excess accumulation above the level given by the investment function leads to a fall in output, and deficit accumulation similarly leads to a rise in output.

Solution of the One-Country Model

The equilibrium is determinate, as we have five equations (1 to 5) and five unknowns, $A, P, C, X, and M$. The equilibrium is stable if an increase in output increases actual accumulations. The solution is illustrated in Fig. 56. As in Fig. 52 (page 297), output is measured along the horizontal axis, and the components of output on the vertical axis. For the sake of simplicity in the figure we add together the consumption and investment function, so that for each level of output, "home absorption," $H = C+A$, and we have a "home absorption" function, $H = F_c(P)+F_a(P)$, represented by the "home absorption curve," Hh. We draw an imports curve, Mm, representing the imports function, and an exports curve, Xx, representing the exports function. We now draw the "exports requirements curve," $X_r x_r$, as follows. At any output, say OP, where imports are Pm, home absorption is Ph, and output is also equal to Pp (p being on the 45° line), we measure $mx_r = hp$. Px_r is then the exports requirement, X_r, at this level of output—that is, the amount of exports required if the given output is to be the equilibrium output. By the construction we see that $X_r = M+P-$

$(C+A)$, and therefore if the identity (1B) is to be satisfied we must have $X_r = X;$ that is, the actual exports must equal the export requirements in equilibrium. The point of equilibrium then is given by the intersection of the exports curve, Xx, with the exports requirements curve, X_rx_r, at the point x_e in the figure. At this point, and only at this point, the excess of imports over exports, x_em_e, is equal to the excess of

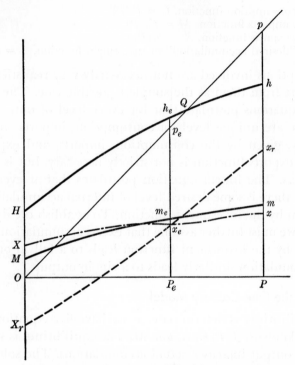

FIG. 56. Foreign Trade Equilibrium, One Country.

home absorption over output, p_eh_e. At larger outputs than OP_e there is a "deficiency" of exports and there will therefore be unwanted accumulations of goods at home leading to reductions in output. At smaller outputs than OP_e there will be an "excess" of exports leading to unwanted decumulations of goods at home and therefore to a rise in output.

The "Export Multiplier"

From this model a number of multipliers of varying degrees of significance can be derived. Suppose, for instance, that there is a spontaneous rise in the exports function, from, say, Xx_e to $X'x'_e$ in Fig. 57, leading to a shift in the equilibrium position from x_e to x'_e. We suppose that the curves are straight lines within the relevant ranges. $x_e x_r$ is the export requirements curve. The exports multiplier, m_x, is the

ratio $\dfrac{x_e y}{zx'_e}$—that is, that change in the equilibrium output per unit shift in exports. Suppose α_m, α_c, α_a and α_x are the "propensities" to import,

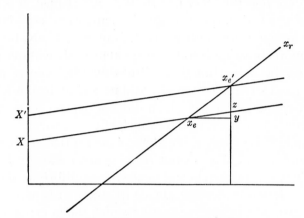

FIG. 57.   The Export Multiplier.

consume, accumulate, and export respectively—that is, the increase in imports, consumption, voluntary accumulation, and exports which result from a unit increase in output. We have, then,

$$zx'_e = yx'_e - yz = x_e y(1 + \alpha_m - \alpha_c - \alpha_a) - x_e y(\alpha_x)$$

i.e.,
$$\frac{1}{m_x} = \frac{zx'_e}{x_e y} = 1 + \alpha_m - \alpha_c - \alpha_a - \alpha_x$$

or
$$m_x = \frac{1}{1 + \alpha_m - \alpha_c - \alpha_a - \alpha_x} \tag{6}$$

We can of course simplify the model somewhat by supposing that exports are an "exogenous" factor given by the outside world, in which case $\alpha_x = 0$, but it does not seem unreasonable to suppose that α_x in fact might be positive.

The "Foreign Investment Multiplier"

In a similar way we could derive "multipliers" for any of the other variables of the system, or even for combinations of variables. We might, for instance, define a "foreign investment multiplier" as the increase in equilibrium output which would result from a unit increase in foreign investment $(X-M)$. Indeed, of the multiplication of such multipliers there seems to be no end. Whether any of these multipliers are useful instruments of analysis, however, is another question, and the student must bear clearly in mind the sharp, and often unrealistic, limitations which must be placed on the system if a multiplier is to be meaningful. A multiplier describes the effect on equilibrium output of a "vertical" shift in one of the behavior functions of the system, *on the assumption that the other functions do not change.* It is the latter assumption which is so questionable in many cases, especially in the case of the foreign trade multipliers. It is most unlikely, for instance, that the imports function could shift spontaneously without any shifts in the other behavior functions. Probably the exports multiplier makes the most sense, as we might assume a shift in the foreign demand for a country's exports which did not depend much on its domestic behavior functions, or have much effect on them.

The principal weakness of the above model is that it is confined to a single country, and hence is not really general enough, for the system of trade is a world system and hence the equilibrium of one country must be affected by decisions made in others. It is particularly unrealistic to assume an exports function which shows exports only as a function of income (or other variables) in the exporting country. It is necessary therefore to expand the model at least to include two countries. As we expand the model, unfortunately, it becomes much more difficult to analyze. These difficulties however are inherent in the subject and must be faced.

The Two-Country Model

Let us consider, then, the theory of a "two part economy"—i.e., a closed "world" economy which is divided into two "countries." It should be observed that this model has an importance far beyond the theory of international trade: it can be applied, for instance, to the study of the relations between any two "halves" of the world economy, such as, for instance, the agricultural sector and the nonagricultural sector, or the consumption goods sector and the investment goods sector. The simplest possible model we can construct of such a two-part economy consists of six equations and six unknowns. Let P_1, P_2 be the total outputs (income) of the two sectors. Let H_1, H_2 be those amounts of product which are willingly absorbed at home in each sector. H_1, that is to say, is equal to the consumption of sector I plus the willing accumulation (home investment) in sector I. Then let M_1 be the imports into sector I, which is the same as the exports from sector II (X_2), and let M_2 be the imports into sector II, which is the same as the exports from sector I (X_1). As there are only two sectors, anything which is an import of one sector must be an export of the other. We now postulate six equations to determine these six unknowns:

Two basic identities, like identity (1):

$$P_1 = H_1 + X_1 - M_1 = H_1 + M_2 - M_1 \qquad (7)$$
$$P_2 = H_2 + X_2 - M_2 = H_2 + M_1 - M_2 \qquad (8)$$

Two behavior functions for country I:

$$\text{a ``home absorption function,''} \quad H_1 = F_{h1}(P_1) \qquad (9)$$
$$\text{an ``imports function,''} \quad M_1 = F_{m1}(P_1) \qquad (10)$$

Two similar behavior functions for country II:

$$H_2 = F_{h2}(P_2) \qquad (11)$$
$$M_2 = F_{m2}(P_2) \qquad (12)$$

An algebraic solution for this system, for the special case of linear functions, is given in appendix 2 to this chapter. A graphic solution is

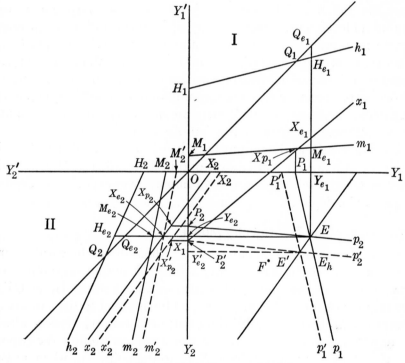

FIG. 58.   A Two-Country Model.

shown in Fig. 58. Linear functions are also used here for the sake of simplicity in drafting, but the graphical method is clearly applicable to nonlinear functions. Output of country I (P_1) is measured along OY_1, of country II (P_2) along OY_2. The components of P_1 are measured along OY'_1, the components of P_2 along OY'_2. Thus the diagram in the field bounded by OY_1 and OY'_1 is the "basic model" diagram for country I, analogous to Fig. 56, page 396. The field bounded by OY_2 and OY'_2 is the similar diagram for country II; it may look a little unfamiliar to the reader because of the location of the axes, but if he will rotate the page 90° and look at it in a mirror he will see that it is essentially the same figure as for country I. H_1h_1 then is the home absorption (consumption plus investment) curve for country I, H_2h_2 the corresponding curve for country II. M_1m_1 and M_2m_2 are the imports curves for the two countries. We now construct the "exports requirements curves," x_1X_1 and x_2X_2, for each country, as before (page 395). In the present figure, with H_1h_1 and M_1m_1 straight lines, X_1x_1 will also be a straight line, so that it is only necessary to find two points on it and join them with a straight line. It will be observed that the export requirements curve intersects the imports curve at a point immediately below the point Q_1 where the home absorption curve intersects the 45° line. The distance $M_{e1}X_{e1}$ ($=H_{e1}Q_{e1}$) represents the amount of foreign investment, or the export surplus which is necessary to prevent unwanted home accumulations at the level of output OY_{e1}. That is to say, at any level of output OY_{e1}, $Y_{e1}H_{e1}$ is all that will be disposed of at home either in consumption or in willing accumulation; the excess of income over home accumulation, therefore, $H_{e1}Q_{e1}$, must be disposed of as net exports if there are not to be unwanted accumulations at home forcing a contraction of output.

For country II, at the output OY_{e2} it will be observed that there is an *excess* of home absorption over output amounting to $H_{e2}Q_{e2}$. This must be taken care of by an excess of imports over exports if stockpiles are not to be depleted.

Equilibrium of the Two-Country Model

We now construct a "P_1 curve," P_1p_1, which shows the equilibrium position of the output of country I for *each* output of country II. This is constructed as follows. For any output of country II, say OY_{e2}, the imports of country II are $Y_{e2}M_{e2}$. This is equal to the exports of country I. To find the equilibrium output of country I, then, which corresponds to the output OY_{e2} of country II, we follow the export requirements curve of country I, X_1x_1, to the point X_{e1}, where at the output OY_{e1} the export requirements of country I, $Y_{e1}X_{e1}$, are equal to the imports of country II, $Y_{e2}M_{e2}$. The perpendiculars to the axes at Y_{e2} and Y_{e1} intersect at E, which is therefore on the P_1 curve. In the present case the curve is a straight line and it is only necessary to find two points on it and join them. Thus P_1 is the point on OY_1 where $P_1X_{p1} = OM_2$.

In an exactly similar way we construct the "P_2 curve," P_2p_2; thus the point P_2 is where the export requirements of country II, P_2X_{p2}, are equal to the imports of I, OM_1. The point where the P_1 curve and the P_2 curve intersect, E, is the point of equilibrium of the whole system, where all six equations (7) to (12) are satisfied. If the curves are linear it is clearly the only point in the field where all the equations are satisfied. OY_{e1} is the equilibrium output of country I and OY_{e2} the equilibrium output of II. At these outputs only are the export requirements of each country equal to the imports of the other.

Shifts in the Two-Country Model

We can now study the effect of changes in the functions of the model on the position of equilibrium. Let us suppose first that there is a "downward" shift in the imports function of country II, reflected in a shift in the imports curve M_2m_2 to a position $M'_2m'_2$ at which there is a smaller volume of imports at each level of output. The export requirements curve of country II likewise shifts downward to the position X_2x_2. The fall in the export requirements curve of country II then "raises" the P_2 curve to the position $P'_2p'_2$. At each level of output of country I there is still the same volume of I's imports and therefore of II's exports, so output in II will now be larger than before at each level of the output of I. Thus P_2 will move to P'_2, where $P'_2X'_{p2}$ is now equal to OM_1. Similarly the fall in the imports curve of II "lowers" the P_1 curve from P_1p_1 to $P'_1p'_1$, as corresponding to each output of II there is now a smaller export from I and therefore a smaller output from I. The position of equilibrium (E) therefore moves to a new position E', at which the output of II is larger and the output of I is smaller. As long as the home absorption functions do not change, the position of equilibrium must lie on the line through EE' (in the present figure a straight line). This line shows all combinations of outputs for which the excess of home absorption over output of one country (e.g., $H_{e1}Q_{e1}$) is equal to the corresponding deficiency in the other (e.g., $H_{e2}Q_{e2}$). The equilibrium point must be somewhere on this line, as the difference between the exports of one country and the imports of the other must be equal to the excess or deficiency of production over home absorption in each country—otherwise there will be unwanted accumulations somewhere in the system.

The "Economic Warfare Line"

The line EE' might well be called the "economic warfare line." It shows how one nation can improve its own output at the expense of another through manipulating the import functions. Thus we saw how nation II, by depressing its import function (say by imposing tariffs, quotas, or other restrictions on imports), might shift the point of mutual equilibrium from E to E', with the expansion of its own output and the diminution of the other nation's output. Similarly by depressing its own imports curve nation I might move the point of equilibrium back up the economic warfare line toward E or even beyond. The reader may wonder at this point what has become of all the much advertised advantages of international trade and specialization noted in earlier chapters. It looks in the present model as if each nation has an advantage in reducing its imports, provided the other nation does not. If each nation therefore acted without regard to the possible effects of its actions on the policy of the other nation, it would seem as if each nation will lower its imports curve until in the final equilibrium each imports curve coincides with the corresponding output axis and there is no international trade whatever!

Retaliation

Two things modify this dismal conclusion. The first is the possibility that each nation may take into account the possibility of retaliation. Thus if nation II was fairly sure that in the event of its restricting imports in the attempt to move from E to E' nation I would retaliate with a sufficient restriction of its imports to bring the equilibrium back to E, there would be some hesitancy at least in starting a restrictive policy; for if both nations restrict imports the final equilibrium as far as employment and total output are concerned may be just the same as it was before, but both nations are actually worse off because the *composition* of their consumption and absorption patterns is worse. Both nations, that is to say, will lose some of the advantages of specialization and trade, and neither will gain anything in employment and output. Unfortunately, however, the fear of retaliation seems to be a very weak motivation in situations of this kind, as the rather similar case of the arms race in international political relations also indicates. The motivation is still weaker as we move from the two-nation case to the many-nation case, for whereas the possibility of retaliation in the two-nation case is quite large, where there are many nations a small nation among them may get away with import restrictions which do not provoke retaliations because their effects are so widespread.

Full Employment Limits Economic Warfare

Fortunately, however, there is a second limitation on the above model which offers some hope for the persistence of international trade. The economic warfare line is only significant within the limits marked out by the full employment or capacity outputs of the two countries. Thus suppose in the figure that OY_{e1} represented the capacity output of country I and OY'_{e2} represented the capacity output of country II. Then only that portion of the economic warfare line between E and E' would be significant, as the system could not move to positions beyond the capacity of either country. That is to say, when any country reached capacity it would lose any further incentive to reduce imports. Unfortunately this does not mean that the process of competitive import restriction might not set in even when there is only a narrow range of possibilities on the economic warfare curve. Thus country II might want to push the position of equilibrium from E to E', and country I then might push it back to E, and country II push it back again to E', all the time through successive lowerings of the import functions. If, however, the range is narrow enough, and still more if the point of full employment for both countries lies *on* the economic warfare curve, the position may be stable, especially if each country takes some account of the possibilities of retaliation, and also perhaps balances the loss from the diminution of trade as such against possible gains in employment.

Effects of Raising "Home Absorption"

Movement along the economic warfare curve through import restriction is not, of course, the only means by which a country can seek to expand its output up to capacity. It can also seek to raise its home absorption curve, either through fiscal or monetary policy or other methods of stimulating consumption and domestic investment. Such a course is twice blessed—if successful, it raises both the income of the nation which undertakes the policy and the income of the other nation as well. Thus suppose that nation II is at a position of less than capacity output, and seeks to raise this output by measures which will "raise" the curve H_2h_2 to give a larger amount of home absorption at each level of output, without change in the imports function. The export requirements curve will again "fall," as home absorption is a negative component of the exports requirement $(P_2 - H_2 + M_2)$. This will "raise" the P_2 curve, say from the position P_2p_2 to $P'_2p'_2$. There will not, however, be any change in the P_1 curve, as there is no change in the imports curve M_2m_2 or in any of the curves of nation I. The position of equilibrium then moves from E to E_h. There is an increase in the equilibrium outputs of *both* nations. We can if we like regard this as a "division" of the benefits of the policy, the international trade situation resulting in a certain diversion of the benefits of the policy from the nation which undertakes it to the nation with which it trades. The amount of this diversion depends on the slope (in this case) of the P_1 curve. Movement along the economic warfare curve is sometimes called the "export of unemployment." Similarly the diversion of the effects of a domestic employment policy through trade might be called the "export of employment."

Mercantilism

The above model throws a great deal of light on the persistence of mercantilist ideas, especially in the world of "practical" men, in spite of the long and trenchant attack by the economists. The virtues of free trade are realized only in a full-employment world—i.e., a world in which the point of capacity outputs for all nations lies on the economic conflict curve, and hence there is no relevant section of the economic conflict curve at all. In a world in which the home absorption functions are not "high" enough to yield this desirable result, the economic conflict curve may have a significant range and the free-trade position therefore becomes theoretically as well as practically unstable. The political instability of a free-trade system rests also on certain other grounds. Any tariff or other restriction of imports is likely to benefit some small group, whereas the injuries are likely to be spread over the society at large. Consequently the benefits of trade restrictions are likely to have a much higher political visibility than the injuries. There is a general presumption because of this that trade restriction will be carried far beyond any possible theoretical optimum, as the political influence of vocal and organized minorities who are aware of possible benefits nearly always outweighs the influence of diffuse and unorganized majorities.[2]

Foreign Investment in the Two-Nation Model

We have still not exhausted the two-nation model, simple as it is. At the position of equilibrium, E, there is "foreign investment" by

[2] There are certain grounds for believing that even in a full-employment system there may be an advantage in trade restriction for the nation imposing that restriction, much as a monopolist can obtain gains for himself at the expense of other members of society by restricting his output. The analysis of this case, however, requires analytical techniques which are developed later.

country I in country II. Country I has an excess of exports over imports amounting to $M_{e1}X_{e1}$, and country II has an exactly equal excess of imports over exports amounting to $M_{e2}X_{e2}$. This excess of exports of country I (or of imports of country II) is the "foreign investment." It is necessary in order to take care of the excess of production over home absorption in country I, $H_{e1}Q_{e1}$, and the corresponding deficiency in country II, $H_{e2}Q_{e2}$. Now, however, the question arises, Suppose that investors are not willing to allow foreign investment to go on at this rate; what then? Suppose, that is to say, we add another behavior function to the system, to represent "willing" foreign investment. This could have many forms. If B_{12} is the net foreign investment of I in II, we might write

$$B_{12} = F_b(P_1, P_2) \tag{13}$$

Or we might suppose simply that B_{12} is given by factors outside the system. In either case we now have seven equations (7–13) and only six unknowns, for B_{12} is given by the identity

$$B_{12} = M_2 - M_1 \tag{14}$$

and is not, therefore, an independent unknown. The system, that is to say, is overdetermined. It would only be by accident that the value of B_{12} at the point E corresponded to the value given by the behavior equation (13). We must face the question as to what will happen to the system if there is a discrepancy between the amount of foreign investment which is necessary for equilibrium (say $M_{e1}X_{e1}$) and the desired amount at these levels of output as given by the behavior equation. If there is such a discrepancy it is clear that some machinery must exist whereby the various functions themselves can be adjusted until the discrepancy is eliminated, and the "internal" equilibrium system as given by the point E is consistent with the "external" equilibrium as given by the desired rate of foreign investment.

The Price System in the Two-Nation Model

Here we see the necessity for a certain reconciliation between the "Keynesian" models of international trade which we have been discussing and the "classical" models in which international adjustments were assumed to be made mainly through the price system. If the overdeterminacy of the model noted above is to be avoided, an additional unknown must be added to the system. The most obvious addition to make is some variable which is representative of the relative price structure of the two countries. The simplest case theoretically is that in which the countries possess different currencies which are exchanged against each other in a free foreign exchange market. The foreign exchange rate then can be introduced as a seventh variable which can be included in the imports functions and also in the foreign investment function. Thus suppose that there is net foreign investment of country I in country II, as at the point of equilibrium E in Fig. 58, and suppose that the amount of foreign investment is "too great" at these levels of output, in the sense that nationals of I are piling up claims on the assets of II in excess of the rate at which they wish to accumulate them. The nationals of I will respond to this situation by trying to exchange these claims for claims on their home assets. That is in the market as a whole people will be trying to get rid of currency II and acquire currency I. This will move the exchange rate, making currency I dearer in terms of currency II. This means that country I will find its imports are cheaper in terms of its own currency, and its imports function will therefore rise—that is, it will take more of the now cheaper imports at each level of output. Similarly country II will find its imports dearer, and its imports function will fall. The point of equilibrium therefore will move from E along the economic warfare curve toward E'. As it moves however the foreign investment of I in II declines. When it has declined to the point where the actual amount of foreign investment is equal to the desired amount, the equilibrium of the seven-equation system has been reached.

Adjustments with Pegged Exchange Rates

Now let us suppose that the exchange rates between the currencies of the two countries are fixed, either because both countries conform to a gold standard, or some other "pegging" arrangement, or because the two parts of the economy are governed by a single monetary system, as would be the case if we were discussing the relations between two parts of a national economy. In this case the adjustments have to be made mainly by shifts in the relative price structure of the two countries or parts. In the case of the traditional gold standard, "unwanted" foreign investment will result in trade moving to the gold points, and gold will flow from the country in which the investment is made to the investing country. If now the result of the gold flow is a monetary expansion in the gold-importing country and a monetary contraction in the gold-exporting country, equilibrating forces will be brought into play. The dynamics of the situation, however, are extremely complicated, as we cannot assume that the domestic

absorption functions will remain unchanged. In the case of equilibrium brought about by changes in the exchange rates it is not
unreasonable to assume, at least as a first approximation, that the equilibrating movement takes place through changes in the imports functions alone. There is in that case a movement along the economic warfare curve, as we have seen, but no shift in the position of that curve.
Where, however, the exchange rates are fixed, so that the equilibrating
factor has to be the general monetary changes in the two areas, changes
in the home absorption function cannot be ruled out. The monetary
expansion in one area may raise, and the contraction in the other area
may lower, the corresponding home absorption function. If the rise in
one is exactly similar to the fall in the other, the position of the economic warfare line will not change. The reader may confirm this by
lowering the line H_2h_2 in Fig. 58 by exactly as much as he raises the
line H_1h_1, and working out the position of the economic warfare line
EE'. What will happen, however, is that the amount of foreign investment corresponding to any particular point on the economic warfare
line changes. In the present case the point of zero foreign investment
moves "up" the line toward the OY_1 axis. The amount of foreign investment which is required at the point of equilibrium E to secure
domestic equilibrium therefore falls as H_1h_1 rises and as H_2h_2 falls. If
this process goes on far enough, equilibrium could be achieved without any change in the import functions. The situation is more complicated, of course, if the change in one home absorption curve does
not exactly counteract the change in the other, so that there is a movement in the economic warfare curve itself.

Other Equilibrating Changes

It should be observed also that there are other possible equilibrating
mechanisms besides the monetary changes. There may, for instance, be
flows of population between the two areas, which will also have the
effect of shifting the home absorption curve—raising it in the country
receiving the immigrants and lowering it in the country losing emigrants. The effects here however are difficult to trace, and may even
move the system away from equilibrium. Thus if with the domestic
equilibrium at E in Fig. 58 and an excess of investment of I in II
population moves from I to II—which is by no means unlikely—the
movement of population may intensify the disequilibrium, raising
H_2h_2 and lowering H_1h_1 and moving the equilibrium point still further from E. The situation is also complicated because in practice
movements of population affect the willingness to undertake "foreign

investment" in the form of immigrants' remittances to their place of origin.

The Dollar Shortage

An interesting application of the above model may be made to the problem of the "dollar shortage" which has dominated discussions of international economic relations since World War II. By the dollar shortage is generally meant a persistent and long-continuing tendency for the export surplus of the United States to exceed the sum which would be required by voluntary foreign investment. This phenomenon leads to import restrictions and restrictions on the use of dollar balances held by their nationals on the part of the "rest of the world," and also to a persistent pressure to enlarge American foreign investment through governmental payments (Marshall aid, military aid, and so on). The two-sector model is of course so much simplified that it cannot hope to explain the multitudinous interactions of the real world; nevertheless it is easy to see how something like a chronic "dollar shortage" might arise, if the position of mutual international equilibrium at E in Fig. 58 involved excessive foreign investment as a condition of stability. The processes by which this excessive foreign investment is eliminated are fairly easily blocked, and probably have been blocked in the past few years. Thus exchange rates have generally been pegged, so that adjustment through this mechanism is blocked. The decline in dollar balances held abroad and the corresponding excess of nondollar balances held by Americans do not now result automatically in changes in the monetary base of the internal banking systems of the respective countries, as they did under the old gold standard. Consequently almost the only adjustive mechanism left consists of restrictions on trade or artificial or political subsidies. The dollar shortage is thus seen to be in part at least the same kind of "shortage" that occurs under price control, where, as we have seen, the fixing of prices below some equilibrium level leads to the conversion of the ever present "scarcity" into "shortages"—the disappearance of stocks without any automatic machinery for correction.

Is the Dollar Shortage "Permanent"?

Some have argued, however, that the disequilibrium in international balances is more fundamental and that there is *no* system of exchange rates, or of national price levels, which could correct the situation. There seem to be two possible arguments in this connection. It might be argued that the dynamic effects of movements in exchange rates would shift the determining functions in such a way that a movement toward an equilibrium system would push the equilibrium itself further away. This argument cannot be more than a short-run argument, as these dynamic effects are bound to exhaust themselves and eventually reverse themselves, but the argument is a potent one in practice against allowing freedom of the foreign exchanges. The world has no desire to repeat the experience of purely speculative fluctuations in foreign exchange rates which characterized the period immediately after World War I.

Hyperemployment and Inflation

The other argument is essentially that the various home absorption and imports functions may be such that the nations reach full employment or capacity output *before* reaching the "economic conflict curve." Suppose, for instance, in Fig. 58 that the capacity outputs of both countries is given by a point F, to the left of the line EE'. At this point country II has a sharp excess of imports and country I a sharp excess of exports; the movement which might bring these to equilibrium, however, would involve an expansion of output in *both* countries, which is by definition impossible. This is the situation of "hyperemployment," and it will inevitably result in inflation. If it results in inflation in *both* countries, the home absorption curves in both countries should fall, which will shift the economic conflict curve toward the origin; if the shift is large enough it will go through the point F, and equilibrium will be established again. As we have seen earlier, however, the effect of inflation on the home absorption function is at least dubious, for investment may be stimulated as much as consumption is restricted; hence inflation may not be adequate to restore the equilibrium. If the inflation is suppressed by price controls the forces tending to restore equilibrium are weakened further. It is not suggested here that the above describes the actual situation. It is, however, a possible interpretation. In all these applications the economic models will be most useful if their limitations are constantly carried in mind. They are intended to be a rough sketch map of the problems of the real world, not a detailed account.

QUESTIONS AND EXERCISES

1. Suppose that a large country were broken up into a number of smaller countries. What would be likely to happen (a) to the total volume of international trade, (b) to the total volume of all trade?
2. Enumerate the similarities and differences between (a) a shipment of

goods from Buffalo to Toronto, and (b) a shipment of identical goods from Buffalo to Cleveland, in regard to as many aspects of these two transactions as you can enumerate.

3. What is meant by the "aggregation problem" in economics, and what phases of it are manifested in the theory of international trade?

4. Suppose the government of Brazil, which has previously bought and sold cruzeiros at a rate of 18 to the dollar, devalues its currency and now buys and sells them at a rate of 36 to the dollar. Trace as many effects of this change as you can on the *distribution* of wealth.

5. What may be meant by the "finance" of international capital movements? In what ways may these movements be financed?

6. Would it be possible for a nation to have a positive balance of trade and a negative balance of payments in the same period? Explain carefully.

7. Why is it generally regarded as undesirable to allow free markets in the foreign exchanges, but desirable to allow free markets in commodities?

8. What weakness in the gold standard system led to its abandonment?

9. Under a universal gold standard system, what effects, both immediate and ultimate, would you expect the following events to have upon the transfer of gold to and from the United States, other things always remaining the same?

a. A great international conference in Washington.

b. A sudden increase in the number of American tourists to Europe.

c. A great boom on the New York stock market, attracting funds from abroad.

d. A sudden increase in the rates of the United States tariff.

e. A great American loan to South America.

10. What would be the effects, both immediate and ultimate, of the above events on the foreign exchange rates under free exchanges?

11. In the system given by equations (1) to (5), what would be the formula for the domestic investment multiplier?

12. What will happen to the model of equations (1) to (5) if the capacity of the system were *below* the point of equilibrium given by the model?

13. What will be the effects on the equilibrium outputs, exports, imports, and foreign investment of the two countries in Fig. 58, page 399, of the following changes (each taken separately): (a) An "upward" shift of the home absorption curve of country I. (b) An "upward" shift in the home absorption curves of both countries. (c) An "upward" shift in the home absorption curve of country I, and a "downward" shift in the home absorption curve of country II. (d) An upward shift in the imports curve of country I. (e) A downward shift in the imports curve of country II. (f) A combination of (d) and (e).

14. Can you construct "multipliers" in the case of the model in Fig. 58?

What would be the formulae for them? Discuss the usefulness of these concepts in such a model.

15. By the "terms of trade" of a nation we mean the ratio $\dfrac{\text{physical imports}}{\text{physical exports}}$. What would be the significance of this ratio for the welfare of a nation? What difficulties may be encountered in the measurement of this ratio? Could this ratio be derived from the information given in Fig. 58?

16. According to the technical definition used in this chapter, economic warfare can only arise between nations if there is less than full employment. Why, exactly?

17. What light does the analysis of this chapter throw on the *stability* of free trade as a system?

18. The Keynesian theory of international trade is sometimes referred to as "neomercantilist." Why?

APPENDIX 1

THE "PAYMENTS PAR" OF FOREIGN EXCHANGE RATES

It can be shown that no matter how many separate countries there are, some system of exchange rates of their currencies can be found at which the whole system of payments will be in balance. Let the countries be A, B, C, . . . N, the names of their currencies "Alpha," "Beta," etc. Then we can construct a payments matrix between them like that in Table 35. Here a_b represents the payments from A to B,

TABLE 35.   The Payments Par

	A	B	C	· · · N
A		a_b	a_c		a_n
B	b_a		b		b_n
C	c_a	c_b			c_n
N	n_a	n_b	n_c		

b_a from B to A, and so on. Let $e_a, e_b, \cdot \cdot \cdot e_n$ be the total expenditures of the various countries. Then $e_a = a_b + a_c + \cdot \cdot \cdot + a_n$ is a sum of "Alphas," $e_b = b_a + b_c + \cdot \cdot \cdot + b_n$ is a sum of "Betas," and so on. The receipts of each country consist of a heterogeneous aggregate of all other currencies. The problem is what system of exchange rates will make the receipts of each country equal in value to its expenditures. Now let β, γ $\cdot$ $\cdot$ $\cdot$ ν be the exchange rates of each currency in terms of "Alphas"; i.e., 1 "Beta" is equal to β "Alphas," and so on. The exchange rate of "Alphas," of course, is equal to 1. Then b_a Betas is worth $b_a\beta$ Alphas, c_a Gammas are worth $c_a\gamma$ Alphas, and so on. We have then, the following equations if these exchange rates are to be a "payments par," representing the fact that the value of the receipts of each country, reduced to "Alphas," is equal to the value of its expenditures reduced to Alphas:

$$
\begin{aligned}
\text{for A:} \quad & b_a\beta + c_a\gamma + \quad + n_a\nu = a_b + a_c + \quad + a_n \\
\text{for B:} \quad & a_b + c_b\gamma + \quad + n_b\nu = (b_a + b_c + \quad + b_n)\beta \\
\text{for C:} \quad & a_c + b_c\beta + \quad + n_c\nu = (c_a + c_b + \quad + c_n)\gamma \\
& \qquad\qquad \cdot\ \cdot\ \cdot \\
\text{for N:} \quad & a_n + b_n\beta ++ \qquad = (n_a + n_b + \quad + n_c)\nu
\end{aligned}
$$

We have apparently N equations and only $N - 1$ unknowns, as a is given. However, because of the properties of the payments matrix one of these equations can always be derived from all the others, so that there are in reality only $N - 1$ independent equations. These can be solved to discover the par values of the exchange rates, β, γ, $\cdot$ $\cdot$ $\cdot$ ν.

APPENDIX 2

ALGEBRAIC SOLUTION OF THE TWO-SECTOR MODEL

If the functions of the two-sector model illustrated in Fig. 58, page 399, are assumed to be linear, it is not difficult to obtain algebraic solutions for the system. Thus suppose we replace the equations (7) to (12), page 399, by the following linear system, using the same notation: Two identities:

$$
\begin{aligned}
P_1 &= H_1 + M_2 - M_1 \tag{1} \\
P_2 &= H_2 + M_1 - M_2 \tag{2}
\end{aligned}
$$

Two home absorption functions:

$$
\begin{aligned}
H_1 &= H_{10} + h_1P_1 \tag{3} \\
H_2 &= H_{20} + h_2P_2 \tag{4}
\end{aligned}
$$

Two imports functions:

$$
\begin{aligned}
M_1 &= M_{10} + m_1P_1 \tag{5} \\
M_2 &= M_{20} + m_2P_2 \tag{6}
\end{aligned}
$$

Solving these equations for P_1 and P_2 we get:

$$P_1 = \frac{(H_{10} + M_{20} - M_{10})(1 - h_2) + (H_{10} + H_{20})m_2}{(1 - h_1)(1 - h_2) + (1 - h_1)m_2 + (1 - h_2)m_1} \tag{7A}$$

$$P_2 = \frac{(H_{20} + M_{10} - M_{20})(1 - h_1) + (H_{10} + H_{20})m_1}{(1 - h_1)(1 - h_2) + (1 - h_1)m_2 + (1 - h_2)m_1} \tag{7B}$$

It should be observed that H_{10}, H_{20}, M_{10}, M_{20} are the amounts of home absorption and imports in the two countries at zero outputs. That is, $H_{10} = OH_1$ in Fig. 58, $H_{20} = OH_2$, $M_{10} = OM_1$, $M_{20} = OM_2$. The coefficients h_1, h_2, m_1, m_2 are the "slopes" or the "marginal propensities" of the various functions. It is clear from equations (7) that if the propensities are constant a "rise" in the home absorption curve of either country (i.e., an increase in H_{10} or H_{20}), a rise in the imports curve (i.e., in M_{10}) of country II, or a *fall* in the imports curve of country I will raise P_1, and that a symmetrical proposition holds for P_2.

The "economic warfare line" is given by the condition

$$P_1 - H_1 = -(P_2 - H_2) \tag{8A}$$

(That is, the excess of home absorption over output in one country must be equal to the excess of output over home absorption in the other.) Substituting the values of H_1 and H_2 from equations (3) and (4) we have

$$P_1 - H_{10} - h_1 P_1 = -P_2 + H_{20} + h_2 P_2,$$
$$P_1(1 - h_1) + P_2(1 - h_2) = H_{10} + H_{20} \tag{8B}$$

If the values of P_1 and P_2 from equations (7) are substituted in this equation it will be seen that the point of equilibrium must always lie on the economic warfare line.

Multiplier formulae can be derived, if desired, for equations (7A) and (7B). Thus we have as the "home absorption multiplier" for country I

$$m_{h1} = \frac{dP_1}{dH_{10}} = \frac{(1 - h_2) + m_2}{(1 - h_1)(1 - h_2) + (1 - h_1)m_2 + (1 - h_2)m_1} \tag{9}$$

In the absence of trade we would of course have $h_2 = m_2 = m_1 = 0$, and the multiplier would reduce to the usual formula (cf. page 299), $\frac{1}{1 - h_1}$. It is not difficult to show that foreign trade reduces the multiplier, as some of the effects of domestic expansion leak out to raise outputs abroad. Thus we have

$$\frac{(1 - h_2) + m_2}{(1 - h_1)(1 - h_2) + (1 - h_1)m_2 + (1 - h_2)m_1} \gtreqless \frac{1}{(1 - h_1)} \tag{10}$$

according as

$$(1 - h_1)(1 - h_2) + m_2(1 - h_1) \gtreqless (1 - h_1)(1 - h_2) + (1 - h_1)m_2 + (1 - h_2)m_1$$

i.e., according as

$$(1 - h_2)m_2 \gtreqless 0$$

In fact, as $(1 - h_2)$ must be positive if the system is to be stable, as m_2 is also likely to be positive, $(1 - h_2)m_2 > 0$ and therefore the multiplier with foreign trade (the left-hand side of inequality [10]) is less than the multiplier without foreign trade (the right-hand side of the inequality).

QUESTIONS AND EXERCISES

1. The following is a payments table for four countries:

	A	B	C	D
A		80	40	100
B	30		60	40
C	40	30		20
D	8	18	22	

Assume that expenditures are made in the national currency. Show that the "payments par" values of the currencies of B, C, D, relative to that of A are 1 of B = 2 of A, 1 of C = 3 of A, 1 of D = 5 of A. Show that if all foreign currencies acquired are exchanged for domestic currency at these rates there is no net change in money holdings. What are the values of the other currencies in terms of B's currency? In terms of C's? Of D's?

Suppose that the values of the currencies were fixed by an international monetary authority at 1 of A = ⅓ of B = ¼ of C = ⅙ of D. What will happen to the holdings of the various currencies by the various countries, assuming that all foreign currencies acquired are exchanged for the domestic currency at these rates? How might the various countries react to these changes? Construct new payments tables showing some possible reactions.

2. The following equations give the home absorption and imports functions for countries I and II, with notation as in appendix 2.

$$H_1 = 13 + \frac{4}{15}P_1 \qquad H_2 = 10 + \frac{1}{3}P_2$$

$$M_1 = 2 + \frac{2}{15}P_1 \qquad M_2 = 4 + \frac{1}{10}P_2$$

a. Calculate the equilibrium values for P_1 and P_2.

b. Calculate the equation of the economic warfare curve, and show that it is satisfied by the equilibrium values of P_1 and P_2.

c. Calculate the home absorption multipliers for the two countries (i) under conditions of foreign trade, (ii) without foreign trade. Check the results by reworking the equilibrium values of P_1 and P_2 on the assumption (i) that H_{10} moves from 13 to 14, (ii) that H_{20} moves from 10 to 11.

d. Develop formulae for the "imports multipliers" and check them with the numerical example.

e. Give a graphical solution of the above system, and show that it conforms with the algebraic solution.

CHAPTER 20

DYNAMIC MACROECONOMIC MODELS

Dynamic Models Concern Paths Through Time

We have seen that an economic model consists of a system of equations with an equal number of unknowns, so that there will in general only be a limited number of values of the unknowns at which all the equations are satisfied. The set of values at which the equations are all satisfied is the "equilibrium" set of values, for with any other set of values some or all of the equations will not be satisfied, and as the equations represent either certain necessary identities or certain relationships which express regular patterns of human behavior, a failure to satisfy the equations will result in a change in one or more of the variables (unknowns) of the system.

It is not enough, however, simply to postulate systems of equations, even though they have solutions. We also want to investigate the dynamics of the process by which the equations get "solved." We want to know how the various variables move through time toward their equilibrium. We need this information not only because it is interesting in itself but also because it is necessary if we are to know the *stability* of the equilibrium. Do the variables move rapidly or slowly, directly or cyclically, or even toward or away from the position of equilibrium? Obviously the significance of the equilibrium position cannot be assessed until these dynamic properties are investigated.

Difference Equations

In order to investigate these dynamic properties it is necessary to transform the equations of equilibrium into a system of *difference equations*. A difference equation expresses a stable relationship between two or more *successive* positions of the same variable. Suppose, for instance, that the value of a loan at interest doubles in a given period, say ten years. Then if x_t is the value of the loan at any date, and x_{t+1} is the value ten years after that date, we can write $x_{t+1} = 2x_t$.

This is a very simple difference equation. If we are given the value of x at any date whatever, we can deduce the value at any other date.[1] Thus if $x_0 = 100$, we know from the equation that $x_1 = 200$. But if $x_1 = 200$, then x_2 must be 400. Similarly x_3 is 800, x_4 is 1600, x_5 is 3200, and so on—each value being double the value before. If the value of the variable is initially such that the same value is repeated period after period, the initial value is said to be the *equilibrium* value of the system. That is, if $x_0 = x_1 = x_2, \ldots = x_n$, and so on, $x_0 = x_e$, the equilibrium value. The equilibrium value is found by putting $x_{t+1} = x_t = x_e$ in the difference equation. In the above case the only equilibrium value is $x_e = 0$. This equilibrium is not, however, *stable* in the above case. A slight variation above (or below) zero will set the system moving away from equilibrium. Consider by contrast the system $x_{t+1} = 0.5(x_t)$. If $x_0 = 1$, $x_1 = 0.5$, $x_2 = 0.25$, $x_3 = 0.125$, and so on. A disturbance clearly results in a movement back to the equilibrium position at zero.

Application to the Basic National Income Model

These concepts can now be applied immediately to a simple national income system. Suppose we assume a linear consumption function, $C_{t+1} = C_0 + cY_t$. That is, we assume that consumption in any one year depends on the income of the year before. The linear form of the equation means that the graph of this consumption function is a straight line. The propensity to consume, c is a constant, and it is assumed that there will be some consumption, C_0, even at zero income. Then we suppose investment (willing accumulation) to be constant at A. We know from the savings-investment identity that $Y_{t+1} = C_{t+1} + A$. Putting together the consumption function and the savings-investment identity, we get a difference equation in national income,

$$Y_{t+1} = C_0 + A + cY_t \qquad (1)$$

The equilibrium value is found by putting $Y_{t+1} = Y_t = Y_e$, in this equation, giving

$$Y_e = C_0 + A + cY_e, \text{ or } Y_e = \frac{C_0 + A}{1 - c}. \qquad (2)$$

An arithmetical example will clarify the dynamics of this system. Suppose $C_0 = 40$, $A = 20$, $c = 0.8$. The equilibrium value is then $Y_e = \frac{60}{(1 - 0.8)} = 300$. Table 36 then shows first the course of the national income if we start from a point below the equilibrium, say 200,

[1] Any other date, to be exact, which is an exact multiple of the unit time interval of the equation.

TABLE 36. Dynamics of a National Income Model
$(Y_{t+1} = 60 + 0.8(Y_t))$

National Income	Y_0	Y_1	Y_2	Y_3	Y_4	Y_5	Y_6	Y_7	Y_8	Y_9
$C_0 + A$		60	60	60	60	60	60	60	60	60
$0.8(Y_t)$		160	176	189	199	207	214	219	223	226
Y_{t+1}	200	220	236	249	259	267	274	279	283	286
$C_0 + A$		60	60	60	60	60	60	60	60	60
$0.8(Y_t)$		320	304	291	281	273	266	261	257	254
Y_{t+1}	400	380	364	351	341	333	326	321	317	314

and then shows the course of the national income if we start from a point above the equilibrium value, say 400. It will be observed that the equilibrium position is stable. A divergence from equilibrium either above or below the equilibrium value sets in motion forces to restore the equilibrium position. It will be observed also that there is

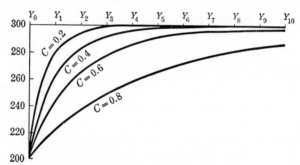

FIG. 59.   Paths to Equilibrium.

no cyclical movement. The national income constantly approaches its equilibrium value at a diminishing rate. Fig. 59 shows the path toward an equilibrium of 300 with propensities to consume of 0.8, 0.6, 0.4, and 0.2. It is evident that the lower the propensity to consume, the more rapid the approach to equilibrium.

Graphic Solution of Dynamic Models

Systems in which the difference equations relate only two successive years can be "solved" by a simple graphic technique. Suppose we measure x_t on the horizontal and x_{t+1} on the vertical axis in Fig. 60. The difference equation relating these two quantities can be represented as a line on this graph. Suppose in Fig. 60 LK is such a line. Now draw the 45° line from the origin, OR, intersecting HK in Q. Q is clearly the equilibrium value, for by construction $OS = SQ$—that is, $x_t = x_{t+1}$. Suppose now that OA is the initial value x_0. If AB is drawn vertically to meet HK in B, $AB = x_1$. If BD is drawn horizontally to meet OA in D, we have by construction $OC = CD = AB = x_1$. If CD

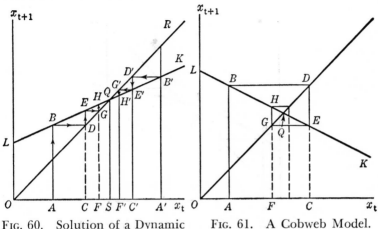

FIG. 60. Solution of a Dynamic Model.   FIG. 61. A Cobweb Model.

is projected upward to meet HK in E, $CE = x_2$. Similarly, $FH = x_3$, and so on toward the equilibrium at Q. Similarly, starting from a position above the equilibrium at A' the successive positions x_0, x_1, x_2, x_3 are OA', $A'B'$, $C'E'$, $F'H'$, etc. The equilibrium in Fig. 60 is clearly stable. If the curve LK is steeper than 45° where it cuts the line OR, the equilibrium is unstable.

A curve which expresses a difference equation may be called a "difference curve." If the slope of the difference curve is negative, as in Fig. 61, the movement toward or away from equilibrium follows a cyclical path. Starting from an initial position $x_0 = OA$, we have $x_1 = AB(= OC)$, $x_2 = CE(=OF)$, $x_3 = FH$, and so on in a "cobweb" around the equilibrium point, Q. The celebrated "cobweb theorem" in price theory is merely a special case of this type of dynamic system. If the slope of the line LK is $-45°$, G will fall on the line AB and the cycle will be repeated indefinitely. If the slope is greater than 45° the cycle will be an explosive one, and the equilibrium will be unstable.

This graphic technique has the advantage that it can be applied just as easily to nonlinear as to linear difference equations. Thus in Fig. 62 we suppose that the difference curve has a diminishing slope. In terms of our economic model this would mean that the marginal propensity to consume diminished with increasing income—a not implausible hypothesis. Under these circumstances the approach to equilibrium from below, following the course *ABCDEF*, etc., is *slower* than the approach from above, *A'B'C'D'*, etc. This would suggest that down-swings of the system would be dramatic and rapid, whereas upswings would be slow and prolonged. There is some evidence that business

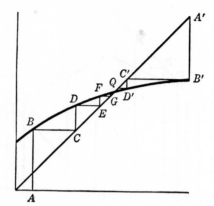

FIG. 62.   A Nonlinear Dynamic Model.

cycles tend to follow this pattern. It is clear also from the analysis that a simple "multiplier" system cannot by itself yield a truly cyclical fluctuation about an equilibrium unless the propensity to absorb is negative—an excessively unlikely hypothesis.

The Accelerator

If therefore there are to be true cycles in a national income model, additional relationships must be introduced. The simplest of these is the "accelerator." This assumes a relationship between the level of investment and the *change* in national income. Let us suppose, for instance, that investment is a constant, K_i plus a constant *proportion, α,* of the change in national income between the two previous years. That is,

$$I_{t+2} = I_o + \alpha(Y_{t+1} - Y_t) \tag{3}$$

The constant a is called the "accelerator," largely because it reflects the assumption that a rise in income accelerates itself through the stimulation which is given to investment. This stimulation is generally supposed to result from the fact that a rise in output requires at least a proportionate rise in the total stock of equipment necessary to produce his output. If the output of this equipment has been just sufficient in he past to replace a given stock as it wore out, the increase in the stock necessitates a temporary increase in the output of equipment proportionally greater than the increase in final product. Thus suppose that 1 machine produces 10 widgets, and lasts for 5 years. If the annual output of widgets is 100, there will be 10 machines, 2 of which will be replaced each year. Now suppose that the output of widgets increases to 120. In the year of the increase 12 machines will be needed, so that the output of machines must jump from 2 to 4; 2 for replacement, and 2 more to bring the total number up to 12. A 20 per cent increase in the output of widgets therefore necessitates a 100 per cent increase in the output of machines. This topic will be examined in more detail on pages 437–438.

The Accelerator Model

To return now to the dynamic model, we suppose as before that there is a linear consumption function, so that consumption is a constant C_0 plus a fixed proportion, β of the national income of the year before. The constant β is the "propensity to consume." We have then

$$C_{t+2} = C_o + \beta Y_{t+1} \tag{4}$$

From the savings-investment identity we derive immediately a difference equation of the second order in national income,

$$Y_{t+2} = C_{t+2} + I_{t+2} = C_o + \beta Y_{t+1} + I_o + \alpha(Y_{t+1} - Y_t) \tag{5}$$

1. No Cycle

The properties of this system can be illustrated conveniently by arithmetical examples. In all these examples suppose $C_0 = 800$, $I_0 = 200$, and $\beta = 0.8$, so that the equilibrium value is the same in each, equal to $\dfrac{1000}{(1 - 0.8)} = 5000$. Tables 37A to 37E show the course of national income with accelerators (a) equal to 0.1, 0.5, 1.0, 1.1, and 2.0. It will be observed that the influence of a *small* accelerator is simply to speed up the movement toward equilibrium. Thus the accelerator comes into play in year 2, when it produces a component of investment equal to the rise in income between years 0 and 1 (200, from 4000 to 4200) multiplied by the accelerator, 0.1: $200 \times 0.1 = 20$. Had it not been for the acceleration, national income would have been 4360 in year 2; because of the investment produced by the rise in income, therefore, the rise in income in the next period is greater. When in-

TABLE 37A. The Accelerator Model ($\alpha = 0.1$, $\beta = 0.8$)

Year	1	2	3	4	5	6	7	8	9	10	11
$C \begin{cases} C_o \end{cases}$		800	800	800	800	800	800	800	800	800	800
βY_{t+1}		3200	3360	3504	3618	3706	3774	3826	3866	3897	3921
$I \begin{cases} I_o \end{cases}$		200	200	200	200	200	200	200	200	200	200
$\alpha(Y_{t+1} - Y_t)$			20	18	14	11	8	6	5	4	3
Y_t	4000	4200	4380	4522	4632	4717	4782	4832	4871	4901	4924
$Y_{t-1} - Y_{t-2}$		200	180	142	110	85	65	50	39	30	23

TABLE 37B. The Accelerator Model ($\alpha = 0.5$, $\beta = 0.8$)

Year	0	1	2	3	4	5	6	7	8	9	10	11	12
$C \begin{cases} C_o \end{cases}$		800	800	800	800	800	800	800	800	800	800	800	800
βY_{t+1}		3200	3360	3568	3758	3902	3993	4040	4056	4053	4041	4027	4015
$I \begin{cases} I_o \end{cases}$		200	200	200	200	200	200	200	200	200	200	200	200
$\alpha(Y_{t+1} - Y_t)$			100	130	119	89	57	30	10	−2	−7	−8	−7
Y_t	4000	4200	4460	4698	4877	4991	5050	5070	5066	5051	5034	5019	5008
$Y_{t-1} - Y_{t-2}$		200	260	238	179	114	59	20	−4	−15	−17	−15	−11

TABLE 37C. The Accelerator Model ($\alpha = 1.0$, $\beta = 0.8$)

Year	0	1	2	3	4	5	6	7	8	9	10	11	12	13	14	15
$C\begin{cases} C_o \end{cases}$		800	800	800	800	800	800	800	800	800	800	800	800	800	800	800
$\begin{cases} \beta Y_{t-1} \end{cases}$		3200	3360	3648	4006	4363	4647	4802	4796	4631	4340	3981	3626	3346	3197	3209
$I\begin{cases} I_o \end{cases}$		200	200	200	200	200	200	200	200	200	200	200	200	200	200	200
$\begin{cases} \alpha(Y_{t-1} - Y_{t-2}) \end{cases}$		200	200	360	448	446	355	193	-7	-206	-364	-449	-444	-350	-186	$+15$
Y_t	4000	4200	4560	5008	5454	5809	6002	5995	5789	5425	4976	4532	4182	3996	4011	4224
$Y_{t-1} - Y_{t-2}$		$+200$	$+360$	$+448$	$+446$	$+355$	$+193$	-7	-206	-364	-449	-444	-350	-186	$+15$	$+213$

TABLE 37D. The Accelerator Model ($\alpha = 1.1$, $\beta = 0.8$)

Year	0	1	2	3	4	5	6	7	8	9	10	11	12	13	14	15
$C\begin{cases} C_o \end{cases}$		800	800	800	800	800	800	800	800	800	800	800	800	800	800	800
$\begin{cases} \beta Y_{t-1} \end{cases}$		3200	3360	3664	4066	4494	4867	5104	5144	4959	4582	4050	3456	2911	2530	2404
$I\begin{cases} I_o \end{cases}$		200	200	200	200	200	200	200	200	200	200	200	200	200	200	200
$\begin{cases} \alpha(Y_{t-1} - Y_{t-2}) \end{cases}$		200	220	418	552	590	513	326	55	-232	-519	-730	-817	-749	-525	-173
Y_t	4000	4200	4580	5082	5618	6084	6380	6430	6199	5727	5063	4320	3639	3162	3005	3231
$Y_{t-1} - Y_{t-2}$		200	380	502	536	466	296	50	-211	-472	-664	-743	-681	-477	-157	$+226$

come is rising, that is to say, the accelerator gives it an additional "push." Similarly, when income is falling, the accelerator also gives it an additional push downward and makes it fall faster. In Table 37A this additional "push" is small enough so that it merely accelerates the movement toward equilibrium.

2. The Damped Cycle

If the accelerator itself is a little larger, however, the "push" will be great enough so that income will shoot up beyond the equilibrium value of 5000. Once this happens the consumption function part of the equation (βY_{t+1}) operates to pull the income down again, and a cycle is set up. If the accelerator is less than 1 this cycle will be *damped*—that is to say, the successive fluctuations will make smaller and smaller swings until the swings finally become imperceptible. This is shown in Table 37B, where the accelerator is 0.5. It will be seen that by the sixth "year" the "push" of the accelerator is sufficient to carry the national income beyond the equilibrium value of 5000, up to 5070 in the year 7; in the year 8, however, the force of the consumption function is powerful enough to overcome the weak accelerator, and income starts to fall. By the year 15, however, equilibrium is practically reached, and the fluctuations become very small.

3. The Constant Cycle

We contrast this with the case of Table 37C, where the accelerator is equal to 1.0. Here the "push" of the accelerator up when income is rising and the "pull" down when income is falling is so great that a perpetual cycle is set up. The accelerator pushes income up so rapidly that the equilibrium point is overshot by year 3; the consumption function brings the rise to a stop at about 6000 in year 6 and income starts to fall again; the accelerator pushes it past the equilibrium again in year 10, but it reaches a minimum of about 4000 in year 13. Arithmetical roundings cause the figures of the table to be slightly inaccurate; it is clear, however, that income will continue to fluctuate between 4000 and 6000 indefinitely.

4. The Explosive Cycle

If now the accelerator is greater than 1.0, but not too great, explosive cycles will be set up, each fluctuation being larger than the next. This is shown in Table 37D, where the accelerator is 1.1. The accelerator carries income well beyond equilibrium up to a maximum at about 6430, then plunges it down to a minimum at about 3005, far below the original value of 4000. The reader may calculate for himself that from this point income will rise to a maximum of about 7808 before it turns once again for a still more violent fall.

5. The Explosion

Finally, if the accelerator is still larger the accelerator effect outweighs the consumption function effect altogether, and income moves always in the direction of the accelerator, though perhaps eventually at a decreasing pace; the consumption function is never powerful

TABLE 37E. The Accelerator Model ($\alpha = 2.0$, $\beta = 0.8$)

Year	0	1	2	3	4	5	6	7
$C\begin{cases} C_o \\ \beta Y_{t-1} \end{cases}$		800	800	800	800	800	800	800
		3200	3360	3808	4742	6462	9410	14222
$I\begin{cases} I_o \\ \alpha(Y_{t-1} - Y_{t-2}) \end{cases}$		200	200	200	200	200	200	200
		—	400	1120	2336	4300	7368	12032
Y_t	4000	4200	4760	5928	8078	11762	17778	27254
$Y_{t-1} - Y_{t-2}$		200	560	1168	2150	3684	6016	9476

enough to reverse the direction into a cycle, not even an explosive cycle. This is illustrated in Table 37E, where the accelerator is 2.0. It will be seen that income rises indefinitely, with the accelerator also rising. These five cases are portrayed graphically in Fig. 63.

Significance of the Models

The economic significance of these dynamic systems is unfortunately much less clear than the mathematical analysis. It must be recalled first that the development of these models in time assumes constancy in the basic coefficients, the propensity to consume and the accelerator. This assumption is dubious even in the case of the propensity to consume. Forecasts of the postwar national income of the United States made in the later years of World War II generally turned out to be very inaccurate, mainly because they were based on values of the consumption function derived from the 1930's. In the 1940's the consumption function apparently took a marked upward shift, for reasons which are easier to perceive after the event than before. Quite a slight shift in the level of the consumption function, however, can create large shifts in the position of equilibrium, especially if the propensity to consume is close to 1.0. If the stability of the consumption function is in some doubt, there is much more doubt about the stability of the accelerator. In point of fact there is not much empirical evidence even for the existence of an accelerator, much less for its stability. Hence models which assume constancy in the accelerator must be used with the greatest caution, and they are not likely to be descriptive of actual economic cycles. The best that models of this kind can do is to show

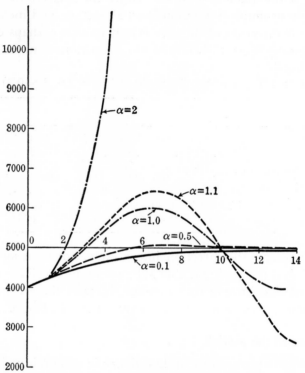

FIG. 63.   Movements of National Income with Various Values of the
Accelerator (Propensity to Consume = 0.8).

how cycles *might* be generated. Whether cycles are in fact generated in the way indicated cannot of course be deduced from the theoretical models themselves!

Expectational Price Cycles

Dynamic models showing the course of market prices over time can be constructed along lines similar to those outlined above. Suppose, for instance, that we modify the "market identity" of page 59 $\left(p = \dfrac{M r_a}{A r_m} \right)$ into the form $p_t = K r_t$, where $K \left(= \dfrac{M}{A} \right)$ is assumed constant and $r_t \, (= r_a/r_m)$ is a parameter expressive of the intensity of net money demand for the commodity. Let us further suppose that this demand coefficient, r_t, is equal to some "normal" level, r_0, plus a factor which is larger if the price is rising, smaller if the price is falling. That is to say, we suppose that people project the trend of prices, so that rising prices lead to the expectation of further rise, and so an increase in demand, while falling prices lead to an expectation of further fall, and so a decrease in demand. If these functions are linear we can write:

$$r_t = r_0 + \alpha(p_t - p_{t-1}) \qquad (6)$$

We have therefore:

$$p_t = Kr_t = Kr_0 + K\alpha(p_t - p_{t-1}),$$

or

$$p_t(1 - K\alpha) = Kr_0 - K\alpha p_{t-1} \qquad (7)$$

This is a simple linear difference equation of the first degree; the course of the price through time can therefore be analyzed by a di-

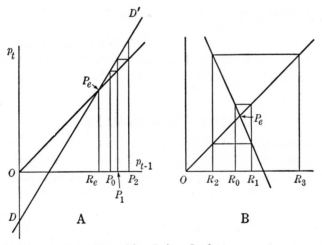

FIG. 64.   Price Cycles.

agram similar to Fig. 61. Thus in Fig. 64A and B the line DD' is the difference curve corresponding to equation (7). If $K\alpha > 1$, the slope of the difference curve DD', $\left(\dfrac{-K\alpha}{1 - K\alpha}\right)$, will be positive, but less than 1, as in Fig. 64A. The equilibrium at P_e will therefore be unstable. If we start from a price above the equilibrium price OR_e, say OP_0, the subsequent prices will be OP_1, OP_2, etc.; the price rises at an accelerating rate. Similarly if we start at a price below the equilibrium the price will fall at an accelerating rate. As Ka gets closer to 1 the line DD' becomes steeper, and the movement away from equilibrium gets faster and faster, until when $Ka = 1$, DD' is vertical, and the equilibrium is perfectly unstable; the price shoots immediately to plus or minus infinity if disturbed from the equilibrium level. With $Ka < 1$ a cyclical pattern will be set up, as in Fig. 64B. If Ka lies between 0.5 and 1 the cycle will be explosive, as in the figure; the course from OR_0 is up to OR_1, down beyond OR_0 to OR_2, up beyond OR_1 to OR_3, and so on. If $Ka = 0.5$ the cycle will be perpetual. If Ka lies between 0 and 0.5 the cycle will be damped, as in Fig. 61. The smaller is Ka, the more rapidly is the cycle damped. If Ka is zero, the price moves immediately to its equilibrium position.

The abrupt transition from high to low to high prices in Fig. 64B is not particularly realistic. However, this is merely the result of expressing the model in the form of a difference equation of the first degree. If we suppose that r_t is a function of $(p_{t-1} - p_{t-2})$, say,

$$r_t = r_0 + \alpha(p_{t-1} - p_{t-2}) \qquad (8)$$

we get a difference equation of the second degree,

$$p_t = Kr_0 + K\alpha(p_{t-1} - p_{t-2}) \qquad (9)$$

The reader can test for himself that this relationship also yields a perpetual cycle if $Ka = 1$, a damped cycle if $Ka < 1$, and an explosive cycle if $Ka > 1$.

POPULATION ANALYSIS

A very important field of dynamic analysis covers the theory of the movements of a population. A population may be defined as any aggregate which can be measured in some common unit, and in which the *age* of each unit can be identified, or at least postulated. The age of a unit is the length of time which has elapsed between some "present" date and the date of "birth," or the entry of the unit into the population. In all ordinary populations it is also generally postulated that each unit has a finite age of "death," or departure from the population. Birth and death in this sense do not necessarily mean the creation or the destruction of the unit in question, but refer to the dates at which the unit begins to conform to, or ceases to conform to, the definition of the aggregate which constitutes the population. Thus if our aggregate is the human population of a finite area, such as the United States, the entrance of an immigrant is a "birth" and the exit of an emigrant a "death" into that population, just as much as physiological births and deaths.

The Survival Function

The dynamic analysis of population movements rests on the postulate of certain stable difference equations. We may, for instance, postulate a stable "survival function," showing how many units survive to each age from a given number of births. Thus of a 100 "births," 90 may survive to be one year old, 85 to be two years old, 81 to be three years old, and so on down to the last tottering survivors. The survival function is thus built up from a series of difference equations,

$$a_1 = k_1 a_0, \ a_2 = k_2 a_0, \ \cdots \ a_n = k_n a_0$$

Where a_n is the number that survive to year n out of a total number of births B_0 in year 0. In the simplest form of the function k_1, k_2 $\cdots$ k_n are constants. The number dying, or leaving the population, out of the group that is r years old in the year t, between the year t and the year $t + 1$ is $a_r - a_{r+1}$, or $k_r a_0 - k_{r+1} a_0$, or $\dfrac{k_r - k_{r-1}}{k_r} a_r$. The survival function can therefore also be expressed as a "death function."

Dynamics of a Stable Population

If now we are also given a "birth function" relating the number of births in any given year to the numbers or composition of the population, the whole course of the population can be charted. The process can conveniently be illustrated by arithmetical examples. Consider, for example, the process shown in Table 38. Each row in this table represents the numbers in a population divided into five age groups. Thus suppose that in year 1 there are 100 units between the ages of 0 and 1 "year," 96 between 1 and 2, 66 between 2 and 3, 56 between 3 and 4, 30 between 4 and 5, and none older than 5 years. The diagonals marked by the arrows show the survival distributions of each "cohort," or group in the population having the same birth year. Thus we suppose that of 100 people between the ages of 0 and 1 at the end of year 1, 80 survive to the end of year 2, 60 to the end of year 3, 40 to the end of year 4, 20 to the end of year 5, and none to the end of year 6. If the "net births" (B) in each year are defined as the number between 0 and 1 year old at the end of the year, then we suppose that the survival function in the above table is given by $k_1 = 1$, $k_2 = 0.8$, $k_3 = 0.6$, $k_4 = 0.4$, $k_5 = 0.2$, $k_6 = 0$. The figures in parentheses at the top of the table show the net births from which the age groups of year 1 are descended, if the survival function is assumed to be constant. Thus if there are 96 units between 1 and 2 years old in year 1, these must be the survivors of a cohort of 120 births in the previous

Table 38. Population Dynamics: Stable Population

Year	0–1	1–2 (120)	Age (Years) 2–3 (110)	3–4 (140)	4–5 (150)	5+	Total
1	100	96	66	56	30	0	348
2	100	80	72	44	28	0	324
3	100	80	60	48	22	0	310
4	100	80	60	40	24	0	304
5	100	80	60	40	20	0	300
6	100	80	60	40	20	0	300

year: $96 = 120(0.8)$. In year 2 then the numbers between 2 and 3 years old must be 72 $(= 120(0.6)$, and in year 3 the numbers between 3 and 4 must be 48 $(= 120(0.4)$, and so on.

The "Death Function"

The same process can also be described by using a "death function." Thus if a number $(0.6)B$ aged 2–3 becomes $(0.4)B$ by the end of the following year, $(0.2)B$ have "died" during that year—that is, one-third of the number aged 2–3. Thus of the 66 aged 2–3 in year 1, 22 will die in the following year, leaving 44 survivors aged 3–4 in year 2.

In Table 38 we have supposed that the number of net births after year 1 is constant at 100 per year. It is evident on this assumption that the population soon settles down to an equilibrium value of 300, in which the same age grouping is repeated year after year. An equilibrium population can be defined as one in which the number of births and deaths per annum is equal and constant, and in which the numbers in each age group are also constant.

Population Dynamics: Increasing Population

Suppose now that the number of births each year is not constant, but is a function of the numbers in the different age groups. As long as this function is known and is stable it is still possible to trace out the course of any population through time. Thus suppose, in Table 38, that following the year 6 the number of births in each year was equal to the total number of units in the 2–3 and 3–4 age groups. In year 7 the number of births would still be 100 $(= 60(40)$ and the population would continue in equilibrium. Suppose, however, that the number of births was equal to the number of units in the 1–2 and 2–3 age groups. The population would follow a course as in Table 39. In this

Table 39. Population Dynamics: Expanding Population

Year	0–1	1–2	2–3	3–4	4–5	5+	Total
6	100	80	60	40	20	0	300
7	140	80	60	40	20	0	340
8	140	112	60	40	20	0	372
9	172	112	84	40	20	0	428
10	196	138	84	56	20	0	494
11	222	157	103	56	28	0	566

table the first figure in each row (after the first) is equal to the sum of the 1–2 and 2–3 age groups of the preceding year. Thus $140 = 80 + 60$, $172 = 112 + 60$, and so on. It is assumed that all those "born" in the course of a year are between 0 and 1 in the following year. The survival function is assumed to be the same as in Table 38. It is evident that on these assumptions the population will increase indefinitely. Every increase in births provides a bigger age group as a base for still more births.

Declining Population

Suppose on the other hand we assume that the number of births in each year is equal to the numbers in the 3–4 and 4–5 age groups. The population will follow the course of Table 40. In this case each cohort

Table 40. Population Dynamics: Declining Population

Year	0–1	1–2	2–3	3–4	4–5	5+	Total
6	100	80	60	40	20	0	300
7	60	80	60	40	20	0	260
8	60	48	60	40	20	0	228
9	60	48	36	40	20	0	204
10	60	48	36	24	20	0	188
11	44	48	36	24	12	0	164
12	36	35	36	24	12	0	143

of births produces less than its own number to replace it, and the population will decline indefinitely.

Algebraic Solution

It is not difficult to formulate the conditions under which populations will expand, contract, or be stationary under stable birth or survival functions. Let a_1, a_2, $\cdot$ $\cdot$ $\cdot$ a_n be the numbers in the N age groups of a population. Then the "birth function" can be described by a series of constants, b_1, b_2, $\cdot$ $\cdot$ $\cdot$ b_n, so that

$$B = b_1 a_1 + b_2 a_2, \cdot \cdot \cdot b_n a_n \tag{10}$$

This is the simplest useful form of the function. Some of the b's may of course be zero, and in a biological population they will be largest in the most fertile age groups. The complication introduced by the necessity for the cooperation of two sexes is neglected here. Now we also postulate a survival function, also as a set of constants, k_1, k_2, $\cdot$ $\cdot$ $\cdot$ k_n, as before. We have therefore the year t,

$$a_1 = k_1 B_{t-1}, \; a_2 = k_2 B_{t-2}, \cdot \cdot \cdot a_n = k_n B_{t-n} \tag{11}$$

It follows, combining (10) and (11), that:

$$B_t = b_1 k_1 B_{t-1} + b_2 k_2 B_{t-2}, \cdot \cdot \cdot + b_n k_n B_{t-n} \tag{12}$$

If now the population is to be stable, $B_t = B_{t-1} = - = B_{t-n}$, and

$$R = b_1 k_1 + b_2 k_2 + \cdot \cdot \cdot + b_n k_n = 1 \tag{13}$$

The Net Reproductive Ratio

The quantity R is a measure of the net reproductive ratio. In an equilibrium population the survival distribution of each cohort of births is the same as the age distribution in any year. We see this in Table 38, where it is clear that the survival distribution, once the population has settled down to equilibrium (the series on the marked diagonals) is the same as the age distribution of the rows: 100, 80, 60, 40, 20, 0. In an equilibrium population, therefore, R measures the number of net births to which each cohort of the population gives rise. If $R = 1$, therefore, the population just reproduces itself: each generation as it dies out leaves a new generation of equal size. If the net reproductive ratio is more than 1 the population will increase indefinitely, as in Table 39, for each generation as it dies out leaves behind it a cohort of larger size than itself. Similarly, if $R < 1$ the population will eventually decline indefinitely, for each generation leaves behind it a smaller cohort than itself.

The Dynamics of Constant Growth Rates

A dynamic equilibrium of population at a constant rate of growth is possible, though only under rather restricted conditions. Consider, for instance, the population of three age groups given in Table 41.

TABLE 41. Population in Dynamic
Equilibrium with a Constant
Rate of Growth

Year	Age (Years) 0–1	1–2	2–3	Total
1	100	40	10	150
2	200	80	20	300
3	400	160	40	600
4	800	320	80	1200

The basic difference equations behind this table are derived from the coefficients of the survival distribution, 1, 0.8, and 0.4, and the coefficients of the birth function, $B_t = 3a_2 + 8a_3$. Thus in year 1 the number of births is $40 \times 3 + 10 \times 8$, or 200; of these 200, 200 survive to be the first age group of year 2, 160 survive to be the second age group of year 3, and 80 survive to be the third age group of year 4. It is clear from the table that the population grows at a constant rate of 2 per annum, and that the number of births and the numbers in each age group grow at the same rate.[2]

Capital Goods as a Population

Population analysis is important not only for the light which it sheds on the development of human populations, but because it can be applied to populations of all kinds, animate and inanimate. In eco-

[2] Suppose the equilibrium population grows at the rate g. Then we must have $B_{t+1} = gB_t$, whence $B_{t+r} = g^r B_t$. Inserting the appropriate values in equation (12) we have (canceling B_t):

$$\frac{b_1 k_1}{g} + \frac{b_2 k_2}{g^2} + \cdots \frac{b_n k_n}{g^n} = 1 \tag{14}$$

Thus given all the b's and k's the corresponding equilibrium rate of growth (or decline) can be derived from equation (14). It is clear from equation (14) that as $g \gtreqless 1$, $R \gtreqless 1$. It should be observed that the existence of an equilibrium rate of growth does not necessarily mean that this equilibrium situation is stable; the system, starting from any arbitrary age distribution, may move toward equilibrium or it may not. The conditions of equilibrium, however, are too complex for the present work.

nomics the analysis is of particular importance in the theory of capital, because capital goods of all kinds can be regarded as populations, provided that a survival function can be postulated. This means that it must be reasonable to suppose stable, or moderately stable, relationships between the *age* of goods and their rates of consumption or survival. In most cases this assumption is by no means unreasonable. Thus automobiles form a population, in which the age of each automobile can be determined with some accuracy and in which "life tables" or "survival tables" can be constructed showing what proportion of the automobiles "born" or produced in any one year will survive into other years, or will "die" (i.e., be scrapped) in other years.

Birth Functions of Capital

Populations of goods differ from biological populations mainly in the totally different nature of their birth functions. In biological populations, as we have seen, it is reasonable to suppose that the number of births in any year is a function of the numbers in the various age groups of the population. Automobiles do not beget automobiles, however, in the way that horses beget horses; the genetic processes of physical capital are complicated, and involve practically the whole economic system. Nevertheless simple birth functions can be postulated in the case of physical capital, yielding models of population movement which throw a great deal of light on the processes of the real world. Suppose, for instance, that "births" (production) of any good fulfill two functions: one to replace those items which have "died" (been consumed) during the period, and second to add to the total stock in response to an increased demand. The first may be called "replacement production," the second "expansion production." Total production in any year will be the sum of these two quantities, the second of which, of course, will be negative in the case of diminished demand. If the demand for the good is assumed constant, so that the total stock is maintained at a constant level, the number of births in any year will be equal to the number of deaths in that year; that is, production will equal consumption.

The "One-Hoss Shay" Cycle

Table 42 shows an interesting model of a population of "one-hoss shays"[3]—that is, goods all of which survive to a given length of life (five years in the table) and then disintegrate. In terms of the preceding analysis the survival function is given by $k_1 = k_2 = k_3 = k_4 =$

[3] Oliver Wendell Holmes, The Deacon's Masterpiece; or, The Wonderful One-Hoss Shay (*Collected Works*, Vol. XII).

$k_5 = 1$, $k_6 = 0$. We suppose that production is 100 units a year for the first six years. It is evident that by the fifth year an equilibrium population has been reached, and that if the total population is maintained at 500 units this equilibrium will continue indefinitely, with 100 units "dying" and 100 "born" every year. Now, however, we suppose an

Table 42. Population Analysis: One-Hoss-Shay Cycles

Year	0–1	1–2	2–3	Age (Years) 3–4	4–5	5–6	Total	Production
0								100
1	100						100	100
2	100	100					200	100
3	100	100	100				300	100
4	100	100	100	100			400	100
5	100	100	100	100	100		500	100
6	100	100	100	100	100	0	500	200
7	200	100	100	100	100	0	600	100
8	100	200	100	100	100	0	600	100
9	100	100	200	100	100	0	600	100
10	100	100	100	200	100	0	600	100
11	100	100	100	100	200	0	600	200
12	200	100	100	100	100	0	600	100
13	100	200	100	100	100	0	600	100

increase in demand for the item in the year 6, leading to an increase in the total population from 500 to 600. This can be achieved only by increasing production in that year from 100 to 200. This "cohort" of 200 gradually passes through the age distribution, being 0–1 years old in year 7, 1–2 years old in year 8, and so on until it finally "dies" in year 11. In each year from 7 to 10, 100 units "die" every year and, as the population is just maintained in numbers, 100 must be "born." In year 11, however, 200 die, so 200 must be produced. This clearly starts the process all over again, and the cycle will be repeated in-

definitely, 200 being produced every fifth year and 100 in the intervening years. Similar cycles will be set up wherever there is a distortion in the age distribution, whatever the cause.

Distortions Follow Too Rapid Increase

It should be observed that the distortion follows from the attempt
to increase the total stock too quickly. If instead of producing 200 in
year 6, 120 were produced in each year thenceforward, a new position
of equilibrium would be reached in year 11 which would be permanent, and there would be no cycle established. This is illustrated in
Table 43. The number in each age group is increased by an equal

TABLE 43. Population Analysis: One-Hoss Shays with Steady Growth

Year	\multicolumn{6}{c}{Age (Years)}						Total	Production
	0–1	1–2	2–3	3–4	4–5	5–6		
6	100	100	100	100	100	0	500	120
7	120	100	100	100	100	0	520	120
8	120	120	100	100	100	0	540	120
9	120	120	120	100	100	0	560	120
10	120	120	120	120	100	0	580	120
11	120	120	120	120	120	0	600	120
12	120	120	120	120	120	0	600	120

amount, and the relative age distribution (the proportion of the total
stock in each age group) is the same as before. Hence no cycle arises.

Damped Oscillations

These conclusions are substantially modified if we relax the assumption that the commodity is a "one-hoss shay," lasting for a certain
number of years and then immediately disappearing from the scene.
Just as in human life not everybody lives to the allotted span and some
exceed it, so in the case of a commodity some pass out of existence
after a short time, while some last longer. Automobiles, like humans,
have a "life table"; some crack up in the first year of their existence,
some are still on the road after twenty years. It is not difficult to show
that the result of this modification of the original assumption is to
give us not a perpetual cycle but a *damped* oscillation—i.e., a cycle in
which the amplitude continually diminishes as time goes on. If there
were no further initial distortions, then, the age distribution would
gradually work itself into an equilibrium again. Actually, of course,
there are likely to be continual new distortions, giving rise to new
cycles.

The Acceleration Principle

The effect of distortions in the age distribution of goods is accentuated by another principle which forms the basis of the "acceleration principle" noted earlier. If one commodity, B, is necessary for the production of another commodity, A, then the fluctuations in the output of A will be reflected by intensified fluctuations in the production of B. Let us refer again to the previous example. Let us suppose that to produce 10 units of this commodity we must have a machine, B. Then, from Table 42, when 100 units of A are being produced, a stock of 10 machines is necessary. When 200 are produced in year 6, however, 20 machines are necessary. If we suppose that the machine likewise has a life of 5 years, and that it had an equilibrium age distribution, it is easy to see in Table 44 that there will be a very large distortion in

Table 44. Population Analysis: The Accelerator

Year	0–1	1–2	Age (Years) 2–3	3–4	4–5	5–6	Total	(Idle)	Production
4	2	2	2	2	2	0	10	(0)	2
5	2	2	2	2	2	0	10	(0)	12
6	12	2	2	2	2	0	20	(0)	0
7	0	12	2	2	2	0	18	(8)	0
8	0	0	12	2	2	0	16	(6)	0
9	0	0	0	12	2	0	14	(4)	0
10	0	0	0	0	12	0	12	(2)	20
11	20	0	0	0	0	0	20	(0)	0
12	0	20	0	0	0	0	20	(10)	0

its age distribution and a consequent recurrent cycle of very large amplitude. In year 4 everything is in equilibrium. Then in year 5 the number of machines must be increased from 10 to 20, in anticipation of the increase in production of commodity A from 100 to 200 units in year 6. Production in that year must therefore be 12 machines— 2 for replacements and 10 to expand the number from 10 to 20. Then in year 6 the number of machines is 20, but there is no need for production at all, as in year 7 only 10 machines will be required to produce the 100 units of commodity A. Hence, there will be no production of machines in years 7 to 10. In year 7 there will be 18 machines, with 8 idle. In year 8 there will be 16 machines, 2 having disintegrated, with 6 idle, and so on to year 10, when 20 machines must be produced as the 12 that were produced in year 6 disappear, leaving none. In year 11 20 machines are required to produce the 200 units of commodity A. Here again a perpetual cycle is set up with 20 machines produced every five years, none at all produced in the intervening years, and an average of 4 machines idle. This is as extreme as a cycle can be. If now we assume that the production of commodity A is spaced out as in Table 43, so that no distortion in its age distribution results, there will still be a distortion in the age distribution of the machine, B, as shown in Table 45. Now a stock of 12 machines is

TABLE 45.   Population Analysis: The Second Accelerator

Year	Age (Years) 0–1	1–2	2–3	3–4	4–5	Total Stock	Production
4	2	2	2	2	2	10	2
5	2	2	2	2	2	10	4
6	4	2	2	2	2	12	2
7	2	4	2	2	2	12	2
8	2	2	4	2	2	12	2
9	2	2	2	4	2	12	2
10	2	2	2	2	4	12	4
11	4	2	2	2	2	12	2
12	2	4	2	2	2	12	2

required in each year to produce the 120 units of commodity A. In the year 5, therefore, the production of machines will increase from 2 to 4 units, and this will be repeated every five years. In this case the fluctuation is not so intense as in Table 44. Nevertheless, if we now suppose that a machine tool, C, is necessary to produce machine B, the fluctuations in the output of the machine tool will be much greater than the fluctuations in output of the machine. Again, it must be remembered that the severity of the fluctuations in the above examples are due to taking the very extreme case of a "one-hoss shay" life table. In fact the smoother life tables òf reality operate to dampen and smooth out these oscillations. Nevertheless, it remains true even in the general case that fluctuations in the output of machine tools are greater than fluctuations in the output of machines, and fluctuations in the output of machines are greater than the fluctuations in the output of the commodities which they make. This principle is called the "acceleration principle" because the demand for machines depends not so much on the demand for their product as upon the *rate of change* in the demand for the product. It is clear that the problem of adjusting the rates of growth of the stock of various kinds of goods so that distortions in the age distributions are avoided is practically insoluble. In this sense, therefore, some fluctuation in economic activity is a necessary cost of economic progress, a cost which will be greater the more rapidly we attempt to advance.

The "Austrian" Theory of Capital

The analysis of capital as a population of goods is of importance in interpreting the "Austrian" theory of capital, associated mainly with the name of Böhm-Bawerk.[4] According to this view, capital is created when "original factors of production" (labor and land) are embodied in goods, and is destroyed when the services of these embodied factors is finally realized. Capital therefore is regarded as a "population of value," into which values are "born" when factors of production are employed and "die" when services are yielded up. The "average period of production" then is the average "age at death" of values— i.e., the average interval of time which elapses between the employment of a factor of production and its final consummation as utility. Thus the bread that I eat today represents services of delivery men this morning, bakers yesterday, millers last month, farmers last year, and so on. The average age of the services embodied in the bread is its average period of production.

In a population in stationary equilibrium the average age at death is equal to the ratio of the total population to the annual number of births or deaths. Thus if 100 units are born into and die out of a population each year, and the average age at death is 30 years, the total population will be 3000.[5] In the stationary state, therefore, the ratio of total capital (the total population of value) to the annual in-

---

[4] E. von Böhm-Bawerk, *The Positive Theory of Capital,* trans. by William Smart, London, 1891.

[5] Suppose an equilibrium population with age groups a_1, a_2, $\cdots a_n$. Suppose that B is the annual number of births or deaths, and all deaths occur at the end of the year. Then $a_1 - a_2$ dies at age 1, $a_2 - a_3$ at age 2, $a_{n-1} - a_n$ at age n. The average age at death then is

$$T = \frac{(a_1 - a_2) + 2(a_2 - a_3) + 3(a_3 - a_4) \cdots + n(a_n)}{B}$$

$$= \frac{a_1 + a_2 \cdots + a_n}{B} = \frac{P}{B}$$

In dynamic equilibrium with a constant rate of growth, g, if a_1, a_2, $\cdots a_n$ are initial age groups the survival distribution for the group a_1 is a_1, ga_2, g^2a_3, $\cdots g^{n-1}a_n$. The average age at death then is

$$T = \frac{(a_1 - ga_2) + 2(ga_2 - g^2a_3) + 3(g^2a_3 - g^4a_4) \cdots + ng^{n-1}a_n}{B}$$

$$= \frac{a_1 + ga_2 + g^2a_3 \cdots + g^{n-1}a_n}{B}$$

In this case $T \gtreqless \frac{P}{B}$ according as $g \gtreqless 1$, though both T and $\frac{P}{B}$ are constants.

come (income of factors [births] or consumption of product [deaths], these being equal) is equal to the average period of production (the average length of life of embodied values). If the average period of production lengthens, this must mean either an increase in the total capital, if income is constant, or a decrease in income, if capital is constant. Attempts have been made (e.g., by Hayek)[6] to interpret depressions in terms of a decline in income necessitated by an overexpansion of the period of production with an inadequate capital stock. The possibility of difficulties of this kind cannot be altogether ruled out. However, ordinary business-cycle depressions seem to be of a totally different nature. The basic difficulty with period of production analysis is that it is strictly valid only in a stationary state, and is too crude an analytical device to deal with the complex motions of dynamic systems.

QUESTIONS AND EXERCISES

1. "The ability to predict future events in any science depends on its ability to discover stable difference equations relating the variables of its universe." Why, exactly? Does this proposition throw any light on the relative success of astronomy, meteorology, and the social sciences in their attempts at prediction?

2. It is argued that without an analysis of the dynamic properties of an equilibrium system it is impossible to judge the *stability* of the equilibrium. Why?

3. It has been suggested that economics should confine its analysis of change to "comparative statics"—that is, the comparison of two equilibrium positions in a model, on the grounds that the actual dynamic processes of the economy involve variables which belong more to the sociologist or the psychologist, such as the speed of rumor, or the velocity of responses to stimuli. Is this a possible explanation of the alleged unsatisfactory nature of dynamic economic models? Is the general suggestion valid?

4. In some older analyses of business cycles much attention is paid to various "leads" and "lags" in the time series of the economy—e.g., a lag of wages behind prices. How would such leads or lags be expressed in terms of difference equations? Experiment with the construction of systems of such difference equations and explore their properties.

5. Expectations play an important role in some types of dynamic analysis. Why? What sort of links might be postulated between present expectations and past experience? Could these links be described in terms of difference equations? If a link can be established between present expectations and present behavior, can we then link present behavior di-

---

[6] F. A. Hayek, Prices and Production, London, 1931.

rectly with past experience without any specific postulation of expectations? Does this mean that dynamic systems are possible without introducing expectations?

6. Consider the following dynamic model:

$$C_t = 600 + 0.7Y_{t-1}$$
$$I_t = 100 + 0.1Y_{t-1}$$
$$C_t + I_t = Y_t$$

$C_t = $ consumption, $I_t = $ investment, $Y_t = $ income in year t.

What is the equilibrium value of C, I, and Y?

Starting with $Y_0 = 3000$, trace the course of the various variables for a period of ten years. Repeat, starting with $Y_0 = 4000$. Use both the arithmetic and the graphic method.

7. Consider the following dynamic model:

$$C_t = 600 + 0.7Y_{t-1} + 0.1K_{t-1}$$
$$I_t = 100 + 0.1Y_{t-1} - 0.1K_{t-1}$$
$$C_t + I_t = Y_t$$
$$K_t = K_{t-1} + I_{t-1}$$

K_t is the total capital stock of the society in year t. The other symbols have the same meaning as in Exercise 6.

Comment on the economic significance of these equations.

What is the equilibrium value of the variables of this system?

Starting with $K_0 = 4000$ and $Y_0 = 3000$, trace out the course of the various variables for a few years.

Can you devise a graphic solution to this system?

Repeat the exercise, substituting

$$C_t = 600 + 0.7Y_{t-1} + 0.2K_{t-1}$$

for the first equation.

What light does this model throw on the "stagnation thesis"?

8. Consider the explosive model of Table 37E, page 425, $Y_t = 1000 + 0.8Y_{t-1} + 2(Y_{t-1} - Y_{t-2})$. Suppose now that the economy reaches capacity output at a level of 7000 so that it is impossible to raise output above that level. Suppose also that there is a "floor" of -1000 below which investment cannot fall, for physical reasons. Trace the course of national income under these restrictions for twenty years. Note that the "booms" are short and the "depressions" long. What feature of the model produces this result? How realistic is such a model?

9. Repeat Exercise 8, with the *additional* assumption that consumption also has a "floor" of 3000 below which it cannot fall.

10. A population of four age groups has a survival function $k_1 = 1$, $k_2 = 0.9$, $k_3 = 0.5$, $k_4 = 0.1$, and a birth function $b_1 = 0$, $b_2 = 2$, $b_3 = b_4 = 0$.

a. Start with an age grouping $a_1 = 180$, $a_2 = 121$, $a_3 = 50$, $a_4 = 7$ in year 0, and trace the course of the population for ten years. At what rate is the population growing?

b. Repeat, with an initial age grouping of $a_1 = 100$, $a_2 = 10$, $a_3 = 10$, $a_4 = 10$. Note that the population exhibits a two-"year" cycle. Why? Is this a realistic model for human or animal populations?

11. A population of four age groups has a survival function $k_1 = 1$, $k_2 = 0.9$, $k_3 = 0.8$, $k_4 = 0.7$. The birth function is $B_t = D_t$, where D_t is the number of deaths in year t.

a. Start with an age grouping $a_1 = 100$, $a_2 = 90$, $a_3 = 80$, $a_4 = 70$, the total population being 340. Trace the course of the population for a few years and show that the population is in equilibrium. (Note: You will find it useful to insert a line for "deaths" between the age grouping of each year.)

b. Suppose now that the total population is suddenly increased to 440 by an additional 100 births. Trace the course of the population for about 20 years, and show that it exhibits a damped oscillation. Why?

c. Repeat the above exercise with a survival function of $k_1 = 1$, $k_2 = 0.5$, $k_3 = 0.2$, $k_4 = 0.1$, and an initial age grouping $a_1 = 100$, $a_2 = 50$, $a_3 = 20$, $a_4 = 10$. Note that the "damping" of the oscillation is much more pronounced. What feature of the model leads to this effect?

CHAPTER 21

ECONOMIC FLUCTUATIONS AND GROWTH

One of the most striking phenomena of the western world is the alternation of periods of prosperity and depression which goes by the name of the business cycle. This is perhaps the most complex problem of modern economic society, and we cannot hope to explore all its ramifications in a single chapter. With the analytical tools now at our disposal, however, it is possible to outline the principal forces at work and to suggest certain remedies.

Is There a Cycle?

It must be emphasized at the outset that the business cycle is an extremely complex phenomenon. Indeed, it has been questioned whether there is any such thing as "a" cycle—whether the so-called business cycle is not merely the result of a combination of accidental irregularities with certain special cycles in particular industries. It is an instructive exercise to construct a completely random time series —e.g., by throwing dice or pennies, picking numbers out of a hat, or counting the frequency of occurrence of a letter in a book. The eye that is accustomed to tracing cycles in the time series of economic life will almost immediately begin to detect evidence of cyclical movements in any purely random series. If we are to prove that there is a business cycle, therefore, we must do something more than show that there are fluctuations in economic quantities such as prices or employment. These fluctuations must be shown also to have some degree of regularity, and also to have a fairly regular period of recurrence. Perhaps the best evidence of the existence of nonrandom fluctuations in economic life, however, is to be found in the connections that are to be observed between the movements of different economic series. Thus it is observable in the record that low prices generally go hand in hand with depression and unemployment; that a fall in prices is usually followed by a fall in wages after a certain interval, and so on.

443

These indications support the belief that economic fluctuations are not random, but follow a more or less regular pattern.

"True" and "False" Cycles

It is still somewhat open to question, however, whether this regular pattern can strictly be defined as a *cycle*. A true cyclical movement is a swing about a position of equilibrium, in which there are forces operating to bring the fluctuating quantity back to the equilibrium once it diverges from it, and in which the momentum of a movement towards the equilibrium point carries the quantity beyond it. The pendulum is the simplest example of such a cyclical movement: the further the bob swings from the equilibrium position, the stronger is the force operating to bring it back, but the very swing that brings it back gives it momentum that sends it swinging to the other side. In a frictionless world this could go on forever. There are undoubtedly some economic cycles (e.g., the hog cycle) of this nature. The business cycle cannot simply be interpreted, however, as the swing of a pendulum. There are some movements in economic life which tend to perpetuate themselves indefinitely unless checked by some outside force. The processes of monetary inflation and deflation are somewhat of this nature. Hence, there may be cyclical movements which are more like the oscillation of a billiard ball between two cushions than the swing of a pendulum—in which a certain movement might go on indefinitely until reversed by some outside influence.

Endogenous and Exogenous Changes

The question must be raised also to what extent the business cycle is the result of accidental historical disturbances, such as inventions, wars, explorations, and discoveries. These external disturbances produce great fluctuations in the economic system, and yet there may be nothing in their essential nature to make them regular. That is to say, the business cycle may be an illusion created by the fact that in the past two hundred years there have been great external disturbances which happen to have come along at moderately regular intervals. This view regards the business cycle largely as an accident of economic development, or rather as a result of the inevitable irregularity of economic development. There is much to be said for this view, especially as it does not necessarily exclude the possibility of genuinely cyclical changes superimposed on the unfolding process of economic history. Indeed, the problem of the business cycle cannot be separated from the theory of economic development—i.e., the study of the time relationships of economic quantities. Economic history, like all history, may be regarded as an amalgam of freedom and necessity. Certain causal factors can be traced through the whole stream of history—A causing B; B, C; C, D; and so on indefinitely. Into this causal nexus there continually strike new factors—original events which arise out of freedom, chance, call it what you will. So in economic development we distinguish between "endogenous" changes—changes which are generated within the economic system itself—and "exogenous" changes, which intrude into the economic system from "outside," such as political or technological events that do not seem to be closely related to economic processes. The question whether in the whole course of historical events there are any "exogenous" changes is a difficult philosophical question which fortunately we do not have to answer. The fact that we can divide events, however roughly, into "economic" and "noneconomic"[1] is sufficient justification for postulating the existence of exogenous changes as far as economic life is concerned.

A "Standard" Cycle

Whatever doubt there may be about the regularity or causation of the cycle, it is possible to describe five states or conditions of the economic system which, if put together in order, would constitute a "standard" cycle.

1. *Depression.* There is first a state of depression, characterized by low output and underemployment of both men and equipment. Prices and wages are likely to be low relative to a condition of boom; but perhaps even more important, the relative structure of prices is badly distorted. The price of finished products is likely to be low relative to the price of labor; the real wages of those employed may be high, for though money wages are low the price of things which workers buy—wage goods—are lower still. The distribution of the national income is sharply distorted. Profits are low or even negative. Interest, because it tends to be fairly constant in dollar terms in short periods, becomes a much larger proportion of national income. The propor-

---

[1] The distinction between what is and what is not "economic" is by no means easy to draw. In so far as all decisions are matters of choice they may be said to be governed by economic principles. Nevertheless, there is an important, if unclear, distinction between those choices which are made consciously and voluntarily, with weighing up of advantages and disadvantages, and those which are made involuntarily, without conscious weighing of alternatives, or which are motivated by the unregulated passions. Thus, the decision of an American middle-class family to have a child is "economic" in the sense that the decision of an Indian peasant is not. Similarly, many political decisions, wars, etc., are made without any clear weighing of alternatives, but with the passions of love and fear, envy and greed, as the main motivating factors.

tion of national income going to wages and salaries is likewise high, in spite of the widespread unemployment. Because of the fall in the absolute real total of the national income, however, the total of real wages and salaries is likely to be less than in the previous period of prosperity. The high real wages of those who are employed are more than counterbalanced by the poverty of the mass of unemployed, and even in the case of the employed the fear of unemployment takes the edge off their greater purchasing power.

The price of raw materials and agricultural commodities is also likely to be low relative to the price of industrial goods. The "terms of trade" between manufacturing and agriculture have moved in favor of manufacturing, but the advantage which this would otherwise give to the manufacturing population is eaten away by the fact that manufacturing output and employment are so low. Agricultural output, however, will be maintained at a fairly high level. Money incomes will be low generally, but the reason for these low money incomes is different in different sectors of the economy; in agriculture, employment and output will not have fallen, and may even have risen above the boom level. The low incomes of the agricultural population are due to the low prices of agricultural commodities. In industry, prices do not fall so much, and the low incomes are due to low output and unemployment. The industries particularly affected by unemployment are the "construction" industries—building, steel, automobile, and so on. Those least affected are the consumption goods industries—food, clothing, and the like. There is very little construction, either of building or machines.

2. *Recovery.* A depression is generally followed by a period of recovery. Employment and output rise, unemployment falls. With the rise in output there is of course a rise in real income. In the early stages of recovery prices are usually fairly stable, so that there is a rise in money income proportionate to the rise in real income. As a proportion of national income, profits rise, interest and wages fall, though the total wage bill in real terms may well increase because the rise in total income outweighs the fall in labor's proportionate share. Investment rises, perhaps in part spontaneously, in part under the influence of rising profits. Bank loans and deposits rise, though rates of interest may remain low or even continue to fall. The *proportion* of national income going to consumption falls due to the rise in investment, but the absolute amount of real consumption probably rises, again due to the rise in real national income. The velocity of circulation of money probably increases, leading to a larger volume of pay-

ments to finance the increased money incomes. The durable-goods industries revive—construction, machinery, machine tools, automobile, durable household goods. The "acceleration principle" noted earlier (page 420) may come into play, leading to still greater growth in investment and in income. Stocks of farm products, raw materials, and inventories of goods of all kinds may diminish; there may be a certain flow of money from household into business balances. Farm prices, and therefore farm incomes, rise with the recovery of industrial employment and output. The whole process may be cumulative. On the monetary side increased expenditures lead to increased receipts, which in turn may lead to increased expenditures, and so on. On the "real" side increased employment leads to increased incomes and increased consumption, which induces further investment and so leads to still larger income. This process may, however, stop short of full employment, or it may go on until full or "optimum" levels of employment and output are reached.

Recovery periods differ considerably in the forces which initiate or sustain them. The impetus may come from innovations, from the exploitation of new fields for investment in new lands, new products, or new methods. The impetus may come merely from the need to replace capital which has been consumed or depreciated during the depression. Or the impetus may come from government expenditure, for instance, on armaments or war. Whatever the impetus, however, the general dynamics of a recovery is likely to follow the lines indicated above.

3. *Full Employment.* The state of full employment, or prosperity, is presumably the most desirable state and an important goal of economic policy. There are no resources that are *involuntarily* unemployed, the owners of which would like to employ them at prevailing prices but can find no employers. In the field of labor this means that at prevailing wages anyone who wants to work could find a job after a reasonable interval of time. Even in a state of full employment there will be, of course, a certain amount of unemployment caused by labor turnover—i.e., by the fact that it takes a certain amount of time to pass from one job to another; but this is "voluntary" in the sense that people are willing to take this risk if they quit the job they are now performing. Output will be at the highest level that could be permanently maintained. A higher level of output than this is possible temporarily, but only at the cost of hidden capital consumption or an overworked labor force. Money income will be approximately stable, or may be rising slowly in proportion to the rise in real income

brought about by economic progress. Prices will also be approximately stable. Costs and receipts, and therefore profits, are at the level that will just call forth an amount of enterprise sufficient to employ the voluntarily employable population. The structure of relative prices will be approximately "normal"—e.g., the relation of agricultural to industrial prices will be such that resources are being driven from agriculture at a rate commensurate with the requirements imposed by the existing rate of technical progress.

4. *Boom.* This halcyon state is not necessarily reached in all its phases during a recovery, and even if reached, is not likely to be stable. Recovery frequently leads not to a stable state of full employment, but to a boom. The rise in expenditures leads to a rise in prices, once full employment approaches in various industries and supply curves become inelastic and begin to shift. This rise in prices, if it leads to expectations of a further rise, may lead, as we have seen, to a flight from money into any and every kind of real capital. Buildings go up everywhere; new factories, new offices, appear; many new businesses are started. Full employment may pass over into "hyperemployment" —i.e., a shortage of labor, where instead of more workers than there are jobs, there are more jobs than there are workers to fill them. Money wages rise but prices rise faster, and real wages fall. Profits are abnormally high, and hence seem to justify the mass of new investment. There is a boom on the stock market; everybody is anxious to get rid of money and hold stocks, so the price of stocks rises rapidly. Banks make loans to almost anyone who wants them, and people spend the money so obtained in buying commodities, securities, or labor.

5. *Recession.* The boom, however, is unstable, and tends to pass into a recession. It becomes apparent after a while that some of the enterprises which have been started in the rosy anticipations of the boom are not going to be profitable. Or it becomes evident that the opportunities for investment are dwindling. When three skyscrapers have been built in the old home town it becomes evident that a fourth would not only be highly unprofitable but would ruin the other three. Indeed, it may be even that the third, which is almost complete, is already seen to be one too many. Consequently, building slows down, unemployment appears in the construction industries, expenditure declines, and incomes decline with it. This means that other enterprises cease to be profitable. Prices begin to fall, and consumers' purchases—and therefore the revenues of businesses—decline. Real wages frequently stay up at first, as profits decline sharply. Many businesses shut down or contract their operations, and unemployment becomes

general, leading to further decline in incomes, further retrenchment of expenditures, and more unemployment. Meanwhile, in the stock market the boom will have come to an end; the price of stocks will begin to fall, creating a flight *into* money, a strong desire to sell stocks, and a catastrophic fall in stock prices. Banks get scared, and try to improve their liquidity position by calling in loans and selling investments. This, however, reduces the volume of deposits, and leads to a further fall in prices; the fall in the prices of assets may soon wipe out the whole of a bank's net worth and cause a wave of bank failures. This leads to further restriction of expenditure, more unemployment, an almost complete cessation of investment, and we are back again in a depression, whence, like a continuous performance at the movies, the show goes on again; only, unlike the movies, we have to sit through it.

Irregularity of Phases

While there is an observed tendency for economic fluctuations to pass successively through the phases outlined above, the movement may be highly irregular and one phase does not necessarily lead immediately into the next, nor is the length of each phase at all definite. Thus a state of fairly stable depression may lead into recovery, or it may decline into a further recession, as in Britain in 1929. Similarly, a recovery may level off, or even turn into a recession, far short of full employment, and even further short of a boom, as in the United States in 1937. Depression may be fairly stable, and recovery slow, as in the thirties, or depression may be unstable and recovery rapid, as in 1921. Prosperity may be fairly stable, as from 1924 to 1929; or it may be highly unstable, as in 1919. Nevertheless, even though the periods and the order of the various elements of fluctuation are highly variable, they represent clearly recognizable conditions of the economic system.

THE ANALYSIS OF BUSINESS CYCLES

It is hardly an exaggeration to say that the main function of macroeconomic analysis, if not of economic analysis in general, is the analysis of the business cycle—this phenomenon being so important and so all-pervading in a market economy as to constitute the principal body of material which has to be analyzed. It would be impossible, therefore, in a single chapter, to give more than a very partial account of the methods of analysis of business cycles, especially as much of the ground has already been covered in previous chapters. What we can do here perhaps is to draw together some of the methods and the problems which arise out of them in a broad conspectus which will show us the wood rather than the trees.

Dangers in "Eliminating the Trend"

We should first perhaps warn the reader against too great reliance on any single analytical method, for every method inevitably involves half-hidden assumptions which may distort the picture of reality in the mind of the investigator. Consider first some of the problems which arise in the mere description of business cycles. It is not within the scope of this work to describe the various statistical methods employed. Nevertheless, we should be on our guard to see that statistical methods do not imply, and indeed create, a picture of reality which may be misleading. A frequent prerequisite for the statistical analysis of cycles, for instance, is the elimination of the trend. The method of elimination is not important; what we must realize, however, is that in eliminating the trend we are assuming that there is one—that is, we interpret the cycle itself in terms of *fluctuations about* or deviations from some "norm" which may be a pure figment of the statistical imagination.

The Trend Values May Not Be "Normal"

There are two reasons for supposing that statistical trend lines may be quite misleading. In the first place the significant *deviation* of the observed variable may not be from any median values, but from some extreme values. Suppose, for instance, that in Fig. 65A, we measure time along OT and some economic variable—say employment—along OA. The irregular line shows the course of the variable through time. Suppose now the dotted line represents what would be "full employment" at each time, as measured, say, by the total labor force. Unemployment is then seen to be always a deviation *below* the norm. Suppose, however, that the statistician persuades us to draw a statistical trend line through the data, as in Fig. 65B. The deviations then appear partly above and partly below the statistical "trend." In this case however the statistical trend may be economically meaningless, because there is an economically significant deviation which is not described by the statistical deviations. The picture of the cycle which is given in Fig. 65B as a series of fluctuations alternating between "too much" or "too little" employment may be quite misleading, if in fact all deviations, or what is even worse, *most* deviations are really below the norm. It thus makes a great deal of difference to our picture of the

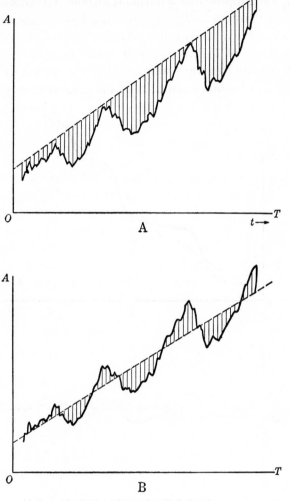

FIG. 65.   Trends and Cycles.

problem itself whether we regard the "trend" as a clothesline from which all the deviations hand downward, as in Fig. 65A, or whether we regard it as a skewer with the actual values lying about as much above as below the line, as in Fig. 65B.

Trends and Growth Curves

A second objection to the elimination of the trend may be almost more fundamental, and is illustrated in Fig. 66. In Fig. 66A we have drawn a time series which consists of three successive "growth curves," P_0P_1, P_1P_2, and P_2P_3. The assumption here is that the variable measured along OA (suppose this is national income) receives some kind of an impetus for growth at P_0—let us say, a new invention. A growth impetus is almost invariably followed by an "ogive" growth curve with the general shape of P_0P_1. Growth is apt to be slow at first, for the impetus takes time to gather weight. After the period of incubation, however, growth becomes rapid, reaching a maximum rate at about

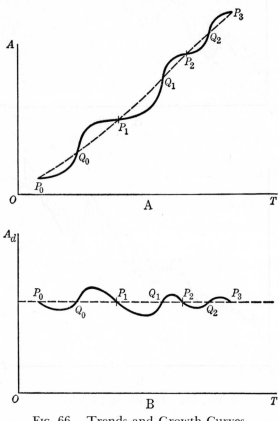

FIG. 66.   Trends and Growth Curves.

Q_0, after which the rate declines as the original impetus works itself out and becomes exhausted. We then suppose a new impetus at P_1, followed by a new growth curve $P_1Q_1P_2$, and a third impetus at P_2 followed by a new curve, $P_2Q_2P_3$. Now suppose that the statisticians persuade us to "analyze the cycle" by drawing a trend line (dotted in the figure) and "eliminating the trend" as in Fig. 66B, where we plot the deviations from the trend line. Then to make matters worse we forget all about the original data and concentrate all our efforts on the analysis of the data as presented in Fig. 66B. It is evident that we have

completely changed our picture of the problem—perhaps unknow-
ingly—by our statistical techniques. Growth and the growth curves
have disappeared; we are analyzing something that looks like a cycle,
and may in fact be nothing of the sort. In this case the growth curve
itself is the significant "trend"; and while it might be important to
discuss deviations from the growth curve, the deviations of the growth
curve itself from an arbitrary statistical trend line may be meaningless, or even positively misleading. Thus the point Q_0 in the growth
curve actually represents the peak of the "growth process," beyond
which the forces making for exhaustion of the growth impulse become
increasingly dominant. In Fig. 66B, however, the point Q_0 apparently
represents the beginning of the "boom." Similarly, the point P_1 in
the growth curve represents the start of a new impulse—this is the
real point of "recovery" from the doldrums of stagnation. In Fig. 66B,
however, the same point P_1 indicates the start of a "depression." These
examples indicate, perhaps, how important it is to make statistics our
servant and not our master!

Dangers in Cyclical Models

Turning now to the dangers which beset the economic analyst as
well as the statistical analyst in this field, we may raise the warning
here also that it is possible to get absorbed in models of cycles to the
exclusion of models of growth. It is easy, as we have seen in the previous chapter, to set up dynamic models of economic systems which
contain cycles. We have seen how difference equation systems even of
the first order can produce cycles which may be either explosive, stable, or damped. The "cobweb theorem" (pages 164, 427) is an important example. The more complex our models, the more variables
we have and the greater the degree of our difference equations, the
more difficult it becomes *not* to get cycles out of the models we construct. We have seen some examples in the previous chapter: the ac-
celeration-multiplier model, for instance (pages 421–426), and the
population process models (pages 428–440). The very multiplicity of
these models, however, means that they must be used with great care,
especially in view of the rather arbitrary assumptions which underly
them all. The multiplier-accelerator model for instance assumes stability in both the consumption function and the accelerator coefficient
—conditions which are certainly not likely to be true of any actual
situation for very long. Population analyses depend on the assumption
of stable survival and birth functions, which again represents a condition which may only obtain for short periods. The rout of the popula-

tion forecasters in the late 1940's and 1950's, when the actual human population growth was almost universally far in excess of what was predicted by all the experts, and of the economic forecasters who predicted large-scale depression following the end of World War II, are examples of the dangers of model building based on insecure assumption in regard to the stability of the various functions and coefficients involved.

The "Sensitivity" (Shiftability) of Models

Nevertheless some important things can be learned from the economic models. All the macroeconomic models are characterized by fairly high degrees of what may be called "sensitivity." The sensitivity of a model I define as the change in the *equilibrium* position of the model which results from a small unit change in one or another of the basic parameters of its behavior equations. Thus the multiplier is a measure of the sensitivity of the "basic model" in respect of changes in any parameter which expresses the "height" of the total absorption function, and, as we have seen on page 299, the closer the marginal propensity to absorb draws toward 1, the larger will be the multiplier. In a system with a large multiplier, then, very slight changes in the underlying behavior functions—for example, in the height of the consumption function or the investment function—will produce large changes in the equilibrium output. This is what we mean when we say that the system is "sensitive." Generally speaking, the sensitivity of a system depends on the difference between the "slopes" of the basic equations. This is seen clearly in Fig. 52, page 297, where we see that as the slope of the total absorption function approximates that of the basic identity (unity), the multiplier gets larger and the system grows more sensitive. In general, systems where the equations of equilibrium can be reduced to two equations whose slopes are nearly equal will be sensitive; if the slopes diverge, and still more if one is positive and the other negative, the system will be insensitive.

One of the important discoveries of macroeconomics is that while price equilibria tend to be insensitive, except in the case of industries of decreasing supply price (see pages 223–225), because the slopes of the demand and supply curves are opposite in sign, income equilibria are highly sensitive for the reasons outlined above. The more sensitive a system is, however, the more likely is it to be subject to large fluctuations in its equilibrium position because of quite small fluctuations in the basic parameters which determine it. Even small and irregular random fluctuations in the basic parameters will lead to an apparently cyclical fluctuation of much greater magnitude in the observed variables because of the time lags involved in moving from one position of equilibrium to another.

A Cycle in the "Basic Model"

This proposition is illustrated for the "basic model" in Fig. 67. Let us suppose a stable consumption function, $C'C$, all the fluctuations being the result of shifts in the level of investment between the two

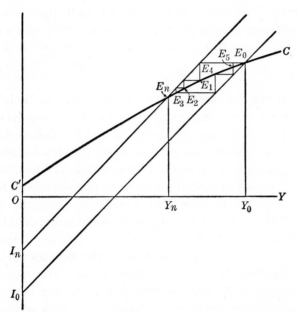

FIG. 67.   A Cycle in the Basic Model.

extremes OI_0 and OI_n. The equilibrium position will shift between E_0 and E_n, depending on the level of investment. Suppose then that the system is in actual equilibrium at E_0 and there is a sudden shift to the lower investment level. The system will move toward the lower equilibrium, quickly at first and then more slowly as time goes on, following a path such as $E_0E_1E_2$, etc. Before the system actually gets to E_n, suppose the investment level shifts to OI_0 again. The system moves toward the upper equilibrium, again quickly at first, then more slowly, following the course $E_3E_4E_5$, etc. Mere sensitivity will not, of course, lead to regular cycles unless there are regular cycles in the basic parameters. The observed business cycle, however, is not particularly regular, and there is not much in the observed data that could not be interpreted in terms of random fluctuations in the basic parameters of a sensitive system.

Sources of Sensitivity: Elastic Money Supply

One of the tasks of economic analysis in this regard, then, is to look round the system for possible sources of sensitivity. The most obvious, and probably the most important, we have already discussed in the form of the multiplier. There are, however, many other sources which might be briefly mentioned. If the money supply is elastic with regard to the price level we may have a monetary equilibrium that is highly sensitive, as we see in Fig. 54, page 319. If the increase in the money stock which follows a unit change in the price level is approximately equal to the ratio $\frac{M}{P}$ (or $\frac{T}{V}$), assuming this to be stable, slight changes in the underlying parameters—for instance, in the "height" of the money supply curve, or in the velocity of circulation—will cause large changes in the equilibrium values of M and P. This is the basic assumption of the Wicksellian system,[1] in which slight changes in the parameters due, say, to interest rate changes, produce indefinitely large shifts in the equilibrium position, so that we always have either a perpetual inflation or a perpetual deflation until the parameters change. This model is helpful also in explaining hyperinflation—the condition of runaway price level which occasionally follows war or revolution, and is mainly an outcome of the breakdown of the tax system. We will return to this question in the next chapter.

Profits-Investment Ratio. Another possible source of sensitivity in the system is the reciprocal relationship which may obtain between profits and investment. If we are going to make a model with an investment function, it would seem reasonable to suppose a behavior relationship between investment and profits. Investment is undertaken mainly in the expectation of profits, and if the expectation of profits is high when profits of the past year have been high, a positive relation may be postulated between profits of one year and investment of the next. There is, however, also another possible relationship between investment and profits: it is not only true that profits create investment; it is also true that, in part at any rate, investment creates profits.[2] At the moment we may observe only that investment means an increase in the net worth of businesses, which is precisely what we mean by profit. If now we also suppose this relationship is stable, we

---

[1] See pages 320, 380–381.
[2] See K. E. Boulding, *A Reconstruction of Economics*, New York, 1950, Chapter 14.

have a model for the determination of both profits and investment, illustrated in Fig. 68. In this figure HEH' represents the "profits-investment" relationship. That is, it shows what amount of investment will be planned for at each level of profit. It is assumed that there must be some profits before any investment is undertaken, and that from the point of zero investment, H, higher profits bring higher investment, but at a diminishing rate. Similarly, the curve KEK' is the investment-profits curve, showing what level of profits is created by each level of investment. The point of equilibrium is where these

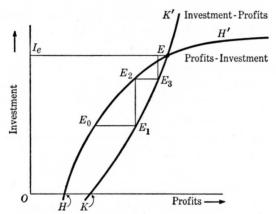

FIG. 68. Dynamics of Profits and Investment.

curves intersect at E. This equilibrium is stable, as will be seen by the dynamic process; if we start from a position E_0, the amount of investment corresponding to E_0 creates profits corresponding to E_1, which induces investment corresponding to E_2, which creates profits corresponding to E_3, and so we move toward the equilibrium point. If the curves intersected in the reverse direction, the equilibrium would, of course, be unstable. Even if there is a position of stable equilibrium, however, the fact that the curves slope the same way means that the system is highly sensitive to change in one or in both of the basic behavior equations. If the profits-investment curve "falls"—i.e., if businessmen become more pessimistic, or less willing to invest at each level of profit—the equilibrium will move down the curve EK, both profits and investment being less than before. If the slopes of the curves are nearly equal a small, "worsening" of the basic behavior equations may mean a large decline in both investment and profits. If now we link this figure with Fig. 67, we see that the decline in investment is multiplied (by the multiplier!) in its effect on equilibrium output or income, so in combination we have a system quite frightening in its possible sensitivity, where a very slight change in the profits-investment function may make all the difference between full employment and severe depression.

The "Boomerang"

Sensitivity, of course, merely explains why little fluctuations in one thing can give rise to big fluctuations in something else. It does not in itself go very far toward explaining the initial fluctuations. We must, therefore, look for another property of economic systems to explain the more or less regular changes in direction of movement which occur in them. This property we might call the "boomerang." This is the element in a system which tends to *reverse* any present direction of movement when that movement has gone far enough. Any system with a "boomerang" in it will have fluctuations. A movement in any direction will be eventually reversed, and will become a movement in the opposite direction, which in turn will be reversed into a movement in the first direction—this successive reversal of direction being what is meant by a fluctuation.

Continuous Boomerangs

There are at least two different kinds of "boomerangs," continuous and discontinuous. The continuous boomerang is the "true" cycle, such as the pendulum in physics or the accelerator-multiplier system in economics. It is characteristic of the dynamics of an *equilibrium* system in which the movement toward equilibrium produces acceleration which drives the system beyond equilibrium, but in which the further the system diverges from equilibrium, the stronger is the force operating in the direction of equilibrium. There are many examples of such systems in economics, and the key to their analysis is the search for "accelerators." The investment-accelerator has already been discussed. The "price-expectations" cycle is an example of the same phenomenon, the accelerator in that case being the movement of liquidity preference or in velocity of circulation in response to expectations projecting current movements of prices. The banking and financial system likewise provides many examples of accelerators. An inflationary movement of the economy is apt to be reinforced by the expansion of bank loans and of the deposits created thereby, and a deflationary movement is likewise likely to be reinforced by the contraction of bank loans and the resulting shrinkage in deposits. If the deflationary movement goes far enough to cause a wave of failures among banks, it is accelerated even further. Not the banking system alone, but the whole credit and financial system, is capable of acceleration effects. The expansion of consumers' credit, for instance, in an inflationary period helps to prolong and accentuate the movement, and its subsequent contraction likewise accelerates the downward movement.

Finance as an Accelerator

The financial system also operates as an accelerator in the investment cycle. When credit is easy, it is easy to "finance"—i.e., spread the ownership of new accumulations of real capital. Entrepreneurs borrow to build buildings, install machinery, or build up stocks of raw materials or half-finished goods. The "real ownership" of these things lies with the lenders and may be very widely distributed; hence it is relatively easy to absorb large stocks of new goods without deflationary pressure. The existence of easy credit, both from banks and from other sources, enables businessmen to create and to hold the title to goods of long life-period which they do not intend to own permanently. A builder, for instance, will build apartment houses with the aid of credit, in the expectation of selling the buildings to investors when they are completed. During the process of construction, the builder holds the title to the values being created, while the lender of credit may be the owner of the equity which the buildings represent. If the expectation is fulfilled and the builder sells the property, he can pay his debt and go on to build more buildings. But if he finds that there is no demand for his buildings on the part of investors, he will be forced either to own and operate the buildings himself, thus changing the character of his business, or, if he wishes to continue his building business, to obtain more capital. If he cannot do that, and if his creditors, who have usually lent on short terms, insist on being repaid, the title of the building may pass to the creditors. All these events are symptoms of crisis. Indeed, it is not too much to say that a boom is a period when bad investments are made, and a crisis is the period when they are found out. It has been argued with some force that the creation of credit makes it easier to make bad investments, for it prolongs the period during which a bad investment can proceed undiscovered. By enabling businessmen to produce in anticipation of demand it also enables them to make more mistakes.

The "Discontinuous Boomerang"

The crisislike character of many of the turning points in economic fluctuations suggests that the model of a "discontinuous boomerang" many also be relevant. This is the "floor and ceiling" phenomenon, where a movement is reversed not because it has passed its equilibrium position, but because it hits a boundary of some sort which cannot be exceeded. Thus we might have a system in which the position of equilibrium lay either at infinity or well outside the limits of the fluctuations, and in which movement proceeded indefinitely until it was stopped by some boundary from which it "rebounds"—the cessation of movement in one direction producing a reversal. Thus we might have systems of such great sensitivity that the equilibrium position always lies outside the possible boundaries of the variables, and movement therefore cannot be reversed by passing beyond the equilibrium position, but can only be reversed by a shock which shifts the equilibrium position of the system from very high to very low values, or the reverse. Thus we may have continuous movements of inflation or deflation which never reach an equilibrium, but which can be reversed by a shock, as in the Wicksellian system (see page 380).

"Floors" and "Ceilings"

An important model involving a system of this kind has been developed in recent years. Suppose, for instance, that, for reasons we shall examine in a moment, full employment can only be maintained if output and investment grow at a certain rate. If this rate is faster than the growth of capacity of the system, it can only be maintained if we start from a period of unemployment. Growth at the full-employment rate, however, cannot then be maintained for very long without the system hitting a "ceiling" when full employment is reached, and the rate of growth must then slacken. The slackening of the rate of growth, however, produces a situation in which there is not enough investment to maintain full employment, and a decline follows, which may be accelerated by the various "accelerators" mentioned above. Decline also cannot go on forever—it will eventually reach a "floor." The exact position of the "floor" is somewhat uncertain, but at least output cannot go below what is necessary to provide "subsistence" for the system! Once the decline has reached the floor, however, it ceases, the accelerators all cease to function and the possibility of growth at the full-employment rate again appears, and the rise starts over again.

The "Warranted" Rate of Growth

The basic question then is whether there is in fact some "warranted" rate of growth which is necessary to maintain full employment. The possibility arises because investment has a twofold function in the economic system. It determines the immediate level of output and income on the assumption of a stable consumption function. But it also contributes to the growth of *capacity,* and hence necessitates still more investment in the next period if full employment or capacity output is to be maintained. The point is illustrated in Fig. 69, which reproduces the principle of Fig. 67. We suppose that we begin with an

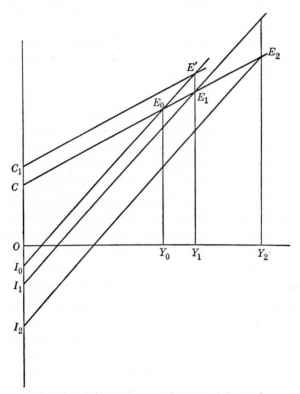

FIG. 69.   The Warranted Rate of Growth.

investment OI_0, and equilibrium output OY_0. Now suppose, however, that as a result of this investment the capacity of the system rises, the new capacity output being OY_1. In order to sustain this level of output, investment must be increased to OI_1. This amount of investment, however, increases capacity output still further, to OY_2, and in order to sustain this output investment must now be increased to OI_2. If full employment is to be sustained, then, it is clear that investment must increase from year to year and output likewise. It is impossible to maintain full employment at a stationary level as long as there is any investment at all. The increase in both investment and output which is necessary is geometric rather than arithmetic, so that the absolute increase in each one increases every year.[3]

Growth Cycles

In this system it is clear that there is only one pattern of growth, or growth curve, of both investment and income which will maintain full employment. Suppose now that this is *not* the growth curve which the economy as a whole can maintain by reason of its rise in population and improvement in techniques. Then clearly the system is in for trouble of some sort. If the full-employment rate of growth is greater than the maximum rate of economic development, the system will fall into cycles of rapid growth followed by depression. From a position of less than full employment, output and investment can grow at the full-employment rate, which is faster than the rate of growth of capacity of the system (the rate of economic development) because unemployed resources are being drawn into the system. Growth at this rate, however, will eventually bring the system to full employment, after which it cannot continue to grow at the full-employment rate, because the rate is now limited by the rate of growth of capacity. If this rate however is below the full-employment rate, full employment cannot be maintained, because investment will have to fall below what is necessary to yield full employment. Hence, instead of maintaining a steady rate of growth at the economic development rate, growth will fall below this rate as unemployment develops, and may even pass into a decline, with a large volume of unused resources. When the decline has proceeded far enough it becomes possible to grow at the full-employment rate once again, and a new revival commences.

This system is illustrated in Fig. 70. Time is measured on the horizontal and national income on the vertical axis. DD^1 we suppose is the "economic development curve" which shows the growth of *capacity* of the system. Suppose now we start a point P_0 and grow at the full-employment rate following the line P_0P_1. In order to maintain full employment at P_1 growth would have to continue along the line P_1P_2. This, however, is impossible because of the limits of the capacity of

---

[3] Suppose the consumption function is $C = C' + cY$, and suppose that a unit of investment leads to an increase in capacity of s. If Y_0, Y_1 are capacity outputs for years 0 and 1, we have $Y_1 - Y_0 = sI_0$. We also have the identity $I_0 \equiv Y_0 - C_0 = Y_0(1 - c) - C'$, whence $Y_1 - Y_0 = s[Y_0(1 - c) - C']$, or $Y_1 = Y_0[s(1 - c) + 1] - C's$. The solution of this difference equation is $Y_n = h^n Y_0 - \dfrac{(h^n - 1)}{h - 1} C's$, where $h = s(1 - c) + 1$. Similarly, it can be shown that $I_1 = hI_0$, whence $I_n = h^n I_0$. In this system, therefore, I must increase at a constant rate, and if $C' = 0$ (i.e., if consumption is proportionate to income), Y will also increase at a constant rate.

the system; from P_0 to P_1 the growth has been possible because of the absorption of unused resources; at P_1 full employment is reached and there are no unused resources. Further growth can only proceed along the line P_1D'. This rate of growth, however, does not demand enough investment to yield full employment; consequently it is not stable, unemployment will develop, and income will fall back along the line P_1P_3. At some point P_3 it will become possible to resume the rapid rate

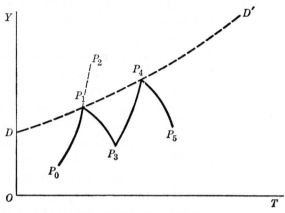

FIG. 70.   Growth Cycles.

of full-employment growth, and income will rise till it hits the economic development curve again at P_4, whence it rebounds to P_5, and so the cycle goes on.

Stagnation in Underdeveloped Societies

This in essence is the theory of economic instability put forward by Harrod, Hicks, and Domar.[4] It is an interesting and in many ways a useful model. It has interpretative value in explaining not only the tendency of a developed society to unemployment but also the tendency of an undeveloped society to stagnation and inflation. Thus suppose that the consumption function is so high that the full-employment rate of growth is *less* than the rate which would be possible through economic development. The society will reach full employment at a level of investment which is less than that which is technically possible. Any attempt to force the growth of the society beyond the full employment level will result in inflation, this being the response of the system to "overabsorption."

[4] R. F. Harrod, *Towards a Dynamic Economics* (London, 1948).
    J. R. Hicks, *The Trade Cycle* (New York, 1950).
    E. Domar, "Capital Expansion, Rate of Growth and Employment," *Econometrica*, April, 1946.

Weaknesses of the Model

The assumptions of this model however must be kept clearly in mind, as they may not be fulfilled in reality, and may lead to quite erroneous conclusions. The basic assumption of this model is that of so many Keynesian models—stability in the consumption function. We do not have to assume, as Harrod and Domar do, that the consumption function is a straight line through the origin (consumption proportional to income). This assumption simplifies the mathematics, but the conclusions are not destroyed if we assume a more general form for the consumption function, as we have done above. If, however, the consumption function is *not* stable, and especially if it exhibits an upward drift in the course of time, the conclusion of the model that investment must grow at a constant rate to maintain full employment is no longer valid. Suppose, for instance, in Fig. 69, that in year 1 the consumption function rises from CE_1 to C_1E'. The full-employment equilibrium will be at E', with a volume of investment still equal to that of the year before, OI_0. Depending on the rate of rise of the consumption function, then, full employment can be maintained at varying rates of growth of investment, even at zero or negative rates.

Upward Drift in the Consumption Function

The excessively gloomy predictions of the Harrod-Domar model therefore are not necessarily true, although any optimism depends on the empirical question whether in fact the consumption function has an upward drift. There is some evidence that it has, at least in the United States, and that the long period of prosperity following the end of World War II is in large measure to be explained by the upward movement of the consumption function. This movement in turn may be accounted for by a number of factors, and it is not easy to identify the contribution of each. Unquestionably the rise in liquid assets, not offset by a proportionate increase in prices, as a result of the cash deficits of war finance had some influence. Another important but much neglected factor is the age distribution of the population. Generally speaking both the young and the old are "low savers"—they generally consume more than they produce. By contrast those in the middle age groups who are in the labor force tend to be "high savers" —they produce more than they consume. A shift in the distribution of the population away from the middle groups toward both the young and the old, therefore, should have an effect in raising the level of the consumption function. This, however, is precisely what has been happening in the United States since 1930. The proportion of old people has been rising as a result of the increase in the expectation of life. The proportion of children has also been rising as a result of increased birth rates. Correspondingly the proportion of people of working age has fallen. In 1930 the proportion of the population in the middle years—say from 15 to 65—was abnormally high; falling birth rates had reduced the number of children, and the effect of the rising expectation of life had not yet worked itself out in rising numbers of old people. This fact alone is almost enough to account for the severity of the great depression.

The Proper Use of Models

The moral of these considerations is that economic models, especially when it comes to the interpretation of a phenomenon as complex as the dynamic fluctuations of the economy as a whole, are aids to thought and not substitutes. We must beware of too great reliance on the too simple model, for the assumptions of such models are always likely to be falsified. Nevertheless, without the aid of these models the complexity of the subject matter leads either to complete bewilderment or to a retreat into the rituals of pure empiricism, and the endless recording of data whose meaning always escapes us, or it leads to thinking with the aid of implicit models which we never openly recognize, and which therefore are all the more likely to lead us astray.

QUESTIONS AND EXERCISES

1. Some writers (e.g., W. S. Jevons) have tried to link business cycles with a 10–11 year cycle in sunspot activity. Later empirical work has largely discredited the theory. Nevertheless, assuming that the sunspot cycle creates a cycle in the yield of crops, how might this affect the economic system according to the various models outlined in this chapter?

2. Professor A. C. Pigou attributes industrial fluctuations to "waves of optimism and pessimism" among businessmen. Trace the possible effects of such waves on the various magnitudes of the economic system.

3. Much emphasis was formerly laid on the rate of interest as a governing factor in explaining cyclical fluctuations of output and income. What effect might a rise or fall in the rate of interest have on (a) accumulation, (b) consumption, (c) production, (d) the quantity of money, (e) velocities of circulation, (f) income?

4. "In order to explain the general business cycle it is not sufficient to explain how there can be cycles in particular industries; we must explain why these particular cycles do not offset each other." Discuss.

5. Suppose the age distribution of automobiles results in a sharp decline in demand for new automobiles in a certain year. What repercussions would this have on the rest of the system; how might the depression in the automobile industry become general; what would have to be done to prevent it from becoming general?

6. Under a gold-standard system a depression in one country spread very quickly to others. By what mechanism? How far do you think this might explain the breakdown of the gold standard? What might a country do to insulate itself from depressions originating abroad?

7. "Any increase in money incomes will raise the demand for labor. The way to cure unemployment, therefore, is to increase the quantity of money." What other things must be true before we can assent to this proposition?

8. The process of recovery from a depression is characterized by a shift to the right of all money demand curves, because of the increasing desire of people to spend. In the early stages of recovery this change in demand is reflected principally in a rise in employment and output. In the later stage (the boom) it is reflected in a rise in *prices*. Show by diagrams that these phenomena can be explained if we assume (a) that in the recovery period supply curves are very elastic and do not shift; (b) that in the boom period supply curves are inelastic, and tend to shift to the left because of increasing money costs.

   Are these assumptions reasonable?

9. A depression manifests itself in agriculture by low prices and stable or even high outputs, and in industry by low outputs and relatively stable prices. How would you explain this difference, and how might this phenomenon be related to various models of the business cycle?

10. Combine in a single diagram Figs. 67 and 68, measuring output to the right of the origin, consumption upward from the origin, investment downward from the origin, and profits to the left of the origin. Describe and investigate the properties of the system diagrammed.

11. In the *Survey of Current Business* (July, 1954, pp. 3–9), published by the United States Department of Commerce, you will find the "Revised Series for the National Income of the United States, 1929–1953." Graph the more important series, and interpret them in the light of the various macroeconomic models. Pay especial attention to (a) the great depression (1929–1937), (b) the 1937–1938 episode (c) the war economy (1939–1945), (d) the postwar economy (1945–1953). Calculate for each year the *proportions* of the various components of the GNP, expressed as a percentage of the total GNP, for the two major breakdowns—(a) sources, and (b) distributional shares. Graph the results.

CHAPTER 22

THE IMPACT OF GOVERNMENT

By far the greatest single economic organization is the national state and its subsidiary organs. This is true even in capitalist society, where, for instance, the government of the United States in 1953 absorbed around 23 per cent of the gross product. It is impossible therefore to regard the economic system as something apart from political organizations, though it is useful to regard the system as consisting of two "sectors," a private sector of nongovernmental organizations and a governmental sector.

The Framework of Legal Prohibitions

The impact of government upon the economy, and especially upon the private sector, is felt through two main channels. In the first place the government in its judicial and legislative aspect sets the legal framework within which private organisms operate. This it does mainly by means of prohibitions enforced by legal penalties—the commandments of government, like those of Moses, are mostly concerned with prescribing the things which we may not do. These prohibitions may affect economic life in very far-reaching ways. There may be, for instance, prohibitions of entire industries, as under the Eighteenth Amendment. The production of dangerous or adulterated commodities may be prohibited, as under the Food and Drug Act. Certain types of securities may be proscribed, as under the Securities and Exchange Act. Various forms of property are defined, and violations of ownership rights prohibited. Certain types of agreements between individuals may be prohibited, as agreements in restraint of trade under the Sherman Act, or yellow-dog contracts under the Wagner Act. Certain types of economic behavior or policy are prohibited, such as price discrimination under the Robinson-Patman Amendment to the Clayton Act, or payments to "stand-ins" for work not performed, under the Taft-Hartley Act.

There may also be restrictions on the prices at which transactions may legally be performed. It may be illegal to buy or sell labor below a minimum wage, and it may be illegal to buy or sell commodities above a maximum (ceiling) price. It may be illegal to hold certain types of assets (e.g., gold). All these legal restrictions set the framework within which private organizations operate. The framework is not absolutely rigid, as indicated by the existence of bootlegging under prohibition or of black markets under price control. Illegality is an *obstacle,* a "cost" of performing the illegal acts, and from the point of view of its effect on the total economic system operates very much like "natural" obstacles.

Transactions of Government

All the activities of government in the setting up and enforcement of prohibitions of one kind or another are negative in that they determine the course of economic activity only indirectly by setting up or removing certain obstacles. There is, however, another economic aspect of government which is "positive" in the sense that it consists of the direct economic relationships which government as an economic organism has with the other organisms of the system. In this sense government is to be regarded merely as a very large and peculiar kind of "firm" with its own system of relationships with the other organisms of society.

Exchanges and Transfers

The transactions of government with private firms or households can be divided into two important classes—*exchanges* and *transfers.* Government and the agents of government make exchanges just like any other economic organism. It purchases labor, and pays wages in return; it purchases goods of all kinds and pays money to the sellers. It also sells certain goods and services—e.g., postal services, war surplus goods—for which it receives payment in money from the buyers. In making exchanges government differs from private organisms only in its ability to neglect to some extent the effect of its exchanges on its asset structure. Governments have two powers which private organizations do not usually possess: the power to tax and the power to create money. Because of these powers the transactions of government include an important class of *transfers,* which differ from exchanges in being one-way transactions. An exchange is a two-way transaction; it involves the mutual transfer of assets between the exchangers. Thus, when a government purchases goods, money passes from the government to the private seller, and goods of equal book-value pass from the seller to the government. From the point of view of the seller the exchange is an asset transformation; he has replaced, say, $50,000 in goods on the assets side of his balance sheet by $50,000 in cash. A government transfer, on the other hand, involves simply the transfer of assets of some kind—usually cash—from the private organism to the government or from the government to the private organism. The commonest form of transfer is, of course, a tax, which is a one-way transfer of money from private individuals or organisms to the government, resulting in a net diminution of the assets of the taxpayer. There are also "negative taxes" in the form of subsidies, which consist simply in a payment of money from the government to a private person or organization, without any transfer in return, thus adding to the assets of the recipient.

Government and the Payments System

Let us consider first the impact of government on the payments of the private economy. The "balance of payments" of government is its "cash budget." If the cash budget is balanced, it means that government is taking in from all sources just as much money as it is paying out to all recipients, no matter whether the payments are transfers or exchanges. If there is a deficit in the cash budget, the government is paying out more money than it is taking in. The difference clearly must be equal to the increase in the cash holdings of private persons and organizations, which in turn is equal to the favorable balance of payments of the private sector of the economy. This conclusion applies strictly only in a closed society; in the case of a single nation it is still true that a deficit in the cash budget of government means an increase in holdings of that government's money, but part of this increase may be held by foreigners. Thus a deficit in the government's budget must result in a "surplus" in all other cash budgets taken together. Similarly, if the government has a surplus in its cash budget it is taking in more than it is giving out, and therefore the private sector will find its stocks of cash diminishing and will find itself with net budget deficits. These principles can be perceived quite clearly from the "payments tables" in Chapter 16. If one of the individuals —say, A—is supposed to be the government, it is clear that A's budget deficit (excess of expenditures over receipts) must be equal to the net sum of all the other budget surpluses (excesses of receipts over expenditures) from the principle that the sum of all receipts must be equal to the sum of all expenditures.

Government's Power to Create Money

Government differs from private institutions, from the point of view of the payments system, mainly because of its much greater capacity for the creation of money or, what is almost the same thing, of readily marketable securities. It should be observed that private organizations possess this power to a limited extent. Thus a firm that wishes to undertake an investment in the course of which it will be necessary for a time to have a deficit in its cash budget as it pays out more than it is receiving may finance this deficit by the creation and sale of its securities, either to the public or to a bank. Governments likewise may create and sell securities, either to private individuals and corporations or to a bank. The effects are very similar in both cases. Where securities are sold to private individuals or to nonbanking corporations, there is a corresponding transfer of money to the body which sells the security. Thus there is a new asset in circulation in the form of the security, but no new money has been created. When, however, a government or any organization sells its newly created securities to a bank, the bank purchases these securities with newly-created bank deposits. Unless its reserve position forces the bank to liquidate some other assets (which is unlikely nowadays), there is net creation of money in the form of bank deposits as well as creation of securities. This is the usual method of financing a governmental deficit in these days, rather than by the creation of government money; the government creates government bonds, which it sells to the banks for deposits to be paid out to private persons and firms. The effect, however, is much the same as if the government had created money directly, except that the banking system increases its holdings of government bonds and its total deposits. The difference between a government and a private corporation lies in the taxing power of government. As long as the people have faith in the government's taxing power, its capacity to issue and sell securities is almost unlimited, as its power to create legal tender is also unlimited. The power of private firms to issue securities depends on the belief of potential purchasers in the profitability of the enterprise. But whereas the profitability of private enterprises depends on their ability to wheedle money out of their customers by offering services, the profitability of government has behind it the big stick of the taxing power.

How Government Can Regulate the Payments Total

We can see now how the fiscal system of government could be used to regulate the total of private payments. If private individuals on balance are trying to accumulate money, the government can prevent the decline in payments which such an attempt involves by having an appropriate cash deficit and so increasing the quantity of money in the hands of the public. If private individuals are trying to "decumulate" money, government can prevent the rise in the payments total which would result by having a cash surplus and so absorbing money from the public. It should be perfectly possible, therefore, given adequate information and a flexible payments system, for government to stabilize the total payments within as narrow limits as it wishes. The simplest way to do this would be through the tax system; if tax levies were automatically reduced whenever the total of private payments fell, and automatically raised whenever the total of payments rose, a "governor" would be introduced into the payments system capable of stabilizing it within reasonably narrow limits.

Obstacles to Adjustable Taxes

It must be confessed that there are severe political and psychological obstacles to the success of such an "adjustable tax plan." In the first place the tax power is rightfully a jealously guarded privilege of a democratic legislature, and the type of administrative discretion which would seem to be involved in a proposal to use the tax power as a stabilizer stands somewhat at variance with the whole parliamentary tradition. This objection could perhaps be overcome by suitably devised safeguards which would limit administrative discretion in regard to tax rates to an automatic procedure linked to some statistical indices approved by the legislature. Even more fundamental, however, than the political difficulty is a psychological obstacle; we are so much accustomed to regarding the tax system as a method of raising money for the government to spend that the idea of using it for quite another purpose is difficult to assimilate. Nevertheless, the principle is so clear, once formulated, that it is to be hoped that its truth will eventually overcome its unfamiliarity.

GOVERNMENT AND EMPLOYMENT

Government Absorption

The effect of government on the total of employment and output is more complicated than its effect on payments. Nevertheless, certain broad principles can be enunciated. In the first place government is highly significant as an "absorber" of output. The net purchases by government (i.e., purchases minus sales) constitute governmental absorption of output. This absorption, like that of households and business, is part consumed and part accumulated. Government purchases, it should be noted, include the labor of civil servants, the product of which can for the most part be regarded as government consumption. From the point of view of employment and output, however, the distinction between governmental consumption and accumulation is unimportant except in the case of material, such as surplus war material, which is accumulated and sold back to the public, or in the case of government investment, for example, in dams and power plants, which competes with and hence may discourage private investment.

Its Effect on Employment

If we can assume simple functions relating total output and private consumption and accumulation, it is not difficult to calculate that amount of governmental absorption which will result in full employment. If at full employment output and incomes the amount of private consumption is c and of private accumulation is a, then the amount of governmental absorption necessary to secure full employment, g, is $g = p - c - a$, where p is capacity (full employment) output. Unfortunately, of course, the problem is by no means as simple as this formula would indicate; the consumption-output and accumulation-output functions are not stable enough to be discovered statistically with any degree of confidence, and are also affected by other operations of government—e.g., its balance of payments—and by innumerable obscure psychological and sociological conditions. Thus an increase in governmental absorption designed to create full employment may have such an effect in restricting private accumulation and consumption, if the general sociological atmosphere is unfavorable to governmental expansion, that the net effect even of an expansion of governmental absorption is unfavorable to output. On the other hand, where the expansion in governmental absorption—e.g., in a popular war—is approved by the general community, it may have favorable effects on private accumulation and consumption and may rapidly produce conditions of "pressure economy."

Graphic Solution. The graphic solution to the simple system is shown in Fig. 71, where output is measured along OK, private absorption along OB, and government absorption along OG. BE is the private absorption curve, showing how much will be consumed and willingly accumulated by the private sector of the economy at each level of output. Suppose now that OK is the capacity, or full-employment output. KE then is the amount of private absorption at full employment. We now draw a 45° line from E, to meet the vertical axis in G. OG is then the amount of government absorption required to yield full employment, as only if government absorption is OG will the whole product be absorbed $(KE + OG = OK)$.[1] If government absorption is less than OG, say OG_d, the equilibrium output will be at less than capacity, OK_d. From a position of unemployment there will be

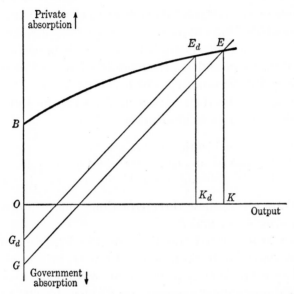

Fig. 71.   Output Equilibrium with Government Absorption (1).

a "government multiplier," m_g, exactly analogous to the investment multiplier of page 296, defined as the increase in the equilibrium output which results from a unit increase in government absorption. If a is the private propensity to absorb (the slope of the curve BE), then as before we have

$$m_g = \frac{1}{1 - \alpha}$$

The multiplier is again a measure of the sensitivity of the system; if it is large, quite small changes in government absorption may produce large changes in equilibrium output.

If government absorption is so large that the equilibrium output in

---

[1] In algebraic terms the model has three unknowns: government absorption, G, private absorption, B, and national output, Y. The three equations are:

1. The basic identity, $Y \equiv B + G$
2. The private absorption function, $B = F_b(Y)$
3. Government absorption given, $G = G$

the basic model is above capacity, there will be inflation, as the economy attempts to consume more than is available for consumption. As we have seen earlier, the inflation will only be "successful" (i.e., self-limiting) if it succeeds in lowering the private absorption curve to the point where there is no longer unwanted decumulation.

Model with Disposable Income and a Government Deficit

The simple model outlined above has one grave weakness: it postulates private absorption (B) as a function of *total* income, whereas it may be more realistic, especially as far as the consumption component is concerned, to suppose that private absorption is a function of "private" or disposable income, Y_d, which is total income, Y minus total tax collections, T. We then have a model with the following equations, G being government absorption:

1. The basic identity, $Y = B + G$
2. The private absorption function, $B = F_b(Y_d)$
3. The definition of disposable income, $Y_d = Y - T$

If G and T are given, these three equations suffice to determine the three unknowns, Y, Y_d, and B.

The system is illustrated graphically in Fig. 72. Disposable income is measured along the horizontal axis from O, private absorption is measured upward from O, government absorption and taxation downward. CE is the private absorption curve. Then let OG be total government absorption, GF be the total tax bill. OF is then the government deficit, for government absorption is what is bought with government expenditure, and is therefore measured in dollar terms by government expenditure. If now we draw a 45° line from OF to cut CE in E, E is the point of equilibrium, OK is the equilibrium disposable income, Y_d, and if a perpendicular EB is dropped to the vertical axis, GB is the total income, Y. From the geometry of the figure it will be seen that all the equations above are satisfied: (1) $GB = OB + GO$, (2) E is on the private absorption curve, $B = F_b(Y_d)$, and (3) $OK = EK + FO = FB = GB - GF$.

Effect of Pure Increase in Deficit

Now let us suppose that there is an increase in the deficit from OF to OF' without any change in government absorption. That is, tax collections fall from GF to GF'. Drawing the 45° line from F' to cut the private absorption curve in E', we find the new position of equilibrium E'. Private disposable income has risen to OK', total income to GB'. It is not difficult to derive "deficit multipliers" in this case. If m_d is the disposable income deficit multiplier and a is the propensity

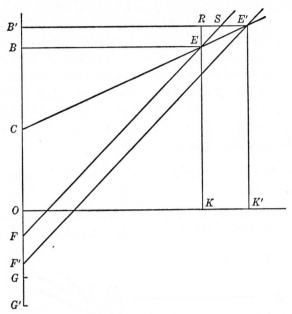

FIG. 72. Output Equilibrium with Government Absorption (2).

to absorb, we have

$$dY_d = KK' = RE' = RS + SE' = ER + FF' = \alpha dY_d + dF,$$

whence

$$m_d = \frac{dY_d}{dF} = \frac{1}{1 - \alpha}$$

If now m_t is the total income deficit multiplier, we have

$$m_t = \frac{dY}{dF} = \frac{BB'}{dF} = \frac{RE}{dF} = \frac{\alpha dY_d}{dF} = \alpha m_d = \frac{\alpha}{1 - \alpha}$$

We recall that α must be less than one if the system is to be stable, so that the total income multiplier will be less than the disposable income multiplier.

Effect of Increase in Deficit, Taxes Unchanged

Consider now the case where there is an increase in the deficit not as a result of a reduction in taxes but as a result of an increase in government expenditure or absorption. The deficit moves as before from OF to OF', but now government absorption also rises by an equal amount from OG to OG', taxes $(G'F')$ being the same as before (GF), so that $FF' = GG'$. The change in disposable income is the same as before, being governed in this model only by the deficit, and not by the volume of government absorption. The change in total income, however, is now equal to the change in disposable income, as taxes are unchanged. The change in total income is $G'B' - GB = BB' + G'G = ER + F'F = RS + SE' = RE' = KK'$, the change in disposable income. In this case then the total income multiplier is the same as the disposable income multiplier.

Effect of Rise in Government Absorption, Deficit Unchanged: The Ricardian Case

Suppose now that we have a rise in government absorption, financed by an increase in taxes so that the deficit remains unchanged (it makes

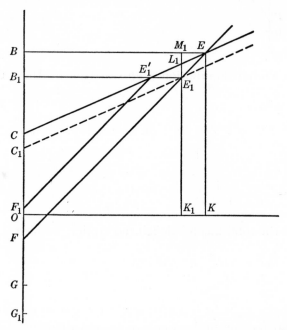

Fig. 73.   Output Equilibrium with Government Absorption (3).

no difference to the analysis, of course, if we assume the deficit to be zero). Now we ask ourselves what must happen to the private absorption function if the equilibrium output is to remain unchanged. This might be described as the "Ricardian" case, as Ricardo always assumed in effect that a rise in government absorption would not raise employment, as private absorption would fall by an equal amount. This is illustrated in Fig. 73, which is essentially the same diagram as Fig. 72. Here we suppose an increase in government absorption from OG to OG_1, and of tax collections from GF to G_1F, so the deficit remains unchanged at OF. Now, however, we want total income to remain unchanged. Private absorption therefore must fall from OB to OB_1, where $BB_1 = GG_1$, in order that the new total income (G_1B_1) shall be equal to the old (GB). This, however, in the absence of other changes requires a fall in the private absorption curve to go through the point E_1, where the horizontal line from B_1 cuts the 45° line FE. C_1E_1 is one such new private absorption curve, though any other reasonable curve which goes through E_1 would be satisfactory. It will be observed that the decline in private absorption at the disposable income OK_1, L_1E_1, is less than the rise in government absorption GG': $L_1E_1 = E_1M_1 - L_1M_1 = B_1B - \alpha M_1E = GG'(1 - \alpha)$

The Principle of Overfinance

Now suppose that the private absorption curve does *not* fall and we ask ourselves what we have to do in order to prevent total income from rising under the impact of expanded government absorption. The answer is clearly that we must diminish the deficit by increasing tax collections. In the figure B_1E_1 cuts the private absorption curve CE in E'_1, and we draw a 45° line from E'_1 to cut the vertical axis in F_1. OF_1 is the deficit (in the case of the figure, a surplus) which is necessary to prevent a rise in total income when government absorption rises from OG to OG_1. That is to say, it is not sufficient to raise merely enough in taxes to cover the increased government expenditure. The rise in tax receipts must be *greater* than the rise in expenditure if total income is not to increase. This may be called the "principle of overfinance." It is, of course, a corollary of the principle already enunciated that expansion of government absorption which is financed wholly by increased taxes is still "inflationary" and will produce an increase of total income. Starting from a position of underemployment, of course, this will probably mean increased real output; from a position of full employment, however, increased government expenditures must be "overfinanced" if they are not to give rise to inflation. It is not surprising in the light of this principle that war nearly always gives rise to inflation, for war requires generally a sharp increase in government absorption. It requires considerable financial virtue not to increase the deficit at such a time, and the amount of financial rectitude required to diminish the deficit, and perhaps to run a surplus, at a time when expenditures are increasing sharply is probably beyond the capacity of any known government.

Application to Effects of Private Investment

The above analysis can also be applied to the study of the effects of private investment as well as of government absorption. In so far as investment is financed either by the creation of new money through the banking system, or by a shift in money balances from business toward households, business in general will have a cash "deficit" analogous to a government deficit. If now household absorption is regarded as a function of "net" household income, that is, gross household income plus increases or minus decreases in the money stock of households, a cash deficit of businesses has the same effect in increasing the money stock of households as a cash deficit of government, for it means that business takes from households less than it pays back to them. Under these circumstances the inflationary effect of investment is augmented. The principle of overfinance also applies to investment. If there is an increase in investment there must be an actual decline in the money stocks of households if equilibrium income is to remain constant. This perhaps is the principal explanation of the frequently observed phenomenon—that full employment tends to pass into a price-wage inflation. If investment increases *from* a position of full employment it is extremely unlikely that the decrease in consumption will just offset the increase in investment. In order for this to happen there would have to be a sharp reduction in household money stocks —something which the existing financial and fiscal system is most unlikely to provide!

Assumptions of the Model

In all these models the warning should again be issued that the validity of their conclusions depends in large measure on the degree to which their behavior functions are in fact stable over time, and the possibility of shifts in these functions must always be kept in mind. Thus the private absorption function assumed in the above analysis may shift for a variety of reasons, many of which may be connected with various aspects of government policy. In the above analysis, for instance, we have been concerned only with the total volume of tax payments, not with the method of collecting taxes, and it will obviously make a difference to the private absorption function whether taxes are levied on income, on sales, on households, on corporations, or on imports. We will return later in the volume to discussions of the effects of particular taxes. Nevertheless the above models provide a rough outline for the understanding of the over-all aspects of public finance, and a method of analysis of the secondary effects through their impact on the primary behavior functions.

WAR FINANCE AND INFLATION

The great rise in government absorption during World War II, at least part of which seems to be permanent, has involved the world in a period in which inflation rather than the unemployment of the over-thrifty thirties is the dominant problem. This inflation has been mainly the result of a volume of government absorption more than sufficient to yield full employment, and inadequately offset by tax collections. The price inflation which results is itself a form of taxation, though often a very arbitrary and unjust form. In a "real" sense taxation is the decline in private absorption which must take place if government expands its absorption from a position of full employment. This decline can be accomplished *either* through the tax system *or* through inflation. It can be accomplished through the tax system by taking enough money away from the private sector to reduce private absorption to what is "available" after government has absorbed the amount of product it wants. Or, if taxes are not high enough to accomplish their proper task, inflation will, as we have seen, redistribute income away from the "low savers" toward the "high savers" and so will lower the total private absorption function (see p. 305).

Open and Suppressed Inflation

Inflationary pressure can take two forms—"open" or "suppressed." In an open inflation there is no control of prices, and they will rise until the redistribution of income is sufficient to accomplish the necessary reduction in private absorption. In "suppressed" inflation prices and money wages are held down by law, and as a result "shortages" develop—the pipelines empty, and consumption is restricted simply because people cannot find things to buy. These shortages can be regularized through rationing, in which consumption is restricted not by high prices but by direct allocation to consumers by means of ration coupons or by a system of priorities.

Whether "open" or "suppressed" inflation is preferable seems to depend on the degree of the inflationary pressure. Price-wage control and rationing in themselves have a high social cost in terms not so much of resources devoted to administration as in the inherent difficulty of administering the system without increasing maladjustments in the *relative* price structure. Unfortunately we cannot control the general level of prices and wages without controlling particular prices and wages—the general level is a statistical abstraction, and law can only operate on the concrete reality of particular prices and wages. The method of price control therefore is always to "freeze" the price structure as it existed at some date, and then set up a machinery for making adjustments and exceptions as the course of time and change in techniques and in demand make the relative price structure of the base date obsolete. The administrative machinery of adjustment, however, is slow and clumsy compared with the swift sensitivity of the free market, and as a result the longer price control operates, the more distorted becomes the relative price structure, and the stronger the temptation to evade the law in "black markets." On the other hand, great as are the difficulties of price control and rationing, they are almost certainly less than the evils of *rapid* open inflation. Inflation, as we have seen, is a very poor equilibrator, because though it probably restricts private consumption, the distribution of income which it brings about increases profits and so probably stimulates investment. The net effect of inflation on private absorption (consumption *plus* investment) may therefore be small, or even perverse. If this is the case, inflation may be quite unable to accomplish the task of restricting private absorption, and may degenerate into "hyperinflation."

Hyperinflation

Hyperinflation is the condition where all the equilibrating effect of inflation is lost, and the value of the monetary unit sinks almost to zero. Such hyperinflations occurred in France after the Revolution, in Germany and Russia after World War I, and in Hungary after World War II. When prices are rising very rapidly, it becomes apparent even to the least speculative that it is folly to hold money for any length of time. People therefore seek to get rid of their money as soon as it is received, for even the wage earner realizes that by the end of a week his money may be worth only half what it is at the beginning. Hence there is an enormous increase in the velocity of circulation, which may even reach the physical limits set by the speed with which people can run from the teller's window to the shop. The increase in the velocity of circulation then reinforces the effect of the increase in the quantity of money, and money incomes and prices skyrocket to figures which may be billions of times their former value. The owners of bonds, mortgages, government debts, pensions, and annuities then lose the whole value of their property, in so far as it consists only of a right to receive certain fixed sums of money, for these sums now become worthless.

The "Lag" in Government Inflation

In a mild government inflation, however, it is usually observed that the velocity of circulation falls a little. Some of the new money goes into hoards and consequently does not affect prices. But once the actual creation of money ceases, the velocity of circulation frequently increases, for the money which has been put away now comes out and is spent. So we often find that the creation of money during a war does not affect prices as much as it might, but that when the war is over, even if the creation of new money ceases, the velocity of circulation increases as the hoards are released, and prices undergo a further sharp rise. This phenomenon was observed after the Napoleonic Wars, and also after World Wars I and II. It goes far to explain the "postwar boom" and the subsequent depression.

Forced Saving

The phenomenon of "taxation through inflation" is a special case of a more general phenomenon. Any rise in prices, whatever its cause, "taxes" the people whose money incomes have not risen in proportion in that it reduces their "real income." This reduction in real income through a rise in prices is sometimes called "forced saving," though the term is not a good one owing to the ambiguity in the word "saving." It may be caused not only by government inflation, but also by a rise in the volume of bank credit, or even by a spontaneous rise in the velocity of circulation. Thus we have seen how an "investment inflation" is something like a government inflation. In this case also there is "forced saving" in the sense that there is a restriction of consumption through the redistribution of real income which the inflation produces. There is a real problem of economic justice here, because when investment is financed by inflation the people who come into possession of the new assets are *not* those whose enforced parsimony made the investment possible. The over-all increase of real assets is always a result of "saving"—i.e., consuming less than is being produced—but the people who have restricted their consumption are not necessarily the ones that own the new assets.

Government Debt

The analysis of Part II is of some assistance in interpreting the significance of government debt. Government debt usually arises when government receipts from taxation and sales of goods and services fall below government expenditures. This gap may be filled in three ways —by the issue of government money (e.g., greenbacks), by the sale of government bonds to banks, and by the sale of government bonds to the general public. Government money may be regarded as a variety of national debt—i.e., as a noninterest-bearing government security. Usually, however, it is not so regarded, and the term "national debt" is reserved for interest-bearing government bonds. The sale of government bonds to banks, as we have seen, is virtually equivalent to the creation of money, for the bonds are exchanged for newly created bank deposits. The sale of bonds to the general public is in its immediate effects equivalent to taxation as far as the payments effects are concerned, for it results in a transfer of liquid funds (cash or bank deposits) from the general public to the government. The sale of government bonds differs from taxation in that the general public does not suffer a diminution in the value of its assets, but merely exchanges one form (money) for another form (government bonds). Where government bonds are redeemable at short notice, they are themselves so liquid an asset as to make this change not very significant. Nevertheless, the purpose of the exchange is to diminish the liquidity of the assets of the general public, and so perhaps relieve inflationary pressure. An individual is somewhat less likely to increase his expenditures if he has, say, $500 in cash and $1500 in government bonds, instead of $2000 cash.

Interest on Government Debt

Government securities usually have to bear interest if people are to be induced to hold them, and this in itself creates something of a problem. The payment of interest on a government bond is an "expenditure"—i.e., a cash outlay of government—and must itself be met by one of the ways suggested above: by taxation, by printing money, or by selling more securities to banks or to the general public. If the government balances its budget, the interest on the debt represents a transfer of money from taxpayers to the debt holders. If everyone who paid taxes owned government debt in proportion to the taxes which he paid, this transfer would mean little, for what each person disbursed in taxes out of one pocket would flow into another of his pockets in the form of interest on his government bonds. In that case the distribution of income would not be directly affected by the amount of the debt. Whether the debt were a million or a billion dollars would make little difference to the structure of incomes. Where, however, the people who pay taxes and the people who own the debt are not the same group, government debt is an instrument for the transfer of income from the taxpayers to the debt holders. The debt holders generally belong to the wealthy and to the middle class. This remains true even when the debt is held largely by banks and insurance companies. In that case the depositors of banks and the policyholders of insurance companies are indirect beneficiaries of the interest payments on the debt. But bank deposits and insurance policies are not held to any great extent by the poorest section of the population, whereas indirect taxation and sales taxes reach down into the lowest income groups. The payment of interest on government debt, therefore, may result in a transfer of income from the very poor to the middle and upper classes—a result which is contrary to most other government policies. This transfer could be prevented by a tax system planned with that end in view, but it is doubtful whether such an objective could be reconciled with other ends of the tax system. Hence, there is strong likelihood that a large government debt will introduce a "regressive" feature into public finance.

The Conversion of Debt

Sometimes a government may reduce the interest payments which it has to make on its debt by the process known as "conversion." This consists in borrowing at a low rate of interest in order to pay off a debt on which a high rate is paid. Suppose that at a time when the rate of interest was high, the government borrowed $100,000,000 at a rate of interest of 5 per cent per annum, the principal to be repaid (or "redeemed") in twenty years. Suppose that at the end of the twenty years the rate of interest was only 3 per cent per annum. Then the government could borrow another $100,000,000 at 3 per cent and pay off the old debt. There would still be $100,000,000 of debt oustanding, but the government would now only have to pay out $3,000,000 in interest in each year instead of $5,000,000.

Advantages of a National Debt

Although a national debt may have certain adverse effects on income distribution, it may have a balance of advantage up to surprisingly large levels. We cannot perhaps agree with Daniel Webster unqualifiedly that "a national debt is a national blessing." Nevertheless, there is much to be said for it. It certainly contributes to political stability—a widely distributed national debt is perhaps the best insurance policy a government can have against the wrath of its people. It may also make positive contributions to economic welfare. In a period when people as a whole wish to "save"—i.e., increase their total assets —but when the increase in real assets which is economically advantageous is not great enough to supply the demand for "savings," an increase in government debt is a useful way to achieve a rise in the total of net worths without accumulation of goods or inflation of prices. In a sense this rise is fictional, for it only arises because government as such has no balance sheet and because noncurrent tax liabilities are not counted as liabilities in private balance sheets. Because of this an increase in government debt results not only in an increase of total assets but also in an increase in the net worths of the public. The issuance of private debt increases assets and liabilities together, and hence does not directly add to net worths. Because the desire to increase net worths in the absence of opportunities for accumulating real capital is one of the principal sources of unemployment, an increase in government debt may result in an increase in output.

Effect on Composition of Assets

Although the increase of the national debt increases the total of net worths, it also has an effect on the *composition* of assets, the effect of which is not easy to assess. The existence of a large volume of safe, liquid assets in the form of government bonds, even though the rate of interest on them be low, may discourage the accumulation of real capital and hence may contribute to the very malady which the growth of the national debt is supposed to cure. On the other hand, the development of a class of *rentiers* living off the interest on the national debt by increasing consumption and diminishing the labor force will have effect in diminishing unemployment as such, though a solution to the unemployment problem which involves the development of a class of respectably but permanently unemployed does not perhaps recommend itself too highly.

Effect on the Banking System

The increase in the amount of government bonds held by banks is a highly significant aspect of the growth of the national debt, especially from the point of view of the control of the monetary system.

The growth in the proportion of bank assets in the form of government securities is a striking result of the methods of war finance employed in World War II. One result of this change is to undermine the control exercised by the Federal Reserve Banks over the commercial banks, because of the great increase in the liquidity of commercial bank assets. The power of the Federal Reserve Banks to affect the reserve position of member banks by means of open-market policy is severely limited by the fact that any sharp reduction in the prices of government securities by Reserve Bank sales would endanger the solvency of the whole banking system. Hence, under present banking laws almost the only curb on a very substantial expansion of bank credit is the conservatism of the banks themselves.

Conclusion

This concludes the present sketch of "macroeconomic" principles and problems. Much still needs to be done in this field, and the frontiers of knowledge are by no means closed. Before we can proceed much further, however, it is necessary to return once more to the "microeconomic" and examine in detail the theory of a single economic organism in its relationships with others. Only by establishing the principles of behavior of the "atoms" of economic society can we develop a truly satisfactory account of the behavior of the groups and aggregates. The laws which we have been studying in this part may be likened to the general laws of the behavior of gases in physics. We must now go beyond the behavior of the mass and discuss the behavior of the molecules which compose it.

QUESTIONS AND EXERCISES

1. "The main economic business of government is to act as a 'Governor'—i.e., to throw inflationary forces into the system when deflation is occurring and deflationary forces when inflation is occurring." Discuss and illustrate.
2. Distinguish between the "regulative" and the "positive" aspects of government intervention in economic life. Then discuss the following proposition: "It is the failure of government to fulfill its positive obligations which forces it to engage in all kinds of unnecessary regulative activities."
3. Define carefully as many meanings as you can which might apply to the word "inflation." Then discuss the following proposition: "Inflation is a deliberate swindle on the part of the government."
4. Under the Treaty of Versailles the German government had to pay a

very large sum to the Allies in reparation payments. What do you think would be the effect of these payments on the foreign exchanges and on the course of international trade?

5. Suppose the government decided to extinguish the national debt by raising a capital levy, i.e., by taking industrial securities from their present owners in a "levy" and giving them to the present holders of the national debt in payment for government bonds. What effect would this measure have on the distribution of national income? Discuss the equity of such a proposal.

6. Discuss the following proposition: "The velocity of circulation is the one uncontrollable element in the monetary system. If we are to control money we must find antidotes for changes in its velocity of circulation."

7. Suppose we have a system like that of Fig. 72, page 475, in which the private absorption function is $B = 35 + \frac{4}{5} Y_d$. The unit of income we suppose is one billion dollars.

a. What will be the equilibrium level of private disposable income for deficits of 0, 5, 10, 15, 20, 25?

b. Suppose now government absorption is 50. What will be (i) private disposable income, and (ii) total national income for total tax collections of 25, 30, 35, 40, 45, 50?

c. Suppose now that government absorption rises to 100, and that the full employment level of total income at the current price level is 250. How much must be collected in taxes if inflation and unemployment are to be avoided?

d. Suppose now government expenditure rises to 125, but that the practicable limits of the tax collection is 100. By how much will private absorption at the equilibrium level of private disposable income have to fall if total income is to be kept at 250?

PART III

ELEMENTS OF THE MARGINAL ANALYSIS

INTRODUCTION

In the first part of this work the two principal weapons of analysis were the concepts of demand and supply. It was assumed that for each commodity or service a supply schedule and a demand schedule could be constructed, the former showing how much would be supplied and the latter showing how much would be demanded at each hypothetical price. It was assumed also that the price of any product tended to reach the level at which the quantity supplied, given by the supply curve, and the quantity demanded, given by the demand curve, were equal. With this slender equipment we have been able to draw a rough picture of the whole complicated system of economic relationships.

Now the analysis must go deeper. It will no longer suffice to assume merely that demand and supply curves exist, that some are elastic and some inelastic, or that some rise and fall. The underlying forces which give shape to these curves, which determine their elasticity, and which give rise to changes in their position must now be investigated. The assumptions of perfect competition, on which much of supply and demand analysis is based, must also be scrutinized. Perfect competition is rare in the actual world. Indeed, as ideally represented in economic theory, perfect competition does not exist anywhere outside the imagination of the economists, although the organized commodity and security markets approximate the ideal case. Over large areas of economic life other systems of market relationships—monopoly, monopolistic competition, and oligopoly—are of great importance. The analysis must therefore be extended to include these conditions. Even here our analysis of demand and supply will be by no means useless, and the existence of monopolistic elements in the system will modify, but not destroy, the conclusions of the more simplified analysis of perfect competition.

The principal analytical tool of Part III will be the theory of an individual economic organism. We shall first consider the theory of the individual firm, particularly with a view to discovering how an individual firm is likely to react to its environment. We shall also

489

examine the theory of an individual industry. The theory of the firm and of the industry will make clear what forces lie behind a long-run supply curve under perfect competition. The theory of the firm will show us what determines the supply curve of its individual product; i.e., what determines how much a single firm is willing to produce at each price. The theory of the industry will enable us to sum these individual supply curves to obtain the total supply curve for a commodity. The theory of the individual firm and industry will also show us what underlies the demand curves for factors of production. Then closely related to the theory of an individual firm will come the theory of an individual consumer, and with it the study of the forces which determine the position of demand curves.

The theory of the individual firm will also enable us to solve problems relating to monopoly and imperfect competition; it is, indeed, the ultimate foundation on which the greater part of economic analysis is built.

CHAPTER 23

THE NATURE OF BUSINESS ENTERPRISE

The foundation of the study of the supply of commodities is the study of their sellers, and the foundation of the study of the demand for commodities is the study of their buyers. Sellers and buyers may be of many kinds. There is the "occasional" buyer or seller—the widow who sells off her household goods, the church which sells an occasional supper, the unwary buyers at an auction or rummage sale. Then there are the sales of "original producers" and the purchases of "ultimate consumers," which are important in considering the demand for consumers' goods and the supply of factors of production. The most important buyer and seller in our present economic order is, however, the business enterprise, or "firm." The great bulk of finished and intermediate products is sold by firms. The great bulk of the services of factors of production is bought by firms. It is essential, therefore, to understand the essential functions of such an organization.

Inputs, Outputs, and the Process of Production

A firm may be defined as an institution which buys things, transforms them in some way, and then sells them with the purpose of making a profit. The things a firm buys we shall call "inputs." The things it sells we shall call "outputs." The process whereby the things it buys are transformed into the things it sells we shall call the "process of production." In any process of buying to sell again a process of production is always involved. This is true even where the physical nature of the commodity does not change in the process. A wheat merchant, who buys wheat at one time and place and sells the identical wheat at another time and place, is organizing a process of production just as much as the miller who takes wheat and grinds it into another substance—flour. Wheat in Liverpool in September is a different commodity from wheat in Chicago in June, just as flour is a different commodity from wheat.

Profits

Now, why does a firm do this? Why does it buy, transform, and sell? The answer is, to make profits. To understand the nature of a firm, then, we must understand exactly what is meant by "profits." For if it is the business of a firm to make profits, then clearly a firm will try to make as much profit as it can. This principle of the *maximization of profits* will guide us all through our discussion of the theory of the firm. It is important, therefore, to know what is the "profit" which a firm tries to maximize.

"Virtual" Expenses and Receipts

The common concept of profit is that it is the difference between the money received by a business and the money paid out. Here, however, careful thought is needed. We must try, if possible, to separate the business as such from the things which people do for the business. We can see the importance of this in an example. Suppose there are two farmers, each working identical farms. Farmer A owns his farm; Farmer B does not, but pays $500 a year rent for it. Both farmers from the sale of their crops receive a sum of $3000 a year. Both pay out, for labor, seed, equipment, repairs, etc., a sum of $1000. Farmer A pays out a total of $1000 and has an excess of cash receipts over cash expenditures of $2000. Farmer B, because he has to pay $500 for his land, pays out altogether $1500; he has an excess of cash receipts over cash expenditures of only $1500. Is Farmer B's farm less profitable, therefore, than Farmer A's? Clearly not, for they are identical farms. The mere difference between the farmer's cash receipts and his cash expenditures in a given time, which we may call the "net cash receipts," is not a measure of profit, for we must take into account the things the farmer owns himself which contribute to the business. In this example we should say that the farmer who has a net cash receipt of $2000 receives $500 in his capacity as landowner of his own land, and $1500 in his other capacities.

Take another example. Suppose there are two similar grocery stores, one of which is owned by the shopkeeper who runs it while the other is a chain store with a paid manager. The owner-shopkeeper and the paid manager are equally good at their jobs; the paid manager receives $3800 a year. The net cash receipts of the chain store are $2200; the net cash receipts of the independent grocer are $6000. Yet in this case if all the other circumstances were similar we should say that the two stores were equally profitable. In order to calculate his profits the

THE NATURE OF BUSINESS ENTERPRISE 493

independent grocer should make an allowance for the services which he renders to his own business.

It is evident that our first definition of inputs as things which are bought by a business is too narrow, if we take it in a literal sense to mean things for which money is paid to outsiders. Inputs must also include things which the proprietor of a business "buys from himself." The payments which a business makes for inputs (called "expenses") include not merely actual expenses paid out to other people. They include also the "virtual expenses"—the payments made by the business to the proprietor *not* in his capacity as proprietor but in his capacity as the supplier of some input used in the process of production which the business conducts. In the first example the payment of $500 for rent in the case of Farmer A might be regarded as a payment from himself as a farmer to himself as a landowner. Similarly, the $3800 paid for the services of management to the owner of an independent grocery store may be regarded as a payment from the grocer as the owner of a grocery business to himself as the manager of his own store.

The Business Defined by the "Process"

It is evident, therefore, that the *process,* not the individual who conducts it, is what defines a business or an enterprise. From the point of view of determining the profitability of an enterprise, it does not matter whether the businessman himself owns any, all, or none of the inputs or sources of inputs which are necessary for the process. A business, therefore, is a *process* whereby certain inputs, valued in dollars in some way, are transformed into outputs, also valued in dollars in some way. Just as there are inputs supplied by the owner of a business, the value of which is a "virtual," not an actual, expense, so there can be outputs consumed by the owner of a business, the value of which forms "virtual," not actual, receipts. Again, in the case of our two identical farmers, suppose each grew $100 worth of potatoes, but suppose Farmer A sold all his on the market, while Farmer B ate his at home. Farmer A's net cash receipts, because of this fact, would be $100 more than Farmer B's. Nevertheless, we should not say that Farm A was more profitable; the potatoes of Farm B, even though eaten at home, constitute output of the farm just as do the potatoes of Farm A.

Profit and Valuation

Can we then define the *profits* of a business in any period of time as the difference between the dollar value of the outputs, including those

sold and those not sold, and the dollar value of the inputs, also including those bought and those not bought, during the interval of time in
question? The answer is yes—again if we are careful about what inputs and outputs mean.

Imagine again two identical farms at the beginning of a year. During the year each yields $3000 worth of agricultural produce. The
value of the land, labor, seed, etc., used on each farm during the year
is $1200. During the year Farmer A buys a tractor for $800, which is
still worth $800 at the end of the year. His net cash receipts during the
year will be only ($3000 − 1200 − 800) or $1000, while Farmer B's net
cash receipts will be $1800. We still would not say, however, that
Farm A was less profitable than Farm B. Evidently we must take into
account not only the final commodities produced by the farm but also
the addition to the value of the possessions of the farm. In the above
case the "revenue" of the farm during the year was $3800—$3000
representing commodities sold or used, $800 representing an increase
in the value of the farm equipment. To use another example: suppose
that the net cash receipts of Farmer A were $1000 and the net cash
receipts of Farmer B were $1800. Farmer A, however, kept his farm in
good condition all the year—weeding his fields, fertilizing his ground,
repairing his buildings and equipment—and Farmer B neglected to
do all this. That is to say, Farmer A spent the $800 necessary to keep
up the value of his farm, and Farmer B did not, with the result that
his farm was worth $800 less than it was at the beginning of the year.
Evidently this $800 loss of value from the $1800 net cash receipts of
Farmer B should be deducted in order to compare his profits with
those of Farmer A.

Values as Virtual Expenses and Receipts

Evidently in calculating the profits *of a given year* we must include
the value of the property possessed by the business at the beginning
of the year among the virtual expenses for the year, and the value of
the property of the business at the end of the year among the virtual
receipts for the year. Otherwise it will appear as if businesses which
are running down the value of their property are making great profits,
while businesses which are building up the value of their property are
making small profits or even losses. That is, in calculating the profits
for a given year we must think of the business as if it "bought" from
itself all the things it owned at the beginning of the year and all the
things it supplied to the business in the course of the year. These
must be added to the actual payments of cash in the purchase of inputs

to find the total of "virtual" expenses. Then we must think of the business as if it "sold" to itself all the things it owned at the end of a year and the things produced by it and used by its owners; and these must be added to the cash received from the sale of outputs in order to find the total of "virtual" receipts. Then the "profit" in that year is the difference between the total receipts and the total expenses as above defined. For example, suppose a boot polish firm had property valued at $20,000 at the beginning of the year. Suppose that it spent in the actual or virtual purchase of inputs a sum of $10,000. Its property at the end of the year was worth $21,000 and the receipts, actual or virtual, which it obtained from the sale of its output amounted to $11,000. Then the "profit" in that year would amount to $(21,000 + 11,000 − 20,000 − 10,000), or $2000. This is the sum which would accrue to the owners of the business in that capacity, as a result of the year's transactions.

The Rate of Profit

Even now, however, we are not quite out of the wood. Can we always say that if two businesses each show a profit of $2000 in a given year they are equally profitable? Clearly not, if one of them starts off with a much greater value of property than the other. If one business, for instance, has property worth $20,000 and makes a profit of $2000 in one year, the *rate* of profit in that year amounts to 10 per cent per annum. If a business which started off with property worth $40,000 makes a profit of $2000 in the year, the rate of profit is only 5 per cent per annum. The second business is evidently less profitable than the first. It is the *rate* of profit, therefore, by which the profitability of different enterprises must be compared. Nevertheless, if it can be assumed that the value of the property of an enterprise remains constant, which is frequently the case, then the greater the *annual amount* of profit, the greater will be the rate of profit. In such a case we can assume without much difficulty that a firm wishes to make its annual profit as great as possible.

Difficulties of Valuation

It is evident that profit cannot be calculated without valuation— valuation on the one hand of inputs and outputs which are supplied or used by the owners themselves, and on the other hand of property which the business possesses. All these valuations are subject to some degree of error. Consequently, the calculation of profit for any one year likewise involves some degree of error. As the annual profit depends directly on the difference between the value of the firm's property at the beginning of the year and its value at the end of the year, errors in these valuations—especially if they are in different directions —may create very large errors in the calculation of the annual profit. We cannot at this stage discuss the methods and the theory of the valuation of property. It is sufficient to note that whatever methods are adopted, a certain margin of error is always possible.

Profit as the Reward of Ownership

Now that "profit" has been defined, the next question is, "Who gets it, and for what?" The answer is that profits, in the sense in which we have defined them here, go to the owners of the business, i.e., the owners of the things which the business, as an entity, owns. Almost any process of production involves the creation of things that are valuable. Consider, for instance, the production of cloth. It starts by breeding and feeding sheep. Services of land and of labor, with some equipment, are bought at this stage, and the result is a sheep—a valuable object which, in a society like ours, must be owned by someone. The sheep is sheared; the wool is baled, transported, combed, washed—all the time growing in value as it approaches the stage of its final usefulness. Then the wool is spun into yarn, which also has value. The yarn is woven into cloth, which also has value. It is evident that this is a process of production whereby certain services of land, labor, and equipment are gradually transformed, over a period of time, into cloth. A piece of cloth is the result of the cooperation of sheep raisers, sheep land, sheep-farming equipment, transport workers and equipment, wool washers and carders and their equipment, wool salesmen and brokers, spinners and their equipment, and finally weavers and their equipment. This cooperation is possible only because the result of the activity of all these persons and their equipment can be "embodied" in a physical object—wool or yarn or cloth. Somebody has to own this wool, yarn, or cloth as it passes through all the multitudinous stages of production. Similarly, somebody has to own the equipment —the sheds and shears, the factories and looms—with which the operations are carried out. It is the owners of these properties who receive profit; it is they who are the "capitalists." Moreover, it is these owners who are the "employers"—who employ the labor and the equipment involved in the process of production.

The Capitalist as the "Real" Employer

We must be quite clear as to what we mean by "employer." An employer is not the personnel manager, the man who actually does the hiring and firing, for he is merely working on behalf of some other person. Who, then, is this other person—the "real" employer? He is the "capitalist," the person or institution which owns the money paid to workers (or to the owners of any other input which is bought) and which owns the *product* of the work after it is done. We have seen earlier that any purchase, whether of labor or of anything else, is essentially an *exchange*. When a worker is employed for a week, in the first instance there is an exchange of a week's labor for, let us say, $50 in money. At the beginning of the week the employer had at least $50 in money; the worker had the possibility of doing a week's work. At the end of the week the worker has $50 in money; the employer has the *result of the work*. The result of the work will be some commodity which, if the labor has been applied fruitfully, has become more valuable on account of the work done. That is to say, the employer has exchanged $50 in money for at least $50 worth of "goods" created by the worker's labor. Suppose the worker is a weaver; in a week he may have converted a pile of yarn worth $100 into a pile of cloth worth $160. In that case the employer will have profited by the exchange, if the wage of the worker is $50, for he has exchanged $50 in money for $60 in goods. At the end of the week, therefore, the employer, because he is an employer, owns goods. In fact, the act of being an employer is the act of transforming money into goods—and of course, by a correlative process, of transforming goods into money by the sale of output.

Production as the Creation of Goods

Thus, any process of production which takes time necessarily involves the creation of valuable objects—goods. The person or institution which buys the inputs that go to make up the process, of necessity comes to be the owner of these goods. The purchase of any input gives to the purchaser a good which he did not have before, and, what is more, it gives him a good which would not have existed at all if he had not purchased the input. Unbought labor results in nothing. The weaver does not possess so much "weaving" which he can sell to the employer any time he likes. Weaving can only come into existence as it is sold or bought; in other words, if the "weaving" of one week is not bought it simply ceases to exist—so much is lost which might have been produced. Consequently, the purchase of labor is more than the purchase of a commodity; it involves the creation of a commodity which would not have been brought into existence if the labor had not been bought. If a purchaser of wheat does not buy in a certain week, the wheat that he might have bought is still in existence and may be bought at some other time or by some other person. If, however, a buyer of labor does not buy in a particular week, the labor he might have bought cannot be bought again; it has perished in the drought of idleness. Labor is the most perishable of all commodities. It must be taken in the instant of its birth, or it vanishes from the earth.

Why Does Profit Exist?

Profit, then, is received by the owner of the commodities, i.e., of the valuable objects, which are the result of a process of production, and the owner owns these commodities because he is the purchaser of inputs. The questions immediately arise, *"Why* does the owner of goods receive an income because of that ownership?" "Why does profit exist?" In other words, how does it come about that the value of the *outputs* in a process of production is greater than the value of the inputs, for profit, as we have seen, is the difference between the value of the outputs and the value of the inputs. Why does not the competition of businessmen force down the prices of outputs and raise the prices of inputs until these values are equal and there is no "profit" in the proper sense of the term?

Even if profit in this sense were abolished, management would still be paid, for management is an item of input; labor would be paid, the suppliers of the services of equipment would be paid, though only enough to cover the value of the inputs used in making the equipment. Why, we may ask, should the capitalist, i.e., the owner of the goods in the process, receive an income, as apparently he does nothing *active* in this capacity? Notice that we are not here suggesting that the independent grocer should get nothing for his labor, or that the private businessman should get nothing for his management; all these things are inputs, and will have to be paid for. But can we truly say that ownership, plain and simple, is an input? This can be seen most clearly in the case of a corporation. Here the owners, represented by the holders of ordinary shares, play practically no part in management; they merely get a dividend check (perhaps) every quarter. The American Telephone and Telegraph Company could still operate, could still provide telephone service, even if it paid nothing to its stockholders, for the stockholders know nothing about telephones except how to talk into them, and they contribute nothing to the working of the company. They neither hire, fire, manage, repair, discover, nor work for the company. All they do is *own* it; and their ownership, apparently, entitles them to such profits as it may receive.

That is to say, they own, collectively, the things which belong to the company; they own the factories, the machines, the equipment, the wires and exchanges and telephones, the stocks of goods in process, and the money which belongs to the company.

Employment as an Exchange of Money for Goods

This perhaps will give a clue as to the real function of ownership. Because the stockholders are the owners of the money which the company possesses, they are also the employers—the real purchasers —of all the things which it buys. Every time an agent of the company buys anything, whether he is a repairman buying a length of wire or a personnel manager hiring a trouble shooter, the company, and through it its owners, has relinquished the possession of a certain amount of liquid funds and has acquired the possession of a certain amount of things having value. As a result of the purchase of a coil of wire for $5, the corporation owns $5 less money and an extra coil of wire. As a result of the purchase of $50 worth of labor, the corporation owns $50 less money and the result of that labor.

Risks of Ownership

Now, people will not make an exchange of money for something which is bought with money unless they feel that the exchange is worth while—unless, that is to say, they feel that it is better to possess the *good* than to possess the money. Possessing goods has certain risks and inconveniences attached to it which are not attached to the possession of money. Although it is true that the purchasing power of money may change, the risk of change of the purchasing power of any particular goods is even greater. A thousand dollars in money, of course, may be worth less next year than it is this year, in terms of what it will buy. If we hold money, therefore, we stand to lose in the purchasing power of what we own by a rise in the general level of prices. But if we possess a commodity—such as wool—we stand to lose not merely if the general price level falls but also if the price of wool falls relative to other things. It is therefore usually considered that a greater risk is involved in the possession of goods than in the possession of money.

There are also other inconveniences. If I possess money—liquid funds—my possessions are immediately exchangeable for anything that is on sale. In any emergency I can transform my possessions immediately into any form I like. This is an attribute which we have already met, called "liquidity." Goods, however, are not "liquid"— i.e., they are not readily exchangeable and are not, therefore, so useful in an emergency. Suppose, for instance, that there is a sudden change in demand, so that the goods which a firm has been producing suffer a sharp fall in price. A firm which is highly illiquid—which has a large part of its capital locked up in the form of goods—will not be able to adjust to this situation; it will not be able to dispose of the goods it has in stock, and hence will not have the money to pay out in the production of other goods more in demand. A firm which is liquid —which has a comfortable proportion of its assets in the form of money—will be able to start production of new commodities and will be able to survive the shock of readjustment. Liquid assets are like "reserves of health"—they enable an economic body to survive adverse changes in its environment.

Profit as a Reward for Owning Nonliquid Goods

If people are not paid for owning goods, therefore—i.e., for having been employers, purchasers of inputs—they will try to transform these goods into money, for money is usually the most convenient form of property to hold. The attempt to transform a great volume of goods into money, however, will cause stupendous disturbances in the economic system. Suppose, for example, that the prices of outputs and of inputs stand in such a proportion that there is no profit to be made by the owners of goods—i.e., by capitalists—the value of outputs being just equal to the value of inputs. The owners of goods will not be satisfied with this condition; if the possession of goods brings no reward to counterbalance its inconveniences and risks, the possessors will attempt to turn their holdings into money. They will cease buying inputs; for a purchase, as we have seen, is an exchange of money for goods, and the owners of money will prefer to keep it rather than to exchange it for goods. They will also attempt to sell all the output they can; i.e., they will attempt to sell off the goods they own. In other words, they will attempt to "liquidate," i.e., transform their property, by exchange, from the form of goods to the form of money. The result will be a fall in the demand for inputs, leading, if the market is competitive, to a fall in their price. There will also be a rise in the supply curves of output as businessmen try to liquidate their stocks. This increase in the desire to exchange goods for money will cause a fall in the prices of goods, which will make the holding and acquisition of goods even less profitable and will accentuate the fall in demand for input and the rise in the supply curves of output. This in its turn will lead to a still greater fall in prices.

Evil Results of a Failure of Profits

It is evident, therefore, that the disappearance of profits would result in very serious disturbances to any free competitive system, disturbances so serious that it is doubtful whether the system could remain unchanged. If all prices, including the prices of input, were flexible, then the disappearance of profits would involve the system in a dizzy and apparently bottomless deflation of prices. If, as is in fact the case, certain prices—for instance, the price of labor—are inflexible, the result will be large-scale unemployment, until the price fall is checked by the increasing scarcity of goods. We cannot go into the details of the phenomenon at this point, but we can readily see that if profits are insufficient to compensate the owners of goods for the risks and unpleasantness involved, the actions of these owners will run the economic system into very serious trouble. Owners must be paid in order to prevent them from trying to turn too many of their goods into money. But almost every process of production involves the existence at any moment of a stock of goods—sheep, wool, yarn, cloth, factories, machines, and so on. These things must be owned by someone; even in a communist society they are owned by the state. And the owners are of necessity the employers of factors of production. The function of exchanging money for inputs, i.e., the employing function, is essentially the same function as ownership. And it is in order to induce people to fulfill this function that in a capitalist society profits have to be paid.[1]

The Vertical Division of the Process of Production: Integration

One other fact about the process of production we must notice. Production is not usually under the control of a single business from start to finish. We could, of course, imagine a process in which the only inputs bought were the services of land and labor; in which every implement was made and owned by the business which used it; and in which all raw materials were extracted by the same business. This state of affairs, however, is practically unknown; the nearest approximation to it might be found in primitive societies where fishermen,

---

[1] It should be pointed out also that the result of low profits in business enterprise might result in a "flight" of capital into consumption capital as well as into liquid assets. If the profits of business become low enough, the capitalist may prefer to hold his assets in the form of houses, jewels, stamp collections and so on—especially if there is any long-run trend toward higher prices. The broadest generalization would seem to be, therefore, that profit is necessary in order to prevent capitalists from trying to shift thir assets into forms more attractive than the assets of business enterprise, whatever these more attractive forms may be. I am indebted to Professor W. T. Baxter for this observation.

for instance, might catch fish, using nets which they had made themselves, from boats which they had built themselves—fish which they themselves then sold to the ultimate consumers. But in modern economic society virtually all enterprises buy some things which have been made by other enterprises. Some of the inputs of any given enterprise are the outputs of other enterprises. Coal, for instance, is the output of a coal mine but the input of an electric light plant. Wheat is the output of a farmer, the input of a miller. Flour is the output of a miller, the input of a baker. Looms may be the output of a loom factory, the input of a cotton mill. So we could go on through innumerable instances.

This is but another illustration of the principle of specialization which we noted in Chapter 2. If the farmer specializes in the production of wheat and the miller specializes in the grinding of wheat into flour, both become expert at their jobs and so produce more flour between them than they could if each farmer tried to grind and each miller tried to grow his own wheat.

The process whereby more and more related processes are brought under one control is called "integration." If a steel mill, for instance, purchased a coal mine or an iron ore mine, coal and iron ore being inputs of steel production, or if it purchased a pressing mill, raw steel being the input of a pressing mill, we should say that the process was being "integrated." Frequently economies are to be gained by such integration of *control,* while retaining the advantages of specialized managers in the conduct of each operation.

The Pricing of Intermediate Products

Even in this case, however, the individual process retains a certain individuality of its own. The owner of a coal mine plus a steel mill will want to have some estimate of how profitable these enterprises are separately, as well as how profitable is the whole complex. In order to do this he will have to set a price upon the coal which passes from the coal mine to the steel mill, even though no money passes in the transfer. We can imagine the owner paying money to himself as coal owner, from himself as steel mill owner, for the coal which is used; the payment for the coal is a virtual expense for the steel mill, a virtual revenue for the coal mine. He will presumably set a price on the coal equal to the price at which he could buy it outside, in order to calculate the profitability of each enterprise. If the price were set above this, the steel mill would appear less profitable, the coal mine more profitable than it should be; if the price were set too low, the coal mine would appear less profitable, the steel mill more profitable than it should be. If, of course, the commodity were unique, so that no outside market existed, the case would be a little more difficult; but this is rare. In such a case we should probably say that the "correct" price was that which would make the profitability of the two enterprises equal. The higher the price assigned to coal, the more profitable would be the coal mine, the less profitable the steel mill. Obviously, there will be some price of the intermediate product at which the profitability of the two enterprises is equal.

Not Fundamentally Affected by Integration

Whether processes are integrated or not does not make much difference to the principles which we have outlined in this chapter. If processes are "disintegrated"—i.e., if intermediate products, in which there is a competitive market, pass from one enterprise to another as the output of one process and the input of another—there will be a tendency for the actual prices of these products to adjust themselves to the point where the real profitability of all enterprises is the same. For if the price of coal is so high that coal mines are more profitable than the enterprises which use coal, the coal industry will expand and the price of coal will fall. If the price is so low that coal mines are less profitable than other industries, the output of coal will contract and the price will rise. The integration of processes may interfere somewhat with the competitive nature of the markets for intermediate products. Nevertheless, the principle still applies that the price of the intermediate product will tend to be fixed at the point where the profitability of the enterprise which produces it is equal to the profitability of the enterprise which uses it.

QUESTIONS AND EXERCISES

1. Define carefully, in your own words, the following terms: (a) a firm, (b) input, (c) output, (d) virtual receipts, (e) actual receipts, (f) profit, (g) intermediate products, (h) capitalists.
2. Would you say that the following institutions were "firms"? (a) a village blacksmith, (b) a college, (c) an orphan asylum, (d) a government, (e) a city, (f) a municipal electric power plant, (g) a consumers' cooperative society.
3. "Call no man happy until he is dead; call no firm profitable until it is liquidated." Discuss.
4. What aims, from a financial point of view, would you endeavor to strive after, if you were (a) the general manager of a department store, (b) the

treasurer of a college, (c) a farmer? Try to define these aims carefully in quantitative terms.

5. The following table gives financial information about two farms:

	Farm A	Farm B
Total cash receipts	$ 8,000	$11,000
Total cash outlays	6,000	7,000
Value of land, buildings, and equipment, Jan. 1	25,000	30,000
Value of land, buildings and equipment, Dec. 31	26,000	29,500

Both farmers own their own land, buildings, and equipment. Farmer A could get a job working for another man for $2000 a year. He has no wife. Farmer B could get another job at $1800 a year. He has a wife who works half time on the farm, and who could earn $1200 a year if employed full time elsewhere. Which is the more profitable farm?

CHAPTER 24

FORMS OF BUSINESS ORGANIZATION

The principles outlined in the preceding chapter will enable us to understand more fully many of the phenomena of economic development and organization. Before going on to study in detail the theory of the conduct of the firm, therefore, we may profitably pause to consider how the organization of the firm, and of the function of enterprise, has developed, even at the risk of some digression.

Development of Specialized Occupations

Generally speaking, the story of economic development is one of increasing specialization. As soon as any kind of social life appears, there must be specialization. Even in tribal society some people are hunters, some fishers, some farmers, some priests, and some chiefs. In primitive society, however, the specialization is almost all along commodity lines; that is, men are divided into "industries" or "occupations," but within each occupation there is little specialization. The fisherman will own his boats and nets, do his own sailing and marketing; the farmer will own his implements and land and sell his own crops. In such a society the services of enterprise as such are not clearly distinguished from the services of labor and equipment. The "income" which any group gets from the exchange of its product is a payment for all the services performed in the production of the commodity sold.

Development of Intermediate Products

The next stage in development seems to be the growth of markets for intermediate products. A craft of boat builders splits off from the fishermen; implement makers begin to form a trade of their own; the shepherd and the spinner and the weaver establish separate trades. The commodities exchanged now include not merely final consumption goods but intermediate products—boats, plows, wool,

505

yarn, cloth, and so on. When society gets to this stage, the institution of *money* becomes a necessity. Very primitive specialization is possible on a barter basis, but as soon as intermediate products begin to be bought and sold the barter system breaks down. Usually some commodity in common demand, such as cattle, comes to be the unit of account. (Note that our adjective "pecuniary" comes from the Latin *pecus,* meaning cattle.) Quite complex civilizations can flourish on this "craft" basis, in which each craftsman performs only part of a process, working perhaps with materials which he has brought from another craftsman and perhaps selling his product to yet another craftsman to work up further. Ancient civilization, and even medieval civilization, was built in part on this level of specialization. The typical "firm" was a craftsman, or a group of craftsmen, buying their own raw materials, owning their simple tools, working in their own homes, and selling their own product.

The Specialization of Enterprise: First in Agriculture

Enterprise as a specialized activity probably began first in agriculture, in the development of specialized ownership of domestic animals and of slaves, who from an economic point of view can also be regarded as a kind of domestic animal. The owner of the great estate was the first capitalist. Even in the ancient world the specialization of ownership as such was common. The landed aristocracy did not derive their incomes from activity of their own; they derived them from the sheer fact of ownership, like a shareholder in a modern corporation. The landowner, both ancient and modern, was frequently an absentee from his estate; the work of detailed management was done by hired managers, just as absentee stockholders hire managers to manage the business which they own. It is interesting to notice, however, that the great estate does not seem to be, in the long run, a more efficient way of producing agricultural commodities than the small personal "craft" farm. The persistence of the peasant proprietor—who is worker and employer and owner all rolled into one—through all civilizations into modern times is one of the most striking facts of history. In agriculture at least there do not seem to be many important advantages attached to large-scale operation, except under rather unusual circumstances. This is probably because the management of agricultural processes cannot be reduced to a routine; the farmer must take opportunity as it comes, and cannot wait for orders.

The Domestic System

In industry the specialization of enterprise begins with what is called the "domestic system." This is a system in which the individual craftsman still works in his own home and with his own tools, but the activities of marketing are taken over by a specialized merchant or middleman. This is what we should expect, for of all the activities which a purely independent craftsman has to perform, marketing is least like his other activities. An independent weaver, for instance, has to buy his own yarn and sell the cloth which he makes from it. Both these activities may be troublesome to him, for his skill at weaving is totally different from the skill required in buying and selling. Consequently, those weavers who find that they are more skilled at buying and selling than at weaving may specialize in the trade of buying and selling—i.e., they may become merchants. A merchant clothier of the fifteenth century in England bought yarn, gave it out to weavers to weave, paid them for their work, and took the cloth they wove. Notice now the subtle and significant change which has taken place in the status of the weaver as he is transformed from an independent craftsman to a domestic worker. Although he works in his own home and with his own loom he is in effect an employee of the merchant, for he does not own the yarn on which he works or the cloth which he produces. It is *because* the merchant owns the yarn and the cloth that the weaver is an employee. The merchant does not buy cloth from the weaver, for the weaver does not own the cloth; he buys the *labor* of the weaver and the services of the weaver's looms and workrooms.

The Factory System

The next step is more spectacular but not, perhaps, really so significant as the change from the craft to the domestic system. This is the development of *factories*. The factory is a child of power; as long as the only power used in production was the power of human or even of animal muscles, there was little point in collecting workers and their implements together into factories. But once devices were discovered, first for using water power and later for using the power of coal and steam, the difficulties of transporting power led to the building of factories and the aggregation of workers into industrial towns. As power could not go to the worker, the worker had to go to the power. However, the power supplied by a single water wheel or a single steam engine was sufficient to drive a number of machines. For purely technical reasons an efficient source of power could not be devised which was small enough to drive a single machine. This fact in itself was probably enough to make factory production profitable. Another development which favored the growth of factories was the increasing specialization of processes, making it convenient to have a number of machines of different types located in the same building so that materials in process could be passed quickly and cheaply from one operation to the next.

The Private Entrepreneur

The growth in the size of the industrial unit, or "plant," led to a great expansion of the form of enterprise run by a manager-capitalist, or "small businessman." The small businessman generally owns the capital of his business; that is, he owns the raw materials and equipment used in the course of the process. He also directly supervises the management of the enterprise. He himself performs the operations of purchase and sale; he personally supervises the workers and is responsible for the efficient cooperation of the various inputs which he uses. In this form of enterprise the worker is a worker pure and simple who sells nothing but the only thing he owns—his labor. The employer is also completely specialized, performing none of the common tasks of labor himself but confining himself to the operations of buying, selling, and supervising.

There is no necessary physical reason why this type of enterprise should have been the result of the growth of factory methods. It is conceivable that the factory system could have been introduced by workers' cooperatives in which the capital equipment and raw materials were owned by the workers themselves, acting as a group. Although the ownership of the capital of the productive processes was now outside the reach of a single worker, owing to the great size of the capital involved, it might not, perhaps, have been impossible for a group of workers to own their own factories, machines, and raw materials. In some fields, as we shall see, the cooperative form of enterprise has been successful. In the field of manufacturing industry, however, it has been an almost complete failure. For reasons connected with the natural differences and capacities of men, the form of enterprise which is owned and guided by those who are not employed by it has been the most successful.

The Partnership

As the size of the unit of enterprise increased, the form of the enterprise developed. The first stage in this development was the *partner-*

ship, in which two or more persons owned a business between them. Partnerships are of several kinds. In one kind each partner owns an equal share in the business and takes an equal responsibility for the conduct of the business. In another kind some partners own large shares, some small shares, of the business. In yet another kind some partners take an active responsibility for the conduct of the business and other partners merely contribute ownership, i.e., are "sleeping partners." The fundamental principle of the partnership, however, is the same in all cases. In so far as any one of the partners perform services (e.g., of management) for the business, he should be paid for those services just as any input has to be paid for. Then any excess of the value of outputs over the value of inputs, i.e., any "profit," should be divided among the partners in proportion to their share in the capital of the business.[1] This is an example of the principle of the preceding chapter—that profits belong to the owners of the capital invested in the enterprise which makes them.

Defects of the Partnership

There are two features of the partnership which frequently cause inconvenience. One is the fact that a partnership is merely an agreement between individuals and not an organization which exists apart from the individuals who compose it. Hence, important decisions can rarely be taken without the consent of all the partners. This limits severely the number of people who can participate in a partnership. Hence also, if one of the partners dies or wishes to withdraw from the partnership, the whole agreement must be redrawn.

The other inconvenient feature is that the partners are usually liable, each individually, for all the debts of the business. Thus, if a partnership fails, all the property of the partners, whether it pertains to the business or not, passes into the possession of the business when it is liquidated. Suppose, for instance, that Mr. A and Mr. B were equal partners in a business which failed with debts amounting to $50,000 and assets amounting to $20,000. Suppose that Mr. A's property outside the business amounted to $10,000 and Mr. B's amounted to $20,000. Then Mr. A would have to hand over all his property to satisfy the claims of the business, and Mr. B also would have to hand over all his property, in spite of the fact that their original shares were equal. In this case the creditors would not lose, for they would be able to draw upon not only the property of the

---

[1] This rule is by no means universal. The forms of the partnership are legion, for there is a wide choice in the terms of the contract which is drawn up. The above-mentioned form is, however, the simplest and most logical.

business itself but also the personal property of the partners. This feature is called "unlimited liability."

Intermediate Forms

In order to remedy these defects many forms of business organization have been tried. For instance, there are limited partnerships, in which the liability of some of the partners is limited to the share of capital which they hold. In this case if the business fails, the limited partners do not lose their personal property outside the business. The difficulties which arise because the partnership is merely an agreement between individuals are avoided in the form of organization known as the joint-stock company, in which the organization is permanent, management may be delegated by the owners to one or more directors, and the shares of ownership are transferable. In this case the organization exists apart from its owners, who may change, and the owners do not have to take any active part in the management. However, the joint-stock company may still have unlimited liability. In that case the shares of ownership involve the owners in responsibility for the debts of the company even up to the extent of their whole personal capital.

The Corporation

The most highly developed form of organization, and one which is perhaps most characteristic of the present time, is the corporation. The corporation is a joint-stock company with limited liability. In England it is usually called a "limited liability company." It is a "legal person," which exists, can buy, sell, own, borrow, or lend as an entity apart from the stockholders who own it. The debtors of a corporation can lay claim only to the property which belongs to the corporation as such. They cannot lay claim to the private property of the shareholders, except in some special cases.[2]

Although the stockholders theoretically own the corporation, as a group they seldom play an active part in the management of the organization. They elect a board of directors, each stockholder having a number of votes in proportion to the number of shares which he owns. To these directors the stockholders delegate the responsibility for the success or failure of the organization. The directors in their turn delegate the day-to-day management of the corporation to paid

[2] Some states provided for the "double liability" of stockholders in the case of banks, where the stockholders may be called upon for twice the value of their stock if the bank is liquidated.

managers and reserve to themselves only the right of decision on fundamental matters of policy.

The Corporation a Legal Concept

It should be remembered that the corporation is a *legal* rather than a strictly economic concept, and is as much a part of the political organization as of the economic organization of society. The corporation is in fact, if not in theory, one of the brood of smaller leviathans which cluster around the great leviathan of the state. That is to say, it is an instrument of local economic government, much as the county or town authorities are instruments of local political government. It is not, perhaps, far-fetched to draw an analogy between the relationships of corporations to the state today and the relationships of the feudal lords to the king in medieval times. The king granted certain rights and privileges to the barons because he could not otherwise administer his kingdom. The power of the barons in theory derived from the king, but in practice frequently the king was controlled by the barons. Similarly, the great corporations are the "barons" of modern life. Their privileges are in theory derived from the state. Again, however, in practice the "barons" may control the "king." Between the formal structure of political and legal relationships and the real structure of power and policy making there is usually little correspondence. Law is fiction; power is personal, though law is the framework within which power works.

Economic Consequences of the Corporation

The corporation, therefore, is not necessarily to be identified with any particular form of economic organization, such as "big business." It is true that the corporate form of organization is particularly appropriate for large-scale enterprises. It may be equally appropriate, however, in small-scale enterprises. Whenever men unite in an enterprise which they wish to keep in some measure separate from their other concerns, and in which they wish to be able to delegate responsibility, the corporate form is usually the most satisfactory. Nevertheless, the legal institution of incorporation has had important economic consequences. It has in particular permitted an enormous extension of specialized financial relationships, providing for almost every degree of risk or of ownership in which an investor might wish to indulge. The variety of corporation securities is almost inexhaustible, ranging from mortgage bonds, ordinary bonds, cumulative preference shares, ordinary preference shares, ordinary shares, even down to nonvoting ordinary shares. This variety has in itself elaborated the possibilities of fraud, for the financial structure of a corporation can become so complex that no investor, unless he is a financial genius, can find out what assets really correspond to the equity that he possesses.

The Pyramiding of Control. Another important consequence of the corporate form is the development of the "holding company" and the "pyramiding" of control. Because of the "dollar democracy" of the corporation (one share, one vote) any person or group who could control even 51 per cent of the voting stock could control the corporation. Suppose, for instance, that Corporation A had $1,000,000 in voting stock. Anyone who controlled $501,000 of this could control the corporation. Suppose now that a corporation (B) was floated, with a capital of, say, $501,000, for the purpose of holding stock in A. Anyone who held $251,000 of stock in B could control both B and A. Similarly, if another corporation (C) was formed to hold the stock of B, anyone who held $126,000 of stock in C would control both B and A. The corporate form, therefore, makes it relatively easy to build up vast industrial "empires" of control, such as the Insull empire, on a relatively small amount of actual ownership.

The Survival of Older Forms of Enterprise

It must not be thought that the older forms of enterprise have been superseded altogether by the newer forms. Although one type of enterprise may be dominant at one period of history and another at another period, examples of almost all previous forms can be found at any one time. In our day the independent craftsman, selling the product of his labor directly to the consumer and working with his own tools and equipment, still survives in the person of the village barber and the city shoeshiner. The domestic system still survives in many industries—in the clothing industry, for instance, where shirts are "put out" to be finished at home, or in the cattle-feeding industry where the stock are frequently owned by the dealer who buys and sells them. The small independent employer is to be found in most industries. In agriculture the independent farmer still predominates, and the small family "works" is still the mainstay of many a town. Nevertheless, it would be true to say that the dominant form of business organization in our day is the corporation.

The Cooperative Society

Through all these many forms of organization one principle holds: *profits,* the difference between the value of outputs and the value of inputs, belong to the owners of a business in proportion to the share which they own. This principle applies even to another form of busi-. ness organization—the cooperative society—which has risen into importance in the past hundred years and which may be of even greater importance in the future. A cooperative society is a business owned by the people who purchase from it, or who sell to it, in the proportion of the amount of their purchases or sales. In the case of a corporation the ultimate owners of the property of the corporation, and therefore of the profits which it makes, are stockholders—people who may not and usually do not buy from the corporation. A cooperative society may be defined as a corporation which is financed entirely by fixed-interest securities ("bonds") and in which the ownership resides in the people who buy from it or sell to it. Its profits, consequently, also belong to the people who buy from it or sell to it, in proportion to the amount which they have bought or sold. That is, profits are distributed in the form of a "rebate" or "dividend" given to each member in a fixed proportion not of the capital stock which he owns but of the purchases or sales which he has made.

The Consumers' Cooperative

A consumers' cooperative is a retailing business, purchasing inputs in the form of wholesale goods, of the labor of storekeepers and managers, of the services of stores, and so on; selling outputs in the form of commodities to consumers across the counter. Its profits belong in the first instance to the business as such, just as in the case of the corporation—i.e., any addition to the net value of the property of the business is profit. These profits, however, must at some time be distributed among the members. Whereas in the case of the corporation the profits are distributed among the owners according to the proportion of the capital stock which each owns, in the case of the cooperative the profits are distributed among the members in proportion to the amount of purchases which they have made. There are also marketing cooperatives, especially in agriculture, which are distributing businesses buying products from the farmers, often processing them in some way, and selling them again to other merchants or to consumers.

Factors in Its Success. The consumers' cooperative has been a very successful form of business organization in Europe, rather less so in the United States. There is nothing inherently superior about the cooperative as a form of organization. Under certain circumstances, and in certain fields, it seems to be superior to other forms; in other circumstances and other fields it is not. The success of the cooperative form of organization in the retail field in Europe is due to a number of causes, some of which were peculiar to the times, others of which are more fundamental. Thus the consumers' cooperative movement in Europe came at a time when considerable economies were possible in the large-scale organization of retailing; the movement seized these economies and consequently made large profits. Part of the profits it used for paying dividends to its members; part were used to finance its expansion. The success of the cooperatives in Europe also seems to be due in part to the class structure of most European countries. The more rigid the class structure of society, the more difficult it is for a man with ability who originates in the working class to attain a managerial position. There may then be a large untapped reservoir of managerial ability among the working classes. The cooperative movement is frequently able to tap this ability, and consequently to obtain its managers at very low wages.

The Divorce of Ownership from Management

In any business the ultimate control of policy is supposed to lie with the owners, for it is their property which is being handled and their money which is being spent. Nevertheless, in those forms of business in which ownership is separated from management the danger always exists that the management will wrest the real control of the business from the owners. Even in such a simple form as the partnership it is possible for an active and unscrupulous partner to run the business for his own ends, while his "sleeping partner" sleeps on unaware. In the case of the great corporations the stockholders are almost inevitably "sleeping partners." There is a form of election of directors by the stockholders, but the latter are frequently ignorant of the details of the business, and the real control of the corporation passes into the hands of a small clique. This is not to say that the management of corporations is necessarily corrupt or not in the stockholders' interests. It does mean, however, that once an owner relinquishes the management of what he owns, he also relinquishes his control and takes an unavoidable risk of bad or corrupt management. The unjust steward is a risk that anyone must take who yields his property to stewardship.

Exists Even in Cooperatives. The same difficulty arises also in connection with cooperative societies. In the case of consumers' cooperatives the members, being the owners of the profit, elect the directors just as the stockholders elect the directors in a corporation.

Where the number of members is large, the knowledge that each member can have about the affairs of the society is slight, and the control which the membership exercises over the management is inevitably weakened. The danger of corrupt management is probably less in a cooperative society than in a corporation, for the opportunities for personal profit are less. However, the danger of inefficient management is a real one, as many cooperative societies have found to their cost.

The Planned Economy

All the forms of business organization which we have described grow up in a free society, i.e., a society in which it is not illegal for private individuals or groups to buy and sell and make profits. There is, however, an alternative way of organizing economic life. This is the "planned economy," or the communist[3] state. In this society the state takes over the property of the whole community (barring a few unimportant items of personal property like clothes, toothbrushes, etc.). The private possession of property outside minor personal items is prohibited. Hence the state becomes the sole "employer," in the sense in which we have used the term, the sole stockholder in all corporations, and the sole owner of the assets of the cooperatives. That is to say, if the state represents the people in it on an equal basis, every member of a society possesses an equal share in the property of that society. We can think of the communist state as if it were a gigantic corporation, owning all the property of the society, employing all the people of the society, and in turn being owned (theoretically) by all the people of the society, each having an equal share.

Is Profit Wicked?

In such a society would profit cease to exist? Some Communists have thought so and indeed, one of the arguments advanced in favor of the communist state is that profit-making is wicked, and the mere ownership of property ought not to entitle the owner to an income for which he apparently does nothing. The discussion of this proposition

[3] I have used the stronger term "communist" rather than the milder and more general term "socialist" in order to distinguish those regimes as "communist" which deny *in principle* the right of private property in the means of production from those regimes which sometimes call themselves "socialist" but which are essentially social-democratic, using the apparatus of the state to redistribute income, to provide social security, and even to control key industries, but which do not advocate the abolition of all private property. Unfortunately the term "communism" has come to have a very specific meaning in our society as that form of organization dominant in Soviet Russia. It should be understood that I use the term in a more general sense to mean any society organized as a "one-firm state" in the ostensible interest of the working class.

is so important historically that we may well digress a little to examine it.

Marxism

The view that profit is unrighteous has a long history. Its most important exponent, however, was Karl Marx, and it is with his view that we shall deal now. It was not merely excess profit, or monopoly profit, that Marx denounced, but *all* profit. Using our terminology, he would say that the mere ownership of goods, the mere act of buying input and selling output, should not entitle anyone to an income. In support of this view he drew upon a theory of value which owes its origin to Adam Smith and Ricardo—the labor theory of value. This theory says that in a state of equilibrium things exchange in proportion to the quantity of labor which has gone to make them. "If among a nation of hunters, for example, it usually costs twice the labor to kill a beaver which it does to kill a deer, one beaver should naturally exchange for two deer."[4] In its modern form it states that things exchange in proportion to their costs of production; we shall examine this theory later. In the hands of Karl Marx it underwent a subtle transformation. To reduce it to the simplest language possible, it became the theory that as labor created all things which have value, labor (i.e., the working class) ought to possess all things which have value, and therefore the whole product of economic life should go to the working class.

Exploitation and Surplus Value

The appeal of this doctrine is obvious and helps to explain how such a book as Karl Marx's *Das Kapital,* probably the least intelligible book on an economic subject ever perpetrated, came to have influence so wide as to become the Bible of a quarter of the inhabited globe. The worker sees the houses, the factories, the machines which belong to the capitalists, and says to himself, "I and my kind made these, but he owns them; why?" He looks at the total social income of goods and services and says to himself, "I and my kind made these; yet I and my kind get only part of them; part goes to the people who own these instruments which I also have made. Why?" The worker in effect says to the owner of property, "You eat the bread which I have baked, and drink the wine which I have pressed, and you sleep on silk which I have woven. What have you given me in return?" And Marx would answer, "Nothing." That is to say, the income of the owners of prop-

---

[4] Adam Smith, *Wealth of Nations,* Book 1, Chapter 6.

erty is "surplus value" which has been obtained by exploitation of the workers. It is income, so to speak, which has been taken from the workers by a kind of force or fraud, because of the superior bargaining power of the employers who own the implements without which the worker cannot work.

Profit Would Not Disappear in a Communist State

The answer to this situation, say the Communists, is to make the state the sole employer and the sole property owner, for then and only then will the workers as a class receive the whole of what they produce. Without going into the rights and wrongs of this argument, let us now consider whether the institution of profit, as an economic quantity, would disappear in a communist society. Clearly, profit would disappear in the sense of a private income, for there would be no private property. Nevertheless, it would still have to be *calculated* in each industry, if the state wished to use its resources in the best possible way. The state, like any other corporation, would be faced with the problem of putting its resources to the best possible use. It would have to decide how big each industry should be. It would have to decide what kinds of things to make. In other words, as the employer, it would have to decide *what* people should be employed and what things should be created by them.

Labor by itself is an amorphous mass which does not create anything; it must be organized into a process of production, and the person or institution which takes the final responsibility for the way in which labor is employed is the one who owns the goods that labor produces. It is the owner of property—whether a private individual, corporation, or state—who has to decide what form that property shall take, whether it shall be in the form of beehives or bananas. This is a very necessary and positive function which must be performed by somebody. In a free capitalist society the responsibility for its performance rests with the owners of private capital. They may evade or shift this responsibility, but in that case they cannot complain if they lose their property, either through depressions or through confiscation.

Communist Accounting

In a communist society the responsibility lies with the state, but the principles which the state ought to follow in fulfilling it are essentially the same as the principles which should be followed under private capitalism. If a communist state is to run itself intelligently it *must* have some system of accounting in terms of a standard unit of value (dollars); it *must* have some way of discovering the relative profitability, to society, of all the multitudinous forms of industry which it commands. And it must be able to transfer resources, by economic or other forms of pressure, from industries which are unprofitable to industries which are profitable. This is the task which should fall upon the shoulders of private capital in a free society. Thus, the argument of the Marxist from the labor theory of value is fallacious. It is not true that values, it is not even true that things, are created by labor and by labor alone. Labor must be organized in a process of production to produce things, and it must be organized in the production of *the right things*—i.e., things which are wanted—if these things are to have value. It is production of the right things which is or should be the contribution of capital and of the profit system.

The Communist Controversy

The economist as such cannot make a final resolution of the great controversy of our age between the communist and the capitalist societies, for the controversy involves much more than economics, and stems indeed from wide differences in basic philosophy. Nevertheless economics can help to point out what the dispute is *about*. It is not a dispute about whether certain functions exist in society; about whether capital is "barren" or "productive"; about whether profit is a payment for services rendered to society or is merely stolen from the workers. It is a dispute about how a certain function ought to be performed—the function which is implied in the ownership of property, the function of the employment of factors of production. Until this is understood the argument will be utterly barren.

QUESTIONS AND EXERCISES

1. Cooperatives are often defended on the grounds that they are "nonprofit-making" institutions. Criticize this argument.
2. Explain carefully the differences between a communist society and a capitalist society.
3. "What we think about communism will depend more on our political views than on our economic views." Discuss.
4. If exchange is recorded as an exchange of equal values—i.e., the value of the thing given up being equal to the value of the thing received—how can pure exchange ever give rise to profit?
5. Consider the truth of the following statement: "Profit in the true sense of the word cannot exist unless the operations of business result in the increase in the value of property."

6. "The main clue to the interpretation of economic history is the growth of specialization." Discuss and illustrate.

7. A and B are equal partners in the ownership of a business. In one year the cash receipts are $50,000, the cash outlays $30,000. The total value of the business at the beginning of the year was $100,000, and at the end of the year it was $99,000. Partner A performs the services of management, valued at $5000 per year. Partner B is a "sleeping partner" as far as management is concerned, but he owns the shop in which the business operates. The rent of the shop is $10,000 a year. What will be the total incomes received by each partner out of the business? What rate of profit will each earn on his capital invested in the business?

8. Suppose the above business is a cooperative store, renting the shop and hiring the manager. Keeping the figures as in Exercise 7, suppose further that $40,000 of the total cash receipts are received from members in payment for goods received, and $10,000 are received from nonmembers. What rate of dividend per dollar of purchases would the store be able to pay? What amount of dividend would a member receive who spent $100 at the store in the course of the year?

CHAPTER 25

GENERAL PRINCIPLES OF THE MARGINAL ANALYSIS: TRANSFORMATION FUNCTIONS

Perhaps the most important single instrument of analysis of the individual economic organism, whether firm or household, is the marginal analysis. Most of the remainder of this work will be devoted to developing the ramifications of this analysis, so that it will be advisable at this point to consider what it is that we are going to do, especially as there is a good deal of misunderstanding of the purposes and limitations of the marginal analysis even among economists.

Transformations and Revaluations

We have already defined the economic organism as a *process of production*. We can now widen the concept somewhat and regard the essential processes involved as processes of *transformation*. Suppose we think first of all of the economic organism as defined by a balance sheet, consisting of a number of items of assets and liabilities—cash, goods, debts, etc., as in Chapter 14. Then the processes which the organism undertakes can all be described in terms either of *transformations* of one balance sheet item into another, in terms of *consumption*—i.e., the simple disappearance of some quantity from the balance sheet—or in terms of *revaluation* in which some item in the physical balance sheet is given a new value in terms of the unit of account (for example, a new dollar value). Revaluation, that is, is a change in a valuation coefficient.

Market and Production Transformations

The principal types of transformations are *market* transformations, or exchanges, and *production* transformations. In the market transformation something is given by one organism to another in return for something else. Thus when a firm makes a sale of butter to a household the firm diminishes its butter stock and increases its money stock, the household increases its butter stock and diminishes its money stock—all this, of course, as of the moment of sale. The transaction would be reflected in the firm's physical balance sheet as a decrease in the butter item and an increase in the money item. Similarly a purchase, say of milk, by the same firm would be expressed as a rise in the milk stock and a decline in the money stock. Most market transformations involve money as one of the items, though exchanges of goods for goods (barter) are occasionally found, and exchanges of goods for debt are common. Thus when goods are sold on credit the transformation consists of a decline in the goods stock and a rise in accounts receivable, not in cash. When debts are paid back the transformation consists of a rise in the money stock of the creditor and a decline in accounts receivable.

It is important to observe the difference between transactions merely involving exchange and those which involve the creation and destruction of credit or debt. When goods are bought and sold for cash there is an increase in the buyer's goods stock just equal to the diminution of the seller's goods stock, and a diminution in the buyer's money stock just equal to the increase in the seller's money stock. Thus suppose 100 bushels of wheat are sold for $200: the buyer's wheat stock rises and the seller's wheat stock falls by 100 bushels; the buyer's money stock falls and the seller's rises by $200. What has happened is a redistribution of the total stock of assets, both wheat and money, among the various parties. When, however, goods are sold for credit, the seller loses goods and gains accounts receivable; the buyer gains goods and also "gains" an item on the negative side of the balance sheet, an account payable. Thus if 100 bushels of wheat are sold on credit for $200, in the seller's balance sheet this is recorded as a decline in wheat and a rise in accounts receivable, with no change in his total assets; but in the buyer's balance sheet this is recorded as a rise in wheat on his assets side and a rise in accounts payable on his liabilities side, both his assets and his liabilities rising by $200. In this case there is not merely a redistribution of existing assets but the creation of new assets, the account receivable (or payable), though there is not any creation of net worth.

"Cost" in Production Transformations

Production transformations consist in the loss of assets which are used up in processes of production and the corresponding gain in the assets produced. Thus suppose a cheese factory produces 100 tons of cheese. There will be an addition to its assets of the 100 tons of cheese produced. There will also, however, be various subtractions from its assets as a result of the process of production. There will be a decline in milk and other raw materials. There will be a decline in money stocks, as money has been paid out in wages to workers. There will probably be a decline in machinery and equipment as a result of wear and tear. Under some circumstances, or for some purposes, as we shall see later, we may wish to include certain interest or profit charges. The whole list of such subtractions may be called the total *physical* cost of the 100 tons of cheese. If now we reduce this list to a sum of dollars or other unit of account by multiplying each item by a valuation coefficient and adding, the result is the *total cost* of the cheese.

Profit as an Increase in Net Worth Through Revaluation

In ordinary accounting practice the cheese would be valued at its total cost until it is sold. If now it is sold for more than its total cost, there is a *profit* or net revenue. The exchange transformation consists of a diminution in cheese stocks and an increase in money stocks. Suppose now that the total cost of the cheese was $500, and that the cheese is sold for $600. The cheese stock diminishes by a value of $500, but the money stock (or perhaps the accounts receivable) increases by $600. In this transaction there is clearly an increase in net worth—that is, in the sum of asset values, positive and negative—of $100. It is this increase in net worth which constitutes "profit." We can think of it either as consisting in a revaluation of the cheese at the moment of sale from $500 to $600, or as an exchange in which the value of what is received is greater than the value of what is given up. The former is perhaps the more accurate way of looking at the event, especially from the point of view of the whole economy, because in the accounts of the *buyer* the transaction will be recorded as a simple exchange of $600 in cash for $600 worth of cheese. We can therefore keep to the convention that exchange is always of equal values if we suppose that the sale of the cheese actually consists of two events—a revaluation and a subsequent exchange.

Asset Consumption: Fixed Costs and Dividends

The other type of "event" in the history of an economic organism, which we have called "consumption," also deserves some illustration and further comment. There are two principal forms of asset consumption as distinct from transformation. The first consists of items of asset diminution or cost which cannot easily be assigned to any *specific* output, production, or asset increase. The depreciation of machinery, for instance, frequently takes place even when the machine is idle, and, indeed, may even take place more rapidly when the machine is idle than when it is working. Items such as rent and interest also frequently are independent of any specific quantity of output, and would involve deductions from assets even if no output at all were produced. These are the items which the accountant calls "overhead" or "oncost." In economic terminology their total value is generally called "fixed cost"—fixed cost being that total cost which is independent of the amount of output produced. It should also be observed, however, that in their effect on the balance sheet of the firm, distributions of profit in dividends have exactly the same effect as fixed cost items. If a dividend of, say, $100,000 is paid to stockholders, the result on the balance sheet is a $100,000 diminution of cash on the assets side and an equal diminution in net worth on the other side. The same would be true for, say, a $100,000 item representing depreciation of plant and equipment. The problem of how and for what purposes we wish to include either dividends or profit earnings in "cost" is a difficult one, and one to which we will return.

Transformation Functions

We have now defined the economic organism by its balance-sheet variables and observed the various types of transactions in which it can engage. It should be observed that so far the theory applies just as well to households as it does to firms, with the proviso that there may be more difficult problems of measurement in the case of the household because of its more rough-and-ready accounting methods. The next step in the analysis is to define the *transformation functions,* sometimes called opportunity functions, which define the *attainable* positions to which a firm can move in the structure of its assets, liabilities, or other relevant variables. The list of values of all relevant variables as of any moment we call its "position."[1] It can generally move to other positions, but not to all conceivable positions. Some positions, that is to say, are attainable and some are unattainable in view of the present environment of the firm. The transformation functions define the boundary between the attainable set of positions—i.e., those which

---

[1] When there are only two variables a "position" can be represented by a point in a plane figure with the two variables measured on the axes. A position involving three variables can be represented by a point in a three-dimensional diagram related to three axes measuring the three variables. Similarly a position involving n variables can be thought of as a point in n-space, each variable being measured along one of the n directions.

can be obtained within the limitations of the present environment—and the unattainable set of positions which cannot be obtained unless the environment changes.

Like transformations themselves, transformation functions are of two kinds—market functions and production or cost functions. The market functions show those positions which can be reached by exchange with other economic organisms. The production and cost functions show those positions which can be reached by internal transformations, e.g., of raw materials into finished goods.

The market transformation functions are of three kinds—"perfect," "imperfect," and "pluperfect." A "perfect market" means that the rate of exchange or price does not change no matter how great the *quantity* of assets exchanged. In an "imperfect market" the rate of exchange, the price, or the "terms of trade" in some sense *worsen* for the organism as the quantity exchanged becomes larger. The case of the "pluperfect" market is rarer, but is sometimes found, in which the rate of exchange or the terms of trade in some sense improves or becomes more favorable to the organism as the quantity exchanged becomes larger.

Exchange Opportunities: Perfect Markets

These concepts are illustrated in Table 46. Here we suppose that we are dealing with the firm in its simplest possible form—a pure exchanger, or speculator, who holds nothing but money and one commodity, say, wheat. We suppose that at a certain moment he owns $400 of money and 600 bushels of wheat. The question is what other combinations of wheat and money are open to him; this clearly depends on the nature of the exchange opportunities, or "markets," which face him. In Table 46 we show the possibilities if he has a "perfect market" at a price of $2 per bushel. This means that he can buy or sell as much wheat as he wants, always at a price of $2 per bushel. Given the price of wheat and the amount bought or sold in items 1 and 2 of the table, we can calculate the money value of the wheat bought and sold and hence the amount of money given up or acquired for each quantity of wheat bought or sold. This is often called the "total revenue" and is shown in item 3, obtained by multiplying each quantity of wheat bought or sold by the price and reversing the sign. Then for each quantity of wheat bought or sold we can find the wheat stock by adding purchases or subtracting sales from the initial stock assumed (600 bushels); thus the purchase of 100 bushels of wheat raises the wheat stock to 700 bushels (item 4). Then for each quantity of wheat bought

Table 46. Exchange Opportunities Under Perfect Markets

1. Wheat sold (−) or bought (+) (bu.)	+400	+300	+200	+100	0	−100	−200	−300	−400	−500	−600
2. Price of wheat ($)	2.00	2.00	2.00	2.00	2.00	2.00	2.00	2.00	2.00	2.00	2.00
3. Money bought (+) or sold (−) ($)	−800	−600	−400	−200	0	+200	+400	+600	+800	+1000	+1200
4. Wheat stock (bu.)	1000	900	800	700	600	500	400	300	200	100	0
5. Money stock ($)	−400	−200	0	200	400	600	800	1000	1200	1400	1600

Table 47. Exchange Opportunities Under Imperfect Markets

1. Wheat sold (−) or bought (+) (bu.)	+400	+300	+200	+100	0	−100	−200	−300	−400	−500	−600
2. Price of wheat ($)	2.40	2.30	2.20	2.10	2.00	1.90	1.80	1.70	1.60	1.50	1.40
3. Money bought (+) or sold (−) ($)	−960	−690	−440	−210	0	+190	+360	+510	+640	+750	+840
4. Wheat stock (bu.)	1000	900	800	700	600	500	400	300	200	100	0
5. Money stock ($)	−560	−290	−40	190	400	590	760	910	1040	1150	1240

Table 48. Exchange Opportunities Under Pluperfect Markets

1. Wheat sold (−) or bought (+) (bu.)	+400	+300	+200	+100	0	−100	−200	−300	−400	−500	−600
2. Price of wheat ($)	1.60	1.70	1.80	1.90	2.00	2.10	2.20	2.30	2.40	2.50	2.60
3. Money bought (+) or sold (−) ($)	−640	−510	−360	−190	0	+210	+440	+690	+960	+1250	+1560
4. Wheat stock (bu.)	1000	900	800	700	600	500	400	300	200	100	0
5. Money stock ($)	−240	−110	40	210	400	610	840	1090	1360	1650	1960

or sold we can also find the money stock by adding acquisitions to or subtracting disbursements from the initial stock of 400. Thus after 100 bushels of wheat have been bought, $200 of money has been given up, and the stock is 400 − 200 or $200. This gives us item 5.

Imperfect Markets

Now under *imperfect* markets we suppose that the more wheat is purchased, the *higher* the price which the purchaser has to pay and the more wheat is sold, the *lower* the price which the seller has to accept. This fulfills the condition of "worsening" of the market environment as the organism moves away from its initial position, since higher purchase prices and lower sales prices are less favorable to the organism than lower purchase or higher sales prices. This is shown in Table 47, where the items have the same meaning, and are derived in exactly the same way as in Table 46; but we assume that instead of a constant price for all volumes of sales or purchases, the price rises with the volume of purchases and falls with the volume of sales, as in item 2.

"Pluperfect" Markets

Under "pluperfect" markets the more wheat is purchased, the lower the price which the buyer has to pay and the more wheat is sold, the higher the price which the buyer receives. This fulfills the assumption that conditions become more favorable as movement takes place. This case is shown in Table 48. The negative values of the money stock here mean that the marketer is borrowing money, the negative values appearing as liabilities (debts) in his balance sheet. Similarly, we could extend the table to show negative values for wheat, if the marketer can "borrow wheat"—i.e., increase his money stock beyond his net worth by selling wheat futures. It is unlikely, of course, that perfection in the market would be maintained at these negative values, if only for the reason that some "worsening" of the market in the form of interest payments is to be expected.

Graphic Illustration. The graphic illustration of these principles is shown in Fig. 74, which reproduces the data of Tables 46 to 48. Thus in 1A we show the transformation function with a perfect market (constant price), $P_m P_0 P_w$. Money stock is measured on the vertical axis, wheat stock in bushels on the horizontal. P_0 is the initial position of the firm ($400 and 600 bushels). From P_0 the firm can move toward P_m (and beyond) by selling wheat and acquiring money, or can move toward P_w (and beyond) by buying wheat and disbursing money. The line $P_m P_w$ corresponds to items 4 and 5 of Table 46. We observe that it is a straight line as long as the price is constant, for every unit gain or loss of wheat is obtained with an equal loss or gain of money. The slope of the line $P_m P_w$ is the price of wheat, or the ratio of exchange. Fig. 1B shows the corresponding sales-purchase curve (SNP) (items 1 and 2 of the table), which indicates the price at which each quantity of sales or purchases can be made. In the case of perfect mar-

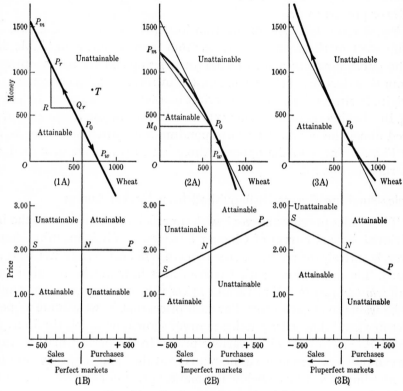

Fig. 74.   Exchange Opportunities.

kets the sales-purchase curve is a straight line parallel to the quantity axis, indicating that no matter what the quantity purchased or sold the price is the same. In this figure the origin O corresponds to the initial point P_0 in Fig. 1A: sales are measured to the left, purchases to the right, of the origin to correspond to the positions in Fig. 1A.

Imperfect markets are shown in Figs. 2A and 2B in a corresponding way. Then $P_m P_0 P_w$ is the transformation curve, plotted from items 4 and 5 of Table 47. It will be observed that in this case the curve bends back from the perfect markets curve into a shape concave to the origin, illustrating the "worsening" of the position with increase in the volume of either sales or purchases. The price or ratio of exchange at any point—e.g., P_m—is the slope of the line joining the point to the point P_0. Thus the price at P_m is M_0P_m/M_0P_0. Fig. 2B shows the sales-purchase curve, SNP. This is now no longer horizontal but is sloped, indicating that price is lower at larger volumes of sales and higher at larger volumes of purchases. In most actual markets, of course, the curve is likely to exhibit a certain discontinuity at the point of zero sales or purchases, N.

Fig. 3A similarly shows the transformation curve for the case of pluperfect markets, and is derived from items 4 and 5 in Table 48. The curve now has a steadily increasing slope as we move upward from P_0, a decreasing slope as we move downward, and is convex to the origin. It always lies above the perfect market line, except at the point P_0, illustrating that the market gets more favorable the further we proceed along the curve. The corresponding sales-purchase curve, SNP, in Fig. 3B slopes in the opposite direction to the curve of imperfect markets in Fig. 2B.

Sales-Purchase Curves Distinguished from Market Curves

These sales-purchase curves have a superficial resemblance to the individual market curves of Chapter 5, page 51. Their meaning, however, is entirely different, and the two kinds of curves must not be confused. The individual market curve shows how much an individual will *want to* buy or sell at various prices if he can buy or sell as much as he wants to at each price. For each price, that is, we assume a "perfect market." The sales-purchase curves show how much the individual is *able* to buy or sell at various prices. In the perfect markets case he can buy or sell as much as he wants to at the "market price," but he cannot buy at any price below the market price nor can he sell at any price above the market price.

Transformation Curves as "Attainability Boundaries"

We can see now how the transformation curves or functions constitute "boundaries" between attainable and unattainable positions. Thus in Fig. 1A the firm is able to reach any position downward and to the left of the transformation line P_mP_w by exchange or by combinations of exchange and "consumption" (throwing away, giving away, or distributing assets "outside" the firm). Thus we could move from P_0 to the position R by exchanging to the point Q_r and then giving away Q_rR of wheat, or by exchanging to the point P_r and giving away P_rR money, or by moving by exchange to any point between Q_r

and P_r and giving away the appropriate quantities of money and wheat. Under no circumstances, however, starting from the point P_0 and with a market transformation curve $P_m P_0 P_w$, could the firm get to the position represented by, say, the point T. All positions downward and to the left of the line $P_m P_w$, therefore, are attainable; all positions upward and to the right of the same line are unattainable. Similarly the corresponding market transformation functions in Figs. 2A and 3A separate the area (or "set") of attainable positions from the set of unattainable positions. The sales-purchase curves likewise can be interpreted as attainability boundaries, as we see in Figs. 1B, 2B, and 3B; though in this case the attainable is below the boundary on the sales side and above the boundary on the purchase side, with the vertical axis itself also forming an attainability boundary.

Production and Cost Functions

Corresponding to production transformations we have production transformation functions, generally called "production functions." These are the boundaries which define the possible combinations of inputs and outputs, and we will return to their study in a later chapter. Meanwhile we will go straight to the consideration of the *cost functions* which are derived from the production functions by a process of summing the *values* of the input quantities used or assets consumed in the production of various quantities of output.

Special Meaning of "Cost"

The word "cost" has a special meaning in economics, which must be emphasized if the student is to understand economists as well as economics. In the business world itself the meaning of "cost" is rather loose. In the case of a small private business it is frequently used to denote the mere cash outlays. A small shopkeeper may regard all the income which he gets out of his shop as an excess of revenue over cost, although much of this income is really a "virtual" payment for an input, as we have seen. In accounting practice, also, the meaning of "cost" is not perfectly definite. The general custom is to include in the total cost of any given quantity of product the value of all physical input—both goods and services—which are employed in the process. That is, "cost" in accounting usually means the sum total of the payments, actual or virtual, for the inputs used in the process. This sum we shall call the *total outlay*. In accounting practice "cost" does not usually include *interest,* or *profit* payments. There is considerable controversy on this point, much of which is mere disputing about names. Probably the best rule which can be deduced from accounting practice is that interest or profit is counted as a cost only when the accountant is quite certain of its amount. As such happy certainty is rare, we can say that with some exceptions "cost" for the accountant means what we have called "outlay."

For the Economist "Total Cost" Includes "Normal Profit"

When the economist refers to the "total cost" of producing a given quantity of product, however, he does not refer merely to the sum of the value of inputs used. Total cost for the economist is equal to the value of inputs used *plus* the normal profit or interest which the capitalist expects to receive. There are excellent reasons for inventing such a concept, as we shall realize later. It is perhaps unfortunate that it bears the ambiguous name of "cost," but as we have a good word, "outlay," to denote the total value of inputs, we shall commandeer the word "cost" for our own purposes.

"Total Revenue" and "Actual Profit"

Some more definitions here will prepare the way for further discussion. By "total revenue" in a process we mean the total value of the outputs (whether sold or used by the producer) which are produced by the process. The total revenue, that is to say, is a sum of dollars, like the total outlay and the total cost. The difference between the total revenue and the total outlay we shall call the "actual profit." It is this sum which accrues to the capitalist as a result of the use of his capital in the process. The relations between these various concepts can perhaps be clarified by a system of equations:

$$\text{Total revenue} - \text{total outlay} = \text{actual profit}$$
$$\text{Total outlay} + \text{normal profit} = \text{total cost}$$

Therefore:

$$\text{Total revenue} - \text{total cost} = \text{actual profit} - \text{normal profit}$$
$$= \text{net revenue} \qquad (1)$$

The difference between the actual profit and the normal profit is called the "net revenue." It might perhaps better be termed "extraordinary profit." When the net revenue is zero, the actual profit is equal to the normal profit—i.e., the process is just normally profitable. When the net revenue is positive, the process is abnormally profitable. When the net revenue is negative, the process is abnormally unprofitable.

The Significance of "Normal Profit"

The question now arises, What is meant by "normal profit"? It can best be defined as the least sum which must be paid to the capitalist to persuade him to allow his capital to be used in the process. As we saw in Chapter 24, the capitalist, the owner of the valuable things in which a process is embodied, is the person ultimately responsible for the employment of inputs. Consequently, the fate of a process depends mainly on the decisions of the capitalist. If the actual profit in a process is so small that the capitalist does not feel it to be worth continuing, then it will not be continued. The ultimate fate of a process, therefore, depends on whether it can maintain its total cost at a level equal to or less than its total revenue. Any process with a total revenue persistently smaller than its total cost is doomed, if it already exists; and if it does not exist, it will probably never be born except through faulty calculation.

Normal Profit Depends on the Type of Capital

What, now, determines the normal profit in a process? The answer is that the normal profit is equal to what the capitalist could get with his capital if he used it in some other way, less an allowance for the difficulties and trouble of transferring it, and plus or minus allowances for any "nonmonetary advantages" of the type described in Chapter 10. The normal profit in a given process depends, therefore, on how far the capital can be transferred to another process, as well as on the opportunities for investment outside the process. In some processes capital can be transferred easily. If the goods in which the capital is embodied are readily salable, as they usually are, for instance, in retail trade, the capitalist can easily exchange them for some other kind of goods, usually, or course, by selling them for money and exchanging the money for the other more profitable goods. Thus, if a department store finds that one department is not paying its way, it can easily replace the unprofitable goods by more profitable goods. Where capital is "liquid," then, or easily transferable, the "normal" rate of profit in any one process will be about equal to the rate in other processes of a similar kind. But if the capital is embodied in goods which cannot be sold and which have a long life, the rate of profit in such enterprises may sink far below the general level before the capitalist will cease to operate the process. It is better to get little than to get nothing; and in some enterprises the capital, once invested, cannot be transferred to another enterprise, however profitable. The owner of a railroad, for instance, will continue to operate it for a considerable period of time at very small rates of profit, simply because he cannot turn his railroad into a nylon mill or other profitable enterprise.

Long and Short Runs

The distinction between processes from which capital can be easily transferred and processes in which capital is immobile is the basis for an important distinction between "short-run" and "long-run" effects. During a relatively short period of time, say, a year, only a small profit is necessary to induce the owner of immobile capital to use his capital in a given process. The owner of a railroad will continue to operate it for a short time even if the sum of profit returned to him is almost nothing, for he cannot use his rails and rolling stock in any other way, nor can he sell them or liquidate them at all except by using them. If, however, a man is considering building a railroad and using it over a period of thirty years, then the expected profit in such an enterprise must be at least equal to what is made in alternative processes. A capitalist will not put his money into a railroad which he expects will earn 6 per cent per annum if he can put his money into something else which will earn 8 per cent per annum and which has the same nonmonetary advantages.

In defining total cost, therefore, we must always have reference to a specific period of time. The shorter the period of time considered, and the less mobile the capital in the process, the less will be the "normal profit" as we have defined it, and therefore the less will be the "total cost."[2]

Total Cost as Determined by Alternatives

We must think of total cost, therefore, first in relation to a specific period of time, second in relation to a specific output. We have seen that the "profit" part of total cost is determined by the returns in alternative uses of capital. It is equally true, though not perhaps so apparent, that the "outlay" part of total cost is also determined by the returns to factors of production in alternative employments. In calculating the total outlay the quantity of each input used is multiplied by its price. The price of each input, however, must be equal to the price which it can receive in other occupations, subject to con-

[2] The term "normal profit" is sometimes used to mean that profit sufficient to keep capital in an enterprise over a period long enough to insure that all the capital of the enterprise is mobile. In many problems, however, this period of time is too long to be particularly significant. In view of the necessity for specifying a period of time in each problem considered, it has been thought best not to confine the term "normal profit" to the extreme case of the long run.

siderations of mobility and nonmonetary advantages studied in Chapter 10. We must think of the total cost of producing a definite quantity of a commodity—say, a million gallons of milk—in a given time—say, six months—as the least sum which will keep all the necessary factors of production, and all the necessary capital, in the milk industry. This sum depends on the profitability of *alternative* occupations. Thus, conditions in one industry affect the total costs of other industries. If milk production becomes unusually profitable in a given area, this will raise the total cost of production of sheep, not only because the unusual profitability of milk production will raise rents and wages but also because sheep producers will not be content with a low rate of return on their own labor and capital if they can get a higher rate of return in milk production.

Cost as Supply Price

We now see more clearly why the economist needs a "total cost" concept which includes "normal profit." The concept of cost which is of most interest to the economist is that which is equivalent to the concept of "supply price"—that price or total value which is just sufficient to attract resources into the production of a specified quantity of a product. The supply price of a given quantity must be that price which is sufficient to attract capital into the occupation as well as other factors. It must therefore be larger than the price which would merely yield enough to cover the value of the inputs by an amount sufficient to cover "normal profit."

Ambiguity of the Word "Cost"

We must now provide ourselves with more cost concepts. Much confusion arises in thinking about cost if we do not realize that the expression "cost of production" is extremely ambiguous, even in ordinary speech. We have already examined some of the difficulties inherent in the definition of the total cost of producing a specified quantity of goods. "Cost of production," however, frequently means not a sum of dollars, such as the total cost, but the *cost per unit*.

Even in the definition of the cost per unit there is ambiguity. Suppose we are asked how much it costs to run our automobile. We might answer first, "$500 a year." Such an answer would not satisfy an eager inquirer, however, for he would want to know how many miles we ran in a year. Obviously, an automobile which runs 10,000 miles for $500 "costs less" in some sense than one which runs 5000 miles for the same amount. If we run 10,000 miles for $500, the "cost per mile" is then 5 cents. Still our inquirer is not satisfied. What do we include in the $500? Gas and oil? Of course. Repairs? Yes. Taxes, insurance? Yes. Wear and tear of tires? Depreciation? Perhaps. Interest on our capital invested? We have seen how to answer these questions in calculating the total cost.

But, our interrogator goes on. "Do you mean," he asks, "that it costs you a dollar every time you take the car out for twenty miles?" Well, no; some of these costs included in our total cost would have to be paid even if we did not take the car out at all. Taxes and insurance, for instance, some depreciation, and garage rent. When we take the car out for twenty miles, then, we perhaps should only include the charges for gas and oil, and some depreciation of tires and chassis—perhaps 40 cents in all. "Then running the car costs only 2 cents per mile?" Yes. "But a while ago you said it costs 5 cents a mile." It is evident that there is some further ambiguity here about the idea of "cost." Perhaps, therefore, it will be necessary to make some clear definitions.

Some Definitions

The *total cost* of producing a given output has already been defined. The total cost is usually divided into two parts, one called the *total fixed cost,* and the other the *total variable cost.* The total fixed cost is that part of the total cost which would be incurred even if no output were produced. The total variable cost is that part of the total cost which depends on the output. In our illustration of the car which cost $500 for 10,000 miles, part of this $500 would have been incurred, assuming that we have the car, even if the car is never taken from its garage. Taxes, garage rent, some insurance, some depreciation due to obsolescence, and so on, may amount, let us say, to $300. This is the total fixed cost. The other $200 for gas, oil, repairs, running depreciation, etc., is the total variable cost. We have, therefore

$$\text{Total cost} = \text{total fixed cost} + \text{total variable cost.} \qquad (2)$$

The *average total cost* is the total cost divided by the output to which the total cost pertains. In our example, with a total cost of $500 we obtain an output of 10,000 miles of transport. The average total cost, therefore, is:

$$\frac{\text{Total cost}}{\text{Output}} = \frac{10,000 \text{ miles}}{\$500} = 5 \text{ cents per mile.}$$

Similarly, the average fixed cost of a certain output is the total fixed cost divided by the output; in the example, $\dfrac{\$300}{10,000 \text{ miles}}$, or 3 cents per mile. The average variable cost of a certain output is the total variable cost divided by the output; in our example, $\dfrac{\$200}{10,000 \text{ miles}}$, or 2 cents per mile.

Dividing equation (2) through by the output, we have:

$$\text{Average total cost} = \text{average fixed cost} + \text{average variable cost.} \quad (3)$$

The Marginal Cost

We must now introduce a new concept, the forerunner of many of its kind. When our inquisitive friend asked us how much it cost to take the car out we said, "Two cents a mile." He might think at first that we referred here to the average variable cost of running the car. But that is not the case. When we said that going out for 20 miles cost 40 cents we meant that because we went out for 20 miles, 40 cents was *added* to our total bill for the car, i.e., to the total cost. This concept is called the *marginal cost*. It may be defined as the amount which is added to the total cost when the output is increased by one unit. Over a range of output, e.g., from 5000 to 5020 miles, the marginal cost may be defined as the increase in the total cost divided by the corresponding increase in output. In our example, suppose our "output" of miles rose from 5000 to 5020, and our total cost rose from $350 to $350.40. Then the marginal cost of that 20 miles is 40 cents, or 2 cents per mile. We shall see that if the average variable cost does not change as output changes, the marginal cost and the average variable cost are equal. This is not so where the average variable cost changes as output changes. We should always think of marginal cost as something *added* to the total cost by the addition of a unit of output.[3] If we say that the marginal cost of milk, for instance, is 50 cents per gallon, we should think of a gallon being added to the output of milk and of 50 cents being added in consequence to the farmer's total cost.

Variation of Cost with Output

There is yet another ambiguity in the expression "cost of production." When our friend asked how much it cost to run our car, we said first, "five cents a mile," this being the average total cost of running 10,000 miles. Suppose, now, that in the period in question we have run not 10,000 miles but 30,000 miles. In order to do this we would have to drive faster, more furiously, more frequently. We would burn more gas and oil per mile, there would probably be greater wear and tear on the tires and more repairs. It is reasonable to assume that the average

[3] Or as something subtracted from total cost by the subtraction of a unit of output.

total cost of 30,000 miles might well be greater than the average total cost of 10,000 miles—say, 6 cents per mile. Similarly, if we had run only 1000 miles our average fixed cost would be high, and the average total cost would also be high—say, 20 cents per mile. It is evident that there is no such thing as "the" cost per mile of running an automobile, no such thing in general as "the" cost of production of a commodity. In the general case all the cost quantities, with the exception of the total fixed cost, change as the output changes. Except in a special and unlikely case, therefore, it makes no sense to say simply, "The cost of production of milk is 40 cents per gallon." If we are to be accurate we must say, "The average total (or average variable, or marginal) cost of production of a particular ten thousand gallons of milk is 40 cents per gallon."

Cost Schedules

We suppose, then, that each volume of output has its own total cost, or supply price, and that the total schedule of such quantities is the total cost schedule, or the total cost function. From this all the other cost quantities can be derived. An example is given in Table 49, the figures of which are not supposed to be realistic, but are chosen for their illustrative value. We will return to the firm of Table 46, now supposing, however, that it is a wheat *producer,* and that its total cost schedule is shown in Table 49, columns 1 and 2. The total fixed cost

TABLE 49. Cost Schedules

1	2	3	4	5	6	7	8	9
Out-put (bu.)	Total Cost ($)	Total Fixed Cost ($)	Total Vari-able Cost ($)	Average Total Cost ($ per bu.)	Average Variable Cost ($ per bu.)	Marginal Cost ($ per bu.)	Wheat Stock (bu.)	Money Stock ($)
0	100	100	0	∞	?		600	300
50	225	100	125	4.50	2.50	2.50	650	175
100	290	100	190	2.90	1.90	1.30	700	110
150	350	100	250	2.33	1.67	1.20	750	50
200	410	100	310	2.05	1.55	1.20	800	−10
250	470	100	370	1.88	1.48	1.20	850	−70
300	530	100	430	1.77	1.43	1.20	900	−130
350	595	100	495	1.70	1.41	1.30	950	−195
400	665	100	565	1.66	1.41	1.40	1000	−265
450	745	100	645	1.66	1.43	1.60	1050	−345
500	880	100	780	1.76	1.56	2.70	1100	−480

(column 3) is equal to the total cost at zero output, assumed to be $100. Total variable cost (column 4) is total cost less total fixed cost. Average total cost is obtained by dividing each total cost figure by the corresponding output (column 5). Average variable cost is obtained by dividing each total variable cost figure by the corresponding output (column 6). Marginal cost (column 7) is obtained by dividing each *addition* to total cost by the corresponding addition to output. Thus when output rises from 0 to 50 bushels, a rise of 50 bushels, total cost rises from 100 to 225, a rise of $125. Marginal cost, therefore, in the range for 0 to 50 bushels is $125 per 50 bushels, or $2.50 $\left(\dfrac{125}{50}\right)$ per bushel. In column 8 we show what will happen to the wheat stock of the firm, assuming that it starts with 600 bushels, if various quantities of output are produced and nothing is sold; the stock of course equals the initial stock plus the output. Column 9 shows what will be the money stock after various outputs have been produced. The money stock is the initial stock (assumed to be $400) less the total cost. We assume that all the total cost is paid out in the form of money.

Cost Curves

These schedules are shown graphically in Fig. 75. Fig. 75A shows the asset transformation curve (columns 8 and 9 of Table 49). P_0 shows the initial position. If in the period there is a fixed cost, P_0P_1, this drops the position to P_1. Then if there is *production*, this leads to an increase in the wheat stock with a corresponding diminution of the money stock following the curve P_1P_2. In Fig. 75B we have the total cost curve, OC_1C_2 (columns 1 and 2 of Table 49). OC_1 is the total fixed cost. The same curve measured from the line C_1F is the total variable cost curve. Thus at an output OT, TK is the total cost, TF is the total fixed cost, FK is the total variable cost. Then in Fig. 76C we show the marginal cost curve, m_1m_2 (columns 1 and 7 of Table 49), the average variable cost curve, v_1v_2 (columns 1 and 6 of Table 49), and the average total cost curve, c_1c_2 (columns 1 and 5 of Table 49).

The Average-Marginal Relationship

We wish to note first some points in regard to the geometry of these curves. In the first place we can see that the asset transformation curve, $P_0P_1P_2$, is simply the mirror image of the total cost curve, OC_1C_2, because total cost represents money given up for wheat produced. We should note next that the marginal cost curve passes through the lowest points of the average total and average variable cost curves. That is to say, when the average cost is at a minimum it is equal to the marginal cost. This is no accident but a necessary property of this relationship. It can be proved by reference to Fig. 75B.

Thus at any output OA the total cost is AB and the average total cost is $\dfrac{AB}{OA}$, which is the slope of the line OB, or tan BOA. As B moves along the total cost curve, the slope of the line OB is evidently falling until the point K, at an output OT, where OK is a tangent to the total

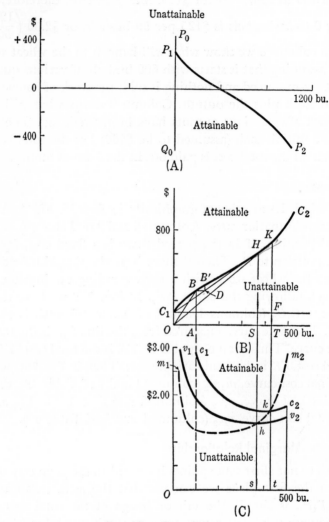

FIG. 75.   Cost Curves.

cost curve. If now we move the point B beyond K the slope of the line OB (i.e., the average total cost) again begins to rise. K therefore is the point of minimum average total cost. Now the marginal cost is the slope or steepness of the total cost curve itself. Thus suppose we move a short distance from B to B'; the marginal cost in this range is the increase in total cost, DB', divided by the increase in output, BD, which is the slope of the line BB'. As B and B' move together this ratio approximates to the slope of the curve itself, or of the tangent to the curve. At B it is evident that the slope of OB is greater than the slope of BB'—i.e., average total cost exceeds marginal cost, as we can see also by referring down to Fig. 75C. At K, however, the slope of the total cost curve at K (the marginal cost) is equal to the slope of the tangent OK, which is also equal to the average total cost. Marginal cost is therefore equal to average total cost at the point of minimum average total cost, K. In an exactly similar way, by drawing a tangent from C_1 to the total cost curve at H we can show that H is the point at which average variable cost is a minimum and also is equal to marginal cost. The points H and K in Fig. 75B correspond exactly to h and k in Fig. 75C.

These propositions are special cases of a more general proposition relating "average" and "marginal" quantities, which we may call the "average-marginal relationship." It states that when any "average" quantity is falling, the corresponding "marginal" quantity is smaller than it; whenever an "average" quantity is rising, the "marginal" quantity is greater than it; and whenever the "average" quantity is constant, the "marginal" quantity is equal to it.[4]

Average Fixed Cost

Another point to notice is that the average variable cost curve gets closer to the average total cost curve as output increases. This is because the vertical distance between them, e.g., v_2c_2 in Fig. 75C, measures the average fixed cost, which continually declines with increase in output as the constant total is spread out over a larger number of units of output. The average fixed cost curve (not shown in the figure) is a rectangular hyperbola.

Drawing Marginal Cost Curves

When a marginal cost curve is drawn from arithmetical figures, the simplest method of reasonable accuracy is to plot the marginal cost at

[4] The "average-marginal relationship" can easily be proved by algebra. Let a be the average total cost of x units, a_1 the average total cost of $x+1$ units. Then the total cost of x units is ax, and of $x+1$ units is $a_1(x+1)$. The marginal cost of the $(x+1)$st unit is $a_1(x+1)-ax$, or $(a_1-a)x+a_1$. If the average cost is constant as output changes, $a_1=a$, and the marginal cost is equal to the average cost, a_1. If the average cost is increasing as output increases, $a_1>a$, $(a_1-a)x$ is positive, and the marginal cost is therefore greater than the average cost. If the average cost is decreasing as output increases, $a_1<a$, $(a_1-a)x$ is negative, and the marginal cost is less than the average cost.

the mid-point of the range over which it is calculated. Thus in Table 49 the marginal cost over the range from 0 to 50 bushels is $2.50. In plotting this on a graph it should not be plotted at either end of the range, but at 25 bushels. For perfect accuracy we should plot the total cost curve, draw the tangents at various points, and measure the marginal cost at these points by the slopes of these tangents. This refinement, however, is usually more trouble than it is worth, and the approximate method given above is accurate enough for most purposes. Plotting the marginal cost at either end of the range over which it is calculated, however, will lead to noticeable errors in the graphing. These considerations apply to the construction of all marginal curves.

Cost Functions as "Attainability Boundaries"

All the functions defined above represent in some sense "attainability boundaries." Thus in Fig. 75A all positions within the area bounded by $Q_0 P_1 P_2$ are attainable, for we can always obtain output at *greater* cost than that shown by the production opportunity line. Points outside this area cannot be attained by *production,* though they may of course be attainable by exchange. Similarly, in Fig. 75B the total cost curve separates the attainable area above from the unattainable area below, as again any given output can be achieved at greater total cost than that shown by the total cost curve, but not at less. Each point on the total cost curve, that is, represents the *least* total cost for which the corresponding output can be produced. We shall return to the problem involved in finding this least cost later. Similarly, in Fig. 75C each curve separates the attainable values which lie above it from the unattainable values which lie below it.

The Optimum

The analysis cannot, of course, stop at the transformation functions. It is useful to be able to separate the attainable from the unattainable positions of the organism. We want to know more, however. We want to know where, within the field of the attainable, is the "best" position. We need, therefore, a theory of the optimum—i.e., of the principles according to which the organism *selects,* out of all the positions which are open to it, the preferred or optimum position. In order to do this it is necessary to have some *principle of ordering* or ranking the various positions, in order to be able to pick out that position which heads the list—i.e., which is the best of the set. The marginal analysis is an important special case of this general principle of ordering in which the optimum position is defined as the position giving the *maximum* value to some variable (the "maximand") which ranks the various positions, in the sense that any position associated with a higher value of this maximand outranks any position with a lower value. As we shall see, the marginal analysis proper only applies when the maximand function is continuous at the maximum. The theory, however, can be widened to take care of discontinuous functions. In the elementary theory of the firm it is generally assumed that profit, or net revenue, is the maximand—i.e., that the optimum position is that at which profit is a maximum. We shall develop this case with considerable elaboration. It must not be thought, however, that we necessarily assume that firms in fact select the position of maximum profit. The *principle* of the marginal analysis, and the techniques involved in it, do not, however, stand or fall on the realism of this special case. Profit maximization is a special case of the more general theory of the optimum, and though we shall find it useful for a while to confine our attention to the detailed consequences of the assumption of profit maximization, we shall broaden the assumptions later.

QUESTIONS AND EXERCISES

1. Using the terminology of the first part of the chapter we might say that the total cost curve of Fig. 75 could be divided into three sectors— "pluperfect," "perfect," and "imperfect." Where would you mark the boundaries between these three sectors, and how would you define these terms? Would it help to define the concepts in the case of the market transformation curves if we employed a concept of "marginal revenue" analogous to "marginal cost"? Figs. 1 and 2 of Fig. 74 correspond to Figs. A and B of Fig. 75. What in Fig. 74 would correspond to Fig. 75B?
2. The concept of an "attainability function" defining the boundary between possible or attainable positions and impossible or unattainable positions is a perfectly general one. As an exercise in the method of plausible topology, discuss the probable shapes of the possibility boundaries in fields with the following axes:
    a. The legal weight of the golf ball and the average score of golfers.
    b. The average speed of automobiles and the number of fatal automobile accidents.
    c. The area of a country and the proportion of national income derived from exports.
    d. The ratio of Negroes to whites in a census tract and the number of mixed marriages per thousand population.
    e. The national income of a country and the percentage of national income devoted to defense.

3. Suppose the following schedule represented the average variable cost schedule of an automobile, over a period of six months:

Miles Run	Average Variable Cost (Cents per Mile)
1,000	3.0
2,000	3.0
3,000	3.0
4,000	3.0
5,000	3.02
6,000	3.05
7,000	3.10
8,000	3.175
9,000	3.278
10,000	3.410
11,000	3.573
12,000	3.775
13,000	4.023

Suppose that the total fixed cost in this period amounted to $100.

Calculate, for each thousand miles from 0 to 13,000 (arranging the results in tabular form): (a) The total variable cost. (b) The total cost. (c) The average fixed cost. (d) The average total cost. (e) The marginal cost.

On one graph (A) draw the total cost curve and the total variable cost curve. On another graph (B) draw the average total cost curve, the average variable cost curve, the marginal cost curve, and the average fixed cost curve.

From the graph find the point of minimum average total cost and determine how many miles should be run in order to operate the car at the minimum average total cost. Show that at this point the average total cost and the marginal cost are equal.

4. In the above example, suppose that a benevolent uncle offered to pay the owner of the car 5 cents for every mile driven. Calculate the total revenue and the net revenue accruing to the owner of the car under these circumstances, for each thousand miles from 0 to 13,000. On graph A draw the total revenue curve and also the net revenue curve, showing the net revenue at each number of miles. How many miles will the owner of the car have to run in order to get the greatest net revenue? Show, on graph B, that at this number of miles the marginal cost is 5 cents per mile.

5. Using the cost figures in Table 49, page 536, calculate the most profitable (or least unprofitable) output when the price is $1.20, $1.40, $1.60, $1.80, $2.00. (Use graphs.) What do you deduce from these results about the effect of the price of a product on its output?

6. The table on page 543 shows five different total cost curves.
In each case calculate the following schedules: (a) Total variable cost. (b) Average Total Cost. (c) Average Variable Cost. (d) Marginal Cost. On separate figures for each case draw the curves corresponding to these

Output (tons)	(1)	(2)	Total Cost ($) (3)	(4)	(5)
0	1000	1000	1000	1000	1000
10	1100	1024	1221	1050	1050
20	1157	1061	1335	1100	1100
30	1180	1120	1410	1150	1150
40	1200	1190	1464	1200	1200
50	1226	1287	1509	1250	1250
60	1264	1388	1538	1300	1300
70	1315	1512	1555	1350	1350
80	1385	1670	1570	1400	Inf.
90	1480	1870	1583	1450	Inf.
100	1700	2160	1595	1500	Inf.

schedules. Show that in each case the average-marginal relationship is sustained. Show that in cases where there is a minimum value for either average total or average variable cost, the marginal cost is equal to the average cost at its minimum value. Is this true also in case (5)? Suppose now that in cases (1), (2), and (3) the total cost went to infinity at an output of 80 tons. What does this do to the various curves? What would be the *meaning* of such an assumption and how realistic do you think it might be?

CHAPTER 26

THE PROFIT-MAKING PROCESS AND THE
THEORY OF MAXIMIZATION

We have already thought of the firm as defined by a *process* by which assets are continually transformed and retransformed through production and exchange. Before going on to the theory of maximization of profits we may wish to examine further the nature of this process from the point of view of how the transformation of assets results in the making of profits.

Dynamics of a Marketer

Let us return, then, to our simple example of the wheat marketer, and consider a succession of purchases and sales at different prices, shown in Table 50. Given the initial money and wheat stock ($400

TABLE 50. The Profit-Making Process

Position Day	P_0	P_1 1	P_2 2	P_3 3	P_4 4	P_5 5	P_6 6
Price		2.00	3.00	2.50	2.00	3.00	2.00
Wheat bought (+) or sold (−)		+100	−600	+400	+400	−700	+400
Money paid in (+) or out (−)		−200	+1800	−1000	−800	+2100	−800
Wheat stock	600	700	100	500	900	200	600
Money stock	400	200	2000	1000	200	2300	1500

and 600 bushels, as before) we can immediately calculate, as in the last two lines of the table, the successive "positions" of the physical balance sheet. These are represented in the points P_0, P_1, · · · P_6 in Fig. 76A. P_0 is the original position. On the first day the exchange opportunity line is P_0P_1, and we suppose the firm moves to P_1 by buying wheat. Then next day the price is higher; the opportunity line

544

is P_1P_2, and the firm sells wheat, moving to P_2. The third day the price is lower and the firm buys along the new opportunity line P_2P_3 to P_3. The fourth day the price is lower still, but the firm still buys along the new line P_3P_4 to P_4. So we go on. It is clear that these operations are profitable, for by the time we get to P_6 we have reached a position with the same amount of wheat as we started, and a good deal more money. The "profitableness" of the operations consist in moving through a succession of swings "outward" in the figure, so that on the whole we are increasing our assets. If the operations were unprofitable —as of course they may be—the firm will find itself moving "in" toward the origin. It might find itself, for instance, buying dear and selling cheap, following a path such as $P_6P_5P_4P_3$ · · · etc.

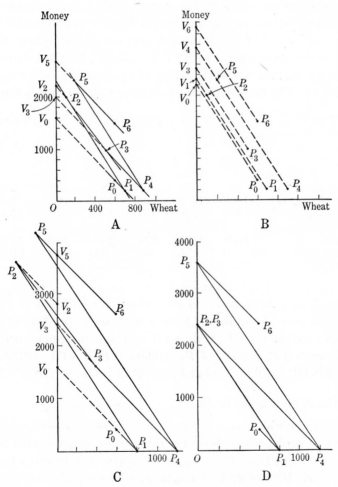

FIG. 76.   The Profit-Making Process.

The Profit-Making Process

This process of moving "out" in an asset space (which in general will be of many dimensions) through a succession of transformations is the essence of the profit-making process. Profit making, that is, is the process of "growth" of the whole asset complex. If we are to measure this growth, however, we must reduce the n-dimensional asset complex to a single dimension of a unit of account, say, "dollars." This can only be done by *valuing* all the physical assets by multiplying their quantity by a coefficient of valuation. This is exactly the same index-number problem which we have met earlier (page 277) in the measurement of economic aggregates, though it is not generally recognized as such, even by accountants! Let us assume here a very simple method of valuation, which corresponds roughly to the accountants' "FIFO" method (see pages 266–268). We will suppose that all wheat stocks are valued at the initial price of $2 per bushel. The total value of the wheat stock, and the net worth (value of wheat plus money), are shown in Table 51. The successive positions of net worth are shown in Fig.

TABLE 51.   The Calculation of Profit: Wheat at $2 per Bushel

Position Day	P_0 1	P_1 2	P_2 3	P_3 4	P_4 5	P_5 6	P_6
Wheat stock	600	700	100	500	900	200	600
Value of wheat stock	1200	1400	200	1000	1800	400	1200
Money stock	400	200	2000	1000	200	2300	1500
Net worth	1600	1600	2200	2000	2000	2700	2700
Total profit	0	0	600	400	400	1100	1100

76A by projecting valuation lines from the various positions to the money axis at a slope equal to the valuation coefficient of $2. Thus from P_0 we project the line P_0V_0 at a slope of $2 per bushel to meet the money axis at V_0; OV_0 is then the corresponding net worth. Thus the net worth at P_0 and P_1 is OV_0 ($1600), at P_2 it is OV_2 ($2200), at P_3 and P_4 it is OV_3 ($2000), and at P_5 and P_6 it is OV_5 ($2700).

Difficulties in Measuring Profit

The paradoxical nature of the measurement of net worth (and therefore of profit, which is simply the growth in net worth) is shown in the movement from P_2 to P_3, which apparently results in a loss of $200, because 1000 bushels of wheat are sold for $2.50 and are valued at $2. Nevertheless it is clear from subsequent events that the movement from P_2 to P_3, and again to P_4 (which registers no gain or loss), actually lays the foundations for the subsequent gains at P_5 or P_6, and that if the firm had not moved down from P_2, at an apparent loss, it would not have made the subsequent gains. The dependence of the measure of profit on the system of valuations is brought out clearly in Table 52, which represents the physical data of Table 51 but values

TABLE 52.   The Calculation of Profit: Wheat at $3 per Bushel

Position	P_0	P_1	P_2	P_3	P_4	P_5	P_6
Wheat stock	600	700	100	500	900	200	600
Value of wheat	1800	2100	300	1500	2700	600	1800
Money stock	400	200	2000	1000	200	2300	1500
Net worth	2200	2300	2300	2500	2900	2900	3300

the wheat stocks at $3 instead of at $2. Comparing the course of net worth with that in Table 52, we see that at the higher valuation the loss from P_2 to P_3 is turned into a gain, and that the great gain from P_4 to P_5 is wiped out! The course of net worth is shown in Fig 76B.

What Determines Profit?

It should now be easy to see that the larger the *swings* in a profitable succession of transformations, the greater the total profit. Suppose, for instance, that with the price history of Table 50, we double the purchases and sales. The result is shown in Table 53. Comparing the total

TABLE 53.   Calculation of Profit: Larger Transactions

Position	P_0	P_1	P_2	P_3	P_4	P_5	P_6
Wheat sales (−) or purchases (+)		+200	−1200	+800	+800	−1400	+800
Money paid in (+) or out (−)		−400	+3600	−2000	−1600	+4200	−1600
Wheat stock	600	800	−400	+400	+1200	−200	+600
Money stock	400	0	3600	1600	0	4200	2600
Value of wheat Stock at $2	1200	1600	−800	800	2400	−400	1200
Net worth	1600	1600	2800	2400	2400	3800	3800
Total profit	0	0	1200	800	800	2200	2200

profit figure (net worth minus initial net worth) of tables 53 and 51, we observe that at any time the profit in table 53 is double what it is in Table 51.

In the present case it is clear that if there were no limits on the amounts bought and sold, and if markets remained perfect indefinitely, and if the future course of prices was certain, then profits could be made at an infinite rate by buying indefinitely large amounts when the price was going to rise, and selling indefinitely large amounts when the price was going to fall. That is, the larger the "swings" the larger the profit, and if there is no limit on the magnitude of the swings, there is no limit on the magnitude of the profit.

What Limits Profit?

1. *Boundary Conditions.* We know in fact, of course, that the swings cannot be indefinitely large, and profits are always finite. We must ask ourselves, then, what *limits* the size of the swings, or successive transformations? There are two main answers. One is the development of imperfections on the market and the other is the presence of uncertainty. The simplest kind of imperfection we might call a "boundary" imperfection. This is a point at which the exchange opportunity suddenly disappears. Suppose, for instance, that in the previous example there was no possibility of borrowing, either money or wheat. The market opportunities would be bounded sharply by the two axes—i.e., all movements would have to be confined to the first quadrant. The maximum profit is then obtained if we follow the following principle: move to the money axis (i.e., hold all assets in the form of money) whenever the *next* change in price is a fall, and move to the wheat axis (i.e., hold all assets in the form of wheat) when the next change in price is a rise. This is illustrated in Table 54 and

TABLE 54.   The Profit-Making Process: Boundary Limits

Position	P_0	P_1	P_2	P_3	P_4	P_5	P_6
Wheat stock	600	800	0	0	1200	0	600
Money stock	400	0	2400	2400	0	3600	2400

Fig. 76D. We observe that a mere fall in price is not sufficient to cause a move to the wheat axis. When price falls at position P_2 from $3 to $2.50, we do not move at all, because the price is going to fall further. If we refer back to Fig. 76A we can readily see that if the firm had not moved to position P_3 from P_2, but had stayed at P_2 on that "day" and then had moved toward the wheat axis to a new position 4, profits would have been higher. In P_6 I have brought the position to the original wheat stock in order to compare it with the other examples;

in a continuing process it would, of course, go right on to the wheat axis, assuming that a rise in price is forthcoming. All that this principle amounts to, of course, is the familiar one of "getting in at the bottom and out at the top." The principle can be applied to any boundary condition—thus there may be a maximum amount of debt possible, in which case the boundaries may lie in the fourth or second quadrants.

2. *Market Imperfections.* Any imperfection of the market will have the same effect of eventually checking purchases or sales, even if the imperfection manifests itself gradually. Let us take first a simple case in which we have an imperfect purchase market but a perfect sales market. This is shown in Fig. 77. Here again we suppose a pure wheat

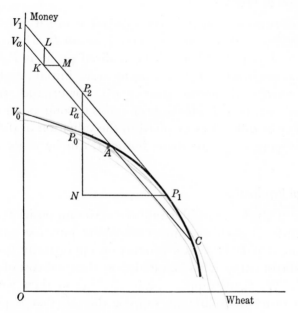

FIG. 77.   Profit Maximization.

marketer as before, with an initial position P_0. Suppose that he can purchase wheat only under an imperfect market, with the price rising the more he purchases, and an exchange opportunity boundary $P_0 A P_1 C$. We suppose further that he anticipates a rise in price, or in general a change in the exchange opportunity favorable to selling, so that he first moves down the line $P_0 A P_1 C$. The question is, How far will he go? If he goes to A and then the price rises to give him a sales opportunity line $A V_a$, he can move back along the line $A V_a$. If, however, he goes further, to P_1, he can move back along a "higher" sales opportunity line, P_1V_1. If he goes still further, to C, he finds he must again move back along a lower sales opportunity line, CV_a. It is clear that the best position along P_0AP_1C is P_1, where the line V_1P_1 is tangent to the purchase opportunity curve at P_1. This proposition is independent of any method of measuring profits, or any system of asset preferences, so long as none of the assets involved are "discommodities"; for if we take any point K on a sales opportunity line AV_a which is not tangent to the purchase opportunity line, we can find a range of points LM on the tangent sales opportunity line P_1V_1 which show larger quantities of *both* assets than the point K, and hence must be preferred to it.

Maximization of Profit

If now we suppose that the firm sells just as much as it previously purchased, NP_1, so that it moves to the position P_2 where the initial stock of wheat is restored, then the realized profit is P_0P_2. This is clearly a maximum when P_2P_1 is tangent to the initial purchase curve; if the firm moved initially to either A or C, for instance, the realized profit would only be P_0P_a. If the firm moves to some point other than P_2, there may be difficulties involved in the valuation of the stock and the measurement of profit; these, however, can be neglected at this stage.

Optimum of Production

Fig. 77 will also serve to illustrate the optimum position of *production* as well as of exchange under imperfect purchase markets. We suppose now that P_0AP_1C is a production opportunity line, derived from a total cost curve. That is, we suppose the total cost of producing NP_1 is P_0N. We again suppose perfect selling markets with straight sales opportunity lines, and we suppose that all that is produced is sold. Again it is clear that the optimum amount of product is NP_1, where the sales opportunity line is tangent to the production opportunity line at P_1. Realized profit again is P_0P_2.

The "Marginal Conditions"

In both the above cases the slope of the line P_0AP_1C at any point is the *marginal cost,* whether we think of it as simple purchase or as production. It represents, that is, the increase in money sacrificed per unit increase in wheat obtained. The slope of the sales opportunity line P_1V_1 is the selling price of wheat. At P_1, then, we have the condition that price is equal to marginal cost. This is the first we have encountered of what will be a long series of *marginal conditions*. These are equalities which must be fulfilled at the position of the organism at which the maximand is maximized. If they are not fulfilled the organism is not at its optimum position. Thus in the present case if we stopped at a position such as A where the marginal cost is less than the price, by increasing purchases (or production) we would be giving up less in money cost than we would be receiving in the value of the wheat added. If, for instance, marginal cost at this point were $1 when the price was $3, increasing wheat by 1 bushel either by purchase or by production, and then selling the wheat thus obtained, would increase the money stock by $2, leaving the wheat stock unchanged—i.e., there would be a realized profit of $2 in each additional bushel bought or produced and then sold. If on the other hand marginal cost were $4 when the price was $3, this would indicate that the firm had gone too far in purchase or in production, and that if it had produced or purchased a bushel *less* it would have been better off, for the extra bushel actually diminished the realized profit by $1. If, however, when the marginal cost is *less* than price, it pays to *increase* purchases or production, and when marginal cost is *greater* than price, it pays to *diminish* purchases or production, the maximum profit must be at the point where marginal cost and price are equal.

Maximization with Imperfect Selling Markets

Let us now extend the analysis to the case where the selling market is imperfect. Let us return to the case of the previous chapter, Table 49, page 536, and suppose that the firm faces an imperfect market for its product, as in Table 47, page 525. The combined tables are shown in Table 55. Columns (1), (2), and (6) are the same as columns (1), (2), and (7) of Table 49. Column (3) shows the price at which each output can be sold; this is the sales curve. Column (4) shows the total revenue, obtained by multiplying each output in column (1) by the price at which it can be sold in column (3). Price is sometimes called "average revenue," and the sales curve the "average revenue curve," because it bears the same relation to total revenue that average cost does to total cost. We have, that is, Average Cost $= \dfrac{\text{Total Cost}}{\text{Output}}$, and Price $= \dfrac{\text{Total Revenue}}{\text{Output}} =$ Average Revenue. Column (4) is the net revenue, obtained by subtracting each total cost figure from the corresponding total revenue figure. This is the "realized profit," or the increase in money stock if all the output is sold. Column (7) is the "marginal revenue," a concept exactly analogous to marginal cost. It is defined as the increase in total revenue per unit increase in output. Thus over the range from 0 to 50 bushels the increase in total revenue is $125; marginal revenue is then $125 for 50 bushels, or $2.50 per bushel. We see now from the table that the net revenue is a maximum (about $70) when the marginal cost and the marginal revenue are equal, between

TABLE 55.   Profit Maximization

1	2	3	4	5	6	7
Output (bu.)	Total Cost ($)	Price or Average Revenue ($ per bu.)	Total Revenue ($)	Net Revenue ($)	Marginal Cost ($ per bu.)	Marginal Revenue ($ per bu.)
0	100	2.60	0	−100		
					2.50	2.50
50	225	2.50	125	−100		
					1.30	2.30
100	290	2.40	240	−50		
					1.20	2.10
150	350	2.30	345	−5		
					1.20	1.90
200	410	2.20	440	30		
					1.20	1.70
250	470	2.10	525	55		
					1.20	1.50
300	530	2.00	600	70		
					1.30	1.30
350	595	1.90	665	70		
					1.40	1.10
400	665	1.80	720	55		
					1.60	0.90
450	745	1.70	765	20		
					2.50	0.70
500	880	1.60	800	−80		

300 and 350 bushels. This again is no accident, but a necessary condition.

Graphic Illustration.   The figures of the table are reproduced in Fig. 78. In Fig. 78A we plot the total cost curve, T_c, and the total revenue curve, T_r, from columns (2) and (4), and the net revenue curve, N_r, from column (5). The net revenue is also equal to the vertical distance between the total cost and total revenue curves. Thus at any output OK, $KL = CR$. Net revenue is zero at B_1 and B_2. These correspond to what are sometimes called "break-even points." OT is the total fixed cost. In Fig. 78B the curves va_r and vm_r are the average revenue and marginal revenue curves, from columns (3) and (7). The curves aa_c and mm_c are the average total cost and marginal cost curves from columns (5) and (7) of Table 49. It will be observed that the net revenue is a maximum, KL, at output OK ($= ok$) where the marginal

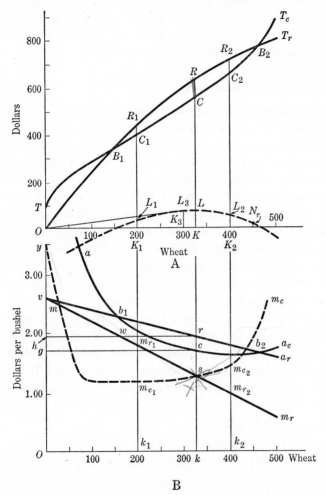

Fig. 78.   Profit Maximization with Imperfect Markets.

cost and marginal revenue curves intersect at s; that is, where marginal cost equals marginal revenue. Marginal cost is the slope of the total cost curve, and marginal revenue is the slope of the total revenue curve. At an output such as ok_1, where marginal cost ($k_1 m_{c1}$) is less than marginal revenue ($k_1 m_{r1}$), the total revenue curve is steeper than the total cost curve and the two curves are clearly *diverging* with increase of output; i.e., net revenue is getting larger as output increases, and is therefore not at a maximum. Similarly, at an output such as ok_2, where marginal cost exceeds marginal revenue, the total cost curve is steeper than the total revenue curve and the curves are converging with increasing output—i.e., net revenue is increased by *diminishing* output, and again is not at a maximum. At output OK the total cost and total revenue curves are parallel, and net revenue therefore is neither increasing nor decreasing.

The "Second-Order Conditions"

It will be observed that marginal cost and marginal revenue are also equal at the point m. This point, however, represents a minimum value of net revenue, not a maximum. The equality of marginal cost and marginal revenue means simply that net revenue is neither increasing nor decreasing with output. This is true both at maximum and at minimum points, or anywhere where net revenue is not changing with output. For a maximum not only must marginal cost equal marginal revenue, but the marginal cost curve must cut the marginal revenue curve from below. That is, at slightly smaller outputs than the optimum, marginal revenue must be larger than marginal cost, and at slightly larger outputs it must be smaller. This is what is known as "second-order condition" for a maximum.[1]

Under perfect markets marginal revenue and price are identical, as we have seen, so that the maximum condition reduces to the equality of *price* and marginal cost already noticed. With imperfect markets, however, price is greater than marginal revenue, and at the point of maximum net revenue price (kr) is greater than marginal cost (ks).

Further Geometric Properties

One or two further points of geometry should be noticed. The distance cr in Fig. 78B is the difference between the price and the average total cost, or the net revenue per unit of output. This is not generally at a maximum when the net revenue is a maximum. If we draw OL_3 to touch the net revenue curve in Fig. 78A, OK_3 is the output at which

---

[1] The student who is familiar with the differential calculus will recognize the marginal analysis as an example of the theory of maximization. Thus we have: net revenue (N) = total revenue (R) − total cost (C). The conditions for maximizing N with respect to output (q) are (1) the first-order condition, $\dfrac{dN}{dq} = \dfrac{dR}{dq} - \dfrac{dC}{dq} = 0$, or $\dfrac{dR}{dq}$ (marginal revenue) $= \dfrac{dC}{dq}$ (marginal cost), and (2) the second-order condition, $\dfrac{d^2N}{dq^2}$, negative—i.e., the excess of marginal revenue over marginal cost must be declining.

the net revenue per unit is a maximum. We see that this will always be at a smaller output than OK where the net revenue is a maximum, unless the maximum net revenue is itself zero—i.e., if the net revenue curve touches the horizontal axis from below. Then K_3 and K would coincide. Net revenue in Fig. 78B is measured by the area of the rectangle $crhg$—this being the net revenue per unit of output (cr) multiplied by the number of units of output (gc). Total revenue is the area of the rectangle $okrh$ and total cost is area $okcg$.

Total revenue is also equal to the area under the marginal revenue curve, being the sum of all the individual marginal revenues. Thus suppose the marginal revenue of the first unit of output were $2.60 and of the second unit $2.59. The first unit would add $2.60 and the second $2.59 to total revenue, so that the total revenue at the end of the second unit would be $(2.60 + 2.59)$. That is, in Fig. 78B total revenue at output ok is also the area $ovsk$, $=$ area $ohrk$. Subtracting the area $ohwsk$ from both these areas, we have area $hvw =$ area wrs. If the marginal revenue curve is a straight line, the triangles hvw and wrs are not only equal in area but congruent. In that case, $hw = wr$. This gives us a convenient method for constructing the marginal curve corresponding to an average curve. If the average curve is a straight line, the marginal curve will also be a straight line passing through the point at which the average curve cuts the vertical axis, v. If from a point on the average curve r we drop a perpendicular rh to the vertical axis and bisect rh in w, vw is the corresponding marginal curve. Even if the average curve is not a straight line the construction can be used to find the marginal quantity corresponding to each average quantity. Thus if vr were *tangent* to an average curve at r, ks would be the corresponding marginal quantity. The area under the marginal cost curve is similarly the total *variable* cost, if the marginal cost of the first unit of output excludes the fixed cost. If the marginal cost of the first unit includes the fixed cost, then the area under the marginal cost curve is the total cost. In this case the area *between* the marginal cost and marginal revenue curves is the net revenue. Thus in Fig. 78B, at an output ok_1 net revenue would be the area $mm_{c1}s -$ the area vmy, where y is the point at which the marginal cost curve cuts the vertical axis. The point m is clearly a maximum *negative* value of net revenue. As we move beyond m the positive area increases; at s it is a maximum; beyond s—e.g., at the output ok_2—the area $sm_{c2}m_{r2}$ represents a subtraction from the value at s. This constitutes another proof that s, the point where marginal cost and marginal revenue are equal, is the point of maximum net revenue.

The Firm Without Limits

Up to this point we have assumed that the only factor limiting the operation of the firm has been "imperfection" in some sense—either imperfection of the selling market, of the buying market, or of the production opportunity or total cost curve. If all markets were perfect and if the firm never ran into increasing cost, there would be no limit to the extent of its operations, either in marketing or in production— it would always pay to increase output. We see this clearly in Fig. 79A,

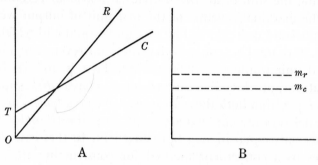

Fig. 79. The Firm Without Limits.

which shows a firm with a perfect market for output and constant marginal cost. OR is the total revenue curve, TC the total cost curve—and it is clear that there is no maximum position of net revenue, which increases indefinitely with increase in output. The marginal cost curve, m_c, and the marginal revenue curve, m_r, are shown in Fig. 79B; these are parallel, and never meet. It is clear that if there is to be a maximum position of net revenue, then either the marginal revenue curve must turn down—i.e., there must be imperfection in the selling market—or the marginal cost curve must turn up—there must be "increasing cost."

Uncertainty as a Limit

There is, however, another factor which may limit the operations of an economic organization *before* the limits of imperfection have been reached, and which therefore might provide limits even in the extreme case of Fig. 79. This is the factor of *uncertainty*. Up to this point we have assumed implicitly that the various opportunity functions were certain. In fact this is rarely, if ever, the case. To return first to the example of the pure marketer of Fig. 76. He moves in the direction he does along any of his market opportunity lines in anticipation of a change in price. Thus he moves "down" from P_0 to P_1, buying wheat because he thinks the price is going to rise. If he is absolutely sure the price is going to rise, and if there are no market imperfections, we have seen that it will pay him to go as far as he can in the direction of acquiring wheat and getting rid of money. However, he is never *quite* sure. Suppose that in fact he is disappointed, and the price falls. Then the further he has gone in the purchase of wheat, the worse off he will be; he should have gone the other way, selling wheat and acquiring money. As he moved down from P_0, then, his chance of gain increases if things turn out as he hopes—but also his chance of loss increases if things do not turn out as he hopes. He will stop, generally, at the point where the chance of loss, if things turn out badly, is greater than he can stand. That is, there is some point beyond which he feels the risk of being wiped out if things go badly outweighs any possible gain, no matter how great.

The Principle of Increasing Risk

The "principle of increasing risk," as Mr. Kalecki calls it,[2] is of particular importance when the firm has liabilities—i.e., when its total of assets is greater than its net worth—for then an unfavorable movement in its asset values leads to a much larger unfavorable movement in its net worth, as we saw on pages 378–379. The problem is illustrated for the simple marketer in Fig. 80. P_0 is the initial position in a wheat-money field. We suppose the exchange opportunity line is $P_0AP_1P_2$. Note that the slight steepening of the line at A represents interest on the debt incurred to purchase wheat beyond his net worth. If now he anticipates that the price will rise to, say, the slope of P_1V_1, if he goes to P_1 the first day, and then sells the next day, moving, say, all the way to V_1, his gain will be V_0V_1. If he goes to P_2 and then sells at the high price, he will move to V_2, with a greater gain (V_0V_2). Obviously, the further he goes downward along the opportunity line on the first day, the greater his profits on the second day—if things turn out as he *hopes*. Suppose, however, that things turn out badly, and the price falls, and that also he is forced to liquidate his debt. If he has moved to P_1, incurring a debt P_1C, he will have to sell at least CB of wheat to pay off the debt; and if the remainder of his wheat stock is valued "at market" (this now being below cost), his net worth will be OW_1—a severe loss of V_0W_1. If he goes to P_2 and the worst happens, he will be wiped out altogether, and his net worth falls to zero. It is clear that a reasonably cautious man would be extremely hesitant to go be-

[2] See Chapter 18, page 379.

yond the point P_2, no matter how attractive the gains hoped for, if the loss feared amounted to irretrievable disaster.

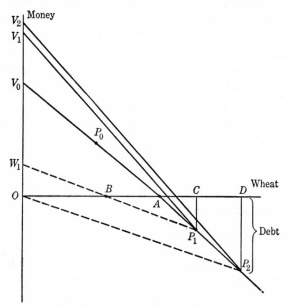

FIG. 80.   Uncertainty as a Limit.

The "Fear of the Worst" as a Limit

This is not to say, of course, that disaster will never be risked. It does mean, however, that equal possible gains and losses are not of equal significance—that even if moving along an opportunity path increased equally the possibility of both gains and losses, the fear of loss would eventually outweigh the hope of gain. At this point the movement will cease, even though it is not checked by imperfections in the market or in cost curves. Exactly the same kind of considerations apply to movement in expectation of a fall in price; suppose, for instance, that the marketer moves into the second quadrant, borrowing wheat (i.e., selling wheat futures) in order to increase his money stock. If his expectation is disappointed and the price of wheat rises, he may again suffer severe losses, and perhaps even be wiped out, when he has to purchase wheat to make good his undertaking to deliver. Uncertainty, therefore, results in what are apparently "boundary maxima," which may operate even when imperfections in the opportunity functions yield "true" maxima. That is, we may stop an operation, whether marketing or production, before the point of maximum profit under *favorable* anticipations, because of the fear of the losses which would result if things turn out badly. We may hesitate, for instance, to produce as much as would yield maximum profits if our best expectation is fulfilled, because to do so would involve a position of illiquidity which would risk some disaster, such as loss of control of the enterprise, if things turned out badly and we were not able to dispose of the product at a profit.

Asset Preferences as Limitations

What this means is that the movement of an enterprise will be limited by certain *asset preferences*—i.e., there will be certain proportions of various kinds of assets in its total position which the firm will not care to violate. These preferences may be "boundaries"—i.e., the firm will not mind certain proportions being in excess, say, of some boundary figure but will get seriously disturbed if the proportions fall below the boundary. A good example of such a preference boundary is the reserve ratio of a bank. As we have seen, banks are most unwilling to allow the ratio of reserves to deposits to fall below a certain minimum. Indeed, there is usually a legal limit to this ratio. All firms, however, keep an eye on various aspects of their asset *structure,* especially their liquidity position, in view of the uncertainties of the future. Some assets depend for their value on a narrow range of future circumstances; if things turn out only slightly worse than expected, they may lose all or the greater part of their value. These we will call "specific" assets. Other assets will retain their value even though the future turns out very differently from what is hoped—these are "flexible" assets. Generally speaking, "fixed" assets—buildings and machinery—tend to be more specific, and raw materials and money are "flexible," though there may be exceptions to this rule. An increase in uncertainty itself will tend to shift asset preferences toward flexible and away from specific assets, simply because with flexible assets there is less chance of disaster if things go wrong and there is a better chance of being able to take advantage of presently unforeseen opportunities. In particular the demand for liquid assets (e.g., bank deposits and government bonds) is strongly influenced by the prevailing state of uncertainty—the less certain the future, the greater the demand for liquid assets, which are, as it were, a sort of insurance against the unforeseeable.

The flexibility or specificity of assets is strongly affected, as far as the individual firm is concerned, by the nature of the market for them. Generally speaking, assets which have perfect markets are more flexible than those which have imperfect markets. With perfect markets, even if price changes unfavorably, there is no difficulty in changing the proportions of the assets in the total structure, because they can be exchanged in indefinitely large amounts without difficulty or loss due to the mere amount exchanged. Assets that have sharply imperfect markets, however, are likely to be specific to the firm, for they cannot be transferred into other assets in large quantities without loss. Because of this a firm with imperfect markets may stop short of the point of profit maximization under favorable expectations, because of the danger of getting "stuck" with unsalable assets if markets take a turn for the worse.

QUESTIONS AND EXERCISES

1. In Fig. 76, page 545, the profit-making process seems to be identical with the process of growth of assets—i.e., of accumulation. How could a firm make profits and still not accumulate assets over the years? How would this be represented in the diagrams?
2. Recalculate the net worth of the various positions in Table 50 (or Fig. 76A, page 545) at valuation coefficients of $0.50, $1, $1.50—up to $3.50. Tabulate the results. Can you draw any conclusion from this table?
3. Prove that the increase in net worth per unit purchase of commodity is equal to the valuation coefficient of the commodity less the marginal revenue. Prove as a corollary that in a perfect market it will be profitable to sell when the valuation coefficient is greater than the price, and to buy when the valuation coefficient is less than the price.
4. The following table gives the total cost and total revenue functions for an enterprise:

1 Output (Tons)	2 Total Cost ($)	3 Total Revenue ($)
0	200	0
5	215	45
10	225	90
15	231	135
20	236	180
25	242	225
30	249	270
35	257	315
40	274	360
45	306	405
50	340	450
55	385	495
60	450	540
65	535	585
70	644	630

Calculate and tabulate the following additional schedules: (a) the total variable cost, (b) the average total cost, (c) the average variable cost, (d) the marginal cost, (e) the average revenue (price of product), (f) the marginal revenue, (g) the net revenue. Draw the corresponding curves on a diagram similar to Fig. 78, page 553. What kind of market for its product does the firm have? Show that in this case the maximum net revenue is where marginal cost equals price. Show that in this case the maximum net revenue *per unit of output* is at the output where average total cost is a minimum. What will be the optimum output (assuming maximization of net revenue) when the price is $6, $7, $8, $9, $10? Draw up a schedule showing the optimum output at various prices. Could this schedule be derived directly from those previously calculated? Why does the marginal cost curve exhibit irregularities when the average cost curve is apparently smooth?

5. The following table shows six marginal revenue schedules:

Sales	Marginal Revenue					
	1	2	3	4	5	6
0	100	100	100	100	100	100
1	100	90	80	90	99	90
2	100	80	60	81	97	82
3	100	70	40	73	94	76
4	100	60	20	66	90	72
5	100	50	0	60	85	70
6	100	40	−20	55	79	70
7	100	30	−40	51	72	72
8	100	20	−60	48	64	75
9	100	10	−80	46	55	76
10	100	0	−100	45	45	76

a. Calculate the corresponding total revenue schedules and the average revenue schedules in each case.

b. Plot on squared paper the total, average, and marginal revenue curves in each case.

6. A wheat marketer can buy or sell in unlimited quantities at $2 per bushel, can borrow money at 1 per cent per month, and can sell next month's wheat futures at $1.98. He has no wheat but $40,000 of money. Draw his exchange opportunity line, from the second to the fourth quadrants. The following month the price rises to $3. Calculate his net revenue for various quantities of wheat bought in the first month and sold in the second (say 10, 20, 30, 40 thousand bushels, and also for various quantities of wheat futures sold (say 10, 20, 30, 40 thousand bushels). Repeat with a price of $1 in the second month. Calculate the exact point in each case at which his net worth would be reduced to zero. Call this the "wipe-out point." (Note that when he sells futures his "cost" is positive, being an addition to his money stock, and his "revenue" is negative, being the subtraction from his money stock when he buys the wheat to fulfill his contract to deliver—i.e., pay back his "wheat

debt.") What will be the effect of a rise in the rate of interest on the wipe-out point? Is there an analogy to the rate of interest in the case of selling wheat futures? Does this example throw any light on the possible effects of a rise in the rate of interest on the behavior of a marketer?

CHAPTER 27

THE DERIVATION OF SUPPLY CURVES
FROM COST CURVES

Our first important application of the marginal analysis will be to show certain possible relationships between the cost curves of firms and the supply curves of competitive industries.

In deriving a supply curve for a product we have to explain two things: First, how and why does the output of a single enterprise change in response to changes in the price of its product? Second, how does the *number* of enterprises change as the price of their product changes?

The Supply Curve of an Individual Enterprise

The analysis of marginal cost in the preceding chapter will almost immediately give the answer to the first question. It was there shown that the most profitable output of an enterprise with a perfect market for output is that at which the price of the product is equal to its marginal cost. Assuming, then, that an enterprise tends to produce the most profitable quantity of output, we know that high prices will permit the output to expand to a point where the marginal cost has risen to the high price, and that low prices will force the output to contract until the marginal cost has fallen to the low price. Thus the marginal cost schedule, or curve, itself shows immediately what will be the most profitable or least unprofitable output at which to produce, for a series of hypothetical prices.

Suppose we have in Fig. 81 a marginal cost curve, *MC,* and an average total cost curve, *ATC,* of an enterprise with a perfect market for its product. Suppose the price of the product is *OL;* the marginal revenue curve and the average revenue curve will coincide, and will be *LR. R* is the point of maximum net revenue (see page 553), where marginal cost equals marginal revenue equals price. *LR* then is the optimum output. At a lower price, *OK, KQ* is the optimum output

563

—smaller than *LR*, if the marginal cost curve is positively sloped. Similarly, at the price *OH*, *HP* is the optimum output. At this price, however, where *HP* touches the average total cost curve, the price is equal to average total cost at the optimum output, and net revenue is zero. This means, as we have seen earlier, that the firm is just normally profitable (page 530). At a price below *OH*, say *OJ*, *JN* is the most profitable output, but even at the most profitable output net revenue is negative and the enterprise is making less profits than are necessary to keep it alive. Obviously, then, at prices less than *OH* the

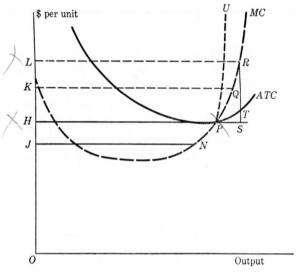

FIG. 81.   The Supply of Product from a Firm.

enterprise, at least in the long run, will produce nothing. At the price *OH* it will produce *HP*, and at higher prices it will produce more, following the marginal cost curve *PR*. The supply curve of product from the enterprise, then—i.e., the relation between the price of the product and the amount which the enterprise will produce—on the assumption of maximization of net revenue, is *OHPR*. The price at which a certain quantity will be supplied is called the "supply price" of that quantity. The supply curve relates supply price to quantity supplied; it must not be confused with the "sales curve" which relates price to the amount that can be sold. The supply curve concept is strictly valid only on the assumption of perfect markets for output.

The Supply Schedule for an Industry

If the supply schedules of all the firms, actual or potential, associated with the production of a given commodity are known, the supply schedule for the commodity as a whole can be deduced by simple addition. Table 56 gives the supply schedules of four firms which comprise an "industry." Firm A is a "low-cost firm." Its minimum average cost is $4 per unit of output, attained when it has an output of 25 units. Consequently it will produce nothing at a price lower than $4, but it will come into the industry as soon as the price rises to that level and will start producing 25 units of output. When the price rises to $6 per unit, Firm B, which is the second most favorably situated in respect to its costs, will enter the industry. Firm B starts with an output of 30 units, at which its average cost is at a minimum of $6. At a price of $6, then, the schedule shows that Firm A produces 43 units, this being the output at which its marginal cost is equal to $6, and Firm B produces 30 units, 73 units in all. Similarly, at a price of $10 per unit, Firm C enters the industry, making the total output 168

TABLE 56.   Derivation of Total Supply Schedule

Supply price ($ per ton):	0	2	4	6	8	10	12	14	16	18
Output (tons)										
Firm A	0	0	25	43	55	63	70	75	80	85
Firm B	0	0	0	30	50	65	75	83	87	90
Firm C	0	0	0	0	0	40	60	75	85	90
Firm D	0	0	0	0	0	0	50	65	75	82
Total	0	0	25	73	105	168	255	298	327	347

units; at a price of $12 per unit Firm D enters the industry, making the total output 255 units, and so on. It is evident that as the supply price rises, the output of the industry increases for two reasons: (1) the output of each existing firm increases, and (2) new firms enter the industry.

What Determines the Elasticity of Supply?

The schedule showing the relationship between the price and the total output of an industry is what we have previously called the "supply schedule." The question now arises, What determines the elasticity of this schedule? What determines the response of output to a change in price? The answer is that the supply will be more elastic if (1) a given increase in the output of the single firms produces only a small increase in the marginal cost of production in the firm, and (2) a given increase in the price makes it profitable for a large number of new firms to enter the industry. If it is easy for the individual firm to expand its output, as reflected in the fact that this can be accomplished without much increase in the marginal cost, and if it is easy for new firms to enter the industry, then the supply will be elastic, for a given increase in price will result in a large increase in output. If, on the other hand, it is difficult for the individual firm to expand its output, as reflected in the fact that it cannot expand without suffering a considerable increase in the marginal cost, and if it is difficult for new firms to enter the industry, then the supply will be more inelastic.

Perfectly Elastic and Perfectly Inelastic Supply

The supply will be perfectly elastic over a range of output if either the existing firms can expand output without any rise in the marginal cost or there are a number of firms whose minimum average cost is equal to the price of the product, so that a small rise in that price will bring these firms into the industry and a small fall will drive them out. The supply will be perfectly inelastic if the existing firms are producing at their absolute maximum capacity, so that an increase in output will result in an infinite increase in the marginal cost, and if no new firms can come into the industry.

The Equilibrium of an Industry

We can now formulate the general condition for the equilibrium of an industry. An industry is said to be in equilibrium when there is no tendency for it to expand or to contract. It will be in equilibrium, therefore, if the least profitable firm in it (commonly called the "marginal firm") is normally profitable. If the profits of the least profitable firm are less than normal, this firm and others in like case will eventually leave the industry. Their departure will lessen the total output, which will raise the price of that output, making the remaining firms more profitable. Firms will continue to leave the industry until the least profitable firm is normally profitable. In this condition the least profitable firm would gain no advantage in moving out of the industry, and the industry therefore will cease to decline. If, on the other hand, the least profitable firm is making profits above normal, this probably means that a new firm coming into the industry would also be able to make profits above normal. Consequently, there will be a tendency for new firms to come in, and the industry will expand. As it expands, its total output will rise and the price of its product will fall, making the profits of existing firms less, and lessening the temptation for new firms to come in. When the profits of the least profitable firm are normal again, the industry will cease to expand, for any new firm coming into it will probably make less than normal profits.

Graphic Derivation of the Normal Supply Curve

Just as we have derived the normal supply schedule of an industry from the cost schedules of its component firms, so we can derive the normal supply curve from the cost curves of the component firms.

Fig. 82 shows the average cost curves (AC) and the marginal cost curves (MC) for four single-product firms comprising an industry. Firm A has the lowest minimum average cost, Firm D the greatest. The exposition is confined to four firms for the sake of convenience; in fact, of course, a perfectly competitive industry would have a large number. From the cost curves we can derive the normal supply curve for the product of the industry, as follows: When the price of the

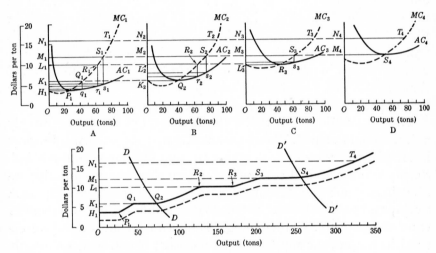

FIGS. 82 and 83.   Derivation of the Supply Curve.

product is less than OH_1, nothing will be produced. At a price equal to OH_1 Firm A will find it profitable to enter the industry, and will produce at an output measured by H_1P_1 (Fig. 82A). As the price rises from OH_1 to OK_1, the output of Firm A rises from H_1P_1 to K_1Q_1, following its marginal cost curve. Transcribing this movement to Fig. 83 (the supply curve) we see that the quantity supplied rises from nothing to K_1Q_1 as the price rises from 0 to OK_1, following the curve $OH_1P_1Q_1$. At the price OK_1 Firm B will enter the industry, for OK_1 is equal to its minimum average cost. It produces at this price an amount K_2Q_2. The total quantity supplied by the industry at this price is therefore $K_1Q_1 + K_2Q_2$, or K_1Q_2 in Fig. 83. As the price rises from OK_1 to OL_1, the output of both firms increases, following their marginal cost curves, till at the price OL_1 their combined output is $L_1R_1 + L_2R_2 (= L_1R_2$ in Fig. 83). At this price Firm C comes into the industry, and the total output increases by an amount L_3R_3 to L_1R_3 in Fig. 83. At a price OM_1 the fourth firm enters the industry. The supply curve for the industry, therefore, is the curve $OH_1P_1Q_1Q_2R_2R_3S_3S_4T_4$ —etc., of Fig. 83.

The Elasticity of Supply

It will readily be seen from the figures that the elasticity of the supply curve depends on the two aforementioned factors. The first is the slope of the marginal cost curves, for the steeper the marginal cost curves are, the steeper the supply curve will be. The second is the difference between the minimum average cost of successive firms on the cost scale. Thus, a rise in price of $4 per ton is necessary, after Firm B has been brought in, to bring in Firm C. The supply in this range is more inelastic than in the next price range, where a rise of only $2 per ton in price is sufficient to bring in Firm D. If we think of the succession of firms from A to D as a "ladder" of costs, then the steeper the ladder, the more inelastic the supply.

These conclusions tally well with the concept of elasticity of supply as it was used in Part I. We see now clearly that the elasticity of supply is a measure of the *ease* with which an industry may be expanded. A steeply rising marginal cost curve is a sign that an enterprise is running into increasing difficulties as it tries to expand its output. A steeply rising "cost ladder" means that it is difficult for new firms to enter the industry. If, therefore, it is difficult for an industry to expand its output, the supply will be inelastic; if it is easy, the supply will be elastic. If the "cost ladder" is horizontal, or nearly so—i.e., if the cost curves of all the firms lie at about the same level—there will be perfect elasticity of supply.

LONG-RUN AND SHORT-RUN SUPPLY

The Period of Adjustment

We have already noticed that our definition of cost, and therefore of supply, must always have reference to a specific length of time. This is necessary because adjustments take time; consequently, the shorter the period of time under consideration the less adjustment can be made. In any situation there is a period so short that no adjustments can be made to changing circumstances; this we may call the "instantaneous" period, though it may cover a finite period of clock time. At the opposite extreme there is what is called the "long period"; this again is no very definite number of days or years, but is a period long enough to permit all adjustments to be completed. In between these two periods are an indefinite number of "short periods" representing various temporary adjustments which are not in themselves complete. Suppose, for example, that a man is proceeding along a road at a steady pace when suddenly the road is blocked by a landslide ahead. For a brief moment the change in circumstances produces no change in the man's behavior; he continues walking along the road at the old pace; this is the "instantaneous" period. Following that come various "short-run" adjustments to the new situation. He may stop altogether and take stock of the situation, he may scramble over the obstacle at a reduced pace, he may turn back to find another road, and so on. If the road is a well traveled one, however, there will be an ultimate, long-run adjustment to the landslide: the obstacle will be cleared away, or the road will be rebuilt over it with perhaps a heavier gradient than before.

Instantaneous and Long-Run Adjustments

Similarly, in the problem of supply we can distinguish three broad "periods of adjustment," with three different types of cost and supply curves. At one extreme there is the "instantaneous" period, so short that no adjustments can be made. Cost curves in this period are vertical, and supply curves perfectly inelastic. A change in demand or a change in price produce no change in output; the wheels of production grind on from force of habit in exactly the old fashion. At the other extreme there is the "long run"—the period long enough to allow all adjustments to be made; long enough, for instance, to allow for the liquidation of plant and equipment and their replacement by other forms. The long-run supply curve is likely to be the most elastic of all the supply curves, for it represents the maximum possible adjustment of output to price or demand. The long-run supply curve also has the property of being *reversible*. That is to say, if the conditions of long-run cost are unaltered, the same supply curve shows the reactions of output either to a rise or to a fall in price. Thus, if $H_1 T_4$ in Fig. 83 is a long-run supply curve, it will show with equal accuracy the effect either of a rise in demand from DD to $D'D'$, or of a fall in demand from $D'D'$ to DD. If cost curves are unchanged and an industry is in equilibrium, a rise in demand followed by a fall in demand to its original position will eventually return the industry to its initial equilibrium.

The "Short Run" and the Concept of "Capacity"

Between the instantaneous "no adjustment" and the long-run "full adjustment" there lies the indefinite morass of the "short period." Short-period supply curves present many difficulties, mainly because the analytical apparatus so far constructed is not fitted to deal with the kind of dynamic problems that characterize temporary adjustments. The analysis up to this point has been essentially static in character, and hence is best suited to the solution of those problems of long-run equilibrium where the adjustment is not a function of time but is complete, and therefore independent of particular time periods. Care must be taken, therefore, not to load too much on an inadequate analytical apparatus in the interpretation of short-run adjustments.

When economists talk about "the" short run they usually mean a period of time too short to make changes in the quantity of plant and equipment—i.e., in the "capacity" of an industry—but long enough to make changes in the degree of utilization of that capacity. In point of fact, of course, adjustments in capacity and in the utilization of existing capacity are likely to proceed simultaneously, so that it is impossible to take any definite period—say, a year—and call it the "short period." The actual adjustments made in a short period of time —e.g., to changes in demand—depend very much on the expectations of the future. Thus the adjustment which may be made to a change in demand or in price expected to be temporary might be very different from that made to a supposedly permanent change.

Short-Run Cost Curves

If now we assume that firms are operating under "short-run" conditions so that they have a more or less definite "capacity" set by the size of their plant and fixed equipment, certain conclusions about the shape of the short-run cost curves follow. Until capacity output is reached, there is no particular reason to suppose that variable and marginal costs will rise much, if at all, with increasing output. It is not, in fact, an unreasonable assumption to suppose that as long as a firm is operating under capacity, its average variable and marginal costs are constant.[1] When the limit of capacity is reached, however, the expansion of output can only be obtained at greater and greater cost. In the most extreme case we may suppose that marginal and average variable costs are constant until the point of capacity output is

---

[1] Most of the empirical studies of cost curves confirm this assumption. See Joel Dean, *The Statistical Determination of Costs*, University of Chicago Press, 1936.

reached, at which point they become infinite. Such a case is illustrated in Figs. 84A and 84B. Fig. 84A shows the total cost curve, *ABD,* where capacity output is *OC.* Fig. 84B shows the corresponding average variable cost curve and marginal cost curve, *abd,* which in this case are identical, and the average total cost curve, *efd.* It is evident that under these extreme assumptions the firm will either produce at capacity or not at all, if it has perfect markets for its output. If the price of the product is above *cb,* the firm will continue to produce in the short run. With the price between *cb* and *cf* it will not be making enough profit to justify its permanent existence, but it will nevertheless be better to produce than to shut down, as long as its capacity remains unimpaired. Thus, if in Fig. 84A the revenue curve is *OM,* the "loss" at capacity production *MB* is less than the loss at zero production *OA.* If, how-

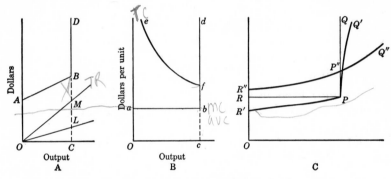

FIG. 84.   Short-Run Cost and Supply Curves.

ever, the price falls below *cb* of Fig. 84B, so that the total revenue curve is, for example, *OL,* it will pay to shut down completely; the loss at zero output, *OA,* is less than the loss at any positive output. The short-run supply curve of the individual firm is therefore the line *oabd* in Fig. 84B, indicating that at all prices below *oa* (or *cb*) the firm will produce nothing, and at all prices above *oa* it will produce at the capacity output, *oc.*

The Short-Run Supply Curve

If now all the existing firms in the industry have the same average variable and marginal costs when producing at less than capacity, the short-run supply curve of the industry will also have the right-angled shape such as *RPQ* in Fig. 84C, with the angle at the capacity of the whole industry, *RP.* If the various firms in the industry, as may be quite possible, exhibit a "cost ladder," so that there are some firms with a higher marginal cost at capacity than others, the short-run supply curve for outputs less than the capacity of the industry will not be perfectly elastic, but will be something like $R'P$ in Fig. 84C. If the capacity of the firms in the industry is not quite definite, so that instead of having a right angle at b in Fig. 84B we merely have a sharp bend, with costs rising rapidly after a certain output but not immediately becoming infinite, the short-period supply curve beyond the point of approximate capacity will not be absolutely vertical, but may be something like PQ'. As long as the problem is a short-run problem, there will be some sense to the concept of "capacity," and the supply curve will have a definite kink or angle in it around the capacity output. The longer the period of adjustment, however, the more possible it becomes to expand the "capacity" of an industry, and the less meaningful therefore the concept of capacity becomes; in the long run, therefore, the "kink" disappears from the supply curve and it takes on a shape more like $R''P''Q''$. It will be observed that the long-run supply curve has been drawn to cut the vertical portion of the short-run curve at P''. This is necessary because at the point P the price is below the minimum average *total* cost of the constituent firms; hence the long-run supply price of the capacity output RP must be more than OR—must, in fact, be sufficient to cover the fixed as well as the variable costs of the various firms.

As we have seen, firms will continue producing once they have a certain capacity established, even if the price of their product falls below the minimum average total cost, provided that the price exceeds the minimum average *variable* cost. They will not *expand* their capacity, however, unless the expected price is at least equal to the average *total* cost of the product of the expanded capacity. Because of this there is a certain asymmetry between the response to a rise or to a fall in demand in a given time period. A rise in demand which is thought to be permanent may attract new firms, or may cause old firms to expand their capacity, in a relatively short time. A fall in demand, however, will not result in a decline in capacity until the equipment on which the capacity is based wears out; the equipment will continue to be employed for a long time even though its full costs are not covered by the price of the product. That is to say, the "short run" may be a much longer period of time when the adjustment is a contraction than when it is an expansion, particularly where the equipment or "fixed capital" is long-lived relative to its period of construction.

One important result of the asymmetry of short-run supply is that industries with highly fluctuating demands tend to suffer from chronic overcapacity. A rise in demand is thought to be permanent, and results in a rapid expansion of capacity; a subsequent unexpected fall in demand does not lead to a rapid reduction of capacity, but results rather in a long period of unprofitable production, if the firms in the industry have perfect markets, or perhaps in much idle capacity if the industry is monopolistic.

The chronic overcapacity of the construction industries (e.g., steel, housing, etc.) is responsible for a good many of the woes of capitalist society and may, at least in part, be attributed to the above phenomenon. Such an industry is like a beetle trap—easier to get into than out of. There is little wonder that it tends to become overcrowded.

ECONOMIC RENT

In Part I (page 211) we made a brief examination of the concept known as "economic rent." Our analysis of cost will enable us to make a more thorough study of this elusive but important idea. We saw in Part I that economic rent came into being when a supply curve was less than perfectly elastic; for then, at a price which was high enough to call forth the necessary quantity, some of the suppliers would be paid more than was strictly necessary. By "economic rent" we then meant the excess amount paid to any supplier above the minimum sum necessary to keep him supplying.

Net Revenue as "Economic Rent"

Now, when an industry has a number of firms some of which have high costs and others low costs, it is evident that if the price is high enough to keep the high cost firms in the industry, it will be greater than is necessary to keep the low-cost firms in the industry. The low-cost firms, then, are apparently receiving more than is strictly necessary to keep them operating; they are the recipients of "economic rent." The net revenue of such a favored firm is the measure of this "economic rent" or surplus, for when the net revenue is zero a firm is just normally profitable, and if the net revenue is positive the firm is receiving more than is necessary to keep it alive. Fig. 82, page 567, will serve also to illustrate this concept. When the price of the product is as low as OH_1, even the first firm has a zero net revenue. If the price rises to OK_1, the net revenue, or economic rent, in Firm A rises to the area $K_1Q_1 \times Q_1q_1$, as in Fig. 78, page 553. If the price rises to OL_1, the economic rent in Firm A is the area of the rectangle $L_1R_1 \times R_1r_1$, the economic rent in Firm B is the rectangle $L_2R_2 \times R_2r_2$, and there is no economic rent in Firm C. If the price rises to OM_1 the economic rent in Firm A is $M_1S_1 \times S_1s_1$, in Firm B is $M_2S_2 \times S_2s_2$, in Firm C is $M_3S_3 \times S_3s_3$, and in Firm D is nothing. An increase in demand, therefore, where the supply is not perfectly elastic, will increase the economic rents in all the firms. If, for instance, the demand in Fig. 83 were the curve DD, only two firms would be in the industry, the price would be OK_1, and only the first firm would enjoy an economic rent. If the demand rose to the position $D'D'$, the price would have to rise to OM_1 to overcome the barrier of increasing cost, four firms would be in the industry, and the first three firms would be receiving economic rent. In a perfectly competitive industry there will of necessity be a large number of firms—we merely use four firms as a convenient expository device.

No Economic Rent with a Perfectly Elastic Supply

If all the cost curves of all firms in an industry are identical, the supply curve will be perfectly elastic. Such an industry would be described as an industry of "constant cost." It should be noticed that to have an *industry* of constant cost it is not necessary for the individual enterprise to have constant costs. It is possible for the average cost and the marginal cost of each enterprise to vary with its output, and still the industry as a whole may have constant costs and a perfectly elastic supply curve. If in Fig. 82 the minimum average cost of all the firms were on the same level, the industry would be a constant-cost industry even though for each firm a rise in price would lead to a rise in cost. In this case an increase in demand would result in the addition of new enterprises to the industry, but not in any increase in price, and not, therefore, in any increase in cost. In such an industry there are clearly no "economic rents." The price of the product will be determined by the minimum average total cost of each firm. Each firm will then be normally profitable when the industry is in equilibrium, no matter how great the demand or how great the output of the industry. There will be no "net revenues" except in periods of transition when the industry is moving from one point of equilibrium to another.

Who Gets Economic Rent?

In the discussion of the present chapter we have assumed implicitly that the "net revenue" accrues to the owner of the business. In fact, one or more of the factors of production employed by the business may receive part or all of the "economic rent" resulting from the favorable position of a business. We shall return to this topic in the next chapter, when we have discussed more fully the nature of the individual enterprise.

THE EFFECT OF A CHANGE IN COST CURVES

With the analytical tools now at our disposal we can go to work on a proposition stated briefly in Part I (page 179). It is that a fall in the average cost of production of individual enterprises *at each output* will result in an increase in supply, i.e., in a movement of the supply curve of the industry to the right.

Change in "Cost" and in the "Cost Curve"

In the case of demand there is a vital distinction between a "change in demand" and a "change in the quantity demanded." A change in demand means a shift of the whole demand curve, a change in the quantity demanded at each hypothetical price. A "change in the quantity demanded" means a change in the quantity demanded *as a result of* a change in price, the demand curve itself remaining unchanged. Similarly in the case of cost curves, a shift in the whole cost curve of an enterprise must be distinguished from a change in cost which is due to a change in output. In the first case there is a new cost of production at each hypothetical output. In the second case the cost curve is unchanged, but the cost changes because of a "movement along the curve." The first we shall call a "change in the cost curve" to distinguish it from a mere "change in cost."

Fall in Cost Curves Equivalent to an Increase in Supply

We shall show in the next chapter that an improvement in the techniques of production will lower the average total cost at each hypothetical output, i.e., will lower the average total cost curve. An improvement in techniques will also probably lower the marginal cost at each output, although this result is not absolutely necessary. In any case, however, a study of Figs. 82 and 83, page 567, will show that an improvement in techniques, a fall in the price of inputs, or anything resulting in a lowering of the cost curves will cause a movement of the supply curve to the right, and therefore, probably, a fall in price and a rise in the industry's output. Suppose that for some reason every cost figure in Fig. 82 fell by $2 per ton. That is, every cost curve, both marginal and average, moved $2 per ton downward toward the output axis. Then the supply curve, Fig. 83, would also move downward by $2 per ton to the position marked by the dotted line. A fall in the cost curves, therefore, results in a fall in the *supply price* of each quantity of output. If cost curves fall, that is to say, the industry will be prepared to supply any *given* quantity of output at a smaller price than before. This means also that at any *given* price the industry will be prepared to supply a *larger* quantity than before. A fall in the supply price at each output is equivalent to what we have called an "increase in supply," i.e., a rise in the quantity which will be supplied at each price. In terms of geometry, a movement of the supply curve downward toward the output axis is the same thing as a movement to the right away from the price axis. It is this movement to the right which we call a "rise" in supply.

COST AND THE OUTPUT OF AN INDUSTRY

Specialization Lowers Cost Curves

Cost analysis will also help to clear up another problem relating to the equilibrium of an industry—the problem raised by the fact that the *size* of an industry may affect the productive efficiency of the firms which compose it, and may therefore affect the cost curves of these firms. We have already observed many applications of the great principle that the degree of specialization depends on the extent of the market. This principle frequently applies to a whole industry. The larger the industry, the more extensive will be the specialization within it. In primitive agriculture, for instance, each farmer makes many of his own tools and implements, raises his own seed, rears his own stock, and builds his own buildings. In a highly developed agricultural industry the farmer buys most of his tools, implements, power, stock, and seed from other firms. The increased specialization may then result in a general increase in productive efficiency and therefore in a general lowering of the cost curves.

Increasing, Constant, and Decreasing Supply Price

In an industry of this type, then, an increase in demand for the product may cause not a rise but a fall in its price. If we could assume that the cost curves of an industry were unchangeable, then of course all supply curves would be positively sloped, and any rise in demand, if supply were not perfectly elastic, would result in an increase in the price of the product—the increase being necessary in order to expand the output of the industry over the "hurdle" of the high costs of the new firms. If, however, an increase in the output of an industry *itself* brought about a general lowering of cost curves of all the firms connected with it, a rise in demand would go hand in hand with a rise in the supply, i.e., with the movement of the supply curve in Fig. 83 to the right, brought about by a general fall in cost curves. If the movement of cost curves is slight, the result of a rise in demand may still be a rise in the price of the product. If the movement of cost curves is a little greater, the rise in demand may have no effect on price. If the movement of the cost curves is greater still, the rise in demand may produce a fall in price. In the first case the industry would be called one of "increasing supply price"; in the second case, one of "constant supply price"; and in the third case, one of "decreasing supply price."

Graphic Illustration. These principles are illustrated in Fig. 85. In each diagram *DD* and *SS* represent the demand and supply curves of an industry in equilibrium. *SS* here may be called the "given-cost supply curve." It shows how much will be produced by the industry

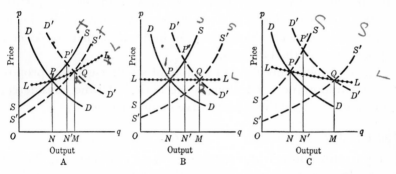

Fig. 85.   Increasing, Constant, and Decreasing Supply Price.

at each price, on the assumption that the industry has a definite series of cost curves. Now suppose demand rises. The demand curve shifts to *D'D'*. If the cost curves of the industry do not change, the price will rise to *P'N'*, the output to *ON'*. This we may call the position of given-cost equilibrium.

Greater output, however, will make possible a greater degree of specialization within the industry. Production will be more efficient and cost curves will fall. The given-cost supply curve, therefore, will shift to the right. As it shifts, the output will increase and the price will fall. As output increases, costs may fall still further, and the given cost supply curve will shift farther to the right until finally it comes to rest at the position *S'S'*. In this position the price is *MQ*, the output is *OM*, and the supply curve *S'S'* is derived from that set of cost curves which is consistent with the output *OM*. This position is the "long-run equilibrium" of the industry. For every possible rise or fall in demand, whether great or small, there will be a series of points such as

Q. These points lie along the beaded curve *LL*. This we may call the "long-period supply price curve." It tells us what, in the final adjustment, when the cost curves are consistent with the equilibrium output, will be the price and the output corresponding to each possible level of demand.

If now a rise in demand, and therefore in output, causes only a small movement in cost and short-period supply, as in Fig. 85A, the curve *LL* will slope upward, though with a greater elasticity than the short-period supply curves. If the rise in output causes a larger movement in cost curves and in short-run supply, as in Fig. 85B, the curve *LL* may be a straight line parallel to the output axis. That is, the long-period supply price curve will be perfectly elastic, and the industry will be one of "constant supply price" in the long run. If a rise in output causes a large fall in cost curves the result may be as pictured in Fig. 85C, where the long-period supply price curve slopes downward and has a negative elasticity. This would be an industry of "decreasing supply price" in the long run.

These propositions are an example of another general proposition of great importance: The longer the period of time considered, the more elastic will be the supply curve of any product.

The Effects of Uncertainty

Up to this point in the chapter we have assumed that the various cost and revenue functions are certain and known, and that therefore the maximization of net revenue is a reasonable rule of economic behavior. We may now wish to inquire what modifications the presence of uncertainty introduces into the analysis. Suppose, for instance, returning to Fig. 81, page 564, that the entrepreneur hopes for a price of *OL,* but fears that the price might be only *OH*. If he follows only his most hopeful expectation he will of course produce *LR* (= *HS*). Suppose now, however, that he produces *LR* but the price in fact turns out to be *OH*. He will then make a "loss" (negative net revenue) of *HS* × *ST*, whereas had he been more cautious and only produced *HP* he would at least have made normal profits. Uncertainty, then, is likely to make producers commit themselves rather less than they would at each expected price if they were quite certain of realizing the price. That is, the supply curve from the firm will be more inelastic than the marginal cost curve above the point *P*—say, *PU* rather than *PR*. From the point of view of the entry of new firms also the presence of uncertainty will make prospective new firms hestitant to commit themselves. This makes for "steepness" in the cost ladder, and hence also for more inelastic supply curves, especially in the short run. Thus we see that the presence of uncertainty modifies the above analysis, but does not affect its basic principle. It is noticeable that a reduction of uncertainty—e.g., by government guarantees of price in agricultural production—has a marked effect in increasing the elasticity of supply. A guaranteed low price may be more effective in calling forth output than the uncertain prospect of a high price.

SOME APPLICATIONS OF THE FOREGOING ANALYSIS

"Fixing Price According to Cost of Production"

We frequently hear the complaint that the price of a certain commodity is "below the cost of production" and that the government should step in and fix a "fair" price which will be "equal to the cost of production." The milk industry, and agricultural production in general, seem to be particularly subject to this complaint. Our analysis of cost will show the fallacy in most of these arguments. We have seen that there is no such thing as "the" cost of production of a commodity. There are as many costs of production as there are firms, and as many costs of production within a firm as there are different quantities of output. When, therefore, an industry demands that the price of its product be fixed so as to cover "the" cost of production of the commodity, the question at once arises, *"Whose* cost of production?" We have seen that in equilibrium the price of the product of a competitive industry is of necessity equal to the marginal cost of production in all firms and to the average total cost of production in the marginal firms. How, then, does the complaint arise that the price is "below cost"?

Low Prices a Symptom, Not a Cause

The answer seems to be that a cry for fixing prices generally arises from an industry which is larger than its equilibrium size. In such an industry there are a number of "submarginal" producers who are making less than normal profits and who therefore should leave the industry and employ their resources elsewhere. The "cost of production" which is not "covered by the price" is the average cost of these submarginal producers. If the price could be "fixed" to cover the cost of production of these producers, the industry would be permanently "too large," would be prevented from finding its position of equilibrium, and there would be a permanent maldistribution of resources. Low prices and unprofitability in any industry are a *symptom* of a deep-seated economic complaint. To treat the complaint of maldistribution of resources by fixing prices is like treating jaundice by painting the patient pink.

In any case the fixing of prices at a level high enough to keep the submarginal producers in the industry cannot be achieved unless there is restriction of production by all, or most, producers below the level which would be most profitable to each individually. As we saw when studying demand and supply in Chapter 8, if prices are fixed above the level at which the quantity demanded and the quantity supplied are naturally equal, then unless there is control of production the output of the industry will increase to a point where the whole output cannot be sold at the fixed price. Then either the price-fixing scheme collapses or rigid control of production must be introduced.

The Case for Intervention

The above argument is not, however, necessarily a proof that government should keep its hands off the affairs of a competitive industry. If the submarginal producers find it very difficult to transfer themselves to another industry, or if all producers have about the same cost curves, the "automatic" mechanism may not work at all well. The "automatic" adjustment of an industry by the forcing out or the attraction of submarginal or supermarginal producers is something that works best when there is a moderately inelastic supply, a steep "cost ladder" between different firms, and consequently a relatively small number of firms which are actually on or around the margin of profitability at any one time. In such an industry any overexpansion is easily remedied by the dropping of a few firms, and the automatic adjustment takes place without a great deal of personal suffering. If, however, the "cost ladder" is almost horizontal and the supply very elastic, but firms find it difficult to leave the industry, then the adjustment to a new equilibrium may take a long time and cause a good deal of suffering. Indeed, in such a case there may be no movement toward equilibrium at all, but a perpetual cyclical movement, the industry swinging continually between overexpansion and overcontraction. If the "cost ladder" is steep and there is a fall in the price of the product, most firms will still be able to continue in operation with some reduction in "economic rent," and only a few firms will find their position in the industry untenable. But if the "cost ladder" is horizontal, a fall in price will make almost *all* the firms in the industry unprofitable. This sad condition will remain until some firms are forced out.

Now, however, it is not clear *which* firms should be forced out. Suppose that with 10,000 milk farmers almost all milk production is unprofitable, while with 9000 milk farmers the price of milk would be great enough so that almost all milk production would be profitable. If there are 10,000 milk producers, evidently the only final answer to the problem of the industry, apart from the monopolistic exploitation of the consumer, is to get rid of a thousand milk producers. But who is to be driven out, if all ten thousand of them are about equally profitable? It may be that they will all hang on to the industry at an unprofitable level of prices for some time, and then quite suddenly two or three thousand may get disgusted and quit the business. This may make production highly profitable for those who remain, until the high profits once more attract large numbers of new producers.

"Efficiency" and Profitability

A further problem arises where the least "desirable" producers are the most tenacious. An unprofitable situation in the milk industry may result in forcing out the clever producers who are able to seek opportunities elsewhere, leaving the slothful and insanitary back-country muck-dairymen in possession of the industry. According to our definitions, in this case the technically efficient dairymen, with their spotless sheds and tested cows, might well be "high-cost" producers, while the technically inefficient producers might be "low-cost." That is to say, technical inefficiency may be balanced, and more than balanced, by the low alternative cost of the skill and enterprise involved. During the depression, for instance, it was a curious sight to see coal mines fitted with the very latest in technical equipment lying idle because they could not meet the competition of the hill scratchers who dug coal out of the mountains with pickax and bucket. It is evident that there may be a conflict between economic efficiency, as measured by low alternative cost, and engineering efficiency, as measured by some physical standards. Where such a conflict exists there is often a tendency to overemphasize the engineering aspect of the problem at the expense of the economic. A good example of such overemphasis is found in the breeding of farm animals. Too often animals are bred for arbitrary "points" rather than for economic efficiency, and the ritualistic ideals of the dog show predominate to the exclusion of the more humdrum calculations of the accountant. In this kind of conflict we should constantly be on the watch for the specious allurement of purely technical ideals. Nevertheless, there may be a case for government intervention where the commodity produced by the technically inferior methods is itself inferior and where the public does not have an adequate opportunity for judging its inferiority. It might, for instance, be undesirable to let economic efficiency triumph over technical efficiency in the milk industry, if the technically inefficient plants produced unsafe milk and the public were not capable of judging its quality. The case for regulation here, however, rests on grounds other than the instability of the industry.

The "Infant Industry" Argument for Tariffs

An important application of our analysis of long-period supply and of industries of "decreasing supply price" is found in one of the few theoretically sound nationalistic arguments for a protective tariff. If an industry of decreasing supply price inside a country is small, its cost curves will be high and it may be at a comparative disadvantage in international trade. If there is complete free trade, then, the industry will never grow in the country concerned, because its larger foreign rivals will always have a cost advantage over it. If, however, the industry is protected from foreign competition by a tariff when it is young, it will grow; and as it grows the cost curves of the firms in it will fall, until it stands in a position of comparative advantage in respect to foreign industries. Then the tariff can be withdrawn and the industry can stand on its own feet. The price of the product may then be lower than it would have been without the tariff, and consumers will benefit from the economies of specialization.

The "infant industry" argument applies equally well to the case of a subsidy given to a small, struggling industry in the hope that it will eventually grow to a size where it can stand on its own feet. Indeed, there are many reasons for preferring a subsidy to a tariff as a means of protecting infant industries. Subsidies are more direct in their effects, and their costs are more obvious. For this reason industries themselves are likely to prefer tariffs, the cost of which is obscured by the complexity of its expression, appearing as it does in higher prices and depressed export markets which may not seem to be very clearly related to the tariff which produces them. Both subsidies and tariffs, however, are difficult to get rid of once they have been established, for vested interests with political influence grow up behind them. Even, therefore, when the "infants" have grown to lusty maturity, it is difficult to wean them from the government pap which has nourished them. For this reason, if for no other, there is something to be said for J. S. Mill's dictum that even though there may be oc-

casional sound arguments for a protective tariff, politicians could
never be trusted to know when these occasions arose!

QUESTIONS AND EXERCISES

1. What would you expect to be the effects of a tax on pigs on (a) the price
of pigs, (b) the number of producers in the pig industry, (c) the cost of
production of pigs? Assume that it is easy to get into and out of the pig
industry.

2. "It is possible for the supply curve of a single enterprise to be inelastic,
and yet for the supply curve of the industry of which the enterprise
forms a part to be perfectly elastic. Similarly, it is possible for the supply curve of an industry to be inelastic in the short run, and yet perfectly elastic in the long run." Discuss and illustrate.

3. In the course of the expansion of the automobile industry there was a
tremendous expansion of output and an equally remarkable reduction
in the price. How do you account for this fact, when we usually assume
that an increased output will result only from a *higher* price?

4. "It is seldom, if ever, true to say that the price of a product is determined by its cost of production. It is much truer, though not the whole
truth, to say that the cost of production is determined by the price."
If this is so, what is the "whole truth"?

5. Discuss the correctness or completeness of the following statements:
a. An industry is in equilibrium when no firms are leaving it and no
firms joining it.
b. A firm is in equilibrium when it is producing at its lowest cost.
c. No extraordinary profits can be made in a perfectly competitive
industry.
d. A firm must be making profits if the price of its product is equal to
or greater than the marginal cost of production.
e. In an industry which is in equilibrium the least profitable firm will
be making normal profits.
f. The price of a product will tend to be equal to (i) the marginal cost
of *all* firms in the industry, (ii) the average total cost of the marginal
firm in the industry.

6. If new firms join an industry, they will compete for factors of production employed by the other firms and will therefore raise the prices
of these factors of production. What effect will this have on the cost
curves of firms already in the industry? What effect on the supply curve?
How far does this element (which we have hitherto neglected) affect
the validity of our analysis?

7. The proposal is often made for a "scientific" tariff which will "equalize
the cost of production at home and abroad." How would you criticize
such a proposal in the light of our analysis of cost and of comparative
advantage?

8. "The farmer demands a living price for milk." Discuss.

9. "It is not an exaggeration to say that, at the present day, one of the main dangers to civilization arises from the inability of minds trained in the natural sciences to perceive the difference between the economic and the technical." (Lionel Robbins, *The Nature and Significance of Economic Science,* 2nd ed., p. 34.)

Discuss this statement with particular reference to (a) the problem of war, (b) government agricultural policy, (c) architecture.

10. Illustrate graphically the proposition that fluctuating demands may lead to chronic overcapacity in an industry that has large fixed capital.

CHAPTER 28

PRODUCTION FUNCTIONS AND COST FUNCTIONS

We have seen (page 529) that one of the basic transformation functions of an enterprise is its *production function,* which shows what quantities of inputs (factors) can be transformed into what quantities of output (product). The total cost of any quantity of output is simply the *value* of the inputs given up in its production. Clearly, then, production functions and cost functions must be closely related—indeed, the properties of the cost functions are for the most part derived from properties of the production functions. The main purpose of this chapter is to discuss the properties of production functions, and to show how the properties of cost functions are derived from them.

Production Relationships

In the first place inputs and outputs are related in a qualitative way. If we put turnip seed into the sea we will not get potatoes as a result; but if we put seed potatoes into land we probably will get potatoes. The production of any commodity involves certain techniques, i.e., certain *kinds* of inputs which must be used in order to get the *kind* of output wanted. Any process of production, then, is much like a recipe in a cookbook: take this and that and the other thing, cook in a slow oven for five hours, pour off the juice, and serve in ramekins. Indeed, cooking is a very good example of a process of production, for it clearly involves taking certain "inputs"—raw materials in the form of ingredients, the time of the cook, the heat of the oven, and so on—mixing them all together, and producing a product.

Quantitative Relations

A cookbook, however, would not be much use if it were merely qualitative, if it merely said, "Take sugar and butter and flour, mix them together, and bake." Besides telling the cook what *kinds* of things to put into a recipe, it also tells her what *quantities*. The process of production has a quantitative as well as a qualitative aspect, for inputs and outputs are closely related in *quantity*. Small quantities of input will yield only small quantities of output. If the *proportions* of inputs are varied, the quantity or quality of outputs will also be varied. Generally, these quantitative relationships are fairly definite. If we put 4 eggs, 2 cups of milk, 3 cups of flour, ½ cup of melted butter, 4 teaspoons of baking powder, and 1 teaspoon of salt into a waffle mixture and obey the instructions, we should expect to get ten waffles out of it, no more and no less. If we got twenty waffles or five waffles we should be not merely surprised, but indignant. Similarly, when an iron manufacturer goes to his cookbook, or whatever the equivalent is in the iron industry, and mixes so much ore, so much lime, so much coke, and so much heat for so many hours, he knows almost exactly how much iron he will get as a result. In some processes, like agriculture, the result is less certain. The farmer may plant so much seed potato on so many acres and give it so many hours of attention; but he may raise either a fine crop of potatoes or a fine crop of blight. From year to year the results of the application of agricultural recipes varies. Nevertheless, this variation is due merely to changes in "inputs" over which the farmer has no control, such as the weather. The farmer is merely a "cook" working with a remarkably unreliable oven. Even here, however, over a number of years, the farmer knows pretty well what size of crops he will get in response to various quantities of seed, land, and labor used. We shall not go far wrong in assuming that in any process the quantity of output is determined by the quantities of input of all kinds which go into it.

The Physical Production Schedule

For any process of production, then, we can draw up a schedule showing the relations which may exist between input and output quantities. This may be called the "physical production schedule." Just as we should read a demand schedule: "If the price were p then the amount purchased would be q," so we read the physical production schedule: "If we put a units of this input with b units of that input with c units of the other input, we shall get x units of output." Now there will be a large number of kinds of inputs and outputs in most processes. This makes the study of these relationships more difficult, as we now have a large number of "dimensions," or kinds of quantities, instead of only two as in the demand schedule. However, let us take the simplest possible case first.

A Simple Case: One Variable Input

Suppose a process of production uses two inputs, which we shall call "labor" and "land," and produces a single output, which we shall call "potatoes." Let us assume at first that the quantity of land to be used by the process cannot be varied, and is equal to 8 "acres," or land units. A land unit will be an area of land for a given time—say, an acre for a month. In this case the quantity of labor applied to the 8 acres of land can be varied, and the quantity of output depends on the quantity of labor applied. The unit of labor will be the work of one man for a given period of time—say, a "man-hour," or a "man-month." For shortness we shall call the labor unit a "man." In these examples we are not considering the time at which these inputs are applied. That part of the analysis will come later; here our concern is merely with the relationships between the *quantities* of inputs and outputs.

A Total Product Schedule

Just as we can construct a schedule to show the relation between, say, output and cost, so we can construct a schedule to show the relation between the quantity of labor applied to our 8 acres of land and the quantity of product which will result in each case. This is shown in columns 1 and 2 in Table 57, and is called the total product sched-

TABLE 57.   Productivity Schedules

1 Quantity of Labor Applied to 8 Acres of Land (Men)	2 Total Product (Tons)	3 Average Physical Productivity (Tons per Man)	4 Marginal Physical Productivity (Tons per Man)
0	0	?	
1	8	8.0	8
2	24	12.0	16
3	34	11.3	10
4	40	10.0	6
5	42	8.4	2
6	44	7.3	2
7	46	6.6	2
8	48	6.0	2
9	49	5.4	1

ule. This schedule should be read as follows: If no labor is applied to the 8 acres, there is no product; if one unit of labor is applied, there will be a product of 8 tons; if two units of labor are applied, there will be a product of 24 tons, and so on. The successive figures on the schedule denote alternative ways of using the 8 acres.

Average and Marginal Productivity

We saw how from the total cost schedule two other important schedules could be derived—the average total cost and the marginal cost schedules. Similarly, from the total product schedule two important schedules can be derived—an average physical productivity schedule (columns 1 and 3) and a marginal physical productivity schedule (columns 1 and 4). The average physical productivity of an input is defined as the ratio of the total product of a process to the quantity of the input necessary to produce that total product. Thus if 2 men produce 24 tons of potatoes, the average physical productivity is 12 tons per man. The marginal physical productivity of an input may be defined most simply as the increase in the total product resulting from the addition of one unit to the quantity of the input employed, under the condition that the quantities of all other inputs do not change. Thus the addition of the first man in Table 57 increases output from 0 to 8 tons; if the quantity of labor used is increased from 1 to 2 men, the product increases from 8 to 24 tons, i.e., by 16 tons; a further increase of one man, from 2 to 3, increases the product by 10 tons; and so on. If the quantity of input increases by a and the quantity of output responds by increasing x units, the marginal physical productivity over the range in question is $\frac{x}{a}$.

The "Law of Diminishing Returns"

There are several important things to notice about Table 57. The first is that both the average physical productivity and the marginal physical productivity rise at first, reach a maximum, and then fall as the quantity of labor applied to a fixed quantity of land is increased. This is, of course, a property of the figures for the total product assumed in our illustration, but it represents a principle of great importance, usually described as the "law of diminishing returns." As the expression "diminishing returns" is a loose one, capable of several meanings, we shall avoid it as far as possible, and refer to this principle as the *law of eventually diminishing marginal physical productivity*. It could also be stated as a law of eventually diminishing *average* physical productivity, for if one eventually diminishes, so does the other.[1] The expression is clumsy, but it is better to be clumsy than vague.

Its Exact Statement. Note that it is a law of *eventually* diminishing marginal physical productivity. It may be stated thus: As we increase the quantity of any one input which is combined with a fixed quantity of the other inputs, the marginal physical productivity of the variable input must eventually decline. It must be clearly understood that when we say "increase" the quantity of one input we mean in different experiments. To find the effect of a fourth man working with 8 acres we must not start working with 3 men and then add a fourth when the process is halfway through. We must take first 8 acres and 3 men and see how many potatoes we get. Then in a separate experiment we must take 8 acres and 4 men and see how many potatoes we get. The difference in the output is the marginal physical product of the fourth man. In this sense, then, the first man put to the 8 acres gives us 8 tons of potatoes, the second man gives us an additional 16 tons, the third an additional 10 tons, the fourth an additional 6 tons, the fifth an additional 2 tons, and so on. The more labor added to our 8 acres, the more potatoes we have.

But the output of potatoes does not increase in proportion to the quantity of labor used. That is, the output rises at a decreasing rate. If we increase the number of men on our acres to a large enough number, we shall find that eventually the addition of more labor does not enable us to get any more potatoes. The land has reached the physical limits of its productive capacity, and the marginal physical productivity of labor is then zero. If we add still more men they may get in each other's way and trample down the plants, and an extra man may actually reduce the yield of potatoes. If a thousand men had to work on 8 acres the crop would probably not be large! The marginal physical productivity may then be negative.

The Law Applies to Any Factor of Production

The law of eventually diminishing marginal physical productivity is a general law applying to any factor of production or input whatsoever. It is perhaps easier to visualize a varying number of men being applied to a fixed quantity of land. The law applies, however, if a fixed number of men are spread out over varying quantities of land. Sup-

[1] This statement is not absolutely true. It is possible for the marginal physical productivity to be increasing as the quantity of input increases, even when the average physical productivity is decreasing, if the latter is decreasing slowly at a decreasing rate. But this case is so improbable that it can be ruled out with safety.

pose that we have only 5 labor units ("men") to work with, but that we can spread them over as much or as little land as we like. By conducting a series of experiments we might then be able to construct a table such as Table 58, which would show how much product could be produced by 5 "men" on varying quantities of land.

Table 58 is similar to Table 57, with land in the place of labor. The average physical productivity of land and the marginal physical productivity of land are calculated as are the corresponding concepts for labor. It will be observed in this case also that the average and marginal physical productivities at first rise and then decline as the quantity of land is increased. Just as the physical productivity of labor must

TABLE 58. Land Productivity

1	2	3	4
Number of Acres to Which 5 Men Are Applied	Total Product (Tons)	Average Physical Productivity of Land (Tons per Acre)	Marginal Physical Productivity of Land (Tons per Acre)
0	0	?	
1	7	7.0	7.0
2	15	7.5	8.0
3	20	6.67	5.0
4	25	6.25	5.0
5	30	6.00	5.0
6	35	5.83	5.0
7	39	5.57	4.0
8	42	5.25	3.0
9	45	5.00	3.0

decline because of the physical limitations on the product from a given area of land, so in this case the fact that there is a definite physical limit to the amount that a fixed quantity of labor can produce, no matter how much land it has to work on, means that the physical productivity of land will eventually decline as labor is spread over a larger and larger area.

Productivity Schedules and Cost Schedules

The next task is to show how cost schedules can be derived from the productivity schedules in the simple case where only a single input can be varied in quantity. If we know the prices of the inputs used and the quantities of input necessary to produce a given quantity of product, we can calculate immediately the total outlay required to produce such a quantity. Table 57, page 587, for instance, shows that a product of 8 tons can be obtained with 8 acres of land and 1 unit of labor. If, then, the price of land were $20 per unit and the price of labor $20 per unit, the total outlay on 8 tons would be $160 for land plus $20 for labor, or $180. So we could calculate the total outlay for each quantity of output; and if we knew the normal profit at each output, we should have the whole total cost schedule. In this example we assume that normal profits are zero—the problem of allocating normal profit is difficult and must be left to a later stage of our analysis. The inclusion of normal profit in total cost, however, makes no great difference to the argument of the present chapter, and the exposition will be simplified by assuming that total outlay and total cost are identical.

TABLE 59. Derivation of Cost Schedules

(Assumptions: Land = $20 per unit, labor = $20 per unit. Variable quantities of labor working with 8 acres of land.)

1	2	3	4	5	6	7	8
Total Product (Tons)	Quantity of Labor	Outlay on Labor (Total Variable Cost) ($)	Outlay on Land (Total Fixed Cost) ($)	Total Outlay (Cost) ($)	Average Total Cost ($ per Ton)	Average Variable Cost ($)	Marginal Cost ($ per Ton)
0	0	0	160	160	∞	?	2.50
8	1	20	160	180	22.5	2.50	1.25
24	2	40	160	200	8.33	1.67	2.00
34	3	60	160	220	6.47	1.76	3.33
40	4	80	160	240	6.00	2.00	10.00
42	5	100	160	260	6.19	2.38	10.00
44	6	120	160	280	6.36	2.73	10.00
46	7	140	160	300	6.52	3.04	10.00
48	8	160	160	320	6.67	3.33	20.00
49	9	180	160	340	6.94	3.67	

The total cost schedule derived from the product schedules in Table 57, on the assumption that land costs $20 per unit and labor costs $20 per unit, is shown in Table 59. A close examination of the schedule will show that *because* increasing quantities of labor produce a less than proportionate increase in the total product, after a certain point an increase in the total product can only be obtained under the penalty of increasing average cost. The average total cost in the table reaches a minimum of $6 at an output of 40 tons.

Cost and Product Curves

The graphic treatment of these various relationships is shown in Fig. 86. At the top left of the whole figure we plot the total product curve, $OMNPR$, with labor measured on the horizontal and product on the vertical axes. This is columns 1 and 2 of Table 58. From this, in the lower left of the figure we derive the average physical product curve, $a_p nr$, and the marginal physical product curve, $m_p mnpcd$, from columns 1 and 3 and 1 and 4 of Table 58. At any quantity of input OH the marginal physical product is the slope of the total product

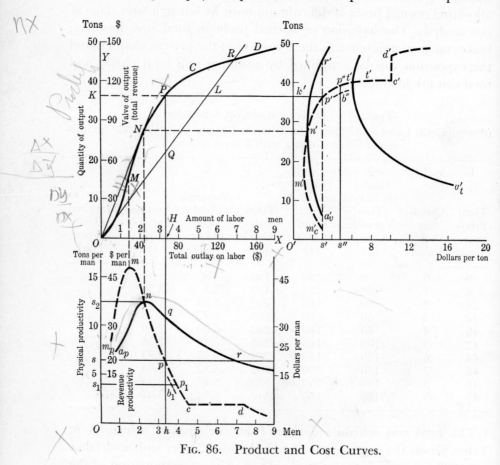

FIG. 86.   Product and Cost Curves.

curve at the corresponding point P, and the average physical product is the slope of the line OP (not drawn in figure) or HP/OH. We now relabel the horizontal axis OX so that the scale now reads "total outlay on labor." We suppose here the price of labor is \$20 per unit, so that 1 unit represents an outlay of \$20, 2 units of \$40, and so on. Perfect markets are of course assumed throughout. The curve $OMNPR$ now represents the *total variable cost curve*, with total variable cost measured along OX and output along OY. If the figure is held up to a mirror the reader will see that the curve has much the same shape as the total cost curve of Fig. 75, page 538. If the origin were moved to the left a distance equal to the total fixed cost, the curve would then represent the total cost curve. From this total variable cost curve the marginal cost curve, $m'_c m'n'p'c'd'$, is derived in the top right figure. This is from columns 1 and 8 of Table 59. The average variable cost curve, $a'_v n'r'$, and the average total cost curve, $a'_t t'$, are similarly derived from the total cost curve, or from columns 1 and 7 and 1 and 6 of Table 59.

We can now notice several things about the relationships of these curves. (1) The point of inflection of the total cost or total product curve, M, is the point of maximum marginal physical product, m, and also the point of minimum marginal cost, m'. (2) The point where the tangent from the origin, ON, touches the total product or total cost curve at N is the point of maximum average physical product, n, and also the point of minimum average variable cost, n'. This assumes of course that only one factor varies. (3) It will be observed that the "average-marginal relationship" holds for the relations of average and marginal physical product, as well as for average and marginal cost. That is, the marginal physical product curve cuts the average physical product curve at its highest point, just as the marginal cost curve cuts the average cost curve at its lowest point. (4) In the range of input quantities where marginal physical product is rising $(m_p m)$, there is a corresponding range of output quantities where the marginal cost is falling $(m'_c m')$. Similarly, where marginal physical product is falling, in the range mc, marginal cost is rising in the range $m'c'$. In a range where marginal physical product is constant with respect to input (cd), marginal cost is constant with respect to output $(c'd')$ and the total product, or total cost curve, is a straight line (CD). We thus see the intimate connection between the principle of eventually diminishing returns and the principle of eventually rising cost. Exactly similar propositions hold for the relation of average physical product and average variable cost.

Revenue Curves

Now let us suppose that there is a perfect market for the product at a price of $3 per ton. Assume no fixed cost. Measuring dollars along OX, the straight line OR is the total revenue curve. The net revenue is at a maximum, PL, at the output OK. Here the price $k'p'$ is equal to the marginal cost, $s'p'$ being the marginal (and average) revenue curve. The curves OR and $ONPCR$, however, can be given another significance. Suppose now we relabel the vertical axis OY, multiplying each quantity of output by its price, so that 10 tons becomes \$30, 20 tons \$60, and so on. Then with the OX axis measuring the quantity of labor (men) and the OY axis measuring dollars, the line $OMNPR$ is now a total revenue curve, showing what *value* of product is produced with each quantity of input. The line OR now is a total cost curve, showing the total cost of each quantity of input. That is, at any input OH the total cost of the input is HQ. When both axes register dollars OL is a 45° line—i.e., in dollars $HQ = OH$. At the input OH, then, HP is the total revenue, HQ is the total cost, and QP is the net revenue. We also have, however, as OL is a 45° line, $QP = PL$; i.e., QP is also the maximum net revenue. Moving down now to the bottom left-hand figure, we again relabel the vertical axis, multiplying each ton by its price—in this case \$3. Thus 15 tons per man becomes \$45 per man, and so on. The curves of the figure now represent the average (a_pnr) and the marginal (m_pmcd) *revenue* product. At any input oh, hq is the average revenue product—i.e., the total revenue divided by the quantity of input—and hp is the marginal revenue product, i.e., the increase in total revenue which results from a unit increase in input. If now os is the price of the input, assuming a perfect market, we see that the quantity of input at which net revenue is a maximum is oh ($= sp = OH$) where the price of the input is equal to its marginal revenue product.

The Marginal Conditions for Input

This is another application of the general marginal principle. In the general case where the market for input is not perfect the principle may be expressed as follows: Net revenue can be increased by increasing input if the marginal revenue productivity of the input is greater than its marginal cost, and can be increased by decreasing input if the marginal revenue productivity is less than the marginal cost. This method of statement implicitly takes care of the "second-order conditions" (see page 554) and ensures that the condition defines a maximum, not a minimum. The marginal cost of input is of course the increase in the total cost which results from a unit increase in input. A simple arithmetical example will illustrate the point. Suppose at a certain level of employment of input (say, labor) the marginal revenue product of labor were \$50 per man-week, and the marginal cost of labor were \$40 per man-week. That is to say, the addition of a man-week to the total amount of labor employed would increase the total revenue by \$50 and would increase the total cost by \$40.

Clearly the increase in labor employed would increase net revenue by (50 − 40) or $10, and it will pay to increase the quantity of labor employed. As this quantity is increased, however, the marginal revenue productivity will decline, and if the market is imperfect the marginal cost will rise. When, say, the marginal revenue productivity has declined to $45 per man-week and the marginal cost of labor has risen to $45 per man-week, it will no longer pay to increase employment, for an increase in employment adds just as much to revenue as it does to cost and there is no increase in net revenue. If now the firm goes beyond this point, to where, say, the marginal revenue productivity is $40 and the marginal cost is $50, it will clearly pay to reduce employment back to the point of equality of marginal revenue productivity and marginal cost of input.

Where the market for input is perfect, as we have seen (page 524), the marginal cost of input and its price are identical, so that the marginal condition becomes the one formulated above—price equals marginal revenue productivity.

SOME APPLICATIONS: RENT IN THE INDIVIDUAL ENTERPRISE

In the preceding chapter we noticed that in any industry with a less than perfectly elastic supply curve those firms with lower costs apparently received a positive net revenue, described as "economic rent." We must now examine this phenomenon further, for it seems as if the existence of economic rent would conflict with the principle of equal advantage as applied to profits. We shall prove that any economic rent in an enterprise tends to be appropriated by the owners of "specific" inputs. A specific input is defined as one which is perfectly inelastic in supply to the enterprise concerned, for which the entrepreneur can find no substitutes, and which is absolutely necessary for carrying on his business.

Specific Inputs Absorb Economic Rent

Suppose that in the example in this chapter a potato producer is working with 8 acres of land, and that the position and quality of this particular plot of land are such that the potato producer is earning extraordinary profits—i.e., he receives an economic rent. In that case the owner of the land would be able to raise the price of land services until he had appropriated all the extraordinary profits of the potato grower, leaving him with normal profits. The potato grower will not be forced off the land unless the landlord tries to exact a rent which will leave less than ordinary profits, i.e., which will result in a negative net revenue for the grower. If, for instance, in the example in Table 59 the price of potatoes were $6, the farmer would evidently be "breaking even," or earning normal profits, at the minimum average cost output of 40 bushels. At this point his net revenue is zero, as the total fixed cost ($160) is just equal to the excess of total revenue ($240) over total variable cost ($80). If, however, the price were less than $6 per bushel the farmer would be making less than normal profits if the rent were $20 per acre, and the landlord would have to reduce the rent if he is to hold the farmer on his land. Similarly, if the price were above $6 per bushel the landlord would be able to raise the rent above $20 per acre without driving the farmer away.

Calculation of Economic Rent

Thus the economic rent at any given price is equal to the difference between the total revenue and the total variable cost at the most profitable output, as this is the total fixed cost which would make the net revenue zero. The principle is illustrated in Fig. 87, drawn from Table 59. Output is measured along OX (or ox), total cost along OY, average or marginal cost along oy. OTD is the total variable cost curve, $m_c't'$ is the marginal cost curve, $a_v'A_o$ is the average variable cost curve, and $a_t'A_{20}$ is the average total cost curve when land rent is $20 per acre. These curves are identical with the corresponding curves in Fig. 86, except that the axes are reversed to make them look more familiar. Suppose now that the price of the product is os ($6). To calculate the economic rent we draw st' to cut the marginal cost curve in t'; st' ($= ok$) is then the most profitable output. The total revenue is then $ok \times os$, or the area of the rectangle $okt's$. The total variable cost is $okuw$. The economic rent then is the area of the rectangle $wut's$. Economic rent can also be calculated from the lower part of the figure. Project $t'k$ down to cut the total variable cost curve in T. Draw the tangent to the curve at T, TO_t, to meet the vertical axis at O_t. OO_t is then the economic rent. If the origin is shifted to O_t, then OTD becomes the total cost curve, O_tT the total revenue curve, and it is evident that net revenue is a maximum of zero at the point T.

It will be observed that the average total cost curve, $a_t'A_{20}$, is tangent to the horizontal line st' at t'; that is, the average total cost is a minimum at t'. This is a general property; at each price there will be an average total cost curve (including rent), and the minimum value of the average total cost will be equal to the price. The minimum point of each of these average total cost curves also lies on the marginal cost curve. That is, for each marginal cost curve there is a whole family of average total cost curves, each one corresponding to a given fixed cost. Curves corresponding to a fixed cost or economic rent of 0, 10, 20, are shown in Fig. 87 at A_0, A_{10}, A_{20}.

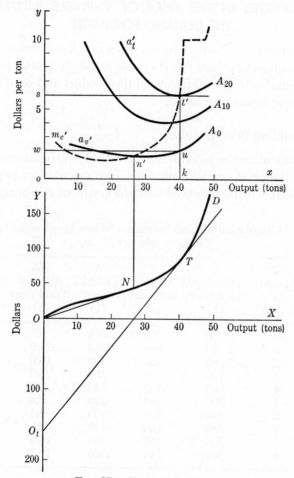

Fig. 87.   Economic Rent.

If now we include the economic rents in our average total cost, we can show that the minimum average total cost of *all* firms, not merely of the marginal firm, will be equal to the price of the product when an industry is in equilibrium. It is the differences in the average *variable* cost curves between different firms which constitute the "cost ladder" in Figs. 82 and 83. If the demand for the product rises, and therefore the price rises, the price of those fixed inputs which receive economic rent will also rise, until the minimum average total cost of each firm is equal to the price of the product. Then the rents of the fixed factors will be greatest in those firms which have the lowest average *variable* cost curve.

CHANGES IN THE PRICE OF VARIABLE INPUTS: THE DEMAND FOR INPUT

In the simple case of an enterprise with one fixed and one variable input we can now consider the effects of a change in the price of the variable input, both on the amount of the product and on the quantity of the variable input purchased.

Effect of Doubling Price of Labor

Let us recalculate the schedules of Table 59 on the assumption that the price of labor is not $20 but $40. This calculation is performed in Table 60. It will be observed that the result of doubling the price

TABLE 60.   Calculation of Cost Schedules When Land = $20 per Unit, Labor = $40 per Unit

1 Total Product	2 Quantity of Labor	3 Outlay on Labor ($)	4 Outlay on Land ($)	5 Total Cost ($)	6 Average Total Cost ($)	7 Marginal Cost ($)
0	0	0	160	160	∞	
						5.00
8	1	40	160	200	25.0	
						2.50
24	2	80	160	240	10.0	
						4.00
34	3	120	160	280	8.2	
						6.66
40	4	160	160	320	8.0	
						20.00
42	5	200	160	360	8.6	
						20.00
44	6	240	160	400	9.1	
						20.00
46	7	280	160	440	9.6	
						20.00
48	8	320	160	480	10.0	
						40.00
49	9	360	160	520	10.6	

of the variable input is to double the marginal cost at each level of output (Table 60, column 7, being compared with Table 59, column 8). The average total cost at each output is increased but not doubled. The average variable cost at each output is doubled, as the student may verify by making the calculations for himself.

The result of a rise in the price of a variable input, therefore, is a general rise in the cost curves of all the firms comprising an industry. However, a rise in the cost curves of all firms will lower (shift to the left) the supply curve of the product (page 575). If there is no change in demand for the product, there will then be a rise in the price of the

product and a fall in its total output, partly because of a decline in
the output of each firm after the rise in the marginal cost curve, partly
because of a reduction in the number of firms. The rise in costs will
push a number of firms which previously had been profitable below
the line of normal profits and drive them from the industry. The rise
in the variable cost curve will tend to lower the rents of the fixed input, and the rise in the price of the product will tend to raise the rents.
The decline in the output of the industry will also go hand in hand
with a decline in the purchases of the variable input. Therefore, the
demand curve for the variable input can also be derived from the
production schedules of the firms in the industry and from the demand for the product of that industry.

Graphic Illustration.   The solid lines in Fig. 88—A_1V_1, A_2V_2, etc.—
represent the average variable cost curves of four firms. The solid lines

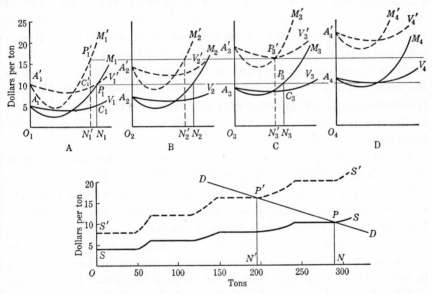

Figs. 88 and 89.   Effect of Rise in Wages.

A_1M_1, A_2M_2, etc., represent the marginal cost curves of the same firms.
The line SS in Fig. 89 is the supply curve of the industry, constructed
from the cost curves after the principles of Fig. 83. DD is the demand
curve for the product, PN the equilibrium price, ON the equilibrium
output of the industry. Firm D is the marginal firm. If the price of
labor now doubles, labor being the only variable input, in each firm
both the marginal cost and the average variable cost will be doubled
at each output. The new average variable cost and marginal cost

curves are shown by the dotted lines, $A'_1V'_1$, $A'_1M'_1$, etc. The new supply curve is $S'S'$ (Fig. 89), where the supply price of each quantity of output is twice as great as before. The new equilibrium price is $P'N'$ and the new equilibrium output is ON', P' being the point where the demand curve cuts the new supply curve. Under these conditions Firm D has to drop out of the industry, and Firm C becomes the marginal firm.

Effect on Rents

What happens to the rents in the individual firms depends on the circumstances of the case. In our example it is evident that the rent of Firm C has declined from $P_3C_3 \times O_3N_3$ to zero, as Firm C is now the marginal firm. In Firm A, however, the rent originally was $P_1C_1 \times O_1N_1$. With the price and output scales the same as those in Fig. 82 this amounts to 5×81, or \$405. After the rise in the price of labor the rent is $P'_1C'_1 \times O'_1N'_1$, which on the same scale amounts to 6.7×78, or \$522. There is no rule, therefore, which will tell us a priori whether the rent in a firm will rise or fall when the price of the variable input rises. It depends on whether the tendency exerted in the direction of a rise in rents by the rise in the price of the product is outweighed by the tendency exerted in the direction of a fall in rent by the rise in variable costs. Probably rents will tend to rise in low-cost firms and fall in high-cost firms.

Fig. 88 shows the effect of the rise in the price of labor on the output of each firm. In Firm A output falls from ON_1 to ON'_1, in Firm B it falls from O_2N_2 to $O_2N'_2$, and in Firm C it falls from O_3N_3 to $O_3N'_3$. If, however, we know the production schedule of each firm, we can immediately find how much labor is needed to produce any given quantity of product and can therefore find how great a diminution in the quantity of labor employed results from the rise in the wage. That is, we could calculate the elasticity of demand for labor. The quantity of labor bought by each individual firm does not decline very greatly, even when the price of labor doubles, for the decline in output in each case is relatively small (e.g., $N_1N'_1$). But the fact that one firm goes out of the industry means a considerable decline in the quantity of labor employed. Indeed, it is probable that the magnitude of the effect of a rise in wages on an industry depends more on its effect on the number of firms engaged in the industry than on its effect on any individual firm. The effect on the number of firms we may call the "industry" effect and the effect on the individual firm, the "firm" effect.

Importance of Elasticity of Demand

We can see immediately from Figs. 88 and 89 that the elasticity of demand for the product is of prime importance in determining the effect of a change in the price of an input (e.g., wages). If the demand for the product is inelastic, a rise in wages will result in a large rise in the price of the product and in little change in the number of firms and in the output of the industry. In that case there will be little change also in the quantity of labor employed. That is, an inelastic demand for a product is likely to result in an inelastic demand for any input which goes to produce it. This proposition has already been stated in Part I, page 205. Conversely, if the demand for the product is elastic, a rise in wages will produce a relatively small change in the price of the product, and a large reduction in the number of firms, in total output, and in the volume of employment of labor.

THE DEMAND FOR INPUT AND MARGINAL PRODUCTIVITY

The demand for input can also be analyzed by means of the marginal revenue productivity curve. We saw on page 594 that net revenue is not a maximum if the marginal revenue productivity of any input is not equal to its marginal cost. When the market for the input is perfect its marginal cost is equal to its price, and the condition for maximum net revenue is that the *price* of each input should equal its marginal revenue productivity. This means that if the marginal revenue curve does not change as the price of input changes, the marginal revenue productivity curve is itself the demand curve for the input, at least below the point of maximum average revenue. Thus in Fig. 86, in the lower part of the figure we have the marginal revenue productivity curve *mnpcd*. If the price of the input (in this case the wage) is *os* (on the dollars-per-man scale), the total amount of input employed (assuming maximization of net revenue) is *sp*. At a lower price (wage), os_1, more will be employed, s_1p_1. When the wage is equal to os_2, the maximum average revenue product, the net revenue is zero; for wages above this level net revenue is negative and the firm will eventually go out of business, so that the long-run demand curve for the input is s_2npcd.

The total demand for the input can be derived by adding up the individual demand curves from each firm. This analysis is essentially similar to the derivation of supply curves from the marginal cost curves of individual firms. It suffers also from a similar defect. A change in the price of an input, as we have seen on page 599, is likely to have an effect on the price of the *product* unless the demand for the product is perfectly elastic. If the price of the product changes, however, this changes the marginal revenue productivity curve, for it (assuming perfect markets for the firm's product) is derived by multiplying the marginal physical productivity (assumed invariant) by the price of the product. Thus a fall in the wage will lower the equilibrium price of the product, and so will lower the marginal productivity curve. Thus suppose in Fig. 86 again the wage falls from os to os_1. As a result of this the marginal revenue product curve itself may fall, and the amount of employment will not be s_1p_1 but s_1b_1. The firm's demand for labor, that is, will be less elastic than the marginal revenue productivity curve. A similar difficulty is found in the derivation of the supply curve. Thus suppose there is a rise in the price of the product from $o's'$ to $o's''$ (Fig. 86, right-hand side). Output rises from $s'p'$ to $s''p''$, following the marginal cost curve. As a result of the rise in output, however, there may be a rise in the price of input, which will raise the marginal cost curve. In this case the output at price $o's''$ will be not $s''p''$ but $s''b''$. Here again the supply curve of product from the firm will be less elastic than the marginal cost curve.

Just as the total elasticity of supply for a product may depend much on the steepness of the "cost ladder" and the "industry effect," so the total demand for an input may depend more on the steepness of the "productivity ladder"—i.e., the intervals between the maximum average productivity of successively less productive firms—than on the steepness of the marginal productivity curve for any one firm. If a large proportion of the output is produced by marginal firms or firms close to the margin, a rise in the price of input (e.g., in wages) will drive a lot of firms out of business and the demand for the input (e.g., labor) will be elastic.

QUESTIONS AND EXERCISES

1. Suppose that the following represented a production schedule for wheat, applying different quantities of labor to 10 acres of land:

Quantity of labor (man-months)	0	1	2	3	4	5	6	7	8	9
Product (bushels)	0	100	220	340	450	540	605	645	665	675

Assuming that labor and land are the only factors of production, and neglecting normal profits, calculate and draw, as in Fig. 86, page 592.
  a. The total product curve.
  b. The average physical productivity curve.
  c. The marginal physical productivity curve.

    d. The total variable cost curve.

    e. The total revenue curve.

    f. The net revenue curve (fixed cost = 0).

    g. The average and marginal revenue productivity curves.

    h. The average variable and the marginal cost curves.

Assume that the price of labor is $80 per unit and that the price of wheat is $1 per bushel. Under these circumstances what is the most profitable output? What is the total economic rent of the land? The rent per acre? With the fixed cost equal to the total economic rent, draw the average total cost curve and show that it reaches a minimum point at the most profitable output.

2. "If it were not for the law of diminishing marginal physical productivity we could grow all the world's food in a flowerpot." Discuss.

3. a. Prove that when the marginal physical productivity of a single variable input is zero, the total product is as great as it can possibly be.

    b. Prove that if the law of diminishing marginal physical productivity holds, in every process of production in which there is a necessary fixed factor there must be some absolute maximum to the amount of product obtainable.

    c. What would be the significance of a negative marginal physical productivity? Would such a case ever occur in practice?

4. Construct an arithmetical example to show that when the average physical productivity of an input does not vary with the quantity, the marginal physical productivity is equal to the average physical productivity and is also constant.

5. "The principle that the marginal cost eventually rises as output increases (the law of increasing cost) is essentially the same as the principle that marginal productivity declines as we increase the employment of an input (the law of diminishing returns)." Discuss.

6. "It is no more true to say that wages are determined by the marginal productivity of labor than it is to say that prices are determined by cost of production." Discuss.

7. When we draw up a production schedule we assume that the *methods* (techniques) of production are given. Any change in techniques operates through changing the whole production schedule. Consider, therefore, the effect of an improvement in the techniques of production of potatoes on:

    a. The production schedule.

    b. The cost curves of potato firms and the potato industry.

    c. The supply curve for potatoes.

    d. The demand curve for potato labor.

    e. The rents of potato land.

    f. The price of potatoes.

    g. The price of potato labor.

8. The following tabulation gives a relationship between the quantity of concentrates fed to a cow and the amount of milk obtained:

Concentrates fed (lbs.)	0	4	8	12	16	20	24
Milk obtained (gals.)	1	2	2.8	3.5	3.9	4.0	3.9

Assume that all other inputs are held constant, and that their total cost is 20 cents. Suppose the cost of concentrates is 3 cents per pound, and the price of milk is 30 cents per gallon.

a. Plot the marginal physical and marginal revenue productivity curves for concentrates.

b. Calculate, using graphs, if necessary:

    i. The most profitable amount of concentrates to feed.

    ii. The most profitable amount of milk to produce.

    iii. The output of milk at which its average total cost is the least.

c. The output at which the average total cost of milk is least is smaller than the most profitable output, which in turn is less than the maximum possible output. Are these relationships generally true? Under what circumstances might they not be true?

d. Are there any circumstances under which a cow with a high maximum yield might be *less* profitable than one with a low maximum yield? Illustrate graphically.

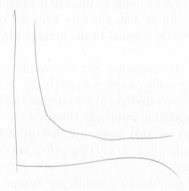

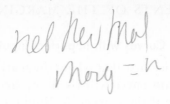
net Rev Mal

Mary = h

C H A P T E R   2 9

PROBLEMS IN THE THEORY OF MONOPOLY

In the two previous chapters it was assumed for the most part that the firm faced perfect markets for both output and input—that is, the prices received for output or paid for input did not vary with the quantities sold or bought. We shall now go on to consider some problems which arise when the firm has imperfect markets for input or output.

The "Pure Monopoly" Level of Analysis

There are several levels on which this analysis can be carried out. We can analyze first what would be the optimum position of the firm under the condition that its transformation functions were stable, certain, and unaffected by any other variables or decisions of the firm. This level of analysis is what is usually called the "theory of pure monopoly," because it would apply to the most extreme form of a one-firm industry. It is better regarded, however, as a level of analysis than as a description of any specific institutions in the real world, for there probably never has been a pure monopoly. All actual firms will find that their transformation functions will be affected in some degree by the value of their various variables, such as profits; if, for instance, they are making very high profits, this will encourage other firms to produce products which are in some degree substitutes for the product of the first firm, which will lower its sales curve, or perhaps its labor force will demand and obtain higher wages, which will raise its purchase curve. It is useful, nevertheless, as a step in the analysis to develop some special cases at the simple "monopoly" level.

The "standard case" has already been discussed on pages 551–555. Here we saw that net revenue would not be at a maximum if marginal cost were not equal to marginal revenue. We shall now proceed to some special applications of this general principle.

mR—mC

Marginal Cost Curves with Imperfect Input Markets

We may notice first that where the markets for input are imperfect, the marginal cost curve will rise more steeply, with given production functions, than if the markets for input are perfect. Let us define the

TABLE 61. Marginal Costs of Labor and Output

			Perfect Markets	
1	2	3	4	5
Output	Quantity of Labor	Marginal Physical Cost	Marginal Cost of Labor	Marginal Cost of Output
0	0			
8	1	0.125	20	2.5
24	2	0.0625	20	1.25
34	3	0.1	20	2.0
40	4	0.166	20	3.33
42	5	0.5	20	10.0
44	6	0.5	20	10.0
46	7	0.5	20	10.0
48	8	0.5	20	10.0
49	9	1.0	20	20.0

	Imperfect Markets		
6	7	8	9
Price of Labor	Total Cost of Labor	Marginal Cost of Labor	Marginal Cost of Output
20	0		
21	21	21	2.62
22	44	23	1.44
23	69	25	2.50
24	96	27	4.48
25	125	29	14.50
26	156	31	15.50
27	189	33	16.50
28	224	35	17.50
29	261	37	37.00

marginal physical cost of output as the increase in physical input which must accompany a unit increase in physical output. Then the marginal (money) cost of output is the marginal physical cost multiplied by the marginal cost of input, the marginal cost of input being the increase in its total money value which accompanies a unit increase in its employment. Thus suppose that at a given output of potatoes the marginal physical cost is 0.1 men per ton; that is to say, the addition of 1 ton to output involves the addition of 0.1 "men" to input. If the marginal cost of labor is $25 per man, this means that the addition of 1 man adds $25 to the total cost of labor. The marginal cost of output then is $2.50 per ton; adding 1 ton to output adds 0.1 men to input, which adds $(0.1 × 25) to total cost. The point is illustrated in Table 61. Columns 1 and 2 show the production function of Table 59. Column 3 is the marginal physical cost in each range of output. Column 4 shows the marginal cost of labor on the assumption that the price of labor is constant at $20 per man; in this case the marginal cost of labor is constant also and equal to its price (wage). Column 5 shows the marginal cost of output, obtained by multiplying columns 2 and 4. It is identical with column 8 of Table 59. Then in columns 6 to 9 we recalculate the marginal cost on the assumption of an imperfect market for labor—i.e., we suppose in column 6 that the price of labor rises with increase in the quantity bought. Column 7 then shows the total cost (price times quantity) of labor, and column 8 the marginal cost of labor, the first differences of column 7. Column 9 then shows the new marginal cost of output, by multiplying column 3 by column 8. Comparing column 9 with column 5, we see that the introduction of imperfection in the input market steepens the marginal cost curve, because the marginal cost of labor rises as the quantity employed rises.

Do Imperfect Markets Lead to Misallocated Resources?

An important consequence of imperfection in the firm's market is that profit maximization now leads to production at a level where the price of output is *above* the marginal cost, and where the price of input is *below* its marginal revenue productivity. As we shall see more clearly later, this is evidence, though not absolutely conclusive evidence, that imperfection in the market leads to misallocation of resources. The price of a product is a measure of the value placed on the marginal result of a certain method of employing resources. The marginal cost is a measure of the value placed by the market on the resources themselves. If then in any line of production the price exceeds the marginal cost, this indicates that the market is placing a higher marginal value on the product of the resources than on the resources used, which would indicate that there would be a social gain in expanding this line of production at least up to the point where price was equal to marginal cost; at this point the "gain" from further expansion as represented by the value of the product is just equal the "loss" as represented by the marginal cost. A similar argument can be used to show that production should be carried to the point where the price of all inputs are equal to their marginal revenue productivities; for if the price of an input is below its marginal revenue productivity, an increase in its use will bring greater gain, as measured by the marginal revenue productivity, than it involves "loss," as measured by the price of the input. Considerable qualifications must be introduced into this argument before it can be accepted as a valid standard for judging social policy. Nevertheless it does suggest one thing that is "wrong" with monopoly—that it results in too few resources going into the monopolized product and too many into other things.

PRICE DISCRIMINATION

A problem of great interest in the theory of monopoly, which can be handled very conveniently by the marginal analysis, is that of price discrimination.

In the preceding sections we assumed that the monopolist sold each unit of his output at the same price. It is not always necessary for him to do so; indeed, it will be necessary only if his customers can easily resell to one another the commodity which he has sold to them. If resale is possible without trouble, the monopolist who sells some of his output at a low price and some at a high price will find that the output sold at a low price will be resold in the high-priced market. Suppose, for instance, that a monopolist sold his product to Mr. A for $10 per ton and to Mr. B for $5 per ton. If resale were possible it would clearly pay Mr. B to buy all he could at $5 per ton and resell it to Mr. A at some price between $5 and $10 per ton. In that case the monopolist would find that he could not sell to Mr. A at the high price, for Mr. A would buy the resold product from Mr. B. The monopolist therefore would be forced to charge the same price to both Mr. A and Mr. B. This is an application of the "principle of arbitrage" noted in an earlier chapter.

If Mr. A and Mr. B do not know each other, cannot meet each other, and cannot trade with each other, resale is impossible and there is nothing to prevent the monopolist from charging each a different price. This practice is known as "price discrimination." It is possible only when a monopolist is faced with two or more separated markets. The problem arises, then, what are the most profitable prices to charge in two or more separated markets? A common example of two separated markets for a commodity is the "home market" and the "foreign market." A monopolist may sell at one price in his own country and at another price abroad, for the people who buy from him in the one market cannot very well sell in the other.

Marginal Revenue Equal in Each Separated Market

This problem is essentially a part of the "sales" problem; i.e., how to get the greatest total revenue from any given total volume of sales. Where there are two or more separated markets, the solution is that the greatest total revenue from a given volume of total sales is obtained when the marginal revenue in each of the separated markets is the same. For clearly, if the marginal revenue in one market is greater than that in the other, it will pay to shift sales (by raising price or lowering selling costs) out of the market in which the marginal revenue is low into the market in which it is high.

Suppose, for instance, that in the "home" market the marginal revenue is $10 per ton and in the "foreign" market the marginal revenue is $15 per ton. Under these circumstances, if a ton of sales is withdrawn from the home market (say by raising the price at home) and transferred to the foreign market (say by lowering the price abroad), the result is a loss of $10 of revenue in the home market but a gain of $15 of revenue in the foreign market, representing a net gain of $5 of revenue from the same *total* volume of sales as before. As such transference proceeds, however, the marginal revenue in the home market will rise as sales are lowered, say, to $12 per ton, and the marginal revenue in the foreign market will fall as sales are increased, say, also to $12 per ton. At this point it will no longer be possible to increase total revenue by transferring sales from one market to the other; the maximum total revenue from a *given* volume of sales has been reached. If the total volume of sales is increased the marginal revenue in each market will decline, but it still remains true that unless the marginal revenue in each market is the same gains can be made by shifting sales from one market to the other.

Marginal Revenue in Each Market Equal to the Marginal Cost

We still need, however, to solve the problem of the optimum size of *total* sales. This also can be done with the marginal analysis.

Let us define the *total marginal revenue* as the increase in the total revenue which results from a unit increase in total sales, divided equally over all the various separated markets. The total marginal revenue is then equal to the arithmetical average of the marginal revenues in the various markets. Suppose that in one market the marginal revenue is $10 per ton and in another it is $8 per ton. Then, by selling half a ton in each market the amount added to the total revenue will be $5 + $4, or $9; $9 per ton is therefore the total marginal revenue. When the marginal revenue in each market is the same, then, each is equal to the total marginal revenue. But the most profitable total output of the monopolist is that at which the total marginal revenue is equal to the marginal cost. Hence at the most profitable output, the marginal revenue in each separated market will also be equal to the marginal cost.

Graphic Illustration. The graphic solution of the problem of price discrimination between two separated markets is shown in Fig. 90. In 90A we have the sales (demand) curve, R_1A_1, and the marginal

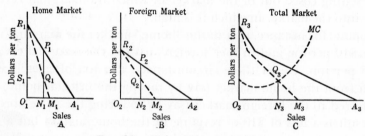

FIG. 90.   Price Discrimination.

revenue curve, R_1M_1, in one market—let us say the home market. In 90B we have the demand curve, R_2A_2, and the marginal revenue curve, R_2M_2, in another market, separated from the first—let us say a foreign market. These curves are drawn as straight lines for convenience, but it is not necessary to assume straight-line curves for this particular analysis. In C we have the aggregate demand curve in both markets, R_3A_3. This shows how much would be sold in both markets at various prices if the same price were to be charged in each market. It is formed by adding the horizontal ordinates of Figs. A and B. Thus $O_3A_3 = O_1A_1 + O_2A_2$. The curve R_3M_3 is similarly the aggregate marginal revenue curve in both markets. It shows how much can be sold in the two markets at various levels of marginal revenue, if the marginal revenues are the same in both markets. This curve is constructed by adding together the quantities sold in the two markets at each level of marginal revenue. Thus when the marginal revenue in both markets is O_1S_1, O_1N_1 is sold in Market A and O_2N_2 in Market B and O_3N_3 ($= O_1N_1 + O_2N_2$) in both markets together. The curve R_3M_3 is *not* the "marginal" curve corresponding to the "average" curve R_3A_3.

The dotted curve MC in Fig. 90C is the marginal cost curve of the monopolist. His most profitable output is O_3N_3, where his marginal cost is equal to his aggregate marginal revenue. He will sell O_1N_1 in Market A, for at this volume of sales the marginal revenue in Market A is equal to his marginal cost. He will also sell O_2N_2 in Market B. In order to sell O_1N_1 in Market A he must charge a price N_1P_1 there, for P_1 is on his sales curve. Similarly, in Market B he must charge a price N_2P_2 in order to sell O_2N_2. It will be observed that the price in Market A is higher than the price in Market B. This is because the demand in Market A is more inelastic, at the equilibrium output, than the demand in Market B.

Higher Price in Less Elastic Market

It can be shown in general that if the elasticities of demand in the two markets are the same, the prices which it will pay best to charge in the two markets will be the same; but if the elasticities of demand in the two markets differ, the higher price will be charged in the less elastic market. It is difficult to prove this without the use of mathematics; a mathematical proof is appended below.[1]

[1] Let p_1 be the price in the first market; p_2 be the price in the second market; q_1 be the quantity in the first market; q_2 be the quantity in the second market; r_1 be the total revenue in the first market; r_2 be the total revenue in the second market; m_1 be the marginal revenue in the first market; m_2 be the marginal revenue in the second market; e_1 be the elasticity of demand in the first market; e_2 be the elasticity of demand in the second market. Then

$$m_1 = \frac{dr_1}{dq_1} = \frac{d(p_1q_1)}{dq_1} = p_1 + q_1\frac{dp_1}{dq_1} = p_1\left(1 + \frac{1}{e_1}\right), \tag{1A}$$

$$\text{for } e_1 = \frac{dq_1}{dp_1}\cdot\frac{p_1}{q_1}.$$

Similarly,

$$m_2 = p_2\left(1 + \frac{1}{e_2}\right). \tag{1B}$$

The expression $(1 + \frac{1}{e})$ is important. We may call it the "coefficient of imperfection," for when the market is perfect, e is infinite and this coefficient is unity; when the elasticity is zero this coefficient is infinite. It is equal, as we see in equation (1A) and (1B), to the ratio $\frac{\text{marginal revenue}}{\text{average revenue}}$.

When the marginal revenues in both markets are equal,

$$p_1\left(1 + \frac{1}{e_1}\right) = p_2\left(1 + \frac{1}{e_2}\right). \tag{2}$$

This is the condition which must be fulfilled if the total revenue from both markets is to be maximized. It is evident immediately from equation (2) that when $e_1 = e_2$, then $p_1 = p_2$. Now we know that a monopolist will never sell at outputs where the demand is rela-

We have seen that the more elastic is the demand schedule, the less is the divergence between the marginal revenue and the price. When the marginal revenues in the two markets are equal, the price will be higher in the less elastic market, for in that market there will be a greater divergence between the price and the marginal revenue than there will be in the more elastic market.

Price Discrimination Between Different Quantities

Besides charging different prices to different buyers or in different markets, a monopolist may also charge different prices for various quantities of the same commodity sold to a single buyer. He may, for instance, charge a high price if the buyer buys small quantities, and a lower price if the buyer buys large quantities. This device is used sometimes in retail stores as a special price policy ("five cents each, three for a dime"). It is also used by electricity companies and other public utilities, as a regular price policy.

Marginal Outlay Determines Purchases

The effectiveness of this device rests on the fact that the quantity which determines whether a buyer will expand his purchases is not the *price* he has to pay (the average outlay) but the amount which an additional unit purchased will add to his total bill—the "marginal outlay." If, for instance, I am considering whether or not to install an electric cooker, I shall calculate the cost of electricity used in running it according to the amount which each extra unit adds to my electricity bill. What I pay for electricity used for lighting and other purposes should not influence my decision. If the electricity company charges me, let us say, 6 cents per unit for lighting and 3 cents per unit for cooking, I may find it worth while to buy as much electricity as if the price were 3 cents for all units, and the company will be able to extract from me a greater sum than if it had charged a flat rate for all units. This principle is illustrated in Table 62.

The first two rows of this table show a demand schedule of a consumer for electricity. They show that if the price is 8 cents per unit,

---

tively inelastic (e between 0 and -1), for then, it is clear from equations (1A) and (1B), the marginal revenue will be negative. As marginal revenue is equal to marginal cost at the most profitable output, and as marginal cost is always positive, the marginal revenue at the most profitable output must also be positive; i.e., the demand must be relatively elastic (e between -1 and $-\infty$). When the demand is relatively elastic in both markets, equation (2) shows that the price will be higher in the less elastic market. For instance, if $e_1 = -2$ and $e_2 = -10$, e_1 being the less elastic market, then from equation (2) $p_1 = \frac{9}{5} p_2$;

p_1, the price in the less elastic market, is greater than p_2.

he will buy only 20 units; if the price is 7 cents, he will be a little more extravagant and buy 40 units; if the price is 6 cents, he will buy 80 units, and so on. The third row shows how much he will increase his consumption for each unit change in price. Suppose the electricity company charges 8 cents for the first 20 units used and 7 cents for the next 20 units used. The consumer will buy his first 20 units at 8 cents, for he thinks that it is worth paying 8 cents per unit, let us say, to light

TABLE 62. Price Discrimination Between Different Quantities

1. Price of electricity (¢ per unit)	9	8	7	6	5	4	3
2. Consumption (units)	0	20	40	80	200	400	600
3. Increase in consumption (units)		20	20	40	120	200	200
4. Differential revenue (¢)		160	140	240	600	800	600
5. Total differential revenue (¢)		160	300	540	1140	1940	2540
6. Total flat-rate revenue (¢)		160	280	480	1000	1600	1800

two of his rooms. If the price came down to 7 cents per unit he would light two more of his rooms and consume 40 units. But if the company charges 7 cents for this additional 20 units, he will still find it worth while to light his two other rooms. Therefore, if the company charges 8 cents for the first 20 units and 7 cents for the next 20 units, the consumer will buy 40 units in all; he will pay 160 cents for the first 20 and 140 cents for the second 20 (shown in the fourth row of the table) and will therefore pay 300 cents for the 40 units. If, however, the electricity company had charged a flat rate of 7 cents for all units bought, the consumer would still have bought 40 units, but he would have paid only 280 cents for them, as shown in the sixth row of the table. Similarly, if the company charged a flat rate of 6 cents per unit, it could induce the consumer to buy 80 units, and would receive 480 cents; but if the company charges 8 cents for the first 20 units, 7 cents for the next 20 units, and 6 cents for the next 40 units, the same consumer will still be persuaded to buy 80 units, but will pay the company a total of 540 cents for these 80 units. So we can go on all through the table.

This Is Possible Only If Buyers Cannot Resell

If a monopolist could shade his price according to quantity to follow the consumers' demand curve exactly, his marginal revenue would be equal to the price that he charged for the last unit bought, for he could increase his sales by offering to sell an extra unit at a lower price without lowering the price of the other units he sells. In practice, of course, it is not possible for a monopolist to adjust his price scale accurately to the demand of each buyer. Nevertheless, the practice of charging lower prices for larger quantities is very common. It may, of course, be combined with the practice of charging different prices to different buyers; thus an electricity company may have one scale of prices for commercial buyers and another scale of prices for domestic buyers. It should be•noticed that this type of discrimination also is possible only if the buyers are unable to resell what they have bought. If resale is possible, then, as we have seen, any buyer who buys at a low price will undercut the monopolist himself by reselling to those buyers who have to pay a high price to the monopolist. This principle applies as much to the practice of charging different prices for different quantities as

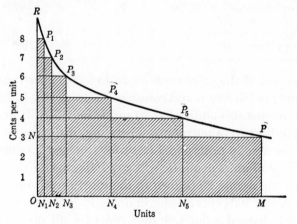

FIG. 91.   Price Discrimination.

it does to the practice of charging different prices to different people. If buyers can resell, it will pay some of them to buy large quantities —thus getting the product at a low price—and to resell some of their purchases to those who buy only small quantities and who therefore would have to pay a high price to the monopolist. If a householder could retail electricity to his neighbor, it would obviously not pay the electricity company to charge smaller prices for larger quantities, for such a policy would merely encourage people to buy large quantities of electricity for resale.

Graphic Illustration.   Fig. 91 illustrates the process of discriminating according to quantity. *RP* is the demand curve of a single buyer of electricity. If the seller wishes to sell an amount equal to *OM*, he can achieve this end by charging a flat rate of *ON*, in which case the total revenue will be *OM* × *ON*, or the area *OMPN*. But if he charges N_1P_1 for the first ON_1 units, N_2P_2 for the next N_1N_2 units, N_3P_3 for the next N_2N_3 units, and so on, and *MP* for the last N_5M units, he will still be able to sell an amount OM, but his total receipts from this consumer will be the shaded area of the figure. Evidently, if the gradations could be made in infinitely fine steps, the "stairs" of the shaded area could be made smaller and smaller until the total receipts amounted to the whole area under the demand curve, $RPMO$. The maximum possible gain from quantity discrimination, then, is the area NRP. This is sometimes called the "consumers' surplus." It represents the difference between what a consumer pays when there is a flat rate for all quantities and the maximum amount which can be extracted from him by skillful pricing. The seller must be careful, however, not to schedule a reduction in price at a quantity which is greater than that which would be bought by the consumer at the preceding price on the schedule. Suppose, for instance, that the electricity company scheduled a price of 8 cents for the first 20 units, 7 cents for the next 50 units, 6 cents for the next 100 units, and so on. A consumer with the demand curve in Fig. 91 would stop short at 20 units and would never extend his purchases into the low-price quantities, because at 7 cents a unit he would only purchase 40 units altogether. Not unless his total purchases at 7 cents amounted to at least 70 units would he be tempted to purchase more by reason of the 6-cent price for quantities greater than 70 units.

Discontinuous Cost Functions

Some interesting problems arise in the theory of the firm when the various cost and revenue functions are discontinuous—that is, exhibit sharp jumps, corners, or changes. There are several cases where discontinuous functions are plausible.

It has been argued,[2] for instance, that when a plant is engineered for a certain capacity output, marginal cost is likely to fall over the whole range of output up to capacity and then to rise very sharply. This is illustrated in Fig. 92. AMC is the marginal cost curve, AVC the corresponding average variable cost curve. We suppose that the plant is engineered to a capacity output at OK, and that marginal (and average) cost falls continuously toward capacity but then rises immediately to infinity. In this case if the marginal revenue curve cuts the vertical line MVC at any point above V, the maximum net revenue is at capacity output. With a large range of fluctuation of demand, therefore, the output of the firm is completely inelastic; the firm will either produce at capacity or not at all. This does not mean, of course,

---

[2] W. J. Eiteman and G. E. Guthrie, "The Shape of the Average Cost Curve," *American Economic Review*, December, 1952, pp. 832–838.

in perfect or imperfect competition, that the "industry" demand must be inelastic, because of the possibility of shifts in the number of firms.

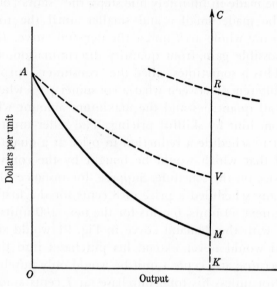

FIG. 92.   Discontinuous Cost Curves.

Discontinuous Sales Functions

Another interesting possibility of discontinuity is in the firm's demand or sales functions. Suppose, for instance, that the firm produces a multiple-use commodity, in which the demand is very elastic in each use up to a point of "saturation" after which demand becomes very inelastic. In the extreme case the demand curve will be a step function, as in Fig. 93. Above the price OA we suppose nothing will be sold; at OA the first "use" comes into play, and AB will be sold. Lowering the price below OA does not expand sales beyond AB until the price OC' is reached, when sales expand suddenly into the second use, to $C'D$. A third use comes in at price OE', expanding sales to $E'F$, and so on. The total revenue curve corresponding to this sales (average revenue) curve is shown in the lower part of the figure, $obcdefg$, assuming no price discrimination. Thus at sales equal to ob' total revenue suddenly drops from $b'b$ ($=$ area $OABB'$) to $b'c$ ($= OC'CB'$) as sales are pushed into the second use.

The Discontinuous Marginal Revenue Curve

The marginal revenue curve in this case is very curious. It may be visualized best perhaps if we imagine ourselves driving a little car over the saw teeth of the total revenue curve and observing its changes in angle; from o to b marginal and average revenue are the same, equal to OA. At b the slope suddenly changes from OA to minus infinity, and the marginal revenue curve rushes off from B through B' to minus

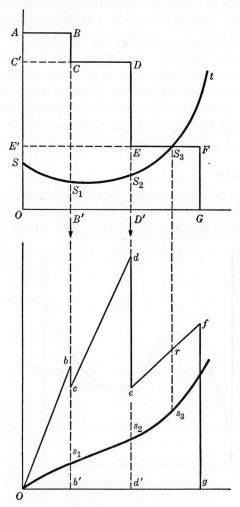

FIG. 93. Discontinuous Sales Curves.

infinity. At c the slope is again reversed to a positive number $(B'C)$ and marginal revenue rushes back from minus infinity at $B'C$. From c to d marginal revenue is again constant at $B'C$; at d it again goes off to minus infinity, and returns to $D'E$ at e.

Relative and Absolute Maxima

Suppose now that we have a marginal cost curve St. This strictly cuts the marginal revenue curve at three points S_1, S_2, and S_3. Indeed, it cuts the marginal revenue curve *twice* at each of the points S_1 and S_2, once on its way down to minus infinity and once on its way back! This curious phenomenon has, however, a very simple interpretation, as we see from the total revenue and total cost curves in the lower part of the figure. At the output ob' there is both a relative maximum net revenue at b and a relative minimum at c. Similarly, there is a relative maximum at d and a relative minimum at e. There is also a relative maximum of the conventional type at r, corresponding to the point S_3 in the upper figure. There is no way of telling which of the three relative maxima, b, d, and r, represents the highest absolute value of the net revenue except by inspection. In the figure d is clearly the absolute maximum; this however is a mere accident of the functions selected.

Boundary Maxima

In the two previous cases the *formal* conditions of the marginal analysis have survived the discontinuities of the functions; that is, the maximum position is still formally at a point where marginal gain is

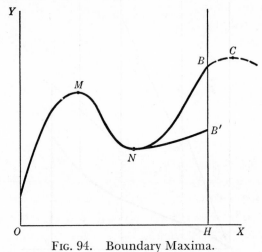

Fig. 94.   Boundary Maxima.

equal to marginal loss, even though the formal condition loses much of its significance when the functions are discontinuous. In the case of the "boundary maximum," however, not even the formal condition is retained. A boundary occurs when there are limits imposed, say, by law or custom, beyond which some variable is not allowed to go. Minimum wage laws, usury laws, price controls, output quotas, are examples of such boundaries. If the greatest value of the maximand (say net revenue) is found at the boundary, it is said to be a boundary maximum. At the boundary, however, the marginal conditions may not be satisfied at all. The case is illustrated in Fig. 94. The maximand is measured along OY, some related variable along OX. We suppose this has a boundary at OH. In the figure there is a regular relative maximum at M, where all the marginal conditions will be fulfilled. There is likewise a relative minimum at N. The boundary maximum at B, however, is clearly the highest possible value of the maximand. If the boundary did not exist there might be another relative maximum at C. Because of the boundary, however, B is the best position, in spite of the fact that the marginal conditions are not fulfilled there. It should be observed, however, that the mere presence of boundaries does *not* mean that the boundary itself is the maximum. Thus in Fig. 94, if the maximand went from N to B' instead of to B, M would be the absolute maximum and the organization would not proceed to the boundary but would stop at M.

EFFECT OF A FALL IN DEMAND

The marginal analysis throws some light upon the effects of a change in demand for the product of a monopolist. We will discuss the effects of a fall in demand; an exactly similar analysis, of course, holds for a rise. As the general demand curve of the public for the product of a monopolist is the same as his sales curve, a fall in demand means a shift in the sales curve to the left. The marginal revenue curve will therefore also move to the left and will intersect the marginal cost curve at a point representing a smaller output. A fall in demand for the product of a monopolist will thus cause a reduction in the output of the product. In general there will also be a reduction in the price of the product, although circumstances are conceivable in which a fall in demand may lead to a rise in the price of the product. In Fig. 95A, RA and RM are the sales curve and the marginal revenue curve before the fall in demand, ON is the equilibrium output, and NP is the price, at which the marginal revenue is equal to the marginal cost, NQ. MC is the marginal cost curve. After the fall in demand, $R'A'$ is the new sales curve, $R'M'$ the new marginal revenue curve. The marginal revenue is now equal to the marginal cost, $N'Q'$, at the output ON' sold at a price $N'P'$. There is evidently a fall in output from ON to ON' and a fall in price from NP to $N'P'$. The extent of the fall in output depends on the slope of the marginal cost curve. If the marginal cost curve is steep there will be a small fall in output. If the marginal cost does not change much as output changes, however, the output will have to fall a good deal before the marginal cost is again equal to the marginal revenue.

Fig. 95B shows a case in which a fall in demand causes a rise in the price of a monopolist's product. In this case the symbols have the meaning assigned to them in Fig. 95A. But the marginal cost falls with increasing output in the significant range, and therefore a very large decline in output, from ON to ON', results from the fall in demand.

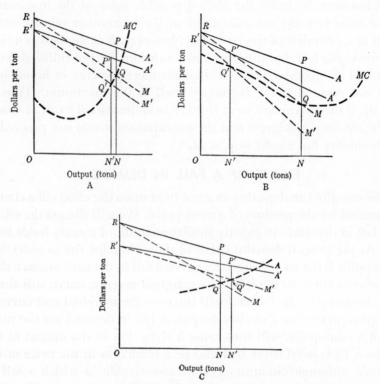

FIG. 95.   Effect of a Fall in Demand on Monopolist.

The decline in output is so great that it permits an actual rise in price —from NP to $N'P'$.

Another interesting special case is shown in Fig. 95C. Here demand falls from RA to $R'A'$, but it also becomes more elastic. This might happen, for instance, if the fall in demand was caused by the appearance of a substitute product. In this case the marginal revenue curves, RM and $R'M'$, actually cross; and if the marginal cost curve cuts them to the right of their point of intersection, the fall in demand actually results in a *rise* in output—in this case from ON to ON'. It still, however, results in a fall in price. The student should compare these various results with those obtained under perfect competition.

Why Does a Monopoly Have Rigid Prices?

We see from these examples that there is likely to be a larger reduction in price and a smaller reduction in output when the marginal cost is rising sharply with increased output. This condition, however, is characteristic of a firm working at full capacity. Where a firm is working at an output well below the capacity of its plant, the marginal cost curve will be flat or may even slope downward as in Fig. 95B. When a monopolist is working with "excess capacity," then, a fall in demand may lead to a still further reduction in output and a still greater "excess capacity," and will not lead to much fall in price. This conclusion has a good deal of importance for the theory of economic fluctuations. One important feature of our society which tends to intensify depressions is that when the money demanded for industrial goods declines, the prices of these goods fall little and their output therefore declines greatly. This may in part be due to conventional price policies; businessmen may not wish to go to the trouble of adjusting their prices to meet new conditions. We now see, however, that the policy of rigid prices may have a foundation also in self-interest. If most plants are working under capacity their marginal cost curves will be flat or even negatively sloped, and a fall in demand will result in a large fall in output and little or no fall, or even a rise, in price, as can be seen from Fig. 95B.

TAXATION

The effect of taxes on a monopolist, as on any firm, depends principally on whether the tax is a fixed sum or whether its total amount varies with output.

A Fixed Tax

The effect of a fixed tax is shown in Fig. 96A. OQC is the total variable cost curve. OPR is the total revenue curve. In the absence of fixed costs, ON is the output at which the net revenue, QP, is a maximum. If the fixed input is not owned by the monopolist himself, a rent may be charged equal to QP, or OK. The total cost curve is then KP; the most profitable output is still ON, at which the monopolist's net revenue is zero. If, now, a fixed tax equal to OK' is laid on the monopolist, there is no change in the most profitable output, ON, for there is no change in the *marginal* cost curve and none in the revenue curves, so that the marginal cost will still be equal to the marginal revenue at the output *ON*. But the economic rent will be reduced from *QP* (= *OK*) to *Q'P* (= *K'K*). The total fixed charge cannot exceed the sum *QP*. Therefore, if there is a tax equal to *QQ'*, the total cost curve including the tax but excluding rent will be *K'Q'C'*, and the rent will be that sum which will make the total fixed charge equal to *QP*, or *Q'P*. A lump-sum tax on a monopoly, then, is equivalent to a tax on economic rent. Unless it exceeds the economic rent, it will

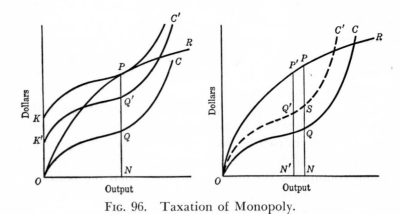

Fig. 96.   Taxation of Monopoly.

not affect the output of the monopolist, unless, of course, the parties concerned are not following their own interest. Even a lump-sum tax may affect the output of a monopolist if it forces him to devote greater attention to *finding* his most profitable output. If the tax exceeds the economic rent, it will force the monopolist out of business and reduce the output to zero.

A Variable Tax

The effect of a tax which varies in total amount with output is shown in Fig. 96B. Suppose there is a specific tax on each unit of the commodity produced. The total cost, including the tax, is now greater than before at each output; but instead of increasing by a fixed amount, it increases by an amount which is proportionate to the output. That is, at large outputs the tax is greater than at small outputs. If in Fig. 96B the original total cost curve is *OC*, the total cost curve after the tax will be *OC'*. The effect of a specific tax is similar to the effect of a rise in the price of input. The marginal cost curve rises, for the marginal cost at each output is increased because of the tax. The output will therefore tend to decline, and the price of the product will rise. The rent of the monopoly will also decline. In Fig. 96B the original output will be ON, where the net revenue or rent is a maximum at QP. After the imposition of the tax the slope of the new cost curve, OC', at the output ON' is greater than that of the old cost curve; i.e., the slope of OC' at S is greater than that of OC at Q. In other words, at the old output, after the tax, the marginal cost has risen. But previously the marginal cost was equal to the marginal revenue at this output. Now, however, as the marginal revenue has not changed, the new marginal cost must be greater than the marginal revenue. The net revenue can therefore be increased by reducing the output to ON', where $Q'P'$ is the new maximum net revenue, ON' the most profitable output. The amount by which a given specific tax will reduce the output and raise the price will depend on the character of the demand for the monopolist's product. If the demand is very elastic, there will be a large reduction in output and a small rise in price. If it is not very elastic, the reduction in output will be smaller and the rise in price larger.

Conclusions Modified

The presence of discontinuities and boundaries may, of course, modify these conclusions in regard to changes in demand and taxation. Generally speaking, positions of maximum profits at boundaries or at discontinuities tend to be rather insensitive to changes in the environment, and may survive considerable changes, for instance, in levels of demand or of taxation, without shifting. Thus suppose in Fig. 95A the marginal cost curve were vertical (at capacity output, as in Fig. 92); it is evident that a fall in demand would not affect output at all, as long as the firm was producing. No matter what the demand, within wide limits the firm would produce at capacity. Taxes, even variable taxes, would have a similar effect.

The conclusions of the elementary marginal analysis in regard to the effect of changes in environment may be modified also if account is taken of the asset preferences of the firm. The assumption underlying simple profit maximization is that the firm is concerned only with the gross increase in total value of its assets and is indifferent to the structure and composition of these assets. If, however, the firm is concerned for the composition of its assets—for example, if it wishes to preserve some proportion of liquid to nonliquid assets—it may well prefer a position with less than maximum total profit but in which the composition of assets resulting from the operation is superior to that which would emerge at the profit maximum position.

In a case of this kind even a fixed tax is likely to affect the output and sales positions of a firm, at least in the short run, because of the effect of the tax on the composition of assets. If the tax is collected in money, this has the immediate effect of making the firm less liquid, and hence it may attempt to recover its liquidity by cutting down production and selling off inventory, even under a fixed tax.[3]

QUESTIONS AND EXERCISES

1. "A perfect monopoly is almost as inconceivable as perfect competition." Discuss.
2. "A monopoly price is one which is raised above the competitive level." What do you understand by the "competitive level"? Is the price charged by an unrestricted monopolist necessarily above the competitive level? If not, how could you tell whether the price of a monopolist was or was not above the competitive level?
3. "A monopoly is most likely to be successful in the case of commodities whose demand is relatively inelastic." Discuss.
4. Prove that a monopolist will never wish to produce at an output where the elasticity of demand for his product is numerically less than one. (Note: Prove first that when the marginal revenue is positive, the elasticity of demand is numerically greater than 1.)
5. "In making any decision the businessman merely has to ask himself whether his proposal will add more to the total revenue than to the total cost. If it does, he will proceed with the proposal in question. Otherwise he will not." Discuss, in the light of the marginal analysis.
6. Analyze the effect of an increase in demand for the product of a monopolist on (a) his price, (b) his output, (c) his demand for inputs.
7. Who is injured by the existence of a monopoly?
8. Compare and contrast the results of monopoly and of perfect competition.
9. Milk cooperatives usually charge a higher price for milk in the "liquid" market (for direct consumption) than for milk in the manufacturing market (for butter and cheese). Why? What assumptions does it imply about the demand in these two markets?
10. Discuss in detail the effects of a subsidy given to a monopolist (a) when the subsidy is a fixed amount irrespective of output; (b) when the subsidy is a fixed sum on each unit of output produced; (c) when the subsidy is a fixed percentage of the price of each unit produced; (d) when the subsidy is progressive, i.e., increases per unit as the output increases.
11. Prove that the maximum tax which can be extracted from a monopolist without driving him out of business is greater in total when the tax is a fixed sum than when it is a specific tax on each unit of output.

[3] For a detailed discussion of this problem, see K. E. Boulding, *A Reconstruction of Economics* (New York, 1950), pp. 104–107.

12. Suppose a monopolist is selling a product at its most profitable price at $20 per ton. Suppose that (a) a specific tax of $10 per ton is laid on the commodity, and (b) an ad valorem tax of 50 per cent of the price of each unit of the commodity is imposed. Compare and contrast the results of these two taxes. (Note: Treat the ad valorem tax as a deduction from revenue, as on page 145.)

13. The following table shows the marginal revenue and marginal cost schedules for a monopolist producing a patented refrigerator:

Output of Refrigerators (Units)	Marginal Revenue ($ per Unit)	Marginal Cost ($ per Unit)
0		
100	200	100
200	185	95
300	171	91
400	158	93
500	146	96
600	135	100
700	125	105
800	116	112
900	108	122
1000	101	137
1100	95	157

a. Calculate, for each output, the total revenue, the price of the product, the total variable cost, the average variable cost, and the net revenue.

b. Draw on one graph (A) the marginal cost curve, the marginal revenue curve, the sales curve, and the average variable cost curve. What is the most profitable output?

c. What is the maximum amount which the owner of the patent could exact from the monopolist without driving him out of business? Is this economic rent? Explain.

d. Calculate the average total cost, at each output, on the assumption that the total fixed cost is equal to the maximum amount receivable by the owner of the patent. Draw on graph A the average total cost curve. Show that it touches the sales curve.

e. On another graph (B) plot the total variable cost curve, the total revenue curve, and the total cost curve, calculated according to the assumptions in d. Compare graphs A and B, and note any significant conclusions.

f. What will be the effect of (a) a flat tax of $40,000, (b) a flat tax of $50,000, (c) a tax of $30 on each refrigerator, on the refrigerator company?

g. In the case of the above refrigerator company, what subsidy (per refrigerator) would expand the output to 950 refrigerators? Assuming that the net revenue is all economic rent, what fixed tax would now leave the concern normally profitable?

14. The following table shows two straight-line demand curves facing a monopolist in two separated markets, A and B.

Price	0	10	20	30	40	50	60	70	80	90
Sales in A	90	80	70	60	50	40	30	20	10	0
Sales in B	150	120	90	60	30	0	0	0	0	0

a. Plot the sales curve and the marginal revenue curve for each of these markets, and the aggregate sales curve and the aggregate marginal revenue curve, as in Fig. 90.

b. For *each level* of marginal revenue, 0, 10, 20, . . . 80 use the above graphs to calculate:
  i. Sales in Market A.
  ii. Sales in Market B.
  iii. Aggregate sales in both markets.
  iv. The price in market A.
  v. The price in market B.
  vi. The total revenue from market A.
  vii. The total revenue from market B.
  viii. The aggregate total revenue from both markets.
  ix. The aggregate average revenue from both markets per unit of sales.

Assume that price discrimination is practiced so as to maximize the total revenue from any given volume of sales. Arrange the results in tabular form.

c. Suppose that the average variable cost in this firm is constant with respect to output. For various levels of this constant average variable cost (10, 20, 30, etc.) calculate (i) the total variable cost and (ii) the total economic rent (net revenue), at various levels of output 0, 10, 20, · · · 120, assuming that there are no fixed costs. Arrange results in tabular form.

d. Plot on a single sheet, with sales (ouput) along the horizontal and revenue along the vertical axis, the family of net revenue curves corresponding to various levels of average variable cost.

e. Show that the maximum net revenue is always at that level of output where marginal cost is equal to the aggregate marginal revenue.

15. A monopolist with the demand curves of Exercise 14 is now prohibited by law from charging different prices in different markets; he must now charge a uniform price for all sales.

a. Calculate, for levels of output 0, 10, 20, · · · 120:
  i. The uniform price at which each quantity can be sold, using both markets.
  ii. The total revenue from each level of output.

   iii. The marginal revenue at each level of output.
   iv. The total variable cost and the net revenue (assuming no fixed
   costs) on the assumption of various constant average variable cost
   levels, e.g., 20, 25, 30, 35, 40, 45.
Arrange results in tabular form.
b. Plot on the same figure the family of net revenue curves at various
levels of average variable cost derived from the figures in a(iv). Comment on any peculiar features of this family of curves, comparing them
with the family of curves derived in Exercise 14, part (d).
c. Plot the aggregate demand curve of the monopolist from the figure
in a(i). On the same figure plot the marginal revenue curve which corresponds to this aggregate demand curve. How does this curve differ
from the aggregate marginal revenue curve of Exercise 14? Interpret
the peculiarities of the family of net revenue curves derived in b. by
reference to the marginal revenue curve. Show, in particular, that
where a marginal cost curve cuts the marginal revenue curve in three
places, the net revenue curve will exhibit two maxima.
d. Plot on one figure:
   i. The total revenue curve under price discrimination from Exercise 14, b(viii).
   ii. The total revenue curve under uniform pricing from Exercise 15,
   a(ii).
Comment on the relationship of these two curves.
e. Assume again that average variable (= marginal) cost is independent
of the volume of output. Plot on another figure curves showing the
equilibrium output at various levels of average variable cost, (i) under
price discrimination, and (ii) under uniform pricing.
f. On another figure plot (i) the price in A, (ii) the price in B, and (iii)
the average price, from Exercise 14, b(viii), all under price discrimination, and (iv) the price under uniform pricing, for various levels of
constant average variable cost.
16. In the light of the above two exercises, write an essay on the effect of
   compulsory uniform pricing on a monopolist who has previously been
   practicing price discrimination, with especial reference to the effect on
   prices and sales.
17. In Fig. 93, what would be the total revenue curve and the marginal
   revenue curve under conditions of perfect price discrimination? How
   would price discrimination affect output in this case? Can the results
   of this case be generalized?

CHAPTER 30

IMPERFECT COMPETITION

We have now treated in some detail two extreme cases—perfect competition on the one hand and pure monopoly on the other. Both are important in actual economic life, for some industries, notably those producing the standard raw materials of commerce, operate under conditions close to perfect competition, and others, like the "public utilities," operate under conditions close to pure monopoly. Probably, however, the bulk of economic activity is carried on in industries whose condition lies somewhere between these two extremes, in which neither the conditions of perfect competition nor the conditions of pure monopoly are completely observed. This state of industry is known as "imperfect competition."

Forms of Competition

Within the general field of imperfect competition three important cases can be distinguished whose results differ significantly; we shall call the first "monopolistic competition," the second "perfect oligopoly," and the third "imperfect oligopoly." In all cases of competition, whether perfect or imperfect, we assume freedom of entry of firms or of other resources into the industry. The four cases of competition are then defined by ringing the changes on two fundamental conditions: the homogeneity of the product and the number of firms. When many firms are producing a homogeneous product the result is perfect competition. When many firms are producing heterogeneous products, and the product of each firm is similar to but not identical with the product of other firms in the same industry, the condition is known as monopolistic competition. When a *few* firms are selling a homogeneous product there is a condition which may be called *perfect oligopoly*. When a few firms are selling heterogeneous products there is a condition which may be called *imperfect oligopoly*. Where there are only two sellers the condition is known as "duopoly."

628

Definition of an "Industry"

It must be confessed that the various "states of the market" distinguished above are not sharply divided one from the other, and that what we have in fact is a complex continuum of market conditions. The concept of an "industry" is as vague as it is useful; we can hardly ever draw sharp lines around a given number of firms and say that here is an "industry" within which a certain kind of imperfect competition prevails. What, for instance, is the "steel industry"? Does it include those firms which make frames for automobiles? If so, how far does one have to go down the process of production before the "steel industry" passes into the "automobile industry"? Worse still, does the "steel industry" include firms producing close substitutes for steel, such as aluminum? The C.I.O. evidently thinks so, for the aluminum workers are now included in the United Steelworkers of America! It is evident that what we have in reality is a mass of firms rather than a collection of "industries," each firm entering into complex competitive relationships with other firms in increasing circles of diminishing intensity. It is possible to describe the situation of the market solely in terms of the cross-relationships of firms, without relation to the concept of an "industry."[1] Nevertheless, the concept of an "industry" is useful for purposes of discussion. It may be defined as a group of firms closely related in the competitive process by reason of the great substitutability of their respective products, and distinguished from other firms by a "gap" in the range of substitute products.

Levels of Abstraction in Competition Models

These various "models" of different forms of competition can be regarded not only as corresponding roughly to different states of actual markets but also as different levels of abstraction. We have seen that the analysis of the firm under "monopoly" is really the analysis under the condition that the market functions relating sales or purchases to price structure are not only "given" for the firm but are independent of any other variables related to the firm itself. Thus no matter how high the profits of a "pure monopoly," the market functions will not be affected. At the next stage of analysis we may suppose that the market functions of the firm depend on some other variables—say profits —and that if profits are above normal new firms will be attracted into the "industry" and the market functions of old firms will move to the "left" (less can be sold or purchased at each price). This is the analysis

[1] See Robert Triffin, *Monopolistic Competition and General Equilibrium Theory*, Harvard University Press, 1940.

of "monopolistic competition." "Perfect competition" is simply a special case of the above analyses when the market functions are perfectly elastic. Then a still later stage of the analysis involves the assumption that not only do the market functions in fact depend on other variables, but that the firm knows this and plans accordingly. This assumption gets us into problems of oligopoly.

MONOPOLISTIC COMPETITION

Product Differentiation

Consider first the case of monopolistic competition. This condition is characterized by a number of firms large enough so that the policy of one firm does not appreciably affect the policy of another firm producing a similar product. It is also characterized by "product differentiation," or heterogeneous products. That is to say, the product of any one firm is not a perfect substitute, in the mind of the buyer, for the product of any other firm. A good example is the breakfast food industry, where a number of firms are selling products which are similar, in that they satisfy the same kind of want, but which differ among themselves somewhat in character and name. Grape Nuts, Shredded Wheat, Wheaties, and Kix are all breakfast foods and are all to some extent substitutable one for the other. But not one of them is perfectly substitutable for any other—the differences between them are important enough so that each buyer at any one time will have a definite preference for one rather than another, even when both are the same price. The result of this "product differentiation" is to give each firm something of the position of a monopolist, for, as we have seen, a monopolist is none other than a firm whose product is different from that of any other firm.

The Sales Curve in Monopolistic Competition

A firm in monopolistic competition, therefore, will find that its sales curve is not perfectly elastic. If it cuts its price it will gain sales from other firms, but only to a limited extent; if it raises its price it will lose some but not all of its sales to other firms. We should note how this property of the sales curves depends upon the *differences* between the product of the firm in question and that of other firms. If the buyer thinks that there are no differences in the products of different firms, then if one firm shades its price even fractionally below the others, all the buyers will rush to the cheaper firm; if a firm raises its price even fractionally above the general level, buyers will rush away from it to the other firms. Where, however, there are differences in the product of different firms, each firm will have a group of buyers who prefer, for one reason or another, the product of that particular firm and who will not be driven away from it even if it raises its price above the general level. Suppose that at a price of $10 per ton a given firm, A, had 1000 buyers. If it raised its price to $11 per ton it might drive some of them away—but not all—to Firms B, C, D, etc. Suppose at $11 a ton it had 800 buyers. At $12 a ton it would drive still more buyers away—but again, perhaps not all; it might have 500 buyers. At $13 per ton it would drive away all but the most faithful, and would perhaps have only 100 buyers. Similarly, if it cut its price to $9 per ton, it would attract the most "faithless" buyers from Firms B, C, D, etc., but would not attract them all.

Kinds of "Differences"

These "differences" may be of many kinds. We may prefer to buy from one firm rather than another because of the nice smile with which the product is sold, or the pleasant surroundings; because of the past reputation of the firm; because of our personal relationships with the seller; because of an attractive name, an attractive package, or simply because of distance.

Differences of Location

This last source of difference—the distance between firms—is an important one, and as it is fairly simple we shall do well to examine it more closely. Suppose that two firms, A and B, are situated 100 miles from each other in the middle of a perfectly flat plain over which transport costs per mile are the same in any direction. They both charge the same price at the factory—say, $10 per ton—for their product, and the cost of transport of the product is 1 cent per ton-mile.

The "Boundary of Indifference"

Evidently, under these circumstances buyers at all points which are equidistant from both firms will not care from which firm they buy, i.e., buyers on the line LKL' in Fig. 97, where K bisects AB and LL' is perpendicular to AB. Thus any buyer at L, 75 miles from both A and B, will find that A's price (factory price plus transport) is $10.75, and that B's price is also $10.75. Any buyer situated to the left of the line LL', however, will prefer to buy from Firm A; any buyer situated to the right of LL' will prefer to buy from Firm B. The two firms therefore only "compete," in the sense that they can sell to the same buyers, along the line LL'. All buyers to the left of LL' are A's special preserve, and all buyers to the right of LL' are B's special preserve. Now suppose that A cuts his factory price to $9.80 per ton. At the

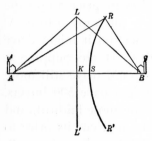

point K he now sells for $10.30 while B still sells for $10.50 per ton. He will therefore attract a certain number of B's buyers to himself, but only a limited number. At S, where AS is 60 miles and SB is 40 miles, A's price will now be $10.40 (9.80 + 0.60) and B's price will also be $10.40 (10.00 + 0.40). With the new prices, therefore, S is on the boundary between A's preserve, and B's preserve, and the new boundary line will be RSR'. This is now not a straight line but a hyperbola, for it must fulfill the condition that for any point R, $AR - BR = 20$ miles, or $2 \times KS$. If AR, for instance, is 80 miles and BR is 60 miles, A's price at R will be $10.60 and B's price will also be $10.60.

Fig. 97. Monopolistic
Competition.

Effect of Unilateral Price Change

It is evident that the reduction in price made by A has resulted in a transfer of some, but not all, of B's buyers to A. To be precise, A has gained and B has lost all those buyers who are situated in the area between the lines LL' and RR'. The greater the difference between A's price and B's, the greater this area will be, and the greater will be A's gain in sales and B's loss. Notice, however, that it is the *difference* in price which is significant. If A cuts his price to $9.80 and B immediately cuts his price also to $9.80, the boundary line between their two markets remains at LL', and neither firm gains or loses buyers.

No matter how great the number of firms, they will divide up the market area among them, so that each has a definite area within which it sells and a boundary line on which it competes with other firms. No matter how great the number of firms, it is also still true that if one firm cuts its price while the others do not, it will gain buyers at the expense of the others, provided, of course, that there are buyers in the "market area" so gained. Although we have illustrated this principle in terms of spatial differences, it clearly applies to other differences as well.

Where Should a New Firm Locate Itself?

Now consider a rather different problem. Suppose Firm A is established at the position marked A, and B is a new firm which decides to come in and share A's market. A, for instance, may be a Woolworth store, already established on the main street of a town and B another five-and-ten, seeking a site for its shop. Where will be the best place for Firm B to establish itself? Obviously it will wish to obtain as large a market as it can; that is to say, it will want to push the line LL' as far over toward A as it can. So it will try to locate itself as *near* A as it can. If it can establish itself right next door to A, but not so near that buyers will not care whether they buy from A or B, it will have obtained for itself the largest share of A's market. If we suppose that buyers are very sensitive to differences in costs of transport, so that they will neither walk past B to get to A nor walk past A to get to B, then if A and B are next door to each other, B will get all buyers who live to the right of the place, and A will get all buyers who live to the left of it. Similarly, if A and B are established at a certain spot, the best place for Firm C is as near to both of them as it can get without destroying the difference in situation altogether.[2]

The "Principle of Minimum Differentiation"

This is a principle of the utmost generality. It explains why all the five-and-tens are usually clustered together, often next door to each other; why certain towns attract large numbers of firms of one kind; why an industry, such as the garment industry, will concentrate in one quarter of a city. It is a principle which can be carried over into other "differences" than spatial differences. The general rule for any new manufacturer coming into an industry is "make your product as like the existing products as you can without destroying the differences." It explains why all automobiles are so much alike, and why no manufacturer dares make a car in which a tall hat can be worn comfortably. It even explains why Methodists, Baptists, and even Quakers are so much alike, and tend to get even more alike, for if one church is to attract the adherents of another, it must become more like the other but not so much alike that no one can tell the difference. It explains the importance of brand names in commercial, social, and even religious life, for the best way of making a product as much like other products as possible without destroying the differences is to make it physically similar to the others but to *call* it something different, and to try to build up by advertising a preference in the mind of the buyer for the *name* of the product. Thus it also explains the importance of

[2] It should be noted that the process of concentration of firms does not go on indefinitely; there are circumstances in which even C will not want to settle close to A and B but will start a new center. When D, E, F, etc., are brought into the picture, the situation becomes very complicated, and secondary and tertiary centers tend to be established.

advertising, for a great part of advertising is little more than an attempt to establish a brand name in the minds of the public.[3]

The Profits of Differentiation Not Permanent

We shall now prove two important propositions in connection with monopolistic competition. The first is that if there is freedom of entry into a monopolistically competitive industry, that industry will not in the long run show profits which are above normal. This is because of a principle already discussed under conditions of perfect competition, that if an industry has freedom of entry and a relatively large number of firms, any profits above normal will attract new firms into the industry, while if profits are below normal, firms will be driven out. The entry of new firms will lower profits by increasing the output of the industry and lowering the price of its product. The departure of firms from the industry will raise profits by lowering the total output of the industry and raising the price of its product. As long as there is freedom of entry, this principle applies, whether there is perfect competition or monopolistic competition.

The only difference under monopolistic competition is that we cannot say simply that the entry of new firms causes the price of the product to fall, for there is no one price, and each firm has a range of prices at which it may sell. Even in an industry which is in monopolistic competition, however, the entry of new firms will lower the sales curve of each firm already in the industry. That is, after a new firm has entered, each of the old firms will find that at each possible price it can sell less than before, or—what is the same thing—that in order to sell the same amount as before it has to charge a lower price. This will reduce the profits of each firm. The entry of new firms will go on until it does not pay new firms to enter. The profits in the industry are then "normal."

Exception Where the Number of Firms Is Small

We must make one qualification of this principle. It will apply strictly only where the output of each firm is small relative to the output of the industry, i.e., where the average cost in each firm begins to rise at a fairly small output. In an industry in which the average cost falls in each firm over a long range of output (e.g., the automobile industry) the most profitable size of each firm is large, and such an industry may have a small number of large firms. Here the addition of another firm might reduce the profits of all firms to a point well

---

[3] Cf., Hotelling, *Economic Journal*, Vol. 39 (1929), pp. 41 ff.

below normal. Therefore, even if the profits of existing firms are above normal, it will not pay a new firm to come in. The extreme case of this situation is the type of industry in which there is a "natural monopoly"—in which one firm may be profitable, but the firms must be so large that two firms will be unprofitable. In such a case the firstcomer may enjoy profits undisputed for a long period of years. The railroads before the development of road transport were to some extent in this position, for very few routes had so much traffic that two railroads on the same route could be profitable.

The Necessity for Innovation

The temporary nature of above-normal profits, even in industries in which there is a high degree of monopolistic competition, goes a long way toward explaining the constant tendency in capitalism toward innovation. The situations in which unusual profits can be made permanently are rare. In most cases unusual profits may be obtained by the *first* firms in a new industry, but they will constantly be eaten away by imitators who are attracted by these unusual profits. Consequently, in the search for profits capitalists are constantly attempting to put new products on the market, or even variations of old products, in order to reap what we may call the "profits of innovation."

Monopolistic Competition Results in Production with Decreasing Average Cost

The second proposition concerning monopolistic competition is that when an industry in this situation has reached equilibrium, with profits at the normal level, the size of each firm is smaller than the size at which the average cost is at a minimum, so that each firm will be producing under conditions of "decreasing average cost." In perfect competition we saw that when the industry was in equilibrium and profits were normal each firm was producing at the output where its average cost of production (including rent) was a minimum. In monopolistic competition, however, firms are producing at their most profitable output when they could still reduce their average cost by increasing output. It is not difficult to see why this should be so. Under perfect competition each firm can sell as much as it wants at the market price. The only thing which limits a firm, then, in its desire to expand output, is the fear of rising costs, so that a firm cannot possibly be producing at its most profitable output if it could lower its average cost by expanding its output. But in monopolistic competition a firm is limited in its desire to expand output not merely by the fear of rising costs but by the fear of falling revenues, i.e., by the fact that it cannot sell as much as it wishes at the going price but must lower its price (or raise its selling costs) in order to sell more. Consequently, it will stop expanding its output at a point where its average cost is still falling, if its marginal cost is equal to its marginal revenue. Beyond this point, although its average cost falls, the fall in cost is more than counterbalanced by the fact that in order to sell the increased output the price must be lowered or the selling cost raised.

Example: The Retailing Industry. The industry which provides the services of retailing is a good example of monopolistic competition. Almost every store has a certain clientele which would buy from it even if its prices are somewhat higher than those of surrounding stores. Thus, physically identical commodities may sell for different prices even in neighboring stores. This would be impossible under perfect competition, and is a proof that an element of monopoly is present. The profits in the retail business are not unusually large, however, for it is usually an easy business to enter. If profits were above normal in any line of retail trade or in any locality, new stores would quickly open up and reduce profits to normal. Indeed, it may be that profits are actually below normal in the retail trade on account of the unshakable and unwarranted optimism of the small capitalist with a few thousand dollars.

The result of monopolistic competition, therefore, is not that profits are large but that the number of stores is greater than would be the case if perfect competition prevailed. Almost every retail store could lower the average cost of its services if it had a larger volume of sales. In most cases, however, it does not attempt to get this increased volume of sales, in spite of the lower cost, because of the loss in revenue involved in obtaining the increased volume. The loss in revenue may be due to lower prices or to increased selling cost, but it should be noticed that in either case this loss would not be present under perfect competition. If the industry were perfectly competitive, some of the weaker stores which are protected under monopolistic competition by the "faithful clientele" would be driven out. The remaining stores would expand their outputs to the point where the average total cost (including rent) of their services was a minimum. Monopolistic competition, however, enables the relatively inefficient firms to make normal profits, and so keeps these firms in the industry. It also enables all firms to maximize their profits at a level of output which is inefficient in terms of costs. These are "wastes" of monopolistic competition for which the consumer must pay in the form of higher prices.

Graphic Illustration. The theoretical solution of the problem of an individual firm in monopolistic competition is essentially the same as the solution for pure monopoly. The only difference between the two cases lies in the solution of the problem of equilibrium in the industry as a whole. An industry in monopolistic competition partakes of the character of a perfectly competitive industry in so far as there are a large number of firms and unrestricted entry, for then it is impossible to prevent the entry of new firms if the industry is abnormally profitable. Consequently, in equilibrium the marginal firm will have normal profits and a zero net revenue. The position of the marginal firm in imperfect competition is shown in Fig. 98C or 99D. It will be seen immediately from a study of Fig. 98C that the most profitable output, O_3M_3, is smaller than the output at which the average total cost is least.

Equilibrium of an Industry in Monopolistic Competition

We cannot construct a "supply curve" for an industry in imperfect competition as we can for one in perfect competition, for there is no *single* price at which all the product is sold; even in equilibrium each firm may charge a different price. But a construction similar to that in Fig. 82, page 567, can be applied to the case of monopolistic competition. Although there is now no single supply or demand curve, we can still interpret a general rise in demand, say, for breakfast foods as a whole, as meaning a rise in the sales curves of all the firms connected with the industry. Figs. 98 and 99 show the cost and revenue curves (average and marginal) for a series of firms in an industry in monopolistic competition. In each case the dotted curve marked C is the marginal cost curve, the dotted curve marked R is the marginal revenue curve, the solid curve marked V is the average variable cost curve, and the solid curve marked S is the sales curve, or average revenue curve. In Fig. 98 the position of the curves is such that Firm C is the marginal firm, or the "no-rent firm." This firm's most profitable price is equal to its average variable cost, and therefore its fixed factors receive no rent. Firms A and B bear rent. Fig. 99 gives the effects of a "rise in demand" for the commodity. The rise in demand means a rise in all the individual demand curves (sales curves) of the various firms. It will be seen that Firm D is now brought into the industry, whereas in Fig. 98 Firm D would not be in the industry in equilibrium because even at its most profitable output (O_4M_4) the price (M_4P_4) is less than the average cost (M_4Q_4). The rise in demand clearly raises the output of each firm—e.g., of Firm A from OM_1 to $O'_1M'_1$.

It will probably raise the price charged by each firm—e.g., from M_1P_1 to $M'_1P'_1$. As we saw earlier in Fig. 95B, the rise in price, though probable, is not an absolutely necessary result. The rise in demand will increase the rents in the industry, as may be seen by comparing the rectangle $P_1Q_1 \times O_1M_1$ with $P'_1Q'_1 \times O'_1M'_1$.

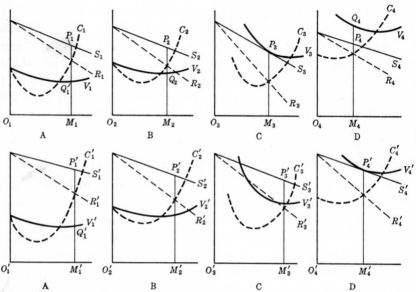

Figs. 98 and 99. Rise in Demand in Monopolistic Competition.

OLIGOPOLY

When a few firms comprise an industry, the condition is known as "oligopoly," from the Greek meaning "few sellers." Oligopoly itself has several widely different forms, but they are all marked by one phenomenon not found when there are many sellers. In oligopoly, each firm must ask itself what will be the effect of its action upon the behavior of other firms. Up to now, in searching for the most profitable output of a firm, we have considered certain data as given. We have seen how, given the physical production table of a process together with the sales curves for output and the purchase curves for input, we can derive from these data what will be the most profitable "position" of the process, i.e., the most profitable quantities of output to produce and of input to use. In the case of oligopoly, however, the sales curve, at least, does not seem to be "given," for the sales curve of any one firm depends upon what the other firms are doing— especially on what sales policy they are pursuing. A firm will find it advisable to pursue one policy if it thinks that the policy of the other firms will remain unchanged. But if it thinks that its own policy will affect the policy of other firms, then it will pursue a different policy. What A does depends upon what B does, which in turn depends upon what A does, and so on ad infinitum.

Example

Suppose that a tobacco company is considering whether or not to put on an aggressive sales campaign for its cigarettes. The success of the campaign will depend largely upon the reactions which it generates in the policy of the other tobacco companies. The first result of the campaign will be, of course, to increase the sales of the campaigning company at the expense of the others. If the others do nothing about this, the first company may find its campaign profitable. If, however, the other companies retaliate by expanding their sales campaigns or by cutting their prices, the original company will find that it has expanded its sales very little, and all the companies lose.

Types of Oligopoly

We cannot solve the problem of oligopoly, then, unless we make definite assumptions concerning the reactions of one policy on another. These assumptions fall into two subdivisions. First we may assume a case in which the product is so homogeneous that a cut in price by one firm will immediately result in an identical price cut by all the other firms in the industry. This is the condition called "perfect oligopoly." Each entrepreneur acts on the supposition that any change in prices which he initiates will immediately be followed by a like change in the prices of his competitors. The second condition is one in which there is some differentiation of the product, so that a cut in price by one firm will not immediately attract all, or the larger part, of the customers of the other firms. In such a case retaliation may be slow, and a firm can fix its price on the assumption that at least for a time the prices of the other firms will not be changed. This condition is called "imperfect oligopoly."

Perfect Oligopoly

1. *Identical Cost Curves and Equal Shares of the Market.* The condition of perfect oligopoly can be further divided into three cases. We shall analyze each case on the assumption of duopoly, i.e., of two firms only; the results can easily be generalized. The first case is that of two firms with identical cost curves and equal shares of the market.

It is illustrated in Fig. 100. The total demand curve for the product of the "industry" is HF_i. As the total sales of the industry at each price are assumed to be equally divided between the two firms, the individual demand curve (sales curve) of each firm will be HPF, where at any price, ON, charged by both firms the amount sold by each firm, NP, will be half the amount sold by the "industry." This sales curve is drawn for each firm with the premise that the same price is charged by both firms, not, as is usual, with the premise that one firm alone changes its price. In perfect oligopoly, as we have seen, it is impossible for one firm to change its price alone. Then suppose BRB' is the marginal cost curve of either firm, both firms having identical cost curves.

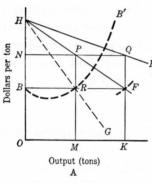

FIG. 100. Perfect Oligopoly, Equal Costs.   FIG. 101. Perfect Oligopoly, Unequal Costs.

The marginal revenue curve for each firm is HG, this being the curve which is "marginal" to the "average" curve HF. Then each firm will set its price at the level ON ($= MP$), where it will sell an output OM and where its marginal cost is equal to its marginal revenue, MR. The total sales of the industry will then be OK ($= NQ$). For the sake of convenience the demand curves are drawn as straight lines, but the analysis does not, of course, depend on this assumption.

Where the demand curve is a straight line, however, we can show in this special case that the price and the output of the industry are the same as would result from pure monopoly. If our two firms are united into one, assuming that no economies or diseconomies result from the union, then the united firm will be able to produce twice as much output for a given marginal cost as either of the old firms. Thus at a marginal cost of OB each of the old firms could produce BR, and therefore at this marginal cost the united firm could produce BF ($= 2BR$). The marginal cost curve of the united firm will therefore pass through the point F. But the point F is also on the marginal revenue curve of the new firm, HF.[4] HF is the "marginal" curve to the "average" curve HQ. The output OK, therefore, is the most profitable output for the new firm, where its marginal revenue and marginal cost are both equal to KF; and the price it charges will be KQ, or MP. In all this analysis we have supposed that at the most profitable output the price is not less than the average total cost. Otherwise, of course, the industry will not exist at all.

2. *Two Firms with Different Cost Curves.* Now consider the case of two firms with different cost curves, as in Fig. 101. Suppose Firm A is a low-cost, or high-capacity, firm, with a marginal cost curve, B_1. Firm B is a high-cost, or low-capacity, firm, with a marginal cost curve B_2. The "capacity" of a firm is measured by the distance of its marginal cost curve from the vertical axis, for the farther the marginal cost curve lies to the right, the greater the output which can be attained at any given marginal cost. We again assume equal shares of the market, so that the revenue curves HQF_i, HPF, and HRG have the same significance as in Fig. 100. On these assumptions Firm A will be best satisfied at the output OM, where the price is MP, and its marginal cost and marginal revenue are both equal to MR. Firm B, on the other hand, would prefer to produce at an output OM', with a price of $M'P'$, where its marginal cost and marginal revenue are both equal to $M'R'$. Here, then, is a conflict of policy between the two firms. The high-capacity firm, however, has a certain advantage, as the price it prefers, MP, is lower than the price preferred by the low-capacity firm, $M'P'$. The high-capacity firm (A), therefore, will set the price to suit its own convenience, and the low-capacity firm (B) will be forced to follow suit, as the prices charged by the two firms cannot differ. If Firm B set its price at $M'P'$, Firm A would be under no obligation to follow it, for Firm A prefers a lower price. If Firm A sets the price at MP, however, the other firm *must* follow it, or lose all its sales. If at the price MP Firm B is unprofitable, it will go out of business and leave Firm A with a monopoly. It is quite possible, however, for Firm B still to be making at least normal profits when the price is MP, even though it is not as profitable as it would be if it could set the price to suit itself. In this case the industry will be stable, and will attract enough firms to make the least profitable firm at least normally profitable.

A Special Problem. An interesting problem arises in connection with the interpretation of Fig. 101. NP shows how much each firm *can*

---

[4] See page 555 for the proof of this proposition.

sell at the price ON. There is no reason to suppose, however, that each firm has to sell as much as it can; if it wishes, it can sell less than the market will take simply by not having the product available when the last buyers come for it. Consequently, the demand curve for Firm B, when Firm A fixes the price at ON, is not HF but NPF. That is to say, Firm B can sell any amount not greater than NP at the price ON; and if it lowers its price, the other firm will be forced to follow and both firms will expand sales following the path PF. The marginal revenue curve of Firm B, therefore, is $NPRG$. If now the marginal cost curve

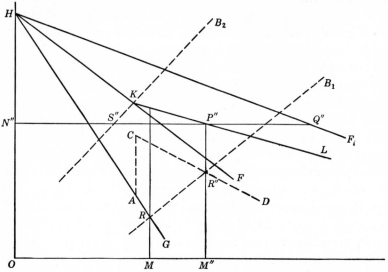

FIG. 102.   Perfect Oligopoly, a Special Case.

of this firm cuts this marginal revenue curve between P and R, no problem arises, and the above analysis stands. If however, as in the figure, the marginal cost curve B_2 cuts firm B's marginal revenue curve between N and P, at S, Firm B will not wish to sell all that the market will take but will only sell an amount NS. That is, Firm B has virtually perfect markets in this range, at the price set by Firm A, and will not wish to produce or sell beyond the output where price is equal to the marginal cost. This means, however, that Firm A now can sell an amount equal to $NP + SP$, or NS', where $SP = PS'$. Firm A's demand curve therefore is no longer HF, but is something like HKL in Fig. 102, K being the intersection of HF with the marginal cost curve B_2, and KL being drawn so that KF bisects any horizontal line such as $S''P''$ between the curve B_2 and KL. The marginal revenue curve corresponding to this demand curve is $HACD$, where CD is the curve marginal to KL. The optimum output of Firm A, OM'', is given by the point R'' where A's marginal cost curve cuts its marginal revenue curve. The price will be $M''P''$; at this price Firm B will only wish to sell an amount $N''S''$, leaving $S''Q''$, which by construction is equal to $N''P''$, to Firm A.

A similar difficulty can also arise in the analysis of Fig. 103.

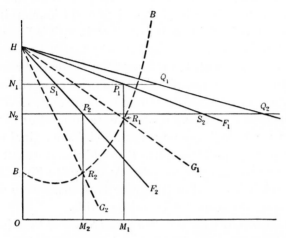

FIG. 103.   Perfect Oligopoly, Unequal Shares of Market.

Price Leadership.   We have obtained from our geometry a result which corresponds closely to reality. Many industries are characterized by the very phenomenon of "price leadership" by the high-capacity firm which we have seen emerging from our theoretical discussion. As we should expect also, the industries characterized by "price leadership" are those in which a simple, homogeneous commodity is produced by a small number of firms. The steel industry and the cement industry are excellent examples. In the steel industry, for instance, the United States Steel Corporation, having the greatest capacity, has been the "price leader," and the other firms have followed the prices it set.

3. *Two Firms with Different Shares of the Market.*   A third situation, where two firms have identical cost curves but different shares of the market, is illustrated in Fig. 103. Here HQ_2 is the demand curve for the product as a whole. We assume that at each price set, both firms selling at the same price, Firm A gets three-quarters and Firm B gets one-quarter of the total sales. Thus at a price ON_1 the total sales are N_1Q_1, the sales of Firm A are N_1P_1 $[= \frac{3}{4}(N_1Q_1)]$ and the sales of Firm B are N_1S_1 $[= \frac{1}{4}(N_1Q_1)]$. The sales curve of Firm A is then HP_1F_1;

the sales curve of Firm B is HP_2F_2. The marginal revenue curve of Firm A is HG_1; the marginal revenue curve of Firm B is HG_2. The marginal cost curve of both firms is assumed to be the same, BB. Then Firm A would prefer to have the price set at the level ON_1, where it could sell an amount N_1P_1 $(= OM_1)$, at which its marginal cost and its marginal revenue were both equal to M_1R_1. Firm B would prefer to have the price set at the level ON_2, where it could sell an amount N_2P_2 $(= OM_2)$, and where its marginal cost and its marginal revenue were both equal to M_2R_2. In this case, therefore, it is Firm B, the firm with the smaller share of the market, which will be able to set the price, for the price which it prefers (ON_2) is smaller than the price which the other firm prefers (ON_1). If the price charged by both firms were ON_1, then Firm A would sell an amount OM_1 (N_1P_1) at which its marginal cost and marginal revenue were equal. But Firm B would then be selling only N_1S_1, an output at which its marginal revenue was greater than its marginal cost. Firm B would therefore cut its price to ON_2 and force Firm A to do likewise. At this price Firm B would sell N_2P_2 and Firm A, N_2S_2. If at this price both firms were at least normally profitable, the situation would be stable.

Price Leadership by a Firm with a Small Share of the Market. This result may seem surprising, for we should perhaps at first sight expect that the firm with the larger share of the market would act as the "leader." We must remember, however, the peculiar assumptions which we have made, in particular the assumption that the marginal cost curves of the two firms are the same. This implies that all the firms have about the same capacity. In that case it is the *least* fortunate firm which is most active in setting the price. In the retail gasoline industry, for instance, when it is passing through one of its intermittent periods of stability, the situation outlined above frequently holds. The price is set by those firms which are not getting a very large share of the market. In the first instance they may have cut their price below that of the more fortunate firms in order to try to attract new customers. The other firms also cut prices to follow suit. At this lower price the firms with the larger share of the market may still be making profits, though not maximum profits—i.e., they would prefer to have everybody charge a higher price. But the firms with the small share would be worse off if everybody raised prices, for having already a small share of the market the reduction in total sales which would follow a rise in price would hit them proportionately harder than it would hit the firms with the larger share of the market. Consequently, the firms with the small share of the market refuse to raise their price, and the firms with the larger share cannot compel them to do so. The relative permanence of cut-rate gasoline in many centers is probably an example of this phenomenon. The stations with the small share of the market, however, can set the price only as long as the capacity of all stations is approximately equal.

In our discussion of perfect oligopoly we have assumed that the share of the market possessed by each seller is not under his control but is determined by chance or by situation. It may be, however, that a firm cannot charge a price different from that of other firms but can make certain efforts to gain larger or smaller shares of the market by increasing selling costs. In such a case the problem becomes one of great complexity, and it is doubtful whether any general propositions can be deduced.

Imperfect Oligopoly

Finally, there is the condition which we call "imperfect oligopoly." It stands intermediate between perfect oligopoly, in which the products of the various firms are so similar that there cannot be more than one price in the market, and monopolistic competition, in which there are so many firms that the action of one does not cause retaliation by others. In imperfect oligopoly the product is differentiated enough so that a price cut on the part of one firm does not immediately result in retaliatory price cuts on the part of other firms. A price cut, therefore, may attract a large volume of new business to the price cutter.

Price Cutting. In such an industry price cutting will be common. The price cutters will not assume that all other firms will cut prices immediately—as in perfect oligopoly—and consequently may formulate their policies on the assumption that other firms will not retaliate. A very unstable situation may then arise. Firm A, let us say, thinks that its marginal revenue is greater than its marginal cost and therefore cuts prices in order to expand sales. This belief is justified only if B does not cut prices. For a time B may not react, in which case he will simply lose business to A. However, with A's price at its new level, B may find it profitable to cut prices even further. But with B's low price A may find it profitable to cut prices still further, and B may retaliate with still another cut.

The full diagrammatic treatment is difficult, but the following illustration will suffice to bring out the main features of the problem. In Fig. 104 the price charged by Firm A is plotted along OX, and the price charged by Firm B along OY. The curve marked I shows the most profitable price that Firm A can charge for each price fixed by

Firm B. That is, if from any point P on curve I a perpendicular to OX is dropped, PH, then OH represents the most profitable price that Firm A can charge when the price charged by Firm B is HP. In the same way curve II shows the most profitable price that can be charged by Firm B for any price charged by Firm A. Suppose Firm A charges a price OH. At this price it will pay Firm B to charge a price HQ $(= KR)$. When Firm B sets its price to KR $(= HQ)$, however, it will pay Firm A to reduce its price to OK. Whereupon Firm B will reduce

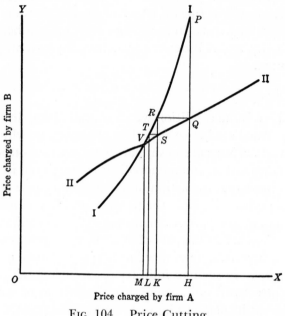

FIG. 104.   Price Cutting.

its price to KS. And so it goes on until finally the point V is reached, where Firm A charges OM and Firm B charges VM. Then it will pay neither firm to cut its price.

The Stability of Imperfect Oligopoly.   The stability of the equilibrium of imperfect oligopoly depends on whether, at the level of prices represented by V, both firms are normally profitable. If so, then a position of stable equilibrium has been reached. But if at this point one or both firms are less than normally profitable, as may well be the case, then either one firm will go out of business, leaving the other with a monopoly, or the two firms will come to an agreement to raise prices; i.e., will again behave like a monopoly. Or—another possibility—each firm may seek to increase its power to raise the price by a further differentiation of the product, thus decreasing the elasticity of its sales curve. If the firms are abnormally profitable at the point of equilibrium, new firms will tend to enter the industry. These new firms will disturb the equilibrium again and may make it unstable; or a new position of equilibrium may be found at which price cutting is unprofitable and yet the least profitable firm is making normal profits.

It will be seen, therefore, that imperfect oligopoly may not allow a position of stable equilibrium. If at the level where it pays nobody to cut price further, all or most of the firms are unprofitable, there may be an agreement to raise prices again. But there will always be a perpetual temptation for individuals to break the agreement and start cutting prices, for if the sales curve is elastic, a price cut may for a time bring in large profits; it is always the *first* price cutter who makes the most profits out of price cutting. Even if a firm knows that other firms will retaliate in time, it may reckon to make a sufficiently large profit from price cutting, before retaliation begins, to make the price cut worth while.

This type of price warfare is frequently found in the retail gasoline industry; indeed, it follows quite a regular cycle. In the fall when sales begin to decline some enterprising gas station decides to cut prices, figuring that the sales it will attract will more than compensate for the low price. But it attracts sales from the other stations nearby, who retaliate by cutting prices also. The first station may cut prices again, and so on until all the stations are selling at a price which is extremely unprofitable to them all. Then someone calls a meeting, and an agreement is made to raise prices, or perhaps the original price cutter is forced out of business and the others raise prices by tacit agreement. This goes on smoothly until someone else decides to cut prices, when the process may start all over again. The "war" need not necessarily take the form of a price war, of course; an increase in selling cost is roughly equivalent to a fall in price, and the "sales war" may easily take the form of competitive advertising.

Selling Costs in Imperfect Competition

The full treatment of selling costs must wait until more advanced techniques of analysis have been presented in Part IV. Nevertheless, some important conclusions can be drawn from the simple propositions (1) that the purpose of sales expenditures is to move the sales curve of the firm to the right, and (2) that the more effective is sales promotion as a method of increasing sales and the less effective is price reduction, the more likely are selling costs to be high. It is clear that a firm with perfect markets will not have any selling costs; there is no point in trying to increase the amount that can be sold at the market price when any amount within the limits of the firm's capacity is salable.

In general, the more homogeneous the product, the less important will selling cost be for the individual firm. Even in the case of perfect competition, of course, selling costs may be expended by an association of the industry as a whole, in an attempt to increase the total demand for the product—the "Drink More Milk" and "Eat More Fruit" campaigns are typical. Such "industry" advertising is also characteristic of perfect oligopoly. Individual selling costs incurred for its own benefit by the individual firm, however, grow in importance as the products become more heterogeneous. In perfect oligopoly, advertising by the individual firm may exist, in an attempt to give the firm a larger share of the market; but if the product is completely homogeneous the market will be divided equally and no amount of advertising will persuade a buyer that the product of one firm is better than that of another. The more "imperfect" oligopoly becomes, the more important becomes individual selling cost.

In monopolistic competition selling costs are extremely important, for the more inelastic the sales curve, i.e., the more differentiated the product, the less effective is a reduction in price as an instrument for increasing sales, and the more effective selling cost is likely to be. Because an increase in selling cost may be a substitute for a fall in price, many of the results of this chapter may need reinterpretation in terms of competitive increases in selling cost rather than in terms of competitive price cutting. Thus a fall in demand may lead to an increase in selling cost rather than to a decline in price, according to the relative effectiveness of these two methods of increasing sales. Similarly, in the case of imperfect oligopoly there may be advertising wars rather than price wars. The cigarette industry is probably a case in point, where, like the Red Queen in *Through the Looking-Glass,* each firm has to run as fast as it can in the direction of selling costs in order to stay where it is. If, however, a fall in price is relatively more effective than an increase in selling cost as a means of expanding output, imperfect oligopoly will lead to price wars rather than to competitive advertising.

Weaknesses of the Models

The reader should not be deluded by the apparent neatness of some of the solutions of this chapter into thinking that the problems of oligopoly and imperfect competition are easy. In fact this represents still one of the least satisfactory fields of economics, in spite of much useful work in recent years. There is, for instance, no adequate theory of the "macroeconomic" impact of various states of the market, nor of the dynamics of these various situations; and until this gap in theory is filled, any over-all appraisal of the effects of these different market forms must be made with great reserve. The most we can say for the marginal analysis in this regard is that the pursuit of various degrees of abstraction in the analysis seems to lead to cases that bear a striking resemblance to conditions which are observed in the real world. For further development of this topic the reader is referred to William Fellner, *Competition among the Few* (New York, 1949), and to Edward Chamberlin, *The Theory of Monopolistic Competition* (Cambridge, Mass., 1933).

QUESTIONS AND EXERCISES

1. It has been proposed to measure the degree of monopoly power possessed by any firm by the reciprocal of the elasticity of its sales curve. Criticize this proposal from both the theoretical and the practical standpoint.
2. Under what circumstances is price cutting likely to arise? How may it be prevented?
3. "One of the greatest evils of modern society is price cutting." "The benefits of economic progress must be passed on to the consumer in the form of lower prices. This can only be done by price cutting." Discuss these two statements.
4. Discuss briefly the truth, falsehood, or completeness of the following statements:
   a. Rent cannot exist except in an industry which is operating under conditions of monopolistic competition.
   b. Firms in an industry in monopolistic competition will be smaller than those in an industry in perfect competition.
   c. The profits of monopolistic competition are not permanent.
   d. No stable position of equilibrium is possible under oligopoly.
   e. In monopolistic competition, when the industry is in equilibrium, the marginal cost will be less than the average total cost (including rent) in all firms.
5. Make a tabular statement comparing and contrasting the conditions and results of (a) perfect competition, (b) monopolistic competition, (c) pure monopoly, (d) perfect oligopoly, (e) imperfect oligopoly.
6. What are the competitive and what the monopolistic elements in monopolistic competition?

7. Analyze, as far as you can, the effect of taxation upon industries in monopolistic competition, in perfect oligopoly, and in imperfect oligopoly.
8. Analyze the situation when two firms in perfect oligopoly have different cost curves *and* different shares of the market.

CHAPTER 31

APPLICATIONS OF THE MARGINAL ANALYSIS: THE REGULATION OF COMPETITION AND MONOPOLY

The previous five chapters have formed a long connected argument in which it has not been possible to follow the general plan of this work in regard to the application of the theoretical models. Now, however, that we have gained a broad view of the marginal analysis it is possible to consider some applications of the theory, especially to problems of the regulation of monopoly and competition.

For a complete analysis of this problem we need first to understand what causes the emergence of different forms of market structure—monopoly, oligopoly, monopolistic competition—and second we need to have some analysis of the "social optimum" according to which these various forms can be judged. The first is the easier problem, and the marginal analysis throws a good deal of light on it. The question is, if the economic system is left to itself, without government intervention, what will be the result? Will there be universal perfect competition, universal monopoly, or a mixed system? The answer seems to be that an unregulated system would soon find itself in a "mixed" condition in which some industries were monopolies, some perfectly competitive, some in monopolistic competition, some perhaps in almost pure oligopoly. The question arises, therefore, "What determines the character of an industry in the absence of state intervention?"

Perfectly Competitive Industries

Two principal factors determine the nature of an industry. One is the character of the commodity which it produces. The other is the character of the process by which its commodity is produced. For an industry to be perfectly competitive, two things must be true. The commodity which it produces must be a relatively simple, homoge-

651

neous, chemical substance, easily graded into a small number of grades, and sold in bulk. Unless this is the case, the product of one firm will not be perfectly substitutable, in the minds of the buyers, for the product of any other firm in the industry, and therefore the market for the output of each firm will not be perfect. Also, the most profitable output of the individual firm must be small relative to the total output coming to the market. This latter condition will be fulfilled only if the average cost of production in each individual firm reaches its minimum at a relatively small output. It will also be fulfilled only if the commodity is readily transportable and if the buyers and sellers of the commodity are in close physical proximity. The average cost of production will reach a minimum in the case of any firm, as we have seen, because of the existence of inputs whose quantity cannot indefinitely be increased. In short periods capital equipment is typical of these "fixed" inputs. In long periods it is the quality of management which is fixed. In any process in which management is a detailed and complex function the point of minimum average cost will come at a relatively small output.

Agriculture as a Typical Competitive Industry

Agriculture and, to a lesser extent, mining provide the best examples of perfectly competitive industries. Most agricultural products are homogeneous substances, easily graded and defined. There is therefore little opportunity for product differentiation, especially by the individual producers of the standard raw materials—wheat, sugar, coffee, etc. The size of the firm is small, for the average cost apparently begins to rise at a relatively small output. This is due mainly to the fact that in agricultural processes management is a detailed and difficult process which cannot be reduced to a simple routine or delegated to employees. The farmer must catch the weather when he can; he cannot work to an eight-hour day or a set of book rules. Consequently, large-scale production has been much less successful in agriculture than in industry.

Natural Monopolies

At the other end of the scale are those industries which are "natural monopolies," in which the size of the firm is so large in relation to the market that there is room for only one firm. As always, the exact definition of what is "natural" and what is "artificial" is no easy matter. No economic life can be carried on without some laws, and laws imply intervention by the state. There are doubtful cases in which firms have obtained monopolies by gaining control of the whole supply of some input necessary for the production of their commodity. The exclusive possession of patents is another possible case. Apart from these examples there are industries in which the productive process exhibits decreasing cost over a long range of output and in which, therefore, large firms will prosper at the expense of small firms until only a single firm is left. Whether this will occur or not depends largely on the physical character of the productive process.

A change in techniques may easily break up a natural monopoly through the introduction of new ways of providing the old commodity. The introduction of the automobile is an interesting example of a technical change leading to a reduction in the size of the unit of enterprise. The railroad was an excellent example of a natural monoply in many cases. It was a form of organization of transport in which the unit of enterprise had to be large or it could not exist. The automobile, on the other hand, is a form of organization of transport which lends itself admirably to small enterprise, whether the business enterprise of the independent trucker or taxi driver or the personal enterprise of the car owner.

Imperfect Competition

Wherever the cost curves of firms are such that the size of the individual firm is large in relation to the size of the market but where there is room for a few firms, imperfect competition in one or another of its forms is likely. Which form it will take depends mainly on the character of the commodity. With a chemically simple, definable commodity product differentiation will not exist, so there will be pure oligopoly and price leadership. Steel is a good example. With a moderately homogeneous commodity in which small differences may exist from firm to firm, imperfect oligopoly with its attendant recurrent price cutting will be the rule. The gasoline industry and some other retail industries tend to fall into this class. With a complex and highly manufactured commodity the product of each firm is likely to be appreciably different from that of other firms in the same "industry," and monopolistic competition will result.

The "Social Optimum"

The analysis of the nature of the social optimum is difficult, and presents problems which may be impossible to solve in an exact form. Nevertheless the marginal analysis throws some light on the nature of *serious* divergences from the social optimum, and legal regulation is most clearly justified where these serious divergences can be detected. It is very difficult to say exactly what is the ideal state of society. It is much less difficult to detect situations which are clearly *not* ideal, and it is usually possible to say something about the direction of change which will improve matters. Therefore it is fortunately not necessary to have a clear or exact theory of the social optimum or ideal in order to be able to say something about desirable directions of change away from situations which are clearly not ideal.

THE REGULATION OF MONOPOLY

The first situation which can clearly be recognized as a divergence from the economic ideal is monopoly. In considering the problem of the regulation of monopoly, then, we must first answer the question, "What is wrong with monopoly?" Why do we have to bother about its regulation? There are many answers to this question. They can, however, be reduced to two principal propositions: that monopoly distorts the distribution of resources among various occupations away from that which is socially most desirable, and that monopoly allows the exploitation of one group by another. If an industry which formerly was operating under perfect competition were suddenly to be organized as a monopoly, its owners would find it profitable to restrict its output and to raise the price of its product. By eliminating those plants which were operating under the highest variable costs and so restricting the output, the owners could obtain a higher price for the product and thus a higher net revenue in the remaining plants. As the net revenue in the eliminated plants would be small in any case, there would clearly be a gain in total net revenue through their elimination. Those resources which were employed in the high-cost plants would be forced out of the industry and either would be unemployed or would have to find employment elsewhere. The fact that they did not seek employment elsewhere before the advent of the monopoly, however, implies that when the industry was perfectly competitive they were in their most advantageous occupation.

The formation of a monopoly, therefore, will drive some resources from the monopolized industry into an occupation which is *less* advantageous to them. Consequently, the "principle of equal advantage" is violated. A monopolist can maintain his own advantages at a level higher than the prevailing level only because he can prevent the movement of those resources which would like to move into his occupation. He can be said to "exploit" these resources. He can also be said to "exploit" consumers, who now have to pay a higher price than before. A monopoly, then, results in a general distortion of the distribution of resources, a smaller amount than is desirable going into the monopolist's occupation and a larger amount than is desirable going to other uses, with the results that, first, there is a general social loss, and second, the monopolist appropriates an unduly large proportion of what is left. A monopolist is like a greedy boy at a table, who not only seizes more than his fair share of the cake but also in the scramble causes some cake to be spoiled.

Dissolution vs. Regulation

There are two broad policies possible in an attempt to deal with the monopoly problem. One is the policy of *dissolution*—that is, the attempt to split up the monopoly into a number of competing firms. The success of this policy is very doubtful. It is rarely possible to split up a monopoly into more than a small number of firms, and competition among such a small number (oligopoly) may have consequences which are even less desirable than monopoly. The alternative policy of *regulation* is therefore much more popular. This involves the acceptance of monopolies as "necessary evils" in some cases and the regulation of their practices and policies by law. Regulation is practiced principally in those industries where there is a strong "natural" tendency for monopoly; i.e., where the optimum size of the firm is so large that the industry if left to itself would all come under the control of a single firm. The so-called public utilities—water, gas and electricity, telephones, railroads, etc.—are for the most part natural monopolies, and there is therefore a reasonable fear that left unregulated in private hands they would prove instruments for the exploitation of the people.

Objects of Monopoly Regulation

It is one thing, however, to say that monopolies ought to be regulated and another thing to say *how* they ought to be regulated. From the point of view of the distribution of income it is fairly clear that they should not ideally be allowed to retain more than "normal" profits, though exactly how "normal" is to be defined in practice, and how above-normal profits are to be extracted from them without changing their policies in other directions, possibly adverse, is also not always clear. When we come to the question of what constitutes the "ideal output" of a monopolist, we find controversy not only in the matter of how to achieve the ideal output, but even in regard to the definition of the ideal.

The problem is illustrated in Fig. 105. Fig. 105A shows the curves of average revenue (AR), marginal revenue (MR), average cost (AC), and marginal cost (MC) of a monopolist. We suppose that average cost is rising with output. For convenience in drawing, all the curves are assumed to be straight lines, but this is not necessary to the argument.

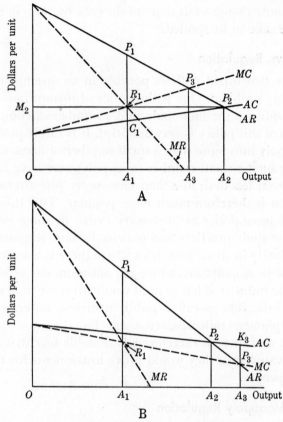

FIG. 105. Monopoly Regulation.

Then the output at which profit (net revenue) is a maximum is OA_1, at which marginal cost equals marginal revenue at R_1 (see page 553). The largest output at which profits are normal is OA_2, where the average revenue (price) is equal to the average cost, and the net revenue therefore is zero (see page 531). If therefore the regulatory commission sets the price at A_2P_2, under the condition that all the output that can be sold at that price must be produced, profits will be normal. The condition is necessary because otherwise it might still pay the monopolist to restrict output and sales below the maximum amount which could be sold at the set price. Thus suppose the price were set at A_2P_2 ($= OM_2$), but that the firm were left free to produce and sell as much or as little as it pleased. The marginal revenue curve to the firm would then be M_2P_2, which intersects the marginal cost curve at R_1, and the firm would still restrict its output to OA_1, even though it now makes smaller profits than formerly ($R_1C_1 \times OA_1$ as against $P_1C_1 \times OA_1$). In the present figure M_2P_2 goes through R_1, the intersection of MR and MC, only because all the curves are straight lines; but even if the curves are not linear, M_2P_2 will cut MC well to the left of P_2, and there would be restriction of output.

Marginal Cost Pricing

Yet another criterion for determining the socially best output has been suggested, by Hotelling, Lerner, and others:[1] that the price should equal the marginal cost. In the figure this would mean an output of OA_3, where the MC curve cuts the AR curve at P_3. The price would then be A_3P_3. The reasons for this proposal are subtle, and cannot be explained in full here. Suppose, however, that the marginal cost is a measure of the value of resources used up in producing an additional unit of the product, and the price is a measure of the value of the product to the consumer. Then if the marginal cost is less than the price, there is evidence that an expansion of the output in question will create more social value (as measured by the price) than the value of the resources used up, and therefore it will be socially desirable to expand output. If the marginal cost is greater than the price, a contraction of output will release a greater value of resources than the value of the product, and there is a presumption that resources should be transferred to other commodities.

There are many objections to this proposal, both theoretical and practical. We may notice, for instance, that the criterion is formally satisfied at R_1 (Fig. 105A) if the price is fixed at OM_2 but the monopolist is allowed to produce any quantity he wants. A condition must be added, therefore, that sales must not be less than the maximum possible at the fixed price. A more serious objection is illustrated in Fig. 105B. Here the meaning of the figure is identical with Fig. 105A except that we have supposed decreasing instead of increasing cost. Under these circumstances it will be observed that P_3, the point where price equals marginal cost, is at a larger output than P_2, the point

[1] For an excellent summary of this proposal and the controversy connected with it, the reader is referred to two articles by Nancy Ruggles, "Recent Developments in the Theory of Marginal Cost Pricing," *Review of Economic Studies,* 17 (1949–1950), 107–126, and "The Welfare Basis of Marginal Cost Pricing," ibid., 29–46.

where profits are normal. This means that if output is pushed to the point where price equals marginal cost, there will be losses (profits below normal) equal to $P_3 K_3 \times OA_3$. If the enterprise is to continue, therefore, a subsidy at least equal to this amount must be paid, and the question arises how this subsidy is to be raised without creating further distortions in the system. The question will be discussed later (pages 824–826).

Difficulties of Marginal Cost Pricing

The practical difficulties are perhaps the most serious: long-run marginal cost is not really in the information system at all, and even if short-run marginal costs can be discovered, serious errors might be introduced by pricing according to short-run marginal costs. It should also be pointed out that under constant cost the MC and AC curves coincide in a horizontal line and that therefore P_3 and P_2 are the same point—that is, the "normal profits" criterion and the "price equals marginal cost" criterion are the same. The longer the period of time considered, the more likely are we to find approximately constant cost conditions, as in the long run most adjustments of capacity can be made. Under these circumstances it is not surprising that the less sophisticated criterion of normal profits has proved a more effective guide for regulation than the sophisticated criterion of equating price with marginal cost.

Difficulties of "Normal Profits" Pricing

Even if the "normal profits" criterion is accepted, the practical difficulties in the way of carrying out such a policy of regulation are enormous, though perhaps not insuperable. One difficulty is the *definition* of normal profit. Presumably, "normal profit" in this connection means a certain *rate of return* on capital, measured as a percentage per annum, which the investor could reasonably have expected to earn had he invested in some other unregulated enterprise of comparable risk. But as we saw in Chapter 23, the definition and calculation of the rate of profit is by no means an easy matter; for in order to calculate the rate of profit over any period of time less than the whole life of the enterprise, *valuations* of the property of the enterprise must be made at the beginning and at the end of the period. It is the making of these valuations which provides most of the difficulties of effective public regulation, for there is no agreement as to the principles according to which they shall be made. We must leave the detailed consideration of these difficulties until we have examined the theory of valuation.

Another practical difficulty is that of identifying the "normal rate of profit" itself. Any figure, such as 6 per cent per annum, fixed by the courts is bound to be arbitrary. It is not only difficult to discover what are the actual profits in the regulated business; it is even more difficult to discover what are the rates of profit in unregulated businesses, and still more difficult to estimate and allow for the differences in risk between various enterprises. But if the figure set by the courts is too high, part of the purpose of regulation is evaded, and if it is too low, there will be little new investment in the regulated industries, and even the old investment will in part be liquidated.

Public Operation of Monopolies

In view of these difficulties public ownership and operation of natural monopolies has been advocated, and in many cases it has been carried out. The Post Office is an excellent example of a business which seems universally to be best administered by the state. In many countries railroads are run by the state; and the municipally owned and operated water, gas, electricity, or transport company is a common occurrence. If the political system is efficient, the operation of monopolies by the state may be the most satisfactory solution of the problem. Where political life is corrupt, however, or even where it is honest but unintelligent, state or municipal operation is no guarantee of maximum social welfare. Even under state ownership, it should be noticed, the principles of profit making are not absent. When *all* the services and costs are valued properly, a government agency should usually be operated at the maximum output at which normal profits can be made. If less than normal profits are made there is evidence either of inefficient production methods or of a misuse of resources.

The misuse of resources involved in unprofitable public undertakings need not, of course, be due to any particular corruption or incompetence of public officials, but may simply be due to errors of forecasts. All investment is made in anticipation of future returns, and these anticipations are by their very nature subject to error. It should be pointed out, therefore, that public ownership involves public acceptance of the risk of loss as well as of the chance of profit. If a privately owned coal mine or railroad turns out to be unprofitable, the owners bear the bulk of the loss. If a publicly owned coal mine or railroad turns out to be unprofitable, the loss is distributed over the whole people in some degree. For this reason public ownership is not quite the unqualified blessing that it might appear to be at first sight: a town, for instance, which has incurred a mass of bonded indebted ness to acquire a transport system which turns out to be a financial burden may well envy its sister community which allowed its defunct trolleys to remain in private hands.

Regulation by Taxation

One possible method of regulation emerges from our analysis which has probably never been tried but is of some theoretical interest. The purposes of regulation are (1) to prevent the monopolist from making abnormal profits, (2) to expand the output of the monopolist beyond the point of greatest private profit. Both these ends might be achieved by the combination of a fixed tax with a variable rebate or subsidy. The effect of a variable subsidy is of course opposite to that of the variable tax studied on page 622. The marginal cost curve will be lowered (if the subsidy is regarded as a deduction from cost) and consequently the monopolist will expand his output under the influence of the subsidy. Any monopoly profits that accrue to him, however, can theoretically be absorbed by the state in the form of a fixed tax, for a fixed tax, as we have seen, should not affect the monopolist's output.

DUMPING AND PRICE DISCRIMINATION

Another important aspect of the monopoly problem we have already noticed (pages 608–615) under the heading of price discrimination, and many problems in the regulation of monopoly arise out of this practice. In international trade the policy of price discrimination between two markets is known as "dumping." A steel combine, for instance, which has a monopoly within its own country may find that the demand for its product at home is less elastic than the demand abroad, for in foreign markets the fact that buyers have alternative sources of supply makes the demand for the product of the monopolist highly elastic. A high price will not restrict sales at home as much as it would abroad, for buyers at home cannot turn to other sellers. Consequently, the monopolist will find it most profitable to charge a high price at home where the demand is less elastic, and a low price abroad where the demand is more elastic. This policy often arouses the anger of competitors abroad, who accuse the company of selling "below cost"; the layman may well wonder how it could possibly pay anyone to sell "below cost." The ambiguity of the word "cost" is well illustrated in this problem. If the monopolist wishes to maximize his profits he will, as we have seen, try to sell that quantity and charge that price in each market at which the marginal revenue is equal to the marginal cost. This means that the price in each market cannot be below the *marginal* cost, for except when the demand is perfectly elastic the price at any volume of sales is greater than the marginal revenue. However, it is quite possible for the marginal cost to be well below the average cost, as it will be if the plant is working at a smaller than optimum capacity. Consequently, it may profit a monopolist to sell at a price below his *average* total cost in some market, provided that the additional revenue received from the sale of an additional unit at least covers the additional cost of producing that unit.

Price Discrimination in Domestic Trade

"Dumping" is found in internal trade as well as in international trade. The milk cooperative, for instance, which sells milk at a high price to domestic consumers and at a low price to butter and cheese manufacturers is "dumping." A celebrated example in the industrial sphere was that of the Goodyear Tire Company, which sold tires under its own name at a high price through the regular channels, and sold the identical tires through a mail-order house, under another brand name, at a lower price! The grocer who used to divide his tea into three parts—one selling at 20 cents, another at 30 cents, and another at 40 cents a pound—was following exactly the same principle. So is the doctor who charges a high fee to a rich patient and a small fee to a poor patient.

In all these cases it should be observed that the price discrimination is possible only because the markets are separated. It is possible on an international scale because of the difficulty of reselling, in its country of origin, material sold abroad. Frequently a tariff on imports of the commodity is necessary or at least helpful to the monopolist in maintaining the separation of markets. Discrimination in the milk market is possible only because domestic consumers cannot conveniently purchase from the manufacturers, or because an agreement or contract forbids the resale of milk sold for manufacture. Discrimination is possible in the retailing business because consumers do not generally buy and sell from each other. A drugstore which follows a policy of "25 cents for one, 26 cents for two!" would soon be run out of business if all its customers hunted in couples, and the above-mentioned tea merchant would soon find his little tricks unprofitable if the Colonel's lady who insisted on "the best" tea at 40 cents ever began to compare notes with Judy O'Grady who bought the same tea for 20 cents. Similarly, doctors can discriminate only because a poor person cannot retail his appendicitis operation to the rich.

Railway Rates

Another interesting, though complex, example of price discrimination is found in the theory of railway rates. Railroads usually charge a low rate per ton on bulky commodities of low value-density, such as wheat and coal, and a high rate on commodities whose value is great in proportion to their bulk or weight. Railroads also charge low rates over long hauls and higher rates over short hauls; they may charge one rate from west to east, and another rate from east to west; they may charge a low rate between two points where there are competing forms of transport and high rates between intermediate points on the same route where there are no competing forms of transport. All this complex structure of rates is an application of the principles of price discrimination which we have outlined. The principle of discrimination in this case goes by the name of "charging what the traffic will bear." If the demand for a particular form of transportation is highly elastic, the rate is likely to be lower than if the demand is more inelastic. Thus in the case of bulky commodities a high freight rate may prevent their transportation altogether; the demand for their transport is therefore elastic, and the rate will be relatively low. In the case of precious commodities transport charges may be only a small proportion of the total cost of getting them to the consumer. Consequently— with transport services regarded as an "input" in the whole process of production—the demand for this input will be inelastic, according to Proposition II of our four propositions on the demand for input, Part I, page 205. The price will be considerably greater than the marginal revenue and will be relatively high. Similarly, when a railroad runs between two points which have water communication, the demand for the transport of those types of freight which can easily travel by water will be very elastic. The cost of transport by rail cannot greatly exceed the cost by water or the freight will travel by water exclusively. The railroad rate will therefore be low compared to the rate on shorter hauls where there is no competition and the demand for transport is inelastic.

The problem of railway rates is complicated by the fact that each class of transport may have a different marginal cost. In each line of traffic, then, the most profitable price is that which will make the marginal revenue equal to the marginal cost of the operations involved. As the marginal costs of different forms of transport differ, it is not true in this case that the marginal revenues in all lines of traffic will be equal. If, however, in any one line the rate is such that an alteration in the rate will increase the total revenue more than it increases the total cost, it will pay to make that alteration.

Discrimination as a Weapon to Achieve Monopoly

In all our discussion so far we have assumed that the monopoly is established, and we have seen that under those circumstances it frequently pays to charge different prices for different units of output. There is another field in which discrimination may be important: this is in the original *establishment* of a monopoly position. A would-be monopolist may discriminate even more than considerations of immediate profit would demand in order to drive a competitor out of business. An oil company, for instance, may drive a competitor out of a certain district by cutting its price far below the point even where the marginal revenue in that market is equal to the marginal cost. By so doing it will reduce its profits temporarily, but this may be an "investment" in the hope of regaining still larger profits later when it has established a monopoly. The problems involved in this type of operation are complex and involve a consideration of the theory of capital. They cannot, therefore, be discussed fully at the present point. An analogous operation is found in the purchases of input as well as in the sale of output. A monopolist, by having, or pretending to have, a highly elastic demand for an input which is sold by another monopolist, may force the seller to sell the input at a price lower than that charged to competitors. The Standard Oil Company, for instance, in its early days frequently obtained special concessions in railroad rates for the transport of oil.

The Movement Against Price Discrimination

In the history of the United States there has been a strong movement to outlaw the practice of price discrimination. The feeling against it arises partly from the fact that it has been used as a method of obtaining monopoly, and also from the fact that in itself it is rightly regarded as a *symptom* of monopoly power. The practice is also associated in the popular mind with "unfair competition," whatever that may mean. Two acts of Congress are specifically directed against it—the Clayton Act of 1914 and the Robinson-Patman amendment to the Clayton Act of 1936. Both, of course, apply only to interstate commerce. Like most legislative enactments they are careless in the definition of what they forbid, and the definition of their prohibitions is still in some dispute. In principle they forbid charging different prices to different buyers except where the price differences are "justified" by cost differences. The idea that price differences must be justified by cost differences is common in the lay discussion of this topic. It overlooks the problem of the ambiguity of the word "cost," however, and is not necessarily a safe guide to social policy. Does it mean that the price of any service should equal its "average cost"? In that case the problem is virtually insoluble, for wherever there is joint cost it is almost impossible to allocate the overhead costs over various products or services. Does it mean that the price of any good or service should equal its marginal cost? Carried to its extreme this policy might deprive the poor of medical services, for a doctor forced to charge the same price to all for his services might have to charge so much as to exclude all below the middle class.

Thus it is not easy to discover all the implications of price discrimination for social policy. Price discrimination may be a method for redistributing real income. The demands of the rich are generally more inelastic than those of the poor, so that a monopolist will usually tend to charge higher prices to the rich than to the poor. This will have the effect of lessening the apparent inequalities of income. But it can also be argued that this method of equalizing incomes is undesirable, and that direct, conscious taxation and subsidy are to be preferred to the "indirect taxation" involved in price discrimination. These problems involve political and social considerations which go far beyond the range of our present study.

SPECIAL CASES OF MONOPOLISTIC ORGANIZATION

Our analysis will enable us to interpret several important types of monopolistic organization. A monopolistic organization is a combination of firms in an industry that is not a natural monopoly. Its object is to establish a price and sales policy giving greater profits than would result from the uncoordinated action of individual firms. As we have seen, the least stable form of competition is imperfect oligopoly, or "cut-throat competition." In industries which have a tendency toward this sort of competition, where the product is fairly homogeneous and the number of firms is relatively small, monopolistic organizations are common. Such industries have a constant tendency to try to escape from imperfect oligopoly either into monopolistic competition through product differentiation, or into perfect oligopoly through price leadership, or into a form of monopoly.

The "Basing Point" System

An interesting example of an industry escaping from imperfect oligopoly into perfect oligopoly is the steel industry. Before about 1900 the American steel industry was a good example of imperfect oligopoly. Prices were generally quoted on the "mill base" system— i.e., the price was quoted at the foundry and the buyer paid this price plus the freight from the foundry. As we saw on pages 631–632, such a system will lead to an imperfect market for the output of each seller. The elasticity of demand for the product of the individual seller will be great, but not infinite; the product will be differentiated, but not sufficiently so to produce monopolistic competition. Such was the case in the steel industry. Price cutting was frequently profitable and frequently practiced. A price cut, say in Pittsburgh, pushed back the "boundary of indifference" between Pittsburgh and, say, Chicago by an appreciable amount and gave to Pittsburgh a number of customers who previously had been in Chicago's market area. In order to escape from this situation the "basing point system" known as "Pittsburgh plus" was established. On this system all steel firms, wherever located, charged the same price for steel delivered at any given location. This price was the Pittsburgh mill price plus the freight charge from Pittsburgh to the buyer. The result of this was to do away with the "market areas," for all firms charged the same price at any given point. This is evidently an example of "price leadership," the leader in this case being the United States Steel Corporation. In the early days the system was established by a so-called gentlemen's agreement. Mr. Gary gave one of his celebrated dinners, and the price of steel quoted by all companies mysteriously adjusted itself to the "Pittsburgh plus" system. Thereby price competition was avoided, and steel firms confined themselves to the apparently less noxious form of competition in services, such as speed in delivery.

Discrimination Under "Pittsburgh Plus"

Under the "Pittsburgh plus" system the firms in Pittsburgh received the same price at the mill for their steel no matter where they sold it. Firms, elsewhere, however, received a lower price at the mill when they sold to buyers between their mill and Pittsburgh than when they sold to buyers on the other side. Suppose, for instance, that the Pittsburgh mill price is $40 per ton and the freight from Pittsburgh to Chicago is $5 per ton. At a point midway between Pittsburgh and

Chicago the price will be $42.50 per ton. Chicago will receive a mill price of $40. At a point the same distance on the other side of Chicago the price will be $47.50 per ton, for $7.50 is the freight from Pittsburgh. Chicago will get this price, but will pay only $2.50 in freight, giving Chicago a mill price of $45. For all points west of Chicago (assuming, what is not quite true, that transport costs per mile are uniform) the Chicago mill price will be $45. This meant in effect a "division of the market," but in a way which would not allow any firm to increase its market by a small amount by price cutting. Chicago was now not anxious to push sales in the eastern area, for such sales brought a lower mill price to her than western sales. Chicago therefore concentrated on the West, Pittsburgh on the East, without there being any movable "boundary of indifference" for buyers between them; for at any point, east or west, both quoted the same price to the buyer.

Cartels

Another interesting form of monopolistic organization is the cartel, or selling agency. A cartel is an organization of a number of producers for the common selling of their product. It differs from the "gentlemen's agreement" or from "price leadership" in that the title to the commodity passes from the hands of the individual producer into those of the cartel itself. The individual producer, however, retains his individuality as a unit of production and enterprise. Cartels are common in both industry and agriculture, though in agriculture they are usually dignified by the name "cooperatives" and frequently are organized according to the cooperative form of business enterprise. The principal problem of the cartel, if it wishes to make monopoly profits, is that of restricting the production of its members without interfering too vitally with their independence of management. If cartels are successful in this, they are usually faced with the possibility of a breakaway by some of their members.

Example: The English Milk Marketing Board. An interesting example of a compulsory cartel is found in the English Milk Marketing Board. Every milk farmer in England must sell his milk by a contract registered with the Milk Marketing Board. His buyer pays the money not to the farmer directly but to the Marketing Board. The board then pools all moneys received from the sale of milk, deducts its expenses, and pays out the rest to the farmer as a "pool price." Previous to the establishment of the board (in 1933) a peculiar variety of imperfect competition prevailed in the milk market. There was a con-

tract agreement between farmers and distributors, without legal standing but very generally observed, at least until 1931. This fixed the
price of liquid milk at a level which was probably higher than would
have prevailed without the collective bargain. It was appreciably
higher than the price which the farmer got for milk sold to be manufactured (i.e., for butter, cheese, etc.). Consequently, the individual
farmer found himself with a sales curve something like *ABCD* in Fig.
106. He could sell any amount up to a quantity *AB* in the "liquid"

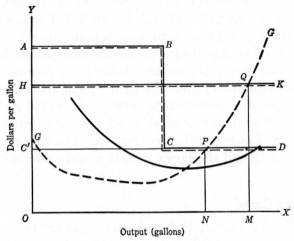

FIG. 106.   Result of Forming a Cartel.

market at the price *OA*. If, however, he produced a "surplus" he had
to sell it in the "manufacturing" market at a price *OC'*. If under these
circumstances *GG* were his marginal cost curve he would produce an
amount *ON*, where the marginal revenue was equal to his marginal
cost, *PN*. The marginal revenue curve is also *ABCD*.

Now, after the cartel has gone into operation, he receives a uniform
pool price, *OH*, which is somewhat less than the old "liquid" price
but greater than the old "manufacturing" price. But he receives this
price no matter how much he sells. The cartel, therefore, has given the
producer a perfect market. If there are no restrictions on entering the
industy, no license fees, etc., the effect of the cartel—a monopolistic
organization—has been, paradoxically enough, to produce "perfect
competition."

Cartels May Increase Transport Costs

Unless the pool prices are adjusted properly for cost of transport,
however, the result may be a distortion of the geographic distribution

of the industry. This in fact happened. Normally it is liquid milk which is produced near the consuming centers, butter and cheese which are produced in the remoter districts. The result of the milk marketing scheme was to shift liquid milk production to the extremities of the island, thus increasing the total expenses of transportation of milk. The dealers paid their own costs of transport and were allowed a deduction from what they had to pay to the board according to the distance the milk traveled. This deduction at first proved to be greater than the actual cost of transport, so that the dealers made a profit on every mile a gallon of milk was carried. The result was naturally to send the liquid milk dealers out into the distant regions—e.g., Cumberland and Cornwall—for the farther they carried the milk, the more profit they made. Any monopolistic scheme is in danger of running into difficulties like this. The basing point system, for instance, results in a good deal of cross-transportation. Instead of each mill serving the area immediately around it, all the mills can sell over the whole country. Consequently, steel may travel farther, on the whole, between the mill and the buyer than it would under a "mill base" system.

Results of the Cartel

The result of the cartel, if there is no control or "rationing" of individual producers, is that individual producers increase their production. The farmer of Fig. 106 will increase his production from ON to OM. If there are no restrictions of entry and no rationing of production, the cartel cannot give the members a profit which is above normal in the long run; for if the cartel succeeds in raising prices to the point where the industry is abnormally profitable, new producers will flock in. The total output of the industry will then increase until it becomes impossible for the cartel to maintain the price any longer. The Brazilian coffee scheme, mentioned on page 142, was an example of an unsuccessful cartel. The cartel, therefore, cannot obtain a monopoly price for its product unless it can both ration the production of its members by "quotas" and restrict entry into the industry. Even here, of course, the profits may not remain with the members, but may be absorbed by the rent owners in the industry. The British hops marketing scheme (established in 1931) is a good example. Under this scheme no one may produce hops unless he possesses a "quota." Hence the expansion of the industry is rigidly controlled. Those who were already in the industry in 1931 were allotted "quotas" of production, i.e., permits to produce a given amount. The result has been that the monopoly profits of the industry have been given to the owners of these "quotas," which have become valuable items of property. Newcomers to the industry can enter only by buying a "quota" from an established producer. The price of the "quota" presumably is such that newcomers will make only normal profits.

Cartels not Necessarily Monopolies

It will be seen from these examples that cartels are not necessarily monopolies, and do not necessarily have the power to exact monopoly prices or to give their members monopoly profits. Two conditions are necessary before a cartel can have monopoly power. First, it must be able to prevent any appreciable sales of its commodity through independent channels; otherwise, if the cartel attempts to raise prices above competitive levels, it will rapidly lose business to its independent competitors. Second, it must be able to control the admission of new members. Even if a cartel controls all sellers of its product, so that there is no problem of competition from independents, it will still be unable to obtain monopoly profits unless it can restrict admission. Otherwise, the existence of monopoly profits will attract members in until profits have been eaten away to normal levels. From the social point of view, therefore, it is very important that cartels, if we must have them, should be "open"—i.e., open to anyone who wishes to join. It is important to note also that the diminution of profits as new sellers join the cartel may be accomplished in two ways, one of which is much more desirable, socially, than the other. If the output of the members is unrestricted the inflow of new members raises the total amount which the cartel has to sell, and hence the cartel must lower the price in order to sell the extra amount. If, however, the cartel has the power to restrict the output of each member, the adjustment to an inflow of new members may take the form of restricting the output of each individual member to the point where profits are not high enough to attract new entrants, not because of low prices but because of high costs. Under this system the cartel invariably results in a waste of resources and in the building up of idle capacity. The German potash cartel was a case in point.

The "Trust" and the "Merger"

The purely voluntary cartel is an unstable institution, for if it obtains a monopoly price by rationing the production of its members, there is a strong incentive for an individual to break away and obtain the benefits of the monopoly price without having to restrict his own production. In the absence of compulsory cartels, therefore, producers in search of monopoly organization have been forced into combinations of a much more drastic kind. The "trust" is an arrangement whereby the ownership, or at least the controlling share in the ownership, of the combining firms is vested in a single corporation, or "trust." The legal form of the trust was made illegal in the United States by the Sherman Act of 1890. Nevertheless, the economic form survives in the "holding company." This is a form of economic organization made possible by the institution of the corporation. The "holding company" is a corporation formed for the purpose of holding a controlling share of the stock in other corporations (see Chapter 24). By this means the policy of the subsidiary corporations may be brought directly under the control of the holding company, even though the subsidiary corporations maintain a degree of independent existence. In the "merger" the constituent corporations lose their identity altogether and are "merged" into a new corporation. Control over the constituent plants thus becomes absolute.

The "Trust Movement"

It is not the place of this volume to go into the elaborate details of what is known as the trust movement. We should, however, notice one or two points. The first is that there are two broad types of industrial combination. The first is the "vertical" combination of firms, one of which uses the product of the other. The combination of an ore mine and a steel mill would be an example. The second is the "horizontal" combination of a number of firms producing the same product. The second generally has more of a monopolistic motive than the first. "Vertical" combination may result in genuine economies and reductions of cost. "Horizontal" combination is likely to result in economies only if a better proportion of management to other expenses can be obtained. The problem of motives in the promotion of combinations is interesting. Frequently combinations have proved less profitable than their constituent parts, and the motive of power or prestige has played an important part in their creation. They are the battlegrounds of the captains of finance, and have often been promoted more for the promoters' than for the owners' benefit. Frequently, also, promoters have capitalized on the expected gains of combination, and then the investors have found that these gains were illusory. Nevertheless, there seems to have been a movement toward larger units of enterprise in many industries inspired by the economies of large-scale production and the elimination of the wastes of monopolistic competition as well as by the desire for monopoly profit.

The Labor Union as a Cartel

Many of the principles we have outlined in connection with organizations of business also apply to interpreting organizations of labor. A labor union is a "labor cartel." A cartel in the usual sense is defined as an organization of sellers for the joint sale of their product. A labor union is an organization of the sellers of labor (workers) for the joint sale of their product (labor). This is not to say, of course, that the cartel aspect of labor unions is their only one; they have many purposes, sociological and psychological as well as economic. But in their economic aspects unions must be understood principally as a subspecies of the cartel. Thus collective bargaining is always a sign of cartelization, for a collective bargain is one in which the terms of sale of the product of many buyers or sellers is arranged jointly by their representatives.

This is not to say, of course, that unions are necessarily monopolies; if they have nonunion labor competing with them (i.e., independent sellers of labor outside the cartel), or even when there is no nonunion labor in the field, if the union is "open" and does not restrict the labor of its members beyond the normal requirements of health and custom, then there is no monopoly. Unions differ from most business cartels in that the proceeds of the collectively arranged sale are not channeled through the organization but are paid to the members directly. Perhaps as a consequence of this, one is less apt to find the more objectionable aspects of cartelization in the labor movement, although parallels to almost all the cartel practices can be found. Thus, there is a certain amount of subsidization of idle capacity in the form of unemployment benefits or the "stand-in" arrangements of the musicians. One also finds unions which restrict entry by means of high entrance fees, onerous apprenticeship requirements, racial discrimination, or even by simple limitation of numbers. When such a "closed union" enjoys a "closed shop" it is very likely to have monopoly powers. Fortunately, these monopolistic situations are confined for the most part to craft unions; where they exist, however, they are a danger not only to the public interest but to the labor movement itself, for it is the labor monopoly that is the breeding ground of the labor racketeer.

THE WASTES OF COMPETITION

We have now said a good deal about the evils of monopoly. It must not be inferred, however, that competition is an unmixed blessing. Competition, like Janus, is a two-faced deity. On the one hand it is lauded by the economists as the mainspring of the economic system, the beneficent—if somewhat stimulating—source of efficiency, through whose operations the resources of society are pushed gently but firmly into those places in which they will do the most good. On the other hand there is a good deal of talk about the "wastes" of competition, about its evil effects on society and upon humankind. On one side it is the hero of the warfare of man against the Wicked Dragon, Monopoly; on the other it seems to be the enemy of the Beautiful Princess, Cooperation. This paradox is soon resolved when we realize that "competition" is a word with a number of different meanings. It may be perfect, oligopolistic, or monopolistic. It may refer simply to that ability of superior processes to displace inferior processes which is the ·necessary condition of any progress. It may refer to a particular condition of a market. It may refer to an interpersonal situation in which the gain of one is a loss to another. It may refer to the biological competition of populations in which a rise in one population causes a fall in the other. With so many meanings it is little wonder that there is confusion.

On the whole it seems fair to say that the major "evils of competition" are associated with the monopolistic aspects of competition rather than with "perfect" competition. These evils may be classified under two main heads: first, the evils which result from the fact that competition means the conflict of interest of one person against another; second, the evils which result from certain *wastes* of competition, such as competitive advertising. Both these evils are peculiarly characteristic of monopolistic competition. Under perfect competition, for instance, there are so many sellers and buyers that the action of any one of them cannot affect appreciably the fortunes of any other. The seven million wheat farmers are in perfect competition one with another; yet no matter what the policy of one farmer—provided he treats his land properly and does not allow weeds to flourish on it—he will not affect one way or another the fortunes of his neighbors. Whenever people speak of competition being "keen" or "intense" they always refer to a state of imperfect competition, in which there are relatively few firms and in which, therefore, the action of one firm, say, in pushing sales or reducing prices, will affect the fortunes of the others.

Competitive Advertising

The "wastes" of competition are also characteristic mainly of imperfect competition. Perhaps the most important of these wastes from a social point of view is that involved in competitive advertising. There is a case for a certain amount of advertising, such as the purely informative advertising which is descriptive of the qualities and prices of commodities. This is a form of consumer education which is necessary if consumers are to make intelligent choices; in fact, it makes competition more nearly perfect. This virtuous advertising, however, does not bulk very large in the total. Most advertising, unfortunately, is devoted to an attempt to build up in the minds of the consumer irrational preferences for certain brands of goods. All the arts of psychology—particularly the art of association—are used to persuade consumers that they should buy Bumpo rather than Bango. Look through the pages of any magazine or newspaper, or listen to any program on the radio, and see how much space or time is devoted to an accurate description of the properties and prices of goods; the amount is surprisingly little. Instead, advertisements seek to associate the commodity in question with something else which the consumer likes or with the avoidance of something which the consumer seeks to avoid. Drinks are portrayed with beautiful flowers, cigarettes with beautiful girls, soaps are associated with love and marriage, and so on. There is very little place in the technique of advertising for the sober, truthful presentation of the qualities and prices of commodities.

This Is Social Waste

There is a strong presumption that much competitive advertising is social waste. There seem to be only two arguments in its defense. From the economic side it might be argued that selling expenses increase the velocity of circulation of money and so increase employment. There are, however, cheaper and more dignified ways of increasing employment, and this argument breaks down completely in a time of full employment, and still more in a time of inflation. On the sociological side it might be argued that advertising has itself an entertainment and cultural value, and that it promotes mass communication in the form of cheaper magazines, newspapers, radio, and television. I am happy to leave this argument to the sociologists. With these possible exceptions competitive advertising does not result in the creation of wealth, for the consumer would spend his money in any case, advertising or no advertising, and he would probably spend it more wisely if there were no competitive—only informative—advertising.

No Competitive Advertising Under Perfect Competition

However, the wastes of competitive advertising are characteristic of monopolistic, not of perfect, competition. In perfect competition, as we have seen, there is no advertising of a competitive nature, for when each firm has a perfectly elastic sales curve it can sell all it wants at the market price and advertising will do it no good. It is useless for a single farmer to advertise "Buy Wheat," for even if his advertising has the effect of increasing the total demand for wheat, his share of that increase will be infinitesimal. It is useless for a single farmer even to advertise "Buy Giles's Wheat," for everyone knows that Giles's wheat is just the same as everybody else's wheat for miles around.

Monopolistic Competition Leads to Faulty Distribution of Resources

Another of the "wastes of monopolistic competition" is that it leads to a faulty distribution of resources and to excess capacity in those industries which operate under it. We proved in Chapter 30 that although perfect competition led to a state of affairs in which each enterprise produced at the output where its average cost (including rent) was least, this is not the case under monopolistic competition. The overabundant multiplication of small shops, of gas stations, of merchants of all kinds—in fact, all those things which are usually called "wastes of distribution"—is attributable to this property of monopolistic competition. Two railroad tracks where one would carry all the traffic; ten milk deliverers in every street where one could do the work much more easily; the litter of gas stations at the exit to every city where a few would sell gas more cheaply; even perhaps the extreme multiplicity of sects, both religious and political—are all evidences of monopolistic competition. If perfect competition could exist in these industries, these evils would disappear. Inefficient distributors would be driven out by the efficient ones, the number of distributors would fall, costs of distribution would be lower, and present wastes would be avoided. As it is, the inefficient distributors now shelter behind their little walls of monopoly and cannot be driven out into occupations where they would be of more benefit to society.

The Evils of Perfect Competition

It may be asked, however, with some justice: Are there not wastes of perfect competition just as destructive to human happiness as the wastes of imperfect competition? If perfect competition is a remedy for our economic ills, how does it happen that the agricultural industry, which perhaps approaches most closely to this idea, is constantly in difficulty? Is not the growth of product differentiation, of advertising, of trusts and combinations, evidence of a desire to escape from the evils of unrestricted competition? These questions deserve examination. Even if monopoly were eliminated and all industries operated under conditions of perfect competition, there would still be economic dislocations. Any change in the structure of consumers' demands, for instance, will tend to bring about a shift of resources from one industry to another. We analyzed in detail in Chapter 12 how this was done. If, now, resources are difficult to shift from one occupation to another, the result of a change in demand may be that one industry is abnormally prosperous for a long period of time and another is abnormally unprosperous. Perfect competition works out to the general good only if resources are easily transferable from one industry to another. Where resources are highly "specific" to a single industry, there may be serious maladjustments of the system for long periods even in a perfectly competitive industry.

At the other extreme an industry may be too sensitive to temporary shifts in its profitablity. An industry in this condition is subject to cycles, such as the hog cycle, which are mainly the result of too easy, and too thoughtless, entry and exit. An industry may also run into difficulties of adjustment if all its firms are very similar, so that the "cost ladder" (page 568) is very flat. If under these circumstances the industry is unprofitable, some firms should get out of it; but as all the firms are so much alike, it is not clear *which* firms should get out. All firms may therefore hang on for a long time in an unprofitable condition in the hope that some other firms will abandon the struggle; then when things are very bad a large number of firms will leave suddenly, and the industry will become highly profitable, which may set off a new cycle.

Maldistribution of resources is not, of course, a *result* of perfect competition; it is likely to occur in all situations, and, indeed, monopoly or monopolistic organization will intensify the evil rather than cure it. But in some cases it can be argued that monopolistic organization will prevent the symptoms of the disease from becoming too unpleasant. It might similarly be argued that a doctor is justified in giving drugs to ease pain even if the drugs retard the final cure of the disease. So, if an industry is overexpanded, the result will be less painful to the individuals concerned if the effects of overexpansion are mitigated, or rather dispersed, by monopolistic organization than if the overexpansion is allowed to produce its entire effect in perfect competition. Even here, however, we must beware of lingering illnesses; it may be better to kill off an industry quickly by perfect competition than allow it to drag out a painful and burdensome existence to a long-delayed end under monopolistic regulation or government subsidy.

Evils of a "Mixed" System

In a system in which some industries are monopolistic and some approach perfect competition certain difficulties arise which might not arise under a system of universal monopoly or of universal competition. In a mixed system, such as in fact we have, serious dislocations of the price structure and unemployment of resources over long periods of time are all too likely to occur. In monopolistic industries prices are likely to be relatively stable, while output and employment fluctuate. In competitive industries output and employment are likely to be stable, while prices fluctuate. Suppose in a competitive industry the supply curve is inelastic. This will almost certainly be the case in short periods, and it may be so even over relatively long periods if there are unusual difficulties in the way of the movement of resources into and out of the industry. Then a fall in demand will bring about a sharp fall in the price of the commodity. The output of the industry will not be much affected. In the case of a monopoly, however, a fall in demand may be met in ways other than a fall in price. Selling costs may be increased and output may be reduced. Consequently, a fall in the demand for the product of a monopolist is likely to result in a small fall in price, or there may be no effect on the price (cf. pages 619–621). But where there is no effect on the price there will be a sharp fall in output and in employment.

These facts are of great importance in interpreting the phenomena of the business cycle. Suppose, for instance, that there is a general fall in the velocity of circulation of money, in bank loans and bank deposits, leading to a fall in money incomes. This is characteristic of the period of recession. Then there will be a decline in the money demands for almost all commodities. This fall in demand, however, will not have a uniform effect on prices. The price of goods produced by competitive industries will decline sharply, but the output will not decline, and may even rise (cf. pages 122, 224). The price of goods produced by a monopolistic industry will fall but little, if at all. The output of these goods, and the employment in these industries, will decline sharply.

How a "Mixed" System Intensifies Depressions

This is a regularly observed phenomenon of depression. In agriculture, for instance, prices fall, often catastrophically, while output and employment may even increase. In the construction industries prices stay up, but output and employment suffer a disastrous slump. The disparity between the two halves of the system produces evil secondary effects, intensifying the depression. Because of the reduced incomes of farmers and the high prices of industrial products, the purchases of industrial products fall still further, causing more industrial unemployment. Because of the industrial unemployment the demand for farm products falls still further, causing a greater fall in agricultural prices. If, now, industrial prices had been flexible and had fallen with the fall in demand, prices all round would have declined, but output and employment would have been maintained. Prices would reach a new stable level at that point at which the "demand for money" was satisfied.

The Flight from the Free Market

It is impossible to study the history of industrial combinations, of the labor movement, of the protectionist movement, of the agricultural organization movement, and of the socialist movement without realizing that all these historical movements of the past hundred years or more are in one sense aspects of a larger movement which can be described as the "flight from the free market." While the leaders of western capitalism have been giving lip service to the principle of competition, they have been busily engaged in building up associations of all kinds for the purpose of limiting competition. A movement as universal as this cannot merely arise from what Adam Smith calls the "wretched spirit of monopoly"; there must be more fundamental causes. One of these causes, we have already seen, lies in the fact that an unregulated and unorganized economic order may produce not perfect, but imperfect, competition over large areas of economic relationships. There may, however, be even deeper causes. We have seen in Part I how the completely unregulated market is subject to erratic and meaningless fluctuations in prices arising from "self-justified anticipations." The deflationary phase of these fluctuations is extremely destructive to enterprise and employment. In some part the "flight from the free market" in all its forms can be interpreted as an attempt —perhaps in large part unconscious—to "protect" smaller groups from a general deflationary movement. Thus, the protectionist movement in commercial policy is in part an attempt to protect an individual nation from world deflation, and the failure of free traders to convince the world of practical men by arguments which would seem to be academically unimpeachable may be in great measure due to their failure to recognize the short-run deflationary effects of tariff removal and the inflationary effects of tariff imposition. Similarly, the labor movement in its economic aspects is an attempt to protect the organized worker from general deflationary movements, and the same may be said of agricultural and industrial combinations. In even broader terms it is an interesting question how far the strength of socialism is derived from experiences with the instability of the free market, and especially from the recurrent failure of capitalism to provide full employment. There are questions here which it is easier to raise than to answer: nevertheless it is clear that the "monopoly problem" is not going to be solved by preaching against or even by legislating against monopoly, unless at the same time something is done to counteract by other methods the deflations which have undermined confidence in the ability of the free market to do its proper job. On the other hand, it may also be true that a genuine solution of the instability problem is impossible in a monopolistic economy. As we have seen in Part II, the nightmare of the monetary stabilizer is a situation in which attempts to raise employment by monetary expansion result in a rise in money prices and wages rather than in a rise in output and employment. Hence, it may well be that in a monopolistic economy the only way to get full employment is to have a continuous inflation—a highly unsatisfactory state of affairs. The attack of the economists on monopoly has been ineffective mainly because economists have not seen that there was a real social question which monopolistic organization was trying to answer. The tragedy of our present situation is that monopoly is not only the wrong answer; it is an answer which may prevent the right answer being found.

QUESTIONS AND EXERCISES

1. "Under a system of perfect competition there would be waste of resources, for we cannot prevent people from making bad investments. Monopoly does nothing to prevent these wastes, though it may prevent the consequences of bad investment from falling on those who ought to bear them. In addition, monopoly produces many wastes of its own." Discuss.
2. Pure monopoly may be preferable to imperfect competition. Why, and under what circumstances?
3. Which is the greater evil, the fluctuation of prices or the fluctuation of outputs? Does your answer support the institution of monopoly?
4. What is conveyed to your mind by the phrase "unfair competition"? Give examples. Try to define "fair competition."
5. "The tariff is the father of the trust," Do you agree?

6. "The monopolistic organization of industry is an expedient necessitated by the wastes of competition." Discuss.

7. "The troubles of the milk industry stem from the fact that the market is too competitive at the producers' end, and too monopolistic at the distributors' end." Discuss.

8. Suppose every industry were a pure monopoly. Would all industries then be able to make monopoly profits?

9. "A system cannot remain half slave and half free. Likewise, a system cannot remain half competitive and half monopolistic." Discuss.

10. What similarities and differences are there between the practices of:
   a. Industrial cartels
   b. Labor unions
   c. Agricultural cooperatives

11. The following causes have been suggested for the growth of organization in labor, in business, and in agriculture:
   a. The need to protect groups against deflation
   b. The desire for monopoly profits
   c. The growth of skills of organization and the development of a class of professional organizers.
   d. Growth of a moral feeling that cooperation is ethically superior to competition.
   Can you suggest any other causes? How would you rate these various causes according to their importance? If you feel that your information is not sufficient to justify rating the causes, what sort of information would you need?

12. Suppose the mill price of steel at Pittsburgh is $40 per ton, and the freight rate is $0.01 per ton-mile. Assume that Chicago is 500 miles from Pittsburgh. On the "Pittsburgh plus" system draw up a schedule showing (a) the price of steel, (b) the price received by Pittsburgh mills at the mill, (c) the price received by Chicago mills at the mill, for points at hundred-mile intervals on a line drawn from Pittsburgh through Chicago to a point 500 miles west of Chicago. Illustrate the schedule with a diagram, plotting distance along the horizontal axis and price along the vertical axis.

CHAPTER 32

THE ELEMENTARY THEORY OF CONSUMPTION

The preceding chapters have been devoted mainly to the problems of the individual firm and industry from the point of view of supply. We have examined the forces which determine the position of supply curves and also the modifications introduced into our analysis by the existence of monopoly and imperfect competition. Our next task is to turn to the other part of the analysis of price determination, to the theory of demand. In all the analysis thus far we have assumed ultimate demands to be given factors in the system of economic quantities. We have, it is true, investigated the demand for the inputs purchased by enterprises, but even there we referred ultimately to an assumed demand curve for the product. It is now time to inquire as to the behavior of the supreme mover of the economic order—the ultimate consumer, for whom all goods are made and toward whom all economic activity is directed.

Utility as the Product of Consumption

However, we do not step into a strange and unfamiliar world. The forces which move the action of a consumer and the laws which govern his intelligent choices are remarkably similar to the forces and relationships which guide an individual producer. Nor is this fact surprising. A consumer may most conveniently be regarded as a little "firm" at the final stage of the process of production. He buys consumers' goods as a firm buys inputs, and like the firm he transforms them into a final product whose worth may in some manner be estimated. The final product of the consumer, however, is not a physical product to be seen, tasted, and handled. It is a psychological product, technically known as "utility." Just as a producer buys labor, land services, and raw materials and transforms them into a physical product, so a consumer buys food, clothing, and amusements and out of

680

them builds the edifice of his satisfactions. Utility, therefore, is the ultimate product of all economic activity—indeed, in its broadest sense, of all human activity whatever. Just as labor is bought in order to produce coal, and coal in order to produce steel, and steel in order to produce automobiles, and automobiles in order to ride down to the drug store and buy ice cream, so the ice cream is bought in order to produce those inner delights and satisfactions which its passage engenders. All physical goods are valuable only because they serve to produce utility. All physical goods, even final consumption goods, are really intermediate products. At the head of every process of production stands the satisfaction of a want. It is this want-satisfaction that gives the process meaning. The "process of consumption," therefore, is not something separate and distinct from production; it is the final act in the economic drama, the culmination of a long series of processes held together by intermediate products.

THE UTILITY SCHEDULE

The Consumer as a "Firm"

If, then, the consumer is a little "firm," buying inputs in the form of consumers' goods and producing "utility," or "want-satisfaction," or whatever we care to call it, as a product, how much of the theory of the firm can be applied to the consumer? For the present we shall make the assumption, for purposes of exposition, that utility is a quantitatively measurable substance. In fact this is not so, and we shall see later how to escape from this unrealistic assumption. But for the moment suppose that we can strap a galvanometer to the seat of the emotions and record quantitatively the amount of enjoyment or utility which is produced under the stimulus of the consumption of various quantities of a commodity. Let us suppose that we can define a unit of utility called a "util." Then just as we construct a series of experiments to show how the quantity of product varied with the quantity of labor applied, listing the results in a physical production schedule (Table 57, page 587), so we could conduct a series of experiments to find how great a total utility a consumer would register under the stimulus of various quantities of consumers' goods. Table 63, columns 1 and 2, represents such a schedule. Here it is assumed that the consumption of all other goods does not change, and a series of experiments with different quantities of a variable commodity ("food") shows what in each case will be the total utility registered. We have assumed in the table that as the quantity of food rises, the total utility derived from its consumption rises also, but not proportionately. Total utility rises at a decreasing rate, and as the quantity of food increases to the point of satiety, between 7 and 8 pounds, the total utility reaches a maxi-

TABLE 63.   Utility Schedules

1 Quantity of Food (Lbs.)	2 Total Utility (Utils)	3 Marginal Utility (Utils per Lb.)	4 Marginal Rate of Substitution ($ per Lb.)
0	0	10	0.50
1	10	20	1.00
2	30	18	0.90
3	48	15	0.75
4	63	11	0.55
5	74	7	0.35
6	81	3	0.15
7	84	0	0.00
8	84	−4	−0.20
9	80		(Marginal utility of money = 20 utils per dollar)

mum. Beyond that point any increase in our consumption of food makes us sick, or at least gives us a smaller total satisfaction than before.

Marginal Utility

The *marginal utility* of any quantity of commodity is the increase in total utility which results from a unit increase in consumption. Comparing Table 63 with Table 57, page 587, we see that the total utility corresponds to the total product, and the marginal utility to the marginal physical productivity. The *form* of the schedules is also similar. Just as the marginal physical productivity at first rises, reaches a maximum, and then falls off, so in Table 63 the marginal utility rises, reaches a maximum, and then falls continuously as the quantity of commodity increases. Corresponding, therefore, to the "law of diminishing returns" or the "law of eventually diminishing marginal physical productivity" is an exactly analogous law, the law of eventually diminishing marginal utility.

The more exact proof of the law of diminishing marginal utility must be left to Part IV. But even at this stage we can show that it is a reasonable assumption. It may be stated as follows: As a consumer increases the consumption of any one commodity, keeping constant the consumption of all other commodities, the marginal utility of the variable commodity must eventually decline. If I go to one movie a month I shall probably get a good deal of satisfaction from it. One movie may whet my appetite so that two movies might give me more than twice as much satisfaction. But probably the third movie will not increase my satisfaction as much as the second, the fourth not as much as the third, the fifth not as much as the fourth, and so on.

Reasons for Diminishing Marginal Utility

1. *Commodities Are Imperfect Substitutes.* There are several good reasons for supposing that the marginal utility of a commodity falls eventually as the quantity consumed increases. The first is that commodities are not perfectly substitutable one for the other. That is to say, there are certain appropriate proportions in which commodities tend to be consumed. We should be worse off with an ounce of butter and no bread, or a loaf of bread and no butter, than with half an ounce of butter plus half a loaf of bread. In a series of experiments successively increasing the consumption of butter while keeping the consumption of bread and other things constant, we should find that when the "best proportions" of butter to bread had been passed, successive ounces of butter would add less and less to our enjoyment. As our consumption of butter increases with a constant amount of bread, pretty soon we do not have enough bread to spread our butter on.

2. *Satiability of Particular Wants.* Another fundamental reason for assuming a diminishing marginal utility is that no *particular* want is insatiable. No matter how great a quantity of other things we might consume, our consumption of salt, for instance, will never rise above a certain quantity. Even if we could consume as much of a commodity as we wished without any sacrifices, we should still not consume an infinite amount. The point of satiety in consumption is the point where the total utility cannot be increased by further consumption, and therefore the marginal utility is zero. But at smaller quantities of consumption the marginal utility is positive, and total utility is rising. Between a level of consumption where the marginal utility is positive and a higher level where it is zero, then, the marginal utility must have been declining.

THE DERIVATION OF DEMAND CURVES

In Chapter 28, pages 601–602, the demand curve of an individual firm for input was shown to be derived from its productivity curves. An exactly similar analysis can be applied to the derivation of the demand of an individual consumer for consumption goods. At this

stage of our analysis we shall derive the demand curve for one commodity—"food"—on the premise that the consumption of other
commodities remains unchanged. We shall remove this unrealistic
assumption in Part IV.

The Marginal Utility of Money and the "Marginal Revenue of Utility"

The first problem, then, is to find an equivalent for the concept of
the "marginal revenue product" of page 594, in terms of utility, for
we have seen that "marginal utility" is analogous to "marginal physical
productivity." This problem is solved if we can assume a relationship
between a sum of utility and a sum of dollars. In order to turn the
marginal physical product into a marginal revenue product we multiply by the marginal revenue of output; thus if the marginal physical
product is 8 tons per man and the marginal revenue of output is $4
per ton, adding a man will increase output by 8 tons and revenue by
$32, and the marginal revenue product is $32 per man. The problem
therefore is to find a concept in the theory of consumption analogous
to the concept of marginal revenue in the theory of production. Such
a concept is found in the idea of the *marginal utility of money*. This
is the increase in total utility which results from the addition of one
"dollar" to the total expenditure of a consumer. Suppose the marginal
utility of money is 20 "utils per dollar." Then adding one "util" to
the total utility is equivalent to adding one-twentieth of a dollar to
the total expenditure. The reciprocal of the marginal utility of money,
then—in this case $\frac{1}{20}$ per util—may be called the "marginal revenue
of utility," as it measures the equivalent, in monetary terms, of the
addition of one util to the total "utility product." It is the "marginal
revenue of utility" which is analogous to the "marginal revenue" (of
product) in the theory of production.

Marginal Rate of Substitution

If, then, the marginal utility of a commodity is multiplied by the
marginal revenue of utility, or, what is the same thing, if the marginal
utility of a commodity is divided by the marginal utility of money, a
quantity analogous to "marginal revenue productivity" is obtained.
To take an arithmetical example. In Table 63 the marginal utility of
the third unit of food is 18 "utils per pound." Suppose that the marginal utility of money is constant, and equal to 20 utils per dollar.
Then the increase in the consumption of food from 2 to 3 pounds is
equivalent in utility to an increase in money expenditure of $\$1\frac{8}{20}$, or

$0.90. (One pound = 18 utils: 20 utils = $1; therefore one pound = 18 utils = $0.90.) This quantity has been called the marginal rate of substitution;[1] it is related to the marginal utility just as the marginal revenue productivity is related to the marginal physical productivity. The marginal rate of substitution, then, is that sum of money which will afford the same satisfaction as one unit of the commodity in question. The marginal rate of substitution also varies with the quantity of consumption; its schedule is shown in column 4 of Table 63 on the assumption that the marginal utility of money is constant, and equal to 20 utils per dollar. If the marginal utility of money is not constant, as will in fact be the case unless the commodity in question is only a small part of the consumer's total expenditure, we can still construct a relative marginal utility schedule if we know the schedule giving the marginal utility of money for each quantity of "food" consumed.

Demand Schedule Identical with Marginal Rate of Substitution Schedule

Just as the demand schedule for input is identical with the marginal revenue productivity schedule, so the demand schedule of a consumer is identical with the marginal rate of substitution schedule. For whatever the price of the commodity (if it has a perfect market), the consumer will consume that quantity at which the price is equal to the marginal rate of substitution. If he is consuming an amount at which the price is less than the marginal rate of substitution, he can increase his total utility by consuming an extra unit. Suppose in Table 63 that the price were $0.35 per pound, and the consumer consumed only 3 pounds, the marginal rate of substitution being $0.90 per pound. Under these circumstances, by consuming an extra pound the consumer will give up $0.35 in money, but will gain in utility an amount which he thinks would be worth a sacrifice at $0.90. Obviously, then, he will gain in utility by buying and consuming an extra pound; and as long as the price is less than the marginal rate of substitution, he will be able to increase his total utility by increasing his consumption, for the gain from the increased consumption is more than the loss from the sacrifice of money. To put the matter in another way: again referring to the conditions in Table 63, if the price were $0.35 per pound and the marginal utility of money were 20 utils per dollar, we see that a sacrifice of $0.35 would be equivalent to a loss of 20 × 0.35, or 7

[1] This quantity is sometimes called the "relative marginal utility." The term "marginal rate of substitution" is used because the quantity measures the amount of money which could be *substituted* for one unit of commodity without causing any gain or loss in utility.

utils. If, therefore, the marginal utility is greater than 7 utils per pound, there will be a gain in total utility from expanding consumption. If the marginal utility were 18 utils per pound, for instance, the increase of a pound in consumption would cause a gain of 18 utils and a loss of 7 utils for the $0.35 given up. The consumer would therefore expand his consumption to include the sixth pound, whose marginal utility is 7 utils per pound. In Table 63, columns 1 and 4 give the demand schedule of the consumer for food on the assumption that he does not change his consumption of other things.

No Assumption of Measurable Utility

Although for purposes of exposition we assumed a quantitatively measurable utility, in fact this assumption is not necessary to the argument. The "marginal rate of substitution" is a magnitude measured in "dollars per ounce" which does not contain the imaginary "util." We can therefore postulate a marginal rate of substitution schedule without making any assumption regarding the cardinal measurement of utility. The only assumption necessary is that the utilities of a quantity of money and a quantity of commodity can be *compared*. We must be able to say that this quantity of money has a utility greater than, equal to, or less than the utility of a certain quantity of commodity. But we do not have to assume that we can measure by *how much* the utility of one thing is greater than that of another.

Utility an Intensive Magnitude

A magnitude such as utility is termed an "ordinal" magnitude as distinct from a "cardinal" magnitude. A cardinal magnitude, such as length, weight, or time, is one in which the ratio of two quantities is subject to exact numerical calculation. It makes sense to say that "A is 2.756 times as long, or as heavy, or as voluminous, as B." Length, weight, and volume are therefore cardinal magnitudes. It makes sense to say that "A is brighter, or redder, or wetter, or rougher, than B." But unless we adopt an arbitrary standard of measurement from some cardinal quantity, it does not make sense to say that "A is 2.756 times as bright, or as red, or as wet, or as rough, as B." Brightness, redness, wetness, roughness are all ordinal magnitudes as far as their ordinary meaning is concerned. Such magnitudes can only be measured quantitatively by selecting, more or less arbitrarily, some cardinal magnitude which is connected with the ordinal magnitude. Brightness can be measured in terms of foot candles, redness in terms of the proportion of light waves of a certain wave length, and so on. But all these measurements are to some extent arbitrary. Utility, therefore, does not stand alone as an ordinal magnitude; there are many such, even in the physical sciences, and the difficulties of measuring utility are not fundamentally greater than the difficulties involved in measuring any other ordinal magnitude.

THE DIVISION OF EXPENDITURE

We cannot in the present chapter develop fully the theory of the consumer who is faced with the problem of consuming many commodities. We shall, however, indicate the main lines along which the solution of this problem is found. Suppose a consumer is faced with the problem of spending a given amount of money in a given time —say, $5000 in a year. He must divide this total expenditure among a large number of competing uses. He must spend some on bread, some on butter, some on shoes, some on coats, some on travel, and so on through the thousand and one varieties of expenditure. The problem is to formulate a principle which will indicate the "best" distribution of a given expenditure among a number of alternative uses.

The Weighted Marginal Utility

Let us again assume for purposes of exposition that total utility can be measured in terms of "utils." Then the "weighted marginal utility" of a commodity may be defined as the increase in the total utility of the consumer which results from a unit increase in *expenditure* on the commodity in question. The weighted marginal utility is equal to the marginal utility divided by the price of the good concerned. Suppose the marginal utility of food at a certain level of consumption was 18 utils per pound and the price of food was $0.35 per pound. Then the weighted marginal utility would be $\frac{18}{0.35}$, or 51.4, utils per dollar. That is to say, an increase of 1 dollar in the expenditure on food would increase purchases by $\frac{1}{0.35}$, or 2.86 pounds; and as an increase in consumption of 1 pound increases the total utility by 18 utils, an increase in consumption of $\frac{1}{0.35}$ pounds will increase the total utility by $\frac{18}{0.35}$, or 51.4 utils.

The "best" division of expenditures is that at which the weighted marginal utilities in all lines of expenditure are equal. In other words, the expenditure of an extra dollar in all lines of expenditure must have the same result in increasing utility. Otherwise it would pay to transfer expenditure from commodities where the weighted marginal utility is low to commodities where it is high. Suppose for instance that the weighted marginal utility of food is 50 utils per dollar, when the weighted marginal utility of cloth is 30 utils per dollar. In that case if the consumer spends a dollar less on cloth he will lose 30 utils, and if he spends a dollar more on food he will gain 50 utils. The transfer of a dollar from cloth to food will result in a net gain of 20 utils, and therefore the transfer will be made.

As the transfer proceeds, however, the marginal utility of food falls, for the amount purchased is increasing, and the marginal utility of cloth rises as the amount purchased diminishes. The weighted marginal utility of food will likewise fall, say, to 40 utils per dollar, and the weighted marginal utility of cloth will rise, say, to 40 utils per dollar. At that point nothing is gained by transferring expenditure from cloth to food, and the total utility is therefore maximized.

The Equimarginal Principle: General Applications

1. *To Expenditure of Time.* This is a general principle of great importance; we may call it the *equimarginal principle*. Stated in general terms it runs as follows: In dividing a fixed quantity of anything among a number of different uses, just so much will be apportioned to each use to cause the gain involved by transferring a unit of dividend into one use to be just equal to the loss involved in the uses from which the unit of dividend is withdrawn. It obviously applies no matter how many the number of uses to which the dividend can be put. It applies no matter what the dividend is. It applies to the expenditure of twenty-four hours a day of time as well as to the expenditure of money. In considering whether or not to go to the movies we must balance the advantage (utility) to be derived from the two hours spent in the movies against the advantage to be received from two hours spent in some other way (reading, studying, gardening, or in bed). The principle of diminishing marginal utility applies here as much as to the consumption of commodities; if we have been to the movies six times during the past week, the marginal utility of time spent at the movies will be low, and if we have been neglecting our studies and have an examination coming up soon, the marginal utility of time spent in study will be high. Consequently we are likely to choose study rather than the movies; what is gained by devoting two hours to study will be greater than what is lost by not going to the movies. If, on the other hand, we have been burning a lot of midnight oil and have not been to the movies for a month, the marginal utility of movies may

be high, and that of study may be low, and we shall choose the movies.

2. *To the Distribution of Assets.* The equimarginal principle applies not only to the distribution of income, whether of "money" or of time, but also to the distribution of assets among various forms, liquid or illiquid. Thus an individual who possesses, say, $10,000 worth of assets of one kind or another—bank notes, bank deposits, savings deposits, bonds, stocks, real estate, furniture, clothes, utensils, household goods, stocks of food, and so on—is faced with the problem of the way in which the total value of his assets is to be divided among the many asset forms. The redistribution of assets is of course accomplished by exchange: if a man feels that he has too much in the form of cash and not enough in the form of shirts, he has the recourse, usually of going out to buy shirts—a process which increases his stock of shirts at the expense of his stock of cash. Or, anticipating an inflation, one may exchange cash and bonds for stocks; or anticipating a deflation, exchange stocks and real estate for cash and bonds. As long as an individual feels that the psychological gain from expanding his holdings of one form of asset by one dollar's worth is greater than the psychological loss from contracting his holdings of another asset by a dollar's worth, it will be worth his while to shift his distribution of assets by exchanging the more for the less valued form. The individual will only be in equilibrium, as an asset holder, therefore, when his psychological valuation of an extra dollar's worth of any form of asset is the same. This is the equimarginal principle.

3. *To Resources in General.* The apportionment of the general resources of a society among various alternative uses is the most fundamental of all economic problems, and its formal solution is again an example of the equimarginal principle. The ideal apportionment is clearly that in which there is nothing to be gained by transferring marginal units of resources from one use or occupation to another. This involves us, however, in some notion of "social utility" which is not possible to define very exactly, though the concept clearly has meaning. But however social utility is defined—a task which we may well leave to the political scientist, the sociologist, or the philosopher —the equimarginal principle still holds. The best distribution of resources is that in which the marginal social utility in each use is the same.

Limitations of Equimarginal Principle

1. *Indivisibility of Goods.* There are some qualifications and limitations of the equimarginal principle which must be noticed. The first

is that it can only be fully satisfied if the resources (money, time, etc.) divided and the commodities bought with these resources are divisible into very small parts. Where a commodity is indivisible—like a house or a car—only certain quantities of it can be bought; consequently, expenditure on these things and our holdings of them can increase only in large jumps. In a given period of time a man can buy one car or two cars; he cannot buy $1\frac{1}{2}$ cars. He can spend, say, $2000 or $4000 on cars (if cars all cost $2000 each); he cannot spend $3000. Perhaps, however, the weighted marginal utility of money spent on cars would be equal to the weighted marginal utility of money spent on other things only when $3000 is spent on cars. If, therefore, the man buys only one car for $2000, he will feel that he is spending a little too much on other things in comparison with automobiles. If he spends $4000 he will feel that rather too much is going toward cars and not enough toward other things. It is like trying to build a number of towers of equal height with building blocks of different sizes; the towers built with big blocks are sure to be either a bit too tall or a bit too short. Wicksteed[2] suggests that this is responsible for the fact that we all feel that we would be a lot better off if we had just a *little* more money, no matter how much we have. On those items of expenditure in which the units are large we tend to spend a little too much, and we therefore feel that this expenditure, although not justified at our present income, would be quite justified at a rather higher income level. But of course even if we get a larger income we still find it impossible to adjust our expenditures exactly according to the equimarginal principle, and so still feel that we could do with just a little more!

2. *Indefinite "Budget Period."* Another thing which limits the application of the equimarginal principle is the fact that our "budget period" is not definite. The equimarginal principle assumes that we have a definite quantity of resources (say, time or money) to spend. But of course we only have a definite quantity within a definite period of time. That period of time which we usually reckon in calculating how much income, for instance, we have to divide may be called the "budget period"; it is usually a year, though it may be any period. Many things which are bought within one budget period, however, are used in another budget period—e.g., cars and furniture. When buying an armchair I do not merely compare the benefits received from this chair in the current year with the loss involved in giving up the things on which I otherwise would have spent the money, for I

---

[2] Wicksteed, *The Common Sense of Political Economy,* Chapter 3.

must take into account the benefits to be enjoyed in many years to come. Consequently, some "capital accounting" enters into even the consumer's budget. The flexibility of the budget period, we should notice, to some extent modifies the difficulty introduced into economic adjustments by the indivisibility of commodities. In one year it may be true that either $2000 or $4000 must be spent on a car, but over two years it is quite possible to spend $3000 by buying three new cars over the two years. The longer the "budget period," therefore, the less troublesome becomes the fact of indivisibility. But no matter how long the budget period, some indivisibility will occur.

THE EQUILIBRIUM OF THE CONSUMER

The equimarginal principle gives an excellent answer to the question of how to dispose of, or arrange, a *given quantity* of resources in the best possible way. It is not, however, a complete solution to the problem of the equilibrium of the consumer. Just as in the theory of production we first state the problem of the "least cost combination" —how to get a *given* output at the least total cost—and then go on to discuss what determines the most profitable output itself, so in the theory of the consumer we have not only a problem of the best way to divide *given* resources but also questions relating to the size of the resources to be divided. This question presents itself at several levels. There is the question of what determines the consumer's total expenditure of money in a given period. Total expenditure, we know from the balance of payments identity, must be equal to total receipts of money during the period less the increase in the consumer's money stock; hence we can push the discussion further to the question of what determines consumer's receipts and consumer's "hoardings" or "dishoardings." There is a further question of what determines consumers' income, outgo, and saving (i.e., increase in net worth). The equimarginal principle will yield *formal* solutions to all these problems. The exact relationships, however, are complex and must be investigated.

What Determines Earnings?

The most fundamental problem is perhaps that of determining the distribution of individual's time between "work" and "leisure." This distribution determines that part of income which may be called "earnings," and like any other distribution of a resource it falls under a general equimarginal principle. Thus, "work" means the sale of the services of resources which a man owns, such as the sale of the

692   ELEMENTS OF THE MARGINAL ANALYSIS

services of his body in "labor." "Leisure" means the use of his resources for his own enjoyment. Everyone has twenty-four hours a day to "spend" according to the equimarginal principle, as we have seen on page 688. Part of this may be devoted to earning a money income, part to occupations which do not bring in money, that is, to "leisure." With freedom to choose how much time to spend on each, a person will so divide his time between "work" and "leisure" that the gain in utility resulting from a small unit increase in one exactly balances the loss in utility resulting from a small unit decrease in the other. If, for instance, to use a numerical example, we spent 6 hours on work and 18 hours on leisure, and if with this distribution of time the marginal utility of time spent on leisure was 10 "utils" per minute and the marginal utility of time spent on work was 12 "utils" per minute, it would pay us to transfer a minute from leisure (thereby losing 10 "utils") and to add that minute to work (thereby gaining 12 "utils"), a net gain of 2 utils. It would pay to transfer time from leisure to work until the rising marginal utility of time spent on leisure met the falling marginal utility of time spent on work. Similar considerations apply to the distribution of other resources—e.g., land—to "earning" or "nonearning" uses.

The Distribution of Earnings Between Saving and Consumption

The problem of what determines the individual's total income will be studied further in Part IV. Even if income is given, however, there is still a problem of the allocation of income between consumption and "saving" (i.e., accumulation). Formally, we can again invoke the equimarginal principle; we can regard accumulation as one method of disposal of income, and say that the equilibrium distribution of income between consumption, or between the various lines of consumption and saving, is that at which the marginal gain from an increase in consumption is just equal to the marginal loss from the resultant decline in accumulation. It is not satisfactory, however, to leave the matter there; we need to know something of the *nature* of the gain or loss (utility) functions involved, for only then can we know whether people will think it worth while to save much or little.

Factors Affecting Saving

1. *Size of Income.* The most obvious factor affecting saving, whether as an absolute quantity or as a proportion of income, is the size of income itself. Saving is a "luxury." At very small incomes the imperious demands of subsistence press upon the scanty means and

saving is impossible; indeed at very low levels of income saving is negative, the minimum consumption being larger than income. At larger incomes we would expect saving to be larger, both in absolute amount and as a proportion of income.

2. *"Rainy Day" Saving*. The amount saved by a consumer is likely to depend also on the expected future time shape of his income. If he thinks his future incomes are going to be larger than his present incomes, the incentive to save will be small. If he expects his incomes to be smaller in the future, the incentive to save will be great. Such saving may be called "rainy day" saving. Saving for old age is its most typical form. If this were the only type of saving, in a stationary population there would be no *net* saving, for the old would spend what the young saved. In this type of saving we save to redistribute our consumption over the span of our life, and not primarily to accumulate a capital fund. It usually results in the accumulation of a capital fund by an individual only if he anticipates that his present income is larger than his future income will be. If we knew that our future income was going to be larger than our present income, it would be rational to "dis-save" in the present—that is, to "decumulate" or borrow in the present in order to increase our consumption and to accumulate or pay back loans in the future when our income is large. The young heir who borrows in anticipation of coming into his fortune later is therefore following exactly the same principle as the thrifty peasant who saves for his old age. "Rainy day" saving derives its justification from the principle of the diminishing marginal utility of outgo. If this principle holds, then we will gain on balance by taking a dollar from a year of large income and adding it to a year of small income. That is, we shall gain by making our outgo more equal in all the years of our life. If the schedule relating outgo and total utility were the same in all the years of our life, and if the rate of interest at which we could borrow or lend were zero, we should adjust our saving so as to make our outgo in each year equal. If our outgo in one year were greater than in another, in the above case, what we should lose in utility by withdrawing a dollar of outgo from the high outgo year would be less than what we should gain in utility by adding a dollar of outgo to the low-outgo year.

3. *Certainty of Future Incomes*. In the third place the amount an individual will save depends upon the certainty with which his future income can be anticipated. This type of saving necessarily involves building up an individual fund of capital. It derives its justification from the fact that an individual whose income suddenly disappears

through, for instance, the loss of his job is in a much worse position if he has no capital fund to draw from. A man who possesses, say $100,000 worth of property has much less need of life insurance than a man who possesses no property. Other things being equal, we should expect a man with a safe job to save less than a man with an uncertain job. This may be called "insurance saving." It must not be confused with the insurance premium itself in its pure form, which is a form of expenditure—the purchase of a "consumption good" known as "protection." Pure insurance does not result in the building up of an individual capital fund; "insurance saving" does.

4. *"Shiftlessness."*   In the fourth place the amount of saving depends on the carefulness with which the future is anticipated, i.e., on the degree to which present income is preferred merely because it is present, because we have not the imagination to visualize future needs. This is a nonrational element of "time preference" which we may call "shiftlessness." The more shiftless we are, the more we live only in the present, the less likely are we to save even in times of relatively high income, although if we had the imagination to do so we would be better off over our whole life. The element of shiftlessness often goes along with an uncertain or casual income, but it should not be confused with the effects of uncertainty itself. Uncertain incomes in themselves should promote saving. In so far, however, as they go hand in hand with a careless attitude about the future, the element of shiftlessness involved may serve to make people with uncertain incomes actually save less than people with equivalent safe incomes.

5. *Interest Rates.*   Finally, the amount saved depends on the *result* of saving, i.e., on the real rate of interest which saving will bear, and on the certainty with which that rate of interest may be anticipated. If the real rate of interest on invested funds is high and safe, a consumer may generally be expected, on purely rational grounds, to save more than when the rate of interest is low or uncertain. That is, a high safe rate of interest will encourage saving. However, in this problem it is risky to make a priori judgments of this nature, based on the doubtful assumption that saving is "postponed consumption."

"Nonrational" Saving

Saving is perhaps the least "rational"—i.e., the least planned—of all the forms of disposal of income. For one thing, the phenomenon of saving and of capital accumulation is surrounded by all manner of social taboos—e.g., the taboo against the squandering of capital, and the feeling that saving is done, not to spend again, but to provide a fund from which a perpetual income may be drawn for one's descendants. Again, saving is frequently not a "planned" part of the budget but a "buffer" which adjusts changes in outgo to changes in income. That is to say, the standard of life of the consumer has a certain inertia of its own; once a certain standard is established it takes some time to make the consumer adjust himself to a different one. When the money income of the consumer is rising or when prices are falling, his standard of life will frequently lag behind the rise in the purchasing power of his income; he will find himself saving. Conversely, if the consumer finds that his money income is falling or that prices are rising, he will for a time maintain his old standard of life, even though it means that he may consume more than he gets. The amount which a consumer will save in a given time may consequently depend as much upon the rise or fall of his income or the prices of the things he buys as upon the rational calculations which he makes in planning his budget. It has been suggested by Duesenberry,[3] for instance, that the highest previously attained income may be an important variable in the savings or consumption function. The studies of consumer behavior by the Survey Research Center[4] confirm the hypothesis that income is an important determinant; they also bring out the wide variations in individual behavior in this regard and the many variables which may be involved. Age, family status, occupational status (farmers and small businessmen save more than others of comparable income), asset totals and distributions all are significant variables.

Liquidity and Hoarding

In the above discussion we have used the word "saving" to mean the increase in the consumer's net worth, "income" to mean gross additions to, and "outgo" to mean gross subtractions from his net worth, income being the value of his production, outgo the value of his consumption, saving the value of his total accumulation. In the complete picture of the consumer's behavior we also need to consider the *forms* in which he holds his assets—e.g., whether liquid or nonliquid—and also his expenditures and receipts. An expenditure is a transfer of an asset from a liquid to a nonliquid form; a receipt is a transfer from nonliquid to a liquid form. Thus, when a consumer makes a purchase, he diminishes his stock of money and increases his stock of the thing purchased. Purchase and expenditure are thus not the same things as consumption, though they may be followed by it. Similarly, when the

[3] James S. Duesenberry, *Income, Saving, and the Theory of Consumer Behavior* (Harvard University Press, 1949).

[4] See the annual "Survey of Consumer Finances" in the *Federal Reserve Bulletin*.

consumer makes a sale, he increases his stock of money and decreases his holdings of the thing sold; receipts are not the same thing as income, though they are closely related to it.

Besides the problem of income, outgo, and saving, then, there is an additional problem of receipts, expenditure, and "hoarding"—hoarding being the change in the consumer's stock of money. Consumers make expenditure mainly in order to replace what they have consumed; hence, for some purposes the assumption that consumption and consumers' expenditure are identical is not wholly unrealistic. Nevertheless, we cannot afford to neglect the possibility that consumers make expenditures not merely to replace what they have consumed, but in order to change the form of their asset holdings. For instance, a consumer feels that he is holding too much money; he will increase his expenditures beyond his consumption and so expand his holdings of nonliquid and diminish his holdings of liquid assets. Conversely, a consumer who wishes to increase his liquid assets will diminish his expenditures even though his consumption may not be diminished; the result will be to increase his liquid assets at the expense of his nonliquid assets. The formal solution of the problem of expenditures and asset forms again lies in the equimarginal principle: the equilibrium distribution of assets between different types—e.g., liquid and nonliquid—is that at which the marginal gain of adding to one type is just equal to the marginal loss of the thereby necessitated subtraction from another. This equilibrium is perpetually disturbed by consumption and production, which add to and subtract from assets of different kinds, and it must continually be restored by expenditures (purchases) and receipts (sales).

CHANGES IN DEMAND

We can now examine, in so far as our analytical techniques allow, the forces which lie behind a change in consumers' demand. We have seen previously how a change in demand is a fundamental force operating to change the system of prices, costs, and outputs. Now we must look for forces which underlie a change in consumers' demand itself.

Change in Tastes

A consumer's demand curve will shift if his tastes change. A change in taste toward an increased desire for a commodity will be reflected in a shift in the total utility curve upward, as in Fig. 107A. At each quantity of the commodity the total utility will be greater than before.

At a quantity ON, for instance, the original total utility was NP. After an increase in desire for the commodity the total utility will be NP'. If OP is the original total utility curve, OP' is the curve after the increase in desire. This new total utility curve will probably be steeper than the old, at each level of consumption. As the steepness of the total

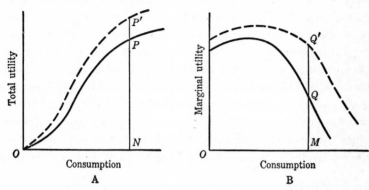

FIG. 107.   Effect of a Change in Taste.

utility curve is the marginal utility, the marginal utility will also be increased at each level of consumption—say, from MQ to MQ' in Fig. 107B—when OM units are consumed. The marginal utility curve, therefore, will move upward and to the right. The marginal rate of substitution curve will do likewise, as the marginal rate of substitution is equal to the marginal utility multiplied by an almost constant figure —the marginal revenue of utility. But the marginal rate of substitution curve is the same as the demand curve of the consumer for the commodity in question. An increase in desire for a commodity will therefore shift the demand curve of an individual consumer upward and to the right; i.e., will cause an increase in his demand.

Change in Income

From our utility curves we can also prove that a rise in a consumer's money income will raise all or most of his demand curves. A rise in money income will operate principally by lowering the marginal utility of money. It may have a significant effect on the marginal utility curves themselves, but that problem is reserved for the next part. Here we can show that even if a change in money income does not affect the total and marginal utility curves for a commodity, the change in the marginal utility of money is sufficient to affect the demand. It is generally assumed that the marginal utility of money declines with an increase in money income; i.e., that a dollar "means less" to a rich man than to a poor man. A rise in money income will therefore increase the marginal rate of substitution of a given level of consumption of most commodities, for if the marginal utility does not change, it is now divided by a smaller sum in order to calculate the marginal rate of substitution.

Suppose, for instance, that at a certain level of consumption of "food" the marginal utility was 20 utils per pound. If the marginal utility of money were 40 utils per dollar the marginal rate of substitution would be $0.50 per pound. If a rise in money income lowered the marginal utility of money to 30 utils per dollar, the marginal rate of substitution of the same quantity of food would be $0.67 per pound. A rise in money income therefore raises the whole marginal rate of substitution curve upward and to the right and causes a rise in the consumer's demand for commodities. We saw the importance of this assumption in discussing the theory of money; we now see its grounds.

Changes in Saving

Changes in the consumer's propensity to save also have an effect on demand curves similar to that produced by a change in money income. With an increased desire to save, the relative marginal utility curves and the demand curves will fall, mainly because of the rise in the marginal utility of money. Changes in the propensity to save frequently offset changes in money income or in prices, especially in the short run where savings act as a "buffer." For instance, a rise in money income or a general fall in prices will often increase saving rather than expenditure. The rise in the propensity to save will offset the tendency for demand curves to rise as a result of increased money income.

Changes in Asset Preferences

Changes in demand for commodities (or securities) may also come about as a result of changes in the "asset preferences" of individuals. If, for instance, there is a rise in "liquidity preference," so that people now wish to hold a greater proportion of their assets in liquid form, the result will be a decrease in the demand for commodities, i.e., in the willingness to purchase at a given price, even though consumption might remain unchanged; people will allow their stocks of commodities to run down, and will try to build up their money stocks. Changes due to asset preferences will not generally be of long duration, and for purposes of long-run analysis they may perhaps be neglected. Over short periods, however, changes in asset preferences may be very important in explaining changes in demand.

THE ELASTICITY OF DEMAND

We can now proceed to a further understanding of the forces which determine the elasticity of consumers' demand for a commodity. The elasticity of demand for a single consumer depends mainly on the *steepness* of the marginal utility curve. The steeper this curve, i.e., the faster marginal utility declines with increase in consumption, the faster will the marginal rate of substitution decline and the less elastic will be the demand of the consumer for the commodity in question. In this problem also there is a close analogy between the forces which determine the elasticity of the demand of a single consumer for a product and the forces which determine the elasticity of a single producer's demand for input. The demand for input is more elastic, the greater are the possibilities of substitution. Likewise, the demand for a consumption good will be more elastic, the better its substitutes. If a commodity has good substitutes in consumption, a rise in its price will cause the consumer to turn to the substitutes, and so will diminish greatly his consumption of the dearer commodity. We saw that the demand for input was more elastic, the greater the part played by the input in the process of production. Similarly, the demand for a consumption good will also be more elastic if it absorbs a large proportion of total expenditure. Thus a commodity like salt, on which we spend a very small part of our total income, is likely to have an inelastic demand.

The "Industry Effect"

Corresponding to the "industry effect" in the case of supply is a similar effect in the case of demand. We saw that the elasticity of supply depended in great part not only on the effect which a rise in price had on the output of an individual firm but also on the effect of a rise in price on the *number* of firms. Similarly, the elasticity of the *total* demand curve of all consumers for a product depends not merely on how a change in price will affect the purchases of an individual consumer, but on how a change in price will affect the *number* of consumers. Many commodities have an almost completely inelastic demand as far as the demand of a single consumer is concerned and yet have an elastic total demand because a change in price causes a large change in the *number* of purchasers. The demand for a magazine is a good illustration. Largely because of the indivisibility of the unit, and because the expenditure on any one magazine forms a small part of total expenditure, the demand of a single individual for a given magazine is probably almost perfectly inelastic within the range in which he is willing to purchase it. If I am willing to buy one copy for 15 cents, probably I should not be induced to buy two copies even for a price of 1 cent, or even for no price at all. Nevertheless, the total demand for a magazine may be highly elastic, because although a reduction in price will not cause any one individual to buy two copies where previously he bought one, it may cause a large number of individuals to buy one copy who previously had not purchased the magazine.

QUESTIONS AND EXERCISES

1. "Utility" does not connote mere pleasure or physical satisfaction. It refers to the satisfaction of *any* want, physical or spiritual. The theory of utility does not merely apply to mundane matters; it applies to such things as friendship, love, forgiveness, honesty, and peace of mind as much as to the things more usually regarded as "economic." Discuss and illustrate.

2. "High Heaven rejects the lore of nicely calculated less or more" (Wordsworth). Why?

3. "Saving is the least rational thing we do." Discuss the meaning of the word "rational" in respect to consumption.

4. Which of the following sentences best expresses the law of diminishing marginal utility?
   "The more you have of anything, the less you want it."
   "The less you have of anything, the more you want a good deal of it."
   "The more you have of anything, the less you want more of it."
   "The second drink is never as good as the first."
   "The more you have of anything, the more fun you get out of it."
   "Desire grows by what it feeds on."

5. Make a tabular statement, comparing and contrasting, as far as you can, the theory of production with the theory of consumption.

6. In discussing the demand for input we stated that the marginal revenue productivity curve of an individual firm *below the point of maximum average revenue productivity* was the demand curve. Is there any similar condition in the derivation of the demand for a consumer's good?

7. a. Using the figures of Table 63, page 682, calculate the sacrifice of total utility resulting from the money given up in the purchase of 1, 2, · · · 9 lbs. of food, assuming that the price of food is $0.35 per lb. Tabulate, and calculate the *net gain* in utility for each amount purchased. Show that the net gain is greatest at the point where the price is equal to the marginal rate of substitution.
   b. Repeat for a number of different prices of food, and show that for any price above $0.80 it does not pay to buy food at all.
   c. What must be assumed about the nature of the utility function if

food is a "necessity," so that there is *no* price above which food will not be bought?

d. Suppose that with a marginal rate of substitution table as in Table 63, columns 1 and 4, the marginal utility of money is constant at 10 utils per dollar. Repeat parts (a) and (b), calculating the new total utility schedule. Show that the results are not affected by the level of marginal utility of money assumed, and discuss their significance.

8. Draw a set of curves showing how an individual's saving might be expected to vary with (a) income, (b) future income, (c) certainty of future income, (d) the age of the consumer, (e) the number of children in the family, (f) the rate of interest, (g) the cost of living. Draw a corresponding series of curves to show how his consumption might be expected to vary. Can the consumption curves always be deduced from the savings curves? If so, how? What is the relation between the savings or consumption functions of individuals and the over-all consumption function of a society? How is a change in the distribution of income likely to affect the over-all consumption function?

CHAPTER 33

EQUILIBRIUM, PROCESS, AND POLICY

We have now reached a point in the analysis where it may be profitable to try to bring together what we have so far accomplished and to look briefly at its usefulness and limitations in the solution of economic problems. There are many important techniques of analysis which we have not yet explored. Nevertheless, the essential concepts of pure economics are now in our possession, and before proceeding to further refinements we shall do well to survey the ground already traveled.

Economic Models

Economic analysis consists essentially in the construction of "models" which have relevance to the study and interpretation of economic life. A model is a simplified system of variables, with far fewer variables and relationships in it than are found in real life. It is fairly easy to test models for their internal logic and consistency. Relevance is more difficult to establish. It is tested, however, by two criteria: understanding and prediction. A model which increases our ability to predict is clearly relevant. Even if predictions fail, however, a model which enables us to understand why they fail may be of importance.

Equilibrium Models

There are two broad classes of economic models: equilibrium models and process models. On the whole it has been the equilibrium model which has dominated this analysis. Thus in the first chapter we asked, "Why is the price of butter 80 cents a pound?" It may be argued that we have avoided this question and turned our attention to answering another question altogether—what determines the "equilibrium price" of butter? There is reason for this shift of emphasis from any actual price to a hypothetical "equilibrium" price. It is usually more interesting to know where a train is going than to know exactly where

702

it is at any moment. The "equilibrium" position of any price, wage, firm, industry, or system is the position toward which it is tending. The importance of equilibrium analysis, then, is that it enables us to discuss the *directions* of change. If a train is in New York and its "equilibrium" position is in Chicago, we are reasonably confident that the general direction of its motion will be westward, even if it unaccountably decides to travel north for the first hundred and fifty miles. Thus, to the question about the price of butter there are two possible answers within the framework of the equilibrium model. One is that the price of butter is 80 cents a pound because nobody who has the power to change that price wants to change it. Then it is the "equilibrium price." The other answer is that there are forces operating to change it to, say, 75 cents a pound, but that they have not yet had time to work out. That is to say, there are people who both want to do and can do things which will change the price of butter, but who have not yet had time to do them. In this case also it is important to know what the equilibrium price is, even if it merely represents the goal of a journey.

Process Analysis

There is, however, a third possible answer to the question about the price of butter. It is that the price is what it is today because of what it was yesterday, or on some past day or days. If there is a *stable* relationship between the price today and the price yesterday, then if we know the price on one day we can deduce the price on all other days. The stable relationship is what we mean by a difference equation (see pages 416–420), and the derivation of time series from difference equations is process analysis. These processes may or may not lead to equilibrium values. If the difference equation is such that a price of 80 cents today results in a price of 80 cents tomorrow, we have an equilibrium situation, and many processes lead to such equilibria. Some processes, however, such as the growth of a capital sum by compound interest, do not lead to equilibrium but to perpetual growth, unless the growth itself continually reduces the rate of interest. There are processes of inflation and deflation also which do not seem to lead to equilibrium. These cases, however, are rare, and the fact that most processes converge toward an equilibrium value is ample justification of the use of equilibrium models, even though it is always necessary also to investigate the processes by which equilibrium is reached and maintained. Indeed, the *stability* of an equilibrium cannot be determined without knowing the processes which maintain it.

Particular Equilibrium

A price is in equilibrium, then, when nobody who wants to act so as to change it has the power, and when nobody who has the power to change it wants to do so. That is, a price is in equilibrium when those who have incentive to change it have no opportunity and those who have the opportunity to change it have no incentive. Similarly, a firm is in equilibrium when there is no opportunity to act so as to increase its profits and no incentive to act so as to lower them. An industry is in equilibrium when those who have opportunity to expand or contract it have no incentive to do so and when those who wish to expand or contract it have not the opportunity. The equilibrium of a single firm, a single individual, a single industry or group of industries, is known as "particular equilibrium."

General Equilibrium

The equilibrium of any particular part of the system, however, is always determined by certain external data. A firm in perfect competition, knowing the prices of its products and of its inputs, will seek to discover the equilibrium quantities of input and output, and for each set of prices there will be a corresponding set of equilibrium quantities. For the economic system as a whole, however, there are no external prices or even fixed external quantities. All prices and quantities are decided by individuals, choosing what they believe to be the best alternative in the given circumstances. But in the case of most individuals at least part of the external circumstances which govern their decisions consist of the results of the decisions of others. That is, the decisions of some organisms form the opportunities of others. A firm, say, fixes a price; but the price it fixes is part of the data on which its customers base their decisions. The final problem of the theory of equilibrium, then, is to investigate the consistency of the equilibrium positions of the various organisms in the system. This is the problem of *general* equilibrium. It has to deal with the ultimate determinants of the system of prices and quantities of all commodities.

Mutual Determination in General Equilibrium

What we have in economic life is not so much a system of causation as a system of mutual determination. Suppose that our system had only three organisms, A, B, and C. The position of A would be determined in part by certain things belonging to the system as a whole, in part by the positions of B and C. Similarly, the position of B would be determined in part by the positions of A and C, and the position of C would be determined in part by the positions of A and B. This looks at first like circular reasoning. In fact it is not, for given the circumstances which belong to the system as a whole and the schedules or functions which show how the position of each organism is related to the position of the other two, we can find the equilibrium position of all three. A mechanical analogy is that of three balls in a bowl. The equilibrium position of any one ball depends first on the shape of the bowl and on its own size and second on the position of the other two balls. Nevertheless, there is a perfectly definite position of equilibrium of all three balls lying in a trefoil arrangement in the bottom of the bowl. The same is true no matter how many balls there are, in the absence of friction (imperfect competition!). Even if friction is introduced into the picture, there is still a limited range of possible positions of equilibrium.

Ultimate Determinants of the System

We can carry the analogy even further. In the mechanical problem of the balls in the bowl we need to know three sets of data before the problem can be solved: (1) the size and shape of the bowl, (2) the size, shape, and number of balls, and (3) the principle of equilibrium—in this case the principle of the balance of the forces of gravity and of reaction. In the problems of economic equilibrium it is also necessary to know (1) the external obstacles to the production of want-satisfactions, (2) the nature of the wants and resources of the organisms concerned, and (3) the principle of equilibrium—that is, the situation under which the net balance of forces produces no change. General equilibrium models can be set up with varying degrees of generality, depending on what we regard as "given"—i.e., as external obstacles to the system. The "givens" of the less general model should become variables to the more general.

The "Market Model"

Thus we can set up a model of a pure market in which the "givens" consist of the quantities and distribution among the marketers of the stocks of all exchangeables, both goods, securities, and money. Then the wants of the marketers can be expressed as preference ratios (see pages 59–60), and the "principle of equilibrium" is that of "clearing the market," a principle which may be expressed in several ways. We may say, for instance, that the equilibrium price system is that at which the quantities offered for sale and the quantities demanded for purchase of all commodities are equal. Another way of putting the same thing is to say that at the equilibrium price system the sum of what marketers are willing to hold of all exchangeables is equal to the quantity which is there to be held, or is present in the market.

The "Normal Price" Model

We can now go on to release the assumption that the stocks of exchangeables are constant, and develop a model of the general equilibrium of "normal price." In this case the basic "obstacle" or limitation of the system is the existing quantities of factors of production. The "nature of the organism" is represented by the production functions and utility or preference functions of the firms and households in the system. The principle of equilibrium is the principle of maximum advantage, especially in the form of the principle of equal advantage. The existing set of prices of all goods and services determines the distribution of income among occupational groups and industries. If this distribution is such that there are people who feel that their position can be improved by moving their resources, whether labor, land, or capital, from their present occupation to some other, equilibrium has not been reached, for resources will move. The movement of resources, however, will itself change the set of prices, diminishing those in areas into which resources are moving, raising those in areas out of which resources are moving, and this adjustment of prices will itself move the system closer to a position of equal advantage.

Normal price models can be constructed in considerable variety, depending on the nature of the assumptions. Thus we can distinguish between short-run and long-run equilibrium—the former in which fixed capital, for instance, is assumed not to be mobile between occupations, the latter in which it is. We can also distinguish between competitive and monopolistic equilibria, depending largely on the degree of mobility of resources assumed. The principle of equal advantage does not state that advantages are to be equal in all occupations, but only that movement will take place from less to more advantageous occupations when movement is possible. The institutional framework of a society may limit movement and so any equilibrium is relative to this framework; large differences in advantage may exist, but if movement is prevented the situation may be regarded as an equilibrium.

The Stationary State

The most "long run" of the normal price models is that of the stationary state. This is a condition where population is constant in numbers, age composition, and skill, and where stocks of capital goods are likewise constant in size and composition. People are born and die, and goods are produced and consumed, but births equal deaths and production of each good equals its consumption. Prices are stable; so is the quantity of money and of all other assets. The question as to whether interest and profit can exist in a stationary state is somewhat in dispute; if it exists, however, it must be stable in amount.

The Subsistence Theory

The model of the stationary state implies that population growth is a function of economic variables, especially real incomes, and also that capital growth is also a function of, say, the rate of profit. This is the essential assumption of the "classical" model, associated especially with Malthus and Ricardo. If the stationary state is to be stable, in the sense that all economic processes lead toward it, it must also be assumed, at least beyond a certain point, that increase in population leads to a decline in real income per head, and the increase in capital stock leads to a decline in the rate of profit. This is the essence of the unjustly despised "subsistence theory," both of wages and of profit. The proposition that per capita incomes will be lower at larger populations, techniques and natural resources being constant, is an application of the "law of diminishing returns" (page 588). Applying larger and larger quantities of labor to fixed natural resources (land) will eventually result in declining average physical product.

The subsistence theory is illustrated in Fig. 108. Here the population is measured horizontally, and the per capita real income, or "standard of life," is measured vertically. Curve AA shows what standard of life can be maintained at each level of population. The population at which the standard of life is a maximum (NB) is called the optimum population (ON).

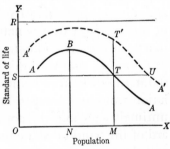

FIG. 108.   The Subsistence Theory.

The subsistence theory of wages of the classical economists is based on the assumption of some such curve as AA, plus the assumption that there is some standard of life at which the population (in particular, the working population) will just maintain itself. This standard of life is the "subsistence level." It is not a level of physical subsistence necessarily, for, as Ricardo himself recognized, the "subsistence level" may be purely conventional. It depends on the degree to which low income prevents the successful rearing of children. We assume, then, that there is some standard of life below which the people will raise so few children that the population will decline and above which the people will raise so many children that the population will increase. Suppose OS is this standard of life. Then ST is the population at which this standard can be maintained. If the population is smaller than ST (= OM), it will grow, and the standard of life will decline to OS. If the population is larger than ST, it will decline, and the standard of life will rise to OS. The subsistence level, therefore, is an equilibrium level of the standard of life, a very long-run equilibrium, it is true, but nevertheless valid as a statement of tendency.

The Dismal Science

It is not difficult to see how this theory led to conclusions which justly earned for political economy the title of the "dismal science." For if it is the subsistence level which determines the long-run equilibrium of the standard of life, there is no *ultimate* hope for the advancement of mankind through an improvement in the techniques of production. If techniques of production improve, there will be a rise in the average physical productivity for each quantity of labor applied. That is, the whole curve AA will rise to a position $A'A'$, indicating that at each level of population a higher standard of life can be maintained than before.

Suppose, then, that with a population OM (= ST) in equilibrium at a subsistence level MT (= OS) a sudden improvement in techniques or the discovery of new natural resources or land raised the curve AA to a position $A'A'$. The standard of life would of course increase from MT to MT'. But alas, this blessing would be merely temporary. The standard of life MT' being above the subsistence level MT, the population would set itself to breeding, children would cease to expire at untimely ages, and the population would grow. As it grew, the standard of life would decline until finally the population had risen to SU and the standard of life had sunk once more to the subsistence level, OS. The effect of an improvement in the productive effciency of labor, therefore, in the absence of any change in the subsistence level, is eventually to allow a larger population to exist, but in precisely the same state of misery as before. This is the nightmare of the Reverend Mr. Malthus, and a real nightmare it is in many stages and types of society. Shelley was unjust when he remarked that he would "rather be damned with Plato and Lord Bacon, than go to Heaven with Paley and Malthus." Malthus was also a reformer, but one who saw where the only possibility of reform lay—in the raising of the subsistence level itself by the voluntary restriction of births.

Overpopulation

In many societies today, and in most societies of the past, the Malthusian nightmare is a grim reality. The disappointing results of the industrial and agricultural revolutions of the eighteenth and nineteenth centuries are perhaps in part due to the vast increase in population which they sponsored. The chronic destitution of hundreds of millions of people in Asia and the failure of improved techniques to improve their lot perceptibly may also be attributed to the evil influence of propagation restrained only by the checks of famine, pestilence, and war. Indeed, the fantastic difference in the standard of life between the western and the eastern worlds is due more than anything else to the differences in population density in relation to natural resources. If the United States had a population of a thousand million the majority of her people would be reduced to the starvation level simply because the limited land area, however highly cultivated, could not be forced to feed adequately such a mighty legion of mouths.

Population in Developed Countries

In the 1930's it looked as if a new danger threatened the western world—that of race suicide. In many civilized countries the growth of economic consciousness, and especially of economic calculation in the planning of family size, coupled with easy methods of birth control, had brought the net reproductive ratio[1] down below 1, and it looked as if the populations would eventually die out. In terms of Fig. 108 it looked as if the subsistence level had risen, say, to OR, above the maximum possible standard of life. In that case no equilibrium is possible short of zero, for no matter what the size of the population, it will not be willing to produce enough children to reproduce itself. These fears seem to have been largely dissipated by the remarkable increase in birth rates and reproduction rates in the forties and fifties; in the United States, for instance, the number of births in the 1940's

[1] The net reproductive ratio is usually defined as the average number of surviving female children per woman of childbearing age. Assuming constant sex ratios, if the net reproductive ratio is 1, each generation as it dies off leaves a generation of equal size, and the population will settle down to stationary equilibrium. If the ratio is more than 1, population must grow as each generation more than replaces itself; if it is less than 1, population must decline as each generation fails to replace itself (see page 432).

was about double the number in the 1930's. In no small degree this seems to be a result of rising real income, and we therefore face the possibility that the "Malthusian specter" may be a real one for the developed as well as for the undeveloped countries. In the undeveloped countries the Malthusian pressure arises because economic calculation is not present in the production of children. Even when economic calculation is present, however, a sufficient rise in income may bring most families to the point where they can afford three or four children. In developed societies nearly all children survive, so that a four-child family pattern may lead to a very rapid rate of population increase. Thus we may have two Malthusian problems—one in societies where people have children because they cannot afford them, and one in societies where they have them because they can.

The "Subsistence Theory" of Profits

The idea of a stationary state implies something like a "subsistence theory" of profits as well as of wages. If we suppose that capital is accumulated because of the hope of profit, then the cessation of accumulation must depend on the diminution in profit rates as accumulation proceeds. If we suppose that there is some rate of profit at which there is no accumulation, above which there is positive accumulation, and below which there is decumulation, and if we further suppose that an increase in the total stock of capital, other things being equal, will diminish profits, then the growth of capital is seen to be very much like the growth of population. Fig. 108 will now illustrate capital growth as well as population growth, measuring the rate of profit along OY and the total capital along OX. If AA is the "profit curve" and OS is the "subsistence rate" at which accumulation just ceases, capital will grow to OM. Technical change, of course, may raise the profit curve to $A'A'$, in which case capital will grow further to SU. The classical economists believed that the real wage of the human population depended directly on the total capital stock—this is the essence of the "wage fund" theory. The dynamic course of a society was then seen as a "race between population and capital." If capital grew faster than population, wages rose and profit declined. If population grew faster than capital, wages fell and profits rose. No matter how many times, however, the population curve was raised by the growth of capital, or the capital curve raised by the growth of population, or both curves by technical discoveries, the time would eventually come when the limits of change had been reached and both wages and profits were stable at the subsistence level.

The Example of Ireland

This "Ricardian" model is useful in explaining many dynamic processes in economic history. The history of Ireland is an admirable example of the Ricardian dynamic at work. When the potato was introduced into Ireland in the seventeenth century, the population was about two million or less. Under the stimulus of the increased yield of foodstuffs per acre the population rose to over 8 million by 1841. The failure of the potato crop in 1845 and 1846 led to famine, starvation, great mortality, and emigration which finally reduced the population to a little over four million by 1911, a level at which it has remained, largely because a rise in the conventional "subsistence level" has been reflected in a very late age of marriage.

Stagnation in the Stationary State

The Ricardian model is not, however, wholly satisfactory because of its neglect of the possibility of stagnation as the stationary state is approached. In the stationary state, as we have seen, there can be no net saving or investment, so that consumption must be equal to production. It may be, however, that the consumption function does not permit zero net saving at full employment, in which case the stationary state will be characterized by underutilization of resources and unemployment. The possibility of stagnation in this sense depends on the extent to which the consumption function rises as time goes on and as capital increases. If the rise is sufficient, then a stationary state with full employment is not impossible. It cannot be assumed, however, that the appropriate rise is automatic. It depends on the institutions of the society as well as on the more basic economic principles, and hence there may be a strong case for public policy directed toward raising (or even in some cases lowering) the consumption function as investment proceeds and capital accumulates.

Dynamic Equilibria

The question of the application of the equilibrium concept to dynamic processes themselves is worth some attention, even though we cannot explore it fully. A process through time may be said to be in dynamic equilibrium if the rates of change of its essential variables are constant. Thus, a population is in dynamic equilibrium when it is increasing (or decreasing) at a constant rate, in such a way that its birth and death *rates* (per cent per annum) are constant, though of course not equal one to the other. Then the age distribution, the proportion of individuals in each age group, is likewise constant, although the total number of individuals changes. Similarly, an economic system might be said to be in "dynamic" equilibrium if its total stock, including both things and people, changed at a constant rate (per cent per annum) and if the rates of production and consumption of all items of the stock increased at the same rate. It may be doubted whether such a conception of dynamic equilibrium is of great importance in interpreting economic change, for there is no "natural" tendency for society to conform to it. It is a much more artificial concept than that of the stationary state, for the latter is at least a historical possibility, whereas there is no particular reason why a society should ever be in dynamic equilibrium.

"Expectational" Equilibrium

In the progress of an economic system through time another aspect of the equilibrium concept becomes important. This we may call "expectational equilibrium": a condition in which the expectations of the various organisms of society are mutually compatible and are fulfilled. The data upon which all economic judgments are based are in part expectations of future circumstances. Thus the farmer in planting a crop is guided by what he expects the future price to be, for it is that price, and not the present one, which will determine the profitability of his enterprise. Similarly, in purchasing equipment a businessman will look to his expectation of future prices as well as to the current prices, and if he expects future prices to be lower, he will defer his purchases. A problem immediately arises as to the compatibility of the expectations of the innumerable individuals of society. Suppose, for instance, that a farmer bases his decisions on the expectation that the price of wheat is to be $2 a bushel in six months, and a miller bases his decisions on the expectation of a price of $1.80. It is evident that both these expectations cannot be correct; at least one must be disappointed. Disappointment, therefore, is the symptom of "expectational disequilibrium." However, the concept of disappointment is not perfectly clear. In so far as expectations are vague, disappointments are vague also. Hence the presence of uncertainty makes the concept of expectational equilibrium not a "point" but a "cloud," shading away into varying degrees of disappointment.

Disequilibrium in the Business Cycle

By far the most important source of expectational disequilibrium lies in the fact that the stream of goods coming on the market at any one moment is the result of *past* decisions, whereas the demand for these goods is determined by the expectations of the future. Consequently, it may very well happen, and frequently does happen, that the stream of goods coming on the market does not "fit" the present structure of demand. The goods were produced in anticipation of a demand which does not now exist. A good example of such disappointments occurs in the business cycle. During the boom businessmen are optimistic and expect a greater demand for their products than actually exists when the products begin to come on the market. The crisis occurs when there is a general discovery that expectations of demand have been too optimistic. The goods realize lower prices than had been expected, businessmen take losses and become pessimistic, and a depression follows.

Difficulties of Expectational Equilibrium

In expectational equilibrium, then, a society would so distribute its resources that current output could always be sold at the expected prices. The whole history of capitalism proves that expectational equilibrium is very difficult to attain, for the failure to attain it is that most characteristically capitalist phenomenon, the business cycle. It is easy to see the reason. Decisions to produce are taken by one set of people; decisions to invest, i.e., to own goods, and to consume are taken largely by another set of people. The greater the division of labor in this regard, the more likely are expectations to be disappointed, for each group acts more or less independently of the others.

NORMATIVE ECONOMICS

A distinction is frequently made between "positive" economics, which contents itself with analysis and description, and "normative" economics, which goes on to judgment and prescription, and which attempts to state not only what is or what might be but what ought to be. Some economists have argued that economics as a discipline should confine itself to positive statements about what is and should avoid discussions of normative statements about what ought to be. In so far, however, as the method of economics is applicable to the clarification and analysis of normative statements, there seems to be no reason why it should not be applied. In their writing also economists have seldom confined themselves to positive statements, but have usually gone on to suggest normative implications of their analysis.

The "Welfare Function"

A normative statement takes the form A is better than B. It implies therefore that the various alternatives in which we are interested can be *ordered* on a line so that any alternative on one side of any point is regarded as "better" than any alternative on the other side of it. This is what is generally meant by a "welfare function." In economics we can postulate a welfare function such that all alternative positions of the economic universe (i.e., all combinations of prices, outputs, incomes, and all other economic quantities) can be ordered or arranged in this manner. The combination or position at the head of such a list is the "optimum" position. All value judgments imply an ordering of this nature. Immediately, of course, we run into the difficulty that the welfare functions of different individuals are different. One individual may even have different welfare functions, depending on the role he is playing. He may say, "A is worse than B for me, but better than B for the country." Economics cannot say which of all possible welfare functions is itself the "best." It has been shown by Kenneth Arrow[2] that it is not even generally possible to "add up" or otherwise combine the welfare functions of different individuals into a "social welfare function" to which they will all voluntarily consent. Other social sciences may be able to say something about the way in which compromise social welfare functions are derived from discussion and political activity. The contribution of economics, however, lies mainly in the analysis of the formal properties and plausible general characteristics of welfare functions, especially those which involve economic variables. These properties and characteristics are similar to those of utility or production functions.

"Value Analysis"

We can, therefore, perform something with the tools of economic analysis which might be called "value analysis," and which should be of use in clarifying the choices involved in economic policy. It is necessary first to identify certain broad characteristics of systems which can be regarded as significant from the welfare point of view. These characteristics, or "subordinate ends," must be capable of rough measurement, and must be related to a welfare function in the sense that we can arrange the various values of the subordinate end in an order of "goodness." Thus we might distinguish the following subordinate ends of economic policy: (1) the rate of economic progress; (2) the short-run stability of employment, incomes, or prices; (3) equality in the distribution of income; (4) absence of waste in the allocation of resources among different industries and occupations; (5) width of freedom of personal choice in regard to commodities, occupations, or

[2] Kenneth Arrow, *Social Choice and Individual Values* (New York, 1951).

modes of life; (6) the degree of satisfaction with the human relations involved in economic processes. This list is by no means exhaustive; it covers, however, a good deal of the territory.

Possibility Functions Relating "Ends"

The task of value analysis then is twofold. It is to examine the "possibility functions" which limit the achievement of these subordinate ends. We want to know, that is to say, what combinations of these subordinate ends are possible or compatible. We may not be able to plot the whole range of this function, but we need to know something about its marginal properties. We need to know, for instance, at least roughly, what we have to give up of one end in order to gain more of another. If, for instance, we achieve greater equality of income, does this mean that we must accept a slower rate of economic progress; if we increase the rate of economic progress, does this mean that we have to pay for this in a certain rate of inflation or in the restriction of individual choice or in the development of strained human relations and cultural disintegration; if we have wide freedom of personal choice, does this involve us in wider fluctuations of employment? The answers to these questions depend on the empirical nature of the system as it is; they do not involve any judgments about the welfare function, or what ought to be. Without some knowledge of the possibility function, however, our welfare judgments may be irrelevant. There is no point in wanting the impossible or in crying for the moon, and the essence of the intelligent value judgment is the selection of the best out of all *possible* situations.

Welfare Orderings of "Ends"

In order to find the "best" situation, however, we must have a welfare function, and even though we cannot specify that any particular welfare function is the "right" one we can explore certain general properties of welfare functions as a safeguard against partial and uninformed judgments. Thus we can assert with some confidence that no single subordinate end can serve as a measure of welfare as long as there are others which may compete with it or complement it. A "law of diminishing returns" is likely to apply to the welfare ordering of any *single* end, such as economic progress, if the quantity of other ends is held constant. If we suppose for a moment that "goodness" can be measured along the O_y axis of Fig. 108, and a subordinate end, say the rate of economic progress, along the OX axis, the welfare function may be expected to have the general shape of the curve AA. At smaller values of the "end" an increase in the end increases welfare, but the rate of increase diminishes with increase in the quantity of the end achieved; there is a maximum "goodness" beyond which increase in the end actually diminishes welfare. Every virtue is a vice if carried to excess, and every vice a virtue if in small enough quantity. In considering, therefore, whether we want "more" of any particular objective we must consider first what is the "cost" of this increase in terms of other objectives given up, and second what valuation we place on these gains and losses. The formal solution is, of course, that we should push each objective to the point where we estimate the marginal gains involved in pushing it further to be just equal to the value of the marginal losses involved in the other objectives sacrificed. Formally, that is, the choice between progress and stability, or between equality and liberty, is not essentially different from the choice between ham and eggs.

Economic Progress

To develop explicitly the implications for economic policy of the above principles would require a separate volume. It may not be inappropriate, however, at this point to illustrate in somewhat greater detail the nature and relationships of some of the subordinate objectives of economic policy mentioned above. We may begin with the concept of economic progress, as perhaps the most important single end of economic policy. Economic progress is not easy to define or to measure. Nevertheless, almost all would agree that it can be observed in history. There are clearly observable "chains of improvement." The candle replaces the rushlight, the oil lamp the candle, the gaslight the oil lamp, the electric light the gaslight. Similar chains lead from the oxcart to the truck, from the sedan chair to the automobile, from the sickle to the combine-harvester. Other chains of development we are not quite so sure about—the chains, for instance, that lead from the Parthenon to the First National Bank Building, or from Chartres to the First Methodist Church, or from the Beatitudes to last Sunday's sermon. It is evident that economic progress is something real, but that not all change is progress.

Economic Progress as Improvement in Means

The dilemma is resolved if we define economic progress as an improvement in the means used to obtain a given end. That is to say, whenever a change occurs which enables man to obtain a given quantity of *ends* with a smaller quantity of *means,* or what is the same thing, to obtain a larger quantity of ends with a given quantity of means, then we can affirm that economic progress has taken place. In the most general terms, that is to say, we have defined economic progress as the ratio $\dfrac{\text{Ends produced}}{\text{Means used}}$. This ratio is the most general measure of what is meant by "efficiency"; it may be called the "efficiency ratio." The significance of the efficiency ratio clearly depends on the definition of "ends" and of "means." Ends are the "output" of a process; means are the "input." The efficiency ratio, therefore, is the output per unit of input. It will depend on what we include in output and input, and how we measure them. The simplest case of a means and ends relationship is one in which output and input are both physically measurable. In this case the efficiency ratio measures what is called the *technical efficiency* of the process. Thus, engineers have a concept of the technical efficiency of an engine, measured by the output of available energy per unit of input of fuel or fuel energy. Similarly, the technical efficiency of a cow might be measured in terms of the output of milk per unit of input of feed.

Technical vs. Economic Efficiency

Technical efficiency, however, is not the same thing as economic efficiency, for the inputs and outputs which are of interest to the technicians are not the *whole* inputs and outputs of the process. Thus, an engine may be very efficient in the engineering sense and yet may be economically quite useless, either because of its cost or because its output of energy does not come in a usable form, or because it is inconvenient in size, or because it requires so much labor to attend and maintain it, or for many other reasons. Similarly, a cow may be a very efficient transformer of feed into milk, and yet may be highly inefficient economically, either because she has a short length of life, or is unusually subject to disease, or requires an expensive type of feed, or an unusual amount of attention.

Although it is easy to see that technical and economic efficiency are not the same, it is less easy to define what we really mean by economic efficiency. Efficiency, it is true, is "output per unit of input." But what are the significant concepts of output and input from the economic point of view? The ultimate product or output of all economic activity is, as we have seen, an intangible, unmeasurable, but nevertheless real quantity which we call "utility." The ultimate resource which we have to spend in the production of utility is human time; it is the inexorable fact that a day is only twenty-four hours long which ultimately limits our ability to do what we want. The most significant concept of economic efficiency, therefore, is that of the production of utility per man-hour of life. This, however, is not a quantity which is amenable to statistical analysis or to social aggregation; utility is a treasure locked in each man's mind, and we have no key that will enable us to bring these treasures out and add them together. If we are to discuss economic progress from a social or statistical point of view, therefore, we must find a concept which is perhaps less ultimately significant for the individual, but which is more measurable than utility. This we may find to some extent in an index of physical output, arbitrary as any such index must be. A rise in output per man-hour of human productive activity, therefore, may not unreasonably be regarded as an expression of economic progress.

Some qualification would have to be introduced into this proposition where the increase in output per man-hour was accompanied by an increase in the disutility of labor or in a decline in utilities elsewhere in the system. Such disutilities and utilities are not measurable, but we do in fact make judgments about them.

Structure in Economic Progress

We can therefore use the rate of change of an index of physical output per man-hour as a rough measure of economic progress. Use of this measure, however, must not blind us to the importance of the change in the structure of the economy as economic progress proceeds. The over-all effect of a rise in output per man-hour of some particular commodity depends on two things—the *importance* of the commodity, that is, the proportion of its output to the total output, and on the elasticity of demand for the commodity. It is clear that the more important is a commodity, the greater the total effect of a rise in its output per man-hour. Technical progress in wheat growing has much more significance than a similar technical progress in the production of caviar.

The effect of technical progress in the production of one commodity on the distribution of resources among industries depends on the elasticity of demand for that commodity. If the demand is inelastic there will be a transfer of resources to the production of other commodities. Suppose, to take an extreme case, that the demand for wheat is perfectly inelastic and that a technical discovery makes it possible to produce a bushel of wheat with the average expenditure of 2 instead of 3 man-hours. The result will not ultimately be an increase in the output of wheat, for there will not be any expansion in consumption. The same amount of wheat will be produced as before with a smaller expenditure of man-time. One out of every three men previously engaged in the production of wheat will be shifted to other occupations. The price of wheat will fall relative to the prices of other commodities, and this fall in price will drive out the surplus resources from the wheat industry. A technical improvement in an industry whose product enjoys an elastic demand, however, may result in a transfer of resources toward the improved industry. Suppose that a technical improvement in the automobile industry makes it possible to produce an automobile with a total of 1500 man-hours instead of 2000. However, if the fall in the price of automobiles which results increases their sales from 1,000,000 a year to 1,400,000, there will be an increase in the total number of man-hours annually employed in the automobile industry from 2 billion (2000 × 1,000,000) to 2.1 billion (1500 × 1,400,000).

Importance of "Necessity" Industries

An important corollary of these propositions is that the development of "luxury" industries depends upon technical progress in the "necessity" industries. Again we may refer to the peculiar position of agriculture. Agriculture for the most part produces commodities which are the "means of subsistence," without which we could not live at all. If the labor of an agriculturalist produces only enough food for himself and his family, there cannot possibly be any specialized industry. The existence of nonagricultural occupations therefore depends on the existence of a "surplus" from agriculture, i.e., a surplus of food over and above what the agriculturalists themselves eat. The extent of specialized industry depends on the size of this surplus. If an agriculturalist produces enough food for three people, society need have only one-third of its population in agriculture and can have two-thirds in other occupations. This proposition throws a good deal of light on the course of economic history. It is no accident that the development of towns in the Middle Ages was accompanied, and to some extent preceded, by the development of improved methods of agriculture (e.g., the three-field system). It is no accident either that the industrial revolution of the eighteenth and nineteenth centuries was preceded and accompanied by an agricultural revolution—the introduction of root crops, four-course rotation, horse-hoeing husbandry, and scientific animal breeding.[3]

[3] It is an instructive exercise in the interpretation of economic history to consider how far the discovery of root crops (e.g., the turnip) is responsible for the development of the past three centuries. Root crops did two main things: they eliminated the "fallow field"

Importance of Transportation

Another corollary to be noticed is that technical developments in transportation have a peculiarly great effect on economic progress. The "extent of the market," i.e., the number of people who can exchange one with another, depends largely on the methods of transportation. Where transportation is poor the market is local; where it is good the market may be world-wide. Consequently, improvements in transportation may make possible improvements in methods of manufacture and distribution which otherwise would have been out of the question because of the limitation of the market. Even without any technical *discoveries* in other industries, an improvement in transportation by allowing greater specialization may result in technical progress in these industries, in the sense of output per man-hour. The development of transportation particularly affects the growth of cities. Poor means of communication mean small cities; the great cities of the present day owe their existence largely to the development of cheap transportation. It is no accident that the greatest cities are on coasts and rivers and that the cheapest transportation is by water.

"Costs" of Economic Progress

In the evaluation of economic progress as an objective, account must be taken of its "costs" both among its causes and its effects. The causes of economic progress lie deep in the institutions and psychological characteristics of a society—in the nature of the family, the practices of child rearing, the basic institutions of religion and government, and that indefinable "spirit" which makes the difference between a stationary, traditional society and a dynamic and progressive

---

and made possible scientific animal breeding. The fallow field was necessary to eliminate weeds, and the practice of planting roots in rows between which horses could hoe the ground made the fallow field unnecessary. Also the roots enabled the farmer to feed his stock through the winter and thereby prevented the monstrous slaughter at Christmas. This made selective breeding possible, with astounding results. The increased production of food probably was the principal cause of the amazing fall in mortality, and especially in infant mortality, in the middle years of the eighteenth century, to which most of the rise in population of the western world is due. The extra food enabled more babies to live and thus provided the inhabitants for the industrial cities. The new techniques enabled agriculture to produce a large surplus and thus made it possible to feed the hungry mouths of the new towns. Even if there had been no startling changes in industrial techniques, therefore, it is probable that the agricultural revolution itself would have produced many of the phenomena which we usually associate with the industrial revolution. It is possible that the vast developments in agricultural techniques which are now proceeding may foreshadow a new revolution in economic life as great as that of the last century.

one. The economist brings no special competence to these areas. He can point out, however, that economic progress almost always involves the accumulation of capital, which in turn involves a cost in terms of consumption foregone. The proposition is all the more incontrovertible if, as in strict logic we should, we regard human bodies and minds as capital, and the rearing, training, and education of these bodies and minds as investment. The rate of economic progress, therefore, will be limited sharply by the "cost" conditions which limit the accumulation of capital.

Accumulation Difficult in Poor Societies

The conditions may be of two kinds. In poor societies the physical difficulty of accumulation is very great. Accumulation, as we have seen, is the excess of production over consumption. Where the level of production is low, the insistent demands of the bare necessities of consumption press continually against meager outputs, and any accumulation is very difficult. There must be, in fact, in each type of society some level of output below which accumulation is impossible, for as soon as anything is produced, the urgent need for consumption swallows it up. This explains the great difficulty experienced by any poor society in making progress; the degree of "abstinence" (i.e., restriction of consumption) necessary for accumulation represents a disutility greater than can be endured. Below a certain critical point, therefore, the level of which depends, of course, on the character of the people and the society concerned, progress is impossible. The society treads an endless treadmill of poverty; low production makes it impossible to accumulate, and without accumulation there can be no increase in production. This is seen most clearly in relation to "human capital"; a society with a low food output will suffer from malnutrition, which will sap the energies of the people and make them incapable even of applying techniques which they know to increase their production of food. We do not even have to go outside the boundaries of the United States to find communities in this condition, and it is the condition in which the majority of mankind still finds itself.

Unemployment in Rich Societies

On the other hand, once a certain critical point has been passed, progress becomes almost inevitable. Once it becomes possible to accumulate, accumulation increases output and hence makes more accumulation all the more easy. The greater the output of a society, the less disutility is involved in the "abstinence" required for accumulation. A savage society will have to deprive itself of dire necessities in order to accumulate; our own society need only restrict its consumption of superfluities. As accumulation proceeds, and as a society gets richer in consequence, a new factor emerges which restricts further accumulation and growth in wealth—unemployment. We have already examined some of the complexities of this problem in Part II, and we need not repeat that analysis here, save to mention that its structure, and especially its monetary institutions, may create a situation in which a society is unable to accumulate and consume as much as it can produce. This is the limitation with which we are most familiar, and it bulks larger in our imaginations. Nevertheless, if we are to have a proper sense of proportion, we must realize that the greatest part of the world's problem is not unemployment, but lack of productivity.

Significance of Foreign Investment

In this connection the institution of "foreign investment" or the "export of capital"—conceived in its broad sense as investment by one region in another—is of great importance. A region "exports capital" if it exports a greater value of goods and services than it imports; conversely, a region "imports capital" if it imports a greater value of goods and services than it exports. By this means some accumulation of one region may be *located* in another, even though still owned by the inhabitants of the first. Thus, Americans might export machinery to Brazil, not receiving anything in return but in some way retaining the ownership, if not the title, of the machines concerned. A capital import by a backward area may easily be the means of lifting it over the critical point of no accumulation, and may set it on the upward spiral of progress. Similarly, a capital export by a rich area may help it to stave off unemployment and may result in the production of goods which otherwise, for lack of a market, might never have been produced at all. When properly applied, therefore, capital export and import are twice blessed, and may help to solve the problems both of excess and of deficiency.

Progress and Stability

Let us now take a brief look at some possible relations between economic progress and other subordinate ends of economic policy. There is some reason to suppose that high rates of economic progress are likely to produce short-run instability in the economy, both inflation when investment proceeds faster than is consistent with a stable price level, and depression when investment takes a cyclical downswing in a society accustomed to high rates of saving. There is some possibility, on the other side, that fluctuations up to a point may contribute to economic growth, through the weeding out of inefficient firms and processes and the stimulus which comes to investment through necessity in hard times. Both these possible relationships are highly speculative, but their possibility is disturbing. It may be that if we are too successful in promoting growth we do so at the cost of violent instability, and if we are too successful in promoting stability we shall end in a nirvana that stultifies growth.

Progress and Equality

Another important objective of economic policy is that of making the distribution of income more equal. If the utilities of income to different individuals could be compared, the total social utility would be maximized when the marginal utility of income to each individual is the same. Suppose, for instance, that the marginal utility of A's income was 5 utils per dollar, and of B's income was 8 utils per dollar. Transferring a dollar from A to B would result in a loss of 5 utils to A but a gain of 8 utils to B—a net gain of 3 utils to society as a whole. It would therefore pay to transfer income from A to B until their marginal utilities were equal. This is as far as the marginal analysis carries us. We cannot draw from this proposition the conclusion that all incomes should be equal, for it is probable that the utility functions of different people are different. A man for whom the marginal utility of income declines rapidly with rising income should therefore have a smaller income than one for whom marginal utility declines slowly. In other words, they should be richest who most enjoy riches. We may well feel, however, that the task of deciding who enjoys riches most is one that can hardly be left to the judgment of a legislature, and that so refined a principle is incapable of instrumentation.

Progressive Taxation

Nevertheless, the principle of diminishing marginal utility of income is used, with some reason, to justify the principle of progressive taxation. Although we cannot assume that the utility schedules of all men are the same, they are probably not widely different. Consequently, it is not unreasonable to assume that a dollar taken from a rich man and given to a poor man increases its total utility by the transfer. In effect, this is what progressive taxation achieves. What degree of inequality is regarded as proper is a matter for the moral judgment.

The Dynamics of Equality

There are undoubtedly cost relationships between progress and equality though what they are is again a matter for speculation. In rich societies greater equality of income, by providing mass markets and increasing consumption, may favor economic growth by lessening unemployment. In a poor society, however, economic growth may require quite sharp inequalities, and too great equality might condemn the society to stagnation. A society of uniform mass poverty can hardly hope to accumulate or to concentrate resources in the hands of the innovators. At first economic growth frequently seems to accentuate inequality, as those few who participate in it draw away toward higher incomes from the mass of the society which still remains in the primitive condition. The end result of economic growth, however, seems to be a more equal distribution at the higher level, when all members of the society have been caught up in the more productive culture. As the pioneering middle class moves out of the morass of universal and equal poverty, inequality increases; but if the progress continues, the whole society is gradually drawn up into the plateau of universal and relatively equal comfort—a condition which we would be happily approaching in the more advanced countries, were it not for the specter of war.

The Attack on Economic Rent

A premature attempt at too great an equalization of incomes, then, may destroy productive activity and may hamper economic growth by taking away its rewards. Out of our analysis, therefore, comes a piece of advice to the lawmaker: wherever possible, attack economic rent. Economic rent we have defined as any payment to the owner of a factor of production in excess of what is required to keep that factor in continuous service. If such an excess is absorbed by taxation or regulation, there will be no diminution in the quantity of the factor supplied. But if taxation digs deeper than this surplus and attacks the actual "supply price" of the factor, the quantity supplied will be adversely affected. The advice is good; the difficulty is, of course, to find the economic rents. We certainly cannot assume either that economic rent is peculiar to the income from land or that the income from land is all economic rent. A great deal of labor income is economic rent, and in part the services of land are a "produced" commodity with a quite definite cost. We cannot even assume, with Henry George, that increments in land values are "economic rents." The increment of land value may be in many cases the reward of pioneering; and if full taxation of land values had been in effect in the nineteenth century, it is probable that the great westward expansion of the United States would never have taken place, for the expectation of rising land values was one motive which inspired the pioneers to invest their lives and comforts in the development of an empty continent. It is probable that a properly constructed income tax falls to a very large extent on economic rents. In so far as it applies to all occupations it does not affect *relative* profitabilities, and so cannot be escaped by shifting occupations. It may have some effect in reducing activity where the amount of labor offered by an individual is within his control, especially where the marginal rates of taxation are high. It may have some effect in discouraging risky innovation, especially where this may lead to highly irregular incomes, as the high tax rates of the successful years are not offset by the losses of poor years. There does not seem to be much direct evidence, however, that these effects are serious at the degree of progressiveness which prevails in the American tax system, though in so far as the deleterious effects are cumulative they may not show up in the short run.

Progress and Misallocation

Economic progress, as we have seen, inevitably involves the redistribution of resources among various occupations. Such redistribution, however, is inevitably accompanied by losses to the owners of resources, whether capital or labor, in a declining occupation and gains to those in an expanding occupation. The best solution to this problem is mobility—that is, rapid redistributions of resources in accordance with new structures of demand. Sometimes, however, mobility may not be possible, or may be costly, as in the case of highly specific equipment or skills. Such unavoidable losses may properly be charged as part of the cost of economic progress, and it seems unfair to make those on whom they normally fall bear the whole burden. If, however, these costs are charged to the innovator, we run grave risks of suppressing progress altogether. Consider, for instance, the philosophy of "equalizing competitive advantage"—a theory which has been applied, for instance, both to the tariff and to the taxation of chain stores. Tariffs are sometimes justified on the grounds that the tariff should compensate for the lower costs of the foreign producer, and chain store taxation is justified on the grounds that chain stores have lower costs than independents. Such a doctrine applied at an earlier date would have taxed railroads to the point where stagecoaches could compete with them, power looms to the point where hand looms could compete with them, and even spades to the point where fingers could compete with them. This is not to say that society has no duty to those dispossessed by technical progress or by changes in demand. But its efforts should be directed toward increasing mobility rather than toward freezing the existing structure by taxes and subsidies, and if compensation is to be given it should be charged to society as a whole.

The problem of evaluating the market structure of a society—that is, its competitive, monopolistic, or oligopolistic nature—is one of great difficulty. From the point of view of allocation and distribution there is a strong case against monopoly, as we have seen (pages 654–660). Too much competition, on the other hand, may be inimical to economic progress, for unless there is some degree of monopoly protection the fruits of innovation cannot be enjoyed by the innovator. This is the justification usually given for patent and copyright laws. Similarly, there are wastes of monopolistic competition in terms of undercapacity operation and competitive advertising, but there are also gains in terms of opportunities for variety and decentralization of control of information.

Progress, Freedom, and Character

Finally we come to the most difficult problem in evaluation, and yet one which cannot be shirked in the total evaluative process. What is the effect of various forms of economic life and institutions on individual freedom, character, and personality? Perhaps all that the economist dare do here is to point to the problem. Does the division of labor, as even Adam Smith suggested, produce narrow, ill-rounded characters? Does the increase of power which economic progress brings merely enable us to damn ourselves all the more easily—to satisfy the evil lusts and ambitions from which poverty would keep us free? Does the increase in the scale of organization which results from economic development impair personal freedom and the intimacy of personal relationships? These are questions to which the economist as such can give no clear answers, but which are nevertheless involved in any final appraisal of economic institutions and policies.

Conclusion: The Dismal Science?

The conclusions of our analysis will be disappointing to the student who seeks a panacea for all our problems. In the days of Malthus, economics earned justly the title of the "dismal science," not because it was dull but because its conclusions were so depressing to those who looked for a bright future for humanity. The Malthusian specter still haunts us, perhaps even in the developed economies. But the Malthusian hope also remains—that if it is expensive tastes rather than the biological urge which limits the growth of population, a stable and rich society is possible. We are still in the thick of the technical revolution, and where it is carrying us no man can say; but if it does not take us to destruction, there is at least a reasonable hope that it may take us to a new level of society as far removed from past and even present civilizations as they were from the barbarism which preceded them, and in which war, poverty, and disease will be effectively eliminated.

There is no cause, however, for undue optimism. If the dark dynamics of population growth does not dash the cup of plenty from our lips, the darker dynamics of national and ideological warfare may do even worse things to us. The hope which many once saw in socialism and in the conscious control of man's destiny has been dimmed by the dreadful spectacle of the communist world—the liquidation of the kulaks, the reliance on slave labor, the shocking disintegration of all decency and simplicity in personal relationships, the monstrous corruption and tyranny of the one-firm state. There is a dismal science of politics as well as of economics, and the attempt to abolish the free market and to set up a planned economy runs into economic and human diseconomies of scale, the substitution of violence and coercion for economic advantage as the prime mover of men, and the unspeakable horror of the manipulative society.

On the other hand, it must not be thought that the economist brings uniformly cheerful tidings to the supporters of capitalism. His results are profoundly disturbing to any who believe that capitalism with its attendant democracy is preferable to any form of planned economy. The optimism of "laissez faire," if it ever existed, is gone. It has become clear that an unregulated capitalism is liable to serious disorganization; it is subject to business cycles and periodic unemployment. It may also suffer from more serious ills: from "secular stagnation" as opportunities for further accumulation get used up, or from a creeping paralysis of political control and monopolistic restriction. It suffers perhaps even more from certain sociological diseases: from a failure to satisfy the deep needs in man for community, for "belonging to" something greater than himself. Hence, nationalism in extreme forms steps into the emotional gap which capitalism creates, and by the very growth of state power the foundations of a society based on a multiplicity of private institutions is destroyed.

We must recognize both the contribution and the limitations of economic analysis. Without a grasp of what it has to offer, we shall miss our way among the intolerable complexities of social life and the labyrinthine paths of history. But of itself it does not claim to provide a complete interpretation of history; we cannot say from economic analysis alone whether, for instance, socialism is inevitable or whether capitalism will survive. It does, however, point toward a certain philosophy of history and toward certain possible lines of human development. It encourages the hope that we may be able to find, somewhere between the ruthless extremes of totalitarian, monolithic socialism, and rudderless capitalism a developing middle way toward a "governed economy," in which the state shall have certain clear and perhaps extensive economic functions to perform in its capacity as a "governor" of the system, but in which the virtues of a "polylithic" society of many diverse and interacting free institutions and free individuals may be preserved.

PART IV

MORE ADVANCED STUDIES IN ANALYTICAL TECHNIQUES

INTRODUCTION

THREE-VARIABLE ANALYSIS

The greater part of the techniques of economic analysis has now been covered in outline. The principal method used has been the graphical method. There is a good reason why the graphic method has proved so useful in economics. Economics deals with certain functional relationships between various economic quantities, such as demand functions, cost functions, and so on. The exact algebraic form of these functions is usually not known. That is to say, we may know that the quantity demanded, (q), depends on—that is, is a function of—the price, (p), but we are not justified usually in assuming any explicit relationship between these two quantities, such as, for instance, $q = 10 - 6p - p^2$. To write almost any significant economic relationship as an explicit equation would be to assume too much. On the other hand, we know *something* about the shape and nature of these functions; to write them as a purely general function, $q = F(p)$ would be to assume too little. Graphic analysis enables us to discuss the relationships of functions of which we know the general character but no more; it is, therefore, extremely well suited to the tasks of economic analysis. It has, however, this severe limitation. A curve in two dimensions can only describe the relationships of two variables. If, therefore, we wish to describe graphically the relationship of three variables, e.g., the quantity of A demanded, the price of A, and the income of the demander, we must use a surface in three dimensions.

Three-dimensional figures are not, of course, so easy to draw or to visualize as two-dimensional ones. Fortunately, in most cases there is a simple method for expressing the shape of a three-dimensional surface in a two-dimensional figure. This is the method of contour lines or "isomers" used in mapping. A contour line or isomer is a line on a plane surface joining all those points on the surface which have some other quantity in common. Thus in a geographical contour map the 100-foot contour is the line which runs through all points on the map which are 100 feet above sea level; it represents the coast line which

731

would exist if the sea rose 100 feet. On a weather map the "isobars" are lines running through all places having the same barometric pressure, an isotherm is a line running through all places having the same temperature, and so on. By drawing a system of contours the shape of any nonre-entrant surface can be described on a plane diagram, and some of the difficulties involved in the construction of three-dimensional diagrams themselves obviated.

We can also represent relationships of three variables in schedule form by drawing a chessboard diagram in which each square represents a certain combination of two quantities, say X and Y, and the third quantity, Z, is written in the square.

CHAPTER 34

THREE-VARIABLE ANALYSIS OF A FIRM

We may conveniently begin our three-variable analysis by considering the relationships between *two* inputs and one output. A simple production schedule of the type illustrated in Table 57, page 587, is not now sufficient to show all the various relationships between the quantities of input and output. If the two inputs are labor and land, it is not sufficient to show how various quantities of labor will affect the product when a fixed quantity of land is used. We need a schedule to show not only how much product is produced with various quantities of labor applied to 8 acres, but how much product results from the application of various quantities of labor to 7, 6, 5, or any other number of acres. Such a schedule is illustrated in Table 64. The horizontal rows of this schedule show how much product (tons of potatoes) will be produced when the various quantities of labor (shown on the bottom row) are applied to a fixed quantity of land (shown at the left of the row). Thus with 8 acres of land 1 unit of labor produces 8 tons, 2 units 24 tons, 3 units 34 tons, and so on. This row corresponds to the production schedule in Table 57. Similarly, with 7 acres of land 1 unit of labor produces 9 tons, 2 units 24 tons, 3 units 32 tons, and so on. The columns of the table show how much product results from the application of various quantities of land to a fixed quantity of labor. Thus 4 units of labor on 1 acre produce 8 tons, on 2 acres 14 tons, on 3 acres 19 tons, and so on, reading up the column. From the complete schedule we can find, therefore, how many tons of potatoes will be produced by any combination of quantities of labor and land. Each of the heavy figures represents the number of tons of potatoes produced by the quantity of land shown at the head of the row and the quantity of labor shown at the foot of the column in which the figure lies. Thus we see that 7 acres of land and 5 units of labor produce 39 tons of potatoes. This table represents not successive results but the results of alternative combinations of the two inputs.

733

TABLE 64.   The Physical Production Table

	0	1	2	3	4	5	6	7	8	9
9	0	7	23	36	41	45	48	50	52	54
8	0	8	24	34	40	42	44	46	48	49
7	0	9	20	32	36	39	41	42	43	44
6	0	10	24	30	32	35	36	37	38	39
5	0	11	22	26	28	30	31	32	33	34
4	0	12	20	22	24	25	26	27	28	29
3	0	12	16	18	19	20	21	22	23	24
2	0	10	12	13	14	15	16	16½	16	15½
1	0	6	7	8	8	7	6½	6	5½	5
0	0	0	0	0	0	0	0	0	0	0
	0	1	2	3	4	5	6	7	8	9

(Left axis: Number of acres of land. Bottom axis: Number of man-months applied. Diagonals marked C, B, A.)

It should be read: *"If* 7 acres of land are used with 5 units of labor, *then* 39 tons of potatoes will result." In this part of our analysis we neglect the uncertainty of the results, and assume that the result of combining definite quantities of inputs can always be predicted by reference to the production schedule.

"Returns to Scale"

We have already examined the law of "eventually diminishing marginal productivity" in Chapter 28. We can see by examining Table 64 that this law applies to each column and to each row of the table. Now, however, a new property of the physical production schedule emerges when there are two variable inputs. We have seen what will happen to the product when one input is increased and the quantity of the other is kept constant. What will happen when *both* the inputs are increased in the same proportion? Instead of running our eye along one of the columns or rows of the table, let us run our eye diagonally from the bottom left-hand corner, i.e., from the zero point. In this way we can see what will happen when both inputs are increased in the same proportion. For instance, following the diagonal marked *B,* we see that with 1 unit of labor and 1 of land 6 tons are produced; with 2 units of labor and 2 of land 12 tons are produced; with 3 units of labor and 3 of land, 18 tons are produced; and so on. That is to say, as *both* inputs are increased in a given proportion, the output also increases in that proportion. Doubling both inputs doubles the output, trebling both inputs trebles the output, and so on. Similarly, diagonal *A* shows that 1 unit of land and 2 of labor produce 7 tons; 2 of land and 4 of labor, 14 tons; 3 of land and 6 of labor, 21 tons; and so on. Along diagonal *C*, 1 unit of labor and 3 of land produce 12 tons; 2 of labor and 6 of land produce 24 tons; 3 of labor and 9 of land produce 36 tons, and so on. The student may entertain himself by following out other diagonals to see whether this rule is universal in the figure.

The Laws of "Returns to Scale." Homogeneity

This property of a table is called, mathematically, "homogeneity." We shall call it the property of *constant returns to scale*. It means that if we take any combination of inputs and outputs and increase all but one in a given proportion, that one must also increase in the same proportion. Increasing all inputs in the same proportion is increasing the *scale* of the process. One thing is a "scale model" of another if all the measurements of the one are the same proportion of the corresponding measurements of the other. If we wished to build a scale model of the Capitol we would make all our measurements a given proportion—say $\frac{1}{1,000}$ of the measurements of the actual building. Similarly, in a process of production, if, when all inputs are changed by a given proportion, the output also changes in that proportion, then one process is a pure "scale model" of the other, and there are constant returns to scale. If, with all inputs changed in a given proportion, the output changed in a greater proportion, we should have *increasing* returns to scale. If, with all inputs changed in a given proportion, the output changed in a smaller proportion, we should have *decreasing* returns to scale. For instance, if, when the quantities of all inputs doubled, the quantity of output more than doubled, we should say that the process showed increasing returns to scale. And if under the same circumstances the output less than doubled, the process would show decreasing returns to scale.

The Confusion of the Two "Laws of Returns"

A great deal of confusion has been caused in economics by the failure to separate these two quite different "laws"—the law of change of marginal or average productivity, and the law of change of scale.

All too frequently economists have meant by "diminishing returns" the principle of eventually diminishing physical productivity, and by "increasing returns" the postulate of increasing returns to scale.

Diminishing Marginal Productivity and Substitution. Two Cases

Now *why* are we justified in assuming a law of eventually diminishing physical productivity? The answer is that the law of diminishing physical productivity is merely a way of expressing the fact that the inputs in a process are *not perfectly substitutable* one for the other. Unfortunately there seems to be no substitute for the deplorable word "substitutable." Nevertheless, the concept of substitutability is one of the most important in the whole of economic analysis. We can see the truth of this relationship by examining two extreme cases.

Fixed Proportions. Table 65 is a physical production table in which the inputs can be used only in absolutely fixed proportions. A possible case of this might be the production of certain alloys where if the ingredients are used in the right proportions, the desired product is obtained, and if they are used in any other proportions, it is not. Table 65 assumes that two inputs, "A" and "B," in equal proportions

TABLE 65. Fixed Proportions

Units of "A"						
5	0	0	0	0	0	30
4	0	0	0	0	24	0
3	0	0	0	18	0	0
2	0	0	12	0	0	0
1	0	6	0	0	0	0
0	0	0	0	0	0	0
	0	1	2	3	4	5
			Units of "B"			

TABLE 66. Perfect Substitutability

Units of "A"						
5	15	18	21	24	27	30
4	12	15	18	21	24	27
3	9	12	15	18	21	24
2	6	9	12	15	18	21
1	3	6	9	12	15	18
0	0	3	6	9	12	15
	0	1	2	3	4	5
			Units of "B"			

will produce an output, but in any other proportions they will produce nothing.

Perfect Substitutability. Table 66, on the other hand, is the physical production table for two inputs which are perfectly substitutable, i.e., which can be substituted one for the other at a given rate without the product being affected. Thus in Table 66, 1 of A and 3 of B, or 2 of A and 2 of B, or 3 of A and 1 of B, or even 4 of A and 0 of B all give the same product: 12. That is to say, we can use any combination of A and B, take away one unit of A and add one unit of B, and go on doing this without changing the quantity of product. Clearly, this could never be the case over the whole range, unless A and B were identically similar, or it would lead us to the preposterous conclusion that we could make a product without any quantity of an essential ingredient! Nevertheless, inputs may be perfectly substitutable over short ranges, though even this is unlikely.

Diminishing Productivity in These Two Cases

What has happened in Tables 65 and 66 to our "law of eventually diminishing physical productivity"? In Table 66 we see that looking along any row of the table the marginal physical productivity of input B is constant and equal to 3. That is to say, if we add 1 unit of B to a fixed quantity of A, the result is always an increase of 3 units of product. There is no "diminishing marginal physical productivity" at all, for the inputs are perfectly substitutable. Looking up the columns, we see that the marginal physical productivity of input A is likewise constant, and does not decline as we increase the quantity of A which we combine with a fixed quantity of B.

Table 65, on the other hand, shows that along any row the product remains at zero as the quantity of input B is increased, until the "correct" proportions are reached. Then the product immediately rises, and immediately falls to zero again as the quantity of B is increased beyond the correct proportions. That is, the marginal physical productivity, at the point of correct proportions, diminishes very rapidly indeed. For instance, with 2 units of A and 1 of B there is no product; adding one unit of B increases the product by 12 units; the marginal physical productivity over that range is 12. Adding another unit of B reduces the product again to zero; the marginal physical product is −12. With infinitesimally small units of inputs which could not be substituted one for the other the rate of diminution of marginal physical productivity would be infinite.

The "Best Proportions"

In the more usual case represented by our original Table 64, page 734, the inputs are substitutable to some extent; i.e., the proportions in which they are used can be varied in some degree. Nevertheless, they are not perfectly substitutable. There will be, as we shall see, some proportion which is the "best," and too great a proportion of either input will yield worse results than the "best" proportions. It is the fact that some *proportions* of input are better than others which gives rise to the law of eventually diminishing marginal physical productivity. As we start adding a variable input to a *fixed* quantity of the other inputs we shall first find that we *approach* the best proportions. The additional units of the variable factor therefore produce more than proportionable returns in product; the marginal physical productivity of that factor is increasing. Soon, however, we reach and then pass, the "best" proportions. As our variable factor is increased from this point the proportions get worse and worse all the time. Consequently, the marginal physical productivity declines, and eventually the addition of more of the variable factor actually lessens the product—i.e., the marginal physical productivity becomes negative.

"Increasing Returns to Scale" Frequently Only Apparent

Thus the problem of "diminishing returns," in the sense of diminishing marginal physical productivity, essentially relates to the problem of the *proportions* of the inputs used. The problem of increasing, decreasing, or constant returns to *scale* has nothing to do with the change in the proportions of the input quantities. Frequently, however, what appears to be variable returns to scale turns out to be nothing but a subtle example of variable marginal physical productivity. For instance, it is often the case that doubling the size of a factory, the number of machines in it, and the number of men and the quantities of materials employed more than doubles the output. We may be tempted to regard this immediately as an example of increasing returns to scale, or, as it is often called, "the economies of large-scale production." However, we have overlooked one kind of input—management. What we have really been doing is to hold constant the quantity of one input, management, and to vary the quantities of all the others. It is possible that the proportion of management to the other inputs was better in the larger factory and that management was being "underworked" in the smaller factory, just as land might be underworked when it had only a small quantity of labor employed on it.

But Genuine Variability of Returns to Scale Is Possible

This is not to say, however, that a genuine variability of returns to scale is not possible in economic life, though its presence is difficult to prove. It is perhaps difficult to see at first why, if we could double *all* inputs, including the "quantity of management," we should not also double the output. Nevertheless, there are examples from nature which show that genuine variable returns to scale exist. For instance, a flea can jump over a scale model of the Capitol, scaled down to the size of the flea. If a flea were as big as a man, however, it could not jump over the Capitol in Washington. Indeed, it could not jump at all. Its legs would break. This is due to the fact that the strength of muscles and bones is proportional to their *cross section,* which is an area. The weight of an object is proportional to its *volume.* Now, as the size of any object is increased according to scale, its volume increases as the cube of the proportionate increase in length, but its areas increase only as the square. Multiply the length, breadth, and height of a flea by 1000 and you will have increased all its areas by 1,000,000, and all its volumes by 1,000,000,000. You will have increased its weight by a thousand times more than the increase in its strength of bone and muscle. No wonder it would break in pieces! Sizes, therefore, and not merely the proportion of the parts, are important in nature and account for the different structures of things of different sizes— for the slender legs of the insect, the tiny legs of the mouse, the sturdy legs of man, the gigantic legs of the elephant, and the flippers of the whale.

The same may be true of enterprises. A moderately large enterprise may be more efficient than a small one simply because it is bigger. Quite apart from the possibility of varying the proportions of the factors, the very size of an enterprise may permit a better or worse use of the factors employed in it. Very large enterprises may be unwieldy, and may even break under their own weight. Very large combinations, for instance, have occasionally broken down because of the sheer weight of bureaucracy necessary to maintain them. The possibility of genuine departures from homogeneity in the production schedule must therefore be taken into consideration. It is quite possible that at small scales there may be "increasing returns to scale," but at large scales "decreasing returns to scale" may be the rule.

Graphic Representation. The graphic representation of Table 64 introduces some difficulties not present in the simple cases in Chapter 28, as here we are dealing with three quantities—labor, land, and product—and consequently have to use three dimensions, length, breadth, and height, in order to represent their relations. Consider the little boxes in Table 64 containing the product quantities. The position of any one of these, relative to the axes OX and OY, shows from what *combination* of quantities of land and labor the product figure within it is derived. Thus the "box" at the top right-hand corner containing the figure 54, shows that nine units of labor combined with nine units of land yield 54 units of potatoes. Now suppose that on each of these boxes we build a little tower, equal in height to the figure in the box. We should then have a solid figure which would give all the

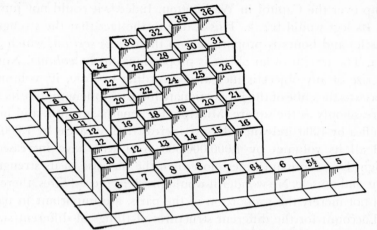

FIG. 109. Physical Production Surface.

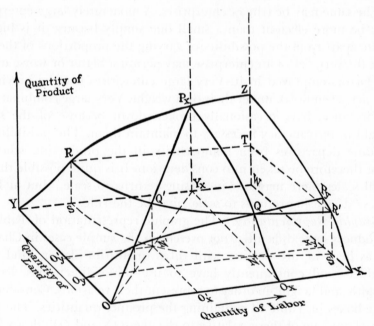

FIG. 110. Physical Production Surface.

relationships between the three quantities, labor, land, and product, just as a figure on flat paper will show the relationships between any *two* quantities. Part of this figure is shown in perspective in Fig. 109.

If the units of land, labor, and product are extremely small, the "steps" in Fig. 109 will be smoothed out and will form a *surface* shaped like Fig. 110. This is the *physical production surface.* Any point on the surface, such as Q, represents a certain combination of labor, land, and product quantities. If we drop a perpendicular, QN, to the base, and drop perpendiculars NO_y to OY and NO_x to OX, then NQ represents the quantity of product produced by an amount OO_x of labor and an amount OO_y of land.

The Total Product Curve

A perpendicular "slice" of this figure parallel to OX, such as $O_yP_yX_y$, gives us a curve O_yQP_y, which is a total product curve like that in Fig. 86, showing the relation between the total product and the quantity of labor when the quantity of land is kept constant and equal to OO_y. Similarly, a perpendicular section such as $O_xP_xY_x$ cut parallel to OY gives us a total product curve O_xQP_x, showing the relation between the total product and the quantity of land, under the condition that the quantity of labor, OO_x, is constant. The "symmetry" of the principle of diminishing marginal physical productivity is evident from the figure; the curves O_yQP_y and O_xQP_x have the same general shape.

The "Iso-Product" Curve

Suppose now that we take a slice parallel to the base plane, such as RTR'; what is the significance of the curve RQR'? This is a line which connects all those points on the surface at which the product is equal to SR; that is to say, it is a "contour line" of the surface. Its projection on to the base, SNS', we shall call an "iso-product" curve or a "product contour."[1] Any point on it represents a combination of input quantities which will produce the same output, SR. Thus, to return to Table 64, all those combinations in the product "boxes" which yield 24 tons of potatoes—for example, 6 of land and 2 of labor, 4 of land and 4 of labor, and 3 of land and 9 of labor—will lie on an "iso-product" curve. Just as isotherms are lines which connect on a map all points having the same temperature, so iso-product curves are lines connecting all points which yield the same product.

[1] This curve is often called the "isoquant," being a curve of equal quantities. As, however, there are many kinds of isoquants, I have thought it better to retain the name given above.

The System of Product Contours

It is clear that just as we can represent a mountain on a flat map by drawing its contours, so we can represent a physical production surface on a flat diagram by drawing its "contours," i.e., its iso-product curves. Thus in Fig. 111 the curve P_6 represents all those combinations of land and labor quantities which produce 6 tons of potatoes; the

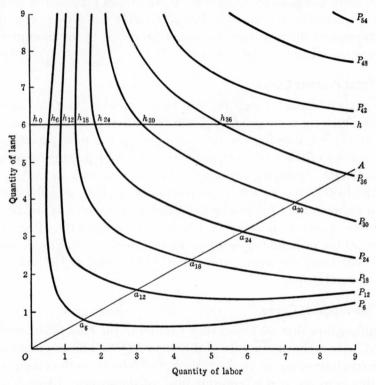

FIG. 111.   Product Contours.

curve P_{12} represents all those combinations of land and labor quantities which produce 12 tons of potatoes; and so on. Those who are accustomed to reading contour maps will readily visualize this figure as a surface—a "mountain" rising up from the origin. Fig. 111, then, is another way of describing the facts described in Table 64.

"Returns to Scale" on the Physical Production Surface

Let us now see how "returns to scale" can be expressed in our figures. With constant returns to scale we saw that increasing *both* labor and land in the same proportion also increases the total product in that proportion. This property of the physical production table is expressed in the physical production surface, Fig. 110, by the fact that any line drawn from the origin, O, to touch the surface will touch it at all points of its length. That is to say, a slice of the surface through the origin perpendicular to the base plane, such as OP_xY_x, will cut the surface in a straight line, OP_x. To put it in another way, if the surface shows constant returns to scale, it must be made by moving a straight line with one end fixed at O and the other end moving over a path such as $YRZR'X$.

This follows from a well-known property of similar triangles. If from any point, Q', on the line OP_x a perpendicular $Q'N'$ is dropped to the base plane, the triangles $OQ'N'$ and OP_xY_x are similar. Therefore, $\dfrac{ON'}{OY_x} = \dfrac{N'Q'}{Y_xP_x}$. Also, dropping the perpendiculars $N'O'_x$ to OX and $N'O'_y$ to OY we see that triangles $ON'O'_x$ and OY_xO_x are similar, and triangles $ON'O'_y$ and OY_xY are similar. Therefore $\dfrac{ON'}{OY_x} = \dfrac{OO'_x}{OO_x} = \dfrac{OO'_y}{OY} = \dfrac{N'Q'}{Y_xP_x}$. That is, a given proportionate increase in both land and labor quantities will cause the product quantity to increase in the same proportion. If the line $OQ'P_x$ were curving upward there would be increasing returns to scale; if it were curving downward there would be decreasing returns to scale.

Properties of the Product Contour Map

Most of the properties of the physical production surface can be represented by means of a product contour map like Fig. 111. The use of such a map is therefore a great convenience, as it enables us to represent a relationship between three variables on a plane figure, and avoids the use of awkward three-dimensional diagrams.

If the production surface is homogeneous (with constant returns to scale), then *any* diagonal from the origin, such as OA, will be divided into equal segments by successive product contours. If the contours in Fig 111 represent a homogeneous production surface and the product contours P_6, P_{12}, etc., cut the line OA at a_6, a_{12}, etc., then $Oa_6 = a_6a_{12} = a_{12}a_{18} = a_{18}a_{24}$, etc. This rule follows from the definition of a homogeneous production surface as one in which equal proportionate increases in both inputs produce equal proportionate increases in output. If there are decreasing returns to scale, successive intercepts on a diagonal will become larger and larger. Then $Oa_6 < a_6a_{12} < a_{12}a_{18} < a_{18}a_{24}$, etc. Similarly, if there are increasing returns to scale the successive intercepts will become smaller. In the case of decreasing returns to scale the "mountain" of the production surface becomes flatter as we climb, and the contours therefore become farther and farther apart. In the case of increasing returns to scale the "mountain" becomes steeper as we climb, and the contours get closer together.

The law of diminishing marginal productivity is illustrated by the intercepts made by successive contours on a line parallel with either axis. Consider the line h_0h. As the quantity of labor increases, with the quantity of land constant as Oh_0, the intercepts h_0h_6, h_6h_{12}, $h_{12}h_{18}$, etc., eventually increase, indicating the fact that to produce successive equal increments of product increasing increments of labor must be used.

Drawing the product contours corresponding to Table 66, we shall find that they are straight lines running diagonally across the figure. If, therefore, the product contours have no curvature, the inputs are perfectly substitutable. The product contours corresponding to Table 65, where no substitution is possible between the inputs, have an infinite curvature, for they have contracted to a point. The curvature of a product contour, then, is a possible measure of the degree of substitution of the two inputs. Where the product contours have a small curvature, the substitution of one input for another (represented by moving along the contour) does not greatly affect the *rate* of substitution. But if a product contour is curved sharply, as one input is substituted for another it takes more and more of the expanding input to replace one unit of the contracting input. This is a sign that the inputs are not easily substitutable.

The "Best Combination" Problem

When there are two variable inputs a problem arises because there are many ways of producing a *given* output. This was not true in the case in which only one input could be varied; Table 57, for instance, shows that to produce 24 tons of potatoes 2 units of labor must be used on 8 acres. This is the only way to produce 24 tons with 8 acres, and it must therefore be the best way to produce 24 tons! Table 64, however, shows that 24 tons of potatoes can be produced either with 8 acres and 2 units of labor or with 6 acres and 2 units of labor, or with 4 acres and 4 units of labor or with 3 acres and 9 units of labor, as well as with an indefinite number of intermediate combinations not shown in the schedule. Now, if the producer decides to grow 24 tons of potatoes, which is the best of all these alternative ways of doing it? We shall not yet inquire why he wants to produce 24 tons and not any other quantity, for that part of the solution comes later. Before the final solution can be given we must know the best combination of inputs which will produce any given quantity of output.

Example.   Table 67, section (a), shows a number of these possible

TABLE 67.   The Least Outlay Combination

(a)	Quantity of labor	2	3.0	4.0	5.0	6.0	7.0	8.0	9	Men
	Quantity of land	6	4.5	4.0	3.7	3.5	3.3	3.1	3.0	Acres
(b)	Labor @ $20 unit	40	60	80	100	120	140	160	180	$
	Land @ $20 unit	120	90	80	74	70	66	62	60	$
	Total outlay	160	(150)	160	174	190	206	222	240	$
(c)	Labor @ $10 unit	20	30	40	50	60	70	80	90	$
	Land @ $10 unit	60	45	40	37	35	33	31	30	$
	Total outlay	80	(75)	80	87	95	103	111	120	$
(d)	Labor @ $10 unit	20	30	40	50	60	70	80	90	$
	Land @ $30 unit	180	135	120	111	105	99	93	90	$
	Total outlay	200	165	(160)	161	165	169	173	180	$
(e)	Labor @ $10 unit	20	30	40	50	60	70	80	90	$
	Land @ $40 unit	240	180	160	148	140	132	124	120	$
	Total outlay	260	210	200	(198)	200	202	204	210	$

◯ = Least outlay combination

combinations. Which is the "best"? Will it pay to produce 24 tons with a lot of labor and a little land or with a little labor and a lot of land or with some combination in between? Obviously, from the point of view of the producer the "best" combination of inputs is that which he can purchase for the least amount of money. In order to find out how much money must be expended (the "total outlay") in the purchase of any combination of quantities of input, however, we must first know the *prices* of these inputs. In Table 67, section (b), then, is calculated the total outlay required to purchase the various combinations shown in section (a), on the assumption that the price of labor is $20 per man-month and the price of land is $20 per acre for the appropriate period. The total outlay on labor in each case is the quantity bought multiplied by the price; the total outlay on land is also the quantity bought multiplied by the price, and the sum of these quantities is the total outlay expended on the purchase of the combination. In the case represented by section (b) of this table it is evident that the "least outlay combination" of inputs is 3 units of labor and 4.5 units of land, where the total outlay is $150.

The "Least Outlay Combination" Depends on the Relative Prices of Input

Now let us see whether the least outlay combination changes when we change the prices of the inputs concerned. Section (c) of Table 67 gives the case in which the price of *both* inputs is $10 per unit instead of $20 as in section (b). It is evident that the least outlay combination is still 3 units of labor with 4.5 units of land, where the total outlay is $75. A proportionate change in the prices of *both* inputs therefore does not change the quantities of input which form the least outlay combination; it merely changes the total expense involved in purchasing the least outlay combination. In section (d), however, the price of land has risen relative to the price of labor, land now being $30 per unit and labor $10 per unit. It will be seen from the table that the "least outlay combination" is now 4 units of labor and 4 units of land, where the total outlay is $160. Similarly, in section (e), where the price of land is $40 per unit as against $10 per unit for labor, the least outlay combination is 5 units of labor and 3.7 units of land. Evidently, as land increases in price relative to labor, the cheaper input (labor) will oust the dearer input (land), and the proportion of labor used will increase relative to the amount of land used. That is to say, when one input increases in price relative to another, the cheaper input is substituted, up to a point, for the dearer input. This, of course, is what we should expect.

The Rule for Finding the Least Outlay Combination

The economist does not rest content with the mere proposition that under most conditions there exists some combination of inputs which is the "least outlay combination." He wants a formula which will enable him to find this combination. The provision of this formula, and of others like it, is the principal task of the marginal analysis.

The Rate of Product Substitution

In the search for this formula we must first define an important concept, *the rate of product substitution*. The rate of product substitution of input A for input B may be defined as the quantity of input A which must be substituted in place of one unit of input B in order to leave the total product unchanged. If the rate of product substitution of land for labor were half an acre per "man," this would mean that subtracting 1 man from the total amount of labor used and adding half an acre of land to the amount of land used would not change the total production (of potatoes in this case). Thus Table 67 shows that 24 tons of potatoes can be produced with 3 men and 4.5 acres of land. If 1 man is added to the quantity of labor and half an acre is subtracted from the quantity of land—that is, 1 unit of labor is substituted for half an acre of land—the result is 4 man-months and 4 acres, which also produces 24 tons of potatoes. In this range the rate of product substitution is half an acre of land per man-month of labor.

The Rate of Outlay Substitution

Corresponding to the concept of a rate of product substitution is the concept of a *rate of outlay substitution*. The rate of outlay substitution of input A for input B is the quantity of input A which must be substituted in place of one unit of input B in order to leave the combined outlay on the two inputs unchanged. If the rate of outlay substitution of land for labor were 2 acres per man, adding 2 acres of land and subtracting 1 man would not change the total outlay on both labor and land.

These Rates Are Equal at the Least Outlay Combination

We shall now prove that the combination of input quantities at which the total outlay incurred in producing a given quantity of product is a minimum, i.e., the least outlay combination is that at which the rate of product substitution is equal to the rate of outlay substitution. Suppose first that the rate of product substitution of land for labor is half an acre per man, and that the rate of outlay substitution is more—say, three-quarters of an acre per man. If, then, half an acre of land is substituted in place of 1 man-month, the product will be unchanged but the total outlay will be less, for it would take three-quarters of an acre of land to replace 1 man-month and leave the total outlay unchanged. If, however, the total outlay can be lessened by replacing labor by land, this will be done, for evidently the point of minimum total outlay has not been reached. Similarly, if the rate of outlay substitution in this case were less than the rate of product substitution, say, one-quarter acre per man-month, the replacement of land by labor will again lessen the total outlay. Apparently the total outlay is not at a minimum unless the rate of product substitution is equal to the rate of outlay substitution. When this is the case the total outlay cannot be diminished either by substituting land for labor or by substituting labor for land.

Rate of Outlay Substitution Equal to Ratio of Marginal Costs for Input

The marginal cost of input is the increase in its total cost which results from a unit addition to purchases (see page 594). Suppose now that the marginal cost of labor is $10 per man-day and of land is $30 per acre-day. This means that the addition of one man-day to the amount of labor purchased adds $10 to the total outlay on labor and the addition of one acre-day to the amount of land purchased adds $30 to the total outlay on land. That is to say, if we give up 1 unit of land we can add 3 units of labor with the money released without adding to total outlay; the rate of outlay substitution is 3 units of labor per unit of land, or $\frac{1}{3}$ units of land per unit of labor.

Rate of Product Substitution Equal to Ratio of Marginal Productivities of Input

In an exactly similar way it can be shown that the rate of product substitution is the ratio of the marginal productivities of input. Thus if the marginal physical productivity of land is 4 tons of potatoes per acre, and of labor is 2 tons of potatoes per man, then adding $\frac{1}{2}$ ($= \frac{2}{4}$) acre of land in place of 1 man-month of labor will leave the product unchanged. Adding the half acre of land will increase the product by 2 tons, for adding one acre would increase it by 4 tons. Subtracting 1 man-month of labor will decrease the product by 2 tons. The result of adding half an acre of land and subtracting one man-month of labor will therefore be to leave the total product unchanged.

The Least Outlay Condition

We can now restate the least outlay condition as follows: Outlay will be least when

$$\frac{\text{Marginal productivity of labor}}{\text{Marginal productivity of land}} = \frac{\text{Marginal cost of labor}}{\text{Marginal cost of land}}$$

When the market for an input is perfect (see page 595) the marginal cost of input is equal to the price of the input, for if the addition to purchases does not change the price of the input, each unit addition to purchases raises the total cost of the input by an amount equal to the price. When, therefore, both inputs have perfect markets we can rewrite the least outlay condition as follows:

$$\frac{\text{Marginal productivity of labor}}{\text{Marginal productivity of land}} = \frac{\text{Price of labor}}{\text{Price of land}}$$

Geometric Solution. The problem of finding the least expensive way of producing a given quantity of product can be solved by the use of product contours. Our first task is to devise a construction whereby we can represent the *total outlay* on two inputs together in relation to various combinations of inputs. In Fig. 112 the quantity

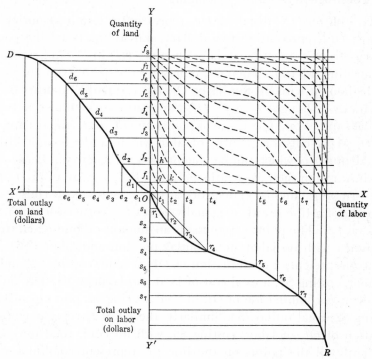

Fig. 112.   Construction of Outlay Contours.

of labor is measured along OX, the total outlay on labor along OY'. Then the line OR is the *total outlay curve* for labor; it shows how the total amount spent on labor varies with the amount of labor bought. If the price of labor is constant this curve will be a straight line through the origin. In Fig. 112, however a more general case is shown with three possible market situations. As the quantity of labor increases from O to Ot_5, the price gradually falls, indicating a condition in which the enterprise is getting a "reduction for quantity." The price of labor at any point on the outlay curve—e.g., at r_4—is the slope of the line Or_4, or $\dfrac{t_4 r_4}{Ot_4}$. From the quantity Ot_5 to Ot_7 we assume that the price is constant. The outlay curve, $r_5 r_7$, in this range is a straight line whose projection passes through the origin, O. Above the quantity Ot_7 we assume that the market is imperfect, i.e., that as the firm tries to buy more and more labor the price rises against it. This is reflected in the increasing steepness of the outlay curve after r_7. The outlay curve for land, OD, is treated similarly. The slope of a total outlay curve at any point is the marginal cost of the input.

The Construction of "Outlay Contours"

Mark off on OX' distances Oe_1 representing 1 unit of outlay (one dollar), Oe_2 representing two dollars, and so on. Draw the perpendiculars from e_1 meeting the outlay curve OD in d_1, and from d_1 to OY meeting OY in f_1. Then Of_1 represents the quantity of land which can be bought with \$1. Similarly, Of_2 represents the quantity of land which can be bought with \$2, Of_3 the quantity which can be bought with \$3, and so on. The range of points on OX, t_1, t_2, t_3, etc., are similar; Ot_1 represents the quantity of labor which can be bought with \$1, Ot_2 the quantity which can be bought with \$2, and so on. Perpendiculars drawn from their axes at the points f_1, f_2, f_3, etc., and from t_1, t_2, t_3, etc., form a rectangular framework as in the figure. Now consider the meaning of a line drawn diagonally across the corners of this framework, as f_3t_3. The point f_3 represents an amount of land equal to Of_3, combined with no labor; total outlay on land and labor is \$3. The point h represents a combination of Of_2 of land, costing \$2, and Ot_1 of labor, costing \$1; a total cost of land and labor of \$3. The point k represents a combination of Of_1 of land, costing \$1, plus Ot_2 of labor, costing \$2; total outlay, \$3. Similarly, the point t_3 represents a combination of Ot_3 of labor, costing \$3, with no land; total outlay, \$3. Evidently all the points on the line f_3t_3 represent combinations of input quantities which can be bought for a total sum of \$3. Likewise, all the points on the line f_4t_4 represent all those combinations of input quantities which can be bought for \$4; and so for the whole system of dotted lines in the figure.

Just as we called the line joining all those points representing combinations of input quantities which produced the same product an "iso-product" curve or a "product contour," so we can call the dotted lines of Fig. 112 "iso-outlay" curves or "outlay contours." They represent the contours of a "total outlay surface" in which the total amount spent on purchasing any combination of input quantities is measured vertically.

It will be observed that when both markets are imperfect the outlay contours are concave to the origin, as in the top right-hand corner of the figure. When in both markets the price is smaller for larger quantities (a state which we have called [p. 526] a "pluperfect" market!), the outlay contours are convex to the origin, as in the bottom left-hand corner of the figure. When both markets are perfect the outlay contours are straight lines. The outlay contours are the contours of a three-dimensional "outlay surface," in which the total outlay of any combination is measured vertically above the plane of Fig. 112. The surface is generated by erecting the outlay curves OR and OD in a vertical plane above OX and OY respectively, and by moving one curve at right angles to its plane with its origin moving along the other curve.

"Least Outlay Combination" Is Where Outlay and Product Contours Touch

In Fig. 113 a product contour (PP_1P_2) is superimposed on a system of outlay contours. For the sake of simplicity we suppose that the markets for input are perfect throughout, so that the outlay contours

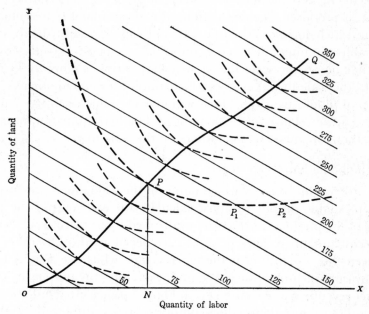

FIG. 113.   The Scale Line.

are straight lines. Let the product contour represent all those combinations of input quantities which will produce 24 tons of potatoes. Then the *cheapest* combination of inputs which will produce this amount is given by the point P, where the product contour is touched by an outlay contour. The outlay contours are marked with the total outlay which they represent; thus the point P_2 represents a combination which can be bought with $200, P_1 a combination which can be bought with $175; P a combination which can be bought with $150. Evidently, as long as we stick to the dotted product contour we cannot find any combination of input which will give us 24 tons of potatoes and which can be bought for less than $150. To take a quantity of labor represented by ON and a quantity of land represented by NP, therefore, is the cheapest way of producing 24 tons of potatoes. For any other quantity of potatoes also, we can draw a product contour and find the point where it is touched by an outlay contour.

The "Scale Line"

A line OPQ drawn through all these points shows all the combinations of quantities of labor and land that are cheapest for producing the amount of potatoes which they do in fact produce. This line may be called the "scale line,"[2] for it shows how the quantities of labor and land will rise as the scale of the enterprise rises, i.e., as more and more output is produced. A combination of labor and land represented by a point which does not lie on the scale line cannot possibly be the most profitable combination to take, for from any point—say P_1—which does not lie on the scale line it will be possible, simply by moving toward the scale line along a product contour, to find another combination of input quantities which will give the same quantity of product at a lower total outlay. The most profitable combination of quantities, therefore, must lie somewhere on the scale line.

The Final Solution

In order to find exactly which point on the scale line represents the most profitable output we must calculate for each output the total value of the product (its quantity multiplied by its price) and also the total cost (quantity times price of each input used). The difference between these quantities is the net revenue, which we assume to be the measure of profitability. We find, therefore, the output at which the net revenue is a maximum (as in Fig. 78, page 553), then returning to Fig. 113 we find the product contour corresponding to this output. The point where this product contour cuts the scale line and is touched by an outlay contour shows the most profitable quantity of

[2] The "scale line" is frequently called the "expansion path." The term "expansion path," however, is somewhat misleading, as it suggests that as a matter of historic fact a firm will expand along this line. This is not necessarily true; the scale line is merely a *construction* line by which the most profitable point in the field of the diagram can be discovered.

land and labor to employ. On the base of Fig. 113 we can erect a total revenue surface, showing the total revenue or value of product corresponding to each combination of labor and land. Similarly, we can erect a total cost surface, showing the total cost corresponding to each combination of labor and land. The point where the vertical distance of the revenue surface above the cost surface is greatest is the absolutely most profitable combination of the two factors. The contours of the revenue surface will be identical in shape with the product contours, as each product contour, representing as it does all combinations of land and labor which produce a given output, must also represent those combinations which produce the value of that output. Thus if the price of 24 tons of product is $10 per ton, the 24-ton product contour is also the $240 revenue contour. Provided that all other costs are held constant, the outlay contours will be identical in shape with the cost contours.

On the Scale Line, the Rates of Substitution for Product and Outlay Are Equal

The condition which indicates when we are on the scale line, i.e., which tells us that there is no cheaper way of obtaining the quantity of product being produced, is the condition described on page 748, that the ratio of the marginal physical productivities of the two inputs should be equal to the ratio of their marginal costs. We can see this by considering the significance of the *slopes* of the product contours and outlay contours. The slope of one of the product contours is the *rate of product substitution* of land for labor at that point. When the product contour is steep it means that a great deal must be added to the quantity of land in order to make up for the loss of one unit of labor. If the product contour is flat it means that only a little land need be added in order to make up for the loss of one unit of labor, and still keep the same quantity of product. We have already seen on page 748 that this slope is equal to the ratio $\dfrac{\text{Marginal productivity of labor}}{\text{Marginal productivity of land}}$.

The slope of an outlay contour is the *rate of outlay substitution* of land for labor; it measures how much land must be substituted for one unit of labor in order to keep unchanged the total amount spent on land and labor together. If the outlay contour is steep that means that a lot of land must be added to take the place of one unit of labor, in order to keep the same total outlay. If the outlay curve is flat it means that only a little land is needed to take the place of one unit of labor in order to keep the same total outlay. We can show (page 749) that the rate of outlay substitution of land for labor is equal to the ratio $\dfrac{\text{Marginal cost of labor}}{\text{Marginal cost of land}}$.[3]

At a point where a product curve and an outlay curve are tangent their slopes are identical—that is, the rate of product substitution is equal to the rate of outlay substitution and the condition

$$\frac{\text{Marginal productivity of labor}}{\text{Marginal productivity of land}} = \frac{\text{Marginal cost of labor}}{\text{Marginal cost of land}}$$

is fulfilled.

The Scale Line Enables Us to Separate Problem of Proportions from Problem of Scale

One great advantage of the scale line as a weapon of analysis is that it enables us to divide the problem of production into two rough parts—the problem of the *proportions of input quantities* on the one hand, and the problem of the *scale of operations* on the other. If the scale line is a straight line through the origin, then any point on it represents a definite *proportion* of input quantities—a proportion represented by the slope of the line itself. In Fig. 113 the steeper the scale line, the greater the proportion of land used and the less the proportion of labor. If the scale line is not straight we cannot make any simple separation of the problem of proportions from the problem of scale. We can still distinguish, however, between swings of the scale

---

[3] In terms of Fig. 112 the marginal outlay at any point measures the *slope* of the total outlay curve at that point. Thus between, say, a purchase of Ot_1 and Ot_2 units the total outlay rises from Os_1 to Os_2. Therefore a rise of s_1s_2 dollars of outlay is caused by the increase in purchases of t_1t_2 units; the marginal outlay is $\dfrac{s_1s_2}{t_1t_2}$ dollars per unit. But this ratio is the slope of the outlay curve in the range r_1r_2.

Consider now the slope of an outlay contour—say, the contour f_3t_3 between h and k. The slope is equal to $\dfrac{qh}{qk}$ which in turn is equal to $\dfrac{f_1f_2}{t_1t_2}$. Now we know also that:

$$\text{Marginal outlay on labor between } t_1 \text{ and } t_2 = \frac{s_1s_2}{t_1t_2}$$

$$\text{Marginal outlay on land between } f_1 \text{ and } f_2 = \frac{e_1e_2}{f_1f_2}$$

But we know by the construction that $s_1s_2 = e_1e_2$. Therefore:

$$\frac{\text{Marginal outlay on labor}}{\text{Marginal outlay on land}} = \frac{f_1f_2}{t_1t_2} = \text{slope of } hk.$$

But $\left(\dfrac{f_1f_2}{t_1t_2}\right)$ is the number of units of land which have to be substituted for one unit of labor in order to keep the total outlay constant in the range from h to k. In other words, it is the rate of outlay substitution of land for a unit of labor, and is also the slope of the outlay contour in that range.

line itself, which correspond roughly to changes in proportions, and movements along the scale line, which indicate changes in scale.

APPLICATIONS TO THE CASE OF PERFECT MARKETS FOR INPUT

We can now apply this analysis to some problems involving perfect markets for input.

Equal Proportionate Change in Prices of All Inputs Causes Change in Scale Only

If the prices of the inputs change *in the same ratio,* there will be no change in the position of the scale line and hence, roughly, no change in the proportions of the inputs used. If, for instance, the prices of labor and land both double, there will be no change in the rate of outlay substitutions; $^{3}\!/_{10}$ is just the same as $^{6}\!/_{20}$. The slopes of the outlay contours will not therefore be changed, although there will be a change in the total outlay which each contour represents, i.e., in the "height" of the contour. The scale of the process is likely to decline, but there will be no change in the proportions of the inputs used.

Change in Relative Prices of Inputs Also Changes Proportions Used

If, on the other hand, the price of labor changes in a different ratio from the price of land, there will be a change in the rate of outlay substitution, and the proportions of input—the slope of the scale line —will change. Suppose the price of land increases from $10 to $15 per acre while the price of labor increases from $30 to $60 per man-month. The rate of outlay substitution of land for labor will rise from 3 acres per man-month to 4 acres per man-month. That is to say, the outlay contours will all become *steeper.* Consequently, they will touch the product contours at a point above the old point, where the product contour is also steeper. That is, the scale line will also become steeper; the result of an increase in the price of labor relative to that of land is to increase the proportion of land taken and to decrease the proportion of labor. This is what we should expect; the input which has become relatively cheaper is substituted in place of the input which has become relatively dearer.

Graphic Illustration. This is illustrated in Fig. 114. P_1P_0 (dotted) represents a product contour, $C_0C'_0$ an outlay contour touching the product contour at P_0. OP_0 is then the scale line. Suppose the price of labor rises relative to the price of land. The outlay contours become steeper; $C_1C'_1$ is one of the new outlay contours, which touches the

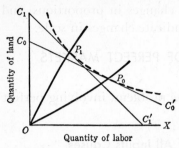

FIG. 114.   Effect of a Relative Rise in the Price of Labor.

product contour at P_1. OP_1 is the new scale line. Obviously, the result has been to increase the proportion of land used at the expense of labor; the relatively cheaper land is substituted for the relatively dearer labor.

Change in Proportions Depends on Product Substitutability of Inputs

It is clear from Fig. 114 that the extent of the change in the proportions of inputs with the change in relative prices depends on the curvature of the iso-product curves. If these are very slightly curved there must be a long swing from P_0 to P_1 before the rate of product substitution is equal to the new rate of outlay substitution. If the curvature is sharp the swing will be correspondingly small. The curvature of the iso-product curve is, however, a measure of the degree of substitutability of the inputs (page 736). The more substitutable the inputs, therefore, the more the proportions of inputs will shift in response to a given change in relative prices, and the less stable will be the position of the scale line.

Scale Line Unstable in "Pluperfect" Markets

To return for a moment to the general case of Fig. 112, it is easy to see that the position of the scale line, and therefore the proportions of inputs used, will be much more unstable when the markets for input are "pluperfect" than when they are perfect or imperfect. In the bottom left-hand corner of the outlay map in Fig. 112 it will be seen that the outlay contours are convex to the origin. But the product contours also are convex to the origin because of the law of diminishing marginal productivity. It would be possible, then, when for both inputs large reductions in price could be obtained with increased purchases, that the outlay and product contours might almost coincide. If they coincided over some range, the position of the scale line would be indeterminate within that range, and a very small shift in the conditions of the problem would cause a large shift in the scale line and in the proportions of the inputs used. Imperfection in the input markets, however, actually increases the stability of the scale line and makes large shifts in the proportions of input quantities unlikely.

Conditions of Constant Average Cost

With the analytical equipment now at hand it is not difficult to show that if the production function is homogeneous, markets are perfect,

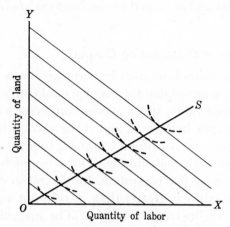

FIG. 115.   Constant Average Cost.

and all inputs are variable, the average outlay, or average cost, will be constant. In Fig. 115 a system of product contours (dotted) and cost contours (solid) is reproduced as in Fig. 113. The product contours in this case, however, represent a production schedule with constant returns to scale. Here it can be proved that the scale line, OS, is a straight line from the origin. It is a well-known property of any homogeneous system of curves, such as the product contours in Fig. 115, that any straight line from the origin will intercept them at points where their *slopes* are equal, and that, conversely, any line connecting the points on the various curves which have a given slope is a straight line through the origin. But by definition we know that on the scale line the slope of each product contour is equal to the slope of the outlay contour at that point. And we know also that when the markets for input are perfect the slope of all outlay contours is constant. The slope of any product contour, therefore, at the point of intersection with the scale line is equal to the given slope of the outlay contours, i.e., to the ratio of the price of the two inputs. So the scale line must be a straight line through the origin. It follows that a given proportionate rise in output is best attained by increasing both inputs in the same proportion. If the prices of input are constant, the total outlay will increase in this same proportion also. For instance, a doubling of the quantity of product will be obtained by doubling the total outlay or the total cost. The total cost curve, instead of being curved as in Fig. 78, page 553, will be a straight line from the origin, such as OQR in Fig. 79. In that case the average cost and the marginal cost are the same at all outputs and are equal to the constant gradient of the total cost curve.

Why Do Costs Rise with Increasing Output?

The above conclusion is of great importance, for in all our analysis of supply we have assumed that the average total cost was *not* constant, but had a minimum value. If the average total cost were the same at all outputs, no matter how great, and if the market for output were perfect at all outputs, there would be nothing to prevent an enterprise from increasing its scale indefinitely. There would be no output at which the net revenue is a maximum, for the net revenue, provided the price of the product is greater than its constant average cost, will always increase with increase in output. The marginal cost will be constant and equal to the average cost, and will always be below the price of the product. If the market for output is perfect, then, an enterprise is prevented from expanding indefinitely only by the fact of rising marginal cost as output expands. But how can marginal cost rise? Only if (1) the prices of inputs rise as more are purchased, (2) one or more inputs are fixed in quantity so that the law of diminishing marginal productivity comes into play, or (3) there are decreasing returns to scale at higher outputs. In short periods both (1) and (2) are likely to be true. Over long periods it is a little more difficult to explain why marginal cost should rise with increasing output, for the usual fixed costs—e.g., plant and equipment—can now be varied as plans are made for many years ahead. Even here, however, there may be one element of input which cannot be increased indefinitely—the element of management. This fact in itself would be sufficient to explain the long-run equilibrium of the single enterprise. Even excluding the factor of inexpansible management, we can still fall back on the assumption of diminishing returns to scale at high outputs to explain why firms do not grow indefinitely.

Extension to Case of More Than Two Inputs

One advantage of the scale-line method of analysis is that it enables us to extend our discussion easily to cases where there are more than two inputs. For three inputs we can construct a three-dimensional diagram with product "contour" surfaces and outlay "contour" surfaces. A product contour surface on such a figure will show all combinations of quantities of three inputs which cooperate to produce a given quantity of product. There will be a system of these surfaces, something like the skins on a quadrant of onion. Similarly, the outlay contour surfaces with perfect markets will form a system of planes lying diagonally athwart the three axes, like the pages of a tilted book. The outlay contours will touch the product contours along a line in 3-space, each point of which represents the cheapest combination of inputs to use in producing a given output. Thus there will be a scale line in our three-dimensional figure. We can also extend the analysis to four or more inputs, though visual geometry fails us here. The scale line is always a "line," even in "n-space," and each point on it represents a definite combination of input quantities, no matter how many inputs there are. The general conclusions developed for two inputs hold also in the case of many inputs. If the production function is homogeneous and the markets for input are perfect, the scale line will always be "straight," and the average total cost will be the same at all outputs. A relative rise in the price of any input will swing the scale line over away from the axis along which the input is measured and will therefore tend to alter the proportions of the inputs in favor of those whose prices have not risen. Similarly, an equal proportionate rise in the prices of all inputs will not change the position of the scale line, though it will in general change the scale itself.

QUESTIONS AND EXERCISES

1. Discuss fully the "laws of returns" in relation to the art of cooking.
2. Assume that Table 64 exhibited constant returns to scale.
   a. Draw as many diagonals as you can, like A, B, and C, passing through figures representing proportional increases in all inputs and outputs.
   b. What would be the output of potatoes when (i) $2\frac{1}{2}$ units of labor are applied to 3 acres, (ii) $1\frac{1}{2}$ units of labor are applied to $3\frac{1}{2}$ acres?
3. Construct a table similar in form to Table 64, page 734, and derived from the data given therein, to show the marginal physical productivity of labor for each quantity of land and of labor. Construct a similar table showing the marginal physical productivity of land for each quantity of land and labor. Show that in each case the law of eventually diminishing marginal physical productivity holds.
   Can we formulate a law to describe the change in the marginal physical productivity of one input as the quantity of the other is increased?
4. The yield of agricultural crops per acre is considerably higher in Europe than in America, although the soil is intrinsically no more fertile. How could you connect this fact with the fact of Europe's dense population?

How would you expect yields per man-hour to differ in the two continents? Yields per acre and per man in American agriculture have been rising sharply since the middle 1930's, while agricultural employment has been falling and arable acreage has remained roughly constant. How might these changes be interpreted in terms of a production function?

5. Show graphically the effect of an equal proportionate rise in the price of all the inputs of an individual firm on the following: (a) the total outlay curves, (b) the outlay contours, (c) the least cost combination of inputs, (d) the scale line, (e) the marginal cost curve, (f) the average cost curve, (g) the equilibrium output.

Show also the effect on (a) the normal supply curve, (b) the price, and (c) the output of the product.

Show also the effect on (a) rents of fixed inputs and (b) the number of firms in the industry.

6. In the physical production schedule of Table 64, assume that the price of labor is 60 per unit, the price of land is $20 per acre, and the price of potatoes is $20 per ton. Assume that normal profit is zero. Then calculate for each one of the 81 combinations of input quantities shown in Table 64, the net revenue resulting from the employment of the combination. Tabulate the results in a similar table. Notice that the net revenue increases indefinitely as the quantities of land and labor increase; there is no maximum value. Why?

CHAPTER 35

THREE-VARIABLE ANALYSIS OF A FIRM
(Continued)

THE MARGINAL PRODUCTIVITY METHOD

The analysis of the optimum position of an enterprise with two or more inputs can be attacked by another method, involving the concept of marginal productivity. We have already seen (page 594) that if there is only one variable input the enterprise will not be at its most profitable point if the marginal revenue productivity of the variable input is not equal to the marginal cost of the input. This condition also holds in the case in which more than one input is variable, for each of the variable inputs. If the quantities of all the inputs are such that for any variable input the marginal revenue productivity is, say, greater than the marginal cost of the input, the net revenue can be increased by increasing the employment of the input. In those circumstances a unit increase in the quantity of the input employed will increase the total revenue more than it will increase the total cost. If, therefore, the marginal revenue productivity of any variable input is *not* equal to its marginal cost, the enterprise is not producing with the most profitable quantities of input and output, i.e., is not in equilibrium. It must be understood, however, that a change in the quantity of one input will change the marginal productivity *curves* of the other inputs, for the marginal productivity of one input depends on the quantities of the other inputs used with it.

Geometric Illustration. These principles are illustrated geometrically in Figs. 116 and 117. In Fig. 116 it is assumed that the quantity of land is held constant, at an amount equal to OH in Fig. 117. In Fig. 116 the quantity of labor is measured along OX, dollars along OY. The curve OPQ is a total revenue curve. A quantity of labor ON, with the fixed quantity of land, yields a product which sells for an amount NP. (This is essentially the same as the $ONPCR$ of Fig. 86, page 592.) We suppose for simplicity that the inputs have perfect

markets; the total cost of labor curve will then be *ORS*. The slope of
ORS is the marginal cost, in this case equal to the price of labor. As
all other inputs are assumed fixed, the total net revenue will be a

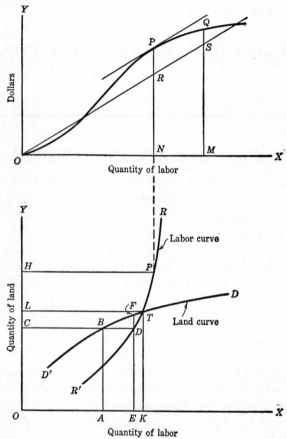

FIGS. 116 and 117.   Marginal Productivity Analysis.

maximum when the difference between the total revenue and the
total cost of labor is a maximum. This is at the quantity of labor *ON,*
where the marginal productivity of labor, equal to the slope of the
curve *OPQ* at *P,* is equal to the marginal cost of labor, equal to the
slope of *ORS* at *R*. The excess of revenue over labor cost, *RP,* is a
maximum at this point, and as all other costs are supposed constant
the total net revenue will likewise be at a maximum.

The "Labor Curve" and the "Land Curve"

In Fig. 117 the quantity of labor is plotted along *OX,* the quantity
of land along *OY*. If *OH* represents the quantity of land to which

labor was applied in Fig. 116, *HP* (= *ON* in Fig. 116) will represent the most profitable quantity of labor to use with the quantity of land *OH*. Similarly, for any other quantity of land—e.g., *OC*—there will be some quantity of labor which will be most profitable—say, *CD*. *D*, *P*, and other such points lie on a curve, *RR′*, which may be called the "labor curve." Any point on it represents a quantity of labor which it is most profitable to employ with a given quantity of land. In an exactly similar fashion, again applying the principle that with a given quantity of labor the most profitable quantity of land to use will be that at which the marginal cost of land is equal to its marginal revenue productivity, we can obtain a curve *DD′*, the "land curve." Any point on the "land curve" indicates a combination of input quantities such that, with the quantity of labor given, the quantity of land is the most profitable to use.

Graphic Solution. Most Profitable Combination Is Where Land and Labor Curves Intersect. The point where these two curves intersect, *T*, shows the most profitable combination of land *and* labor, assuming that the quantities of both these inputs are variable. Suppose we start with a certain quantity of labor, *OA*. The most profitable quantity of land to use with this quantity of labor is *AB* (= *OC*), where *B* lies on the "land curve." But with a quantity of land equal to *AB*, or *OC*, the most profitable quantity of labor to use is *CD*, where *D* is on the "labor curve"; it will pay to increase the purchase of labor. But with a quantity of labor equal to *CD* (or *OE*) the most profitable quantity of land to use is *EF*, where *F* is on the land curve. So we go on, continually approaching the point *T*. Then *TL* is the most profitable quantity of labor to use with an amount of land equal to *TK;* and *TK* is the most profitable amount of land to use with the amount of labor equal to *TL*. The net revenue cannot be raised by increasing *any* of the input quantities. The point *T*, therefore, is absolutely the most profitable combination possible, and the output corresponding to the product contour which passes through *T* is the most profitable output. It must be emphasized that both the scale line method and the marginal productivity method are *constructions* for finding the point *T*, and should give exactly the same result; sometimes one and sometimes the other will be found the most convenient.

THE DEMAND FOR INPUT

Both the scale line method and the marginal productivity method can be employed to analyze the problem of the demand for input for a two-input firm. We suppose, of course, perfect markets for input,

otherwise the concept of a demand for input—that is, a function relating the price of input to the quantity purchased—loses its clarity.
We cannot now assume that the demand for an input is identical with
its marginal value productivity curve (page 601), because the position
of this curve itself, for any given input, depends on the amount of
other inputs employed. We must therefore analyze the effects of a
change in the price of one input on *all* the variables of the enterprise.

Analysis by the Scale Line

The effect of a change in the price of one input in an enterprise
using more than one variable input can be analyzed into two parts.
There will be a "substitution effect"; i.e., a rise, say, in the price of one
input will cause a substitution of a cheaper for the dearer input. The
proportions of inputs will change to the disadvantage of the one which
has suffered the rise in price. Such a change is reflected geometrically
by a shift in the scale line away from the axis of the dearer input, as
shown in Fig. 114, page 756. The second effect we may call the "scale
effect." If the price of even one variable input rises, the marginal cost
of the product at each output will rise. The marginal cost will therefore meet the price at a smaller output than formerly. The rise in the

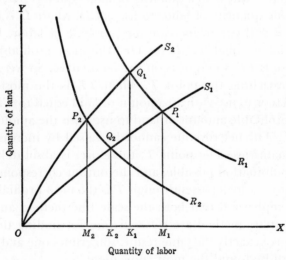

FIG. 118.   Derivation of Demand Curves for Input.

price of input, by increasing costs, will act to reduce the scale of the
enterprise. Both substitution effect and scale effect are illustrated in
Fig. 118.

Here the quantity of labor is measured along OX, the quantity of land along OY. OS_1 is the original scale line; OS_2 is the scale line after the price of labor has risen, as in Fig. 114, page 756. R_1 is the product contour representing those combinations which produce the most profitable output before the price change; the point where OS_1 cuts this product contour, P_1, gives the best quantities of labor and land to employ—M_1P_1 of land and OM_1 of labor. R_2 is the product contour representing those combinations which produce the most profitable output after the rise in the price of labor; it is nearer the origin than R_1, indicating that the most profitable output is now smaller than before. Where this cuts OS_2, P_2 shows the most profitable quantities of labor and land to employ—M_2P_2 of land and OM_2 of labor. If there were no "scale effect" the new point of greatest profit would be Q_1, where the quantity of labor employed was OK_1 and the quantity of land K_1Q_1. Evidently with this condition an increase in the price of labor would cause a decrease in the purchase of labor and an increase in the purchase of land. If there were no "substitution effect" the new point of greatest profit would be Q_2, where the quantity of labor employed was OK_2 and the quantity of land was K_2Q_2. In this event the scale effect alone would bring about a reduction in the quantities of *both* land and labor when the price of labor rose. If the price of labor rises, then, both the substitution effect and the scale effect combine to cause a decline in the quantity of labor bought. The substitution effect will make for a rise, the scale effect for a fall, in the quantity of land bought. If, therefore, the scale effect is small compared to the substitution effect, a rise in the price of labor may cause a rise in the quantity of land bought. If the scale effect is large compared to the substitution effect, a rise in the price of labor may bring about a fall in the quantity of land bought as well as a fall in the quantity of labor.

Substitutability and Importance of Inputs

We have seen (page 756), that the substitution effect—the rotation of the scale line—will be small if the product contour is sharply curved, great if the product contour is but little curved. The magnitude of the substitution effect, therefore, depends, as we should expect, on the degree to which the inputs can be substituted. If they must be used in inflexible proportions, there will be no substitution effect at all.

The magnitude of the scale effect depends mainly on the degree of *importance* of the input in question. If the input plays a large part in the process, the scale effect will be large; if it plays a small part, the scale effect will be small. The more substitutable the inputs and the more important the inputs in question, the greater will be the decline in employment which follows from a given increase in the price of an input—i.e., the more elastic will be the demand for the input. Thus we have proved Propositions II and IV (page 206, Part I), as far as concerns the demand for input of an individual firm.

The "Industry Effect"

In considering the demand for input by a whole industry, we must take into account a further effect—the effect on the profitability of the industry, and on the entry or exit of firms, of changes in the price of an input. Referring to Fig. 88, page 599, we see that a rise in the price of one input would raise all the cost curves of each firm. The rise in costs would drive Firm D out of the industry, thus reducing the total demand for all the factors used. Besides the "scale effect" on the output of each firm, a rise in the price of an input will have an "industry effect" on the number of firms in the industry. This industry effect will be large if the input is an important one, thus confirming the proposition that the demand for an input will be more elastic, the more important the input. This effect will also be large if there are a large number of firms "on the margin," i.e., if the industry approaches the condition of "constant cost." It will also be large if the demand for the product of the industry is elastic, small if the demand for the product is inelastic. As firms drop out, the total output of the industry falls and therefore the price of the product rises. If the demand for the product is inelastic, a small fall in output will cause a large rise in the price of the product, which will offset the rise in costs and so prevent more firms from dropping out. If the demand for the product is elastic, there will not be so much of this offsetting effect of a rise in price, and more firms will have to drop out following a rise in costs before the industry is normally profitable again. This proves Proposition III on page 205. Proposition I on page 204 also follows as a result of the "industry effect." If there is a rise in the demand for a product, the price will rise, new firms will come into the industry, and the demand for the inputs will rise.

It should be noticed that if the prices of all inputs rise in the same proportion there is no substitution effect. There is, however, a scale effect and an industry effect, so that the employment of all inputs will fall. This proposition is true only if the "industry" is "small" so that the effect of its factor payments on the demand for its product can be neglected.

Analysis of Demand for Input by Marginal Productivity Analysis

There is another method by which the demand for input from an individual firm may be analyzed—the method involving marginal productivity analysis as used on pages 761–763. Figs. 119A and 119B

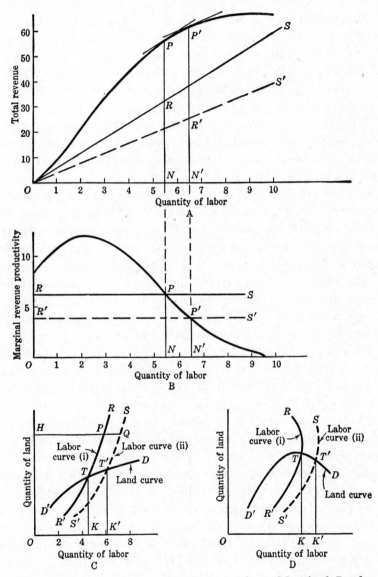

FIG. 119.   Derivation of Demand for Input from Marginal Productivity Analysis.

show the effect of a change in the price of one input on the quantity which will be bought, on the assumption that the quantity of other inputs used remains unchanged. Fig. 119A is similar to Fig. 116, page 762; the quantity of input ("labor") is measured along the horizontal axis, and the total revenue derived from the sale of the output produced by each quantity of labor along the vertical axis, assuming that the quantity of other inputs ("land") is constant. OPP' is the total revenue curve. When the price of labor is equal to the slope of the line ORS, the best quantity of labor to employ will be ON, where the marginal revenue productivity of labor is equal to its price. When the price of labor falls to an amount equal to the slope of the line $OR'S'$, the quantity which it will pay best to employ will rise from ON to ON'. This is shown also in Fig. 119B, where the quantity of labor is plotted along the horizontal axis as before, and the marginal revenue productivity of labor on the vertical axis. At a price of labor equal to OR the quantity of labor at which the marginal revenue productivity is equal to this price is ON, or RP. At the price of labor equal to OR' the quantity employed will be ON', or $R'P'$. It is evident from Fig. 119B that the *steeper* the marginal revenue productivity curve in the region PP', the smaller will be the effect of a given change in the price of labor on the quantity which will be bought. That is, if the marginal revenue productivity falls rapidly as the quantity of labor employed increases, only a small increase in employment is necessary to bring the marginal revenue productivity down to the new level. We saw, however, on page 737, that the marginal physical productivity of an input declines rapidly when the input is not highly substitutable for others. A change in the price of a nonsubstitutable input, therefore, will cause little change in its employment. That is, the demand for an input will be less elastic, the less substitutable it is for others.

Fig. 119C shows the effect of a change in the price of labor on the "land curve" and the "labor curve" of Fig. 117, page 762. A change in the price of labor will not affect the land curve, for it will not change the marginal revenue productivity curves for land. With a fixed quantity of labor the "fixed cost" will have changed, but this fixed cost plays no part in determining how much land shall be employed with the fixed quantity of labor. A fall in the price of labor, however, will move the labor curve to the right, from RR' to SS', for, as we have seen, with each given quantity of land (e.g., OH) the best quantity of labor to employ has increased (e.g., from HP to HQ). The final point of equilibrium, then, with both land and labor variable, has moved from T to T'. The effect of a fall in the price of labor has been to raise the quantity of labor used from OK to OK' and to raise the quantity of land used from KT to $K'T'$. If the land curve bends back on itself, as it well may do, so that it has a negative slope in the range TT', the effect will be to lower the quantity of land used. This is illustrated in Fig. 119D. These two cases correspond to the two cases on page 765.

JOINT PRODUCTS

By means of the methods of the present chapter it is also possible to analyze the problem of joint products. A firm is said to produce joint products when as a result of a *single* process two or more products are made. In such a case the concept of the average total cost of a single product has virtually no significance. Suppose, for instance, that a farmer produces 15 tons of wheat and 10 tons of straw from his wheat-field, at a total cost of $500. The average total cost cannot now be calculated by dividing the total cost by the output unless the total cost can be "allocated" in some way to the two products. Usually, however, it is impossible to allocate the total cost. It is impossible, for instance, in the above example, to say that $400 went for producing the wheat and $100 for producing the straw. The marginal cost of each product still is significant. The marginal cost of wheat is the increase in the total cost of producing both wheat and straw when the production of wheat is increased by one unit without increasing the production of straw. The marginal cost of straw is the increase in the total cost of producing both commodities when the production of straw alone is increased by one unit.

If the commodities can be produced only in a fixed proportion, the problem of the most profitable output differs in no essential from the like problem in the single-product firm. Output can be measured in composite units, such as 1 ton of wheat plus 1 ton of straw, in the fixed proportions in which they must be produced. Then the most profitable output is that at which the marginal cost of a composite unit is equal to its combined price.

If, however, the commodities may be produced in variable proportions, the problem is more complicated. The most profitable situation now is that combination of outputs of the two commodities at which the marginal cost of each is equal to its price. In all this argument, of course, perfect markets are assumed. If the marginal cost of one product is less than its price, it will be possible to increase profits by increasing the output of that product.

The graphic solution of the problem is essentially similar to that of finding the most profitable combination of input quantities. It can be approached either by the "scale line" technique or by the marginal cost technique. Thus in Fig. 113, let OX and OY measure the quantities of the two products, A and B. Then the dotted lines represent cost contours, or isocost curves for these products, showing what combinations would be produced at a given cost.[1] The slope of such a cost contour is the rate of cost substitution of the two products—the amount of product B which can be substituted for one unit of product A without changing the total cost. This is equal to the ratio of the marginal cost of A to the marginal cost of B. The solid lines in the figure now represent revenue contours, and show what combinations of product quantities yield given total revenues. In perfect competition they will be straight lines whose slope is equal to the ratio of the price of A to the price of B. Then a scale line can be drawn, showing the best way to increase the output of both commodities. It is the locus of the points of tangency of the cost and revenue contours, as in Fig. 113. For all combinations on the scale line the ratio of the marginal costs of the two products is equal to the ratio of their prices.

The problem may also be solved by figures such as Fig. 117, page 762. If in these figures we again measure the quantity of product A along OX, and the quantity of product B along OY, then a curve such as $R'R$ can be drawn (the "A-curve") showing what is the most profitable quantity of A to produce for each given amount of B. With a production of B equal to OH, for instance, HP is the quantity of A at which A's marginal cost is equal to its price. Similarly a "B-curve," $D'D$, can be drawn showing the most profitable quantity of B to produce for each given amount of A. The point T where the two curves intersect is the most profitable combination of the two products, for only at this point is the marginal cost of each one equal to its price.

Most of the conclusions of the study of two inputs apply to the case of two outputs. Thus it can be shown that a rise in the price of only one output has a "substitution effect"—moving the most profitable combination to a point where a greater proportion of the higher-priced product is produced—and has also a scale effect, raising the whole scale of the enterprise. Thus a rise in the price of one joint product will always tend to raise its output. The output of the other product will be increased or decreased according as the scale effect or the substitution effect predominates—the scale effect raises and the substitution effect lowers its output. If the price of both products rise in the same proportion, there is no substitution effect, but the scale effect operates to raise both outputs.

---

[1] The cost contours in the present case will be concave to the origin, as normally the marginal cost of each product increases with its output.

Joint Products Under Monopoly

Some interesting modifications of the above analysis follow when the markets for the two products are imperfect. The cost contours as before will be concave to the origin. The revenue contours, however, will no longer be straight lines, as the prices of the products now depend on the outputs, and will generally fall as the corresponding output rises. The revenue contours will be convex to the origin in the significant region. The revenue surface which they describe is no longer a plane inclined to both horizontal axes, but a "dome." There will be some combination of outputs at which the marginal revenue of both products is zero and the total revenue is a maximum. This is the top of the "dome." The revenue contours will make rough circles around this point. Only that part of the field between the origin and the top of the "dome" is relevant, for an enterprise will never expand to outputs where marginal revenue is negative. The slope of a revenue contour at any point is now equal to the ratio of the marginal revenues of the two products, not to the ratio of their prices. A point is on the scale line if the ratio of the marginal costs of the two products is equal to the ratio of their marginal revenues. The most profitable combination of outputs is that at which the marginal cost of *each* product is equal to its marginal revenue. This is again the point where the "A-curve" and the "B-curve" intersect; but each curve is now defined by the condition that for a given production of one product, the most profitable output of the other is that at which its marginal cost and marginal revenue are equal.

Some interesting problems arise when the demand for the two products is not independent. In such cases it can be proved that the total revenue surface, showing the total revenue receivable from any combination of output quantities, is more like a "ridge" than a "dome." If the two products compete in consumption, so that the greater the purchases of one the less the demand for the other, the total revenue surface becomes a ridge running roughly from a point on one axis to a point on the other. If the two products are complementary in consumption, so that the greater the purchases of one the greater the demand for the other, the total revenue surface becomes a ridge like a hog-back hill or a Napoleon hat, running outward from the origin between the two axes, roughly at right angles to the "ridge" formed by competitive demand. In the extreme case of two products which can be consumed only in given proportions (e.g., right and left shoes) the ridge contracts to a razor edge and becomes a simple total revenue curve for the joint commodity.

SELLING COST

Up to now the problem of selling cost has been virtually neglected; this is the problem of how much to spend on advertising, salesmen, free samples, door-to-door canvasses, and so on. Under perfect markets the "selling problem" does not arise. When a firm has a perfect market, it can sell all it wants at the market price, and there is no point in advertising. When a firm has an imperfect market, however, it is limited in the quantity it can sell; the market does not take with open arms everything which the firm has to offer but quickly becomes gorged, so that in order to increase sales at least one of two things must be done. Either the price must be lowered in order to tempt buyers into buying more or the buyer must be persuaded to buy more at each price. The process of persuading the buyers to buy more at each price is called "sales promotion." The total of expenses plus normal profit involved in sales promotion is called "selling cost." Those expenses (plus normal profits) which are not specifically connected with sales promotion are called "production cost."

Distinction Between Selling Cost and Production Cost

The total cost of producing a given output may therefore be divided into two parts—total selling cost and total production cost. The exact point of division is not always easy to determine. Nevertheless, we may roughly define the selling costs as those which are incurred specifically in order to make the buyers buy more of the product at any given price; production costs are the residue. There will always be some costs which are difficult to apportion; should the cost of a cellophane wrapper, for instance, be included among production costs or selling costs? However, the distinction is made in practice, and, like most distinctions, the fact that it is not perfectly clear does not impair its usefulness.

The Total Selling Cost

As the main purpose of selling costs is to affect the revenue (through affecting the volume of sales), it is convenient to treat selling costs not under the cost side of the business but under the revenue side. The selling problem, like that of production, can be divided into two parts. There is first the problem of how to use a *given* expenditure on selling costs most effectively. This is analogous to the problem of how to produce a *given* quantity of product with the least cost. We cannot here go into the various techniques of selling. We shall simply assume that there are several ways of spending money on sales promotion in order to obtain a desired result, the desired result being that a certain quantity should be sold at a certain price. The least expensive method of producing this desired result will naturally be chosen; its cost will be called the *total selling cost* of selling a given quantity at a given price. In the second place, even if we knew the least total selling cost which would sell each possible output quantity at each possible price, we should still have to determine the most profitable combination of price, selling cost, and quantity of output.

TABLE 68. Relationship Between Price, Total Selling Cost, and (1) Output, (2) Total Gross Revenue, (3) Total Production Revenue

Total selling cost (dollars)	0	1	2	3	4	5	6
140	92 / 0 / -140	90 / 90 / -50	78 / 156 / 16	70 / 210 / 70	50 / 200 / 60	40 / 200 / 60	37 / 222 / 82
120	90 / 0 / -120	88 / 88 / -32	75 / 150 / 30	65 / 195 / 75	49 / 196 / 76	39 / 195 / 75	35 / 210 / 90
100	88 / 0 / -100	85 / 85 / -15	70 / 140 / 40	60 / 180 / 80	48 / 192 / 92	37 / 185 / 85	30 / 180 / 80
80	85 / 0 / -80	80 / 80 / 0	65 / 130 / 50	50 / 150 / 70	45 / 180 / 100	35 / 175 / 95	25 / 150 / 70
60	80 / 0 / -60	70 / 70 / 10	60 / 120 / 60	45 / 135 / 75	40 / 160 / 100	30 / 150 / 90	20 / 120 / 60
40	70 / 0 / -40	60 / 60 / 20	50 / 100 / 60	40 / 120 / 80	35 / 140 / 100	28 / 140 / 100	15 / 90 / 50
20	60 / 0 / -20	50 / 50 / 30	40 / 80 / 60	35 / 105 / 85	30 / 120 / 100	25 / 125 / 105	10 / 60 / 40
0	50 / 0 / 0	40 / 40 / 40	30 / 60 / 60	25 / 75 / 75	15 / 60 / 60	5 / 25 / 25	0 / 0 / 0

Price of output (dollars per ton)

The Selling Cost Table

In order to do this we first construct a table such as Table 68. Each of the "boxes" in this table represents a certain combination of price and total selling cost, the price being found at the bottom of the column in which the box stands and the selling cost at the head of its row. The box in the top right-hand corner of the figure represents a combination of a price of $6 per unit with a total selling cost of $140. The first (uppermost) of the figures in each one of the boxes represents the quantity of product (tons) which can be sold if a price is charged equal to the price at the foot of the column and a selling cost is incurred equal to the figure at the head of the row in which the box lies. Thus with a price of $6 per ton and a total selling cost of $140, a quantity amounting to 37 tons could be sold; with a price of $5 and a total selling cost of $120, 39 tons could be sold, and so on for each box of the table.

Total Gross Revenue

The center figure in each box is obtained by multiplying the first figure, representing the quantity of output sold, by the price at which it is sold, found at the bottom of the column. This gives what may be called the *total gross revenue*—the total revenue which is received, in the first instance, from the sale of the quantity of output shown in the box. Thus with a selling cost of $140 and a price of $6, 37 tons can be sold; 37 tons at $6 per ton is $222, and so for all the other boxes of the table.

Total Production Revenue

The bottom figure in each box represents what may be called the *total production revenue*. It is found by subtracting the selling cost at the head of the row from the second figure in the box, representing the total gross revenue. That is, the total production revenue is equal to the total gross revenue less the selling cost. This is the revenue which is passed back, as it were, from the selling department to the production department. It is the revenue figure in which the production department is primarily interested. Thus with a selling cost of $140 and a price of $6 a gross revenue of $222 is obtained; but as $140 of this has been spent in selling costs, only $82 remains to be passed on to the production department.

"Diminishing Returns" of Selling Costs

It will be noticed that the first figure (sales) in each box is an assumed figure; i.e., it is part of the data on which the businessman has to work. The other two figures are derived from the first. In constructing the system of "first figures" (i.e., the relationship between price, selling cost, and the quantity which can be sold), we have made two important assumptions which are illustrated in the figures chosen. The first is that the greater the price with a *given* total selling cost, the less will be the quantity which can be sold. This is what is meant by an imperfect market. If the market were perfect, so that an indefinitely large quantity could be sold at the market price, the selling cost problem would not arise at all. The second is that the quantity which can be sold at *any given price* increases as the total selling cost rises, but that it increases at a *decreasing rate*. Obviously, as the aim of selling costs is to enlarge the quantity which would be sold at any given price, it is reasonable to assume that the greater the selling costs, the more will be sold. But for every commodity there must be some point of saturation beyond which higher selling costs will produce no increase in the total quantity sold. Although at first, then, successive increases in the total selling cost may produce greater and greater increments in the quantity sold, after a certain point unit increases in the selling cost will result in smaller and smaller increases in sales until the point of saturation is reached. This principle is somewhat analogous to the "law of diminishing returns." If the increase in sales which results from a unit increase in the total selling cost is called the "marginal productivity of selling costs," then the principle may be stated as one of "eventually diminishing marginal productivity of selling costs."

Various Ways of Selling a Given Output

Now, consider the boxes which have been marked by a ring in Table 68. These boxes represent different combinations of price and selling cost, all of which have one thing in common: they all enable the seller to sell 50 tons of output, as evidenced by the first figure in each box. Evidently, in this case if nothing is spent on selling costs, the seller will have to give the product away in order to get rid of 50 tons. If $20 is spent on selling costs, $1 per ton can be charged and 50 tons can still be sold. If $40 is spent on selling costs, the price can be $2 a ton and 50 tons can still be sold. If $140 is spent on selling costs, the price can be as much as $4 per ton and 50 tons can still be sold. As the price rises, the total selling cost must also be increased if the same amount as before is to be sold.

The "Best" Way of Selling a Given Output

Again considering the "ringed" boxes, only this time looking at the bottom figures, we see that the box with diagonal shading shows the greatest total production revenue of any of the ringed boxes. If 50 tons are sold with a selling cost of $80 and a price of $3, the total production revenue received will be $70. If 50 tons are sold at a lower price —say, $2—and at a lower selling cost—$40—only $60 will be received in total production revenue. If 50 tons are sold at a high price—$4— and with a high selling cost—$140—again only $60 will be received in production revenue; the great selling cost more than outweighs the advantage of the high price which it makes possible. Evidently, the best way to sell 50 tons is at a price of $3 and with a selling cost of $80.

Similarly, the best way of selling 40 tons is with a price of $4 and a selling cost of $60, the best way of selling 25 tons is with a price of $5 and a selling cost of $20, and so on for any quantity of output. A small figure like Table 68 will not enable us to find very accurately the best way of selling intermediate quantities of output—say, 42 tons—but this could easily be remedied by making a larger and more detailed table. Those boxes which represent the best combinations of price and selling cost for producing a *given* output are shaded.

Graphic Illustration. Just as a three-dimensional "physical production surface" was constructed from the physical production data in Table 64, page 734, so three-dimensional figures can be constructed from the data in Table 68. We need not bother to try to draw these figures, for they can be represented perfectly well by contour lines.

The "Sales Contour." The ringed boxes in Table 68 represent all combinations of price and selling cost which will enable the seller to sell 50 tons. In Fig. 120A this is represented by a "sales contour," S_{50}. The coordinates of all points on this line represent combinations of price and selling cost which will allow 50 tons to be sold; similarly, the coordinates of all points on S_{40} represent those combinations of price and selling cost which will allow 40 tons to be sold; and so on for the whole system of "sales contours," which are the contours of a "sales surface."

"Production Revenue Contours"

From the data given by these sales contours we can calculate, in the way shown in Table 68, the total production revenue obtained from each combination of price and selling cost. These figures are represented in the bottom figure in each box of Table 68. They can be shown by a system of "production revenue contours," as in Fig. 120B;

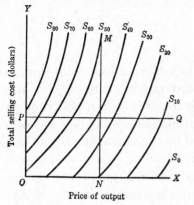

Fig. 120A.   Sales Contours.

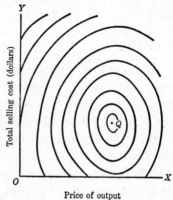

Fig. 120B.   Production Revenue Contours.

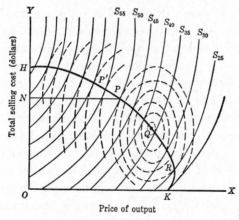

Fig. 120C.   The Theory of Selling Cost.

the coordinates of any point on one of these contours represent a combination of price and selling cost which will yield a given production revenue. There will be some point, Q, representing a combination of price and selling cost at which the total production revenue is a maximum. In Table 68 this maximum value is $105, at a selling cost of $20 and a price of $5. To get a production revenue of rather less than this —say, $100—it is possible with the same price to have either a greater or a smaller selling cost, or with the same selling cost a greater or a smaller price. The contour which gives the combinations yielding

$100 production revenue will therefore circle around the point Q; similarly, for all the other production revenue contours. These "circles" will not necessarily be smooth; they will probably be quite crooked. However, for simplicity in the diagram they are drawn smoothly.

The "Sale Line"

Fig. 120C combines the system of sales contours (solid lines) with a system of production revenue contours (dotted lines). For any sales contour, S_{50}, the point where it is touched by a production revenue contour, P, is the point whose coordinates show the best way of selling the quantity of output represented by the sales contour—in this case, 50 tons. That is to say, the best way of selling 50 tons of output in this case is with a price equal to PN and a selling cost equal to ON, for no other way gives a greater production revenue. Similarly, we can find the best combination of price and selling cost for selling any other output. All these points lie on a line $HPQK$, which we may call the "sale line." It is somewhat analogous to the "scale line" in Fig. 113, page 751, in that it shows the best way of expanding or contracting sales. The best way to expand sales from, say, 50 to 55 tons is to move from a combination of price and selling cost represented by the point P to a combination represented by the point P'. Evidently, if the sale line is steep, the best way to increase sales is to raise selling cost a lot and reduce price a little. If the sale line is flat, the best way to increase sales is to raise selling cost a little and reduce price a lot. If the sale line is vertical, as at R, the best way to increase sales is to raise selling cost without lowering price. if the sale line is horizontal, the best way of increasing sales is to reduce price without raising selling cost. It is just conceivable that the sale line might bend backward, as in the figure between K and R. In such a region the best way to expand output is to increase both price and selling cost. This might be the case if an increase in selling cost is extremely effective in expanding sales while a change in price makes little difference to sales.

Why Sales Promotion Is Preferred to Price Cutting

We can now see why businessmen who are not in perfect competition and who therefore have a selling problem frequently prefer to increase their selling cost rather than to cut prices. That combination of price and selling cost which is absolutely the most profitable must lie somewhere on the sale line between K and Q, for only in this range is the total production revenue increasing as sales increase. If sales are pushed beyond the figure whose sales contour passes through Q, then as sales go up the total production revenue actually decreases. Obviously it could not pay to push sales to this point. In the range between K and Q, however, the sale line is likely to be relatively steep, as we see from the figure and as we have seen from our arithmetical example. Consequently, in the range of output in which the most profitable position is likely to lie it will probably pay better to concentrate on sales promotion rather than price cutting as a means of expanding output. This is not, of course, necessarily so—it is quite possible for the sales curve to be flat in this range if price cutting is effective in expanding sales and sales promotion is not. This seems to be the case in some businesses. Nevertheless, there will be a certain dominant tendency for sales promotion to be more effective in this range than price cutting.

One further conclusion of interest arises from this analysis. It is that probably the best way of expanding sales is not by increasing selling costs alone, or by cutting price alone, but by a combination of the two. This need not be so if the sale line is vertical. A vertical sale line, however, is a special case and is probably not common.

The Final Solution

We can now bring together all the various elements of the monopoly problem into one final solution. First is the problem of *production*, solved by means of the scale-line analysis. From this we obtain a total cost curve, each point of which represents the total cost of the best way of *producing* a given output. Next is the problem of *selling*. This manifests itself as the best way of *selling* a given output—the best combination of prices to different people or for different quantities, or the best combination of price and selling cost, as found by the sale-line analysis. Then for each output we can postulate a *total production revenue*, this being the total revenue which is passed on to the production side of the business after all selling expenses have been met. And just as each total cost is the *least* total cost with which a given output can be produced, so each total production revenue is the *greatest* production revenue which can be obtained by selling a given quantity of output. We can then draw total cost and total production revenue curves, and find where the difference between them is greatest, or we can derive from them marginal cost and marginal production revenue curves, and find where they intersect. Either of these methods gives the most profitable output. Then we can go back to our scale-line figures and find out what is the best way to produce this output, and we can go back to our demand and sales figures and find out what is the best way to sell this output. Then the problem is mathematically solved! We may notice that all the analysis in Chapter 28 is valid if we interpret the marginal revenue to mean the marginal production revenue, and the price to mean the average production revenue. Our more detailed analysis, as usual, extends but does not destroy the simpler constructions.

Mathematics and Business Judgment

This "solution" may seem highly abstract and unreal to the student, especially if he is acquainted with the actual practice of the business world. It may be doubted whether even the most enlightened businessman would recognize a marginal revenue curve if he saw one, much less a scale line! Nevertheless, the student should not lightly assume that because this mathematical treatment is unfamiliar in the business world it is valueless. Most of the things we have assumed as data in solving our problem—the demand schedules, cost schedules, and so on—which in fact determine the profitability of a business, are only imperfectly known even to the best of businessmen. The businessman never knows exactly how, for instance, a change in price or in selling cost will affect sales, nor does he know exactly how much his costs will change if he increases his output. He must, of course, have some idea of these relationships or he cannot make any intelligent decisions. But the data on which he works are subject to so many errors of estimate that his decisions belong rather to the nature of an art than of a science.

This is particularly the case in the selling problem, for it is usually impossible to tell what has been the exact effect of a sales policy even after it has gone into effect. Luck and chance play a great part in business, as does the indefinable but vital factor of intuitive judgment. If the data of the problem were as well known as we have assumed, business would not be an art but a mere mechanical performance. In fact, the businessman is more of an artist than a mathematician. But it is important to understand the mechanics which underlie the art of business, just as it is important to understand the mechanics which underlie, let us say, the art of music. Economic theory is to business much as the theory of sound is to music. Just as a man can be an excellent musician without a detailed knowledge of the theory of sound, so a man can be an excellent businessman and remain totally ignorant of the whole body of economic analysis. But that is no argument against either the theory of sound or economic theory!

SOME APPLICATIONS OF THE THEORY OF SELLING COST

Taxation

The application of the theory of selling cost to problems of taxation is interesting. The analysis of Chapter 29 with regard to the effect of taxation applies perfectly if we replace "price" by "average production revenue," and marginal revenue by "marginal production revenue." Thus, Fig. 96 shows that a lump-sum tax will not lead to a change in output or to a change in "average production revenue." There will therefore be no change in price or selling cost if the monopolist is already selling his output in the most economical way. A variable tax will reduce the output and raise the "average production revenue."

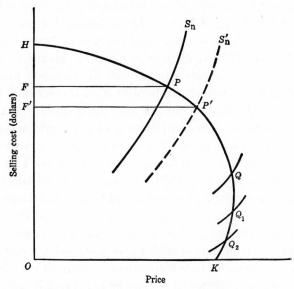

FIG. 121.   Taxation and Selling Cost.

In this case there will be an effect on both price and selling cost, illustrated in Fig. 121. Here selling cost is measured vertically and price horizontally, as in Fig. 120C. HK is the "sale line." Suppose S_n to be the "sales contour" showing all those combinations of price and selling cost which will sell an amount equal to the originally most profitable output. Then OF is the total selling cost, FP is the price. Let S'_n be the sales contour for the smaller output which is most profitable after the tax is imposed. The new price will be $F'P'$, and the new selling cost OF'. The effect of the tax in this case is evidently to raise the price from FP to $F'P'$ and to lower the selling cost from OF to OF'. It is possible, however, that a tax may take out all its effect on the selling cost. If, for instance, the tax shifted the most profitable output from the one represented by the sales contour Q to the one represented by Q_1, there would be no change in price but a considerable reduction in selling cost. A case is even conceivable in which a tax causes a monopolist to reduce his price. A tax which reduced the most profitable output from the one represented by Q_1 to the one represented by Q_2 would have this effect, the sale line being re-entrant in this range.

Effect of a Change in Demand

Our theory of selling cost leads us to broaden our concept of the "demand" for the product of a monopolist. We must now think of the demand not as a simple relationship between the price and the quantity bought, but as a threefold relationship between price, selling cost, and quantity bought. That is, the "demand" for the product of a monopolist really consists of the whole system of "sales contours," as in Fig. 120A, page 777. A "change in demand" means a shift in this whole system. In the simple case a "fall in demand" means that a smaller quantity than before can be sold at each price. For a monopolist, however, a "fall in demand" means that a smaller quantity than before can be sold at each combination of price and selling cost. A fall in demand therefore means that the whole surface, which the sales contours represent, has fallen toward the base plane. The whole system of sales contours in Fig. 120A will move upward and to the left; thus S_{60} might occupy the place now held by S_{80}, and so on. After the fall in demand more must be expended in selling cost in order to sell a given output at the original price, or a lower price must be charged in order to sell a given output with the original selling cost.

That is to say, in order to sell any given output either a lower price must be charged or a greater sum must be expended in selling cost, or both, than before the fall in demand. In any of these cases the result will be a decline in the total production revenue. At each output, therefore, the total production revenue, the average production revenue, and the marginal production revenue will be less than before; the average and marginal production revenue curves will have shifted downward and to the left. We have already analyzed the results of this in Fig. 95, page 620. There will usually be a decline in output and usually (though not always) a decline in the average production revenue. In the case of Fig. 95 itself, of course, the average production revenue and the price are identical.

Where selling cost is taken into account, the problem is more complicated. It is illustrated in Fig. 122. Price is measured along OX; total selling cost along OY, as in Fig. 120C; H_1K_1 is the original "sale line" before the fall in demand; S_1 is the sales contour corresponding to the original output. The effect of the fall in demand will probably

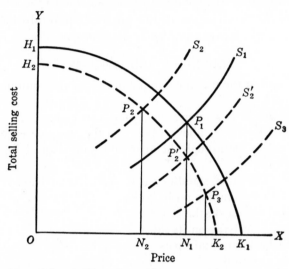

FIG. 122.   Selling Cost After a Fall in Demand.

be to shift the sale line downward and to the left, to the position H_2K_2, for the sales contours in Fig. 120A, page 777, and the production reve-nue contours in Fig. 120B, have all shifted to the left. Conditions are possible in which a fall in demand will not change the sale line, or will change it in the opposite sense, but they are not the most probable. The fall in demand will also have shifted the sales contours to the left. Let S_2 be the new sales contour corresponding to the original output. Then if the output did not change, the point which describes the best way of selling that output would shift from P_1 to P_2. In this case, evidently, there will be a considerable fall in price, from ON_1 to ON_2, and only a slight change in the selling cost, from P_1N_1 to P_2N_2. In fact, unless the marginal cost curve in Fig. 95 rises very steeply, the out-put will decline. If it declines only a little, it remains true that the principal result of a fall in demand is a fall in the price, and not in the selling cost. If it declines sharply, say, to the figure whose sales contour is S'_2, then P'_2 shows the best price and selling cost. The price may be unchanged at ON_1, but the selling cost will fall sharply to $N_1P'_2$. In exceptional cases where the fall in demand brings about a very large fall in output it is conceivable that the sales contour might shift to S_3, in which case the fall in demand would lead to a great fall in selling cost and an actual rise in price! Further complications of this topic arise out of the question whether the fall in demand affects principally the price or the selling cost at which a given output can be sold. It is conceivable, for instance, that the public might become less susceptible to the charms of advertising and more susceptible to the charms of low prices. However, we have probably pursued these abstract ramifications as far as our clumsy techniques will allow.

QUESTIONS AND EXERCISES

1. As an exercise in the use of contour lines, draw the contours of the following objects:

   a. A cone with its apex above the center of its base.

   b. A cone with its apex above a point on the circumference of its base.

   c. A half-cone, cut through the apex and center, and lying on the flat triangular side.

   d. A similar half-cone, standing on its semicircular base.

   e. A half-sphere, standing on its base.

   f. A football at rest on the ground.

   g. A baseball bat lying on its side.

   h. A saddle-back mountain pass.

   i. A square pyramid.

   j. A corkscrew.

2. Compare and contrast the theoretical problems presented by (a) the production of a given quantity of physical product, (b) the obtaining of a revenue from the sale of a given quantity of physical product.

3. Draw in perspective the three-dimensional figures represented in contour form in Figs. 120A and 120B. Draw representative sections of these figures showing (a) the relation between the sales and the total selling cost, price being constant; (b) the relation between price and sales, selling cost being constant; (c) the relation between production revenue and selling cost, price being constant; (d) the relation between production revenue and price, selling cost being constant.

4. Show that as the market for a firm's output became more nearly perfect, the sales contours in Fig. 120A would become steeper and farther apart. What would the sales contours be like for a firm with a perfect market for output? What would its production revenue contours be like? Why must we assume that selling costs would be ineffective in a perfect market?

5. Continue exercise 6, page 760, by drawing a ring around the maximum value of the net revenue in each row of the table. Join these rings by a line. This line is the "labor curve" in Fig. 117. It shows the best quantity of labor to use with each quantity of land. Similarly, ring the maximum values of the net revenue in each column of the table. The line joining these rings is the "land curve" of Fig. 117. Why do these curves not intersect?

6. The following table is a physical production function, showing the number of bushels of potatoes obtained with various amounts of land and labor

Units of Land	Bushels of Potatoes						
7	460	574	660	725	775	820	860
6	442	557	636	707	760	800	838
5	411	536	615	683	747	779	812
4	370	498	577	638	694	736	770
3	322	436	520	576	613	643	668
2	265	360	418	470	519	554	574
1	156	245	307	345	371	391	402
0	1	2	3	4	5	6	7

Units of Labor

a. On squared paper, with labor on the horizontal and product on the vertical axes, draw the family of seven physical production curves corresponding to the seven units of land. Label this Fig. 1.

b. On another sheet of squared paper draw the product contours, with labor on the horizontal and land on the vertical axis, corresponding to quantities of product 100, 200, . . . 800. Label this Fig. 2. Use the curves of Fig. 1 to get the exact amount of labor corresponding to various amounts of land and product.

c. Suppose the price of potatoes at all outputs is $1 per bushel, labor is $100 per unit, land is $50 per unit. Then: (i) Draw the outlay contours in Fig. 2, touching the product contours, and draw the scale line through the point of tangency. (ii) For levels of output 100, 200, . . . 800 calculate the least total input cost, the net revenue, and the marginal cost. (iii) At what level of output and inputs is net revenue a maximum?

d. Find the point on each of the curves in Fig. 1 at which the slope of the curve is equal to the price of labor. From these points plot the "labor curve" on Fig. 2. In a similar way draw the "land curve." Show that these curves intersect at the point of maximum net revenue found in (c).

e. For each of the cells in the physical production table calculate the net revenue, and pick out the largest net revenue figure. Does this correspond with the results of parts (c) and (d)?

f. Repeat parts (c), (d), and (e) on the assumption that the price of labor is $100 per unit and the price of land is $100 per unit.

g. Repeat parts (c), (d), and (e) on the assumption that the price of labor is $50 per unit and the price of land is $50 per unit.

h. Comment on these results.

7. a. In a figure like Fig. 112, page 749, plot the output of one joint product (A) along OX, the total revenue derived from its sales along OY', the output of the other joint product (B) along OY, and the total revenue derived from its sales along OX'. Draw total revenue curves for

each product, on the assumption of perfect markets for output. Construct the corresponding revenue contours, and draw a perspective drawing of the revenue surface which they represent.

b. Repeat the exercise on the assumption that the market for one product is perfect and for the other product is imperfect.

c. Repeat the exercise on the assumption that the market for both products is imperfect. Show that a dome-shaped revenue surface results.

d. Repeat the exercise on the assumption that the two products are (i) competitive in demand, (ii) complementary in demand. (Note: In this case the construction lines forming the network from which we draw the contours are not straight lines, but curved. They are themselves the contours of surfaces showing the revenue derived from a *single* product for each combination of quantities of *both* products.)

8. The following schedule shows the total cost, in thousands of dollars, of producing various quantities of two products, A and B, in a single process.

Quantity of B	Total Cost ($000)								
800	540	600	670	750	840	940	1050	1170	1300
700	455	520	595	680	775	880	995	1120	1255
600	375	445	525	615	715	825	945	1075	1215
500	300	375	460	555	660	775	900	1035	1180
400	230	310	400	500	610	730	860	1000	1150
300	165	250	345	450	565	690	825	970	1125
200	105	195	295	405	525	655	795	945	1105
100	50	145	250	365	490	625	770	925	1090
0	0	100	210	330	460	600	750	910	1080
	0	100	200	300	400	500	600	700	800
					Quantity of A				

Suppose the price of product A is $1200 per unit, and of B is $500 per unit. Find the most profitable output of *both* products by the following methods:

a. Calculate from the table the net revenue at each combination.

b. For each quantity of B draw the marginal cost curves of A, and find at which output of A the marginal cost is equal to the price. From these results draw the "A-curve." In a similar manner draw the "B-curve." Find the most profitable output combination from these two curves.

c. Draw, by interpolation, the cost contours corresponding to the above table. Draw on the same figure the revenue contours. Draw the scale line. Calculate the net revenue for each combination on the scale line, and find where it is a maximum.

Repeat the exercises with different prices for A and B, and study the effects of these price changes. Can you construct a supply curve of either of these two products? Discuss the problem of supply when there are joint products.

CHAPTER 36

INDIFFERENCE CURVES AND THE THEORY OF OPTIMUM CHOICE

In the theory of the firm as developed up to this point we have assumed that the "best" position of the firm is that which in some sense maximizes profits. This limitation must now be removed, as it is clearer that in many cases firms are prepared to sacrifice profits for other things such as security or liquidity. It is clear also that profit maximization is quite inappropriate as a theory of the household, where we have already had to invoke the principle of maximization of "utility" (Chapter 32). What we are looking for, in fact, is a general theory of optimum choice—that is, of the conditions which underly the "best" position of any organization whether firm, household, government, church, school, or society.

The Preference Scale

A theory of optimum choice involves putting together two sets of relationships, one which describes what there is to choose among and the other which enables us to select out of the possible choices that which stands highest on some scale of value or preference. We have already seen how production functions, cost functions, and market functions impose limitations on possible choices. In essence they divide the universe into combinations of quantities that are available and that are not. We have called them "availability" or "possibility" functions. We now want to find ways of describing the preference, value, or welfare functions which indicate the *ordering* of the various conceivable combinations of quantities according to some scale of "better or worse," "up or down." Such an ordering is all that is necessary in order to pick out the "optimum"—that combination of quantities which stands higher on the "up-down" scale than any other. This "up-down" scale is a quite general notion. It may refer to personal preference, to moral values, to group or social preferences, to anything where it makes sense to say that one set of things is "better" or "worse" than some other set.

The analysis of the previous two chapters indicates a convenient way of representing the preference function for combinations of two

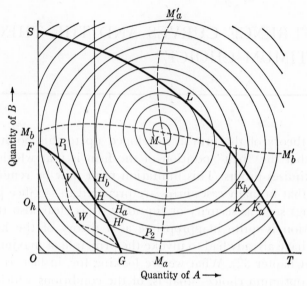

FIG. 123.   An Indifference Curve System.

quantities, A and B. In Fig. 123 we measure A along the horizontal, B along the vertical axis. A and B can be anything we like, so long as they are quantities which are objects of preference or valuation. They may be quantities of commodities consumed, or assets held, or prices, or profits, or characteristics of any kind—even virtues and vices, if they are reasonably measurable. The solid circular lines in the figure then represent contours of a three-dimensional figure in which the third dimension measures the position of the various combinations on the scale of preference. This measure is what in Chapter 32 we have called "utility," for historic reasons, though "preferability" would be a much better name.

Indifference Curves

These contours or lines of equal preference are called "indifference curves" because they represent combinations of quantities which are neither better nor worse than each other but are indifferent. If two points P_1 and P_2 are on an indifference curve it means that the combinations represented have equal values on the scale of preference which the set of indifference curves describes: we "don't care" whether we have a lot of B and little A, as at P_1, or a lot of A and little B, as at P_2. As drawn in the figure the indifference curves are roughly circular around the point M. This means that M is the absolute maximum of utility, the absolutely most preferred point, the top of the "utility mountain," or the point of satiety. This point may, of course, be a long way off or even at infinity, but the most general case is the one drawn. The line $M_bMM'_b$ is drawn through those points where the indifference curves are vertical. It shows the maximum preferability quantity of B for each quantity of A. Similarly, the line $M_aMM'_a$ is drawn through those points where the indifference curves are horizontal. It shows the most preferable quantity of A for each quantity of B. These two lines divide the field into four quadrants. In that bounded by M_bMM_a, both quantities are "commodities" in the sense that as we increase the quantity of either, the quantity of the other being held constant, we move to preferred positions. Thus moving from H to H_a we increase A, keeping B constant, and we move to a "higher" indifference curve, that is, to a preferred position. If we visualize the three-dimensional "mountain," then as we move from H to H_a we are moving "uphill." Similarly, moving from H to H_b also means moving to a preferred position. In the quadrant bounded by $M_aMM'_b$ A is a "discommodity" though B is still a commodity. That is to say, moving from K to K_a increases A but is a move "downhill" on the utility mountain to a lower indifference curve or a less preferred position. Moving from K to K_b is still moving to a preferred position. In similar ways we can verify that in quadrant $M_bMM'_a$ A is a commodity but B a discommodity, and in quadrant $M'_aMM'_b$, both A and B are discommodities.

The "Possibility Curve"

Now suppose we impose on this figure a "possibility curve," FHG, which divides the field into possible or attainable combinations which lie within the area $OFHG$, and impossible or unattainable combinations which lie outside that area. The problem now is which is the preferred or optimum position among all those which are possible, as clearly the unattainable is not particularly interesting. The answer is the point H, where the possibility curve is touched by an indifference curve. Again visualizing the utility mountain, it is clear that H is the highest point on the mountain which can be reached as long as we have to stay within the "possibility fence" FHG. At any point such as H' where the possibility curve cuts an indifference curve, it is possible to move to a higher indifference curve while keeping to the line *FHG.*

The Marginal Conditions for an Optimum

At this point of mutual tangency H the slopes of the two curves are equal. The slope of the indifference curve may be called the *rate of indifferent substitution.* It is the amount of B which could be substituted for one unit of A without moving to a more or less preferred position. That is to say, it is the amount of B which is equivalent, in preferability, to one unit of A. This quantity is frequently called simply the "marginal rate of substitution," but it seems wise to qualify the term to distinguish it from other rates of substitution. The slope of the possibility curve may be called the rate of alternative substitution, or the (marginal) alternative cost of B for A. It is the maximum amount of B which can be substituted for one unit of A. That is, it is the maximum addition to B which can be obtained by the sacrifice of one unit of A. The condition for an optimum is then that the marginal rate of indifferent substitution should be equal to the marginal alternative cost. This is not, however, a sufficient condition for an optimum. Suppose, for instance, the possibility line were SLT. The point L where the marginal conditions are fulfilled is only an optimum if we have to stay on the boundary SLT; if, however, we can move inside the boundary, we will move to the absolute maximum M, simply by discarding some of A and B. Suppose again that the possibility line were $FVWG$. The marginal conditions are satisfied at both V and W where the possibility line touched an indifference curve. V is a relative maximum, but W is a relative minimum. It is not an absolute minimum, as both G and F are on lower indifference curves than W. In all these problems, therefore, it is never wise to rely on the marginal condition alone; the whole field should be examined as far as possible to see where the optimum lies. Basically the problem is one of *selection* of some "highest" point within the possibility area. The marginal conditions are merely aids in this process.

Analogy with Production Functions

In the quadrant bounded by M_bMM_a the similarity to the production function figures of Chapter 34 (e.g., Fig. 111, page 742) is striking. We can think of "utility" as the "product" of the other two quantities. If for a moment we suppose that utility is cardinally measurable, "marginal utility" is seen to be a concept analogous to marginal productivity. A vertical section of the three-dimensional figure plotted in Fig. 123 along the line O_hK gives a total utility curve, as in Fig. 107A. The slope of this curve at any point is the marginal utility of A. The marginal rate of indifferent substitution is then equal to the ratio of the marginal utilities of A and B, just as the rate of product substitution is the ratio of the marginal productivities.

Utility as an Ordinal Magnitude

One of the virtues of the indifference curve analysis, however, is that it applies to many problems where cardinal measurement of utility is not necessary. If we are given a field of indifference curves and a possibility area, all we need to know to find the optimum point is the *ordering* of the indifference curves. That is to say, we need to know of any two indifference curves which is the "higher"—i.e., which represents a superior position—but we do not need to know *by how much* one is higher than the other. This is what is meant by saying that utility is an "ordinal" rather than a "cardinal" magnitude—we must be able to rank or order the various utilities represented by the indifference curves in order from "low" to "high," but we do not have to specify the magnitude of the intervals between them. In geometric terms, we can suppose that the indifference curves are contours of a utility mountain whose general shape we know but whose height we do not know. We can transform the mountain by compressing it or stretching it as much as we like, provided that all points which were previously on the same level remain on the same level, and any point which was previously above another remains so. Maximum properties in general survive transformations of this kind—the top of the mountain is still the top no matter how much we stretch or compress it according to the above rules. This is why confining utility to an ordinal magnitude seems to make so little difference to the analysis.

APPLICATIONS TO THE THEORY OF THE FIRM

Indifference curve analysis can be applied to the theory of the firm to release it from the previous assumption of profit maximization. Thus in Fig. 124 we suppose three possible cases. Profits are measured on the vertical axis, and some other variable of significance to the firm, A, on the horizontal axis. It does not matter for the present purpose what this variable is. It may be size of enterprise, it may be uncertainty, liquidity, security of control, public reputation, or quality of labor relations. We suppose in each case a profits' curve which is a possibility function relating profits to A. This we suppose has a maximum value for profits at M. All combinations of amounts of profit with amounts of A within the curve are attainable; outside it they are unattainable. In each case three indifference curves of a field are drawn.

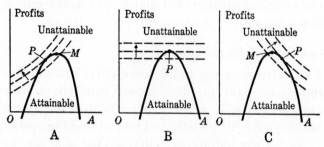

FIG. 124.   Utility Maximization in the Firm.

In Fig. 124A these indifference curves slope upward, indicating that A is a discommodity, as in quadrant $M_aMM'_b$ of Fig. 123. Profits must increase in order to compensate for an increase in the disagreeable A. The optimum position is at P where an indifference curve touches the possibility boundary. This point is below the maximum profits' point M, and at a smaller value of A. It is not worth going on to M because the gain in profits is accounted of less worth than the increase in the discommodity A which would accompany it.

In Fig. 124B the indifference curves are horizontal, indicating that A is neutral—that is, we do not care at all whether we have more or less of it. In that case the optimum point P coincides with the point of maximum profit.

In Fig. 124C, A is a commodity, and the indifference curves slope downward—we are willing to sacrifice profits in order to get more of A. In this case the optimum point P is below but to the right of M, indicating that we are willing to go beyond the point of maximum profits for the delights of getting more A. The principle of maximizing profits is thus seen as a special case in which the firm is indifferent to all those variables which are related to profits in a possibility function.

Utility Maximization for an Exchanger

The indifference curve analysis is useful in indicating formal solutions to many problems in the theory of the firm, whether of simple exchange, production, or inventory. In Fig. 125, for instance, suppose that we have first a pure exchanger, as in Fig. 78, page 553. The axes represent stocks of wheat and of money held. Suppose the exchanger starts from a position P_1, and has an exchange opportunity line MP_1W. We can find his optimum position on this line by drawing a field of indifference curves of which one is shown touching the exchange opportunity line at Q. Q is then the optimum point and the exchanger will move to it by selling wheat. The character of his indifference curves depends on his expectations of price changes. They will become

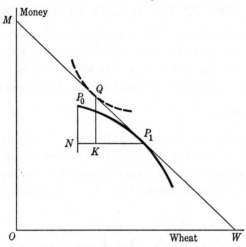

FIG. 125.   The Inventory Problem.

steeper the more he expects the price of wheat to rise, and flatter the more he expects it to fall. The slope of an indifference curve in this figure is the rate of indifferent substitution of money for wheat—that is, the quantity of money which he regards as just compensating for giving up one unit of wheat. If he expects the price to rise, wheat will become more attractive and money less; he will want more money as an equivalent of a unit of wheat than before, and the rate of indifferent substitution will rise. The optimum position will therefore move toward W.

The Inventory Problem

The same figure can be used to solve the problem of inventory on the theory of production. We now suppose the firm starts from P_0 and follows a production opportunity curve P_0P_1. It will move to P_1 where this curve is touched by an exchange opportunity line, as shown on page 549. The firm now moves back along the exchange opportunity line to Q, where it is touched by an indifference curve. Then NP_1 is the amount produced, P_1K is the amount sold, and NK is the amount added to inventory in the period for which the curves are appropriate. An expected rise in price will move the point Q down the curve as before; less will be sold in the present period and more will be added to inventory. An expected fall in price will move the point Q up the curve; more will be sold and less will be added to inventory—indeed, more may be sold than is produced and there may be withdrawals from inventory.[1]

APPLICATION TO THE THEORY OF THE HOUSEHOLD

The theory of the household is a peculiarly important field for the application of indifference curve techniques, as there is clearly no "objective maximand" such as profits which can be maximized, and we must fall back on a more general theory of the optimum.

The Budget Problem

Let us take first what might be called the "budget problem"—that of dividing a fixed income or sum of money in the best possible way between competing lines of expenditure. Let us suppose first that there are only two commodities bought—say, "food" and "clothing."

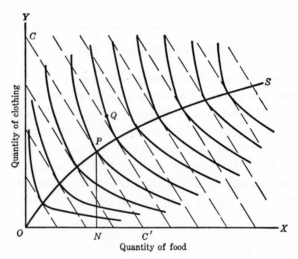

FIG. 126.   The Standard of Life Line.

The solid lines in Fig. 126 show the indifference curves of a consumer for combinations of these goods. Now let us suppose that the household has a fixed amount of money to spend on the two goods. If the whole sum is spent on clothing an amount, say, OC can be bought; if the whole sum is spent on food an amount OC' can be bought. All other combinations of quantities of food and clothing which can be

---

[1] The above type of analysis can be extended to cases of imperfect markets. For this extension the reader is referred to K. E. Boulding, *A Reconstruction of Economics*, New York, 1950, Chapter 6.

bought with the given sum lie on the line CC', which will be a straight line if the markets are perfect. This is an "outlay contour" as in Fig. 112; it is also a "possibility boundary" as the household cannot reach points beyond it as long as it is confined to the given total outlay. The optimum point is where it is touched by an indifference curve at P. There will be a family of such outlay contours corresponding to different total outlays. The locus of their points of tangency with the indifference curves is the line OPS. This is analogous to the "scale line" of Fig. 113. We may call it the "scale of living" or "standard of life" line, for it shows the best way of increasing purchases as the total outlay of the household increases. Given the total outlay of the household and its standard of life line, the optimum consumption pattern is found at the point of intersection of the standard of life line and the appropriate outlay contour.

The "Standard of Life" Line When There Are More Than Two Commodities

The analysis can be extended, like the scale-line analysis, to cover the case of three commodities if the quantity of the third commodity is measured on the vertical axis. Then instead of indifference curves we have indifference surfaces, looking rather like the skins of an onion; instead of outlay lines we have outlay planes, rather like the pages of a book. The point where an outlay plane is touched by an indifference surface represents that combination of *three* commodities which gives the greatest satisfaction, and which we can buy with the total outlay represented by the outlay plane. The locus of all such points is again a standard of life line, but in three dimensions instead of two. Any point on the line now represents a combination of quantities of three inputs which is the best combination for a given total outlay. Similarly, with any number of commodities, n, we can construct analytically, if not geometrically, a standard of life line in n-space, each point of which shows the best combination of commodities which can be purchased with a given total outlay.

Proof of the Equimarginal Principle

If we suppose for the moment a cardinally measurable utility, it can easily be shown that the principle of equality of marginal rates of substitution is identical with the "equimarginal principle" developed in Chapter 32, page 688. We have seen that the marginal condition for an optimum is that the marginal rate of indifferent substitution should equal the marginal rate of alternative cost. For two commodities A and B, however, the marginal rate of indifferent substitution is the ratio of their marginal utilities, and in perfect markets the marginal rate of alternative cost is the ratio of their prices. If for instance the price of A is $1 per unit and of B is $4 per unit, giving up one unit of B releases money which can be applied to purchase 4 units of A, total outlay being constant. We can write the marginal condition for the optimum, then:

$$\frac{\text{Marginal utility of B}}{\text{Marginal utility of A}} = \frac{\text{Price of B}}{\text{Price of A}}$$

Rearranging this equation we have:

$$\frac{\text{Marginal utility of A}}{\text{Price of A}} = \frac{\text{Marginal utility of B}}{\text{Price of B}}$$

This is the equimarginal principle of page 688. Although in this form it apparently requires the assumption of a cardinally measurable utility, this is merely a matter of form, not of substance; and as we see, the principle can be stated in the form of equality of marginal rates of substitution in a manner that does not imply more than ordinal measurement of utility.

Release of the Budget Limitation

Let us now release the budget limitation, and suppose that the total expenditure or outlay of the household is itself variable. Expenditure (E) is equal to receipts (R) minus "hoarding," or the increase in the money stock, H; $E = R - H$. An increase in expenditure can therefore come either out of an increase in receipts or out of dishoarding (a decline in money stocks). Receipts and expenditure here refer to inflows and outflows of *money* from the household. They should not be confused with the concepts of income (I) and outgo (O). Income is the gross additions to net worth of the household, which may be in the form either of money receipts or of other receipts, in the form, for example, of commodities, securities, or claims. Similarly outgo is the gross subtractions from this net worth, especially in the consumption of commodities. Saving (S) is the net increase in net worth, and is therefore equal to $I - O$. Saving consists of two parts—the increase in money stocks, H, and the increase in nonmoney assets, A, so that $S = H + A$. Strictly speaking, receipts and expenditures should be considered as part of the exchange process and regarded as asset transfers. Thus when a man earns income in the form of wages, this is reflected first in the building up of a wage claim, which is a kind of security. When he gets his paycheck he in effect exchanges (sells) this wage claim for money. All money receipts, therefore, can be thought of as resulting from a sale and all money expenditures from a purchase.

Household Decisions

There are therefore several sets of related decisions which a household has to make. There is some flexibility first in the amount of income received, depending on the amount of earning effort (work) put forth. There is flexibility in outgo, or saving, whichever way we wish to look at it, though not in both together once income has been fixed, for to fix income and outgo fixes saving, or to fix income and saving fixes outgo. Then if saving has been fixed there is a further problem of the choice between increasing money or nonmoney assets. Then if H has been decided there is a further problem of how large R or E should be—that is, how large the money turnover of the household should be. In farm households, for instance, receipts may be appreciably less than income, as part of the product of the household is consumed on the spot and does not go to market. This is true even of urban households where much time is spent on home repair and maintenance. On the other hand there are some households which indulge in a good deal of buying and selling; a household, for instance, which buys and sells a house in the course of a year will have receipts and expenditures far in excess of its income or outgo. There is a problem here of when does a household become a business. If a household, for instance, makes a regular practice of buying and selling houses, we should probably want to classify this activity as "business."

Earnings and Hours of Work

Let us consider first the problem of the determination of income or earnings from work. Suppose first that a man has the opportunity to work for as many hours as he pleases at a fixed hourly wage. In Fig. 127A the number of hours worked in a day is measured along the horizontal direction, the total income derived from such work along the vertical direction. We can then postulate a system of indifference curves, such as I_1, I_2, I_3, etc., which describe the system of preferences of the individual as between work and income. Any one of these curves —say, I_1—joins all those points which represent equally advantageous combinations of hours of work and income. Thus both the point P_1, representing 4 hours' work and $1.25 a day income, and the point R_1, representing 8 hours' work and $2.50 income each day, are on the same indifference curve, I_1. This means that if the man were offered the choice between working 4 hours for $1.25 and working 8 hours for

$2.50, he would not know which to choose, each alternative seeming equally attractive to him, like the donkey between two bales of hay. This system of indifference curves can also be regarded as the con-

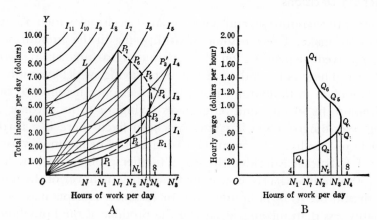

FIG. 127.   Derivation of Supply Curve for Labor.

tours of a three-dimensional utility surface, in which utility is measured in the direction vertical to the plane of the paper. Any student familiar with contour maps will have no difficulty in visualizing the surface as something like a "half-dome" mountain, rising toward the top left-hand corner of the figure.

We have given this system of indifference curves certain properties. We have assumed in the first place that each indifference curve ultimately slopes upward and to the right. This is the graphic expression of the assumption that in order to make anyone do more work per day, it is necessary to offer him a larger total reward. A person might be indifferent regarding the combinations "$1.25 and 4 hours" and "$2.50 and 8 hours." But it would be a strange person who would be indifferent whether he worked 4 hours for a total of $1.25 or 8 hours for a total of $1, as might be the case if the indifference curves had a negative slope. This means simply that labor is a discommodity and we are operating in the quadrant $M_a M M'_b$ of Fig. 123.

In the second place we have assumed that the indifference curves get steeper as the number of hours of work increases. There is a physical limit to the number of hours of work which can be done in a day —say, 16 or 18 hours. At this limit all the indifference curves will be vertical, for there is no point beyond this maximum which can possibly lie on an indifference curve. At the physical maximum, that is, one will always prefer a larger income and will never conceivably prefer longer hours, however great the inducement. It is reasonable, therefore, to assume that the indifference curves, if they are regular in shape, curve upward to a vertical asymptote at the physical maximum number of hours.

There is a further reason for the assumption of a curve with rising slope. It is that after a certain point, at least, successive unit additions to the working day are likely to be more and more distasteful, and less and less pleasant. A man will gladly work an extra hour when he works only three hours a day, irrespective of pay; but it is with a sour face that he faces an extra hour when he has already worked ten. Assuming for the moment a measurable total utility, this means that as the hours of work increase, after a point the marginal utility of work will decline sharply, become negative, and become an increasingly large negative quantity. In Fig. 127A we have assumed that work is a disutility from the very start—though this is not a necessary assumption—and that as the quantity of work done for a *given* income increases, the total utility of work and income together declines with ever increasing velocity. Moving outward from the income axis, OY, along a horizontal line we cross the indifference curves with ever increasing rapidity, indicating that the total utility surface is getting steeper and steeper and the marginal utility of work a larger and larger negative quantity. This result can be achieved only if the indifference curves are curved in the manner suggested.

If, now, the individual receives a fixed hourly wage for all hours worked, the line which shows the relationship between the number of hours of labor and the total income received in one day will be a straight line from the origin. The slope of this line is the hourly wage. OP_1 is the line representing the income-hours relationship when the hourly wage is $\dfrac{N_1P_1}{ON_1}$ or $\text{Tan } P_1ON_1$.

To find the "best" combination of hours and income for any given wage, we find where the income-hours line, e.g., OP_1, is touched by an indifference curve. The coordinates of this point (e.g., P_1) represent that combination of hours and income which gives the individual the greatest total utility consistent with a given hourly wage. This point is on the "highest" indifference curve which the individual can reach under the limitation that he receives only a fixed hourly wage.

The Supply Curve for Labor

It is only a little step now to derive from our system of indifference curves the supply curves for labor. The higher the hourly wage, the greater the slope of the income-hours line. As the wage rises from $\frac{N_1P_1}{ON_1}$ to $\frac{N_2P_2}{ON_2}$, the income-hours line steepens from OP_1 to OP_2, the point of equilibrium shifts from P_1 to P_2, and the number of hours worked changes from ON_1 to ON_2. As the wage rises further to levels indicated by the slopes of OP_3, OP_4, etc., the point of equilibrium changes to P_3, P_4, etc. So we can plot a complete supply curve for labor from the individual, as in Fig. 127B. Here the number of hours is measured horizontally on the same scale as in Fig. 127A. The hourly wage is measured vertically. The the curve Q_1Q_7 is the supply curve for labor from the individual in question. When the wage is N_1Q_1 ($=\frac{N_1P_1}{ON_1}$ in Fig. 127A), the number of hours which the individual is willing to work is ON_1; when the wage is N_2Q_2 ($=\frac{N_2P_2}{ON_2}$ in Fig. 127A), the number of hours worked is ON_2, and so on.

It will be observed that the curve Q_1Q_7 is re-entrant and that the number of hours reaches a maximum, ON_4. At a higher wage than that at which the number of hours is a maximum (N_4Q_4), a rise in wages results in a *fall* in the quantity of work supplied. The curve in Fig. 127B should be compared with the curve in Fig. 41, page 211. Our simple assumptions regarding the indifference curves give a full explanation of how a re-entrant supply curve can exist.

Just as a seller can extract a greater amount of money from a buyer if he charges different prices for different quantities, as we saw in Chapter 29 (page 612), so a buyer of labor can extract a greater amount of labor for a given sum if he offers to pay different sums for different hours. Suppose, for instance, in Fig. 127A that the employer offers to pay an hourly wage equal to $\frac{P_3N_3}{ON_3}$ for the first ON_3 hours worked, and a higher wage, equal to the slope of the line $P_3P'_3$, for each hour worked thereafter. The income-hours line is now $OP_3P'_3$, and the highest indifference curve reached on this line is not I_3 but I_4, if we assume that the line $P_3P'_3$ touches the indifference curve I_4 at P'_3. Such a practice is known as paying "overtime" rates. The figure shows that it may result in extracting from the worker a larger number of hours (ON'_3) than he would be willing to work at *any* wage if the hourly wage were constant!

Fig. 127A also tells how many hours a man will want to work at a given hourly wage if he has income from other sources. Suppose he has an income equal to OK from sources other than labor and that he can earn an hourly wage measured by the slope of the line OP_5. Then a line KL, drawn from K parallel to OP_5, represents the income-hours curve. If this curve touches an indifference curve at L, the coordinates of the point L give the number of hours he will work (ON) and the total income he will earn (NL). We can see immediately from the figure that the larger the income from other sources, i.e., the greater is OK, the fewer hours will be worked.

The Outgo-Saving Decision

With the indifference curve technique we can give at least a formal solution to the problem of the determinants of individual saving and hoarding. Thus in Fig. 128A we show the field of indifference curves

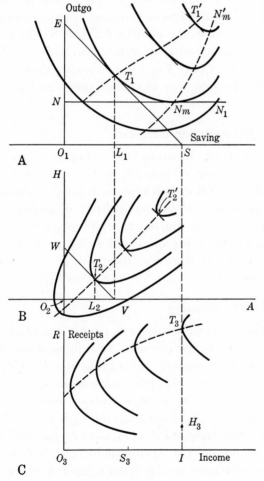

FIG. 128.   Saving, Hoarding, and Receipts.

for combinations of outgo and saving. The hypothesis suggested is that for a given amount of outgo an increase in saving will first increase utility, but utility will reach a maximum and will then decline. This can be seen by following a line such as NN_mN_1, and visualizing the utility surface above it; utility rises from N to a maximum at N_m and then declines as saving is increased further. We suppose, however, that increase in outgo always increases utility, as may be seen by following a vertical line in the figure. The curves as drawn also indicate the hypothesis that the volume of saving at which utility is a maximum is larger at larger levels of outgo. The line N_mN_m', through the minimum points of the indifference curves bears to the right. For each level of income the possibility curve is a straight line making equal intercepts with the axes, such as ET_1S. If all the income were saved saving would be OS; if all were consumed outgo would be OE. The line ETS then represents the identity $I = O + S$. The optimum point is the point of tangency with an indifference curve, T_1, where saving is O_1L_1 and outgo is L_1T_1. The locus of such points is a "scale line," T_1T_1', showing the best way to change outgo and saving as income changes.

The Hoarding-Accumulation Decision

We then project O_1L_1 down to O_2V in Fig. 128B, in which increase in money stock is measured vertically and increase in nonmoney assets horizontally. The line WV then represents the combinations of H and A which are possible with a total volume of saving equal to O_1L_1 ($= OV = OW$). This line touches an indifference curve at T_2, so that O_2L_2 is the optimum value of A and L_2T_2 of H. The indifference curves in Fig. 128B are drawn so that both H and A show a utility maximum as one is increased while the other is held constant.

The Receipts-Income Decision

Finally in Fig. 128C we show the optimum amount of receipts corresponding to each level of income. We suppose a set of indifference curves in the receipts-income field. From the level of income O_3I ($= O_1S$) we draw the vertical line to touch an indifference curve at T_3. IT_3 is then the optimum amount of receipts with the income O_3I. If now we draw $IH_3 = L_2T_2$ (hoarding), H_3T_3 is the optimum amount of expenditure. Similarly drawing $IS_3 = O_1L_1$ (saving), we have O_3S_3 as the optimum outgo. The optimum income, O_3I, we derive from Fig. 127A, given the wage rate. It is not suggested, of course, that these decisions are made in the order named. The analysis is made more difficult also by the possibility that the various sets of indifference curves are not independent—thus a change in the rate of substitution of income for work may well go along with changes in the rates of substitution of saving for outgo and of money for other assets. Nevertheless we must suppose that the whole set of optimum positions is consistent with a set of preferences as above described, provided that each set of indifference curves is consistent with the others.

DERIVATION OF DEMAND CURVES

With the above apparatus we can proceed to a more detailed analysis of the derivation of demand curves from preference (utility) functions. We will first assume the budget limitation—i.e., constancy in total expenditure—and consider the effect of a rise in the price of one commodity or input. The treatment is strictly analogous to that of the demand for input of a firm. Just as a rise in the price of an input has two effects on the equilibrium position of a firm—a "scale effect" and a "substitution effect"—so in the case of a householder a rise in the price of one of his consumption goods will have two effects—a "scale effect," which is called the "income" effect, and a "substitution effect." That is to say, in most cases a rise in the price of a commodity will make a householder buy less of it for two reasons: first, the rise in price makes him *poorer* and so reduces his real income, and second, the rise in price makes him shift his purchases toward the substitutes for the dearer commodity. We shall suppose first that the total expenditure is given and is not changed by the rise in price. We shall again assume that only two commodities are purchased, food and clothing, and shall study the effects of a rise in the price of food. In Fig. 129, then, as in Fig. 126, the quantity of food is measured along OX, the quantity of clothing along OY. Let BC represent the outlay curve for a given total expenditure, $\$t$, when p_c is the price of clothing and p_f the price of food. Then $OB = \dfrac{t}{p_c}$, and $OC = \dfrac{t}{p_f}$. Suppose that the price of food rises to p'_f. The quantity of food which can be purchased with a sum $\$t$ falls from OC to OD $(=\dfrac{t}{p'_f})$. The outlay line therefore moves from BC to BD, as an outlay of $\$t$ will still buy a quantity OB of clothing. Suppose at the old price the outlay line BC is touched by an indifference curve, I_1, at P_1. P_1 will then lie on the "standard of life" line, OS_1, and the consumer will buy a quantity ON_1 of food and N_1P_1 of clothing. When the price of food rises, there is a new outlay line, BD; this is touched by another indifference curve, I_2, at P_2, which lies on the new "standard of life" line, OS_2. The result of the rise in the price of food, therefore, is a reduction in the quantity bought from ON_1 to ON_2. Thus the "law of demand" can be derived from the assumption of a "scale of preference" as embodied in the indifference curves.

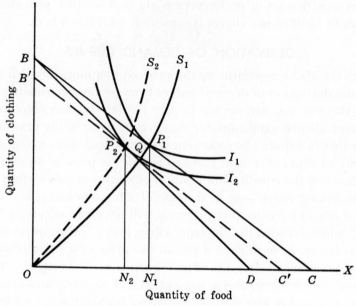

FIG. 129. Derivation of Consumers' Demand.

"Substitution Effect" and "Income Effect"

The fall in the consumption of a commodity which results from a rise in its price is due to a substitution effect—the movement of the scale line from OS_1 to OS_2—and a scale effect—the reduction in "utility" as observed in the passing from the indifference curve I_1 to the lower indifference curve I_2. That is, the rise in price causes a shift to other commodities and also a reduction in real income.

"Industry Effect"

In considering the forces underlying the total demand of all consumers for a commodity we must also note an effect analogous to the "industry effect"; when the price rises, some consumers may cease to consume the commodity altogether, and when the price falls, some consumers who had not previously consumed the commodity will begin to consume it.

Rise in Price Equivalent to Fall in Money Income

Another interesting property of this analysis is that it enables us to define the scale effect of a change in prices in terms of a change in money income. Consider the significance of point Q, Fig. 129, where the standard of life line OS_1 cuts the indifference curve I_2. This represents that combination of food and clothing which would give the same enjoyment as the combination represented by point P_2 (as it is on the same indifference curve); but as it is on the standard of life line OS_1, it also represents the best possible combination to buy at the *old* prices and at an income represented by the outlay line $B'C'$ drawn through Q parallel to BC. The money income which, at the old prices, would give the same satisfaction as the present money income at the new prices is then $OB' \cdot p_c$, or $OC' \cdot p_f$. This is smaller than the actual money income, showing that a rise in the price of even one commodity is equivalent to a loss of money income if prices remained the same. This construction gives us a theoretical solution to the problem of a "cost of living" index number, the change in the cost of living being measured by the reciprocal of the "income equivalent" of a price change. If after a rise in prices the "income equivalent" of $100 at the original price structure is $90—i.e., $90 at the old price structure is equivalent to $100 at the new—then we may say that the cost of living index has risen from 100 to 111.1.

"Poor Man's Goods": A "Backward-sloping" Standard of Life Line

There is one special case of the above analysis which is interesting. If there are two commodities, one of which is a "rich man's good" and the other a "poor man's good" (often called an "inferior good"), the character of the indifference curves will be as in Fig. 130. It will be observed that after a while the indifference curves bend backward and become positively sloped, indicating that the "poor man's good" has become a positive nuisance. It will also be noticed that the point where this happens gets nearer to the X axis as the quantity of rich man's goods increases—the line UU, drawn through the points in the indifference curves where the poor man's good first becomes a nuisance, slopes downward. With such a system of indifference curves the standard of life line, OS, will actually bend backward as in the figure, indicating that as the standard of life increases beyond a certain point, a smaller quantity of the poor man's goods is actually bought. This is true to experience; the rich eat much less margarine and corn pone than the poor.

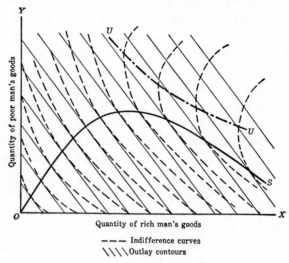

FIG. 130.   Poor Man's Goods.

The Inverse Demand Curve

In this case it is possible for a rise in the price of the "poor man's good" to have a scale effect in the opposite direction to the usual one, so that this rise may actually bring about an *increase* in the quantity bought, because of the decline in the standard of life. This is shown in Fig. 131. Here OP_1S_1 is the original standard of life line. A rise in the price of poor man's goods pushes this line toward the X axis— the substitution effect operating to substitute rich man's goods—and the standard of life line moves to OP_2S_2. The rise in the price of poor man's goods shifts the outlay line from BC_1 to BC_2, for fewer poor man's goods can now be bought for the same money expenditure. At the original prices, N_1P_1 of poor man's goods will be bought, ON_1 of rich man's goods, where P_1 is the point of intersection of BC_1 and OS_1. After the rise in the price of poor man's goods N_2P_2 of poor man's goods will be bought, and ON_2 of rich man's goods, where P_2 is the point of intersection of BC_2 and OS_2. It will be observed that N_2P_2 is greater than N_1P_1—i.e., the rise in the price of the poor man's goods has resulted in an increase in the consumption of them, as it has made people poorer. Thus even an apparent exception to the "law of demand" can be understood by means of the indifference curve analysis. It will be readily appreciated that this exception is likely to be very rare, for the commodity not only must be a poor man's good but it must also play a relatively large part in consumption; otherwise the reverse "income effect" will not be large enough to offset the substitution effect which still, of course, makes for a decrease in the quantity taken when there is a rise in price. Probably the only example is a basic foodstuff, like bread, at a very low level of income.

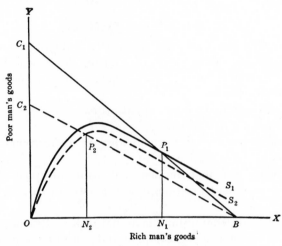

FIG. 131.   Inverse Demand Curve.

Removal of Budget Limitation

The above derivation of demand curves must be modified somewhat if the budget limitation is removed. Thus a rise in the price of "food" is equivalent to a fall in real wages. Consequently, income will change, depending on the supply of labor. If the householder is operating at a point such as P_3 in Fig. 127A, this will diminish his income; the curve BD of Fig. 129 will move down, and the purchases both of clothing and of food will be lessened. Suppose now that beyond P_7, in Fig. 127A, the curve P_1P_7 turned down, so that his income actually rose under the stimulus of the decline in the real wage. The curve BD in Fig. 129 will move up, increasing purchases both of food and of clothing. If this supplementary income effect is large enough, it may lead to an inverse demand curve, with a rise in the price of food actually leading to an increase in the quantity taken—not, this time, because food is an inferior good but because the householder works harder, "work" as opposed to leisure being the inferior good.

It is possible also that a rise in the price of food might lead to changes in saving and in hoarding which would change the total of expenditures relative to income and so shift the position of the budget line *BD* (Fig. 129). If, for instance, the rise in price led to dis-hoarding, expenditures would be increased and the scale effect would lessen the decline in purchases. These changes might also lead to inverse demands, at least in the very short run. These effects, however, are limited to short periods and are of the nature of "once-over" changes; they cannot be the source of permanent changes in demand.

QUESTIONS AND EXERCISES

1. The concept of marginal utility is subject to the objection that it implies a numerical measurement of total utility. How can we get over this difficulty? Translate into terms which do not involve the extensive measurement of utility:

   a. The law of diminishing marginal utility.

   b. The equimarginal principle.

   c. The proposition that a commodity is a "discommodity" if its marginal utility is negative.

   d. The proposition that the marginal utility of "poor man's goods" falls to zero at a smaller consumption when we rise to a higher standard of life.

   e. The law of the diminishing marginal utility of money.

2. With this chapter in view, compare and contrast the analytical tools involved in the theories of production and consumption.

3. Diamonds are often cited as a possible exception to the rule that a higher price makes for a smaller volume of purchases, for a rise in the price of diamonds may increase their value as articles of display. How would you explain this phenomenon according to the indifference curve analysis?

4. "Economics is ultimately the theory of human choices. As such it covers not merely a part of life, but the whole. And the indifference curve is the map of human choice." Discuss.

5. Prove that a man may be induced to work longer hours by means of "overtime pay" than by any straight hourly wage, no matter how high.

6. In Fig. 124 suppose that the variable *A* represents a measure of the over-all size of the enterprise. What types of business character would correspond to the three cases shown? Repeat this question on the assumption that variable *A* measures (a) liquidity, (b) man-days lost in strikes, (c) amplitude of fluctuations in profits, (d) amount paid in taxes, (e) percentage of income given to charity.

7. "The indifference curve is the most potent analytical instrument we possess when we come to investigate the difficult problems of economic welfare." Discuss and illustrate.

8. Apply the indifference curve analysis to the problem of joint demand. How will the indifference curves differ in the case of two commodities

in (a) competitive demand, (b) independent demand, and (c) complementary demand? What kind of demand curves or surfaces (contours) can be derived from these indifference curves?

(Note: The methods in Exercise 7, page 785, can be applied to this problem. Derive the indifference curves from total utility curves, in a construction like Fig. 112.)

9. In Figs. 127 and 128 what might be the effect on the indifference curves and on the optimum positions of the various variables of the following changes:

   a. A general rise in the cost of living.
   b. A rise in the rate of interest.
   c. An increase in income tax rates.
   d. A tax on food.
   e. A decline in frugality.
   f. Expectations of inflation.
   Illustrate by diagrams.

10. Are there any kinds of input in a process of production which correspond to the "poor man's good" (inferior good)? If so, what peculiarities might be encountered in their demand?

CHAPTER 37

FURTHER APPLICATIONS OF INDIFFERENCE CURVE ANALYSIS

THE THEORY OF EXCHANGE AND THE PARETIAN OPTIMUM

With indifference curve equipment we can now return to an earlier problem—the theory of exchange between two individuals.

In the box diagram, Fig. 132, O_aX is the total quantity of commodity H in the possession of two exchangers, A and B, and O_aY is the total quantity of commodity K in their possession. The *distribution* of the two commodities between the two exchangers is shown by a point inside the rectangle O_aXO_bY. Thus at the point P_0, exchanger A has O_aH_a of H and O_aK_a of K; exchanger B has O_bH_b of H and O_bK_b of K. A's quantities are measured by the coordinates of the point relative to origin O_a, and B's quantities relative to origin O_b.

Suppose now that we start from a position such as P_0, and suppose that some price is set at which exchanges can be made. The exchange opportunity line for both parties is a straight line such as $P_0E_bE_a$, the slope of which is equal to the price. Thus suppose we move from P_0 to E_b. This means that A has acquired and B has relinquished LE_b of H, and A has relinquished and B has acquired P_0L of K. The price, or ratio of exchange, is therefore P_0L/LE_b units of K per unit of H, which is the slope of the line P_0E_b. We now impose two sets of indifference curves on the figure. The solid curves such as P_0A_0, E_bA_1, show A's preference function and the dotted curves such as P_0B_0, E_bB_1, show B's preference function. As drawn, A moves to preferred positions as he moves out from O_a, toward O_b, with more goods in his possession; B moves to preferred positions as he moves out from O_b toward O_a. If the figure is turned through 180° it will be seen that B's indifference curves are of the conventional two-commodity pattern relative to B's origin at O_b. We may note in passing that the preference here is for a
810

distribution of the commodities, not for possession alone. If the parties are highly altruistic, so that each worries about the poverty of the other, the indifference curves may exhibit a maximum point within the "box," as in Fig. 123.

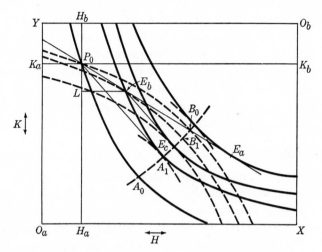

FIG. 132.   The Theory of Exchange.

Dynamics of Exchange

With indifference curves as in Fig. 132 and an exchange opportunity line P_0E_b, exchange will proceed to the point E_b with both parties moving to higher indifference curves and being better off; A's (solid) indifference curve at E_b is higher than the one at P_0, and B's (dotted) indifference curve at E_b is likewise higher than the one at P_0. At E_b, however, B will not wish to exchange any more, and beyond E_b, where the line P_0E_b touches a B-indifference curve, B is moving to worse positions. A would like to go on exchanging at this price up to E_a, where the exchange opportunity line touches one of his indifference curves, but he cannot do this because B is not willing to go beyond E_b. If no further price change is possible, E_b is the point of equilibrium. If, however, the price can be changed (in this case raised) to any level up to the slope of A's indifference curve at E_b, further exchange is possible. Thus suppose the price is raised and the exchange opportunity line shifts to E_bE_c. As we move from E_b to E_c both parties are again moving to higher indifference curves, until again one or the other reaches a point where the exchange opportunity line touches one of his indifference curves and exchange ceases. In the figure E_bE_c has been drawn so that E_c is on a point of tangency both of A's and B's indifference curves. At such a point no further movement can be made which will benefit both parties, no matter what the price.

The Contract Curve

The locus of such points of mutual tangency, $A_0 E_c B_0$ is called the *contract curve*. From any point not on the contract curve an exchange opportunity can be found which will benefit both parties and move them toward the contract curve. No such opportunity can be found for a point on the contract curve. As long as price changes are possible, therefore, the equilibrium point must be on the contract curve, as for any point not on the contract curve a price can be found at which exchange is mutually profitable.

Bargaining Paths

From the point P_0 movement to any point on the contract curve between A_0 and B_0 will benefit both parties. At A_0, A is only just as well off as he was at P_0; B is making his maximum gain from exchange. At B_0 B is only just as well off as at P_0, and A is making his maximum gain. The exact point to which the system will move depends on the actual dynamics of the case—that is, on the succession of prices offered. By perfect price discrimination A can move B down B's indifference curve to B_0, or B can move A down A's indifference curve to A_0. There is one price at which both parties move straight to the contract curve, as on the path $P_0 A_1$, where $P_0 A_1$ is tangent to both indifference curves at A_1. There is nothing in the system to suppose, however, that this price is an "equilibrium price," for any other exchange path within the area $P_0 A_0 B_0$ is equally plausible, depending on the bargaining ability of the two parties. The *final* price at which the two parties reach the contract curve must of course be equal to the marginal rates of indifferent substitution (the slopes of the indifferent curves) of both parties. Even this, however, is not determinate, as it varies from point to point on the contract curve.

Application to Collective Bargaining

This analysis is of general applicability to any bargaining situation, wherever two parties and two "goods" are involved. Thus Fig. 132 might apply to a collective bargain situation in which, say, $O_a X$, measures the wage and $O_a Y$ some other benefit, say, shortness of vacation. The dotted indifference curves now represent the employers' preference function (he likes lower wages, shorter holidays) and the solid lines the union preference function. The origin O_b is not significant here. As before there will be a "contract curve" at the locus of the points of tangency of the two sets of indifference curves. From all points *not* on the contract curve adjustments can be made ("trades") which benefit both parties, and much bargaining in practice consists on finding what these adjustments are. Once on the contract curve, however, movement can only be made which benefits one party and injures another. This involves conflict, whereas "trades" do not.

This analysis illustrates well an earlier proposition (page 31): that exchange involves both a community and a conflict of interest—community of interest in *reaching* the contract curve, conflict of interest in moving one way or the other along the contract curve.

The "Paretian Optimum"

The contract curve describes what is known as the "Paretian optimum" in exchange (after Vilfredo Pareto). It is the condition in which no adjustment is possible which does not make somebody worse off than before. The optimum conditions are perhaps best described in a negative form: the optimum has not been reached if any reorganization is possible which will make some people better off without making anyone worse off. Then the marginal conditions can be stated by saying that if the appropriate marginal rates of transformation between commodities or factors of two parties are *not* equal, keeping either utility or product constant, reorganizations can be made which will improve one party's position without worsening the other.

Seven Marginal Conditions

Seven such "marginal conditions" have been distinguished. (1) In exchange, as we see above, marginal rates of indifferent substitution of two owners should be equal. If owner A can give up $2K$ for $1H$ without feeling loss, and owner B can give up $3K$ for $1H$ without feeling loss, then if A gives B $1H$ and gets from B $2K$, A is no worse off and B is better off, as he would have been willing to give up $3K$ for $1H$. (2) In the reallocation of production: if two producers each produce two commodities the marginal rates of alternative cost should be equal. If giving up the production of $2K$ enables A to produce $1H$, and giving up $1H$ enables B to produce $3K$, then if A produces $1H$ more and B $1H$ less, $2K$ is lost from A but $3K$ is gained from B; no H is lost and $1K$ is gained on balance. (3) In the reallocation of factors: marginal physical productivities of a factor f for all producers should be equal. If $1f$ makes $2K$ with producer A and $3K$ with producer B, shifting $1f$ from A to B will result in a net gain of $1K$ for the same amount of factor employed. (4) In the substitution of factors: two factors f and g should have the same rate of equal product substitution in all occupations. If producer A can substitute $1f$ for $2g$ without loss of product, and producer B can likewise substitute $1f$ for $3g$, then if producer B lets $3g$ go and takes on $1f$, and producer A takes on $2g$ and releases $1f$, there is no change in product and $1g$ is released to make other things. (5) In the substitution of products: for two products H and K the rate of indifferent substitution for any household should equal the rate of equal product substitution for any firm. If household A can give up $2K$ for $1H$ without feeling loss, and producer B can produce $3K$ by giving up $1H$, then shifting production from $1H$ to $3K$ will enable the producer to give the householder $2K$ for $1H$; the household is as well off as before and the producer is $1K$ to the good. (6) In the substitution of leisure for product: the rate of indifferent substitution of factor use for product should equal the marginal rate of reward paid. If it would take an additional $2H$ to induce the owner of a factor to add $1t$ to its use, and if the owner can earn $3H$ by adding $1t$ to its use, then by adding $1t$ to its use the owner is better off. (7) In lending and borrowing (without uncertainty), the marginal rate of time preference should be the same for all individuals. Thus suppose H_1 and H_2 represent "this year's" and "next year's" income. If a lender feels that giving up $1H_1$ is just worth it if he gets $2H_2$, and a borrower feels that getting $1H_1$ is worth it even if he has to give up $3H_2$, then lending $1H_1$ and paying back $2H_2$ will leave the lender as well off as before but will make the borrower better off.

"Trading" Leads to the Optimum

These conditions are not, of course, sufficient to describe a social optimum. If, however, they are violated it means that "trading" of some sort is possible—that is, it is possible to reach bargains which will not make anybody worse off and will make somebody better off. Once they are all fulfilled together, however, all movement implies conflict—i.e., it is only possible to gain at the expense of someone else.[1]

THE THEORY OF A COMPETITIVE MARKET

From the indifference curves of all individuals in a competitive market it is possible to obtain their demand-supply, or market curves,

---

[1] For a more detailed exposition of these marginal conditions, see M. Reder, *Studies in the Theory of Welfare Economics* (New York, 1947), or K. E. Boulding, *Survey of Contemporary Economics*, ed. Bernard Haley (Homewood, Ill., 1952), Vol. II, Chapter 1.

and hence the equilibrium price and quantity exchanged. In Fig. 133 we draw the indifference curves M_0I_0, M_1I_1 of a single marketer showing those combinations of stocks of money and of the commodity concerned to which he is indifferent. His stock of money is measured

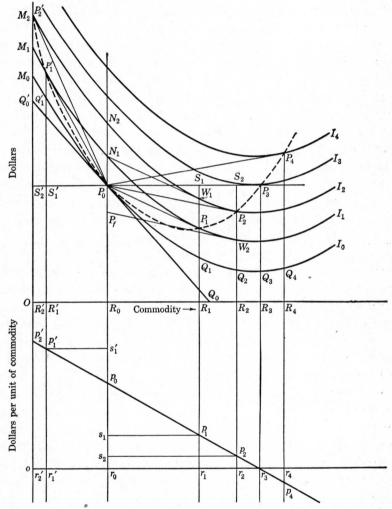

Figs. 133A (above) and 133B (below).   Derivation of Market Curve.

along the vertical axis, his stock of commodity along the horizontal axis. Any one indifference curve, such as I_0, shows all those combinations of holdings of money and commodity to which the marketer is indifferent. Over most of the range it will be observed that the indifference curve has a negative slope, indicating that if money is given up, commodity must be increased to compensate. We have drawn the curves, however, with the slope (i.e., the marginal rate of substitution) diminishing with increase in commodity, indicating that the more commodity a marketer has in his possession the less he values a marginal increase in terms of money. We have drawn the indifference curves sloping positively at high quantities of commodity, indicating that in this range the commodity has become a "discommodity"—i.e., the marketer would have to be offered money in order to persuade him to increase his holdings of commodity. Another property of the indifference curves as we have drawn them should also be noticed; the curves are parallel in a vertical direction—i.e., at a given quantity of commodity the slopes of the curves, or the marginal rate of substitution, is the same no matter how great the quantity of money. This assumption leads to an important simplification of the analysis, though it will be relaxed shortly. It corresponds to an assumption which is important in Marshall's analysis, that the marginal utility of money is constant. If we could assume a measurable utility, the marginal rate of substitution, in dollars per unit of commodity, as we have seen, would be equal to the ratio $\dfrac{\text{Marginal utility of commodity}}{\text{Marginal utility of money}}$. If the marginal utility of money is constant, then the marginal rate of substitution depends only on the quantity of commodity, not on the quantity of money. The implication is that the total quantity of money held by the marketer is so large that changes in his stock of money do not affect his willingness to part with it; hence, his demand for or offer of commodity depends only on his willingness to part with or acquire commodity, not on his willingness to acquire or part with money. It should be observed that the condition that the marginal rate of substitution should be independent of the quantity of money is somewhat broader than the Marshallian assumption; the marginal rate of substitution could be independent of the quantity of money even if the marginal utility of money changed (presumably fell) with increase in the quantity of money, provided that the marginal utility of the commodity changed in the same proportion. Fortunately, however, the indifference curve technique enables us to escape from this grave restriction in a way that the older marginal utility analysis did not permit.

Derivation of Market Curves

From the indifference curves it is not difficult to derive the demand-supply or market curve of the marketer, showing what quantities of commodity he will offer to buy or sell if he is faced with a situation in which he can buy or sell unlimited quantities at fixed prices. Suppose P_0 represents the combination of money and commodity in his possession at the beginning of trading. The straight lines $P_0P'_2$, $P_0P'_1$, Q'_0Q_0, P_0P_1, P_0P_2, etc. are *opportunity lines* showing what combinations of money and commodity are open to the marketer by exchange at various prices, the slope of the line being the price at which exchange takes place. Thus the line P_0P_1 (and its projections, not drawn on the figure) shows those combinations which are open to the marketer when he starts exchanging from the point P_0 at a price $\dfrac{P_1S_1}{P_0S_1}$. Movements to the right from P_0 represent purchases of commodity— the stock of money declines as the stock of commodity increases. Movements to the left of P_0 indicate sales of commodity—stocks of money increase as stocks of commodity decline. It must be emphasized again that all we are considering here is simple exchange; there is no production or consumption, but simply a transformation of the form of assets by buying or selling; the price is the "transformation coefficient" showing how much money can be transferred into or out of one unit of commodity.

The equilibrium position at any price is the point where the opportunity line touches an indifference curve, this being on the highest indifference curve which can be reached as long as the marketer must stay on his opportunity line. Thus, P_1 is the equilibrium point when the price is equal to the slope of P_0P_1. P_0S_1 is the amount of commodity bought; S_1P_1 is the amount of money given up. The locus of all such points, the dotted line $P'_2P'_1$, $\cdots$ P_4, is an outlay-receipts curve with its origin at P_0, showing how much money will be paid out or received for different quantities of commodity bought or sold.

From Fig. 133A the marketers' demand-supply or market curve can immediately be derived, as in Fig 133B. Commodity is measured on the horizontal axis as before, dollars per unit of commodity on the vertical axis. The line p'_2, $\cdots$ p_4 is the marginal rate of substitution curve; its vertical ordinate at each quantity of commodity is equal to the slope of the indifference curves of Fig. 133A at the corresponding point. As we have assumed that the marginal rate of substitution is independent of the quantity of money, the whole system of indifference curves reduces to a single marginal rate of substitution curve, for at a given quantity of commodity all the indifference curves have the same slope. Thus at a quantity or_2 $(= OR_2)$, the slopes of the indifference curves at Q_2, W_2, P_2, etc., are all equal to r_2p_2. Then the marginal rate of substitution curve p'_2, $\cdots$ p_4 is the same as the demand-supply curve of the marketer, because the marginal rate of substitution must be equal to the price when the marketer is satisfied. Thus at a price r_1p_1 the marketer will buy r_0r_1 of the commodity, because when he has an amount or_1, the marginal rate of substitution (the slope of the indifference curve) is equal to the price (the slope of the opportunity line); in other words, the opportunity line is tangent to the indifference curve, as it is at P_1. It has already been shown in Chapter 4 how the total market curve and the market price and quantity exchanged can be derived by summing the market (demand-supply) curves of all the individual marketers, so that from the indifference curves of all the marketers the market price and quantity could be obtained.

A Limiting Assumption Removed

In Fig. 134 we remove the assumption that the marginal rate of substitution is independent of the quantity of money. The figure is essentially similar to Fig. 133, except that the indifference curves are drawn so that the marginal rate of substitution rises with increase in the quantity of money; thus, the slope of the curve at N_2 is greater than that of the curve at N_1. Instead of the whole system of indifference curves now reducing to a single marginal rate of substitution curve we have a whole series of marginal rate of substitution curves in Fig. 134B, m_0i_0, m_1i_1, m_2i_2, etc., each corresponding to an indifference curve in Fig. 134A. In this case higher indifference curves yield higher marginal rate of substitution curves. The demand-supply curve does not now correspond to any single marginal rate of substitution curve. The outlay-receipts curve—the dotted line P'_1, $\cdots$ P_2 in Fig. 134A—is, as before, the locus of the points of tangency of successive opportunity lines $P_0P'_1$, P_0P_1, etc., with the indifference curves. At each point of tangency the price is equal to the marginal rate of substitution. In Fig. 134B, therefore, from each point on the quantity axes, say r_1, we erect a perpendicular till it cuts the marginal rate of substitution curve m_1i_1 derived from the indifference curve at P_1 at p_1; r_1p_1 is then the price at which the market will be willing to buy the quantity r_0r_1. The dotted line p'_1, $\cdots$ p_2 is the marketers' demand-supply curve. It will be observed that the demand section of the curve (p_0p_2) has a flatter slope than the marginal rate of substitution curves, and the supply section $(p_0p'_1)$ has a steeper slope. If the marginal rate of substitution fell with increasing quantities of money, the above relationship would be reversed. The latter case, however, involving as it does an "increasing" marginal utility of money, is extremely unlikely.

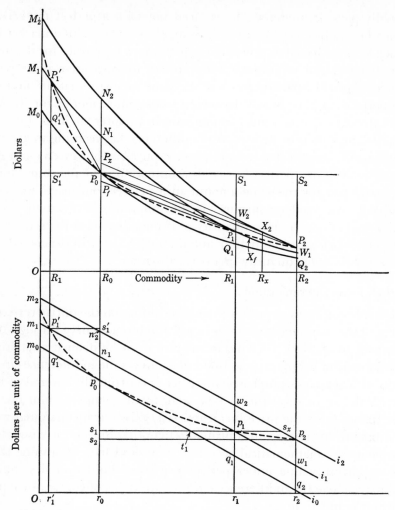

FIGS. 134A (above) and 134B (below).   General Derivation of Market Curve.

ECONOMIC SURPLUS

The above analysis enables us to clear up some confusions relating to the concept of economic surplus. In the Marshallian economics the triangular area bounded by the demand curve, the vertical (price) axis, and the horizontal line at the market price is called the "consumers' surplus." As the concept is related to purchases rather than to consumption, it is perhaps better to call it the "buyers' surplus"; the corresponding concept for sellers may be called the "sellers' surplus." The existence of a demand curve implies that the buyer would be willing to buy smaller quantities than he actually buys at a higher price than he actually pays. If, therefore, he is faced not with a perfect market at which he can buy as much as he likes at a given price, but a market in which he is subjected to price discrimination—a high price for the first unit bought, and successively lower prices for successive units purchased—he will be willing to buy the same quantity that he buys in the perfect market but will be forced to pay more money for it. We have already examined this phenomenon in Chapter 29. The "buyers' surplus" may then be defined as the difference between the total sum which could be extracted from him in the purchase of a given quantity of commodity by "perfect" price discrimination, and the sum which he would pay for the same amount in a perfect (one-price) market. Similarly, the "sellers' surplus" is the difference between the sum which will extract a given quantity of commodity from the seller under perfect price discrimination, and the sum which will persuade him to supply the same quantity in a perfect market.

Perfect Price Discrimination

Under conditions of perfect price discrimination the outlay-revenue curve of the marketer is the same as his indifference curve through the point P_0, for perfect price discrimination must be defined as a situation in which the opportunity line is the same as the indifference curve at P_0. If he expands purchases, the price is continually lowered as his marginal rate of substitution falls, continually tempting him on; if he expands sales, the price is continuously raised as his marginal rate of substitution rises, again continually tempting him to increase sales. For complete mathematical accuracy we should have to assume that the opportunity line under perfect price discrimination lies infinitesimally above the indifference curve—otherwise, of course, the equilibrium is indeterminate.

Buyers' and Sellers' Surplus

Suppose now in Fig. 134 that the marketer expands purchases under perfect price discrimination until he reaches the point Q_1; he will have bought R_0R_1, and will have paid a total amount S_1Q_1. In order to make him buy this amount under a uniform price, the opportunity line would have to be P_0P_1, which is tangent to the indifference curve at P_1. The amount paid under uniform pricing would then be S_1P_1. The difference between the amount paid for R_0R_1 under perfect discrimination and under uniform pricing is P_1Q_1 $(S_1Q_1 - S_1P_1)$. This is the buyers' surplus. Similarly, $Q'_1P'_1$ is the sellers' surplus when the amount sold is $P_0S'_1$.

The Compensating Payment

Another important concept related to that of economic surplus is that of a "compensating payment." This is the sum of money which would just compensate a marketer for a given change in price or in the conditions of the market. Thus, suppose in Fig. 134 that there is a rise in price from $r_2 p_2$ to $r_1 p_1$: the opportunity line shifts from $P_0 P_2$ to $P_0 P_1$. As a result of the rise in price, the marketer is worse off; his position of equilibrium moves from P_2 on indifference curve M_2 to P_1 on the lower indifference curve M_1. The "compensating payment" is that addition to his initial stock of money which will enable him to reach the indifference curve M_2 when the price is equal to $r_1 p_1$. This sum is $P_0 P_x$, where $P_x X_2$ is drawn parallel to $P_0 P_1$, so that it represents an opportunity line, at a price $r_1 p_1$, to touch the indifference curve M_2 at X_2. Similarly, the compensating "tax" for a fall in price from $r_1 p_1$ to $r_2 p_2$, which would make the marketer just as well off as he was before the fall in price, is $P_0 P_f$, where $P_f X_f$ is drawn parallel to $P_0 P_2$ to touch the indifference curve M_1 at X_f. In the general case $P_0 P_f$ is not equal to $P_0 P_x$. The concept of a "compensating payment" is of considerable importance in welfare economics.

If we take the more special case of Fig. 133, in which the indifference curves are parallel, the buyers' (or sellers') surplus becomes equal to the compensating payment which would compensate for the loss of the market, and the change in buyers' (or sellers') surplus due to a change in price is equal to the compensating payment for that change in price. Thus, in Fig. 133, the buyers' surplus when the price is $r_2 p_2$ is $P_2 Q_2$. The payment which would have to be made to a buyer to compensate him for the loss of the market (i.e., for the withdrawal of the privilege of exchanging at the price $r_2 p_2$) is $P_0 N_2$; this is the sum of money which added to his initial stock will bring him to the same indifference curve, I_2, that he can reach by exchanging at a price $r_2 p_2$. If the indifference curves are parallel, $P_2 Q_2$ is equal to $P_0 N_2$. Consider now a change in price from $r_1 p_1$ to $r_2 p_2$. The compensating payment (in this case a tax) is equal to $P_0 P_f$, where $W_2 P_f$ is drawn parallel to $P_0 P_2$ to touch indifference curve I_1 at W_2. The compensating payment $P_0 P_f$ is clearly equal to $P_2 W_2$, which in turn is equal to the rise in buyers' surplus from $P_1 Q_1$ to $P_2 Q_2$, as $P_1 Q_1 = W_2 Q_2$. Similarly, the compensating payment for a rise in price from $r_2 p_2$ to $r_1 p_1$ is $P_0 N_1$, where $N_1 W_1$ is drawn parallel to $P_0 P_1$ to touch the indifference curve I_2 in W_1. We then have $P_0 N_1$ equal to $P_1 W_1$, which is in turn equal to the fall in buyers' surplus, $Q_2 P_2 - Q_1 P_1$.

The "Demand Triangle"

These various concepts may be expressed also in terms of Figs. 134B and 133B. Thus, in Fig. 134A the line S_1Q_1 is the sum (integral) of all the marginal rates of substitution on the curve P_0Q_1; this is equal to the area $r_0p_0q_1r_1$ in Fig. 134B. The line S_1P_1 in Fig. 134A is the total payment made in purchasing r_0r_1 at a price r_1p_1, and is therefore equal to the rectangle $r_0s_1p_1r_1$. The buyers' surplus, therefore, at the quantity r_0r_1 is equal to the area $r_0p_0q_1r_1$ less the area $r_0s_1p_1r_1$, which is the area of the complex quadrilateral $s_1p_0q_1p_1$, or $s_1p_0t_1 - t_1p_1q_1$. In the case of Fig. 133 the buyers' surplus reduces to the "demand triangle," $s_1p_0p_1$, as the condition of parallel indifference curves makes q_1 and p_1 identical points. In the more general case of Fig. 134 the "demand triangle" $s_1p_0p_1$ has no significance whatever. Similarly, in Fig. 134 the total compensating payment at the price r_1p_1 is P_0N_1. $P_0N_1 + S_1P_1$ is the sum of all the marginal rates of substitution between N_1 and P_1, which is the area $r_0n_1p_1r_1$. S_1P_1, as we have seen, is equal to the rectangle $r_0s_1p_1r_1$. It follows that the total compensating payment for the loss of the market at the price r_1p_1 is the area $s_1n_1p_1$, which in this case is greater than the demand triangle. In the case of Fig. 133, however, the lines n_1p_1 and p_0p_1 coincide and the compensating payment is equal to the demand triangle $s_1p_0p_1$.

The Gain from Trade

The concept of a compensating payment can be used to measure the "gain from trade" in a whole market. In Fig. 135, B_1N_1, B_2N_2, . . . M_1S_1, M_2S_2, etc., are the individual demand-supply curves of all the people in a given market. Summing the positive segments of these curves gives us the market demand curve, $B_3H_2H_3N$. Summing all the negative segments gives the market supply curve, $S_3K_2K_1M$. The market price OP is of course that at which the quantity demanded PN is equal to the quantity supplied, PM. If a mirror image of the supply curve is drawn, S_3N, it will cut the demand curve at the market price at N, and we have the familiar Marshallian diagram. If now the marginal rates of substitution of all marketers are independent of their money holdings, the compensating payment for the marketer whose demand-supply curve is B_1N_1 is the area PB_1N_1; similarly, for all the other marketers. The sum of the areas PB_1N_1, PB_2N_2, etc., is therefore the total amount of money which would compensate the buyers for the loss of the market; it is equal to the area $PB_3H_2H_3N$. Similarly, the area $PS_3K_2K_1M$ is the total amount of money which would compensate the sellers for the loss of the market. The total amount of money which would have to be paid to all the marketers to compensate for the loss of the market is the triangular area S_3B_3N; this is a measure of the "gain from trade."

If now we relax the assumption of parallel indifference curves, a simple modification is introduced into the figure; instead of the com-

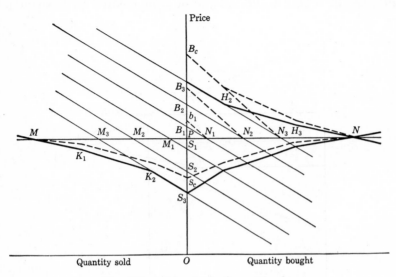

FIG. 135.   The Gain from Trade.

pensating payment to Marketer 1, being represented by the area B_1N_1P, it is now represented by the area b_1N_1P, enclosed by the dotted line b_1N_1—the marginal rate of substitution curve for Marketer 1 at N_1. Similar marginal rate of substitution curves are drawn for the other marketers, and these are summed in the market marginal rates of substitution curves B_cN and S_cM. The triangular figure S_cB_cN now represents the total compensating payment. The assumption of a marginal rate of substitution increasing with increase in the quantity of money leads to a higher compensating payment for buyers but a lower compensating payment for sellers, as buyers are parting with money which is becoming more valuable to them as they part with it, while sellers are acquiring money which is becoming less valuable to them as they acquire it. The compensating payment triangle S_cB_cN is not likely to differ in area very much from the demand-supply triangle B_3NS_3.

Loss from Taxation

The above analysis leads to an interesting proposition in the field of taxation. In Fig. 136 we suppose a tax equal to P_bP_s per unit laid on a commodity whose market demand and supply curves are BP and SP. The volume of transactions shrinks to OQ as a result; the buyers' price is QP_b, the sellers' price QP_s. Starting with the assumption of parallel indifference curves, the payment which would compensate the buyers for the imposition of the tax is equal to the rectangle NN_bP_bP; similarly, the sellers would have to be compensated by a payment of

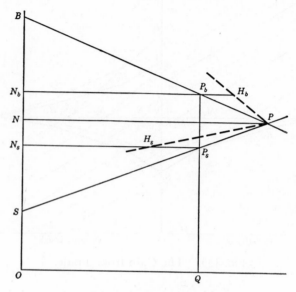

FIG. 136.   Loss from Taxation.

N_sNPP_s to make them as well off as they were before the tax. The total payment which would compensate the marketers for the imposition of the tax is therefore the area $N_sN_bP_bPP_s$. The total receipts from the tax amount to $N_sN_bP_bP_s$. The total receipts from the tax would therefore be insufficient to cover the compensating payment by an amount equal to the triangle P_bPP_s. This is one possible measure of the social "loss" due to the imposition of the tax. If the condition of parallel indifference curves is removed, and if PH_b and PH_s represent the market marginal rate of substitution curves, the total compensating payment would be $N_sN_bH_bPH_s$, and the "loss" due to the tax would be measured by the area of the complex polygon $P_sH_sPH_bP_b$.

TAXATION AND INCOME

The indifference curve analysis can also be used to study relationship of various forms of taxation to the willingness to earn income. In Fig. 137 the dotted lines are indifference curves on a money-hours of work diagram, like that of Fig. 127A, page 798. Suppose the initial amount of money is zero, and that the individual can earn money at a constant wage equal to the slope of the opportunity line OQ_5. Suppose now that we wish to levy a tax on the individual equal to LO. If now we draw LP_5 parallel to OQ_5, all points of equilibrium after the tax equal to LO is paid must lie on this line. The various possible

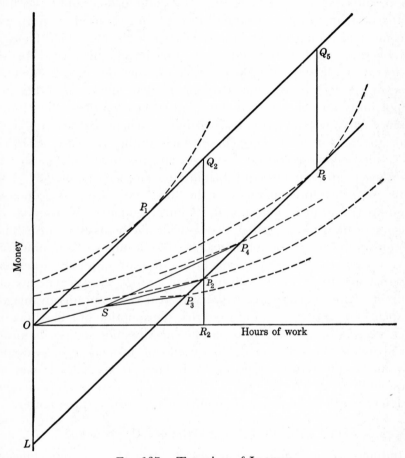

FIG. 137.   Taxation of Income.

schemes of taxation may be represented by different opportunity lines which touch indifference curves at their intersection with LP_5. Thus, OP_2 is the opportunity line of income after tax when the tax is a proportional income tax, equal to a proportion $\dfrac{P_2Q_2}{R_2Q_2}$ of income earned. The line OP_2 touches an indifference curve at P_2. The line OSP_3 represents a progressive income tax; the line OSP_4 a regressive income tax; successive increases or decreases in the rate of tax may be represented by shifts in the slope of the net opportunity line. It will be seen in the figure that a progressive income tax reduces income and effort below the resultant of a proportional income tax yielding the same amount of tax, and also leaves the individual worse off—P_3 is on a lower indifference curve than P_2. A regressive income tax, on the other hand, spurs the individual to greater effort and income, and leaves him better off than a proportional tax; P_4 is at a higher level of effort and income, and is on a higher indifference curve than P_2. The theoretically best tax is a fixed tax independent of the amount earned. If this is levied at the start, the opportunity line net of tax is LP_5. This reaches a higher indifference curve at P_5 than any of the other net opportunity lines. It can easily be seen that P_5 is on the highest indifference curve which can be reached by any scheme of taxation, as it is on the highest indifference curve which can be reached on the line LP_5; and as long as the rate of wages and the total tax collected is unchanged, all points of equilibrium after tax must lie on LP_5. The conclusion therefore emerges that the "best" tax on purely economic grounds is not an income tax at all but a property tax assessed on income-earning power rather than on income actually earned. The administrative difficulties of such a tax make it impossible in practice; nevertheless, the theoretical conclusion at least raises the question whether the administrative advantages of a progressive income tax on individual incomes are worth the very real economic disadvantages of such a tax. It should be observed that the adoption of a fixed tax or even a regressive tax on individual incomes does not necessarily mean the abandonment of the progressive principle as *between* individuals. It would be theoretically possible, for instance, to assess fixed taxes on those individuals with large earning power which are proportionately heavier than those levied on individuals with small earning power.

APPLICATIONS TO THE THEORY OF INTEREST

Indifference curve analysis can also be used to clear up some difficult problems in the theory of "rational" saving and in the long-run theory of interest. In the previous chapter we assumed simply that a preference function existed as between saving and outgo (Fig. 128A). We can now push the analysis further and inquire whether there are any rational grounds for such a preference function.

In a very simple case, assume that a man starts with nothing, has only two years to live, does not want to leave anything to his descendants, and knows exactly what his income is to be in each of the two years. Let his income be n_1 in the first year and n_2 in the second year. Let his outgo be x_1 in the first year and x_2 in the second. Suppose also that he can borrow or lend unlimited amounts at a rate of interest i. What this really means is that he can hold assets in a form which will grow at a rate i per annum; and that if he has liabilities, these too will grow at the same rate. If therefore he saves, the assets which he accumulates grow at the rate i per annum; if he borrows—i.e., "dis-saves" —or increases his liabilities (negative assets), these likewise grow at the same rate.

He saves an amount $n_1 - x_1$ in the first year; it earns a total amount of interest or profit equal to $(n_1 - x_1)i$. His total income in the two years therefore amounts to $n_1 + n_2 + (n_1 - x_1)i$. As he accumulates nothing in the two years, his total income must equal his total outgo. Therefore,

$$n_1 + n_2 + (n_1 - x_1)i = x_1 + x_2,$$

or

$$x_1(1 + i) + x_2 = n_1(1 + i) + n_2. \tag{1}$$

This equation expresses a necessary relationship, under the assumed conditions, between the incomes and outgoes of the two years. It is valid no matter whether the man saves in the first year, consuming the accumulation in the second, or whether he "dis-saves" in the first year, thus incurring debt, and extinguishes the debt in the second.

An arithmetical example may make the meaning of the equation clearer. Suppose that in the first year the income is \$1000 and in the second year \$2200. Suppose that the rate of interest is zero. Then in equation (1) $n_1 = 1000$, $n_2 = 2200$, $i = 0$, and therefore

$$x_1 + x_2 = 3200. \tag{2}$$

That is, the sum of the outgoes is equal to the sum of the incomes. If the rate of interest is equal to 10 per cent per annum, the equation will be:

$$(1.1)\,x_1 + x_2 = 1100 + 2200 = 3300. \tag{3}$$

Suppose, now, that I consume nothing in the first year $(x_1 = 0)$; I will accumulate \$1000, which will be worth \$1100 in the second year. In the second year, therefore, I can consume the \$1100 of accumulation, plus the \$2200 of income, or \$3300 in all; i.e., $x_2 = 3300$. If I consumed nothing in the second year $(x_2 = 0)$, then x_1 would be $\dfrac{3300}{1.1}$, or \$3000; for by consuming \$3000 in the first year I would run up a debt of \$2000, which it would require the whole income of \$2200 to liquidate in the second year.

These equations are linear equations in x_1 and x_2 and can therefore be expressed by straight lines on a graph. In Fig. 138, x_1 is measured in the horizontal direction, x_2 in the vertical direction. The line E_1E_2 then represents equation (2); we may call it an "opportunity line," as it shows all those combinations of outgoes in the two years which are *possible* when the total income is $3200 and there is no interest. The line C_1C_2 in Fig. 138A corresponds to equation (3). In order to make the diagram clear, however, as the shifts in the opportunity line due to changes in the rate of interest are rather small, we have made C_1C_2 represent the opportunity line when the rate of interest is 100 per cent,

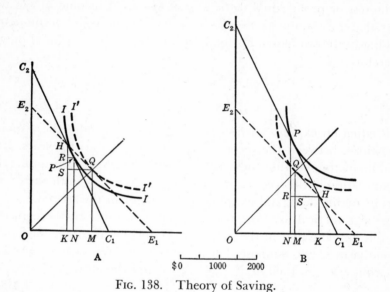

FIG. 138.   Theory of Saving.

and the individual earns $1000 in the first year and $2200 in the second. The incomes are represented by the coordinates of the point H: $KH = \$2200$, $OK = \$1000$. No matter what the rate of interest, the opportunity line will go through H, for obviously one of the possible distributions of outgo in the two years is the same as the distribution of incomes. No matter what the rate of interest, in the above case the individual could always consume $1000 in the first year and $2200 in the second, in which case he would save nothing. A rise in the rate of interest, therefore, results in a swing of the opportunity line on the point H as an axis, the line swinging to a steeper position. The slope of the opportunity line is equal to $(1 + i)$.

The opportunity line by itself is not enough, however, to tell us how much will be saved. We must also have a system of *indifference curves,* or utility contours. Two of these are shown in the figure, $I\ I$ and $I'I'$. For any two points on such an indifference curve, the coordinates of one describe a combination of outgoes just as desirable as the combination represented by the coordinates of the other. We shall examine the derivation of these curves shortly; meanwhile we shall assume that they are negatively sloped, indicating that an increase in the income of one year is counterbalanced by a decrease in the income of the other. We shall also assume that they are convex to the origin.

As before, the individual wishes to obtain that combination of expenditures which will give him the greatest satisfaction, i.e., which will lie on the "highest" indifference curve that his opportunity line reaches. This is the indifference curve which is touched by the opportunity line. The point P, therefore, where the line C_1C_2 touches an indifference curve, $I\ I$, is the "best" combination on the opportunity line C_1C_2. Under these circumstances the individual will consume ON in the first year and NP in the second. He will therefore have to borrow a sum equal to $KN\ (=RP)$ in the first year, and will repay a sum RH in the second.

It can now be easily shown that if the indifference curves are symmetrical, as in Fig. 138, and the interest rate is zero, the best distribution of saving or borrowing is that which makes the outgoes in the two years equal. For if the indifference curves are symmetrical, each must have a slope of $45°$ where it crosses the line $x_1 = x_2\ (OQ)$. Also, if the rate of interest is zero, the opportunity line E_1E_2 will also have a $45°$ slope. At the optimum point Q, where the opportunity line touches an indifference curve $I'I'$, the expenditure in the first year (OM) is equal to that of the second (MQ). An amount $KM\ (=SQ)$ will be borrowed in the first year and an equal amount, SH, will be returned in the second.

Fig. 138A shows that a rise in the rate of interest, shifting the opportunity line from E_1E_2 to C_1C_2, pushed the individual from a higher indifference curve, $I'I'$, to a lower, $I\ I$. That is, a rise in the rate of interest made the individual worse off. This is because the individual's income was concentrated in the second year rather than in the first, and consequently he had to borrow in the first and repay in the second. The rise in the rate of interest, although it made him borrow less, worsened the terms on which he could borrow sufficiently to cause a decline in "welfare." But if an individual has an excess of income in the first year, so that he is a lender, a rise in the rate of interest will benefit him. This is shown in Fig. 138B. Here we assume an income of OK ($2200) in the *first* year and KH ($1000) in the *second*. A rise in the rate of interest then swings the opportunity line from E_1E_2 to C_1C_2. The optimum point rises from Q to P, on a higher indifference curve. Saving (lending) rises from MK to NK, repayments from SQ to RP. It will be observed that the result of a positive rate of interest is that *less* is consumed in the first year than in the second, for the point P always lies above the line OQ.

The Time-Indifference Curves

We have still to ask what determines the character of the "time-indifference curves" as they may be called. These can be derived from the curves showing the total utility derived from a given amount of outgo in one year, if we assume for the moment that utility is measurable. The construction is analogous to that in Fig. 112, page 749, and is illustrated in Fig. 139. The outgo in the first year is measured along OX_1, and the total utility derived from this outgo along OU_1 (downward). R_1S_1 is then the total utility curve for the first year. Similarly, the outgo in the second year is measured along OX_2, and the total

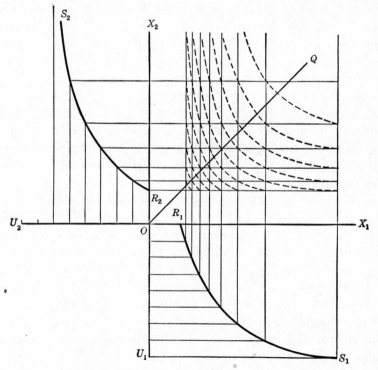

FIG. 139.   Time-Indifference Curves.

utility along OU_2 (leftward). R_2S_2 is the total utility curve for the second year. From these curves we construct a contour framework, as in Fig. 112, and from this derive the utility contours, or indifference curves, marked by dotted lines. It will be seen immediately that if the principle of diminishing marginal utility of outgo applies, these indifference curves will be convex to the origin. For if the marginal utility of outgo (the slope of the utility curve) declines as the total outgo in each year increases, the contours will be steep when outgo in the first year is low, at the left-hand side of the figure, and flatter when outgo in the first year is great. That is to say, when the outgo in the first year is small, quite a small increase in the outgo of the first year will suffice to compensate for a relatively large decrease in the outgo of the second year. The reverse is the case when the outgo in the first year is large.

The above proposition is interesting in that it provides a method of stating the law of diminishing marginal utility of outgo without bringing in the objectionable concept of marginal utility. The slope of the time-indifference curve we may call the *rate of time substitution* of outgo between one year and another. We can therefore restate the law as follows: The rate of time substitution of outgo, or the amount of outgo in year B required to compensate for the loss of one unit of outgo in year A, falls as outgo is transferred to year A from year B.

Time Preference

If the utility curves of the two years, R_1S_1 and R_2S_2, are identical in shape, the contour framework will be symmetrical about the line $x_1 = x_2$ (OQ). If, however, as in the figure, the total utility derived from a given outgo in the first year is greater than that derived from the same outgo in the second, the indifference curves will not be symmetrical about the line OQ, and will have a slope greater than $45°$ at the point where they cut the line OQ. This is what is meant by saying that an individual has a certain "time preference." If we prefer a total outgo of $2000 this year, other things being equal, to a total outgo of $2000 next year, this preference is evidently based on the position in *time* of the outgo and on nothing else. It is therefore a manifestation of "impatience." The greater the "impatience" of the individual, the steeper will be the time-indifference curve at the point where it crosses OQ; i.e., where the expenditures in the two years are equal.

The existence of "impatience" in the time-indifference curves has an effect opposite to that of the presence of a rate of interest. If there is no rate of interest and there is impatience, the individual will choose a combination of outgoes consisting of a larger outgo in the first year than in the second. If the rate of interest is equal to what may be called the "rate of impatience," r, where $(1 + r)$ is the slope of the indifference curve at the point of equal outgoes, the individual will spend the same amount in each year. In that case the slope of the opportunity line $(1 + i)$ is equal to the slope of the indifference curve $(1 + r)$ at the point of equal outgoes.

From the time-indifference curves of an individual we can derive a curve showing how much the amount accumulated in each year will vary with the rate of interest. We shall return to this application later.

Extension to More Than Two Years

We have hitherto assumed that the "time choice" of expenditures lay between two periods of time only. In fact, of course, the choices in this respect cover a large number of years. But many of the conclusions of the simple analysis of two years apply also to the more complex cases if we consider that the first year represents "early" years and the second year "later" years. Moreover, it is not difficult to extend the analysis in algebraic terms to cases involving more than two periods of time. If there are three periods of time to be considered, we can construct a three-dimensional diagram in which the three axes represent the expenditures in three "years," x_1, x_2, and x_3. The incomes of the three years, n_1, n_2, and n_3, are represented by a point, H, in this three-dimensional figure. Through this point we can draw an "opportunity plane" whose slope depends on the rate of interest, just as we drew an "opportunity line" through the point H in Fig. 138. If the rate of interest is zero, this plane will cut all three axes at equal distances from the origin. If there is a positive rate of interest, the plane will cut each axis at a point which is farther from the origin the later the date which the axis represents. "Indifference surfaces" can also be drawn. These will be shaped something like saucers resting on the three sides of the corner of a box. The "best" combination of expenditures will be that in which the opportunity plane touches an indifference surface. Similarly, we can extend the analysis by algebra, if not by geometry, to cases involving more than three time periods.

Supply and Demand for Loans

From an individual's time-indifference curves his supply and demand curves can be derived relating the rate of interest with his borrowings or lendings. This is shown in Fig. 140 for two extreme cases. In each, H shows the distribution of the person's income between the two years. In Fig. 140A the first year's income, OK, is much less than the second year's income, KH; in Fig. 140B the reverse is true. In Fig. 140A the line HP_0, making equal intercepts with the axes, is his "opportunity line" when the rate of interest is zero. At succes-

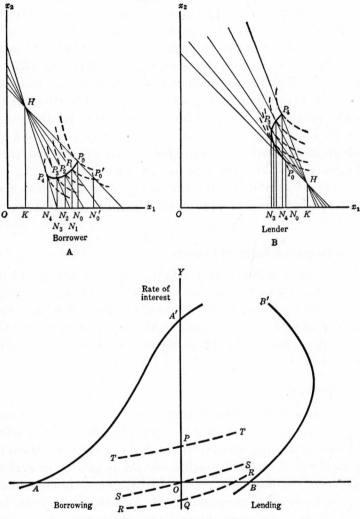

FIGS. 140 and 141.   Theory of Interest.

sively higher rates of interest his opportunity line becomes steeper, shifting to positions HP_1, HP_2, HP_3, etc. The point of tangency of these successive opportunity lines follows a course indicated by the curve P_0P_4. Then at zero rate of interest this individual will borrow a sum KN_0 in the first year. At a rate of interest corresponding to the opportunity line HP_1 he will borrow a smaller sum, KN_1; at a still higher rate he will borrow KN_2; and so on. From Fig. 140A, therefore, we can draw a curve such as AA' in Fig. 141 (not drawn to scale) showing how the amount borrowed declines as the rate of interest increases. In Fig. 140B we carry out a similar analysis for an individual with a larger income (OK) in the first year than in the second (KH). In this case the line P_0P_4 bends backward, and although at low rates of interest a rise in the interest rate induces the individual to lend more, at high rates a rise in the rate may induce him to lend less. The corresponding curve showing the amount he will lend at each interest rate is BB' in Fig. 141. (Compare Fig. 127, page 798.) The curves AA' and BB' may be called the "individual market curves" for the two individuals. By adding together algebraically the market curves of all the individuals in the market (compare Fig. 6, page 67), we shall obtain a "total market curve" for the loan market, such as TT in Fig. 141. If this cuts the OY axis in P, OP is the rate of interest at which there is no *net* desire to borrow or lend on the part of the individuals of the market.

Zero and Negative Rates of Interest

If the total market curve were SOS the equilibrium rate of interest would be zero; if it were RQR the rate would be negative. A negative rate of interest is by no means impossible—indeed, a bank deposit with bank charges is a "loan" made by the depositor to the banker, to whom the depositor pays a charge for the privilege of being allowed to lend money!

Negative Interest

In a society with non-depreciating money it is difficult for rates of interest to become negative, as it is always possible to earn a zero rate of interest by holding money. If, however, money is depreciating either in nominal terms through some tax device or in real terms through inflation, money bears a negative rate of interest and real interest on loans can correspondingly be negative. In France, for instance, because of inflation the real rate of interest on government bonds in the period 1913–1950 averaged about −13 per cent per annum.

Relation to Liquidity Preference Theory

The reader may wonder how the theory of an equilibrium rate of interest developed above is related to the liquidity preference theory of interest developed on pages 369–381. The liquidity preference theory explains the market price of existing securities; it is therefore a "market rate" theory of interest analogous to the explanation of market price under the assumption of fixed stocks. The equilibrium theory of this chapter is a "normal price" theory of interest. Borrowing involves the creation of a security and its sale to the lender. The "normal" equilibrium rate of interest is that at which the *net* rate of creation of new securities is just what the market can absorb without a change in the market rate of interest (see pages 377–381).

Effects of "Impatience" or "Time Preference"

The above method of analysis will give a clue to the effects of changes in "time preference" on the rates of interest. Suppose there is a general increase in preference for early income, i.e., an increase in "impatience." This means, generally speaking, that the system of indifference curves (dotted lines) in Fig. 140 will become steeper at each point, for it will take a larger amount of next year's income to compensate the individual for the loss of a unit of this year's income. The "rate of substitution" of next year's for this year's income will rise at each point. At P_0 (Fig. 140A), therefore, the new indifference curve will be steeper than the one shown and will cut the line HP_0 from above. An "impatient" indifference curve will touch the line HP_0 at a point below P_0, say, at the point P'_0. After the increase in impatience the individual in Fig. 140A is willing to borrow more at a zero rate of interest than before—KN'_0 in place of KN_0. Similarly, at all other rates of interest the individual will wish to borrow more than before, for all the points P_1, P_2, etc., will be pushed farther down their respective opportunity lines by the increase in impatience. Applying a like analysis to Fig. 140B, we can show that an increase in impatience in the case of this individual will also push the points P_0, P_1, etc., farther down the respective opportunity lines and will make him want to lend *less* at each rate of interest than before. A general rise in impatience means a shift of the curves AA' and BB' (Fig. 141) to the left and therefore a shift in the total market curve, TPT, to the left. This will raise the equilibrium rate of interest. A rise in impatience thus causes a rise in the rate of interest.

We may notice that at any equilibrium point, P_0, P_1, etc., the slope of the opportunity line (in Fig. 140) is equal to the slope of the indifference curve, for the individual is not in equilibrium unless the indifference curve touches an opportunity line. We know, however, that the slope of the opportunity line is $(1 + i)$ where i is the rate of interest. The factor $(1 + i)$ is sometimes called the "force" of interest. Similarly, we can define the "rate of time preference" at a point, r, such that the slope of the indifference curve, i.e., the rate of substitution of the income of one year for another, is equal to $(1 + r)$. Then we can say that in equilibrium, for each individual, the rate of interest is equal to his rate of time preference. This does not mean, of course, that "a" rate of time preference "determines" the rate of interest, any more than the marginal productivity "determines" wages or the marginal cost "determines" price. The rate of time preference depends on how income is distributed in time; and it is truer to say that for each individual, in equilibrium, the rate of time preference is determined by the rate of interest than it is to say that interest is "determined" by any rate of time preference. But it is true that the whole *system* of rates of time preference on the part of *all* individuals, as expressed in our system of indifference curves, constitutes the data from which we can deduce the equilibrium rate of interest.

Effect of Capital Accumulation

Although the analysis in these pages is best adapted to problems of the stationary state, it can also be used to throw some light on the effects of progress on interest. Suppose that instead of a stationary state we have a progressive economy in which incomes are rising every year. Then the total of incomes in the "second" year will be greater than the total in the "first." More people, in such a state, would be in the position of Fig. 140A, with larger incomes in the second year, than would be in this position in a stationary state. There will therefore be a greater relative number of individual market curves of the type AA', the total market curve will be farther to the left, and the equilibrium rate of interest will be higher. In a progressive economy the equilibrium rate of interest is likely to be higher than in a stationary state. The greater the rate of progress, the more people will there be in the "borrowing" class with small incomes early, and the higher will be the rate of interest.

Although we have conducted this analysis with respect to two years only, it can be extended to more complex cases. The conclusions worked out for the simple case hold generally. Any complex case can be analyzed by breaking it up into two periods, analyzing it as above, then breaking up each period into two further periods and analyzing it, and so on.

QUESTIONS AND EXERCISES

1. It is a generally observed fact that the rate of interest in "short" investment series is smaller than the rate of interest in "long" investment series. How would you account for this fact, on the lines of the analysis in this chapter?

2. Explain the part played by "time preference" in the theory of interest. What is the relation between the "time preference" concept and the "liquidity preference" concept?

3. Prove that in a stationary society with only two time periods to consider, in which there is no "impatience" or time preference and in which all people have equal incomes in the two "years," the equilibrium rate of interest will be zero and the amount of saving and lending will also be zero.

4. Prove that in a stationary, two-period society, without time preference, the rate of interest will be zero if the distribution of incomes among the people is symmetrical, i.e., if for every person having an income x in the first year and y in the second there is another person having an income y in the first year and x in the second.

5. Prove that in the above society, with a symmetrical distribution of incomes, there will be a positive rate of interest in equilibrium if there is "impatience" or time preference.

6. The results of Fig. 137 have been obtained in part because of certain assumptions which were made in drawing the system of indifference curves. What are these assumptions? Discuss the effect of different assumptions regarding the shape of the indifference curve system on the results obtained. Prove that if the indifference curves are parallel, no tax system can be devised which will increase income and effort. Discuss, in Fig. 137, the relation of the "compensating payment" to the tax.

7. Apply the "compensating payment" analysis to the theory of the tariff. (Use the analysis of Fig. 29, page 147.) Show that the compensating payment is always greater than the receipts from the tariff.

8. Would the "compensating payment" concept have any significance in the case of "long-run" demand and supply curves?

9. From a system of indifference curves, such as in Fig. 132, how can we find the *range of prices* within which exchange is possible? Construct a system of indifference curves under which no such range of prices exists, and under which, therefore, exchange is impossible.

10. Draw, in perspective and in contour forms, three-dimensional figures showing the relationship of quantity demanded and of quantity supplied to both price and income. Analyze the impact of change in income on both price and quantity under different assumptions regarding the shape of the functions.

11. An electricity company charges 8 cents per unit for the first 100 units, 4 cents per unit for the next 300 units, and 3 cents per unit for all subsequent units purchased. Draw the opportunity line facing a consumer under these circumstances. Draw on three separate diagrams systems of indifference curves together with this opportunity line (a) which will make the consumer buy 80 units only, (b) which will make him buy 350 units, (c) which will make him buy 500 units.

Prove that under any circumstances if the consumer pays different prices for different quantities, he would be better off if the company charged a flat rate equal to the average price which he pays under differential pricing, though he would buy less electricity. Discuss the concept of the "compensating payment" under these circumstances.

12. Illustrate all seven of the "marginal conditions" for a Paretian optimum by means of graphs, using indifference curves and equiproduct curves, and draw the contract curve in each case.

CHAPTER 38

TIME, PRODUCTION, AND VALUATION

THE PRODUCTION TIME SCHEDULE

Time Relationships in the Firm

Up to now we have not taken *time* quantities into our analysis in any very explicit fashion. We have assumed that in a process of production outlays are made and revenues received and that the process is most profitable when the revenues exceed the outlays by the greatest amount. We have not, however, concerned ourselves with the *dates* at which inputs or outputs, outlays or revenues, appear.

Inputs and Outputs Have "Dates"

When we constructed the physical production schedule of Tables 57 (page 587) and 64 (page 734), we merely assumed that, given quantities of all the inputs in a process, we could predict a given quantity of output. It is necessary now to consider a fact about these inputs and outputs which we have previously neglected: the fact that they occur at definite points in time. We shall call a point in time a "date," though it may be measured not always from the beginning of the Christian Era but from some "base date" convenient for the problem. For any process of production we can construct a table showing not only the kind of input or output, its quantity, price, and the total outlay or revenue received from it, but also the dates at which each input or output item occurred.

Example. Table 69 is such a physical production table. In this it is assumed that the outlays are made on the date when the corresponding inputs occur, and that revenues are received on the days when the corresponding outputs occur. There is no necessity, of course, for all the output to come at one date as in the example. In general, input items and output items will be strung all through the table. However, the output and the corresponding revenue items will always be expected to be, on the whole, "later" than input and the corresponding outlay items, for as inputs are the physical cause of outputs they precede outputs in time.

TABLE 69.   Production Time Schedule for Potatoes

Time in Months	Kind of Input or Output	Quantity of Input or Output	Price of Input or Output	Outlay (−) or Revenue (+)
1 (March)	Plowing	10 acres	$ 1.50 per acre	−$ 15.00
	Seed Potatoes	2 tons	$10.00 per ton	−$ 20.00
	Land	10 acre-months	$ 0.25 per acre-mo.	−$ 2.50
2 (April)	Harrowing	10 acres	$ 0.50 per acre	−$ 5.00
	Land	10 acre-months	$ 0.25 per acre-mo.	−$ 2.50
3 (May)	Land	10 acre-months	$ 0.25 per acre-mo.	−$ 2.50
4 (June)	Land	10 acre-months	$ 0.25 per acre-mo.	−$ 2.50
	Spraying, etc.	10 acres	$ 0.50 per acre	−$ 5.00
5 (July)	Land	10 acre-months	$ 0.25 per acre-mo.	−$ 2.50
6 (August)	Land	10 acre-months	$ 0.25 per acre-mo.	−$ 2.50
	Digging	10 acres	$ 2.00 per acre	−$ 20.00
	Transport	20 tons	$ 1.00 per ton	−$ 20.00
	Potatoes	20 tons	$ 5.00 per ton	+$100.00

Total Profit in the Production Time Schedule

In the above example the total of outlays is $100, equal to the total revenue; there is no "profit." That is to say, if normal profits are greater than zero, the net revenue in the above process will be negative. In profitable processes the total revenue must be greater than the total outlay. Suppose, for instance, that the receipts from the sale of the potatoes had amounted to $124. The total profit of the process would have amounted to $24. This total profit accrues to the *capitalist* as a result of the performance of the process. It does not include any items of the value of physical input, even if the input is "virtual" input from a source owned by the capitalist himself. Total profit, therefore, is defined as the sum of the values of all outputs, actual or virtual, less the sum of the values of all inputs, actual or virtual. It must be distinguished from the *net revenue,* which is equal to the total profit *less* the "normal" profit.

The Outlay-Revenue Series

The schedule showing the date of each outlay and revenue item is called the "outlay-revenue series." It consists of the first and last columns of Table 69, and is summarized in columns 1 and 2 of Table 70. In column 2 is calculated, in an investment without profit, the

TABLE 70.   The Outlay-Revenue Series and
the Total Capital Invested

1 Date (Months)	2 Outlay (−) or Revenue (+)	3 Total Capital Invested
1	$ −37.50	$ 37.50
2	−7.50	45.00
3	−2.50	47.50
4	−7.50	55.00
5	−2.50	57.50
6	−42.50	100.00
	+100.00	0

"total capital invested" at each date. It is equal to the sum of outlays less the sum of revenues up to the date in question. In the absence of profit each outlay represents an addition to the value of the property of the enterprise equal to the amount of the outlay, and each revenue represents a similar subtraction. An outlay represents a substitution of "real" assets of some kind for "money" assets, and a revenue represents a substitution of a money asset for a real asset. It is conventional in accounting to regard all exchanges as transfers of equal values, so that if an outlay is made of, say $37.50, it is assumed that the $37.50 diminution in money holdings which results from the outlay is counterbalanced by an increase in the value of nonmonetary assets of $37.50. In the present case cash worth $37.50 has been exchanged for potato-potentialities worth $37.50.

Graphic Illustration.   The outlay-revenue series and the capital series can both be illustrated conveniently if the total capital invested is plotted in the vertical direction and the time in the horizontal direction, as in Fig. 142. This figure represents the facts in Table 69. The line *ORABCDEFGHIJKL* shows the total capital invested at various dates. *RA, BC, DE, FG, HI, JK* represent the outlays, *KL* the revenue. It will be seen that the total capital invested after the conclusion of the enterprise is zero, as indeed it should be. If we assume in this case that the enterprise starts off with $100 in money, each outlay represents a shift from money into real assets, and each revenue a shift from real into money assets. Then the line *RABC* · · · etc., represents the distribution at each moment of time between real and money assets.

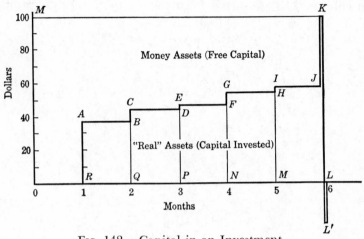

FIG. 142.   Capital in an Investment.

The Allocation of Profit

Where the enterprise has a positive total profit a new problem arises. We cannot now assume that the total capital invested is merely equal to the net past outlays, for according to this calculation the capital invested at the conclusion of the process would be negative. Thus if in the above case the final revenue were $124, by calculating the total capital invested on the method in the previous paragraph we should conclude that the capital after the process was finished was −$24—an obviously ridiculous result. If the final revenue were $124 (= *KL'* in Fig. 142), the total capital at the end of the process would be *LL'*, or −$24. In order to get the correct result we must evidently subtract the sum of profit from the total capital invested. As we shall see, this is a general principle. The total capital invested up to any date may be defined as the sum of outlays incurred and profit allocated, less the revenues received, before that date. Then in Fig. 142 the course of the capital on the final date is given by the line *JKL'L*.

Linear Allocation

It is not always convenient or desirable to allocate all the profits to the final date of the enterprise. Indeed, the principal business of the accountant is to allocate the total profit among the various "months," "years," or other accounting periods over which the course of the enterprise extends. There are many possible ways of doing this. A simple way, though one that is not used in practice, is to allocate the profit equally over the various "months" or accounting periods of the enterprise. If this method were adopted with the outlays in Table 70 and a revenue of $124, the result would be as in Table 71.

TABLE 71. Linear Allocation of Profit

Month	Outlay (−) or Revenue (+) ($)	Profit ($)	Total Capital Invested ($)	Addition to Capital Invested ($)
1	−37.50	4.00	41.50	41.50
2	−7.50	4.00	53.00	11.50
3	−2.50	4.00	59.50	6.50
4	−7.50	4.00	71.00	11.50
5	−2.50	4.00	77.50	6.50
6	−42.50	4.00	124.00	46.50
	+124.00		0	−124.00

Here the $24 profit is allocated equally among the six accounting periods, which give $4 to each "month." Then the total capital invested at any date—say, in the third month—is equal to the sum of outlays up to that date ($47.50) plus the sum of profit up to that date ($12), or $59.50.

Graphic Illustration. This method of allocation can be illustrated graphically if we suppose that the capital grows by a constant amount each month. This is shown in Fig. 143. Again the total capital at each

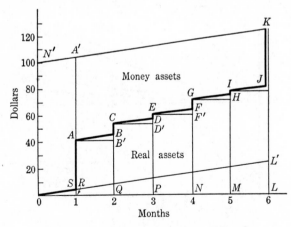

Fig. 143. Linear Allocation of Profit.

844   STUDIES IN ANALYTICAL TECHNIQUES

date is given by the line $OSABCDEFGHIJKL$. The line is constructed as follows: LL' is the total profit. If the profit is apportioned "linearly," i.e., so that equal amounts are apportioned to equal amounts of time, the total profit allocated up to any date is shown by the line OL'. If AB, CD, EF, etc., are drawn parallel to OL' instead of parallel to the base as in Fig. 142, and if SA, BC, DE, etc., are equal to the outlays, then $OSABCDE$, etc., represents the growth of real assets, of capital invested. The line $N'K$ shows the growth of the total value of the enterprise, assuming that it starts with ON' in cash. The distance between $N'K$ and $OSABC$ · · · etc., at any date is the cash holding of the enterprise. Thus at date 1 the cash holding is AA'.

Growth at Constant Rates (Exponential Growth)

The profit-making process, as we have seen earlier (page 546), is essentially the process by which total net worth grows. In the above example we have supposed that the growth takes place at "simple interest"—that is, at a constant absolute amount in each time period. For many purposes, however, it is convenient to regard the growth of net worth as taking place at a constant *rate of growth*, the rate of growth being the ratio of the absolute amount of growth in a unit period to the initial value. Thus if 100 of anything grows to 105 in 1 year, the rate of growth is $\dfrac{105-100}{100}$, or 5 per cent (one twentieth) per annum. Growth at a constant rate is called "exponential" growth. Fig. 144 shows exponential growth curves for \$100—NK for zero growth, NK_2 for growth at 2 per cent per month, NK_4 and NK_{10} for growth at 4 and 10 per cent per month. These curves are also called

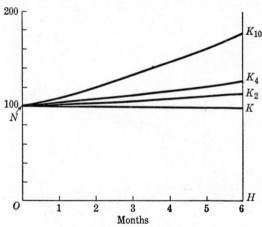

FIG. 144.   Growth Curves.

"compound interest curves," and the growth of value is called "compounding." The reverse process of decline in value looking backward through time is called "discounting." Thus HK_{10} is the compounded value of ON, compounded at 10 per cent per month for six months; ON is the discounted value of HK_{10}, discounted at 10 per cent per month for six months.

The Average Rate of Profit

The rate of profit in a completed enterprise is the "average" rate of growth of total net worth through the history of the enterprise. If the profit allocated to any period is equal to the net worth of the enterprise at the beginning of the period multiplied by the rate of profit as above defined, the rate of profit over the whole enterprise is that which will just suffice to allocate all the profit made. Let us suppose, for instance, that in the potato enterprise mentioned above the total revenue on the sale of the potatoes is $126.54, and the enterprise starts with $100 and holds any money balances idle at zero rate of interest. The figure is chosen for the sake of arithmetic convenience; at this figure the rate of profit is just 4 per cent per month, as may be shown in Table 72. The amount of profit allocated to each month is

TABLE 72.   Allocation of Profit According to a Constant Rate of Profit

1	2	3	4	5	6
				Total	Total
	Outlay (+) or	Total Net	Profit	Capital	Money
Month	Revenue (−)	Worth	Allocated	Invested	Stock
0	0	100.00	0	0	100
1	+37.50	104.00	4.00	41.50	62.50
2	+7.50	108.16	4.16	53.16	55.00
3	+2.50	112.49	4.33	59.99	52.50
4	+7.50	116.99	4.50	71.99	45.00
5	+2.50	121.67	4.68	79.17	42.50
6	+42.50	126.54	4.87	126.54	0.00
	−126.54	126.54		0.00	126.54
Total	−26.54		26.54		

4 per cent of the total net worth at the beginning of the month. At this rate the total profit allocated just equals the total profit made, or $26.54.

Column 1 gives the data. Column 3 shows how the total net worth grows at 4 per cent per month. Profit allocated in column 4 is calculated by multiplying the net worth figure of the preceding month by 4/100. This figure is then added to the net worth of the preceding month to get the total net worth of the present month. Total capital invested (column 5) is the sum of all outlays (+), revenues (−), and profit allocated (+). The money stock (6) is obtained by subtracting outlays and adding revenues to the original stock of $100. The sum of the total capital invested and the money stock is equal to the total net worth.

Growth of Profit Under Conditions of Interest Payment or Receipt

Suppose now that the money stock or the "uninvested capital" of the enterprise can be held in a form which bears interest, and yet be available for outlays. The total profit of the enterprise now includes the interest received, and the money stock (or liquid capital stock) must be assumed to grow at a rate equal to the rate of interest which it receives. These interest receipts can be regarded as additions to allocated profit.

Now suppose that the net worth of the enterprise is less than the maximum value of capital invested. Then the enterprise must incur debt, which can be regarded as negative liquid capital, and interest which is paid on such debt is a subtraction from the profit allocated. Thus suppose that in our example the enterprise starts with a net worth (in cash) of $50, that it can hold liquid capital in the form of a bank deposit at 2 per cent per month interest, and that on outstanding debt it must pay 5 per cent interest—let us suppose for the moment that it operates under the British practice of the overdraft, which is so clearly a negative cash balance. This time, again for purposes of arithmetical convenience, we will suppose that the revenue from the potatoes is $116.01. Table 73 then shows that under these circumstances the rate of profit on net worth is 5 per cent per month.

The calculations of this table need some comment. Profit allocated (column 4) in each month is 5 per cent of the total net worth of the previous month; total net worth in each month is equal to the total net worth of the previous month plus allocated profit. Liquid capital in each month is equal to liquid capital of the previous month, minus outlays (or plus revenues) of that month, and plus interest earned or minus interest paid. Thus in month 1 we have $50.00 − 37.50 + 1.00 = 13.50$. The interest payment in each month is equal to the liquid capital of the previous month multiplied by the rate of interest, assumed to be 2 per cent when liquid capital is positive, 5 per cent when it is negative. The total invested capital is then equal to the total net worth less the total liquid capital, and is also equal to the total invested capital of the previous month, plus outlays and minus receipts, plus allocated profit, and minus interest received and plus interest paid. At the conclusion of the enterprise again invested capital is zero; liquid capital is equal to net worth and has grown by an amount equal to total profit.

Table 73. Allocation of Profit at Constant Rate, Under Conditions of Interest Received and Paid

1	2	3	4	5	6	7
Month	Outlay (+) or Reve- nue (−)	Total Net Worth	Profit Allo- cated at 5%	Total Capital Invested	Total Liquid Capital	Interest Payment (−) or Re- ceipt (+)
0		50.00			+50.00	
1	+37.50	52.50	2.50	39.00	+13.50	+1.00
2	+7.50	55.12	2.62	48.85	+6.27	+.27
3	+2.50	57.88	2.76	53.98	+3.90	+.13
4	+7.50	60.77	2.89	64.29	−3.52	+.08
5	+2.50	63.81	3.04	70.01	−6.20	−.18
6	+42.50	67.00	3.19	116.01	−49.01	−.31
	−116.01	67.00		0	67.00	
Total			$17.00			

Allocation According to External Rates of Interest

Tables 71–73 allocated profit among the various accounting periods of the process according to some purely internal rule without reference to any external conditions. The values so obtained for the total capital invested were purely internal values, derived from the outlay-revenue series alone. In Table 72 and 73 also, the rate of profit is a purely *internal* rate of profit, again derived from the outlay-revenue series alone without reference to outside conditions. In a world in which an investor has many varied opportunities for investment, however, the question arises, Should he not allocate his profit, and so perform his valuations, according to the *external* rates of interest which he could earn in other investments? Instead of finding some constant rate of growth or rate of profit—the 4 per cent per month in Table 72— why should he not calculate the profit allocated to each month by multiplying the total capital invested to date by the current rate of interest in other possible employments of capital? This process is illustrated in Table 74. Here we have postulated a series of external rates of interest, one for each "month," and have calculated the total profit for each month by multiplying the net worth at the end of the previous month by the external rate of interest.

If the total revenue in August were $122.89, the above method would lead to a consistent distribution of the total profit ($22.89) among the various months—consistent in the sense that the total amount distributed by the formula was equal to the total amount of profit earned. If, however, the revenue in August were not $122.89,

TABLE 74.   Calculation of Values by External Rates of Interest

1	2	3	4	5
Month	Outlay (+) Revenue (−)	Rate of Interest (% per month)	Net Worth	Profit Allocated
0			100	
1	37.50	5	105	5
2	7.50	4	109.20	4.20
3	2.50	3	112.48	3.28
4	7.50	2	114.73	2.25
5	2.50	3	118.17	3.44
6	42.50	4	122.89	4.72
	−(?)			22.89

the above method would not give a consistent result. If the revenue in August were more than $122.89, there would be less profit distributed than was earned. Somewhere, therefore, the "surplus" must be accounted for. It could be accounted for by assuming a "capital gain" in August equal to the amount of the surplus. But if the profit calculated at the external rates of interest is regarded as "normal" profit, then any surplus is, as we have seen, an "economic rent." If economic rent is counted as an outlay, then valuation at external rates of interest gives a consistent method for distributing profit.

"Rent" in an Investment

Suppose the total revenue in August was not $122.89 but $132.89. If under these circumstances the profit as calculated from the external rates of interest is the "normal" profit, the excess of the actual profit over the normal profit would be $10. This $10 is the net revenue, or the "rent" in the process. If it is paid to the owner of the rent on the final date of the process, the allocation of profit according to current rates of interest gives a consistent result.

If the "rent" is not all reckoned on the last day of the process, profit will also have to be reckoned on the rent. The arithmetic of this procedure is complicated, although the principle is clear. The total amount of the rent will be less by the amount of interest reckoned on the rent. This is shown in Table 75, where we suppose that the rent is paid at the beginning of the process instead of at the end. In this case the amount of rent paid is only $8.14. If this sum is paid at the beginning of the period, the enterprise will have to start with $108.14

TABLE 75. Valuation at External Rates, Including Rent

1 Month	2 Outlay (+) Revenue (−)	3 Rate of Interest (% per month)	4 Net Worth	5 Profit Allocated
0	8.14 (Rent)		108.14	
1	37.50	5	113.55	5.41
2	7.50	4	118.09	4.54
3	2.50	3	121.63	3.54
4	7.50	2	124.06	2.43
5	2.50	3	127.78	3.72
6	42.50	4	132.89	5.11
	−132.89			——

in cash instead of $100, if it is not to run into debt at the end. The net worth of $108.14 grows to the final revenue of $132.89 at the various external rates of interest. The $8.14 at the beginning of the period is just equivalent to the $10 at the end, at the prevailing rates of interest, and the rent receiver should be indifferent as to which he gets.

THE THEORY OF VALUATION

One of the most important applications of the theory of time relations is to the problem of valuation. This problem has already been noted in Chapter 23. There we saw that the profit made by an enterprise in any one year depended upon the *valuation* placed upon the enterprise at the beginning and at the close of the year. We shall now see that the valuations themselves depend upon the amounts of profit which are allocated to the various "years." That is to say, the problem of allocating the total profit of an enterprise over the years of its existence and the problem of estimating the value of the enterprise at any one moment of time are not two problems but merely different aspects of a single problem.

The "Present Value of the Investment"

The preceding illustrations in this chapter have estimated the value of an enterprise at any date by the addition of all previous outlays and all previous sums of allocated profit and interest paid, and the subtraction of all previous revenues and interest received. This figure we have called the "amount of capital invested." We can arrive at the same figure by adding together the *future* revenues and interest receipts, and subtracting from this total *future* outlays, future profits, and future interest payments. This figure may be called the "present value of the investment," as it is the present value of *future* net receipts. The amount of capital invested is a backward-looking figure, derived from past records. The present value of the investment is a forward-looking figure, derived from the expectations of future receipts and outlays.

Present Value Equal to the Amount of Capital Invested

It is not difficult to show that no matter what method of allocation of profit we use, if *all* the outlays and revenues and dates connected with an enterprise are known—both past, present, and future—the "amount of capital invested" is equal to the "present value of the investment" at any date whatsoever. Any date divides the total outlays, O_t, into past outlays, O_p, and future outlays, O_f. It similarly divides the total revenues, R_t, into past revenues, R_p, and future revenues, R_f; and it divides the total amount of profit, A_t, into that allocated to the past (A_p) and that allocated to the future (A_f), and the total interest, N_t, into that paid or received in the past, N_p, and that paid or received in the future, N_f. Therefore:

$$O_t = O_p + O_f$$
$$R_t = R_p + R_f \qquad (1)$$
$$A_t = A_p + A_f$$
$$N_t = N_p + N_f$$

But we also know that for the whole enterprise, from its beginning to its final liquidation,

$$A_t - N_t = R_t - O_t \qquad (2)$$

Substituting from (1) into (2) and rearranging, we have:

$$O_p - R_p + A_p - N_p = R_f - O_f - A_f + N_f \qquad (3)$$

N_p and N_f here refer to net interest received—interest paid being treated as negative. The left-hand side of equation (3), however, is the total amount of capital invested at the date in question. The right-hand side is the present value of the investment.

The "Present" Included with the "Past"

In the above example we have conceived the "present" as a mere mathematical point of time, so that all outlays and receipts must lie on one side of it or the other. If, however, the "present" is in appreciable period we must adopt some convention in the definition of the amount of capital invested and of the present value of the investment. We shall assume that the "present" (as it shares with the past the property of being known, whereas the future is uncertain) will be included with the "past." Then the amount of capital invested may be defined as the algebraic sum of all outlays, revenues, interest paid($+$), interest received($-$), and allocated profits up to and including the present, and the present value of an investment may be defined as a similar sum subsequent to and not including the present. As interest paid can always be treated as an outlay and interest received as a revenue, in what follows, for the sake of simplicity we shall simply suppose that outlays and revenues are defined to include interest payments, and we shall not distinguish interest specifically.

Calculation of Profit

From equation (3) it is easy to show the relation between the outlays, revenues, profit, and valuations pertaining to any given "year" or accounting period. Let O be the outlay, R the revenue, and A the allocated profit in any one "year." Let O_p, R_p, and A_p be the sums of all outlays, revenues, and profits previous to the date which begins the accounting period in question. Let the value of the investment, or the amount of capital invested, be V on the date that begins the period and V' on the date that ends the period. Then:

$$V' = O_p + O - R_p - R + A_p + A,$$
$$= V + O - R + A; \tag{4}$$

i.e.,
$$A = (V' - V) + (R - O).$$

That is to say, the amount of profit in any one year is equal to the total revenues of that year less the total outlays and plus the amount by which the value of the enterprise has increased. This is the definition of profit used in Chapter 23.

Various Methods of Valuation

All the various methods of valuation, whether used by accountants or not, are based on various methods of allocating profit. The difficulties and uncertainties of valuation also depend on this fact, for the total sum of profit which it is necessary to allocate between the past and the future is itself uncertain until the very date of liquidation of the enterprise. No matter what our *method* of allocating profit, therefore, as long as we allocate any to "past" years the results of our valuation will be uncertain. A possible method of avoiding this uncertainty is the method of valuing "at cost." By this method no attempt is made to allocate profit to past years, but it is all assumed to accrue at some future date or at the end of the process. In this case, therefore, the amount of capital invested is calculated by adding up the past outlays and subtracting any past revenues, without taking any "profit" items into account. Although this method has the virtue of avoiding uncertainty, it also avoids the main problem which the accountant has to solve. For the allocation of profit among various accounting periods is the principal task of the accountant—otherwise accountancy would be mere arithmetic.

Valuation at Market Rates of Interest

Another possible method of valuation is to allocate profit according to the prevailing market rates of interest, as in Table 74. In this case again, to avoid uncertainty we must assume that the "rent" is all allocated to future dates, for the "rent" is an item whose magnitude can only be estimated. Again, this method avoids the main task of the accountant, which should be to allocate "rent" just as much as to allocate "profit." The value at any date is equal to the "compounded" sum of past outlays and revenues. This must be equal to the "discounted" sum of expected future outlays and revenues—including rent. As the expected future outlays are uncertain, the sum of rent is also uncertain.

Valuation at Internal Rates of Interest

Where the accountant is practically certain of the course of future payments in an investment, he may perform the valuation according to the "constant rate of profit" or "exponential" method. Suppose, for instance, that he has to value a bond. Here he knows the past payments, and with almost equal certainty the future payments. He knows, therefore, the rate of profit on the bond over its whole lifetime. Hence he can calculate its value either by "compounding" the past payments or by "discounting" the future payments, as in Table 72. If the rate of profit at which calculations are made is the correct "internal" value, the compounded sum of past payments should, of course, equal the discounted sum of future payments.

Capital Loss and Gain

Yet another method is to allocate the expected profit according to some principle and then to make corrections as it appears that the anticipation was too favorable or too adverse. Suppose the system of linear distribution of profit is adopted, as in Table 71. There is no particular virtue in this method, and it is never used in practice, but the arithmetical calculations are much simpler and any conclusions drawn can be applied immediately to other methods of allocation. Suppose that when a farmer planted a crop of potatoes he expected the value of the crop to be $124, as in Table 71. The allocated profit was then $4 per month. He reckoned on this principle through to June, when the total capital invested, by his calculations, was $71. But a blight attacked the crop, so that its value when sold was lowered from $124 to $106. If he had known this to start with, he would have counted only $1 per month profit, and his capital invested would have amounted to $59 instead of $71. What, then, should he do in these circumstances? The proper thing would seem to be to write down the value of the capital invested from $71 to $59 and thenceforth to calculate profit at $1 per month instead of $4. The new amount of capital invested would then be equal to the value of the investment, as measured by the future revenues, less the future outlays and profits: $(106 − 42.50 − 2.50 − 1 − 1) = $59. This writing down of the capital from $71 to $59 may properly be called a *capital loss,* though it is not always recognized as such in accounting practice.

Capital Loss Distinguished from Capital Depreciation

A capital loss must be distinguished carefully from the capital *depreciation* which occurs as revenues are paid in. When the potatoes are sold the capitalist exchanges 20 tons of potatoes valued at $124 for $124 in cash, and the value of the investment disappears as far as its owner is concerned when he sells the potatoes; but there is no capital loss. A capital loss occurs only when there is an unfavorable revision of future expectations; i.e., when we come to believe that either future revenues are going to be less than we thought, or that future outlays are going to be greater than we thought.

Capital Gain Distinguished from Capital Appreciation

Similarly, if there is a favorable revision of future expectations, if we come to believe that future revenues are going to be greater or future outlays less than we thought, there will be a capital gain. This gain must be distinguished carefully from capital *appreciation* which occurs when outlays are incurred or profits are allocated.

Valuation at "Market" Values

A method of valuation commonly employed in practice is valuation at some "market" price. This method is frequently used in the valuation of "liquid" or readily salable goods. It is not available, of course, for goods which are not constantly bought and sold. It is important to understand its significance. Valuation by market prices is equivalent to allocating the total profit according to variable rates of interest, as in Table 74. Suppose that in this table column 4 represents the market value of the field of potatoes at various dates. We assume, of course, that potato fields are bought and sold frequently, so that a market value can be found by observing the prices in other transactions, even if no actual sales are made of the commodity which we are valuing. Then from these market values a "rate of interest" or a "rate of profit" can be deduced in each month. The *amount* of profit in each month is equal to the capital appreciation less the total outlay. Thus for Month 2 (Table 74) the net worth at market values at the end of the month is $109.20; at the beginning of the month it is $105. The total profit for April is $4.20. The rate of profit is $\dfrac{4.20}{105}$ or 4 per cent per month. Valuation by "market" prices thus runs into the same difficulty that we found in valuation by market rates of interest—it fails to allocate "economic rent."

Valuation at "Cost or Market"

A common rule in accountancy is to value objects at "cost or market, whichever is the lower." Although this is an arbitrary rule, it has a certain basis in principle. In allocating an *uncertain* future profit or rent to present or to past "years" it is better to be as conservative as possible. It is pleasanter for an investor to discover that he has a positive "rent" when a process is liquidated than to discover that his "rent" is negative and that profit which has been cheerfully allocated—and perhaps enjoyed—at past dates has not, in fact, been earned. If the "market" valuation is below "cost" it is an indication that the market expects the process ultimately to be unprofitable. It is perhaps better, therefore, to allocate expected losses than to allocate expected profits. The "cost or market" rule in effect achieves this end, for by making "cost" the maximum it has the result of allocating *no* profits to past dates at all, as we have seen; and by valuing at "market" when market value is below cost, the result is to allocate anticipated losses to past dates.

The Valuation of Public Utilities

Our analysis of profit and valuation throws a certain amount of light on the problem of the regulation of public utilities discussed in

Chapter 31. We can put the problem in this form: How great a *sum* of profit can a monopoly be allowed to earn in a given year in order to give it a normal *rate* of profit? We see clearly that the answer to this question depends upon the valuation placed on the property of the monopoly at the beginning and at the end of the year. The smaller these values, the smaller will be the *sum* of profit which is equivalent to a given *rate* of profit. If, for instance, the value at the beginning of the year is $1,000,000 and the allowed rate of profit is 5 per cent per annum, the corporation will be allowed to earn $50,000. If, however, the valuation is $2,000,000, the corporation will be allowed to earn $100,000. Clearly, a regulated corporation will want to have itself assessed at a high rather than a low value for purposes of regulation. For purposes of taxation, of course, the reverse may be the case.

"Original" and "Reproduction" Cost

Two methods of valuation are important in this connection. One is the method of valuation by "original cost." Strictly, this method implies that no profits are allocated to past dates. It will therefore give a value which is "low" from the point of view of the corporation. The other method is valuation at "reproduction cost."[1] That is, the property is valued not at what it originally cost but at what it would cost to reproduce at present prices of input. If prices have been rising, the reproduction cost is likely to be greater than the original cost, and is therefore likely to be favored by the corporation. But if prices have been falling, the original cost is likely to be greater and will be preferred by the corporation as a basis for rate making.

The "Ideal" Valuation

Probably the ideal valuation method for purposes of rate making is that of allocating profit to past dates according to the "normal" rates of profit at those dates, i.e., according to the method in Table 74. The amount of capital invested up to the present should be reckoned by taking the *compounded* sum of *all* past outlays, whether for "capital account" or not, less the compounded sum of *all* past receipts. This valuation ensures that the enterprise has earned "normal" profits up to the date of regulation. Then profit should be allowed in each year thenceforward at the "normal" rate. Such a method has one flaw which is present in all schemes for the regulation of monopolies. It assumes that the monopoly has a "right" to earn the normal rate of profit no

---

[1] In both cases, of course, allowance is made for depreciation—i.e., for past revenues imputed to the equipment in question.

matter how poorly it is managed or how small the demand for its services. In perfect competition the rate of profit is itself an indication of the efficiency of management, for an enterprise which is poorly managed or which is producing an unwanted commodity suffers losses. But with a regulated monopoly the rate of profit, however defined, is no check on the efficiency of management.

Valuation and the Change in Price Level

One problem raised in an acute form by the regulation of monopoly, but present in any valuation problem, is that of reckoning with changes in the general level of prices. Accounting is usually carried on under the assumption that the value of the dollar remains unchanged, and we have made this assumption all through the present chapter. It is, however, one which is seldom justified in economic history. Consequently, accounting and valuation systems are constantly misleading us as to the "true" or "purchasing power" value of our property and profits. At a time of inflation the dollar value of all goods tends to rise, and hence the dollar value of all property tends to rise. This rise in the dollar value is frequently mistaken for profits, for, as we have seen, profits are the "growth" of the value of property. Such profits are quite illusory unless they are transformed into cash when prices reach a maximum. But they play an important part in the business cycle, for even the illusion of profits is enough to increase the demand for inputs and therefore to increase employment.

At a time of deflation of prices the value of property falls and the accounting system records losses. These losses may be as illusory as the profits of inflation, and yet they may have an equally potent effect. It is hardly too much to say that a revision of our accounting systems in the direction of identifying these "illusory" profits and losses would materially reduce the fluctuations of business.

INVENTORY VALUATION

A difficult problem which can be illuminated in some degree by the above analysis is that of inventory valuation. The problem can best be illustrated with reference to a hypothetical wheat marketer whose experience is illustrated in Table 76. Rows 1, 2, and 3 give the data. It will be observed that we have a "complete" enterprise—that is, one that starts merely with money and finishes with money. Rows 4 and 5 show the wheat and money stocks on each date, assuming that the enterprise starts with $2000 of money. This grows in the course of the transactions to $4287, which is at a rate of 10 per cent per "week," or whatever is the unit time period. Exponential growth of the net worth over the whole period is shown in row 6, and the corresponding profit allocation in row 7. Each sum of profit is 10 per cent of the preceding period's net worth; each period's net worth is the preceding period's

TABLE 76. Inventory Valuation

Date	0	1	2	3	4	5	6	7	8
1. Price of wheat		2.00	2.50	3.00	2.00	3.00	4.00	2.00	2.587
2. Wheat bought (+) or sold (−)		+600	+200	−700	+500	+300	−700	+800	−1000
3. Money paid in (+) or out (−)		−1200	−500	+2100	−1000	−900	+2800	−1600	+2587
4. Wheat stock	0	600	800	100	600	900	200	1000	0
5. Money stock	2000	800	300	2400	1400	500	3300	1700	4287
6. Net worth (exponential)	2000	2200	2420	2662	2928	3221	3543	3897	4287
7. Profit (exponential)		200	220	242	266	293	322	354	390
Value of wheat:									
8. (exponential)		1400	2120	262	1528	2721	243	2197	0
9. FIFO		1200	1700	250	1250	2150	600	2200	0
10. LIFO		1200	1700	200	1200	2100	400	2000	0
Net worth:									
11. FIFO	2000	2000	2000	2650	2650	2650	3900	3900	4287
12. LIFO	2000	2000	2000	2600	2600	2600	3700	3700	4287
Profit:									
13. FIFO		0	0	650	0	0	1250	0	387
14. LIFO		0	0	600	0	0	1100	0	587
Cost of wheat:									
15. FIFO				1450			1550		2200
16. LIFO				1500			1700		2000

net worth, plus 10 per cent. Row 8 shows the value of the wheat stock on this principle; it is the difference between the net worth (row 6) and the money stock (row 5).

"LIFO" and "FIFO"

In rows 9 and 10 we show the value of the wheat stock according to the two most common systems of inventory accounting: "FIFO," which stands for "First in first out," and "LIFO," which stands for "Last in first out." According to the "FIFO" system (which has been dominant, and is now being challenged by "LIFO"), when stock is sold it is supposed that the "oldest" part of the stock is disposed of and hence the cost of the oldest part ("first in") is charged against the revenue from the sales. This means that remaining stock is valued at the cost of the "newest" part—that is, the latest acquired. The alternative system, "LIFO," charges the cost of the "newest" part of the stock against revenues, and hence the remaining stock is valued at the cost of the "oldest" part.

Under both systems purchases of "wheat" do not affect the net worth, as the wheat is immediately valued at cost, so that the value of the wheat acquired is exactly equal to the money given up. Thus for the first two periods the net worth, as shown in rows 11 and 12, remains constant at 2000; the value of the wheat stock is simply the net worth less the money stock (row 5). In period 3, however, when there is a sale of wheat, a difference reveals itself. On the FIFO principle we suppose that the "earliest" acquisitions are sold. Of the 700 bushels sold it is supposed that 600 come from period 1, at a cost of $1200, and 100 from period 2, at a cost of $2.50, totaling $1450 (row 15). The remaining 100 bushels in the wheat stock (row 4) are therefore valued as if they had been acquired in period 2—that is, at $2.50 per bushel, or at $250 (row 9). On the LIFO principle, of the 700 bushels sold it is supposed that the "latest" are charged off—200 from period 2, at $2.50 ($500), and 500 from period 1, at $2 ($1000)—the total cost being $1500, and the value of the 100 bushels remaining in stock being $200, valued at $2, the price of period 1. Similarly, in period 6, on the FIFO principle the cost of the 700 bushels sold is 100 at $2.50 (period 2), 500 at $2 (period 4), and 100 at $3 (period 5), or $1550, the remaining 200 bushels being valued at the price of period 5 ($3)—that is, at $600 (row 9). On the LIFO principle we suppose that of the 900 bushels in stock in period 5, the late acquisitions are sold—300 in period 5 ($900) and 400 in period 4 ($800)—the total cost being $1700 (row 16), and the remaining 200 bushels being valued at the price of periods 4 and 2, that is, at $400 (row 10).

Then the net worth in row 11 is the sum of the value of wheat (row 9) and the money stock (row 5); the net worth in row 12 is the sum of the value of wheat of row 10 and the money stock. The profit figure in row 13 is the increase in net worth in each period from row 11; the profit figure in row 14 is the increase in net worth in each period from row 12.

Graphic Illustration. Table 76 is illustrated diagramatically in Fig. 145. In the left-hand part of the figure time is measured along the horizontal axis, money values on the vertical axis. P_0P_8 shows the growth of net worth by exponential allocation. $P_0H_3L_3H_6L_6H_8P_8$ shows the growth of net worth by the LIFO method (row 12). $P_0H_3F_3$-$K_6F_6K_8P_8$ shows the growth of net worth by the FIFO method. The dotted line shows the money stock; the difference between this line and the net worth line is the value of the wheat stock. In the right-hand side of the figure quantities of wheat are measured horizontally from O', and quantities of money vertically. The path $P'_0P_1P_2$, $\cdots P_8$ then shows the movement of money and wheat stocks in the course of the transactions. By ordinary accounting methods net worth stays at $O'P'_0$ until period 3, when it jumps to OH_3 (LIFO) or OK_3 (FIFO); it makes another jump in period 6 to OH_8 (LIFO) or OK_8

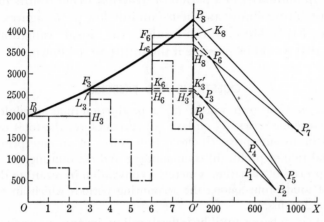

FIG. 145. Inventory Valuation.

(FIFO) and another jump in period 8 to OP_8. By exponential allocation net worth would rise gradually from P'_0 to P_8 following the values of the curve P_0P_8.

Exponential Allocation as a "Test"

Exponential allocation is not, of course, practical, as it would involve a knowledge of the future which the accountant does not possess. Nevertheless it is a useful theoretical construct by which to test the various practical methods. The weakness of conventional accounting—a weakness which is just as characteristic of the LIFO as the FIFO method—is that it allocates no profits to periods involving purchasing, even though the movements of these periods (e.g., from P'_0 to P_2, or from P_3 to P_5) are absolutely necessary preparation for the subsequent gains. Where the period of turnover is less than the accounting period, however, as it generally is in the case with inventories, this weakness is not serious—thus in the present example if the accounting period were 3 "weeks," the results given by conventional accounting would not differ sharply from those given by exponential allocation.

The advantage of LIFO over FIFO is that in some degree it solves the problem of the distortion of accounting results due to general inflation and deflation. We see this in the example, where there is a rather steady inflation up to period 6 and then a return to earlier levels. FIFO expresses this inflation in a steadily rising valuation of inventory; LIFO sticks closer to the original price level. Thus the net worth in period 6 is seen to be more inflated by FIFO (F_6) than by LIFO (L_6). Similarly, in a period of deflation FIFO results in unduly low values for inventory and hence unduly low profit figures. Neither LIFO nor FIFO, however, can result in the "ideal" valuation and allocation that would be possible if the future were known.

QUESTIONS AND EXERCISES

1. Define, in your own words: (a) a production-time schedule, (b) an outlay-revenue series, (c) outlays, (d) revenues, (e) the total capital invested in an enterprise, (f) the present value of an enterprise, (g) the internal rate of profit, (h) compounding and discounting.
2. "The process of valuation is merely a convention in regard to the allocation of total profit among the accounting periods which an enterprise covers." Discuss.
3. "Call no man happy until he is dead: call no investment profitable until it is liquidated." Discuss.
4. If a process of production took no time, i.e., if there were no time interval between inputs and outputs, would it need any capital? If not, could it have any profits?
5. The following represents a time schedule of the outlays involved in building a bridge:

Year	0	1	2	3	4	5
Outlay ($000)	0	130	200	500	150	25

a. At what sum must the bridge be valued at the end of the fifth year in order to make the investment earn 5 per cent p.a. (interest reckoned annually)?

b. Suppose that the rate of interest in other investments were 4 per cent p.a. What would be the total cost of the bridge, counting this 4 per cent as normal profit to be included?

c. Suppose that the following schedule showed the rate of interest in other investments:

Year	1	2	3	4	5
Rate of Interest	10%	9%	8%	7%	8%

Suppose that the bridge was sold for $1,500,000 at the end of the fifth year. How much rent did the investment earn, reckoning the rent as accruing at the time of sale? What, under these circumstances, is the value of the uncompleted bridge at the end of each year? What is the value of the rent at the end of each year? (Use the method in Tables 74 and 75 in calculating the values.)

6. The following represents the outlay-revenue series of an enterprise:

Year	1	2	3	4	5	6
Outlay ($000)	500	400	300	200	100	0
Revenue ($000)	0	100	100	344	600	966

Show, in a table like Table 72, that the rate of profit in this investment is 10 per cent. Calculate (a) the amount of capital invested and (b) the present value of the investment for each date according to the following methods of allocation of profit:

a. All profit reckoned in the year 6.

b. All profit reckoned in the year 1.

c. Linear allocation.

d. Exponential allocation at 10 per cent p.a.

Show that in each case the amount of capital invested is equal to the value of the investment. Assume no interest on cash balances and an initial cash balance just enough to avoid debt.

7. "Valuation is the rock on which all regulation of monopoly splits." Discuss.

8. What problems are raised in the theory of valuation by the fact that the price level changes?

9. The following table shows shifts in holdings of wheat and money of a single marketer in successive periods.

Wheat stock (bu.)	0	400	200	300	100	50	150	400	800	600	0
Money stock ($)	1000	200	700	400	1100	1300	1000	500	100	400	1629

Calculate and tabulate, for each period, (a) the quantities of wheat bought and sold, (b) the quantities of money received or spent, (c) the price of wheat. Show that exponential allocation at 5 per cent per period will just allocate the total profit. Then calculate the net worth, the profit allocated, the value of the wheat stock, and the cost of wheat sold for each period (a) by the exponential method, (b) by the LIFO method, (c) by the FIFO method. Graph the results, and comment.

CHAPTER 39

THE EQUILIBRIUM OF AN
ENTERPRISE IN TIME

Variability of the "Dates" in the Production Time Schedule

In our analysis of the individual firm, as worked out in previous chapters, we neglected many of the problems connected with capital, for we neglected the problems involved in the time relations of production. Even in the preceding chapter we assumed that the "production time schedule" in Table 69, page 840, was a fixed, unvarying schedule. We have not considered at all up to now the fact that a firm may vary not only the *magnitude* of its inputs and outputs, but within limits the *dates* of these inputs and outputs. In a great many processes the dates—at least the relative dates—of inputs and outputs are more or less fixed, so that our preceding analysis applies without much alteration. In some, however, the problem of deciding the dates, of output especially, is very important. This is so in any process in which goods "mature" slowly. The manufacture of wines or cheeses, the growth of timber, even in shorter measure the growth of crops like hay, present a problem not merely of *how much* input and output we shall have, but of *when* we shall have it.

The Maturing of Wines: Arithmetical Example

Take a simple example. Suppose a man buys new wine and lays it away in a cave, so that the only outlay involved in the process is the initial purchase of wine, say for $1000. Suppose the "normal" rate of profit is 10 per cent per annum.

Total Cost. If the wine is kept in the cave for one year, the total cost of the process (in the technical sense of the word "cost"), i.e., the total outlay plus the normal sum of profit, is $1000 outlay plus $100 normal profit, or $1100. If the wine is kept in the cave for two years, the total cost will be $1000 outlay plus $(100 + 110) normal profit, or $1210, and so on for any number of years. This is shown in row 1 of

862

Table 77. The total cost is therefore equal to the compounded sum of the initial outlay, compounded at the "normal" rate of interest.

Total Revenue. Suppose row 2 of Table 77 represents the total value of the wine in each year, if it is sold in that year for consumption. That is to say, if the wine were sold for consumption as soon as it was bought, it would fetch only \$810; if it were sold for consumption one year after it was bought, it would fetch \$1110, for it would be a better wine; after two years it would fetch \$1320; and so on. That is, the figures in this row represent not a present value of a future sale for consumption but what the wine would fetch in a present sale for consumption.

TABLE 77. Time Equilibrium

Year	0	1	2	3	4	5	6
1. Total cost	1000	1100	1210	1331	1464.1	1610.51	1771.56
2. Total revenue	810	1110	1320	1481	1629.1	1775.51	1916.56
3. Net revenue	−190	10	110	150	165	165	145
4. Discount factor	1.0	1.1	1.21	1.331	1.464	1.610	1.772
5. Disc. net rev.	−190	9.1	90.9	112.7	112.7	102.5	81.8
6. Cost differences		100	110	121	133.1	146.41	161.05
7. Rev. differences		300	210	161	148.1	146.41	141.05
8. Rate of cost increase		10%	10%	10%	10%	10%	10%
9. Rate of revenue increase		37%	18.9%	12.2%	10%	9%	7.94%
10. Internal rate of return		11%	14.8%	14.0%	12.8%	12.2%	11.5%

Net Revenue a Maximum Where "Marginal Cost of Time" = "Marginal Revenue of Time"

The net revenue (row 3) is obtained by subtracting the total cost from the total revenue. It will be seen that the net revenue is a maximum between the fourth and fifth years, where the cost difference (row 6) is equal to the revenue difference (row 7). The cost difference we might call the marginal cost of time, for it is the increase in the total cost which results from a unit increase in the time taken. Similarly, the revenue difference might be called the marginal revenue of time, for it is the increase in the total revenue which results from a unit increase in the time taken.

But We Do Not Want to Maximize the Net Revenue. Now, however, arises the question: Do we in fact, in this case, wish to produce so that the net revenue will be a maximum? Might a businessman not prefer a smaller net revenue to the maximum if it accrued to him *earlier?* The answer seems to be yes, for if the normal rate of profit is, say, 10 per cent, then if he received a net revenue of $100 in one year he could put it out to interest and make it turn into $110 by the next year. Obviously, then, if he were confronted with the choice between $100 this year and $100 of the same kind next year, he would prefer the $100 this year, for $100 this year is equivalent to $110 next year.

Maximization of the Discounted Net Revenue

If he wished to compare the net revenues that would accrue in different years, he would have to discount each net revenue back to some convenient date—usually the date of origin. Thus at a rate of 10 per cent per annum the $10 net revenue of year 1 in Table 77 is equivalent to $\frac{\$10}{1.1}$, or $9.10 in year 0; the $110 of year 2 is equivalent to $\frac{\$110}{1.1^2}$, or $90.90 in year 0; and so on for all the other net revenues. So we obtain a table of *discounted* net revenues (row 5) by dividing the net revenue in row (3) by the discount factor $(1 + i)^t$ in row (4). Each of the figures in row (5) represents that sum which, put out at interest at the "normal" rate in the year 0, would grow into a sum equal to the corresponding net revenue. It is evident that the *discounted* net revenue reaches a maximum at a rather earlier date than the net revenue itself; in the table the discounted net revenue reaches a maximum of 112.6+ between the third and fourth years, while the net revenue reaches a maximum between the fourth and fifth years.

This Is a Maximum Where the Rate of Revenue Increase = Rate of Cost Increase

Is there any condition, corresponding to the "marginal cost equals marginal revenue" condition, which will tell us when the *discounted* marginal revenue is a maximum? It is not difficult to find such a condition, and it is illustrated in rows 8 and 9 of Table 77. Here we have calculated two quantities named the "rate of cost increase" (row 8) and the "rate of revenue increase" (row 9). The rate of cost increase is the rate at which the total cost increases from year to year. It is found by dividing the absolute increase in cost between two dates by the total cost at the earlier date. In this case the rate of cost increase is 10 per cent per annum—the rate of interest. The rate of revenue increase is similarly found by dividing the absolute increase in revenue between two dates by the total revenue at the earlier date. Thus between dates 0 and 1 the rate of revenue increase is $\frac{300}{810}$, or 37 per cent; between 1 and 2 it is $\frac{210}{1110}$, or 18.9 per cent; between 2 and 3 it is $\frac{161}{1320}$, or 12.2 per cent; and so on. It will now be observed from the example that the discounted net revenue is at a maximum when the rate of revenue increase is equal to the rate of cost increase. In the present example this point lies between dates 3 and 4. This is a general principle, even with outlays and receipts of many dates. In the above case where the only outlay is at the initial date, it reduces to the proposition that the discounted net revenue is at a maximum when the rate of revenue growth is equal to the normal rate of interest or profit.

Graphic Illustration. The graphic proof of the last-mentioned proposition is shown in Fig. 146. Here time is measured in the horizontal, dollars in the vertical direction. The dotted lines *BB'*, *CC'*,

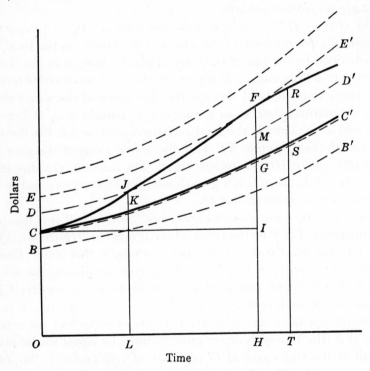

FIG. 146.   The Period of Investment.

DD', etc., represent a system of growth curves accumulating from various present values, *OB, OC, OD*, etc. Growth in each case proceeds at any time at the current normal rate of interest. Thus, *LK* is what a sum *OC* would grow into if it were put out at compound interest in the period between time *O* and time *OL*. We do not have to assume a constant rate of growth, i.e., a constant rate of interest; but the rates of growth in all the growth curves at any one date must be the same, and equal to the rate of interest on that date.

Suppose that in a process like the laying down of wines, an outlay of OC is made at the date O. The total cost of the wine at any future date will be given by the growth curve CC'. This is the total cost curve, for the total cost at any date is equal to the initial outlay plus accumulated interest. The interest may be regarded as a "revenue foregone" because of the fact that a sum OC is locked up in the form of wine when it might have been put out to interest. If, for instance, the wine is kept until the date H, the total cost is HG $(HI + IG)$. $HI (= OC)$ represents the original outlay and IG represents the interest which could have been earned on the sum OC if it had not been spent on the wine. We suppose in this example that once the wine has been bought there are no further outlays.

The curve $CJFR$ then represents the total revenue curve. At any time, say T, the ordinate of this curve, TR, represents the total revenue obtained by the sale of the wine originally bought at the time O. If there are selling costs, TR represents the total production revenue. We assume that the total revenue (i.e., the value of the wine) rises as the wine matures, but at an eventually decreasing rate. If the wine were sold at the date L, the total revenue would be LJ, the total cost LK, and the net revenue KJ. The discounted value at the date O of LJ is OD, where JD is a growth curve. The discounted value of LK at date O is OC, for CK is a growth curve. CD, therefore, is the "discounted" net revenue at date O.

There will be some growth curve, EFE', which will just touch the revenue curve. Let F be the point where it touches, HF the total revenue, HG the total cost, GF the net revenue at that date. The discounted net revenue is CE. CE is the maximum discounted net revenue at date O which can be obtained with the revenue curve $CJFR$.

It can easily be shown that the net revenue (undiscounted) is at a maximum at a later date than H. The rate of growth of the revenue curve at F (the rate of revenue growth) must be equal to the rate of growth of the cost curve at G (the rate of cost growth). But HF is larger than HG. The absolute increase of revenue at F is therefore greater than the absolute increase of cost at G. For example, if the rate of growth at F and at G is 10 per cent per annum, and HF is $1481, the revenue is increasing by an amount equal to $148.10 per annum. If HG is $1331 the cost is increasing by an amount equal to $133.10 per annum. At the date H, then, the revenue is increasing faster than the cost, and the net revenue, GF, is therefore increasing. The maximum net revenue, RS, is found at a date T, where absolute increase of revenue and of cost are equal. The discounted value of RS at date O is clearly less than that of *FG*, even though *RS* is greater than *FG*, for *R* evidently lies on a lower growth curve than *F*.

Maximization of the Internal Rate of Return

Another possible criterion of profitability is the internal rate of return in the enterprise. Row 10 of Table 77 shows the internal rate of return for each period of investment; the internal rate of return, i, being given in this case by the formula $C(1 + i)^t = R$. C is the total initial outlay ($1000) in this case; R is the total revenue produced by the sale of the wine; t is the period of investment. Thus after waiting three years we have $1000 (1 + i)^3 = 1481$, whence $i = 14.0$ per cent. In the table the maximum internal rate of return is 14.8 per cent at a period of 2 years.

The diagrammatic solution of the problem of maximizing the internal rate of return is shown in Fig. 147. For convenience in drawing, the costs and revenues are measured on a logarithmic scale, so that

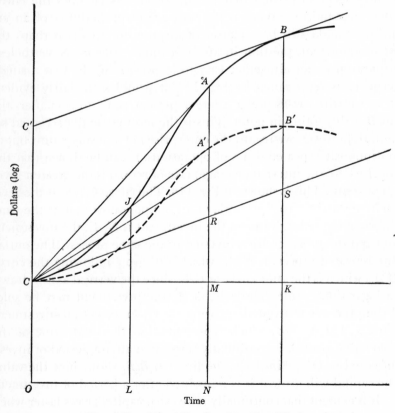

FIG. 147. Time-Production Equilibria.

curves of uniform rate of growth become straight lines. $CJAB$ is the revenue curve showing the growth in the value of output resulting from an initial outlay OC. The internal rate of return at any point J at a time OL is the average rate of growth of capital in the period, which in the logarithmic diagram is equal to the slope of the line CJ. To find the time ON at which the internal rate of return is a maximum, we draw CA to touch the revenue curve at A; the slope of CA clearly represents the highest average rate of growth of capital possible on the given revenue curve. If the normal rate of interest is less than this, the point of maximum internal rate of return is at a shorter period of investment than the point of maximum discounted net revenue, B, for B is the point at which the slope (rate of growth) of the revenue curve is equal to the rate of interest; and if the rate of revenue growth is declining, B will lie further along the revenue curve than A.

What Does the Entrepreneur Maximize?

It may seem surprising that the question, "What does the entrepreneur maximize?" (What is the measure of profitability of an enterprise?) should still be a matter of dispute, for this is perhaps the most fundamental question in all of economic theory. Nevertheless, the question is not altogether easy to answer. If we look at a single enterprise, as represented by Fig. 147, it would seem fairly evident that, as we will always prefer a larger present value to a smaller, the point B is the optimum point. This is the most generally accepted solution. If, however, we regard the enterprise not as a single unit but as a continuously repeated series of operations, it can be shown that the point A where the internal (average) rate of return is the greatest gives the best result. This is shown in Fig. 148. The curve CA_1B_1 is the revenue curve starting from an outlay OC. Suppose now that at the time ON_1, when the selling value of the investment is N_1A_1, the investment is sold and the proceeds are reinvested in the same process. The outlay in the repeated process is N_1A_1, which will grow following the curve A_1WA_2, which is the same curve as CA_1, since the vertical axis is drawn on a logarithmic scale. Similarly, at A_2 the investment may be sold, and the proceeds reinvested, growing to A_3; so we get an investment curve $CA_1A_2A_3A_4$, etc., which represents how the total value of the capital will grow if it is continually reinvested after a period of investment equal to ON_1. Similarly, the line $CB_1B_2B_3$ shows how the value of the capital will grow if it is reinvested after a period of investment OL_1. It is evident that continually reinvested capital grows faster when the period of investment is ON_1 than it does for any other period of

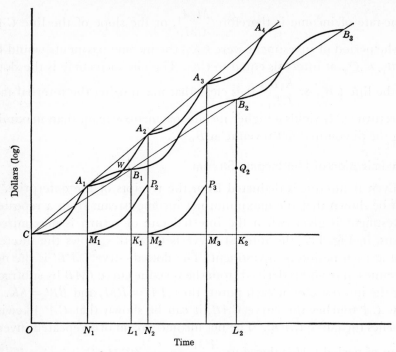

FIG. 148.   Repetition of Processes.

investment, even though there may be certain intervals, as between A_1 and W, where the value under a longer period of investment is greater.

Maximization of Income Stream

It may be said, however, that the entrepreneur does not wish merely to accumulate capital forever; what he wants is an income stream of consumption rather than a maximum rate of accumulation. It is not difficult to see from Fig. 148 what period of investment in a repeated process gives the maximum income stream. Suppose that the entrepreneur at the conclusion of each process withdraws the growth in capital from the enterprise and starts each repetition of the process with the amount of capital with which it began. That is to say, if the period of investment is ON_1 in Fig. 148, the entrepreneur will withdraw an amount M_1A_1 from the enterprise at the time N_1 and will start again with an amount of capital N_1M_1, equal to OC. The course of the capital invested then follows the saw-toothed line $CA_1M_1P_2M_2P_3M_3$, $\cdot$ $\cdot$ $\cdot$ etc. M_1A_1, M_2P_2, M_3P_3 represent a succession of income payments at regular intervals each equal to ON_1. The

time-rate of income is therefore $\dfrac{M_1A_1}{CM_1}$, or the slope of the line CA_1.
If the period of investment were CK_1, the income payments would be K_1B_1, K_2Q_2, at intervals equal to CK_1. The rate of income is the slope of the line CB_1, or $\dfrac{K_1B_1}{CK_1}$. It is clear that maximizing the internal rate of return at A_1 yields a higher income payments stream than maximizing the discounted net revenue at B_1.[1]

Maximization of Net Income Stream

Even if interest is deducted from the receipts of the enterprise, it can be shown that the maximum net income stream from a repeated investment is given when the internal rate of return is maximized. Thus, in Fig. 147, the interest curve is $CRS;$ this shows the interest cost at each period of investment. The dotted curve $CA'B'$ is the net revenue curve and is derived from the revenue curve CAB by subtracting the interest cost at each point; thus $AA' = RM,$ and $BB' = SK.$ If now CA touches the curve $CAB,$ it can be shown that CA' likewise touches the curve $CA'B'.$[2] The net income stream of a repeated investment of period CM is therefore $\dfrac{A'M}{CM},$ or $\tan A'CM.$ This is clearly the greatest net income stream, as CA' has a greater slope than any other line from C to the curve $CA'B',$ such as $CB'.$

Rent in an Investment

The economic rent, in an investment of the foregoing type, is that annual charge which will reduce the maximum internal rate of return

[1] It should be observed that the above argument is only strictly accurate if the vertical axis is measured on an arithmetic, not a logarithmic, scale. The period of investment which yields the largest income-payment stream is, therefore, somewhat smaller than that which yields the most rapid rate of capital growth. The problem arises because we are measuring growth continuously; if it is measured discontinuously, e.g., every year, and if the period of investment is less than the period of compounding, the two criteria give the same result.

[2] Let $OC = c$, $NA = v_1$, $ON = t_1$. Then the equation of the line CA is $v = c + \dfrac{v_1 - c}{t_1} t$, v being revenue, t the period of investment. Similarly, if i is the rate of interest, the equation of CA' is $v = c + \dfrac{v_1 - c - it_1}{t_1} t$. If n is the net revenue given by the curve $CA'B'$ we have $n = v - it$. We have, therefore, $\dfrac{dn}{dt} = \dfrac{dv}{dt} - i$. At the point A the slope of the curve CAB is the same as the slope of the line CA, i.e., $\dfrac{v_1 - c}{t_1}$. At A', therefore, the slope of the curve $CA'B'$ is $\dfrac{v_1 - c}{t_1} - i$, which is the same as the slope of the line CA'. The line CA' is therefore tangent to the curve $CA'B'$.

to the "normal" rate of interest. This is shown in Table 78. Rows 1 and 2 are the same as in Table 77. In row 3 we show what will happen if the wine is sold every second year and the proceeds reinvested in more wine. In two years $1000 grows to $1320; reinvested, therefore, the $1320 will grow to $(1320)^2 (= 1742.4)$ in another two years; if this is

TABLE 78.   Rent and Time Equilibrium

Year	0	1	2	3	4	5	6
1. Total cost	1000	1100	1210	1331	1464.1	1610.5	1771.6
2. Total revenue (not repeated)	810	1110	1320	1481	1629.1	1775.5	1916.6
3. Total revenue (repeated in year 2)			1320		1742.4		2300.0
4. Total revenue (repeated in year 3)				1481			2193.4
5. Net revenue (not repeated)		10	110	150	165	165	145
6. Net revenue (rent) per annum		10	55	50	41.2	33	24.2

sold and reinvested, it will grow to $(1320)^3 (= 2300.0)$ in six years; and so on. In row 4 this is compared with what would happen if the wine is allowed to mature for three years, then sold and the proceeds reinvested for another three years. The rate of growth is slower, as we have gone past the maximum internal rate of return, which in this example is at two years. Thus we see that the period of investment for which the discounted net revenue is a maximum is not that which gives the most rapid rate of growth of capital. Row 5 shows the total net revenue for each period of investment—it is the same as row 3 of Table 77. Row 6 shows the net revenue per annum, obtained by dividing each figure of row 5 by the corresponding number of years. This is the economic rent which corresponds to each period of investment. We see that the maximum economic rent is at year 2, which is also the maximum internal rate of return. If a rent of $55 per annum— or, what is almost the same thing, $110 every two years—is charged against the process the total revenue in year 2 will be $1210 and the internal rate of return (less rent) will be 10 per cent, the normal rate of interest. If the investor adopted a three-year period of investment at such a rent, the revenue would be $1481 − (3 \times 55)$ or $1316. This represents a less than 10 per cent return on the investment. If therefore the maximum rent is charged, the investor is forced to adopt that period of investment at which the internal rate of return is maximized.

The Rate of Interest and the Period of Investment

The above analysis throws some light on the disputed question of the effect of a change in the market rate of interest on the period of investment. If it is assumed that the optimum period of investment is that at which the present value of future net revenue is a maximum, then, assuming a diminishing rate of value growth with increase in the period of investment, a fall in the rate of interest will lengthen the period of investment. Thus, in Fig. 147, a fall in the rate of interest shows itself in a flattening of the line $C'B$, which will clearly move B farther out and will raise the discounted net revenue CC'. If, however, as we have argued above, it is the internal rate of return which should be maximized, then changes in the market—that is, in external rates of interest—should not affect the period of investment. It is to the interest of any investor to have his capital grow as fast as possible, no matter what deductions from this growth must be made for interest. If the rate of interest exceeds the internal rate of return, of course, the investment will not be made, or will eventually be abandoned. A fall in the rate of interest therefore permits investments to be made which have maximum internal rates of return lower than those now undertaken, and if the period of investment in these investments is not the same as the average period in previous investments, the fall in interest rates will change the "average" period of investment through the change in the number of investments—an effect somewhat analogous to the "industry effect" of page 699. There is no reason to suppose, however, that those investments which are now just below the line of profitability at existing rates of interest have either longer or shorter periods of investment than those which are now above the line. A fall in the rate of interest may make more bridge building profitable or it may make more retailing profitable—one with a long, the other with a short, period of investment. It seems impossible to predict, therefore, on a priori grounds, what will be the direction of change of the period of investment under the impact of a fall in interest rates.

More Complex Cases

The case which we have been discussing so far is a very simple one, with a single input and a single output, the value of the output depending on the period of investment. The problem becomes much more complicated when we introduce more inputs and outputs and make the value of inputs as well as of outputs depend on their date of application; and the discontinuities involved make the problem intractible to mathematical analysis. Some indication of the type of problem involved is given in Fig. 149. CQA is a net revenue curve after the deduction of interest, like the curve $CA'B'$ in Fig. 147. Now let us suppose that an outlay of QR at the point Q will result in a new net revenue curve RBQ', the net revenue being the market value

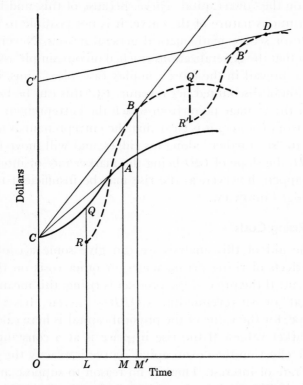

FIG. 149.   Complex Time-Production Equilibria.

of the investment less accrued interest on all previous outlays, less the outlays themselves. The curve $CQRB$ represents the curve of growth of the "own capital" of the entrepreneur if liquidated at each date at market prices. If now the tangent CB has a greater slope than the tangent CA, it will be profitable to make the outlay QR and to expand the period of investment from OL to OM. It should be observed, however, that the point B does not have to be at a greater period of investment than the point A; it would be easy to draw the curve RB so that B is to the left of A instead of to the right. The outlay $Q'R'$ is clearly not profitable, as the resultant net revenue or "own capital" curve never reaches the line CB. We may think of the entrepreneur, therefore, standing with his eye at the point C looking up at a variety of possible "own capital" curves of a saw-toothed nature; the most profitable one is that which makes him crane his head farthest—that which has the highest ridge within his range of vision. The problem is complicated by the fact that there may be innumerable possible outlays of various times and sizes and characters, all of which have different effects on the "own-capital" curve. Because of this, and because of the discontinuous nature of the curve, it is not possible to make any very simple or secure mathematical generalizations. Nevertheless, it can be seen that the generalizations reached on our simple assumptions are likely to prevail in the more complex case, also. Thus, if there is maximization of discounted net revenue, CC' this can be regarded as a raising of the vantage point from which the entrepreneur views the enterprise from C to C'; it is clear that the entrepreneur is now likely to be able to "see further" along his ridges, and will move from B to the point D, the slope of $C'D$ being the market rate of interest. This may not happen, however, as the rise may be insufficient to bring a further "ridge" into view.

Effects of Rising Costs

With the aid of this analysis we can give some account of the probable effects of rising prices, wages, or other costs on the period of investment. If the price of the product is rising, this means that the "own-capital" or net revenue line, $CQRB \cdot \cdot \cdot$ etc., has a generally steeper slope, for the value of the physical capital is here calculated at current market values. If the rise in price is at a constant rate per annum, the effect on the "own-capital" curve is exactly the same as a fall in the rate of interest. There is no reason to suppose any change in the period of investment, for although the "own-capital" curve becomes generally steeper, there is no reason to suppose that further "ridges" are thereby brought into view; as each ordinate changes by a constant proportion, a mere adjustment in the vertical scale of the diagram would restore it to its former condition. If, however, discounted net revenue is maximized, a rise in the price of the product or a fall in the rate of interest is likely to increase the period of investment, as from the vantage point of C' a rise in the whole "range" may bring more distant "ridges" into view.

Consider now the effects of rising prices of input (e.g., wages), other things being equal. The later outlays are now larger than they would have been by the extent of their "lateness." The result is to sink the "later" ridges of the "own-capital" curve more than the earlier; it may easily happen, therefore, that the later ridges sink out of "sight" and the period of investment contracts. Even more difficult to deal with is the situation when the outlays are variable in time position and affect the revenue-growth curves. A shift in relative time-values of input—e.g., rising or falling wages—may then upset the whole system of possible "own-capital" curves and we may find that a completely different arrangement of inputs and outputs now yields a maximum rate of return.

How Much Must Previous Analysis Be Modified?

The foregoing discussion raises the question how far the analysis of earlier chapters must be modified in view of our new principles of maximization. We have seen that the maximization of net revenue is not a proper criterion of profitability, and that the internal rate of return is a better measure. Must we conclude, therefore, that the analysis of the previous chapters must be thrown overboard? Is the maximization of net revenue a useful first approximation, or must it be discarded altogether in favor of more accurate principles?

Fortunately, all is not lost; we do not have to jettison the painfully acquired results of our previous analysis. If the relative dates of the outlays and revenues of a process are *not* variable, the internal rate of return, the discounted net revenue, and the "crude" net revenue are at a maximum under identical conditions. Happily, a great many—indeed, the majority—of processes fall into this category, where the time structure of production is a fact given to the entrepreneur and is therefore not a matter of choice. Even in the cases of processes like forestry, the maturing of wines and cheeses, the raising of meat animals, etc., where the variability of the period of investment is important, most of the conclusions of the previous analysis are to be modified rather than destroyed.

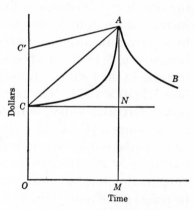

FIG. 150. Technically Determined Investment Period.

Suppose, for instance, that we had a time-revenue curve as in Fig. 150. The net revenue, NA, the discounted net revenue, CC', the internal rate of return $\left(\dfrac{MA}{OC}\right)^{\frac{1}{t}} - 1$, and the annual rent, $\dfrac{NA}{CN}$ are clearly all maximized at the period of investment, $CN (= t)$. The period of investment in such a case may be said to be technically determined; variations in inputs and outputs, etc., may vary the height of $A, AM,$ but will not vary its "date," OM. Any combination of variables, therefore, which maximizes AN automatically maximizes both the discounted net revenue and the internal rate of return. Fortunately for a great many processes this is the case, and we do not need to worry about the problem of the period of investment at all.

Marginal Cost = Differential Outlay × Compounding Factor

In spite of the fact that the conclusions of our previous analysis hold in this case, some extensions of that analysis can be made when we take the dates of input and output explicitly into account. Consider, for instance, a concept such as that of marginal cost. The marginal cost is the increase in the total cost which results from a unit increase in output. The total cost, however, is equal to the total outlay, plus the total of normal profit, which is involved in producing the quantity of output in question. The marginal cost may be analyzed into two parts: the increase in the total outlay, plus the increase in the normal profit, which results from a unit increase in output. Suppose that in Table 77 the length of the process is fixed at three years and that in order to increase the output by one unit the initial outlay must be increased by \$10 from the original outlay of \$1000. Then the total cost will be increased to \$(1010 × 1.331) from \$(1000 × 1.331). That is to say, the increase in the total *cost* resulting from the increase of output by one unit is \$(10 × 1.331). The marginal cost is equal to what we may call the "differential outlay" multiplied by the "compounding" factor, i.e., to the compounded value of the differential outlay. (We use the term "differential outlay" to mean the increase in the total *outlay* which a unit increase in *output* necessitates, as we have already used the term "marginal outlay" to mean the increase in total outlay caused by the increase of one unit in the purchase of *input*.) Similarly, the marginal revenue is the "compounded differential revenue." Our "marginal cost equals marginal revenue" proposition can therefore be restated as follows: A process with fixed time schedules is most profitable when the compounded value of the differential outlays is equal to the compounded value of the differential revenues, both outlays and revenues being compounded to the same date.

Marginal Productivity and Time

We saw on page 595 that with a perfect market for input the net revenue is at its greatest when the price of each input is equal to its marginal revenue productivity. This condition must be modified, or at least reinterpreted, when the inputs and the outputs are separated in time. Suppose an employer is considering whether or not to add another unit to the quantity of labor he uses. If the addition of that unit of labor will add, say, $20 to the total revenue of the enterprise and $20 to the total cost, the net revenue will be unchanged. At a wage of $20, then, the unit of labor will be only just worth adding if the additional revenue and the additional outlay occur at the same date.

Suppose, however, that the addition of a unit of labor will add $20 to the outlay of the enterprise now and $20 to the revenue of the enterprise in three years. The sum of $20 three years hence is not equivalent to $20 now unless the rate of interest is zero. If there is a positive rate of interest, $20 three years hence is worth less than $20 now. For the addition of the unit of labor to be worth while, the *present* value of the addition to the total revenue must be at least equal to the addition to the total outlay. If the addition of a unit of labor added $20 to the total revenue three years hence, and the rate of interest were 10 per cent, this would be equivalent to an addition of only $\frac{20}{1.331}$, or $15 in the current year. Not unless the price of labor were $15 in the current year, therefore, would it pay to add another unit. The condition which tells when the most profitable quantity of labor is being employed, then, is that in which the price of labor is equal to the *present value* of its marginal revenue productivity.

The same formula can be expressed in another way. If we define the marginal cost of input as the amount added to the total cost by the addition of one unit of input, the net revenue will be a maximum when the marginal cost of each input is equal to its marginal revenue productivity. This is the general formula of which the "price equals marginal revenue productivity" equation is a special case, true only when the market for input is perfect and when there is no time interval between input and output. The marginal cost of input is equal to the amount added to the total outlay by the addition of one unit of input plus the addition to the normal profit. This is equal to the *compounded* marginal outlay. If adding a unit of labor adds $15 to the total outlay now, the addition to the total cost, if the revenue is not received for three years, will be $15 × 1.331, or $20. Unless the addition to the total revenue, therefore, is equal to $20, it will pay either to increase or to decrease the quantity of labor employed. It should be observed that the rate of discounting or compounding used in the above formulae depends on the criterion of maximization which is appropriate. If the internal rate of return is maximized, then it is this internal rate which should be used in compounding outlays or discounting productivities. If on the other hand it is the discounted net revenue that is maximized, the market rate of interest is the appropriate rate of compounding or discounting in the cost and productivity formulae.

SCALE AND SUBSTITUTION IN TIME

Another approach to the problem of the equilibrium of the firm in time is to be attributed to J. R. Hicks's *Value and Capital*. In this the theory of "substitution effects" and "scale effects" is carried over to the analysis of the time positions of inputs and outputs by regarding the input or output of each date as a *separate item*. We must, for example, regard labor in one year as a different input from labor in another year, even if they are identical kinds of labor. Then the conclusions which we drew from our "timeless" analysis apply closely to the "time" analysis. For instance, we concluded that a rise in the price of one input had a substitution effect causing the substitution of the lower-priced input for the higher and a "scale effect" causing a general reduction of scale. This is true of two or more inputs which differ in *time* as well as of inputs which differ in kind. Suppose that wages are expected to be lower next year. This will cause a substitution effect— a substitution of next year's cheap labor in place of this year's dear labor—and a scale effect—a general increase in the scale of the enterprise. The substitution effect will operate to diminish the quantity of labor bought this year, and the scale effect will operate to increase it.

Quantity of Input Bought Depends on Anticipated Prices

Thus we reach the important conclusion that the quantity of labor which will be bought this year depends not merely upon the price in this year but upon what employers *think* the price will be next year and in future years. The effect of their anticipation of next year's price upon this year's labor depends on two things: first, on the degree to which this year's labor can be substituted for next year's labor, upon which depends the magnitude of the substitution effect; and second, on the importance of labor in the process, on which depends the scale effect. It will be observed that the substitution effect and the scale effect in the case of a change in expected *future* prices work in opposite directions as far as the effect on the *present* purchases is concerned. Where, therefore, the substitution effect is great, an expected fall in wages will cause a decrease in the purchase of current labor. This is most likely to be the case where the input results in the creation of an easily storable commodity; for then, if labor is expected to be cheaper next year, less labor will be employed this year, inventories will be depleted, and the stock will be replaced next year when labor is cheap. If, on the other hand, the substitution effect is small, where next year's input cannot be anticipated by "producing for stock" this year and where the input in question plays a large part in the business, it is conceivable that the scale effect may outweigh the substitution effect, and an expected decrease in the price of next year's input actually cause an increase in the purchase of this year's as well as of next year's input.

Production of Output Also Depends on Anticipated Prices

Exactly similar considerations apply to the production and sale of output. If the price of next year's output is expected to be lower than that of this year's output, there will be a substitution effect—output will tend to be concentrated into this high-priced year—and there will be a scale effect—a general reduction in scale. Again the substitution effect will bring about an increase in this year's output, and the scale effect will bring about a decline in this year's as well as next year's output; which effect will be stronger will again depend on how far the output is storable. If it can easily be stored it will be easy to increase the sales of one year at the expense of another. The substitution effect, therefore, will be strong. If a rise in price is expected, there will be a diminution in the amount which sellers are willing to sell in the present. Similarly, if the process is such that the dates at which output appears can easily be changed, the substitution effect will also be prominent, and the expectation of a rise in price will cause a diminution of current sales. But if the commodity cannot be stored and if the dates of output cannot easily be changed, the scale effect will outweigh the substitution effect. Then an expected rise in price may cause a rise in current output.

Effects of Expected Rise or Fall Are Unsymmetrical

It is possible that the effects of an expected rise and of an expected fall in price may not be symmetrical. It is probably easier to transfer sales of output from the present to the future than it is to transfer them from the future to the present. Sales can be postponed by storing or by slowing up the process of production. To some extent they can be transferred to the present from the future by selling out of stock or by speeding up production, but there are obvious limits to these operations. The substitution effect in the case of output, therefore, will be greater when a rise in price is expected than when a fall is expected. The anticipation of a future rise in price will probably lead to lessened sales of output now—sellers "wait for the rise." The anticipation of a future fall in price is rather less likely to lead to increased sales now, as current sales may not be so readily expansible.

The Importance of Expectations

It is difficult to exaggerate the importance of expectations in determining the course of economic life. From the foregoing it is clear that the quantity of any commodity which people are willing to buy or sell depends not merely upon its current price but also on what people believe will be the future course of its price. This fact does not destroy the concept of a demand or supply schedule, of course. It does mean, however, that one of the principal determinants of the position of any given demand or supply schedule is the expected future price of the commodity in question and of other commodities. We draw a demand or supply curve on the assumption that expectations do not change; if they do change, the fact is reflected in a shift in the demand or supply curves. The demand for any commodity depends also upon our expectations of the *results* of the consumption or use of the commodity.

This is particularly true of those commodities which are inputs of a process of production, although, as we have seen, all commodities are really "inputs" of some process or other. Our demand for ice cream depends on our expectation of satisfaction to be derived from its consumption. Likewise, the demand for labor depends wholly on the expectation of future benefits to be received as a result of the employment of labor. Labor is employed because the present value of its marginal productivity is at least equal to its wage. But the present value of its marginal productivity is not a realized fact; it is an opinion, an idea, an expectation in the mind of the employer. From some pinnacle of the future we may look back on the past and say, "At this time the present value of the marginal productivity of John Jones was $2 per hour of his labor." But the fact which decides whether John Jones shall be employed at any given time is not this "objective" marginal productivity but the "subjective" marginal productivity; i.e., what some employer, who knows John Jones, *thinks* is his marginal productivity.

What Determines Expectations?

Thus expectations help to determine prices at any time. But what determines the expectations? This is unfortunately a problem about which we know all too little, and it does not seem possible to make any clear a priori judgments about it. Do people expect past trends to continue? If, for instance, prices have been rising, do they expect them to go on rising? There is some evidence that this is the case, especially in regard to commodities in which there is much speculation. On the other hand, it may be that a past rise in price induces people to believe that prices are now due for a fall. The problem of expectations therefore resolves itself largely into the question, How far are people governed in their expectations of the future by their experience of the past? Obviously, the experience of the past is all we have to draw upon in seeking to foretell the future. But just how we shall interpret that experience is a difficult matter. We may, perhaps, venture upon one proposition: The more regular is past experience, the more likely are we to believe that the future will copy the past. If prices have been stable for a long time, we are likely to believe that they will continue so. Businessmen apparently believe that business will continue to prosper for an indefinite future period even on the eve of a crash. The longer the period of a depression, the more difficult it seems to be to emerge from it; for the more it continues, the more people believe that it will continue, and the more people believe that it will continue, the more it continues!

The Elasticity of Expectations

To provide a convenient term to measure this phenomenon, J. R. Hicks has devised the concept of "elasticity of expectations." This is defined as "the ratio of the proportional rise in expected future prices (of a commodity) to the proportional rise in its current price."[3] If a rise in prices is expected to continue at the same rate, the elasticity of expectations is unity. If a current rise in prices leads to the prospect of a smaller price rise in the future, the elasticity of expectations is less than unity. If a fall in price is expected in the future because of a rise in price now, elasticity of expectations is negative.

The Consistency of Expectations

An interesting question raised by the concept of expectations is that of the consistency of current expectations. Suppose, for instance, that Mr. A thinks the price of coal next year will be $12 per ton, while

[3] Hicks, *Value and Capital*, p. 205.

Mr. B thinks it will be $10 per ton. Obviously, both these gentlemen cannot be right, and at least one of them *must* be surprised, either favorably or unfavorably. Unless everyone thought alike, therefore, the nonfulfillment of expectations would of necessity be a constant experience of mankind. Even if everyone had the same expectations, there is no guarantee that they would be fulfilled. Indeed, if everyone has the same expectations there is a practical certainty that they will not be fulfilled. Suppose everyone thought that the price of coal next year was going to be very high—say, $25 per ton. As a consequence of this belief people would seek to shift their purchases of coal into the current year, following the principle of substitution. Cellars and bunkers would be filled; mines would work to capacity. The result would be that next year the demand for coal would fall, and the price would fall, probably far below the $25 per ton originally expected.

Conclusion

We shall not go much further in this volume in the analysis of price determination, though much remains to be done, especially in the study of uncertainty. It is clear that when we take time into our consideration in a specific fashion, much of our previous analysis must be modified. The task of reformulating the theory of monopoly, of selling cost, of imperfect competition, in terms of expectations, capital, and time is one which remains for the future. Nevertheless, the journey we have made has not been in vain, and the conclusions at which we have arrived, though not the whole truth, are of substantial importance. Those movements in demand, cost, and supply which are due to changes in expectations are ephemeral movements; and though expectations change constantly and seem hopelessly unpredictable, they shift around a base of long-run experience. The longer the period over which we consider our effects, the less importance can we attach to expectations as independent causative forces. In the long run, past and future, expectations and their results are all made one.

QUESTIONS AND EXERCISES

1. "Woodman, spare that tree." What financial, as apart from sentimental, reasons could you offer in support of this advice?
2. One of the principal criticisms of the concept of a "period of production" has been that it must be infinite in length, for if we analyze capital goods back into the labor and equipment which made them, and analyze the equipment which made them into further equipment, and so on, there is no place we can stop short of the primordial amoeba. Does this

criticism invalidate the proposition that without a period of production there would be no capital?

3. Can the extension of the theory of the firm to include time as an explicit variable be applied also to the theory of the consumer? Does "discounting" or "compounding" play any part in the consumer's choice?

4. Under what circumstances will the presence of an "elasticity of expectations" give rise to fluctuations in economic activity?

5. In what circumstances are expectations likely to be "self-justifying"— i.e., when will expectations themselves produce, through their effects on human behavior, the thing expected?

6. If an astronomer foretells the movement of the planets, that movement is quite unaffected by the fact that it has been foretold. If an economist, however, forecasts a movement of prices, the fact that he has made the forecast may itself affect the future of prices. Why? Does this fact raise any question about the objective existence of the subject matter of economics? The astronomical universe is "there," presumably, whether there are any astronomers or not. Is that true of the economic universe?

APPENDIX

THE LITERATURE OF ECONOMICS

The body of economic analysis presented in this work is the result of a long and often painful process of thought on the part of many minds through the years. The student of economics cannot appreciate adequately the significance of present-day theory unless he has a substantial acquaintance with the great works of the past and with the history of ideas. The study of past errors is a useful discipline against present errors. The study of how the peculiar circumstances of a past time led its thinkers to ascribe general validity to particular institutions serves as a constant warning against ascribing too much generality to the peculiar circumstances of our own day. Any one author is limited by the scope of his own interests, and the student can never be acquainted with the scope of his subject unless he approaches it through the mediation of many different minds. It is not the purpose of this appendix to outline a systematic history of economic thought, nor an exhaustive bibliography of the literature; rather, is it intended to give some indication to the student of the points of origin of the principal ideas he has encountered in this work, and to guide his interests in further reading. There are several excellent histories of economic thought;[1] and the student would be well advised to read at least one of them, to get the broad historical picture.

Books about great books, however, are no substitute for the great books themselves, and the serious student should not long delay the study of the classical works of theory. The greatest of these, even after more than a century and a half, is Adam Smith's *Inquiry into the Nature and Causes of the Wealth of Nations* (1776).[2] Lacking virtually

---

[1] Alexander Gray, *The Development of Economic Doctrine,* Longmans, Green, 1947; Erich Roll, *A History of Economic Thought,* Prentice-Hall, 1942; Edmund Whittaker, *A History of Economic Ideas,* Longmans, Green, 1940. R. L. Heilbroner, *The Worldly Philosophers,* Simon and Schuster, 1953. T. W. Hutchinson, *A Review of Economic Doctrines,* Oxford University Press, 1953. Joseph A. Schumpeter, *History of Economic Analysis,* Oxford University Press, 1954. Henry W. Spiegel (ed.), *The Development of Economic Thought,* Wiley, 1952.

[2] Cannan's edition (Methuen, 1904) is probably the best. This has been republished in the Modern Library.

884

all the mathematical and graphic techniques of modern value theory, Adam Smith nevertheless perceived, not always with perfect clarity but always with astonishing insight, the essential relationships that lie at the heart of economic life. What I have called the "principle of equal advantage," and the idea of the movement of resources under the stimulus of prices and profits from one occupation to another, which is the central idea of the theory of value and distribution, stems directly from Adam Smith. Chapters 7 and 9 of his Book 1 could be used today with hardly any modification in an accurate elementary text. In his concept of "effective demand" (in modern terminology, the quantity demanded at the normal price) lies the germ of the modern theory of supply and demand. His distinction (unfortunately named, but vital nonetheless) between "productive" labor that was embodied in goods and "unproductive" labor not so embodied was the foundation of the theory of capital. His great defense of free trade against the mercantilists in Book 4 is famous, but it must not be thought that he was a bigoted advocate of "laissez faire." Indeed, almost half the work (Book 5) is a discussion of the proper functions of the state. Then in Book 3 he outlines the much neglected theory of economic progress. Most of all, the *Wealth of Nations* is worth reading for its style and spirit—full of wisdom and the observation of life, universal in the material from which it draws. Of Adam Smith it may often be said that he draws correct conclusions from faulty reasoning, his insight and wide observation affording him conclusions which his imperfect analytical techniques did not enable him to prove. More than any other economist, with the possible exception of Wicksteed, Adam Smith embodies the liberal tradition of humane letters. The student who learns to love his quiet wit and keen but gentle observation of humanity will never degenerate into a narrow-minded specialist.

A writer of very different character, yet in his own way almost equally important, is David Ricardo. The student should read his *Principles of Political Economy and Taxation* (1817)[3] not for its style, which is arid and humorless, nor for its conclusions, many of which are erroneous, but for its crystalline logic. Ricardo's mind cut through the inconsistencies of Adam Smith and reduced economics to a system in which the conclusions followed inexorably from the axioms. Unfortunately, the axioms were not always correct, and the conclusions suffer accordingly, but the student who follows the argument will have an excellent training in the discipline of economic logic. It is to

[3] The magnificent edition of Ricardo's complete works in nine volumes by Piero Sraffa (Cambridge University Press, 1953) is the definitive version. The *Principles* are available in Everyman's Library.

Ricardo that we owe the first faint beginnings of the marginal analysis, in his statement of the law of diminishing returns and his theory of rent. The modern theory of the economic surplus arising in the case of a less than perfectly elastic supply had its beginnings in the Ricardian theory of rent, though its modern applications are much wider than Ricardo imagined.

In reading the classical economists it must constantly be borne in mind that their system is a special case of our more general modern constructions. The relatively little importance given to demand in their theory of value may be traced to their general (implicit) assumption that supplies are perfectly elastic. In such a case, of course, prices do not in the long run depend on demand at all, but are determined by the level at which the supply is perfectly elastic, which in its turn is determined by "the cost of production." Ricardo was perhaps the first to recognize the possibility of what we now call an imperfectly elastic supply in the case of land, and saw that a rise in demand would raise the price at least of foodstuffs by pushing production on to poorer lands. Even Ricardo, however, assumed implicitly a perfectly elastic supply in the case of labor in his subsistence theory.

Ricardo and Torrens between them developed the theory of comparative advantage in international trade, though it was left to an economist of the next generation (Cairnes) to perceive the generality of this principle. With Ricardo, indeed, "model building" enters economics fairly explicitly, even though it is implicit in Adam Smith and Ricardo does not go beyond the mathematical equipment of arithmetical examples.

Another writer of Ricardo's time who is worth reading today is the Rev. T. R. Malthus. He is principally famous for his essays on population (1798 and 1803),[4] in which, however, he does little more than give clearer expression to an idea of Adam Smith (the "pressure of population on the means of subsistence") and supports it with dubious statistics and still more doubtful arithmetic. In the light of modern monetary theory, however, his *Principles of Political Economy* (especially Part II) stands out as a work of remarkable insight, which anticipates many of the Keynesian principles and yet was largely neglected for over a century.

Another writer whose true significance did not appear till a later date was A. A. Cournot (1801–1877), whose *Recherches*[5] (1838) de-

[4] The *Essay on Population* is in Everyman's Library.
[5] *Recherches sur les principes mathématiques de la théorie des richesses* (English translation by N. T. Bacon), Macmillan, 1897; this contains also a useful bibliography of early mathematical economics.

veloped, in mathematical form, much of the modern theory of the firm; the concepts, though not the names, of the marginal analysis were first developed by him. He should be read by any student who has some elementary knowledge of the calculus. The mathematical form of his writing, however, prevented him from having much influence on the economists of his own time, and the classical system, especially as expounded by J. S. Mill,[6] held undisputed sway until about 1870. Karl Marx (1818–1883) stands in a class by himself. *Das Kapital*[7] (1867) is a book which has had a profound influence on the world. It represents an early attempt to develop a theory of the economic system as a whole and of its progress in time. In this attempt, however, Marx was greatly handicapped by the inadequate analytical apparatus which he inherited from Smith and Ricardo; consequently, errors which can be generously interpreted as matters of exposition in the classical economists, such as the labor theory of value, are erected into the foundations of a logical but inadequate system of economic reasoning. Although Marx made little contribution to the broad line of development of economic thought, the student should read at least the first volume of *Das Kapital* or, better still, Borchardt's condensation. To study the errors of a great, if wrongheaded, mind is often more valuable than to skim the platitudes of a small one.

The next important group of writers constitute the so-called "marginal utility school." The ideas of this school were developed at about the same time (c. 1870), independently in England by Stanley Jevons, in Austria by Karl Menger and Friedrich von Wieser, and in France by Léon Walras. With this school began the extended use of mathematics in economic analysis, foreshadowed by Cournot; for though many of its exponents expressed their ideas in literary form, their theories were essentially mathematical in structure. Perhaps the greatest work of this whole school is P. H. Wicksteed's *The Common Sense of Political Economy*,[8] even though it appeared forty years after the first formulations of 1870. This is a book which every student of economics should read, in spite of a certain prolixity and an occasionally labored style. It is couched (often at the cost of being cumbersome) in nonmathematical language, and it provides the most consistent and highly developed exposition of the utility analysis as the foundation of both demand and supply, and as a general theory of choice. Perhaps

---

[6] *Principles of Political Economy* (1848).

[7] The translation by Eden and Cedar Paul in Everyman's Library is very good; the Modern Library edition, containing Stephen Trask's translation of Borchardt's condensation, together with "The Communist Manifesto," is an excellent introduction.

[8] Fourth ed., Macmillan, London, 1910 (reprinted 1924).

Wicksteed's greatest contribution was his demonstration that economics is not merely a matter of the market place or of financial dealings, but is one aspect of *all* human activity—namely, the aspect of choice, or the balancing of alternatives one against another, where limited means have to be apportioned among competing ends. His delightful discussions of how much family prayers should be shortened to speed a parting guest to the train, or of the value of a mother-in-law in terms of how high a cliff one would dive off to save her, should open the eyes of every student to the great *generality* of economic principles. Wicksteed, more than any other, laid the ghost of that shadowy creation, the "economic man." Wicksteed also made valuable contributions to the generality of economic principles themselves, and showed, for instance, the essentially similar derivation of supply and demand, and the universal character of the "law of diminishing returns." The concept of a homogeneous production function, and the distinction between diminishing returns to various proportions of factors and diminishing (or increasing) returns to scale, also owe much to Wicksteed.

The student whose acquaintance with mathematics extends to the elementary calculus should read Jevons's *The Theory of Political Economy,* in spite of the many errors which it contains. Even the nonmathematical student will find much of interest in this work; its freshness of style, its enthusiasm, the sense of discovery, of the opening up of vast new areas of conquest to the human mind, can hardly fail to be inspiring even if, as Marshall pointed out, Jevons was much less of a revolutionary than he himself thought.[9] Much of what the marginal utility school proclaimed is implicit in the classical economists, and, indeed, almost became explicit in the work of Nassau Senior, a contemporary of Ricardo, and was made quite explicit in the unnoticed work of the tragic Gossen (1854). It was not, however, until the productive 1870's that the dependence of value on scarcity in relation to demand, and of scarcity on cost of production, was made quite clear. Von Wieser,[10] in particular, helped to clarify the relationships between the value of finished goods and of factors of production, and showed how the value of factors of production depended on the value of the goods which they produced.

It remained for Walras,[11] however, to bring together the complex relationships of economic life into a single mathematical system of

[9] See Marshall, *Principles of Economics,* 8th ed., appendix I, pp. 813–821.

[10] F. von Wieser, *Social Economics* (Translated by A. Ford Hinrichs), New York, Greenberg, 1927.

[11] Léon Walras, *Eléments d'économie politique pure,* 4th ed., Lausanne, 1900. Translated by William Jaffé, *Elements of Pure Economics,* Irwin, 1954.

mutual determination and mutual interaction. Walras is the Laplace of economics; just as Laplace transformed astronomy from a system in which the movement of each heavenly body was attached to its own particular cause to a system in which the mutual interactions of all bodies upon each other determine the behavior of all, so Walras transformed economics from a system in which each value was attached to its own particular cause to a system in which all values, whether of finished goods, intermediate products, or factors of production, are mutually determined by the interaction of the innumerable forces of desire upon the innumerable resistances of scarcity. The student who for want of mathematical ability cannot read Walras suffers under a severe handicap, and no better investment for the future economist could be recommended than the improvement of his mathematical skills to this point.

The marginal utility school is also important for its contributions to the theory of capital, though the exact significance of these contributions is still somewhat a matter of dispute. The basic idea of their theory of capital is that of a "period of production" between inputs and outputs. Because of this period of production inputs of "original factors" are embodied in intermediate products, which are "real capital." The volume of these intermediate products clearly depends on the length of the period of production. Jevons developed these ideas in a somewhat crude form, but their greatest development is due to Eugen von Böhm-Bawerk, whose *Positive Theory of Capital*[12] is essential to the study of this part of the subject. Another important contributor to this part of the subject was Knut Wicksell (1851–1926), whose little book *Über Wert, Kapital und Rente* (Jena, 1893) systematized the ideas of Böhm-Bawerk and by reducing them to mathematical form brought out their underlying assumptions.

The next great writer in point of time is Alfred Marshall, who may not unjustly be regarded as the father of modern Anglo-Saxon economics. Perhaps his greatest contribution is the development of supply and demand curves and of the concept of elasticity of demand and of supply. These tools of analysis are so essential to the modern economist that he is apt to forget their relative youth. In his *Principles of Economics*[13] Marshall developed a system not unlike that of Walras in essential principles but written in geometrical rather than algebraic language—losing thereby in generality but gaining in practicality. The basic proposition of the system is that the equilibrium output of

[12] Translated by William Smart, Stechert, 1923.
[13] Eighth ed., Macmillan, 1938.

a commodity is that at which the supply price and the demand price of the output are equal (see page 114). Marshall showed how the demand curve depended on the underlying utility relationships, and how the supply curve was related to costs. We are indebted to him for the distinction—useful, if dangerous—between short-run and long-run situations. We owe to him also certain developments of the theory of the firm in monopoly, though he did not succeed in integrating the theory of the firm explicitly into the main body of analysis.

Marshall began an era of great proliferation of economic writings in which we still live and in which, therefore, it is difficult to assess enduring values. As far as the tools of analysis are concerned, we have seen the development of the indifference curve, especially by Pareto, whose *Cours* and *Manuale*[14] are essential reading for the advanced student. In the theory of capital and interest the works of Irving Fisher are to be highly recommended.[15] H. J. Davenport is worth reading for his original point of view and his concept of alternative cost.[16] F. H. Knight's *Risk, Uncertainty, and Profit*, 1921, reprinted by the London School of Economics, 1946, is an important if somewhat unclassifiable work.

Perhaps the most important developments of twentieth-century economics lie in two fields. There has been a great advance in what used to be called the theory of money, but now is frequently called "macroeconomics"—i.e., the theory of the broad averages and aggregates of the whole economic system, such as the general level of prices, of output, of wages, of employment, of interest rates, and so on. There has also been a great advance in extending the theory of relative values to include cases of imperfect competition and monopoly. We seem also to be in the midst of a substantial advance in the theory of the dynamic relationships of economic life, though it is perhaps too early to assess the significance of this development.

Economists up to and including Marshall had many observations regarding the theory of money, but with the possible exception of Ricardo—whose cost-of-production theory of the value of money, however inadequate, at least fitted in with his general system—the theory of money was never integrated into the general theory of value. Although Adam Smith set out on an "inquiry into the nature and causes

---

[14] *Cours d'économie politique,* Lausanne, 1896; *Manuale di economia politica,* Milan, 1906.

[15] *The Nature of Capital and Income,* Macmillan, 1906; *The Theory of Interest,* Macmillan, 1930.

[16] *The Economics of Enterprise,* Macmillan, 1913; *Value and Distribution,* University of Chicago Press, 1908.

of the wealth of nations," the attention of economists in the nineteenth century become increasingly concentrated on the problem of "value" —i.e., of relative prices. The reawakening of interest in the broader problems of macroeconomics begins perhaps with Wicksell, whose *Geldzins und Guterpreise*[17] should be read by every student, and whose *Lectures on Political Economy*[18] are well worth the attention of the more advanced student. Irving Fisher's *The Purchasing Power of Money* is also a landmark, for it gives the first clear formulation of the "equation of exchange" ($MV = PT$). The modern developments in macroeconomics, however, are most closely associated with the work of J. M. Keynes (the late Lord Keynes). His early *Tract on Monetary Reform* (Harcourt, Brace, 1924) is still worth reading, in spite of some out-of-date material. It is an eloquent plea for the stabilization of prices as the object of monetary policy, and contains, along with D. H. Robertson's little book entitled *Money*, the essence of the "oral tradition" on this subject at Cambridge, England, which flowed from the teaching of Marshall. Keynes's major works are the *Treatise on Money* (Harcourt, Brace, 1931) and the *General Theory of Employment, Interest, and Money* (Harcourt, Brace, 1936). These are not easy to read, and are often confused in thought. Nevertheless, the serious student cannot fail to derive substantial benefit from their study; they open up vistas of intellectual exploration which have by no means been fully covered.

The theory of imperfect competition has been developed in two principal works—E. Chamberlin's *The Theory of Monopolistic Competition* (Harvard University Press, 1933) and Joan Robinson's *The Economics of Imperfect Competition* (Macmillan, 1934).[19] The elementary theory of the firm and industry in its modern form, especially as it involves the use of the marginal revenue curve, is to be attributed mainly to these writers. The assumption of perfect competition which underlay so much of the classical economics, and even the Marshallian system, was shown by these writers to be a special case of a more general theory.

The nearer we get to the present day the more important becomes periodical literature as a source of important contributions. The *Quarterly Journal of Economics,* published in Cambridge, Mass., founded in 1885, is probably the oldest periodical specializing in economic theory. The *Economic Journal,* organ of the Royal Economic Society

---

[17] Translated under the title of *Interest and Prices* by R. F. Kahn, Macmillan, 1930.

[18] Translated by E. Classen, Macmillan, 1934.

[19] Another important work in the field is Robert Triffin, *Monopolistic Competition and General Equilibrium Theory,* Harvard University Press, 1940.

and published in London, was founded in 1891. The *Journal of Political Economy* (founded in 1892 and published at the University of Chicago) and the *American Economic Review* (organ of the American Economic Association, founded in 1911) often contain important theoretical articles, but tend predominantly in the direction of applied studies. *Economica* (founded in 1921) is the organ of the London School of Economics. The *Review of Economic Studies* (founded in 1933) is a frequent vehicle for the younger theorists and contains many important articles. *Econometrica* (organ of the Econometric Society, and founded in 1933) is the principal vehicle for articles in mathematical and statistical economics. The *Review of Economic Statistics* (Harvard University) is also important in this field. There are several "local" journals which from time to time have articles of general interest: the *Canadian Journal of Economics and Political Science*, the *Economic Record* (Australia), the *South African Journal of Economics, The Manchester School*, are especially to be recommended. The *Zeitschrift für Nationaloekonomie* (Vienna) and the *Giornale degli economisti* (Italy) are also of importance. *Kyklos* (Zurich) is an international journal with articles in several languages. It would be impossible to attempt a bibliography of the important articles in these journals in the small space of this appendix; the student whose interests lie in any special field will soon have to make such a bibliography for himself. The book reviews in these journals (especially in the *American Economic Review*) in themselves form a most valuable bibliography both for general theory and for all the special fields.

In recent years the publications of specialized economic research agencies, such as the Cowles Commission in Chicago and the National Bureau of Economic Research in New York, and publications of government departments, such as the U.S. Department of Commerce, have become increasingly important, especially on the empirical side of economics.

As we move toward the specialized fields, books, and even good books, multiply to the point where it seems invidious to mention any. In the field of business cycles the works of Wesley Mitchell,[20] in spite of some theoretical and methodological weaknesses, represent the fruits of monumental patience and careful inquiry. Similarly, the principal works of J. A. Schumpeter[21] are important not only for their

---

[20] His last work, *What Happens during Business Cycles*, New York, 1951, is probably the best introduction.

[21] *The Theory of Economic Development*, translation by Redvers Opie, Harvard University Press, 1934; *Business Cycles*, McGraw-Hill, 1939; and *Capitalism, Socialism and Democracy*, Harper, 1942, are important works.

insight into business cycles but into the whole process of economic development. The student of the dynamic process will find important contributions in J. R. Hicks's *Value and Capital* (2nd ed., Oxford University Press, 1946), as well as an admirable exposition of the static theory of value. Perhaps the most important of modern works is Paul A. Samuelson's *Foundations of Economic Analysis* (Harvard University Press, 1947), though it is not accessible to those without a fair mathematical equipment. It contains a definitive account of the theory of maximization, and the first systematic exposition of dynamic theory using the tool of difference equations. Baumol's *Economic Dynamics* (Macmillan, 1951) is a very useful introduction to this field, as is R. F. Harrod's *Toward a Dynamic Economics* (Macmillan, 1948).

The field of welfare economics has shown great activity in recent years. Pigou's *Economics of Welfare* (4th ed., Macmillan, 1932), though now quite out of date, is still the "classic" work in the field. Students interested in modern welfare economics should read works by Reder,[22] Myint,[23] Little,[24] and Arrow.[25] Arrow's work in particular represents a somewhat new departure in economics, using the apparatus of mathematical logic.

The volumes of collected articles published by the American Economic Association are a useful introduction to the periodical literature. The *Survey of Contemporary Economics,* Vol. I and II, also published by the American Economic Association, is a useful guide to recent economic thought and bibliography in many fields.

The list might be continued almost indefinitely, and it is not the purpose of this appendix to provide the student with a complete bibliography. It is hoped, however, that the works mentioned above may provide an essential point of departure for further inquiry.

[22] Melvin W. Reder, *Studies in the Theory of Welfare Economics,* Columbia University Press, 1947.
[23] Hla Myint, *Theories of Welfare Economics,* Harvard University Press, 1948.
[24] I. M. D. Little, *A Critique of Welfare Economics,* Oxford University Press, 1950.
[25] Kenneth Arrow, *Social Choice and Individual Values,* Wiley, 1951.

INDEX

Dollar shortage, 408
Domar, E., 463
Domestic system, 507
Double liability, 510
Duesenberry, J. S., 695
Dumping, 660
Dynamics, of allocation, 190–196
  difficulties of, 152
  of exchange, 811
  models of, 416

Eagerness, 47, 63, 67
Earnings, 691
Economic analysis, definition, 3
  as a "map," 13
  methods of, 10
Economic conflict, 31
Economic dimensions, 241
Economic and noneconomic, 445
Economic organisms, 15
Economic phenomena, 3
Economic progress, 716, 718
Economic quantities, 4
Economic rent, see Rent
Economic surplus, 819
Economic warfare line, 401
Economics, limitations of, 9
  non-Euclidian, 12
  normative, 713
Economy in consumption, 364
Efficiency, 581
Efficiency ratio, 717
Elasticity, absolute, 121, 123
  cross, 135
  of demand, 128, 132, 156, 205, 601, 611,
    699
  of demand and supply, 119–124, 203, 228
  of expectations, 881
  income, 135
  of supply, 127, 209, 213, 219, 221, 222,
    565, 568, 574
Electricity, 612
Employment, as exchange of money for
  goods, 497, 499
Endogenous and exogeneous changes, 444
Ends, 715
Entrepreneur, see Businessman
Equality, 723, 725
Equalizing competitive advantage, 725
Equilibrium, in allocation, 169
  of consumer, 691–698
  dynamic, 711–712
  expectational, 712
  general, 704
  of an industry, 566, 577, 637
  meaning of, 55
  models, 702
  output, 292, 473
  particular, 704

Equilibrium—(Continued)
  paths to, 418
  price, 56, 95, 113
  ratio of exchange, 83
  shiftability of, 299
  two-country, 400
  unstable, 224
Equimarginal principle, 688, 795
Equities, 258
Ever-normal granary, 158
Exchange, 6, 17, 21, 23, 25, 253
  theory of, 810–814
Exchange opportunities, 524
Exchange rates, 75, 83, 406
Exchange system, 308
Exchanges and transfers, 468
Expansion path, 752
Expectation of life, 369
Expectational cycles, 153, 426
Expectational equilibrium, 712–713
Expectations, 97, 880
Expenditures, 322, 687
Expenses, virtual, 494
Explosion models, 425
Exponential allocation, 859
Exponential growth, 844
Export multiplier, 396

Factory system, 507
Facts, 5, 6
Fear of the worst, as limit, 558
Federal Reserve System, 351, 485
Fellner, W., 649
FIFO, 267, 546, 858
Final solution, 779
Finance, 459
Firm, 16, 491
  consumer as a, 681
  supply curve from a, 563–564
  without limits, 556
Fisher, I., 275, 890
Fisher identity, 317, 352, 357
Fisher model, 319
Floors and ceilings, 460
Flow of commodity, 107
Fluctuations, due to fluctuating demands,
  160
  due to speculation, 98
  seasonal, 77
  self-justifying, 97
Forced saving, 481
Foreign exchanges, 81–91, 391–392, 411
Foreign investment, 388, 404, 722
France, 388
Free market, flight from, 677
Freedom, 726
Full employment, 301, 403, 447
Futures market, 99

Investment, effects of, 478
  period of, 865, 874, 875
  present value of, 849
  profits interact with, 457
  See also Accumulation
Investment trusts, 335
Ireland, 711
Isomers, 732
Isoquant, 741

Jevons, W. S., 465, 888
Joint demand, 230
Joint products, 769
Joint-stock company, 510
Joint supply, 227

Kalecki, M., 379, 557
Keynes, J. M., 360, 362, 367, 891
Keynesian controversy, 302
Keynesian system, 292, 405, 464
Knight, F. H., 890

Labor, demand for, 204–208, 598–602, 763–769
  perishable nature of, 498
  supply of, 208–211, 798
Labor curve, 762, 767
Labor theory of value, 516
Labor union, 671
Laissez-faire, 727
Land, nonmonetary advantages of, 189
  productivity schedules, 590
Land curve, 762, 767
Laws of returns, confusion of, 735
Least outlay combination, 745, 746
Leisure, 692
LIFO, 267, 857
Linear allocation of profit, 843
Liquid assets, 333, 339, 500
Liquidity, degree of, 310
  and hoarding, 695
  order of, 311
Liquidity effect, 304
Liquidity preference, 375, 376, 835
Loans, bank, expansion of, 344
  rationing of, 350
Loans, supply and demand for, 832
Long-run adjustments, 532, 569

Macroeconomics, 237, 238
  basic model of, 290, 417, 455, 473
Malthus, T. R., 367, 707, 709, 886
Mandeville, B. de, 367
Margin buying, 104
Marginal conditions, 550, 594, 790, 813, 863
Marginal cost, 535, 553, 607, 748, 876
  of time, 863
Marginal cost pricing, 657–658
Marginal curve construction, 555

Marginal outlay, 612
Marginal productivity, 588, 589, 602, 748, 761, 767
  of revenue, 761, 877
Marginal rate of substitution, 684, 685
Marginal revenue, 551
  total, 609
  of utility, 684
Marginal utility, 682
  of money, 684, 816
  weighted, 687
Market, black, 140
  competitive, 45, 202
  foreign exchange, 82
  home and foreign, 609
  imperfect, 524, 526, 549
  perfect, 524, 755
  pluperfect, 526, 756
Market curve, 51, 528, 815, 819, 834
Market demand and supply, 53–54, 58
Market identity, 59–60, 99, 112, 320, 375
Market schedule, of eager buyer, 51
  of eager seller, 52
  individual, 49
  total, 66
Market structure, determinants of, 651
Marshall, A., 3, 114, 119, 816, 888, 889
Marx, Karl, 22, 887
Marxism, 516
Mathematics and business judgment, 780
Maximization, of internal rate of return, 867
  of income stream, 869–870
  of profit, 541, 550, 551–556
  of utility, 792
  of what?, 868
Maximum, absolute or relative, 617
  boundary, 618
Measurement, as valuation, 309
Mercantilism, 404
Merger, 669
Microeconomics, 257
Middlemen, 21
Migration, 193
Milk industry, 581
Milk Marketing Board, 666–668
Mill, J. S., 582, 887
Minimum differentiation, principle of, 633
Mining, 191
Mitchell, Wesley, 892
Mixed system, 676
Mobility of factors, 219
  See also Immobility
Model, of banking system, 355
  basic, 290, 417, 455
  cyclical, 453
  economic, nature of, 287, 702, 707
  government deficit, 473–477
  international trade, 394–409